YEARS OF DISCORD

Books by John Morton Blum

Joe Tumulty and the Wilson Era
The Republican Roosevelt
Woodrow Wilson and the Politics of Morality
Yesterday's Children (Editor)
The National Experience (Editor)
The Promise of America
From the Morgenthau Diaries
    I. Years of Crisis, 1928–1938
   II. Years of Urgency, 1938–1941
  III. Years of War, 1941–1945
Roosevelt and Morgenthau
The Price of Vision (Editor)
V Was for Victory
The Progressive Presidents
Public Philosopher (Editor)
Years of Discord

YEARS OF DISCORD
American Politics and Society,
1961 1974
JOHN MORTON BLUM

W·W· NORTON & COMPANY NEW YORK LONDON

The text of this book is composed in Linotype Walbaum,
with the display set in Walbaum.
Composition and manufacturing by The Maple-Vail Book Manufacturing Group.

First Edition.

Library of Congress Cataloging-in-Publication Data
Blum, John Morton, 1921–
Years of discord : American politics and society, 1961–1974 / by
John Morton Blum.
p. cm.
Includes bibliographical references and index.
1. United States—Politics and government—1961–1963. 2. United
States—Politics and government—1963–1969. 3. United States—
Politics and government—1969–1974. I. Title.
E841.B59 1991
306.2'0973—dc20   90–49242

ISBN 0–393–02969–7

W.W. Norton & Company, Inc., 500 Fifth Avenue, New York, N.Y. 10110
W.W. Norton & Company, Ltd., 10 Coptic Street, London WC1A 1PU

1 2 3 4 5 6 7 8 9 0

For the liberal spirit, and for its future

Contents

Preface

Unusual political intensity marked the years between the inauguration of John F. Kennedy in 1961 and the resignation of Richard M. Nixon in 1974. As that period began, Americans of substance and stature expressed grave concern about the state of the nation at home and the prestige of the nation abroad. Their anxieties underlay the theme of Kennedy's 1960 campaign—his promise to get the country moving again. Kennedy and his associates on the New Frontier looked to the federal government to provide solutions for protuberant national problems. As they addressed domestic and international issues, their pace and direction failed to satisfy Americans to their political left. Those dissidents succeeded in pushing the administration and the nation to broader efforts at social and economic reform. The agenda Kennedy developed came to fruition under the leadership of Lyndon Johnson. In fashioning his Great Society, Johnson presided over the enactment in 1964 and 1965 of more reform legislation than Congress had passed since 1935.

But unresolved problems of poverty, of segregation and discrimination, and of American involvement in the Vietnam War continued to spur protest on the left. In their anger and frustration, some protesters turned to violence in the cities and on college campuses. Even that violence had identifiable political objectives. It also had significant political effects. The federal government had succeeded in improving the social and economic status of minorities and of the poor. Jealous of those gains, many Americans also resented the turbulence on the left. They responded in a political backlash against the antiwar movement, civil rights agitation, and student demonstrations. The resulting fallout gave Richard Nixon his leverage for reaching the White House. Nixon's controversial undertakings then spawned further dissent and further polarization in American politics. And Nixon's misuse of the power of his office created a constitutional crisis resolved only because of extraordinary efforts on the part of the media, the judiciary, and the Congress.

All in all, from 1961 through 1974 a consciousness of politics and political issues permeated American life. On that account, I have examined the period from the perspective of political history. That approach includes more than elections, legislation, and judicial decisions. It requires consideration of foreign as well as domestic policy. It calls, too, for continual attention to social developments that influenced and reflected politics. A different approach to the period might stress cultural affairs more than I have attempted to. But for the years under review, a time of persisting national discord, political history provides a broad and relevant focus. It also permits a reexamination of American liberalism, for so long since 1974 in political eclipse but now again an apposite source for new and necessary federal action.

JOHN MORTON BLUM

Andover, Vermont

YEARS OF DISCORD

Prologue: 1960

As the 1950s drew toward their close, a mood of dissatisfaction settled on those Americans who still valued the national expectations associated only fifteen years earlier with victory in World War II. Those once bright and beguiling prospects appeared to have dissolved in anxiety and irresolution. Americans in general worried that national power and mission throughout the world seemed near a premature end. Liberal Americans were also troubled because the programs of social justice that Franklin Roosevelt had promised to sponsor remained at a far remove. Recourse to the state—to the authority of the federal government—as the prime agency of reform, so central to Roosevelt's New Deal, had languished for more than a decade.

Those perceptions reflected palpable realities. During the largely prosperous 1950s poverty had persisted throughout the United States. In that decade of assertive national pride, racial prejudice and segregation had continued to belie the American ideal. American leadership in science and technology had been challenged by the success of the Soviet Union in launching the first earth satellite. That feat called into question the adequacies of American education and the ordering of national priorities. Indeed, in the view of many Americans, the Soviet Union was gaining in a global race for prestige as well as power.

By 1960 those conditions had begun to excite rising criticism of national social and economic policies. Much of that criticism emanated from intellectuals who were trying to diagnose and to remedy an American malaise. They were important as interpreters of that malaise, but the problems they identified would have existed and would have engendered serious dissatisfaction even in the absence of interpretation. As it was, the severity of those problems provoked several self-conscious efforts to redefine national purpose. Predictably in a quadrennial year, each aspirant to the presidency, aware of those developments, was trying to identify himself with a potentially winning program of action. As it worked out, John F. Kennedy, the candidate of the Democratic party, offered a message sufficiently persuasive to win election by a tiny margin. His New Frontier, while fresh in spirit, owed much of its content to older liberal expectations that the quest for national purpose refurbished. It owed much also to his evocation of long-standing liberal belief in the beneficent possibilities of positive federal government under the leadership of a powerful presidency.

"The American Century," as Henry Luce first described it in 1941 in an editorial in *Life*, required the American people "to assume the leadership of the world," to accept "wholeheartedly our duty and responsibility as the most powerful and vital nation in the world." As Luce elaborated that concept in the next several years, he contemplated a political, economic, and cultural imperialism. He envisaged a world of nations freed from European domination but content with American hegemony. In that world each nation, following the commanding example of the United States, would be basically republican in government, capitalistic in economics, and Protestant in ethics. That was not exactly the world other Americans expected. Most of them had a greater tolerance for diversity than did Luce and less desire to sustain an imperial commitment. But by and large in 1945 Americans viewed their country, as Franklin Roosevelt did, as one of the great powers responsible for keeping the peace, partly through the agency of the United Nations. Within that context they, too, opposed European colonialism and later Soviet expansion and took special pride in the force of the American example. Those so minded had come to see themselves, as some Americans had since the landing at Plymouth, as an exceptional, an uncorrupted people deserving extraordinary influence, even invincibility. Only a minority looked to quite different kinds of national roles, either isolation from international problems or participation in an evolving united world state.

On domestic matters, Americans of a liberal spirit subscribed to Roosevelt's economic bill of rights, his proposed "new basis of security and prosperity . . . for all." Those rights, as he had enumerated them, included useful employment; sufficient earnings for adequate food, clothing, and recreation; decent housing; a good education; and pro-

Franklin Delano Roosevelt: He proposed security and prosperity for all.

tection from the financial disasters associated with old age, sickness, accident, and unemployment. Americans had long identified those conditions with middle-class status, but personal security had proved elusive during the decade of depression preceding the Second World War. In the prosperous wartime and postwar years more and more Americans reached the ranks of the middle class. Most of them were eager to retain what they had gained. Consequently, they were loath to pay taxes for government programs to provide security for the millions of impoverished, of whom a majority were black or Hispanic, women and children, aged or ill.

For more than two decades national politics had reflected that temper. Since 1939 a loose coalition of Republicans and southern Democrats in Congress had succeeded in resisting social improvements. President Harry S Truman in his Fair Deal had proposed a broad agenda of reform but had spent little influence in its behalf, partly because of his preoccupation with foreign policy. President Dwight D. Eisenhower, who shared that preoccupation, found the social order as it existed basically satisfactory. He made no significant effort to alter it.

The most important change in domestic affairs had originated with the Supreme Court. Its unanimous decision of 1954 in *Brown v. Board of Education* held unconstitutional racial segregation in public schools. That ruling and its implementing decree took the first step toward later decisions that reached the same conclusions about other segregated facilities, public and private. The ensuing counterpoint between the federal courts and civil rights activists spurred the difficult process of desegregation in the United States. But by 1960 that process had resulted in only token gains. Yet few of the middle class then expected the explosions of frustration that soon developed out of the continuing gap between the legal rights of black Americans and the actual circumstances of their lives.

In the eyes of the world, social inequities within the United States contributed to a decline in American prestige that arose primarily for other reasons. Since 1945 Presidents Truman and Eisenhower had accepted the cold war with the Soviet Union as an unavoidable rivalry of national interests, alliances, and ideologies. Both expected, as did most of their countrymen, that the United States would prevail morally and politically. Americans had had continuing confidence in the superiority of their economy, their technology, and their weaponry. But by 1960 that confidence had begun to flag. Three recessions, the most recent still unrelieved, had troubled the country since Eisenhower's first election. His policies had succeeded in braking inflation, as he intended them to, but at the cost of recurrent periods of needlessly high unemployment and uneven economic growth. In contrast, the Soviet economy appeared to be booming. That condition encouraged Soviet Premier Nikita Khrushchev to bluster that the contest between the two nations would hinge on peaceful competition between their social and economic systems. To Vice President Richard M. Nixon, who visited Moscow in 1959, Khrushchev crowed: "We shall bury you."

Soviet accomplishments gave some credibility to that boast. The Soviet Union had long since produced an atomic bomb and in 1953 a thermonuclear bomb. Obviously the United States had no great lead in the understanding or application of theoretical physics. Nevertheless, Americans were stunned in 1957 by the successful Soviet launching of the first earth satellite and the first intercontinental missile. The United States had fallen behind in space technology and weaponry. The fault, in the judgment of many Americans, arose from a failure of education in the sciences, a failure largely attributable to inadequate federal support for education in general. The consequences affected national security, according to the report of the Gaither Commission, which

Eisenhower had appointed, for the Soviet Union would soon possess more missiles than the United States. That report gave rise to fears of a "missile gap," though as the president asserted, none existed.

Soviet achievements also impressed unaligned and underdeveloped nations, where the Soviet Union touted communism as the best means to modernization. In those areas the United States often provoked suspicion because of its alliances with European colonial powers. Even within friendly nations anti-American attitudes seemed to be spreading. Hostile crowds harassed Vice President Nixon during his tour of Latin America. Anti-American riots in Japan persuaded the government there in 1960 to advise President Eisenhower to cancel his planned visit. Episodes like those intensified anxieties about national security and national reputation. Those issues in turn raised anguished questions about "National Purpose."

American social critics, sharing and shaping the mood of their countrymen, had been asking those questions on their own. A small number of them wrote from the left. The anti-Communist crusade of the 1950s had purged the intellectual community of Stalinism, but Marxism, so much a part of the ferment of the 1930s, survived and soon was to

John Kenneth Galbraith:
Economist of wit and insight.

flourish again. Marxist descriptions of the American condition sometimes proved revealing. Indeed, liberal theorists, though they rejected Marxist analysis, recognized the urgency of social change. So it was with John Kenneth Galbraith, an economist of fluency and wit who made his political home with the liberal Americans for Democratic Action. In contrast with some members of that organization, Galbraith practiced a scrupulous anti-anti-Marxism. His primary intellectual forebears were Thorstein Veblen, the incisive, unconventional American sociologist, and John Maynard Keynes, the British statesman and scholar whose *General Theory of Employment* had launched modern economics. In 1958 Galbraith published his influential study *The Affluent Society*. A best seller, the book incorporated the point of view, as Galbraith recalled, that he once expressed in replying to a Polish acquaintance who had asked him if he knew the difference between capitalism and communism. "Well," went the answer, "I will tell you. Under capitalism man exploits man. And under communism it is just the reverse."

With similar irreverence, Galbraith in *The Affluent Society* contrasted the private waste of American consumer culture with the accompanying indifference to public needs. In the spirit of Veblen he prescribed less advertising, less acquisitiveness, and more public spending for schools, slum clearance, and social security. Galbraith also suggested many specific remedies: a national teachers corps to reach the children of the poor, a special attack on poverty in Appalachia, a national program to retrain and relocate unemployed workers, national medical care, nationally subsidized housing, new facilities for urban recreation—all requiring "public effort and public funds" to create a full civic equality. Poverty, Galbraith wrote, could not be made to disappear merely by stepping up the rate of economic growth, though that, too, was necessary. Rather, only salient categorical programs could relieve poverty in the midst of plenty, could correct the existing "social imbalance."

In a more angry vein Michael Harrington, a young socialist with a lucid style and proselytizing zeal, wrote a series of articles later collected in *The Other America: Poverty in the United States* (1962). Harrington documented the prevalence of poverty in the United States among children as well as adults, nonwhite minorities, the aged, migrant workers, the uneducated, and households with women at their heads. He also described the "culture of poverty," the confining cluster of social and psychological characteristics that he saw among disadvantaged groups. That culture was the focus of Oscar Lewis, whose *The Children of Sánchez* (1961) reflected his unobtrusively Marxist anthro-

Social imbalance: Poverty in Appalachia.

pology. In that book and its sequel, *La Vida* (1966), Lewis examined Mexican and Puerto Rican families who carried their poverty with them as they moved in and out of the United States. The adaptations those families made to the needs of survival wherever they lived gave rise, in Lewis's view, to a kind of group anomie from which they could not escape on their own. Remedy for that condition, he argued, required the categorical programs Galbraith had proposed.

Unlike Galbraith, most liberals rejected that remedy. They believed the nation could rely instead on a deliberate, countercyclical federal deficit to shift the economy out of the recession. Recovery would create jobs for millions of the temporarily unemployed and underemployed who would remain at the margin of poverty until they could return to work. Indeed, many national problems originated in the obsession of the Eisenhower administration with a balanced budget. That objective accounted in large part for the president's resistance to increased military spending. A stimulative fiscal policy, in contrast, would increase national income and therefore federal revenues even at lower tax rates. That expansion, as well as the spending to encourage it, would provide the means to enlarge and diversify the American armed forces and also improve their equipment so as to keep up with the formidable capabilities of the Soviet Union. So argued James Tobin, a Yale economist who later won a Nobel Prize for his scholarship, in an article in the *Yale Review*. Economic growth, Tobin went on, would also allow new funding for economic assistance to developing nations and for increased federal support for all levels of education in the United States. Those objectives appealed not only to liberals but also to conservatives anxious about the state of the nation.

In his *Affluent Society* Galbraith predicted that leadership to those ends would emanate from a "New Class" of professional men and women, informed and talented managers of public and private institutions, the lawyers and economists and other specialists with whom they worked—a class exempt from toil and boredom. As Thorstein Veblen and Walter Lippmann had argued many years earlier, the complexities of modern industrial and political institutions required that kind of elite leadership. There remained the question of which elite to trust: the liberal intellectuals and academicians and the politicians who solicited and shared their views or the representatives of business and industry and their political friends. The former in 1960 stood by and large for change; the latter, for the status quo. Whichever governed, the question also remained of how to make them accountable for their decisions.

Those issues agitated the influential prophet of the American left C. Wright Mills. An activist sociologist who became a cult figure for the radicals of the 1960s, Mills believed, with Galbraith, that intellectuals had an obligation to serve as agents for social change. In 1956 Mills published *The Power Elite*. That study attributed the direction of American domestic and foreign policy to three mutually reinforcing groups: the corporate, the governmental, and the military. That "triangle of power," he maintained, "is most important for the historical structure of the present." Mills disdained the political and cultural bases of that structure. "America—" he asserted," a conservative country without any conservative ideology—appears now before the world a naked and arbitrary power. . . . The second-rate mind is in command of the ponderously spoken platitude. In the liberal rhetoric, vagueness, and in the conservative mood, irrationality, are raised to principle . . . in the privately incorporated economy, the military ascendancy, and the political vacuum of modern America."

Critics in the political center rejected Mills's analysis. They saw the problems that disturbed him as both inherent in the nature of politics and subject to gradual solution by resolute men. American political rhetoric did abound with platitudes, but for centuries everywhere political rhetoric ordinarily had, with intermittent flashes of productive debate. American intrusions in recent years in Iran, Egypt, and Guatemala had temporarily involved arbitrary power, but so continuously had Soviet intrusions in Eastern Europe and Asia. No national social and economic system guaranteed international restraint. To be sure, corporate and military influence on national policy worried President Eisenhower, who was to warn his countrymen against it when he left office. But for their part, liberal Democrats had lost much of their traditional suspicions of corporate power, which they believed an alert federal government could successfully control.

One direct rejoinder to Mills appeared in *The End of Ideology* (1960), a collection of essays by the sociologist Daniel Bell. A disenchanted former Marxist, Bell noted the absence of the passion that had marked intellectual life during the 1930s. As he interpreted that change, by the 1950s ideology, especially Marxist ideology, had become too theoretical, too intense and teleological to fit the postwar necessity for accommodation. The ideologist, Bell held, the Communist or religionist, wanted to live "at the level of grandeur." Not so the common individual. Further, there were no longer "transforming moments" that would produce revolution or salvation. The ethics of ends and absolutes, Bell concluded, had now to yield to an ethic of responsibility. That ethic recommended practical political action.

Yet there was also in 1960 a need for a more transcendent cast, for a national purpose that would evoke support for domestic reform without intensifying dormant antagonisms among different classes and ethnic groups. It had, too, to infuse international policies that would protect the national interest without mobilizing chauvinistic hostility to the Soviet Union. Walter Lippmann and George Kennan, two of the most respected commentators of their generation, interpreted the national condition just about identically. Lippmann had been writing important books and columns about public affairs for almost fifty years. "The critical weakness in our society," he now believed, "is that . . . our people do not have great purposes which they're united in wanting to achieve. . . . In our encounter with the Soviet rulers, the question is whether the country can recover . . . a sense of great purpose and high destiny." Kennan, the foremost interpreter of the Soviet Union of his time, had originated the doctrine of containment, the theoretical basis for Truman's foreign policy. Now Kennan doubted whether the United States could compete with the Soviet Union's "purposeful, serious and disciplined society." Following Galbraith, Kennan found the United States "with no highly developed national purpose, with the overwhelming accent of life on personal comfort and amusement, with a dearth of public services . . . with its great urban areas being gradually disinte-grated . . . with an educational system where quality has been exten-sively sacrificed to quantity, and with insufficient social discipline." Strong statements, those, and both emanated from men notable for their essential conservatism, their civility, and their insight.

The sense of inadequacy and dissatisfaction that Lippmann and Kennan expressed motivated three formal investigations of national purpose. The Eisenhower administration commissioned one of those studies; the Rockefeller Brothers Fund, a second; and Time, Inc. in company with the *New York Times*, a third. The participants in those inquiries all were prestigious representatives of the "vital center," the spectrum of political opinion exclusive of the radical left and radical right that the historian Arthur M. Schlesinger, Jr., had defined. Their reports agreed about the continuing threat to the United States from the Soviet Union, suggested no retreat from the cold war, and regis-tered a common concern about national defense and national reputa-tion. They disagreed, however, partly along partisan lines, about the seriousness of national problems and the appropriate role of the fed-eral government in solving them.

The president's commission predictably endorsed his own point of view. Its *Goals for Americans* (1960), written in a grandiloquent and platitudinous prose, expressed confidence in the American system as it was and stressed the importance for the future, as in the past, of per-sonal rather than public responsibility, of states' rights, and of fiscal prudence. The Rockefellers subsidized six reports, published between 1958 and 1960 and compiled in *Prospect for America* (1961). That vol-ume, conventional in its major themes, noted the power of the demo-cratic idea as expressed in an open and pluralistic society with a representative government. "The whole conception of liberty for the individual and freedom of thought and conscience," it stated in a char-acteristic passage, "rests on the conviction that such freedom nurtures intelligence and that this in turn will carry men toward truth and away from error." The democratic vision would release "much human intel-ligence, talent, and vitality," the ingredients necessary for the "excel-lence" that *Prospect* wanted for the nation. Those qualities could flourish in spite of the ability of humankind totally to destroy itself, but national excellence and security both demanded the expenditure by the federal government of increased funds for social, education, and defense pro-grams. *Prospect* also urged a stronger federal promotion of equal opportunity for minorities and for women and a tax reduction suffi-cient to spur the economy, even at the risk of a federal deficit. Translated into specific recommendations, the uncontroversial themes of *Prospect for America* contained implicit criticisms of Eisenhower's domestic policies.

Its section on foreign policy followed the same pattern. In general it reaffirmed old assumptions about American exceptionalism and omnipotence by asserting the disinterestedness of the United States and the nation's ability to discharge global responsibilities. As committed to cold war premises as was Eisenhower himself, *Prospect* called for resistance to Soviet expansion everywhere and, to that end, for gaining and retaining a lead in total economic performance, in all aspects of the arms race, in related technologies, in the development of mobile forces for deployment where needed in limited warfare, and for increased aid to developing nations. Increased expenditures for those purposes were precisely the objectives Eisenhower had deemed unnecessary and imprudent.

The third survey, *The National Purpose* (1960), consisted of a series of statements by individuals that, taken together, followed the general themes of the Rockefeller reports. The contributions took the cold war for granted. Though much of the volume was nonpartisan, some of *The National Purpose* set forth Democratic alternatives to prevailing domestic policies. So it was even with Walter Lippmann, who had twice supported Eisenhower. His essay evoked the memory of Franklin Roosevelt in calling for "concrete measures, practical programs" to reach the goals of a free society. The necessary "innovations would appear with the new generation," he wrote. "For it is not the nation which is old, but only its leaders." Nevertheless, it was one of the older generation, Adlai E. Stevenson, twice Eisenhower's Democratic opponent for the presidency, who spoke most eloquently, as he put it, about "the public aspect of freedom as an organizing principle in a new kind of society." Stevenson saw no inevitable conflict between the private and public aspects of American life. For him they were "the essential pulls of energy in a visionary social order." The federal government, as he saw it, was a "positive instrument designed to secure the well-being of all . . . citizens" and to make the United States a "convincing model of a free society." The government had therefore to clear out the slums, combat juvenile delinquency, improve the schools, make a public shame of racial discrimination, preserve the nation's reserves of water and land, cover the costs of health care, in all erase "the contrast between private opulence and public squalor."

Americans who agreed with Stevenson, with the recommendations of *Prospect for America*, with the antecedent analysis of Galbraith were discontented with the state of the nation. Those who were satisfied for their part viewed the critics as alarmists. So it was that Eisenhower considered Nelson Rockefeller, then Republican governor of New York, a liberal spendthrift unfit for his party's nomination. Eisenhower accepted instead Richard M. Nixon, his vice president. Though Stevenson's programs influenced the Democratic platform, his party turned for its candidate to Massachusetts Senator John F. Kennedy, one of the younger generation on whom Lippmann counted. The presidential campaign that followed, in the perception of the Kennedy partisans, provided a rough political test of strength between the complacent and the concerned.

The issues and the outcome of the 1960 campaign were, of course, more complicated than that, but the Republicans had little choice but to run largely on the record of President Eisenhower, the most popular American of the time. By 1960 the record, though not the man, was subject to attack. Nixon had therefore to identify himself with Eisenhower but also to promise new departures of his own. Privately he chafed at the president's refusal to combat the recession by increasing federal spending. In public Nixon rode the political winds by standing, as did the Democrats, for a larger defense budget in spite of the president's opposition to that course.

On other matters of foreign and military policy, Nixon had little room to maneuver, and usually no wish to. Such had been the case, for one example, after the Soviet Union had shot down an American airplane, a U-2, engaged in high-altitude reconnaissance. On May 5, 1960, just eleven days before a scheduled meeting with Eisenhower in Paris, Khrushchev announced the downing. The State Department replied that the plane had strayed from a meteorological survey. On May 7 Khrushchev disclosed that the pilot had been captured and had admitted he was spying from the sky. The Soviet premier was nevertheless willing "to grant that the president knew nothing about the plane." The secretary of state then contended that aerial espionage was necessary to prevent a surprise attack, and Nixon, wholly of that mind, suggested that the flights would continue. Rejecting Khrushchev's opening, Eisenhower took responsibility for the episode. Khrushchev then destroyed the summit meeting by demanding an apology and punishment for those immediately involved, both of which the president declined. The whole affair was needlessly awkward. Risking a U-2 reconnaissance so close to the date of a summit suggested that Eisenhower did not care to negotiate seriously with the Soviet Union.

Nixon, supporting his chief, seemed just as clumsy as he did. Yet the U-2 flights did have to continue because they furnished indispensable information that no other available technique could provide as fully or as safely. The administration failed in diplomatic tact and finesse. More troubling was its apparent indifference to discussing nuclear disarmament.

The U-2 flights revealed that the Soviet Union, however advanced its space technology, had not in fact deployed any intercontinental ballistic missiles (ICBMs). But that was secret knowledge, as was the American lead in the miniaturization of components for long-range missiles, a lead that at least balanced the superior thrust of Soviet weapons. If Nixon knew about those developments, he could not reveal them, certainly not in response to uninformed Democratic charges about a missile gap. Nixon also failed to persuade Eisenhower to give him public credit for urging a tough policy toward Fidel Castro, whose Communist regime had taken control in Cuba in 1959. Here again, Eisenhower preferred to ignore Democratic demands for action against Castro rather than to disclose secret plans of the Central Intelligence Agency to organize an invasion of Cuba by anti-Castro émigrés.

Eisenhower in any case had always had doubts about Nixon, doubts confirmed in his mind by the vice president's childish shouting match with Khrushchev in Moscow in 1959. Nixon, Eisenhower also believed, should have accepted the cabinet office he had offered him in 1956 in order to remove him from the Republican ticket. Indeed, Eisenhower's personal preference for the Republican nomination in 1960 had been not Nixon but Secretary of the Treasury Robert Anderson, a quiet Texan who never had a chance. Further, Eisenhower was irked by Nixon's repeated claim that he had experience in making major decisions. That contention resembled the Democratic charge, a charge with little basis, that as president Eisenhower had reigned but not ruled. When asked about the "big decisions that Mr. Nixon participated in," the president replied: "I don't see why people can't understand this: no one can make decisions except me." Indeed, Eisenhower in private seemed not much to like Nixon. The president's secretary reported in her diary that he "mentioned again . . . that the Vice President has very few personal friends." She thought the difference between the two men was obvious: "The President is a man of integrity. . . . Everybody knows it, everybody trusts and loves him. But the Vice President sometimes seems like a man who is acting like a nice man rather than being one."

Nixon was trying to seem different from what he had once been. He had made his national reputation while a member of the House Un-

American Activities Committee by his relentless pursuit of Alger Hiss. Whether or not Hiss, a former officer of the State Department, had been a Soviet spy, as Nixon believed, he was sent to jail in 1950 for perjury about his major accuser. In the opinion of the Republican right, that verdict vindicated Nixon. Those so persuaded also put credence in the innuendo by which Nixon had falsely identified his Democratic opponents with Communist causes. Yearning as ever for office, wealth, and fame, a "new" Nixon in 1960 tried to appear more liberal, or at least more flexible, than his reputation. Misled by his tough talk and undisguised nastiness, Democrats had long underestimated his tenacity. More than just another ambitious politician, Nixon was a shrewd and informed professional, dogged in his pursuit of power.

The Democratic nomination went to another tough professional, John F. Kennedy, the only candidate with an effective organization. A veteran of the war in the South Pacific, where he had rescued most of his crew after his PT boat had been sunk, Kennedy was a moderate who had not particularly distinguished himself in the Senate. Adlai Stevenson, who wanted the nomination but would not campaign for it, considered Kennedy too little experienced for the presidency and too susceptible to conservative advice. Stevenson especially questioned Kennedy's failure ever openly to oppose the late Senator Joseph McCarthy, the most vicious of the Red hunters of the 1950s. Kennedy's younger brother Robert had served briefly as counsel to McCarthy's infamous Senate committee, and McCarthy had been a friend of Kennedy's wealthy father, Joseph P. Kennedy, who was notorious for his isolationism during the early years of the Second World War and for his anticommunism thereafter.

Some Democrats who therefore opposed Kennedy had at first favored Senator Hubert H. Humphrey of Minnesota, who had a splendid record of support for civil rights and labor. But Kennedy trounced Humphrey in three crucial, early primaries: in New Hampshire, where Kennedy was favored as a New Englander, but also in Wisconsin, where Humphrey was supposed to have an advantage because he came from a neighboring state, and in West Virginia, a heavily Protestant state, where Kennedy's Catholicism had seemed to put him at risk. Thereafter Kennedy's only important rival was Lyndon B. Johnson of Texas, the majority leader of the Senate, who waited too long to launch his national campaign and entered the convention with few delegates from outside the South.

Kennedy won nomination on the first ballot and then picked Johnson as his running mate. That choice appalled some of his advisers and many liberals. They underestimated Johnson, who had often hidden his talents beneath the role of a crude "good ol' boy." Now Johnson added essential strength to the Democratic ticket, especially in the South, where he undertook a vigorous personal campaign. Eleanor Roosevelt epitomized the dilemma of Stevenson's unreconciled admirers. When Kennedy visited Hyde Park, where he and Mrs. Roosevelt had a private chat, a friend asked her what she thought of the candidate. "He's a nice young man," she replied evasively, "but I can't stand his father." Her friend replied, "Many of us who voted four times for your husband could not stand his mother." Soon thereafter Mrs. Roosevelt declared her support for Kennedy, as Stevenson had gracefully done earlier. As Kennedy himself had quipped, he was the only person who stood between Nixon and the White House.

Though Kennedy and Nixon were roughly contemporaries, Kennedy at forty-three looked much younger than did Nixon at forty-seven. Kennedy emphasized that difference by directing his campaign to the future. He would, he promised, "get the country moving again." His New Frontier addressed issues that had become politically salient, themes that had been rehearsed in *Prospect for America* and *The National Purpose*. In a celebrated speech in the Senate, Kennedy had already criticized French colonial oppression in Algeria and urged the substitution of self-government by emerging nations for colonial rule by European powers. During the campaign he repeated that point in his criticisms of Eisenhower's faltering procolonial policies in sub-Sahara Africa, especially in the Congo. The Soviet Union was also eager to win allies in Africa, as well as in Asia and Latin America, but Kennedy argued that the United States would prevail by assisting the new nations in their quest for a genuine and stable independence. Ideology did not interest him; results did.

The objectives he sought derived from long-standing American cold war doctrines and from the issues that concerned critics of American purpose. One of those critics himself, Kennedy arranged for the publication of a selection of his speeches in a campaign book, *The Strategy of Peace* (1960). Harris Wofford, a campaign aide who assisted in the preparation of the book, later recalled that it deliberately put Kennedy's left foot forward. It was intended to persuade "liberals"—democrats who admired Stevenson and distrusted Kennedy—that the candidate deserved their support. *The Strategy of Peace*, focusing by Kennedy's choice on foreign policy, was nevertheless not so much a liberal as an exhortative book, implicitly critical of Eisenhower's policies largely because Kennedy deemed them inadequate for the continuing national rivalry with communism, particularly with China and the Soviet Union. "Our purpose," he maintained, "is not only to defend the integrity of this democratic society but also to help advance the cause of human freedom and . . . the universal cause of a just and lasting peace." Noble ends, cold war euphemisms that both liberals and conservatives could endorse. Kennedy defined them specifically with frequently ambiguous counterpositions. He recommended working both toward a stronger national defense and toward an agreement with the Soviet Union to suspend nuclear testing. The American military establishment considered those goals contradictory, and the candidate did not attempt to explain how he intended to reconcile them, though he actually had in mind the expansion of conventional forces. Kennedy also called for an end of French colonialism, but he condoned American involvement in place of the French in Southeast Asia. Indeed, he considered South Vietnam, earlier a French client, a "brave little state" and its authoritarian president a true friend. Throughout the book Kennedy stressed general themes that accorded with the spirit of the time, as he knew. It was a time, he held, for anxiety about the state of the nation and for resolute action to improve it. It was a time to mobilize American resources to assist the military and economic development of the emerging nations of Asia, Africa, and Latin America, for otherwise they would be drawn to emulate China, the Soviet Union, and Cuba, which were bent on winning their allegiance. It was a time of dangerous American softness that had allowed increasing "lags" in the competition with the Soviet Union. Those lags included not only the manufacture and development of missiles but also the race in space, the buildup of conventional arms, the rate of economic growth, and the pace of training young scientists and technicians. All that he promised to turn around.

Before he could focus on those and other themes of the New Frontier, Kennedy had first to defuse the issue of his Catholicism. Especially in the rural South, many American Protestants still believed that a Catholic president would serve as an agent of the pope. Fostered by pastors in fundamentalist churches, that bigotry had contributed to the defeat in 1928 of Alfred E. Smith, the only previous Catholic presidential nominee. Kennedy confronted it again. He met the issue directly by accepting an invitation to make a televised address to the Houston Ministerial Association, a Protestant group. In a straightforward speech on September 12, he said he believed "in an America where the separation of church and state is absolute." The religion of a president was his private affair. "I am not the Catholic candidate for President, I am

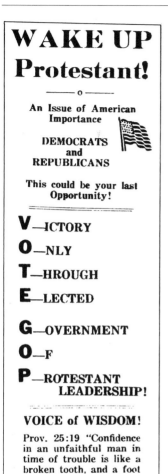

WAKE UP Protestant!

——— o ———

An Issue of American Importance

DEMOCRATS and REPUBLICANS

This could be your last Opportunity!

V—ICTORY

O—NLY

T—HROUGH

E—LECTED

G—OVERNMENT

O—F

P—ROTESTANT LEADERSHIP!

VOICE of WISDOM!

Prov. 25:19 "Confidence in an unfaithful man in time of trouble is like a broken tooth, and a foot out of joint."

Against the candidate who was Catholic.

the . . . candidate . . . who happens also to be Catholic." The address did not eliminate the religious issue, but it won acclaim throughout the country. Sam Rayburn, the Texas Democrat who had long been speaker of the House of Representatives, was enthusiastic: "As they say in my part of Texas, he ate 'em blood raw."

Kennedy also bested Nixon in their initial television debate. Eisenhower and other leading Republicans warned Nixon against the debates, the first of their kind, since Nixon was better known than Kennedy, who could profit from the national exposure. But Nixon was proud of his forensic skill and loath to decline a challenge. Both candidates understood that the impressions they made in their first confrontation would be hard to alter. Kennedy prepared assiduously, reviewing every issue for hours. Speaking first, while he made his familiar points, he appeared youthful, informed, and under a natural self-control. Then Nixon, abjuring his usual pugnacity, said his disagreement with Kennedy was "not about the goals for Americans, but only about the means to reach those goals." That was an honest but a weak response. Nixon also seemed less forceful than Kennedy in answering questions from the panelists selected from the press. Whether because of the studio lighting or because of his makeup, Nixon looked unshaven and drawn. A poll of radio listeners disclosed that they considered the debate more or less a draw, but a majority of those who watched television thought Kennedy had won. The debate did more than give Kennedy quick publicity. His ease in discussing the issues, his "cool nonchalance" cost Nixon any edge he had derived from his claim to greater experience.

Other tactical errors also weakened Nixon's campaign. He exhausted himself by visiting all fifty states, as he had rashly promised to, while Kennedy concentrated on the industrial states with the most electoral votes. Eisenhower's speeches near the end of the campaign helped Nixon in the polls, but the president would probably have helped more if Nixon had enlisted him sooner. Eisenhower's contented view of the state of the nation, still in a recession, heightened and contrasted with the need to get the country "moving again" that Kennedy was stressing. Nixon hoped to win the white South, but Lyndon Johnson's efforts held a majority of that vote for the Democrats. In contrast, Nixon's chosen running mate, Henry Cabot Lodge, Jr., former senator from Massachusetts and ambassador to the United Nations, could not wrest New England from Kennedy.

Kennedy had an instinctive compassion that Nixon could not match. As one of his advisers put it, Kennedy "gained grace . . . by being himself." He did just that in October, when Harris Wofford reported the incarceration in Georgia for a traffic violation of Martin Luther King, Jr., who had become the most powerful and dynamic figure in the movement against segregation. King's pregnant wife, Kennedy was told, was deeply worried. Without consulting his chief political advisers, who would have urged caution, Kennedy telephoned Mrs. King to reassure her. (And without his knowledge, his brother Robert called the Georgia judge to persuade him to set bail for King.) King's father told the press that he had planned to vote for Nixon, but the telephone call to his daughter-in-law changed his mind.

Every change of mind counted, for as the polls predicted, the election was very close. Kennedy received less than half the popular vote, not quite 120,000 more votes than Nixon, but a clear majority of the

HERE WE GO AGAIN

electoral college, 303 to Nixon's 219 (with 15 for Harry Byrd of Virginia). Kennedy ran behind his party, which held both houses of Congress, though the Republicans and conservative southerners retained the strength to block progressive legislation. Kennedy's narrow victory, as Nixon saw it, owed more to dissatisfaction with the economy than to the Democratic campaign. But Kennedy had won the White House. As he realized, he had no effective mandate. Indeed, when those who did not vote as well as those who voted for Nixon were taken into account, the electorate seemed more complacent than concerned. Nevertheless, Kennedy believed what he had told the Democratic Convention: "The New Frontier is here whether we seek it or not . . . unsolved problems of peace and war, unconquered pockets of ignorance and prejudice, unanswered questions of poverty and surplus." To rectify those conditions, he meant to organize and utilize the power of the federal government, of the presidency in particular. He had yet to discover how strong was the inertia he would have to overcome.

1

Legacies

Like any newly elected president, John F. Kennedy could not start his administration with a clean slate. The policies of his predecessor had a momentum that even energetic leadership and intelligent intentions could not quickly reverse. So it was, for one telling example, in the case of the Congo. Kennedy was eager to cultivate the new regimes in Africa, as he was to do successfully in Guinea and Ghana. In his view, Eisenhower had been excessively solicitous of European colonial interests, particularly of Belgian mining concessions in Katanga, a copper-rich province of the Congo. Belgian agents were fanning a secessionist movement in Katanga and encouraging factionalism elsewhere in the nation. Those objectives depended in part on the elimination of Patrice Lumumba, the erratic but determined leader of the Congo nationalists. To that end the CIA station chief in Léopoldville, the Congo capital, had cooperated in the kidnapping of Lumumba, whom he considered a "Soviet instrument."

Kennedy interpreted the disorder in the Congo as an expression of emergent nationalism rather than a product of a Soviet plot. But as had Eisenhower, he pledged his support to the efforts of the United Nations, which the Soviet Union opposed, to restore order in the Congo. He also promised to back a "broadly based government . . . with secession banned." As Kennedy saw it, stability in the Congo had to precede the release of Lumumba and other political prisoners who might prove disruptive. But in Léopoldville the CIA representative interpreted Kennedy's intentions as radical and called for "drastic steps" before the inauguration. With that encouragement, Lumumba's captors murdered their prisoner on January 17, 1961, two days before Kennedy took office.

It was two weeks before that news reached the horrified new president. His distress grew when word of the murder spurred anti-American riots in Africa as well as demonstrations by indignant American blacks in New York. Seizing its chance, the Soviet Union denounced the United Nations and the West as organizers of the murder and promised "all possible help" to the Congolese people. Kennedy responded as he and his advisers believed he had to if Africa was not to be abandoned to Soviet influence. A unilateral Soviet intervention, he warned, would create the "risk of war." He also threw his support to the existing government in the Congo, which was deservedly anathema to the aggressively independent rulers in Ghana and Guinea. Indeed, after the murder of Lumumba and the Soviet effort to exploit it, Kennedy's African policy subordinated sympathy for African nationalism to vigilance against Soviet intrusions. In some degree, the American CIA agent in Léopoldville had contributed to that reversion toward Eisenhower's stance. In larger measure, the exigencies of cold war politics prevailed.

1. WE BAND OF BROTHERS

Eisenhower had naturally commended his own policies to his successor. More partisan than he liked to admit, Ike before the election had disparaged Kennedy as little better than a machine politician. After the election he resented the tendency of the press to treat Kennedy as a savior. But when Kennedy visited the White House for a first briefing, his "warmth and modesty" impressed Eisenhower, as did his attentiveness. Eisenhower on that occasion stressed the importance of reducing the costs of American forces in Europe in order to relieve the increasingly unfavorable American balance of payments. He returned to that theme at their second meeting in January and to the desirability of balancing the budget, both objectives at variance with the Democratic campaign. Privately Kennedy remained dubious about that advice and about Eisenhower's views on Laos. Eisenhower opposed both unilateral American intervention in that country and support for a coalition government there. He recommended instead that the way to keep out the Chinese was "like playing poker with tough stakes." That remark suggested that a nuclear threat would deter China, exactly the course Kennedy wanted to avoid in order also to rule out nuclear retaliation and war. Kennedy came away "from that meeting feeling that the Eisenhower administration would support intervention . . . in Laos." Indeed, Ike had said: "If Laos is lost to the Free World, in the long run we will have lost all of Southeast Asia." By extension in Latin America, Eisenhower went on to urge American support, publicly, if necessary, of anti-Castro guerrillas in Cuba and to describe the CIA training of Cuban refugees for an invasion of the island at an early but undetermined date. Only days earlier he had broken off diplomatic relations with Cuba.

Eisenhower's counsel was less telling than were Kennedy's own convictions and existing political conditions, which worked toward general continuity in policy. The election had provided the new administration with no mandate, and the conservative coalition in Congress was as concerned about balancing the budget as was Eisenhower. With few exceptions, senior career officials in the State Department, the Defense Department, and the CIA were committed to the assumptions and policies of the past. For his part, Kennedy did not much disagree. Still conventional in his economics, he was as yet unpersuaded of the utility at that time of deliberate countercyclical spending, though he did favor a limited increase in defense expenditures, a modest effort to remedy the conditions of poverty, and a slight tax break for industry to stimulate private investment. He and his advisers, like those they replaced, were resolved to resist any expansion of Soviet and Chinese power in Europe or in the third world, as events in the Congo were soon to demonstrate. The national interest, military or economic, was by no means attached to every corner of the world. Nevertheless, the new president, though he said he stood for diversity, viewed the loss of any area on the globe to Communist influences as a loss to the United States. As a Democrat Kennedy also believed he could not afford politically to risk the kind of damage Truman had suffered after 1949 from the unavoidable triumph of Mao-Zedong and the Communists in China. On that account Kennedy rejected the possibility of opening diplomatic relations with the mainland Chinese and was wary of Chinese as well as Soviet ambitions in Southeast Asia.

The strength of their conventional cold war doctrines led Kennedy and his advisers to misread the major address delivered by Soviet Premier Nikita Khrushchev on January 6, 1961, two weeks before the inauguration. While expressing his belief in peaceful coexistence and his horror of nuclear war, Khrushchev predicted the victory of communism through Soviet assistance to wars of national liberation in Asia, Africa, and Latin America, "the most important centers of revolutionary struggle against imperialism." Khrushchev later wrote that he intended that statement for the Chinese, but Kennedy interpreted it as a challenge to the United States.

Kennedy's inaugural address accepted the challenge he discerned and the national sacrifice it would demand. "Let the word go forth . . ." he said, "to friend and foe alike, that the torch has been passed to a new generation of Americans, born in this century, tempered by war, disciplined by a hard and bitter peace, proud of our ancient heritage. . . . [W]e shall pay any price, bear any burden, meet any hardship, support any friend, oppose any foe to assure the survival and the success of liberty." He did not expect the emerging nations always to support American views, he continued, but he hoped they would support their own freedom. He pledged American assistance to impoverished peoples, especially in Latin America. And he matched his tone to his purpose: "Now the trumpet summons us again—not as a call to bear arms, though arms we need; not as a call to battle, though embattled we are; but a call to bear the burden of a long twilight struggle . . . against the common enemies of man: tyranny, poverty, disease and war itself."

That rhetoric obscured the private Kennedy. He was not a fire-eater, though he understood that political leadership occasionally required an oratorical intensity he could produce. Those who knew Kennedy well were struck by his composure, his self-deprecating wit, his sense of irony. J. K. Galbraith found Kennedy "completely content with his own personality." Thus his self-control, one aspect of his "cool" which his admirers tried to imitate. Arthur Schlesinger, Jr., defined Kennedy as a realist disguised as a romantic. He was also physically courageous. He had had to be to undertake his celebrated wartime rescue of his crew and, perhaps even more, to undergo while a senator complicated, dangerous and painful orthopedic surgery for his back. Though his recuperation was slow and though his back continued to bother him, neither the operation nor his Addison's disease—normally a debilitating illness—interfered with his discharge of his presidential responsibilities. "Though the patient," one physician later wrote, "had marked adrenocortical insufficiency, though the magnitude of his surgery was great, and though complications ensued postoperatively, this patient had a smooth postoperative course insofar as no Addisonian crisis ever developed." Addison's disease did not seem to affect Kennedy's womanizing. Still, those close to Kennedy, eager to protect his macho reputation, refused to concede that he had any chronic disease. As if to deny any disability, Kennedy's entourage made much of his "grace

Inaugural ball: The Kennedys enter Camelot.

under pressure"—a quality the novelist Ernest Hemingway had celebrated in his fiction. That, too, was part of Kennedy's "cool."

The Kennedys projected an aura of glamour that their public relations magnified. The new president was young, wealthy, lithe, stylish, articulate. His wife, Jacqueline, was a gracious hostess, fashionably attired, genuinely interested in the visual and performing arts, which she and the president cultivated. Though Kennedy was not an intellectual, he was interested in ideas, particularly their immediate applications.

He was a quick reader and an excellent listener. His personal flair seemed to qualify him to cope easily with matters of state. The Kennedy style, the Kennedy panache, the Kennedy confidence underlay the spirit of Camelot that surrounded the new administration from its beginning. It was a spirit of "can do" but also of elegance and debonair joy. It marked the dinner parties of the most renowned of the New Frontiersmen, and it beguiled journalists and the public alike.

Yet Camelot, in King Arthur's day and in Kennedy's, was a myth. The political realities of 1961 would not succumb to charm. And many of the knights of Kennedy's round table had no interest in seeking the grail. Indeed, Kennedy continued in office two veteran administrators long accustomed to wielding extraordinary independent power: J. Edgar Hoover, the self-agrandizing head of the Federal Bureau of Investigation, and Allen Dulles, the professionally inscrutable chief of the Central Intelligence Agency. Kennedy also chose his advisers so as to have ready access to several different kinds of counsel. The "Irish Mafia"—Kenneth O'Donnell and Lawrence O'Brien, for two—Kennedy's Massachusetts political associates for years, had a large voice in patronage, in relations with Congress and in planning the president's speaking tours. They viewed all issues through the special lenses of Kennedy's personal political interests.

In contrast, the "liberals," men the politicos considered unrealistic, served the president in various capacities, almost always as protagonists of policies somewhat to the left of his usual bent. Among others, they included Adlai Stevenson, appointed ambassador to the United Nations; Chester Bowles, appointed undersecretary of state; and Arthur Schlesinger, Jr., one of the senior White House staff. Bowles, Schlesinger, and Galbraith, now the ambassador to India, had been major figures in the Americans for Democratic Action. Kennedy turned, too, to the more conservative ranks of business and finance, from which he selected Robert McNamara, president of the Ford Motor Company, now appointed secretary of defense, and Douglas Dillon, a New York Republican investment banker who had served under Eisenhower, now made secretary of the treasury. Both McNamara and Dillon were to exercise large influence on national policy. From the academic world, apart from Schlesinger, Kennedy chose three talented Keynesian economists for his Council of Economic Advisers and the impressive dean of the Harvard Faculty of Arts and Sciences, McGeorge Bundy, a professor of government and titularly a Republican, as national security adviser. An economic historian from MIT, Walt W. Rostow, who had conducted several studies for the CIA, served under Bundy. For secretary of state, an office he intended largely to command himself, Kennedy selected Dean Rusk, a bland establishment figure who was the head of the Rockefeller Foundation and a former assistant secretary for Asian affairs during the Truman administration. Kennedy's two closest advisers remained, as they had long been, not least during the campaign, Theodore Sorensen, White House special counsel, and Robert Kennedy, the president's brother, who now became attorney general. The younger Kennedy recruited an extraordinary staff for the Justice Department and provided important counsel on domestic politics, civil rights, and foreign affairs. He also contributed his special mixture of skepticism and compassion both to the councils of the New Frontier and to the playing fields of Camelot.

Many of the men close to Kennedy, particularly the younger men, had grown up in comfortable families; attended prestigious independent boarding schools like Choate, Exeter, and Groton; and graduated from outstanding colleges and universities, Harvard and Yale among them. The privileges they had had and the success they had achieved accounted for the frequent description of them as "the best and the brightest." Latter-day critics of their decisions gave that phrase a pejorative twist. It was meant originally to flatter. But Kennedy and his advisers had other, more significant common elements in their personal backgrounds. For one example, they remembered the New Deal, some with enthusiasm, the others at least with tolerance, as an important era in American reform. They also vividly remembered the Second World War and the episodes of appeasement of Hitler that contributed to its outbreak. Like others of their generation, they had tended, as they continued to, to dress the chiefs of the Soviet state in Hitler's garb and to interpret any compromise with communism as akin to appeasement. The president and the most incisive of his counselors were prepared to accept evidence to modify that view; but the process was to take time, and some senior New Frontiersmen had little inclination to learn. Even the best and the brightest, as their critics sometimes forgot, were necessarily fallible men.

Still, they did have a certain cockiness. They believed that whatever the contest, their administration, their country, their team deserved to be number one. Told that he was often tendentious, one of them had replied, as if for them all, by asking what was wrong with being tendentious. Another new Frontiersman described them all succinctly: "We were activists. We thought the world could be changed. We thought one man could make a difference. . . . Pragmatic, idealistic, activist." For his part, the president liked to quote from Shakespeare's Henry V: "we . . . shall be remembered;/We few, We happy few, we band of brothers. . . . And gentlemen in England now a-bed/Shall think themselves accursed they were not here. . . ." That passage caught the confidence of the New Frontiersmen, many of them young, lieutenants during World War II, now colonels and generals in command. They gladly undertook to invigorate government and to remake the country and the world. Kennedy was not interested in a neat package of proposals. He welcomed differences of opinion among his advisers so that after reflection, he could make his own decisions. The Kennedy system was vulnerable because so much depended on the president himself. But as McGeorge Bundy later recalled, the system usually worked "because we respected each other and we respected the President, and vice versa, the President respected us."

2. IMPEDANCE ON THE HILL

Early and late, Kennedy also respected the constraints of circumstance and attitude that made politics the art of the possible. Asked on one occasion why his negotiations with the president of Panama were faltering, he replied: "He says we've been screwing them all these years, and I agree." He was no less realistic about his opposition in Congress. A majority of Democrats were ready to support the administration's domestic program, but in the House of Representatives the southerners, joined by the Republicans, had the votes to defeat it. Reluctant to ask for legislation he could not get, the president tried to woo the Dixie congressmen. To that end he employed the tools he had: patronage; pleas for party unity; promises of local public works or military facilities. To the dismay of the leaders of the civil rights movement, Kennedy excluded civil rights from the list of measures he recommended. That left him with a familiar Democratic agenda of incremental reforms: increased federal aid for housing and education, federally supported medical care, federal assistance for depressed areas, and an increase in the level and coverage of minimum wages.

To effect those limited but important ends, the administration had first to gain control of the House Rules Committee, a bastion of the conservative southerners. The Rules Committee decided what legislation could reach the floor of the House for debate, and in what order. Dominated by its chairman, the veteran Virginia Democrat Judge Howard W. Smith, the committee had consistently buried reform measures. Smith, cooperating with the Republican leadership, could rely on one other southern Democrat and four Republicans to join him in order to provide six of the committee's twelve votes. The resulting tie, as Kennedy said, guaranteed that "nothing controversial would come to the floor of the Congress. Our whole program would be emasculated."

With Speaker Sam Rayburn leading the fight on the Hill, the administration moved to increase the size of the committee to fifteen. Rayburn could then appoint two liberal Democrats as well as one Republican, who would give the administration an eight to seven majority. But with the assistance of powerful lobbyists, including those of the National Association of Manufacturers (NAM) and the American Medical Association (AMA), Charles Halleck, the Republican leader, fought back. He promised if he won to conduct "business as usual" with Judge Smith and to defeat Kennedy's "radical, wild-eyed, spendthrift proposals." The showdown came with a roll call vote on

January 31, 1961. By a narrow margin, 217 to 212, the administration won. Kennedy knew the apparent victory signified trouble. "With Rayburn's own reputation at stake," he remarked, "with all of the pressures and appeals a new President could make, we won by five votes. That shows what we're up against."

That assessment received an early test in the contest over the administration's education bill. Education, Theodore Sorensen wrote, was "the one domestic subject that mattered most to John Kennedy. . . . He linked education to our military, scientific and economic strength." As a candidate he had stood for generous federal aid to public education. The National Defense Education Act of 1958 had made a small start toward assistance for colleges and universities, but Kennedy had criticized its inadequacies and called particularly for extending aid to public schools. In February 1961 he sent Congress a special message asking for $2.3 billion in grants to the states for use over three years at each state's discretion for the construction of schools or for teachers' salaries, or for both. The president prudently requested only half the funds his special task force on the issue had recommended. To placate the South, he did not make federal aid conditional upon desegregation, a concession deeply disappointing to civil rights advocates. The administration's formula for granting aid took into account both the relative wealth or poverty of each state, a factor favorable to the South, and the average daily school attendance in the state, a factor attractive to states with large cities, most of them Democratic strongholds. The education bill, all in all, was a temperate measure, crafted for success.

On one matter Kennedy would not compromise. During his campaign he had opposed federal aid to Catholic schools. As did many Americans, he believed the Constitution prohibited it, expressly in the injunction of the First Amendment against the establishment of any religion. The cynical had argued that he could in any case be sure of the Catholic vote, but there was much more in his position than that. As president, especially as the first president who was a Catholic, Kennedy was resolved to hold to his interpretation of the law even though many other Catholics disagreed with him. Francis Cardinal Spellman of New York, for one, an eminent conservative in the church, said in January 1961 that it was "unthinkable" to deny any child federal funds offered to other children "because his parents chose for him a God-connected education." Their anxieties aroused by that statement, some of the president's advisers urged him to leave the question to Congress. Instead, in his special message he referred explicitly to "the clear position of the Constitution" against aid to any religious school, Catholic or otherwise. On March 2, 1961, the administrative board of the National Catholic Welfare Congress, a board including eight bishops and archbishops and several cardinals, contradicted the president by calling for "low interest loans to private institutions," which the prelates considered "within the framework of the Constitution." They declared: "In the event that there is federal aid to education, we are deeply convinced that in justice Catholic school children should be given the right to participate."

The administration's fragile political advantage in the House could not sustain the additional weight of the religious issue. With Majority leader John McCormack among those Catholics who deserted the president, the education bill had no chance of enactment. But Kennedy would not alter his course. Protestant opposition to aid to Catholic schools was sufficient to defeat any separate measure for that purpose. And Judge Howard Smith, still a powerful figure, attacked the president's bill as an attempt "to aid the N.A.A.C.P. and complete the subjugation of the South." That illogic would have prevailed on the floor of the House had not the bill died instead, ironically, in the Rules Committee itself. There a Catholic Democrat from New York City joined Judge Smith and the other conservatives in an eight to seven vote that buried the administration's education program. Kennedy naturally resented the religious aspects of the bill's defeat, but he knew where the basic problem lay. In keeping with the views of their colleagues, five Republicans and two southern Democrats on the Rules Committee had voted against the measure. "That's who really killed the bill," Kennedy said, ". . . not the Catholics." Fundamentally the loss reflected the decisions of the voters who had neglected to send to Congress enough supporters for the president they had chosen.

That liability also accounted for the defeat in the House of the administration's bill to increase the minimum wage and extend its coverage. In his campaign Kennedy had made much of those objectives, but opposition in the House forced concessions that trivialized his original recommendations. The Senate, however, supported the president, and the House ultimately accepted a measure close to the administration's standards, though it failed to protect the poor workers. That was also the case of the bill the White House supported for area redevelopment. This relatively noncontroversial measure, richer in promise than in funding, received necessary votes from southern congressmen eager to help the affected Appalachian regions of their states. In contrast they joined conservatives in the House to weaken the manpower development and training bill and prevent its enactment in 1961.

Peace Corps volunteer: Symbol of American hope.

Meanwhile, Kennedy's proposal for Medicare had run up against the fatal opposition of Wilbur Mills, the Arkansas Democrat who was chairman of the House Ways and Means Committee, where the Republicans and southern Democrats controlled a majority. With the AMA financing the lobby against Medicare, that measure failed.

During Kennedy's first year in office the administration could not wholly offset those losses in spite of its most acclaimed initiatives. As Kennedy had put it, "If the free society cannot help the many who are poor, it cannot save the few who are rich." In that light, Robert Kennedy asked David Hackett, a close friend, to give priority attention to juvenile crime. Hackett adopted the ideas of sociologists who argued that reorganization of slum communities would provide the key to eliminating delinquency. Poverty and racial discrimination, in that view, lay at the heart of the problem. So convinced, Hackett and his associates established Mobilization for Youth, an experimental program in New York City that combined vocational training, community centers, and legal services for the poor in order to help them find exits from poverty. Later expanded to other cities, the program involved the poor in shaping their own future, then a novel approach and an important model.

The president early in 1961 also established the Peace Corps under his dedicated brother-in-law Sargent Shriver. That organization recruited thousands of idealistic young Americans to teach literacy and agricultural, mechanical, and other essential skills to farmers and villagers in poor nations throughout the world. Although the culture of the young volunteers sometimes clashed with indigenous mores, the Peace Corps quickly became a symbol of American hope and striving, so popular that it won the endorsement even of Senator Barry Goldwater, the spokesman of the Republican right. The corps also later served as a model for its equivalent for needy domestic communities, Volunteers in Service to America (VISTA), which Kennedy created in 1963. The luster of Camelot that attached to those undertakings nevertheless contrasted with the administration's dull record on the Hill. Indeed, some disappointed critics late in 1961 viewed Kennedy as a younger, Democratic Eisenhower.

3. FALSE STARTS

In foreign and military policy, the new president and his advisers had begun to develop doctrines that in their view contrasted significantly with Eisenhower's, but as in Africa, so elsewhere they were inhibited by their legacies. The resulting interplay between the theoretical and the practicable influenced Kennedy's major decisions particularly during his first year in office.

Averse though they were to ideology, which they associated primarily with the Marxist left, the New Frontiersmen nevertheless developed theories about national security that rested upon assumptions that often deserved more reconsideration than they received. Some of those theories also had a kind of Hegelian quality, an origin at least partly explicable as an obverse of what Eisenhower had stood for. So it was in the case of the doctrine of massive retaliation of Eisenhower's secretary of state John Foster Dulles. Eisenhower had cut the military budget partly on the basis of Dulles's theory that the threat of nuclear attack would deter aggression anywhere in the world. In one case the United States had countered a Chinese challenge to Quemoy and Matsu, small islands controlled by Taiwan, by using that threat. Kennedy and his advisers considered that kind of reaction clumsy and dangerous. The Soviet Union by 1961 was approaching nuclear parity with the United States. Recourse to nuclear warfare over some relatively small and localized issue could result needlessly in nuclear retaliation and the destructiveness of a major war. Consequently, Kennedy sought a new approach to protecting national interests.

The Department of Defense under Robert McNamara worked out the basic principles of the resulting doctrine of flexible response. It called for meeting any conventional attack from the Soviet Union in Europe by the use of conventional NATO forces. But when the Europeans, largely because of the cost, later declined to join the United States in building up those forces, nuclear weapons remained crucial to NATO strategy. Further, those weapons had a major place in McNamara's global strategy, which envisaged their use to strike military rather than civilian targets, though cities nevertheless remained hostages to any ensuing escalation. McNamara's defense budget had to cover the needs of both flexible response and nuclear readiness. Kennedy had, of course, campaigned for more defense spending. Almost immediately he launched a program that included a 45 percent increase in the number of army divisions, a 50 percent increase in the construction of Polaris submarines, a 100 percent increase in productive capacity for Minutemen missiles, and a 100 percent increase in the number of nuclear weapons in the nation's strategic alert forces. That was mammoth expansion even by the standards of the most dedicated cold warriors. The Soviet Union predictably met those developments with larger expenditures of its own. By late 1961 the intensification of the arms race had resulted in only questionable gains in national security.

Neither nuclear war nor conventional forces fitted the requirements of Kennedy's purpose in developing areas of the world. To resist Soviet or Chinese attempts at control or subversion there, he had been attracted to a concept of counterinsurgency that caught the enthusiasm of some of his advisers, Robert Kennedy and Walt Rostow especially. One aficionado of the concept, as it was to be elaborated, described it as "those military, paramilitary, political, economic, psychological, and civic actions taken by a government to defeat subversive activity." As a senior military commander put it, "what the President had in mind was . . . a dynamic national strategy;—an action program designed to defeat the Communist without recourse to the hazard or the terror of nuclear war; one designed to defeat subversion . . . and, even more . . . to prevent it." In "any other form of warfare," the argument continued, "the payoff is measured primarily in the shooting. In the war against insurgency . . . when the shooting starts, the tide of battle has already run far in the wrong direction."

Yet predictably the shooting did frequently start, for the doctrine of counterinsurgency lent itself to distortion and to militarization. The assumptions underlying the theory brushed aside conflicting realities. Few of the emerging nations had genuinely democratic governments committed to social reform. Indigenous resistance to authoritarian clients of the United States therefore reflected legitimate aspirations. To be sure, China and the Soviet Union continually exploited that urge for resistance to their own ends, but nationalism in the developing world sometimes merged spontaneously with Marxist ideology as a function of general disenchantment with European colonial and capitalistic powers. Often indigenous counterguerrilla units, trained and assisted by Americans, were necessary to protect client states from Communist take-overs. It was then a small step from supplying American advice and assistance to supplying American troops and aviators. Indeed, that was the mission of the American counterinsurgency forces, like the Green Berets, that Kennedy organized. Once committed to any area, those forces were quickly exposed to dangers that in their turn created a momentum toward escalation. Even a strong president would find that momentum hard to resist, as Kennedy was to find it hard, for once Americans were engaged in action, their countrymen by and large expected them to win. In practice, counterinsurgency measures soon became indistinguishable from sheer military intervention by the United States.

Kennedy hoped, of course, that American technical and economic assistance to developing nations would help them utilize their resources, improve the standard of living of their people, and strengthen the independence of their governments. In considerable measure, the theory behind those objectives derived from Walt W. Rostow's *Stages of Economic Growth* (1960). That book reflected the assertive self-confidence of its author, who had earlier written an influential study of the British economy in the nineteenth century. Rostow interpreted the British and American experiences as models for economic growth everywhere. Though many eminent economists had strong reservations about Rostow's theorizing, his work came to provide a metaphor for American policy. But Rostow's formulas continually crashed on political obstacles. The patterns of British and American economic development that he discerned had depended in large degree on the economic neutrality or cooperation of democratic governments in countries relatively free of internal strife. That development had depended also on the willingness of the middle class to reinvest much of its earnings in the economy of the nation in which it lived and to share, however grudgingly, both land and income with a working force that would otherwise have been hopelessly impoverished. Those conditions simply did not exist in many of the nations of Asia, Africa, and Latin America. In those countries authoritarian governments, afraid of internal revolt, were controlled by hierarchies of landlords and the military who opposed redistribution of land or wealth; they had only small middle classes, and they tended to expatriate their capital. Furthermore, as Chester Bowles and J. K. Galbraith agreed, economic growth was a "disruptive process" that did not automatically lead to political stability. On the contrary, an increase in gross national product (GNP), unless accompanied by democratization, could widen the gap between rich and poor and, in so doing, foster political unrest. Those conditions accompanied many American programs of economic aid, while military aid, which Congress preferred to supply, almost invariably sustained the status quo. There was no way short of outright American domination to impose enough controls on economic assistance to make that assistance work as Rostow theorized it would. Indeed, Kennedy himself came to describe the "real purpose" of economic assistance as the enhancement of "national security by contributing to the development of economic, political and military strength of countries whose independence is important to our own."

Always attuned to the practical rather than the theoretical, Kennedy recognized that a program of economic aid and cooperation could improve relations between the United States and Latin America and might also induce Latin American governments to move toward social reform, particularly a wider and more equitable distribution of landholdings. In October 1960, after extensive preparation, he had called upon the United States and the nations of Latin America to join together "in an alliance for progress . . . a great common effort to develop the resources of the entire hemisphere, strengthen the forces of democracy, and widen the vocational and educational opportunities of every person in all the Americas." The proposed *Alianza para el Progreso* had a defensive as well as a generous purpose. As Kennedy's task force on Latin America reported in 1961, American policy had "to divide the inevitable and necessary Latin American social transformation from connection with and prevent its capture by overseas Communist power politics." To that end the United States, Kennedy also believed, had to be prepared to provide military support to friendly regimes threatened by communism. Some of those regimes were patently reactionary. Yet the *Alianza,* as its foremost proponents saw it, was designed primarily to promote the interdependent goals of political democracy, economic growth, and social reform. Consequently, its purpose contrasted with

Fidel Castro: Kennedy hoped to topple him.

predictable military expedients. Indeed, the spirit and the potentialities of the *Alianza* were threatened from the first by the invasion of Cuba that the CIA had begun to plan under Eisenhower.

Kennedy could have canceled that operation. The Cuban émigrés training in Guatemala, both disenchanted Fidelistas and vindictive reactionaries, could not have proceeded without American training and equipment. If the operation had been scrubbed, the disappointed Cubans, prone as they were to self-serving rumors, would surely have accused the new administration of timidity. Even for a president zeal-ous of his reputation for courage, that potential accusation should not have been enough to protect a losing tactic. But Kennedy seemed to see Castro almost as a personal enemy. Though without apparent enthusiasm, he appeared from the first prepared to permit the plan-ning of an invasion to go on. He particularly hoped to topple the Castro government before it could gain further strength in Cuba and influ-ence in Latin America. The senior CIA officers advising him, Allen Dulles and Richard Bissell, both holdovers from the past but both also men notable for their previous acumen, expressed total confidence in their plans. The Joint Chiefs of Staff were equivocal. They presup-posed conditions they did not sufficiently spell out to the president, especially control of the air by American planes during and immedi-ately after the landing. The Cuban exiles expected guerrilla assistance and popular approval in Cuba, though at no time did the White House authorize continuing air support or did Cuban security permit a significant uprising. Kennedy for his part had yet to learn how much to discount his various sources of counsel. Like his personal staff, he still "listened with a beginner's credulity to the arguments" of the "eager promoters of the operation."

The president paid little heed to the opponents of the plan. Arthur Schlesinger, Jr., for one, made a case against the scheme on tactical grounds. The United States, he argued, would be held accountable for the success of the invasion, and that success would entail protracted military engagement. General David Shoup, commandant of the Marine Corps, warned that conquering Cuba would require huge casualties. Chester Bowles, the undersecretary of state for political affairs, considered the "Cuban adventure . . . profoundly disturbing." He wrote Secretary of State Rusk: "Our national interests are poorly served by a covert operation . . . when our new President is effectively appealing to world opinion on the basis of high principle. . . . We would be deliberately violating the fundamental obligations we assumed in . . . establishing the Organization of American States. . . . This . . . would be an act of war." But Rusk disagreed with Bowles, and the president, who considered Bowles something of a visionary, rejected the similar advice of J. William Fulbright, chairman of the Senate Foreign Relations Committee. "To give this activity even covert support," Fulbright warned, "is of a piece with the hypocrisy and cynicism for which the United States is constantly denouncing the Soviet Union. . . . This point will not be lost on the rest of the world—nor on our own consciences."

The point did not much move men like Vice President Johnson and Secretary of Defense McNamara, who, as Bowles observed, were innocent of experience in foreign affairs and therefore easy targets "for the military-CIA-paramilitary type answers." Their support confirmed Kennedy's decision, less than two months after the inauguration, to let the invasion proceed.

The operation was a disaster. While the ships carrying the invaders moved toward their beachhead, antiquated B-26 bombers, supplied by the CIA to anti-Castro pilots, took off from Nicaragua to strike Cuban airfields but failed to reach their targets. Cuban photographs of the bombers shattered the CIA's cover story for the flights, but only after Adlai Stevenson, whom the White House had deliberately misinformed, had told a United Nations (UN) committee that the planes were Castro's. By that time it had become obvious that they were not. Only then did Secretary Rusk decide that no second air strike could go

Captives from the Bay of Pigs: They had fought valiantly.

forward from Nicaragua without further embarrassing the United States. Kennedy agreed and canceled any second strike. His decision doomed the already faltering operation.

There was even greater confusion at the Bay of Pigs. Small craft foundered on coral reefs the CIA had not charted. Castro's jet aircraft, which the CIA had underestimated, harassed the landing, sank one ship carrying reserve ammunition, and shot down four overpowered B-26s. Castro's police detained some two hundred thousand suspects who had no chance to resist, much less to help the invaders. For nearly three days the Cubans who had landed fought on, pinned to their position until they were captured or killed.

The ineffectuality of the first air strike had alerted Kennedy to the impending fiasco. He had earlier assured the press that under no conditions would there be "any intervention in Cuba by United States armed forces." In spite of the catastrophic landing, he rejected the military's advice to send in the marines. He knew he had made a grave mistake in authorizing the mission, and he knew better than to compound it. As Theodore Sorensen, Kennedy's special counsel, later wrote, the president had been "stunned by each . . . revelation of how wrong he had been in his expectations and assumptions."

As Bowles and Fulbright had warned, Kennedy had misused Amer-

ican power. Not Castro's often cruel dictatorship, or his commitment
to encouraging revolution elsewhere in the hemisphere, or even his
closeness to Moscow excused the method selected to oppose him. The
problem in Cuba had not been one of national security. Rather, the
problem was psychological, one of national insecurity or at least of the
administration's insecurity, its anxiety about the loss of control over a
small and weak country that the United States was accustomed to
dominating. Success at the Bay of Pigs could have become as embarrassing as failure, just as Fulbright had said, for it would have damaged the reputation of the United States, and it might have provoked
Soviet retaliation in Europe, especially if American troops had been
tied down in Cuba for any considerable time. In the event the failure,
compounded by the clumsiness of the operation, damaged the reputation and the credibility of the president. "How could I have been so
stupid," Kennedy asked Sorensen, "to let them go ahead?" Appropriately he blamed himself. "I am the responsible officer of the government," the president told the press, "and that is quite obvious."

In the wake of the episode American anxiety about Castro grew, not
the least within the administration. Kennedy was determined to find
some way to arrange the release of the 1113 prisoners taken at the Bay
of Pigs, an objective reached only after two years of negotiation. He
immediately took steps to improve his sources of counsel and intelligence. He reorganized his staff by moving McGeorge Bundy into the
White House as coordinator of national security affairs. He had not
included Sorensen or Robert Kennedy in the major discussions of policy preceding the Bay of Pigs; thereafter he counted on their advice in
every crisis. He appointed General Maxwell Taylor, long an advocate
of a tough but flexible military policy, whom he knew and trusted, his
personal adviser on military affairs. Soon Kennedy shook up the Joint
Chiefs of Staff and the CIA, with John McCone, a Republican and an
exceptional administrator, taking charge in the latter agency and Dulles
and Bissell leaving it. He also resumed the regular meetings of the
National Security Council, which he had at first thought unnecessary.
In November 1961 he reorganized the State Department by transferring several officers there in order to bring in some of his own staff
members, including Richard Goodwin, a strong supporter of the *Alianza*,
as deputy assistant secretary for Latin American affairs, and Walt Rostow as head of Policy Planning. One victim of those changes was Chester Bowles, whose friends had talked too much about his virtue in
opposing the Bay of Pigs. Removed as undersecretary, he reluctantly
accepted Kennedy's appointment first as a special representative to

developing areas and then as ambassador to India, a position to which he brought his broad human sympathies.

The departure of Bowles from the State Department removed a liberal dissenter from a position of influence. Though he continued to express his opinion, the hard-liners in the department and elsewhere—especially former Secretary of State Dean Acheson, his admirers, and Secretary Rusk—found Bowles easy to ignore. So did the president, who, as he told one friend, was acting "as his own Secretary of State." No one was listening when Bowles warned that only "self-delusion" permitted the assumption that the shah would carry out "reforms in depth" in Iran; that it was time to take "necessary economic and political steps to prepare for the end of the existing Panama Canal treaty." As before, Bowles proved incisive about Castro. "As a military threat," he wrote, "Castro can be eliminated any time we feel forced to do so. The difficult challenge he holds for us is as a rallying point for anti-American, Communist, and other extreme sentiments." The Alliance for Progress was supposed to contain Castro's influence. But, as Bowles argued, "some of the most economically and politically backward nations in Latin America will be among those most willing to back our anti-Castro position. . . . They will then expect substantial economic assistance from us without regard to . . . internal reforms. . . . If we allow those nations to exploit the Castro situation . . . we will . . . undermine the integrity of the entire program." As Arthur Schlesinger observed, after the Bay of Pigs Kennedy "turned from the people he had inherited in government to the people he had brought in himself." Bowles had been Kennedy's own appointment, but the others the president dropped were holdovers from the past.

The president could not so easily dispose of the rest of his legacy. The humiliation of the Bay of Pigs cost Kennedy prestige with friendly governments in Europe and Latin America. It encouraged the Russians to lower their estimate of his resolve. It persuaded his domestic opponents on the left that he was an old-style imperialist and those on his right that he was afraid of a fight. Vice President Johnson privately concluded, so it later appeared, that Kennedy should have used all the force necessary for success. For his part, the President knew he could not afford another failure. His determination to avoid one accounted for a hardening of his position on issues that Khrushchev was in any case pressing, issues relating to Laos and to Berlin.

4. VIENNA

During the transition between administrations Eisenhower and Kennedy spent more time discussing the "mess" in Laos than any other issue. In the previous five years Eisenhower had prevented Prince Souvanna Phouma, a moderate, from entering a coalition government with the Pathet Lao, a movement of Communist guerrillas receiving support from the Soviet Union. That policy proceeded from the belief that any coalition would take a neutralist position in the cold war, an eventuality Eisenhower was eager to prevent. He still harbored two assumptions, both false or moot: one, that the Communist Chinese in the area were agents of the Soviet Union; the other, that the loss of Laos (or of any other Southeast Asian state) would lead to the loss of the entire area and thus endanger American security. On that account, the CIA set up a pro-Western regime in Vientiane to which the Eisenhower adminstration sent almost three hundred million dollars in aid, primarily military. In the years 1956–1960 Laos received more American aid per capita than did any other country. That bonanza served largely to finance graft and corruption in Vientiane and to subsidize a pro-American army notable for its reluctance to fight.

Though Kennedy was eager to modify Eisenhower's policy, he subscribed, as Ike had, to the theory that made every client country crucial to the outcome of the cold war. If the United States did nothing and the Pathet Lao prevailed, Kennedy feared it would demoralize other small nations, particularly in the area that the United States had prom-

Chester Bowles: Liberal dissenter.

ised to protect, and thereby increase their vulnerability to communism. Eisenhower had put American prestige on the line in Laos, as he had elsewhere, and Kennedy did not intend to damage it. The question of credibility, of the reliability of American guarantees to client states, had its exact counterpart in the Soviet Union, where Khrushchev was no more willing than was Kennedy to risk his or his country's reputation, "grandeur" as he called it. Only in that sense did either major power have a national interest in Laos, a small, undeveloped, mountainous country whose people had no warlike inclinations.

So persuaded, according to his special counsel, Kennedy was loath to send American forces to Laos, though most of the military and intelligence staff he inherited favored that course. His best approach, he concluded, was to negotiate with the Soviet Union to establish a neutralist government. But the predictable opposition to that policy from the American right, which considered it a capitulation to communism, recommended a delay in negotiations until a cease-fire in Laos could stop the gains the Pathet Lao were making. Those factors occasioned the equivocations in Kennedy's statement to the press in March 1961. "Laos is far away," he said, "but . . . its own safety runs with the safety of us all." Yet he would accept, he added, "a truly neutralist government . . . a settlement concluded at the conference table, not on the battlefield." A coalition under Souvanna Phouma, he had been assured by friends he trusted, would adopt a truly neutralist position.

As Kennedy put it to Walter Lippmann at about that time, "We cannot and will not accept any visible humiliation in Laos." The humiliation occurred instead at the Bay of Pigs. That episode also soured Kennedy on those advisers who advocated a military solution in Laos, particularly when they responded to his questions about Laos with confused and bellicose proposals. Kennedy did alert American forces in the area when the Pathet Lao resumed attack, but he also applied heavy diplomatic pressure to bring Khrushchev to negotiate. Because the Russian, too, saw no real national interest in Laos, the tactic worked. When the two men met in Vienna in June 1961, they agreed in principle on a neutralization of Laos. In spite of continuing skirmishing there, in 1962 the United States and the Soviet Union completed a formal accord that established a coalition government under Souvanna. That coalition did not endure because Laos became embroiled in the uninterrupted hostilities in neighboring Vietnam. Still, though its effect was temporary and circumscribed, the experiment represented a small victory for reason and restraint. As Kennedy said to Sorensen in the fall of 1961, "Thank God the Bay of Pigs happened when it did. Otherwise we'd be in Laos . . . and that would be a hundred times worse."

The meeting in Vienna also addressed the conflict of Soviet and American policies in Germany. That question had troubled Soviet-American relations since World War II, when the two nations and Great Britain and France had agreed to occupy Germany, each in a separate zone. During the years that followed, the cooperation the four powers had at first expected gave way to the cold war. The Americans, British, and French merged their zones, the western part of Germany, which they soon thereafter recognized as the independent, democratic German Federal Republic, a crucial member of NATO. The eastern, Russian zone became the Communist German Democratic Republic, a major ally of the Russians in their Warsaw Pact. The city of Berlin, which lay entirely within East Germany, had meanwhile remained divided, as the wartime agreements had foreshadowed, between Eastern and Western rule.

By 1961 Khrushchev faced urgent problems in Germany. The conditions of political freedom and prosperity in the Federal Republic induced increasing thousands of East Germans to flee to the West, most of them through Berlin. Those escapes arose from deep dissatisfaction behind the iron curtain and implicitly criticized Soviet rule. Sensitive to that criticism, Khrushchev doubtless also felt threatened by Kennedy's request to Congress in April for funds to enlarge both nuclear and conventional American forces.

The Bay of Pigs, while heightening Kennedy's concern about losing face, did not deter Khrushchev from accepting an invitation the president had sent him in February for a private meeting, scheduled for June in Vienna. Perhaps Khrushchev expected his customary bluster to shake Kennedy. But except for the agreement about Laos, the discussions at Vienna settled nothing. As Kennedy later told the American people, the sessions were "useful" but "somber." Kennedy stood for preserving the existing worldwide balance of power so as to reduce tensions and diminish chances for a nuclear war. But the status quo that Kennedy postulated conflicted with Khrushchev's Marxist views. Khrushchev argued that the status quo was in flux, with subject peoples reaching toward self-assertion under communism. "Superficially polite," Khrushchev, according to Ambassador Charles Bohlen, who was there, ". . . set forth some hard positions. . . . The President . . . assumed that the position was the . . . fixed position of the Soviet Union. . . . However, he didn't lose his sense of humor and certainly not his nerve." As Kennedy later described their conversation, "We have wholly different views of right and wrong, of what is an internal affair and what is aggression, and . . . where the world is going." Khrushchev believed the force of history, Kennedy said, was "moving his way, that the revolution of rising people would eventually be a Communist revolution. . . . I believe just as strongly . . . that liberty and independence and self-determination—not communism—is the future of man."

Those differences found an immediate expression over the issue of East Germany and Berlin. As he had before Khrushchev in Vienna threatened to sign a separate peace treaty with East Germany that would make Berlin a free city and terminate Western occupation rights there. The East Germans could then cut off access to Berlin from the Federal Republic and contain escapees to the West. The precedent of American solicitude for Berlin and the protection of Western rights in that city moved Kennedy sharply to oppose Khrushchev's threat. When Khrushchev at their last session said that his decision about signing a separate treaty with East Germany in December was final, Kennedy replied: "It will be a cold winter."

Before the Vienna meeting Kennedy had appointed a task force on Germany under Dean Acheson, the major architect of American postwar policy in Europe and still an unrelenting exponent of cold war attitudes. Though the president also listened to his more temperate White House advisers and to Prime Minister Harold Macmillan of Great Britain, he considered Khrushchev's designs on Berlin a step toward the neutralization of West Germany and ultimately all of Western Europe. That reading accorded with Acheson's belief that the Russians were "testing the American will to resist." On that premise and at the urging of Secretary of Defense McNamara, Kennedy requested another increase in military spending, called up 120,000 reservists, and launched a program to build shelters against nuclear attack. The shelter program served only to frighten some Americans and to delude others about their chances of surviving a nuclear war. Further, partly because of pressure from his rivals within the Politburo, Khrushchev announced additional Soviet expenditures for both missiles and conventional arms. But Khrushchev from the first controlled Soviet policy in Berlin so as to prevent a nuclear confrontation with the United States. Now, as he and Kennedy exchanged public statements about Berlin, Kennedy tempered his belligerent rhetoric with conciliatory references to nonmilitary solutions.

The crisis came to a head in mid-August 1961, when East German forces took over most of the crossing points in East Berlin and several days later began building a concrete wall to block further flight to the

West. As Kennedy knew, East Germany had the right to close its border. He wisely allowed Khrushchev that minimum objective. With the governments of West Germany and West Berlin in agreement with his decision, Kennedy limited his protest against the "brutal border closing" to the dispatch to Berlin of fifteen hundred troops, a token force, and to sending Vice President Johnson to reassure West Berliners about the American commitment to their freedom. During September the crisis receded, with Khrushchev drawing back from a separate treaty of peace with East Germany and Kennedy satisfied that he had yielded no American rights in Berlin. The United States and the Soviet Union began official exploratory talks about the city, and Khrushchev initiated a private correspondence with Kennedy. In Germany, as in different ways in Cuba and Laos, the jousting between the superpowers had continued, leaving them no closer than they had long been to either peace or war.

That outcome was not foreordained. General Maxwell Taylor had advised Kennedy early in September that Khrushchev seemed intent upon "using military force, or the threat thereof, to gain his ends in Berlin. . . . Thus far our own defense efforts have been deliberately kept in a low key. . . . I have a strong feeling that the moment has come

The Berlin wall: A "brutal border closing."

to shift into a higher gear." Had Kennedy done so, the storm over Berlin would probably have worsened, with the predictable consequence of strengthening the hands of the militants in the Soviet Union as well as in the United States. As it was, George Kennan, whom Kennedy had appointed ambassador to Yugoslavia, blamed the president and other Western leaders for failing to come forward with new ideas about Germany. In "real anguish of spirit," Kennan wrote Bowles: "It is quite clear that the Russians suspect us simply of stalling; and so long as they suspect that this is our game . . . things are going to continue to get worse." But Kennedy did agree to discuss Berlin, as Kennan hoped he would, though not the neutralization of a reunited Germany that Kennan had long favored. Operating somewhere between the preference of men like Acheson and Taylor, on the one hand, and Kennan and Bowles, on the other, the president, as it worked out, continued essentially along the course Eisenhower had followed. That did not invariably assure a safe landing.

5. "A CAN OF SNAKES"

Kennedy's sense of rivalry with the Soviet Union mixed with his natural competitiveness and his zest for adventure to inform his space program. As a candidate he had fretted about the Soviet lead in the "space race" to which he attributed "world-wide political and psychological" importance. His postelection task force on space warned him the Russians would soon put a man into space, as they did in April 1961, when Yuri Gagarin made the first orbital flight. Kennedy then set up a Space Council with Lyndon Johnson as chairman and followed its recommendations for intensifying the American program. In May he promised that the United States would land a man on the moon "before the decade is out."

The exploration of space had large scientific significance, but unmanned space vehicles would probably have served science as well as or better than did the more costly and glamorous astronauts. Kennedy's emphasis on manned flight, however, suited the military purpose of developing more thrust in American rockets and better technologies for intercontinental missiles. Military considerations were probably paramount, as Kennedy indicated by privately lumping expenditures for space and for nuclear energy with other defense costs. Khrushchev had the identical practice. But the manned space program also neatly fitted Kennedy's "general outlook on life." As he put it in

1962, "But why, some say, the moon? . . . Why climb the highest mountain? . . . We choose to go to the moon in this decade . . . because that goal will serve to organize and measure the best of our energies and skills . . . and 'Because it is there.' " In the same speech he pledged that space would not be "filled with weapons of destruction but with human knowledge." In keeping with that ideal, in 1963 the United States and the Soviet Union both supported a United Nations resolution calling on all states to refrain from placing nuclear weapons in space. Yet the space program of both powers facilitated their ominous competition in guided missiles.

The temptation to use weapons in hand or in reach was making the cold war more and more alarming. Even in seemingly remote areas of rivalry, the convinced cold warriors in Kennedy's entourage searched for new tactics and new devices to press the advantage of the United States. So it was with the excited enthusiasm of Walt Rostow for the employment of indigenous guerrilla forces in Vietnam. Rostow was beguiled, as was the president, by the argument of General Edward Lansdale, a veteran of guerrilla action in the Philippines, who believed that the successful tactics of Mao Zedong in the Chinese Civil War could be turned against communism. To that end Rostow held that the United States should train guerrillas in South Vietnam in order to stamp out the resistance there to the American-sponsored regime of President Ngo Dinh Diem. That proposal seriously neglected many of the conditions in Vietnam. The Soviet Union was indeed sponsoring the Vietcong, the anti-Diem resistance, but it did so for the most part through its client state North Vietnam, which was adamant in its effort to unify the country under its own rule. The Communist government of North Vietnam under Ho Chi Minh was indubitably authoritarian and repressive, but Ho for many years had also been a fervent nationalist, by no means merely a Soviet agent. South Vietnam was an artificial state, a state carved out of the Vietnamese whole. It had no cultural adhesiveness, no tradition of democratic government, but instead a heritage of French colonial rule. Diem and his ruling faction were Catholics, part of a small minority in a country primarily Buddhist in religion. Their government was little less authoritarian or repressive than its rival in the North. Diem's pervasive unpopularity among the peasants of South Vietnam made guerrilla activity against him at best difficult in the areas where they lived. Rostow and like-minded officials in the Pentagon apparently forgot Mao's observation that "guerrilla action would fail if its principal objectives do not coincide with the aspirations of the people."

Kennedy understood the dangers inherent in using American special forces to train pro-Diem South Vietnam guerrillas. But Vietnam was not a precise equivalent of Laos, for there was no conceivable coalition of moderates that Ho would join, and Eisenhower had staked even more American prestige on preserving the division in Vietnam than he had on his clients in Laos. Kennedy was intent upon sustaining American credibility in Vietnam, and he seemed to consider Vietnam politically more important than Laos, perhaps because the Diem government gave an appearance of solidity that contrasted with the instability in Vientiane.

In the spring of 1961 Kennedy sent the vice president to Saigon, the South Vietnamese capital, where in an excess of ebullience Johnson called Diem the Churchill of South Asia. With comparable exaggeration, Johnson on his return to the United States also warned: "We must help these countries . . . or throw in the towel in the area and pull back our defenses to San Francisco." As ever more temperate, Kennedy sent another hundred advisers to South Vietnam to join Americans already there to train guerrillas.

Even that decision violated the Geneva accords of 1954 about Vitenam. Those agreements, signed by the British and French but not the United States, had created the countries of Laos, Cambodia, and Vietnam. They had also divided Vietnam temporarily at the seventeenth parallel. Elections were to be held in 1956 to determine the government of a united Vietnam. But Eisenhower had ignored those agreements in his support for Diem and for the South Vietnamese refusal to permit the elections to unify the country, elections Ho would surely have won. Kennedy's continuing violation of the accords challenged the Vietcong and the North Vietnamese, as well, therefore, as the Soviet Union, and stood in potentially damaging contrast with his more pacific course in Laos.

Worse, American advisers predictably could not solve the problems of Diem's corrupt and inefficient regime. It remained incapable of defeating the Vietcong even though Diem had more than ten times the number of troops. In the fall of 1961 another Kennedy mission to Saigon, now under General Taylor and including Rostow, recommended sending some eighty thousand American troops to South Vietnam. The Pentagon urged the deployment of six divisions, a force of two hundred thousand, which the president considered absurd. To send more troops, he said, was "like taking a drink. The effect wears off, and you have to take another." But he would not risk the possible consequences, in domestic politics and in relations with the Soviet Union, that the collapse of Diem might have entailed. So Kennedy hedged. Though Diem spurned American proposals for political and social reform, Kennedy dispatched still more advisers, as well as American pilots to fly secret sorties out of an air and helicopter base near Saigon. Soon Americans were drawn into the fighting.

In part the President was self-deceived, as he had been in the case of the Bay of Pigs. Because he wanted to believe in the efficacy of counterinsurgency, he responded favorably to the arguments of Lansdale and Taylor and Rostow. But as Robert Kennedy later said, some of the administration's "assumptions in the early sixties about Vietnam were just wrong. . . . We were wrong in that we thought it would be possible to have social and political reform . . . very deep reform." Another of Kennedy's advisers, Roger Hilsman, then went on: "We were all grossly misinformed about . . . the obstacles, that Vietnam culture represents. . . . We go in there thinking that Lansdale has got the picture. . . . He didn't really understand the problem." One who did understand was Ambassador Galbraith. He wrote Kennedy in May 1961 from India in a letter addressed to the general condition of which Vietnam became the most trying example. "Those jungle regimes," Galbraith said, ". . . are going to be a hideous problem for us. . . . The rulers do not control . . . their own people, and they neither have nor warrant their people's support. . . . We must not allow ourselves or the country to imagine that gains or losses in those incoherent lands are the same as gains or losses in . . . France or Italy—or India." The following autumn Galbraith wrote again. He had "no real confidence in the sophistication and political judgment of our people" in South Vietnam. That country, he soon added, was "a can of snakes. I am reasonably accustomed to oriental government and politics, but I was not quite prepared for Diem." Neither really was Kennedy, but because he was unwilling to lose Vietnam and because he had confidence in his closest advisers, he took the drink that, as he knew, would wear off and require another and another. (There were about 2,600 American servicemen in Vietnam in January 1962; 11,300 by the end of that year.) Because Kennedy acted in the name of peace, he also, however inadvertently, deceived the American people, just as Eisenhower had.

Before the end of 1961 the administration's foreign and military policies, based though they were on the cogitation of intelligent and reflective men, had created problems no more tractable than those the president had inherited. Indeed, much of the weight of his legacy remained. Kennedy's advisers, moreover, however much they informed and assisted him, influenced him less than did his own deliberations.

He made a larger impact on them than did they, individually or collectively, on him. At home and abroad the events of the first year after his election revealed him, not surprisingly, as a moderate, close to but not on the liberal tangent of the vital center; as a basically political man, at once tough-minded and cautious about his options, calculating in estimating their probable consequences, but, as in Cuba and Vietnam, by no means immune to error. He was, as his admirers said, a quick learner, but he still had much to learn about his enormous job.

2

Probings

Action, energy, decisiveness—those were the qualities that John F. Kennedy tried to project during the campaign of 1960. Those were the qualities that were supposed to infuse the presidency and, through it, the federal government. In that way he would get the country moving again. That movement, the Kennedy campaign implied, would overcome sluggishness in the economy. It would also, as his telephone call to Coretta King had suggested, enlist federal sympathies behind the cause of civil rights. But the imagery of the campaign created an illusion that the process of governing threatened to dispel. When he took office, Kennedy had formulated no policy to resuscitate the economy. At the most he had leanings toward solutions that his academic advisers were fashioning. Similarly, his sympathies for desegregation fell far short of the positive federal action that the civil rights leaders advocated. To be sure, the new president believed in economic growth and social justice. But for months he hesitated to make the decisions necessary to advance either goal.

1. INTRODUCTORY ECONOMICS

As the somber search for national purpose had indicated, the United States was losing the primacy it had so briefly enjoyed during the years after the Second World War. That loss manifested itself politically in the 1960s in the Soviet advance toward parity with the United States in nuclear and intercontinental weapons and in influence in develop-

ing areas of the world. At the same time the successful revivals of the economies of Western Europe and Japan were ending the superiority the United States had achieved as the only major industrial nation to have gained wealth and markets during World War II.

Those changes occasioned deep anxieties in Washington, not the least about international finance. Before 1960 the world's supply of monetary gold, most of which the United States had accumulated during World War II, had begun to move back to Europe and Japan. That movement occurred because of the heavy payments by the U.S. government for sustaining troops overseas, because of American capital exports to build industrial and commercial facilities abroad, and because Americans had begun to import more goods and export less than they earlier had. The United States, operating as the world's banker, freely converted the dollar earnings and receipts of foreigners and their governments to gold at the fixed and undervalued price of thirty-five dollars an ounce. The Western European nations and Japan had chosen to accumulate large reserves in dollars, rather than convert those dollars to gold, so as to prevent a collapse of the dollar's value relative to their currencies. Such a collapse would have damaged the ability of Americans to import goods from abroad. More important, the policy of holding dollars rather than converting them was designed to avoid offense to the United States, which provided the nuclear shield for Western Europe and Japan. Nevertheless, the accumulated dollar reserves constituted IOUs that the United States might have to pay at any time.

That condition, which had been affecting the American economy for several years, complicated the making of fiscal and monetary policy, major issues by 1962. During the first several months of that year the economy seemed to be resisting the administration's efforts to increase the gross national product and decrease the level of unemployment. Actually those efforts had been inadequate. In deference to the president's essential conservatism about fiscal policy, his postelection task force had submitted a modest program for 1961. In that year the economy improved only marginally, largely because of increases in defense spending, and in 1962 unemployment began to rise again. Kennedy's advisers disagreed about appropriate remedies because, pehaps deliberately, he had chosen two sorts of counselors with markedly different points of view. Secretary of the Treasury Douglas Dillon and his influential subordinate Robert Roosa, an expert on international monetary matters, considered the country's unfavorable balance of payments and the accompanying loss of gold, actual and potential, the foremost economic problem facing the nation. William McChesney Martin, the incumbent head of the Board of Governors of the Federal Reserve System, agreed with them and was also worried about preventing inflation. As they saw it, it was necessary for the Fed to sustain interest rates at the levels then current in order to dissuade Americans from seeking higher returns abroad. But prevailing interest rates, in the view of Kennedy's Council of Economic Advisers (CEA), were so high that they discouraged new industrial investment within the country, with the result that the economy failed to receive the stimulus it needed. Monetary policy, in that light, had been "too little and too limp." As one consequence, unemployment continued to hover near 7 percent.

The members of the Council of Economic Advisers considered that level of unemployment socially intolerable. They based their argument for reducing it on the seminal ideas of the great British economist John Maynard Keynes, whose theories had become dominant among American economists after the huge deficits of World War II had finally lifted the depression of the 1930s, just as Keynes had predicted such deficits would. Public deficits, in Keynes's theory, provided a necessary substitute for private investment essential to restore growth to a lagging economy. Stimulation of the economy, the CEA believed in 1962, could reduce unemployment to about 4 percent and would arise most effectively from a reduction in federal taxes. That reduction would temporarily produce a larger federal deficit but over the next several years would raise the economy to new levels of productivity and income, which would then yield revenues sufficient to balance the budget at the lower tax rates. In the interval the nation could afford the temporary deficits since the ratio of the national debt to gross national product remained low by historical standards, as did the cost of servicing the debt.

Chairman Martin disagreed. He believed that recourse to deliberate deficits would frighten investors and lead them to sell American securities and purchase European replacements, thereby increasing the flow of gold from the United States. Kennedy sympathized with that argument. Though he was not ignorant about Keynesian theory, he had at best a superficial understanding of it, and he was notably cautious about embracing Keynesian policies. Sensitive to Republican contentions that he would be fiscally irresponsible, he worried about the political consequences of federal deficits. As a Democrat he felt especially vulnerable to attacks from Wall Street on that issue. Further, he valued his father's counsel, and Joseph P. Kennedy had long been a conservative about monetary and fiscal questions. As one consequence, the presi-

Walter Heller: Pithy and per-suasive.

dent was also a traditionalist about gold. Anxious about the balance of payments, he recoiled from any suggestion involving a reevaluation of gold—"funny money," his father said. So it was that the president seemed incredulous when a member of the CEA maintained that "fear of the loss of gold should not constitute a barrier to doing something about unemployment."

The council was unanimous in that opinion and persuasive in advancing it. Walter Heller, the chairman of the CEA, later a recipient of the Nobel Prize in economics, had a gift for pithy prose. His lean, witty memorandums, illuminated by metaphor, carried a force in a page or two that the Treasury's tedious, bureaucratic reports could not match. Kermit Gordon, another council member, had sure political sensibilities. He almost always knew just what to tell the president. It was Gordon who eventually assured Kennedy that no nation had ever lost an ounce of gold except because of a political decision by the head of its government. Gordon then cited the case of France under Charles de Gaulle, who regularly attacked American policy in Europe—an example that "brought Kennedy around," according to James Tobin, "though he still felt vulnerable." For his part, Tobin served as the con-science of the council, less visible than the other two, equally effective in defining issues for their collective attention. It was Tobin who requested the study by Arthur Okun about the relationship between gross national product and unemployment. Okun's law, the product of that study, demonstrated that every increase in GNP of 3 percent (later amended to 2.5 percent) would reduce unemployment 1 percent. That was what the council wanted the president to understand and act upon.

One vital route to the president ran through Ted Sorensen, Kennedy's special counsel and closest adviser on domestic issues. In Tobin's judgment "probably the brightest man I ever knew," Sorensen, like Kennedy, examined economics through an acute political lens. To Tobin's explanation of the council's goal for unemployment, Sorensen, dubious, replied: "If you have seven per cent unemployment, you are getting a grade of 93. If you have four per cent unemployment, you are getting a grade of 96. Why on earth should the administration make great efforts with all the fiscal dangers and political dangers, too, to revise its grade from 93 to 96 when they're both A." Sorensen in 1962 still believed, as Kennedy did, that unemployment was essentially a structural problem, subject primarily not to macroeconomic remedies but to specific, targeted programs, like those for area development.

Nevertheless, by 1962 both Sorensen and Kennedy had gained new respect for the council. The president had intended at the height of the Berlin crisis in 1961 to ask for a tax increase to accompany the military program he then recommended to Congress. But the CEA, with the important support of Secretary Dillon, had assured him that no increase in taxes was needed, indeed that any increase would diminish the chances for recovery, and he had accepted that advice. By spring of 1962, with the economy turning down, the council's prediction had proved accurate. A tax increase would have made things worse. Kennedy was not yet ready to advocate the tax reduction Heller was suggesting, but he had growing confidence in the CEA.

2. Big Steel

The president was already approaching the question of inflation as the Council of Economic Advisers recommended he should. Eisenhower had made a major political issue of preventing inflation, which remained insignificant during his terms, but at the cost of several recessions and slow growth in the economy. Kennedy naturally wanted the best of both worlds: steady growth without inflation. At the urging of the CEA, which hoped to spur growth, he decided to rely on persuasion—"jawboning," in the phrase of the day—to stabilize prices and wages. The administration issued guidelines calculated to limit increases in wages to increases in productivity, a formula intended to hold both prices and profits at existing levels.

Kennedy proposed that formula to the steel industry, in which the contract between management and labor was about to expire early in 1962. Steel, at that time a major domestic industry, supplied all other heavy industries, construction and automobiles among them, which would face increased costs were the price of steel to rise. As the president told Secretary of Labor Arthur Goldberg in October 1961, he feared that a resulting general price increase would weaken the dollar and worsen the balance of payments. Goldberg advised him not to intercede with the union. A labor lawyer by profession, Goldberg opposed any reopening of the existing contract or disruption of the normal process of collective bargaining. But with Goldberg's encouragement, Kennedy wrote the chief executive officers of the twelve leading steel companies to ask them to hold the line on prices during the pending negotiations of a new contract and to tell them he was making a similar request about wages to union leaders. For his part, Goldberg persuaded David McDonald, president of the United Steelworkers of America, to assure Kennedy that labor would keep the national interest in mind. The secretary also informed senior steel executives, including Roger Blough, head of the United States Steel Corporation, that he was willing to use his good offices to bring about a moderate settlement.

Before the end of 1961 both Kennedy and Goldberg interpreted the stockpiling of steel as a defensive tactic by management to guard against the chance of a strike. With McDonald agreeable to accelerating negotiations, Goldberg on a national television broadcast in January called for a quick settlement. The president, at a meeting on January 23, 1962, told both McDonald and Blough that the CEA believed a wage increase of 2.5 or 3 percent would fall within gains in productivity and therefore require no increase in prices. European financial reports, Kennedy added, looked upon the steel wage settlement as the most vital economic event in the United States that year. He expected McDonald and Blough to conduct their own negotiations, with Goldberg's assistance if they requested it, but industry, he observed, should keep in mind that it would benefit from an accelerated depreciation schedule the Treasury Department was already preparing to announce.

Negotiations began on February 24, earlier than usual, but broke off on March 2, 1962, with the two sides far apart. Soon thereafter Blough told Goldberg that the union's demand for a wage increase of seventeen cents an hour would be inflationary. Goldberg suggested ten cents an hour, just less than 2.5 percent, as noninflationary. Interested but noncommittal, Blough resumed negotiations with McDonald, to whom Goldberg suggested the ten-cent figure on March 12. On March 31 both sides accepted that amount in principle. Kennedy praised the settlement as "forward looking and responsible . . . obviously non-inflationary."

After the formal agreement was signed on April 11, Blough asked to see the president, who invited Goldberg to the meeting. Upon arriving, Blough handed Kennedy a copy of a press release announcing that U.S. Steel had just raised the price of steel six dollars a ton. "Double cross," Goldberg said; Blough had not kept faith with the administration. He was sorry, Blough replied, that Goldberg felt that way, but he had acted in behalf of his stockholders. Several other steel companies followed his lead.

Furious, Goldberg told Kennedy the next morning that he would have to resign unless the increases were rescinded. The president, angry himself at the industry's deceit, realized that Goldberg's reputation with the steel union was at stake. More important, so were the prestige of the White House and the credibility of the administration's policy on price stablization. At his press conference that day Kennedy alerted the nation to the "unjustifiable and irresponsible defiance of the public interest" by a "tiny handful of steel executives whose pursuit of power and profit exceeds their sense of the public interest." Privately the president put it more succinctly. "My father always told me," he said, "that all businessmen were sons-of-bitches, but I never believed it till now."

The president also ordered an investigation by the Federal Trade Commission to ascertain whether the price increases by the steel industry had resulted from illegal collusion, in which case the government could initiate an antitrust suit. Further, the Defense Department announced it would purchase steel only at the lowest available prices in order to fulfill its responsibilities to the taxpayers. On the advice of the CEA, Kennedy persuaded three of the smaller steel companies to hold the line on prices. After that tough response he arranged a luncheon in New York City for April 13 at which Blough and other steel executives were to meet with Goldberg and Clark Clifford, a Washington Democrat close to former President Truman and Vice President Johnson and universally respected for his legal and political acumen. While they were conferring, Bethlehem Steel rescinded its price increase. Though Blough protested that he had never promised not to raise prices,

"Gunsmoke."

he then gave in. U.S. Steel rolled back its prices late that afternoon.

Kennedy's successful actions during the tempest over steel prices confirmed the uneasiness, even the hostility, with which most businessmen regarded him, as they did most Democrats. "The problem," the president told Arthur Schlesinger, "is that the business community no longer has any confidence in itself. Whenever I say anything that upsets them, businessmen just die. I have to spend my time and energy trying to prop them up." In May investors needed propping up. In the wake of the steel settlement they revealed a disturbing uncertainty about the stock market. Prices fell off early in the month and during two days late in May collapsed farther than they had since the crash of 1929. The financial community and its Republican sympathizers blamed the administration. Though he resented that charge, Kennedy also worried about the market. Walter Heller reassured him. The problem arose, he wrote, because the recovery of the economy had been disappointing, because leading economic indicators had been "dyspeptic," because the balance of payments remained worrisome, and because Wall Street was the victim of its own propaganda about a squeeze on profits. The market had risen on the expectation of inflation, which had not occurred, and the fall in prices would be only temporary, as indeed, it proved to be. Even as Heller wrote, institutions and investment funds were buying stocks at bargain prices. For the long term, Heller added, returning to his steady theme, a tax cut would help the economy and the market, too.

Referring to the same objective, James Tobin recommended a tax cut over the Treasury Department's goal of reforming the revenue system by closing loopholes through which the wealthy avoided taxes. Desirable in the long run, tax reform, Tobin argued, did not preclude an earlier tax cut during 1962, though the Treasury held that without a link to tax reduction, reform would fail in Congress. "Full recovery," Tobin wrote the president, "is more important than tax reform. The risks to the economy from postponing tax cuts are greater than the hazards to tax reform involved in early tax reductions." That Keynesian advice, gospel for the CEA, received an unexpected emphasis from Douglas Dillon, who advocated a moderate budget deficit, which, he believed, would not push up prices during a period, like the current one, of inadequate demand. Kennedy was convinced. At his next press conference he proposed tax reduction in 1962, to be followed by tax reform the following year.

As Walter Heller observed, Kennedy, newly converted, "became more and more . . . intrigued with the idea of giving a whole speech on the topic. In particular, he felt he should deal with the myths . . . blocking the full use of economic tools that could 'get the country moving again.' " The president used that theme in his address at the Yale Commencement on June 11, 1962. Contrary to the mythology of conventional analyses, he said, government spending was not increasing. Since 1945 it had grown less rapidly than other sectors of the economy. Further, federal spending contributed to a widening variety of activities. Yet federal deficits, measured either per capita or as a percentage of GNP, had declined since World War II. Those deficits had not in themselves created inflation. "Some grand warfare of fixed ideologies," Kennedy said, would only disturb "the practical management of a modern economy. What we need is not labels and clichés but more basic discussion of the sophisticated and technical questions involved in keeping a great economic machinery moving ahead."

Though Wall Street considered the speech hostile, the president in a televised press conference in August called for a major tax cut early in 1963. But political factors made him hesitate. Opposition on the Hill, especially from Wilbur Mills, the conservative Democratic chairman of the House Ways and Means Committee, made any changes in taxes unlikely. Shoving the president along, the members of the CEA gave him another informal seminar in their discipline. "The AFL-CIO leaders," Heller pointed out, "emphatically expressed their . . . pessimism . . . their feeling of the great need for an immediate tax cut . . . their concern over the lack of urgency in the Administration's approach." Wrangling over tax reform was delaying tax reduction, Heller continued; the two questions had to be separated because the economy needed stimulation as soon as possible. Eighty percent of business economists favored a tax cut, he added a week later. To convert business leaders to the same view, he drafted the placatory speech Kennedy delivered to the New York Economic Club. "The best means of strengthening demand among consumers and business," the president said, "is to reduce the burden on private income and the deterrents to private investment which are imposed by our present tax system."

That was the most conservative speech since Herbert Hoover, J. K. Galbraith commented, though as he knew, it was really pure Heller. The CEA and its chairman were not Tories, but their conversion of the president to their belief had, in order to succeed, taken on a conservative cast. With less regard for the balance of payments than their critics believed appropriate, Heller, Tobin, and Gordon in 1962 made deliberate deficit spending their preferred tool for spurring the economy. Large public work projects, which Galbraith would have championed, took too long to have the necessary effect, according to Tobin's calculations, and were too unpopular in Congress to win approval, whereas a tax cut would work quickly and win political favor, particularly if it were considered without the predictable friction of special-interest groups lobbying for various tax reforms.

Tobin and Heller were correct about their economic objections, but politically Galbraith considered them wrong, for as he predicted, tax reform would fail in Congress without the inducement of tax reduction. In the opinion of liberal Democrats, tax reform was essential as an instrument of social justice, a device to redistribute income and wealth away from the rich and the upper middle class and toward the poor. The inequities in American society demanded that redistribution. Galbraith remained convinced, too, about the need to eliminate the public squalor he had identified in *The Affluent Society*. To meet that need, the federal government had to spend generously for education, health, housing, and urban renewal, programs that would have required considerable deficits if Congress had been willing to support them. But the CEA and the president in 1962 believed Congress would defeat those programs. Heller and Tobin tendered the advice they did because they considered it the only politically practical advice. As Galbraith conceded, their practicality, which appealed to the president, helped them win his support.

Converted to tax reduction as the means for economic growth, Kennedy, as ever a centrist, nevertheless could not budge the House Ways and Means Committee. That committee, so Wilbur Mills told the president, was "not convinced that we can make a case yet" without being "susceptible to the charge of being fiscally irresponsible." He would not move, Mills continued, unless there was a recession. But a recession, Kennedy argued, would hurt the Democrats in the 1962 elections. Mills allowed that he preferred a tax cut to a recession, but he would wait until confronted with the choice. "That makes sense," Kennedy replied, retreating. They agreed to look at the problem anew in November. Once again the president lacked the votes he needed. Though Heller continued to urge the president to move, it was another year before Mills, with the 1964 election on the political horizon, began to smile upon tax reduction. Tax reform had already lost its chance.

3. International Economics

Kennedy's decision to adopt Keynesian policies for economic expansion moved him to take steps to control the balance of payments problem. As the Treasury Department contended, that problem would worsen if stimulation of the domestic economy pushed up prices, as it might once the existing slack in employment had been overcome. For the long run the Treasury, partly through tax favors, encouraged American multinational corporations to increase their investments in productive facilities in Western Europe. Those investments would enlarge the already considerable presence within the European market of such corporate giants as General Motors and IBM and would yield large returns in European currencies to compensate for the dollars Europeans were earning by exporting to the United States. For both the long and the short term the administration wanted to bring about a reduction in the barriers to American exports, especially agricultural exports, which the Europeans, now formally linked in the Common Market, had erected a decade earlier. At that time the Western European economy had yet to recover from the war. In the era of the Marshall Plan those barriers had been necessary, but during the interval since then the European economy had been growing twice as fast as the American. With European labor costs relatively low, European goods, relatively inexpensive, were pouring into the United States while American goods had difficulty entering the Continent. The identical problem was about to develop with Japan and later with other nations in Asia, where barriers to American exports were even tougher than in Europe.

The State Department in 1961 began to work toward easing transatlantic trade restrictions with its support for the establishment of the Organization for Economic Cooperation and Development (OECD), a joint American and European advisory council. Cooperation became even more exigent when Prime Minister Harold Macmillan informed Kennedy in April that the British government intended to apply for membership in the Common Market. Kennedy welcomed the prospect of an increased British role on the Continent, for it would help offset the prickly leadership of France and West Germany and would also militate toward European political unity. But the addition of Britain to the Common Market with its stiff restrictions on imports might set off a transatlantic trade war with potentially adverse political and economic consequences.

To prevent that development, early in 1962 Kennedy asked Congress for authority to bargain with the Common Market for a mutual reduction in tariffs. In recommending the enabling legislation, the president explained his purpose: "The two great Atlantic markets will either grow together or they will grow apart. . . . That decision will either mark the beginning of a new chapter in the alliance of free nations—or a threat to the growth of Western unity." Congress passed the Trade Expansion Act by large margins in the fall of 1962, but with a revision designed to get Britain into the Common Market.

That objective depended not on American preferences but on the politics of President de Gaulle of France, who could veto Britain's bid for membership. He had long been hostile to the English-speaking powers and suspicious of their special relationship. Those attitudes went back to his wartime exasperation with Roosevelt, who distrusted him, and Churchill, who disliked him. More even than other nationalistic Europeans, de Gaulle also resented what he considered the invasion of the Continent by American corporations and American culture as it was exported in film and advertising and in fashionable goods like blue jeans and Coca-Cola. The Trade Expansion Act indicated an American desire for economic cooperation with Western Europe, but the proposed expansion of the domestic American economy, by portending higher prices for American goods, implied a lack of interest in monetary cooperation. In the absence of that development, Common Market countries would be left with their mounting dollar balances. Those mixed signals fed de Gaulle's suspicions, as did the direction Kennedy was giving to American military policy.

The defense of Western Europe against possible invasion by the Soviet Union consituted the basis of the North Atlantic Treaty Organization— the NATO alliance. The lingering friction over Berlin provided a constant reminder of Soviet ambitions. But Kennedy and Secretary of Defense McNamara believed that the nature of the shield for Western Europe had to change. In their view, the nuclear deterrent on which Eisenhower had based his doctrine of massive retaliation was not really credible, for a nuclear response to a minor Soviet incursion would lead to unlimited destruction. As they saw it, a doubtful deterrent was no deterrent at all. They therefore advocated building up conventional European forces to meet any conventional Soviet attack. But as in earlier years, the NATO nations did not want to spend the money necessary to create an adequate conventional defense. Some of them also believed that a conventional defense, in the new era of intercontinental missiles, would in itself undermine the credibility of a nuclear deterrent to Soviet aggression by calling into question the American nerve to use nuclear weapons and risk nuclear retaliation.

France, furthermore, was eager to become a member of the nuclear club; Great Britain, to retain that status for itself; and West Germany, impatient to gain at least some access to nuclear weapons, a prospect that bothered many of the British. To organize that jumble of nationalistic ambitions without compromising American control of decisions about the use of nuclear weapons, Kennedy and his counselors followed two related courses that had originated with the Eisenhower administration. One related to Great Britain, which had earned special treatment by its role in the wartime construction of the first atomic bomb and as a nuclear power in its own right. Britain by 1958 had its own superbombs but no missiles with which to deliver them. Eisenhower and Macmillan reached an agreement under which Her Majesty's government permitted American submarines, soon to be armed with Polaris missiles carrying nuclear weapons, to use the British base at Holy Loch in Scotland in return for an American promise to supply the Royal Air Force with Skybolt, an air-to-ground missile that the United States was building. That arrangement, as Macmillan saw it, preserved both the "special relationship" between the two countries

On de Gaulle's mind.

and Britain's independent nuclear role. But the agreement excluded other nations. To satisfy the yearnings of President de Gaulle of France and Chancellor Konrad Adenauer of Germany, Eisenhower proposed the creation of a multilateral force (MLF), a small group of ships armed with American nuclear weapons but manned by a mixed force recruited from the various NATO countries. The British were cool to that plan, which conflicted with their own preferred status and brought Germany to the foyer of nuclear power. For his part, Kennedy was dubious about the usefulness of a floating tower of Babel, but he did not withdraw Ike's proposal, which, in each of several forms, held the support of those of his advisers who were most concerned about European affairs.

De Gaulle spurned the idea. France, he insisted, would develop its own nuclear capability, sufficient so that "no one could attack us without running the risk of frightful injury." As he interpreted NATO, it was the price Americans had exacted in return for Marshall Plan economic aid. "My aim," he wrote, "was to disengage France, not from the Atlantic alliance, which I intended to maintain by way of ultimate precaution, but from the integration by NATO under American command." De Gaulle planned to pursue détente with the Soviet Union and eventually with China. Rapprochement with Russia and with West Germany would further his ambition for making France and Paris the center of "the vast area of Europe" reaching from the Channel to the Urals, for a "concert of European states which in developing all sorts of ties between them would increase their interdependence and solidarity." That grand scheme excluded both the United States and Great Britain.

De Gaulle's sense of his own grandeur and its intrinsic place in French destiny made him a difficult man with whom to negotiate. Yet American plans depended upon his approval both of the MLF and of British entry into the Common Market. Kennedy remained determined at the least to sustain the NATO alliance and reduce Western European trade barriers. It was a symbol of the loss of American dominance that by 1962 such important elements of national foreign and economic policy had come to hinge on the will of so majestically temperamental a character as Charles de Gaulle.

4. CIVIL RIGHTS

Since the time of his inauguration, Kennedy's sense of priorities and of political possibilities, as well as the caution of his political advisers, had kept him out of synchronization with the most powerful force for domestic change, the civil rights movement. Involved as he was in foreign affairs and in economic issues, the president seriously underestimated both the moral imperative and the revolutionary zeal of civil rights advocates. Kennedy had an exaggerated and constraining concern about the potential political costs to the administration and to the Democratic party of effective support of civil rights. In 1961, solicitous of southern votes in Congress, he made no recommendation for civil rights legislation, and he appointed to federal courts in the South only white judges acceptable to southern senators and therefore assured of confirmation. Most of those judges sustained segregation. To be sure, Kennedy did appoint more blacks to high federal office than had any of his predecessors, and Robert Kennedy staffed the Justice Department with talented lawyers sympathetic to a moderate course toward desegregation. A moderate himself, the president endorsed the desegregation of public schools and established the Commission on Equal Employment Opportunity with Lyndon Johnson as its chairman. But he did not issue an order desegregating federally supported housing, as he had promised during his campaign. And he rejected immediately the early advice of one staff member who urged him, in contrast with

Segregated water fountains: Symbol of the South.

Eisenhower, "to give clear moral expression to the issues involved." At the most, as one black activist later commented, "Kennedy had the good sense not to oppose the civil rights movement."

For several years Martin Luther King, Jr., the eloquent prophet of equal rights for blacks, had been making the moral aspects of civil rights powerfully clear. He and his associates in the Southern Christian Leadership Conference (SCLC), masters of the techniques of nonviolent protest, were leading sit-ins in the South that advanced the desegregation in that region of buses, luncheon counters, restaurants, and other public facilities. They had expected much more support from Kennedy than they received. They also confronted growing impatience among their followers and increasing rivalry from more militant groups. By 1961 the Congress of Racial Equality (CORE), under the pungent leadership of James Farmer, and the youthful Student Nonviolent

Coordinating Committee (SNCC) were moving to the fore in organizing protests in the South. Both groups were committed to nonviolent tactics, but they were more aggressive in their programs than the administration deemed prudent.

The civil rights activists had taken heart from rulings of the Supreme Court that enlarged the scope of *Brown v. Board of Education* (1954)— the seminal decision that, reversing previous doctrine, found segregation of public schools unconstitutional on the ground that separate facilities were inherently unequal and therefore in violation of the provisions of the Fourteenth Amendment. In *Boynton v. Virginia* (1960) the Court had gone on to rule against segregation of interstate bus terminals. That decision opened the way for CORE in 1961 to sponsor Freedom Rides, in which blacks and sympathetic whites were to travel through the Deep South on interstate buses and disembark at terminals along the way to desegregate them by using drinking fountains, lunch counters, and rest rooms reserved for whites. "Our intention," James Farmer said, "was to provoke the southern authorities into arresting us and thereby prod the Justice Department into enforcing the law of the land."

The meaning of that law was more complicated than Farmer thought. Burke Marshall, the head of the Civil Rights Division in the Department of Justice, a man of formidable intelligence, unfailing courage, and generous sympathies, held to a scrupulous but confining interpretation of the Constitution that limited the police power of the federal government. The Kennedys agreed, convinced that the regular exercise of a federal police power in local situations would violate constitutional restraints against centralization of authority and create precedents subject to perilous exploitation in the future by any would-be Caesar. But King and Farmer interpreted those scruples as excuses for inactivity. They were eager not for legality but for results. Indeed, civil disobedience, a doctrine King preached, had as its objective the undermining of immoral laws.

When CORE undertook the Freedom Rides in 1961, Farmer expected southern bigots to attack the participants and in so doing to attract the national media to scenes of violence that would appall the public and create a crisis the federal government could not ignore. Those expectations, common for the next several years among civil rights leaders eager to mobilize the Kennedys, proved accurate. Hatred and violence greeted the Freedom Riders in May 1961 in savage episodes at Rocky Hill, South Carolina, and Anniston and Birmingham, Alabama. Governor John Patterson, a rabid segregationist, advised the harassed

members of CORE "to get out of Alabama as quickly as possible. . . .
The state . . . can't guarantee the safety of fools." Fearing further attacks
on the demonstrators, the Justice Department provided the airplane on
which they departed.

SNCC leaders remained determined to test federal policy in the face
of southern white militancy. They organized another trip to Birmingham, where the police chief arrested them and transported them out
of the state. Undeterred, they started again for Montgomery, Alabama.
The state police escort accompanying them disappeared as they entered
Montgomery, to which the Kennedys had sent several observers from
the Justice Department. As the passengers left the bus, John Doar,
Burke Marshall's senior assistant, reported by telephone from the scene
that "a bunch of men are beating them. There are no cops. It's terrible.
. . . People are yelling, 'Get 'em, get 'em.' It's awful." Soon exceeding
a thousand people, the mob continued to attack the Freedom Riders.
John Seigenthaler, the president's special envoy to Governor Patterson, tried to help one woman, but several angry whites knocked him
unconscious.

The resulting national publicity and the criticism in European newspapers of American bigotry stung the president and the attorney general, both concerned about the nation's reputation in the period just
before the Vienna summit. The president called upon Alabama officials to "meet their responsibilites." The attorney general had already
ordered the FBI to investigate the violence at Anniston. After the debacle at Montgomery, and over the objection of Governor Patterson, Robert
Kennedy obtained a federal injunction to stop the Ku Klux Klan from
interfering with interstate travel and another requiring the Montgomery police to protect travelers. He also sent about four hundred federal marshals to Maxwell Air Force Base, close to the city.

They were in place to protect Martin Luther King, Jr., when he
reached Montgomery to address a rally on May 21, 1961. A surly crowd
gathered across the street from the church where the rally was to be
held. It began attacking blacks outside the building and throwing stones
through the windows. When federal marshals then arrived, Governor
Patterson at last ordered the National Guard and state police to assist
in dispersing the mob. The next day the SCLC, CORE, and SNCC
leaders in Montgomery rejected Robert Kennedy's advice for a temporary halt to allow tensions to cool. "We had been cooling for a hundred
years," James Farmer said. "If we got any cooler we'd be in a deep
freeze."

The attorney general nevertheless continued to try to forestall trouble. When, on May 24, a group of Freedom Riders left for Jackson, Mississippi, he struck a private bargain with Senator James Eastland of that state. The senator guaranteed an absence of violence in return for Kennedy's promise not to interfere with the arrest of the passengers. That agreement kept order in Jackson, though the Freedom Riders were arrested and fined for exercising their constitutional rights, as were others who followed them that summer not just to Mississippi but also to Arkansas, Florida, Louisiana, and Texas. Forced to act to preserve order, the attorney general also urged the Interstate Commerce Commission to prohibit racial discrimination in interstate facilities, an order the agency issued in September. That victory for the Freedom Riders strengthened the resolve of black leaders to press for further gains and the determination of white supremacists to resist.

The Kennedys were caught between the two groups. The attorney general, as advised by his Civil Rights Division, had attempted in June to persuade civil rights activists to concentrate on a voter registration drive in the South, where the vast majority of blacks remained disfranchised. The registration of black voters, he argued, would develop political strength, which in turn would lead to the end of segregation. The Justice Department, ready to cooperate in that program, had enlisted several philanthropic foundations to finance it. But most young black leaders, suspicious of the administration's motives, hesitated to give up the Freedom Rides. The Kennedys, they believed, were sponsoring a diversion designed to assist the president's reelection. In the autumn of 1961, however, CORE and SNCC decided to go ahead both with their social goals and with voter registration in the Deep South. They interpreted the attorney general's interest as a promise of protection. Further, as James Farmer said, the voter project would require direct action "by which consciousness might be aroused, politicized, and organized." The National Association for the Advancement of Colored People (NAACP) and the Urban League joined the more militant groups in the program. But they still expected more of the Kennedys than they were to receive.

During 1962 the campaigns for voter registration and for desegregation continued to struggle against the administration's constitutional scruples and the president's reluctance to speak out strongly for civil rights. The Civil Rights Division did investigate violations of voters' rights and bring suits to protect those rights, but the preparation of those suits took a long time, as did appeals to United States circuit courts from continually adverse decisions by federal judges in southern district courts, many of them Kennedy appointees. Attorneys in the division admitted they were making little discernible progress. Robert Kennedy in 1962 recommended legislation to abolish the literacy test as a qualification for voting, a step that would have made litigation easier; but civil rights advocates considered that recommendation inadequate, and southern senators, for their part, were resolved to block it, as they did. More important for civil rights activists in the South, local law enforcement officers had a free hand in permitting white supremacists to suppress protests against segregation. Though the Justice Department investigated some cases of police brutality, it was difficult to prove that local police had the specific intent of depriving their victims of constitutional rights. In the period 1959–1964, after some fifteen hundred investigations, the department won only thirteen convictions, all of which carried only light penalties. Even so, the Kennedys were anathema in the white South, where George C. Wallace, the governor of Alabama, promised his devoted constituents: "Segregation now, segregation tomorrow, segregation forever!"

"I began talking about niggers," Wallace said of his political audiences, "and they stomped the floor." They also stomped upon the dedicated men and women, mostly black and mostly young, who were endeavoring to register black voters. All through the summer of 1962 vigilantes of white supremacy in Mississippi were allowed by local police to terrorize representatives of the Voter Education Project, who were often also arrested by the same police, usually on flimsy charges. Blacks who dared register to vote faced loss of their jobs and threats to their families, as well as the calculated delays of registration officials. Beatings, whippings, and other forms of intimidation in Mississippi held the increase in black registration to an insignificant level: The proportion of black voters in the state rose only from 5.3 to 6.7 percent, in contrast with marked gains in the upper South.

The tactic of nonviolent protest also faltered in 1962. In Albany, Georgia, Martin Luther King, Jr., led a yearlong citywide effort to integrate all public facilities. The local chief of police shrewdly prevented white mobs from forming, but he arrested and incarcerated dozens of civil rights demonstrators. That policy deprived national media of sensational news and spared the Justice Department pressure for intervention. To King's distress, the city's public schools, interstate bus terminal, and municipal library remained segregated. In spite of that clear violation of federal law, the president and the attorney general made no helpful gesture. The failure of black nonviolence in Albany contrasted with the success of white violence in Mississippi. The frustration, the dangers, the fears of the young activists were costing many of them their faith in King's methods. Increasingly they were tempted to abandon Gandhian techniques for violence of their own.

5. OLE MISS

One who did not do so was James Meredith, an air force veteran, who applied in 1961 for admission to the all-white University of Mississippi. "I believe," he said later, ". . . that I have a Divine Responsibility to break White Supremacy in Mississippi, and getting in Ole Miss was only the start." The university rejected him, he filed a suit with the help of the local NAACP, and the case was decided in June 1962 by the U.S. Court of Appeals for the Fifth Circuit, which ruled for his immediate admission. After further delays, Associate Justice Hugo Black, an Alabaman, speaking for the Supreme Court in September, ordered state officials to obey the lower court order. But Ross Barnett, the governor of Mississippi, who had called for the nullification of federal law, now asserted on television that he "would not surrender to the evil and illegal forces of tyranny."

The Justice Department had supported Meredith's appeal to the Supreme Court. Forced to deal with Barnett's challenge to federal authority, Robert Kennedy privately worked with James Eastland and other senators to try to resolve the crisis. He also held twenty telephone conversations with Governor Barnett. The governor held his ground. As he put it on September 25, "That's what it's going to boil down to— whether Mississippi can run its institutions or the federal government is going to run things." By that time white extremists were arriving at Oxford, Mississippi, the site of the university. On September 29 the president called Barnett. "I don't know Mr. Meredith," Kennedy said, "but . . . under the Constitution I have to carry out the orders of the Court. . . . I would like to get your help doing it." Later in the day Barnett suggested they "sneak" Meredith in to register at the Jackson branch of the university, but then he changed his mind. A little later he said his highway patrol would "maintain law and order as best we can." But Kennedy had to prepare for trouble. He signed a proclamation ordering those obstructing justice in Mississippi to desist, and he federalized the state's National Guard. On September 30 Barnett agreed to let Meredith register that day if he could "just raise cain about it" to protect his own reputation.

The attorney general believed Barnett had backed down, but as a precaution he assigned some of his senior staff to Oxford under the

James Meredith and federal marshals: Three brave men.

command of Nicholas Katzenbach. They found a crowd gathered around the Lyceum, the university's registration building. Meredith then arrived, accompanied by James McShane, the federal chief marshal, and John Doar—"two of the bravest men I have ever known," Meredith later said. He was secured in a dormitory while federal marshals surrounded the Lyceum, where they planned to register him the next day. With the onset of darkness the growing mob began to throw bricks and bottles, and Katzenbach had the marshals use tear gas to defend themselves. Moments thereafter, according to plan, the president appeared on national television. On the assumption that calm prevailed in Oxford, he gave a conciliatory speech, noting that Americans were free "to disagree with the law but not to disobey it." In Oxford the state highway patrol withdrew, leaving the marshals to control the crowd, now swollen by new arrivals, some of whom opened fire. Katzenbach, alarmed, asked Washington for the troops awaiting orders at their base in Memphis, Tennessee. There ensued a travesty of disorganization during which the president received repeated assurances that the troops were on their way, whereas in fact, they had yet to depart. When they finally got going, they moved with maddening delay. It was dawn before they began to arrive in force. Meanwhile, the marshals held on, though three of them were injured, as were some three hundred in the crowd. Two observers were killed. That morning Meredith registered.

Both Kennedys blamed themselves for believing Barnett and failing to send troops sooner. Burke Marshall thought the president had had no constitutional choice "about refusing in advance to accept the word of the governor of the state." As it worked out, the vacillation of Barnett, the behavior of the mob, the self-restraint of the marshals, and the clear constitutional basis for federal intercession brought the large majority of Americans to recognize the adminstration's course as moderate. Nevertheless, many southerners, by no means only white extremists, were distressed by the president's recourse to the military. For their part, the Kennedys had witnessed a costly demonstration of the intractability of white resistance to even token integration. They were thereafter more alert to the inescapable conflicts that the civil rights movement was engendering, though they were not yet on that account prepared to modify their cautious reading of the Constitution or otherwise to revise their policies. The president remained unwilling to sponsor strong civil rights legislation, and civil rights leaders still despaired over this "lack of moral conviction." That phrase was King's, who also wrote that Kennedy's dealings with Barnett had "made Negroes feel like pawns in a white politician's game." More than ever, he continued, the country needed "vigorous and firm exercise of the powers of the Presidency."

3

Appearance and Reality

Martin Luther King, Jr., often complained about what he considered Kennedy's preoccupation with foreign affairs and national politics. During the fall of 1962, with the questions of the MLF and the Common Market trade barriers pending, and with the off year congressional elections approaching, the president had limited choice. On October 16, 1962, he ceased to have any choice at all. That morning he first saw reconnaissance photographs, taken two days earlier by a U-2. They provided conclusive evidence that the Soviet Union was building bases in Cuba for launching offensive missiles. Too close for effective interception by the existing American early-warning system, those medium-range ballistic missiles (MRBMs), once they became operational, could carry nuclear warheads to targets almost anywhere in the eastern third of the United States. American intelligence had no evidence of nuclear warheads in Cuba, but as the United States later learned, there were twenty of them there and twenty more on the way. As McGeorge Bundy recalled, it was prudent in 1962 to assume they were available. The discovery of the launching pads, in Robert Kennedy's recollection, marked "the beginning of the Cuban missile crisis—a confrontation between the two giant atomic nations . . . which brought the world to the abyss of nuclear destruction and the end of mankind."

President Kennedy had warned Khrushchev against exactly the threat the missiles posed. Both the Cubans and the Russians believed the United States was planning an invasion. Their intelligence services knew about Operation Mongoose, a vast secret scheme authorized after the

Soviet missiles in Cuba: In Washington, shocked incredulity.

Bay of Pigs to destabilize Cuba and eliminate Castro. Robert Kennedy hoped Mongoose would foment an internal revolution to unseat the Cuban leader. The CIA, for its part, was concocting bizarre plots to assassinate Castro. The American military services had also begun to develop their own plans for an invasion. According to his closest advisers, the president did not intend to invade Cuba, but the Cubans and the Russians, privy to the American anti-Castro plans, could not help misreading Kennedy's mind. In July 1962 the Soviet Union had therefore begun a rapid buildup of Cuba's defenses with increasing shipments of first-line equipment, including surface-to-air missiles (SAMs), MiG-21 fighter airplanes, and radar, communications, and electronic gear. As Castro's brother said, "We can now repel an American invasion."

For his part, Kennedy could not ignore the arming of Cuba. Since the Bay of Pigs the Republicans had been criticizing him for his handling of that debacle. In the summer of 1962, condemning Kennedy for permitting the Soviet shipments to Castro, the Republicans, as their speeches continually stressed, designated Cuba as "the dominant issue of the . . . campaign." During the first half of September Kennedy responded in statements characterizing demands for an invasion of Cuba as "irresponsible" and also promising to "watch what happens in Cuba with the closest attention." The president on September 4, 1962, received private assurances from Khrushchev that the Soviet Union would make no trouble for the United States during the election campaign. Kennedy replied immediately by warning the Russians in public against introducing offensive ground-to-ground missiles in Cuba. Robert Kennedy on September 16 repeated that message in private to Soviet Ambassador Anatoly Dobrynin, who delivered further reassurance from Khrushchev. On September 13 the president in another public statement said that if Cuba were to "become an offensive military base of significant capacity for the Soviet Union, then the country will do whatever must be done to protect its own security and that of its allies." There was no misunderstanding between the leaders of the two superpowers. Further, the National Intelligence Estimate of September 19 concluded that the Soviet Union would not place offensive missiles in Cuba, and as late as October 14 McGeorge Bundy said on national television, "I *know* there is no evidence, and I think there is no present likelihood that the Cubans . . . and the Soviet Government would . . . attempt to install major offensive capacity."

1. CRISIS

That very night an American overflight photographed the proof that Khrushchev had been lying, deliberately and successfully deceiving Kennedy. The speed and secrecy of the Soviet action, a major logistical effort, effected a surprise as startling as the Japanese attack on Pearl Harbor in 1941. Khrushchev may have underestimated Kennedy's resolve. He may have counted on better coordination by Soviet bureaucracies in their separate assignments in Cuba and therefore have expected the missiles to be operative before they were discovered. That would have complicated Kennedy's response. Still, Khrushchev should have understood the magnitude of the risk he was taking, a risk for which Cuba itself was too small a stake.

Khrushchev did have a real interest in protecting Cuba, a Soviet client state, the only such in the Western Hemisphere. After the event he found it politically convenient to assert that he had acted to that end. But the installation of sites for Russian MRBMs and the accompanying preparation of larger sites for intermediate-range ballistic missiles (IRBMs) contributed more to Soviet power than to the defense of Cuba. Castro must have realized that the missiles had their only military utility as part of a Soviet first nuclear strike against the United States, a strike that would trigger American nuclear retaliation and, with it, the destruction of Cuba.

The missiles had great military importance for the Soviet Union. As the Kennedy administration had discovered in 1961, and as Eisenhower had known, the United States had a substantial lead over the Soviet Union in its stock of intercontinental ballistic missiles (ICBMs), as well as in long-range submarines and aircraft, the other types of weapons necessary for a direct nuclear attack by one superpower against the other. In the spring of 1962 Secretary of Defense McNamara had referred in public to that advantage, which, he said, "we confidently expect to maintain." The Soviet Union had lagged in building ICBMs because of their expense at a time when the country's budget was strained by the burden of defense in Asia as well as Europe and by the cost of improving civilian conditions of life. To enhance those defenses, the Soviet Union had built a substantial number of MRBMs and IRBMs that could reach targets in Europe and Asia. Nevertheless, under pressure from the military hard-liners in the Kremlin, Khrushchev moved a long way toward rectifying Soviet strategic inferiority by placing the shorter-range missiles in Cuba. The forty-two MRBMs shipped to Cuba, only half of which arrived, constituted two-thirds of Russian missile power at that time. (American military intelligence thought the Russians had twice as many.) With the forty warheads also shipped, those missiles, when they became operational, would more than double the Soviet capacity for a first strike in a nuclear war, and they would assure an element of surprise in that eventuality.

Khrushchev also dispatched to Cuba some forty thousand Russian soldiers and technicians (twice the American estimate) to man the sites, to assemble and operate the missiles, and, not the least, to guard them against the Cubans. Castro, too impulsive for Khrushchev's taste, was to have no control over those weapons. Indeed, for Khrushchev Cuba was a kind of unsinkable carrier from which, as he later wrote, "our missiles ... would have equalized ... the balance of power." He understood the danger of nuclear war. He knew he was ignoring Kennedy's warning against installing offensive weapons in Cuba. Obviously he was playing for very high stakes.

The president understood at once the political and military consequences of Khrushchev's initiative. As Robert Kennedy put it, that accounted for "the dominant feeling ... of shocked incredulity. We had been fooled by Khrushchev, but we had also fooled ourselves." To the American people the president later said that "this sudden, clandestine decision to station strategic weapons for the first time outside of Soviet soil, is a deliberately provocative and unjustifiable change in the status quo which cannot be accepted by this country." It was "a probe, a test of America's will to resist."

If Kennedy backed away, so he reasoned, Khrushchev might seize West Berlin, though the president later mused that "if they doubted our guts, why didn't they take Berlin?" If Kennedy decided to bargain, Khrushchev might demand concessions affecting Germany or the removal of American missiles, obsolete though they were, from Turkey and Italy. Either one of those two outcomes would strain the Western alliance by seeming to sacrifice European for American security. So, too, would an American attack on Cuba, an island to which most European statesmen attached small importance. Such an attack would also alienate Latin Americans, always suspicious of Yankee imperialism, though American inaction would cost the United States face south of the border. Either way Khrushchev gained. The Russian's venture constituted, too, a formal challenge to Kennedy because he had warned so explicitly against it. Above all, it involved an alteration in the status quo, and even the appearance of that change tipped the balance of power, so Kennedy later maintained, arguing that "the appearance contributed to reality."

It was, therefore, under extraordinary political and military pressure that Kennedy reacted to the discovery of the missile sites. Yet he did so with notable caution and control. He proceeded, as did Khrushchev, on the assumption that he was dealing with an essentially rational opponent, though Kennedy worried continually about pushing so hard that the volatile Russian would react impulsively. From the beginning to the end of the crisis the president consulted continually with a group of advisers who formed what became known as the Ex Comm (the Executive Committee of the National Security Council). He first assembled them in the late morning of October 16. They were, according to the president's charge, to "make a prompt and intensive survey of the dangers of all possible courses of action." The group, fifteen in all, included Robert Kennedy, Theodore Sorensen, and Robert McNamara, the three on whom the President most relied, as well as McNamara's senior deputy, Dean Rusk and several others from the State Department, McGeorge Bundy, later the Joint Chiefs, and intermittently Adlai Stevenson and Dean Acheson. They met daily, often several times a day, for thirteen days, sometimes with the president, often without, and they operated with a candor possible because neither rank nor age prevented them from dealing with one another as equals. Almost all of them changed from one position to another as they debated and as new evidence became available, but gradually they divided into two camps, soon to be designated as the hawks—the hard-liners—and the doves—those favoring a more measured course.

At the first meeting, after Rusk had presented a characteristically inconclusive analysis. McNamara spoke to the military options. "If we are to conduct an air strike against these installations," he said, "or against any part of Cuba, we must . . . schedule that prior to the time when these missile sites become operational. . . . If they become operational before the air strike, I do not believe . . . we can knock them out before they can be launched; and if they're launched there is almost certain to be . . . chaos in part of the east coast. . . . Secondly . . . any air strike must be directed not solely against the missile sites, but against the missile sites plus the airfields plus the aircraft which may not be on the airfields but hidden . . . plus all potential nuclear storage sites. . . . This is a fairly extensive air strike. . . . There would be associated with it potential casualties of Cubans . . . most likely in the low thousands. . . . We would have to be prepared, following the airstrike, for an . . . invasion, both by air and by sea." General Taylor, chairman of the Joint Chiefs, added that the United States would also have to prevent further offensive missiles from reaching Cuba, "which means a naval blockade," and would have to reinforce the American base at Guantánamo—all in all, a major military operation.

Further deliberation focused on whether or not to inform or consult NATO or the Organization of American States (OAS) before any action. Bundy worried about "the amount of noise we would get from our allies saying that . . . they can live with the Soviet MRBMs, why can't we." Vice President Johnson said he did not rely on the OAS "for any strength in anything like this." The president, who listened far more than he talked, summarized the options he saw: "[O]ne is the strike just on . . . three bases. . . . The second is the broader one that Secretary McNamara was talking about. . . . Third is doing both . . . and also . . . launching a blockade. . . . And then . . . the fourth question is the . . . degree of consultation." He ordered more U-2 flights to obtain more information, which a secret spy satellite was also gathering. He set up a meeting that afternoon for the State and Defense departments to work out their possible scenarios, political and military. He arranged for a meeting he would join that evening. And before departing, in referring to the preparations necessary for all contingencies, he said: "We're certainly going to do number one; we're going to take out those . . . missiles."

That evening and in ensuing days, at meetings which the president attended and at those he did not, the case for "number one," a surgical strike, crumbled. In the absence of hard evidence that the Soviet Union had sent nuclear warheads to Cuba, the need for a surgical strike against the missile launching pads remained more dubious than any of the Ex Comm contended. More important, the military could not assure the success of a surgical strike. They believed a much larger aerial operation would be necessary, and in that event there was no safe way to warn the Kremlin before the fact, and the bombing was bound to produce casualties among Soviet soldiers guarding the installations. That eventuality forebode Soviet retaliation against either Western Europe or the United States, or both, and, with it, escalation to nuclear war. It was the danger of nuclear war that argued most eloquently against an air strike. The president best expressed that view after the crisis: "Above all, while defending our own vital interests, nuclear powers must avert those confrontations which bring an adversary to the choice of either a humiliating defeat or a nuclear war."

President Kennedy missed a meeting on October 17 because, in an effort to keep appearances normal while he was deciding about policy in Cuba, he was campaigning in Connecticut. That meeting was grim. Aerial photography showed the Russians working much faster than Washington had expected to make the sites operational. The photographs also revealed for the first time three IRBM sites under construction. From those positions missiles with a twenty-two-hundred-mile range could reach almost any part of the United States. As the Russians later admitted, they had selected New York City, Washington, D.C., other centers of population, and major military installations as targets for their missiles.

On the afternoon of October 18, when the Ex Comm met again, American land, sea, and air forces were mobilizing in Florida. Kennedy kept an appointment with Soviet Foreign Minister Andrei Gromyko, who reported his instructions "to make it clear" that the Soviet purpose in arming Cuba was "by no means offensive." Khrushchev prevaricated in the same way to the American ambassador in Moscow. Sustaining their deceit, the Russians obviously did not yet know that the Americans had seen through it. But any resulting American advantages would evaporate as soon as the mobilization in Florida became known or the missile sites in Cuba became operational.

On the evening of October 18 a majority of the Ex Comm had come to favor a blockade instead of an air strike. McNamara had reached that conclusion a day earlier, and the president had been inclining that way. Both were eager to begin with a minimal step, one that would postpone as long as possible an ultimate escalation. A blockade, though an act of war, would give Khrushchev time to draw back. But the Joint Chiefs, except for Marine General Shoup, as they said the next day, still favored an aerial strike or an invasion. Off again campaigning, the president had told his brother Robert and Ted Sorensen to push the group toward agreement in time for action on October 21, a Sunday. Robert Kennedy had become the commanding advocate of his brother's position. He favored a blockade, he later wrote, "not from a deep conviction that it would be . . . successful . . . but a feeling that it had more flexibility and fewer liabilities than a military attack. Most importantly . . . I could not accept the idea that the United States would rain bombs on Cuba, killing thousands and thousands of civilians in a surprise attack." That argument against a Pearl Harbor in reverse irritated Dean Acheson, who contended that the president's responsibility for the security of the American people and the "free world" demanded the destruction of the sites. The attorney general replied that "American traditions and history would not permit such a course of action." A strike would undermine "our moral position at home and around the globe." Acheson stood his ground, with support from Bundy and the other hawks. Robert Kennedy repeated his point. "I said," he recalled, "we were fighting for something more than just survival and that all our heritage and our ideals would be repugnant to . . . a sneak attack."

The president had allowed the debate to go on at least partly to guard against the chance that his committee might otherwise fail thoroughly to explore every possibility. By Saturday, October 20, he had made up his mind privately for the blockade, but at a meeting that Adlai Stevenson attended, Kennedy "sharply rejected" Stevenson's suggestion of offering withdrawal of American missiles in Turkey and evacuation of Guantánamo in exchange for removal of the missile sites in Cuba. Stevenson had missed earlier meetings because he had been in New York on UN business. Now his proposal seemed to Kennedy to be a retreat. The president would not remove the obsolete missiles from Turkey while under pressure from Moscow, though he had earlier wanted their removal, which diplomatic negotiations with Turkey had failed to arrange. "We must be more forthcoming." Stevenson replied," . . . the present situation requires that we offer to give up such bases in order to induce the Russians to remove the strategic missiles." Robert Kennedy "disagreed strongly." Neither brother had liked Stevenson. Now, intending as they were to reject the counsel of the hawks, they berated Stevenson as too weak. "We will have to make a deal in the end," the attorney general told Schlesinger privately, "but we must stand firm now. Our concessions must come at the end of negotiations, not at the start." Just to be sure, Kennedy sent Schlesinger and John J. McCloy, a Republican elder statesman, to monitor Stevenson or, as he put it, "to watch things in New York."

On Sunday, October 21, the president listened while the head of the Tactical Air Command admitted to the Ex Comm that even a major strike might leave some missiles capable of use against the United States. Kennedy then said he would order a blockade. He had already asked Sorensen and others to draft diplomatic notes to the Kremlin, but they could not compose a text that would prevent Khrushchev from out-maneuvering the United States by demanding a meeting or a UN investigation. Either would give him time to complete the construction of the installations. Accordingly the president decided to address the American people on the evening of October 22 to explain the crisis and his plans for a "quarantine," his word for a limited blockade. Concur-rently he would open discussions with the Russians before any naval confrontation could occur. He also sent Acheson to inform the NATO nations and arranged for a meeting of the OAS in order to solicit its support for his policy.

Late Monday afternoon the president told the congressional leaders what was pending. Senators Fulbright and Richard Russell of Georgia argued for an air strike—Fulbright, as he later reflected, because he had not had the benefit of the Ex Comm discussions; Russell, probably because he reflected the personal opinion of Vice President Johnson, who had complained to him privately, in violation of Kennedy's injunction of secrecy. In contrast with the vice president, some of Ken-nedy's critics believed that his speech to the country and his ensuing actions exaggerated the emergency. His text did ring the changes of cold war rhetoric, but otherwise he said little about the Soviet action that was not true and nothing at all in which he did not believe. There had been, as he maintained, a "secret, swift and extraordinary build-up of Communist missiles, in an area well-known to have a special and historical relationship to the United States and . . . in violation of Soviet assurances."

His initial response, the president reported, included the quarantine, continuing surveillance of the buildup, requests for action by the UN and OAS, an appeal to Khrushchev, and preparations for further mea-sures should they prove necessary. As he also said, Americans had been "living daily in the bull's-eye of Soviet missiles located inside the U.S.S.R." Accustomed to the possibility of devastating attack, they now

*Adlai Stevenson at the UN
Security Council: A solemn
and significant speech.*

took the president's speech seriously but without panic. With trivial
exceptions they accepted the crisis, the most serious Soviet-American
confrontation to that date, without altering the pattern of their daily
lives. But the speech marked only the beginning of the test of Kennedy's tactics.

2. RESOLUTION

The OAS unanimously authorized the quarantine, and the NATO
Council supported the president, though de Gaulle, while promising
him support, observed that he had been informed rather than consulted. Stevenson surprised the Kennedys with his powerful statement
of the American case, supported by aerial photographs, to the UN
Security Council. Stevenson introduced a resolution calling for the
"immediate dismantling and withdrawal" from Cuba of all missiles
and other offensive weapons, requesting the secretary-general to send
a UN observer corps to Cuba, and recommending that the United States
and Soviet Union "confer promptly on measures to remove the existing
threat" to peace. "This is . . . a solemn and significant day for . . . the
hope of the world community," Stevenson said. "Let it be remembered

not as the day when the world came to the edge of nuclear war, but as the day when men reached to let nothing . . . stop them in their quest for peace."

For their part, the Russians and Cubans attacked the American quarantine. In his first answer to the president, Khrushchev on October 23 insisted the Soviet arms in Cuba were defensive and accused the United States of aggression against Cuba and the Soviet Union and of violating the UN Charter and the law of the sea. Kennedy had expected no less. On October 24 he began personally to manage the blockade, which went into effect that day.

The president did so with a delicate, prudential touch. At the suggestion of his friend the British ambassador David Ormsby-Gore, he ordered the quarantine line moved closer to Cuba so as to give Soviet ships at sea more time to turn back. As those ships approached, Kennedy decided to let through all except vessels carrying dry cargoes that might include missiles or nuclear warheads. The navy was to shoot, if necessary, only to cripple those ships, not to sink them, and then to board and search them. On October 24 news arrived of a Russian submarine that had moved into position between two ships near the quarantine line. To avoid an incident, the president decided to use an underwater sound message to warn the submarine to surface and, if it

Quarantine: An American destroyer inspecting a Soviet freighter.

refused, to drop only a small depth charge as a further warning. "I think these few minutes," Robert Kennedy later wrote, "were the time of gravest concern for the President. Was the world on the brink of a holocaust? Was it our error? . . . His hand went up to his face and covered his mouth. He opened and closed his fist. His face seemed drawn, his eyes pained. . . . He . . . no longer had control of events. He would have to wait." Within half an hour a messenger reported that the Russian ships had "stopped dead in the water." Soon thereafter the president learned that the fourteen Russian ships closest to the block-ade line had either stopped or turned around.

No more than Kennedy did Khrushchev want to push the crisis to nuclear war. He rejected Castro's plea for a preemptive nuclear strike against the United States. But Khrushchev was determined to prevent American inspection of secret warheads and missiles, which the cap-ture of a ship carrying them would have permitted. Consequently, only one tanker kept coming. The hawks on the Ex Comm wanted to inter-cept it, but the president instead had American vessels shadow the tanker and ordered the navy to let it through. Khrushchev, he reasoned, needed more time: "We don't want to push him to precipitous action. . . . I don't want to put him into a corner from which he cannot escape."

Yet Kennedy also declined a suggestion from the acting secretary-general of the UN for a suspension of the blockade in return for a Russian promise to send no more missiles to Cuba. The Soviet Union had precipitated the crisis, the president held. A peaceful solution required removal of the missiles. Communications with Khrushchev continued almost daily, with daily incidents arising also at sea. On October 25 Kennedy had the navy board a Panamanian cargo ship under Soviet charter. It carried no weapons, but barring some conces-sions from Moscow, the next episode might prove more dangerous. Indeed, the president ordered preparations for an invasion of Cuba should it become necessary. "If we do invade," he said, "by the time we get to these sites, after a very bloody fight, they will be pointed at us. . . . We must accept the possibility . . . those missiles will be fired." They certainly could have been.

In the early evening of October 27 the message for which Kennedy had been hoping at last reached him from Khrushchev. It was "long and emotional," as Robert Kennedy recalled, but it was also coherent. "We . . . understand perfectly well," Khrushchev wrote, while repeat-ing that the missiles were defensive, "that if we attack you, you will respond the same way. . . . I think that you also understand this. . . . We want something quite different . . . despite our ideological differences, to compete peacefully, not by military means." If Kennedy would give "assurances . . . that the United States would not participate in an attack on Cuba" and that the blockade would be lifted, Khrushchev would send no more missiles to Cuba and remove those that were there. "We and you," he continued, "ought not to pull on the ends of the rope in which you have tied the knot of war, because . . . then it will be necessary to cut that knot. Let us take measures to untie that knot. We are ready for this."

But the next morning there arrived a second message, less tractable, more formal, probably a more accurate reflection of the views of the Politburo. It proposed Soviet removal of the missiles in Cuba in exchange for American removal of the missiles in Italy and Turkey, as well as reciprocal pledges by the two powers not to invade their smaller neighbors. The Joint Chiefs, professionally conditioned to propose a military solution, still advised an air strike, with new militancy after they learned that SAMs in Cuba had downed an American plane. "It isn't the first step that concerns me," the president said in rebuttal, "but both sides escalating to the fourth or fifth step—and we don't go to the sixth because there is no one around to do so." Some of the Joint Chiefs, as Kennedy later remarked, were "mad."

While the Ex Comm pondered a draft reply to Khrushchev, Robert Kennedy made the imaginative suggestion that the president ignore the second letter and reply instead to the more hopeful first one. Others supported that idea, which the hawks opposed, until the president sent his brother and Sorensen to prepare the reply they had in mind. As the president then signed it, it called for an immediate cessation of work on the bases in Cuba to be followed by discussions between American and Soviet representatives, in cooperation with the secretary-general of the UN, along the lines Khrushchev had proposed. The Soviet Union was also to remove the missiles from Cuba under UN supervision and introduce no such missiles again, while the United States was to end the blockade and give assurances against invasion of Cuba, as would the OAS. "The United States," the letter said, in the same spirit Khrushchev had displayed, "is very much interested in reducing tensions and halting the arms race; and if . . . you are prepared to discuss a detente affecting NATO and the Warsaw Pact, we are quite prepared to consider with our allies any useful proposals."

Early the next morning, acting as the president's agent, Robert Kennedy told Soviet Ambassador Dobrynin that the United States knew work on the bases in Cuba was continuing, that the shooting down of the U-2 over Cuba would not deter further reconnaissance missions, that if the Cubans or Russians shot at any of those, it would "lead to further incidents and to escalation." "As a statement of fact," not as an ultimatum, the attorney general also said that if the missile bases were not removed, the United States would remove them, and that action might lead to Soviet retaliation and to "not only dead Americans but dead Russians as well." He then explained the terms offered to Khrushchev. Dobrynin inquired about the Jupiter missiles in Turkey and Italy. "There could be no quid pro quo," Kennedy replied, but "within a short time after the crisis was over, those missiles would be gone." That private promise completed the American response to Khrushchev's offer. Both sides had put forward reasonable terms. Though the Kennedys were not optimistic, within a few hours Khrushchev had accepted the deal. The crisis was over, the danger of nuclear war averted, as both principals knew it had to be.

What guided the president through the deliberations, Robert Kennedy wrote, "was an effort not to disgrace Khrushchev, not to humiliate the Soviet Union, not to have them feel they would have to escalate their response." The president "understood that the Soviet Union did not want war," as Khrushchev understood the Americans did not. Each reassured the other about his limited objectives. When it was all over, neither man claimed a victory. "If it was a triumph," as Robert Kennedy concluded, "it was a triumph for the next generation and not for any particular government or people."

The developments of the thirteen days of the missile crisis revealed how much many of the officials of the Kennedy administration had grown since the confused days of the Bay of Pigs, and how little had others. Most impressive were the president and his brother, both of whom demonstrated notable statesmanship under relentless pressure. Sorensen and McNamara also played outstanding roles, and Bundy stood out for his selflessness and loyalty. Secretary of State Dean Rusk, in contrast, contributed less of significance either to the analysis or the resolution of the issues, and the Joint Chiefs, excepting only Shoup, persistently disclosed a professional rigidity. Vice President Johnson, who displayed no larger vision, seemed throughout a restless hawk, disgruntled by the lack of any quick and easy solution.

As the president's supporters maintained, the outcome of the crisis was in part a victory for the doctrine of flexible response. Had massive retaliation been the only American option, the United States would have had either to do nothing or to resort to nuclear war. But the instruments employed for a flexible response owed less to the Kennedy military budgets than his advocates implied. The naval vessels that carried out the quarantine, or their equivalents, had been available before 1961, as had the U-2s that undertook the surveillance of Cuba. Before that date it would have been difficult, if not impossible, to mobilize as quickly or as completely for a possible invasion of Cuba, but that option, of which Khrushchev was aware, was as perilous as Kennedy recognized. Further, the crisis itself might not have occurred when it did had not the Kennedy military program raised Soviet anxieties. It was not so much a doctrine of strategy or of warfare as the clarity of the president's thinking, the prudence of his management, and his horror at the prospect of nuclear war that governed American policy. Even those qualities might have proved inadequate had Khrushchev not also understood the implications of nuclear war and his country's vulnerability in waging one, a vulnerability that predated 1961 and for which he had intended to compensate, at considerable risk, by placing the missile sites in Cuba.

That very risk suggested that senior Soviet officials would not remain content with American nuclear superiority. In the event, there was dubious comfort in McNamara's emerging doctrine of mutual assured destruction (MAD). According to that logic, deterrence depended upon the confidence of each superpower in the ability of its own nuclear forces to survive a first attack and retaliate. Mutual fear of retaliation presumably provided protection for civilian populations. But sustained mutual fear depended on the adequacy, though not necessarily the equality, of each side's arsenal. The sense of inadequacy that prompted Khrushchev to send missiles to Cuba also contributed to his measured response to Kennedy. During the predictable future, no more than the Kennedys or their American critics would the Soviet leaders find nuclear inadequacy tolerable. In the absence of détente, the arms race would continue.

That prospect spoke to the question of American dominance, which the Soviet Union was committed to challenge. There was no way of returning to the temporary American atomic monopoly of the immediate postwar years. Détente offered a less expensive and less dangerous alternative to the arms race, though détente in itself demanded a genuine bargain between effective equals. Khrushchev had suggested the desirability of détente, and Kennedy had encouraged that suggestion; but both were still nervous suitors. Khrushchev, moreover, faced domestic opposition within the Politburo; Kennedy, from American hawks, especially Republican hawks like Richard Nixon, who held that the president had needlessly given away American advantages in the settlement of the missile crisis.

Still, the crisis and its resolution had little apparent effect on the

November elections, which local issues dominated. The results were inconclusive. The Democrats gained four seats in the Senate; the Republicans, two in the House. In the following two years Kennedy would still confront serious opposition on the Hill. The terms for settling the missile crisis also proved difficult to implement. Castro, resentful of the Soviet decisions, refused to permit UN supervision, though the Soviet Union proceeded to remove the missiles and launchers anyhow, with American overflights checking the operation. The United States did not make a formal pledge not to invade Cuba although Kennedy, creeping toward normalization of relations, clamped down on the forays against the island previously ventured by émigrés in Florida. He also withdrew the Jupiters from Turkey, and he began to consider means for approaching détente with the Soviet Union.

Yet Kennedy's concern about appearances as surrogates for reality, the concern that had led him to jump so hard on Adlai Stevenson, constituted an obstacle to overt mutual concessions. Appearances were not realities, as Eisenhower had shown by ignoring the appearance of a missile gap in the secret certainty that none existed. Kennedy had yet to gain the confidence and serenity that inhered in the esteem Eisenhower had commanded. But the resolution of the missile crisis was building the president's esteem. As two of his staff then told him, he "looked ten feet tall." Kennedy replied: "That will wear off in about a week, and every one will be back to thinking only of their own interest."

3. Skybolt

So it was with the British and the French. Throughout the missile crisis Prime Minister Macmillan had rendered Kennedy steady support. But that crisis had diverted the president's attention from Anglo-American relations. Early in November 1962 he accepted Defense Secretary McNamara's proposal to cancel the program to build Skybolt missiles, air-to-surface missiles that Eisenhower had promised to supply to the British. McNamara, who considered other missiles more effective weapons, was eager to cut Skybolt from the budget. But the British had been counting on Skybolt to deliver their independent nuclear deterrent. The unilateral American cancellation of the program wounded British pride and embarrassed the Macmillan government. The *Washington Post* called the "weakness of Skybolt as a weapon less damaging than the weakness in the conduct of American foreign policy."

Kennedy placated Macmillan by substituting for Skybolt the Polaris missile, a weapon for use by submarines. But Macmillan remained dubious about the American proposal for an integrated, multilateral NATO force, a proposal Charles de Gaulle openly opposed. Indeed, de Gaulle, jealous of the independent British deterrent, insisted for France on the "principle . . . of disposing in our own right of our deterrent force." He rejected an Anglo-American offer to receive Polaris on the same basis as the British and proceeded with his own nuclear program.

That decision marked the end of McNamara's hopes for transatlantic integration of both nuclear and conventional forces and the end, too, for State Department hopes for European political union following British entry into the Common Market. Secure in his unacknowledged shelter under the American nuclear umbrella, de Gaulle had shown, as he intended to, that the United States did not dominate him. He soon went on to veto British membership in the European Economic Community. Temporarily in London, continually in Paris, Kennedy had seemed rather less than ten feet tall.

4. SDS

A growing minority of young Americans also had doubts about the president, doubts the missile crisis reinforced. Those young skeptics, convinced that the cold war was unnecessary, blamed its inception largely on the United States. They considered Kennedy reckless in bringing the world so close to a nuclear disaster. They were equally dubious about the sincerity of his administration in its ameliorative approach toward American racism and poverty, which they blamed on systemic conditions they would have liked instantly to have corrected. The vanguard of an incipient youth movement, by 1962 they had begun to formulate their personal, social, and political views and to proselytize among their peers, especially those on college campuses.

The American youth movement of the 1960s reflected in part the universal and recurrent alienation of a younger generation from the values and mores of its elders. The children of the baby boom of the late 1940s and early 1950s constituted an increasing proportion of the total population. By 1962 those who were white and middle-class were moving through high school and college just as their parents, now typically in their forties, were reaching the pinnacles of their various careers as managers, journalists, physicians, attorneys, or even principals of the New Frontier.

That generation—Kennedy's generation, men and women who had

known the Great Depression and fought in World War II—had within
it a large corps of liberals who venerated the New Deal and, with their
more conservative contemporaries, believed with patriotic conviction
in the threat to the United States and to freedom that they saw as
embodied in the Soviet Union and the Communist party. They
responded favorably to the president's cold war rhetoric. Their children, turning away from their parents, more often preferred Kennedy's
expressed idealism. When asked what they could do for their country,
they characteristically mentioned the Peace Corps, not the Green Berets.
By 1962 a small fraction of those young Americans had become critical
of the inadequacies of the president's achievements. They had come to
wonder whether he and the liberals around him, indeed, whether their
parents, too, were not guilty of hypocrisy, a cardinal sin in the pan-
theon of their values—values inculcated largely by the very parents
who now, like Kennedy, fell short of their children's exacting expectations.

American middle-class youth then often had also an unoriginal but
pronounced proclivity to mock their backgrounds. Middle-class life since
the 1940s had become increasingly suburban life, and the suburbs,
especially to the young adults departing from them, seemed stultifying.
There were expensive suburbs for the well-to-do and cheaper suburbs

An American suburb: Cathedral of conformity?

for the lower middle class barely able to afford to escape the ethnic conclaves of the cities. But suburbs in general, in the litany of the young, conformed to the caricatures their youthful expatriates consistently drew. In that version they were cathedrals of conformity, consisting of houses distinguishable from one another only by their colors and inhabited by families pursuing the material comforts of a consumer culture—station wagons, patio furniture, television sets. Most suburban parents in actuality thought of themselves as sensitive to each stage in the development of their children, but in the negative stereotype of the suburbs, parents, perhaps unwittingly, treated their children as extensions of their own egos. They expected their children to succeed in competition with their peers for athletic honors, social success, and admission to prestigious colleges and then professional schools. They also expected their children to conform to the speech, dress, and comportment that they associated with their own advance to bourgeois status or upward within it. There was sufficient truth in the caricature to persuade thousands of suburban children, as they passed puberty and raced toward adulthood, to see themselves as helpless victims, deprived of privacy, of individuality, and, perhaps most grievously, of excitement. Those so persuaded felt alone, alienated from society, separated from one another, eager to find a genuine community based upon morality and love.

On their own terms, the emerging adults of every American generation had felt much that way, but those coming of age in the 1960s had their special contemporary routes and models. One path led to the incipient counterculture; another, to the emerging New Left. Neither excluded the other, and both had their beginnings in the 1950s. During that decade the harbingers of the counterculture built their popularity on vilification of bourgeois attitudes and values. So it was that the poet Allen Ginsberg, an authentic voice of American alienation, poured his mystic soul into "Howl," his protest of 1955 against middle-class restraints on self-expression and sexual gratification. Ginsberg's friend Jack Kerouac wrote his best-selling novel *On the Road* (1957) to recount as fiction his cross continental journey with two companions— an orgy of sex, marijuana, and jazz that terminated in a mystic vision, his "point of ecstasy." Kerouac's flight from boredom and routine, his rejection—and Ginsberg's—of materialism, the work ethic, and monogamy, set the tone for spiritual rebels of the time, who identified their longings with the hip style the two authors exemplified. That style borrowed a vocabulary from the language of inner-city blacks and a uniform from esoteric Asian gurus or, as in the case of dungarees, a half-remembered rural practicality. By 1960 American teenagers were

Allen Ginsberg: Poet of alien-ation.

beginning to make vulgar speech, faded jeans, long and dirty hair, and bare feet into elements of a fashion that spread steadily from California eastward and from New York westward.

Sex, always a teenage preoccupation, constituted one part of the counterculture, as increasingly did drugs, first pot, later in the 1960s also hallucinogens like LSD. A third major ingredient was music. It, too, had earlier roots in the rhythm of black musicians in the 1940s and its incorporation in the pop ballads of Elvis Presley in the 1950s. By 1962 the Beatles, a young singing group in Liverpool, England, were forging the style that made them famous. They swept through Britain in 1963, and a year later Beatlemania reached the United States. The Beatles' rock and roll, its irreverent lyrics and pulsing beat, evoked a fervid, even hysterical response from American youth. "She Loves Me" and "I Want to Hold Your Hand" rose to the top of the list in sales of phonograph records. At the same time Bob Dylan was infusing American folk music with his lyrics of social protest. Before Dylan moved over to rock and roll in the mid-1960s, his early songs—among them "Blowin' in the Wind" and "The Times They Are a-Changin' " carried a political message to the young, both those moving toward the counterculture and those immersed in the struggle for civil rights.

The novelist Norman Mailer, a hero of the rebellious young, had anticipated their new subculture by at least fifteen years in the graphic sexuality and rough language of his early fiction. He had endorsed the hip style in his prescient essay "The White Negro" and in his first two novels—*The Naked and the Dead* (1948) and *Barbary Shore* (1951)— had expressed a Marxism then proscribed in the cold war climate. In those respects, as in his use of drugs, he was a herald of the youth culture of the 1960s and of the New Left, for the decade witnessed a revival of Marxist thought, now stripped of the Stalinist cast of the preceding period.

As they consistently had, American Marxists in the 1960s attributed to capitalism and to its control of the state blame for the persistence of poverty, for the exaltation of bourgeois consumption, for the growth of militarism and American imperialism, and for prolongation of the cold war. That comprehensive indictment provided a party line for the small Marxist youth organizations—the Young People's Socialist League (YPSL) and the Student League for Industrial Democracy (SLID). They were resuscitating a doctrine available for the alienated or angry young, but by themselves they had too little influence to turn the youth movement from cultural to political protest.

Rather, the politicalization of the youth movement resulted primarily from the experience and the example of agitation for civil rights in the South. Young white middle-class Americans from northern colleges participated in growing numbers in the protest against injustice, and they felt the fierce resistance it provoked. In doing so, they saw at first hand the courage of their black contemporaries, the ugliness of white supremacists, and the temporizing of the Kennedy administration. As the protesters viewed it, the New Frontier failed to support their legitimate demands for federal protection against segregationist violence and for immediate federal remedies of ancient southern wrongs. Some northern white students joined their black friends in the independent and more aggressive Student Nonviolent Coordinating Committee, which in 1960 spun away from control by Martin Luther King, Jr., and SCLC. While Kennedy was campaigning for the presidency, the civil rights movement also served as a major catalyst for the emergence from SLID of the Students for a Democratic Society (SDS), the central organization of the white collegiate left. During the next two years the SDS, partly in response to Kennedy's policies on civil rights and Cuba, moved toward a portentous statement of its purposes.

But the SDS was also the product of an increasing uneasiness among college students about American society. During the 1960s enrollment in colleges and universities in the United States climbed to historic highs. In 1946 only two million Americans were attending institutions of higher learning. By 1970 some eight million were. The complexities of American social and economic life required the youth of the country to acquire the business and professional skills that universities instilled, but only a rich society could afford to permit so many young people to defer for so long their beginning of productive work. The privilege of a higher education, until World War II confined to relatively few Americans, was becoming a common part of growing up and a necessary preparation for a satisfying and remunerative career. But many students in college in the 1960s were the first in their families ever to enjoy that experience. And many of them were self-conscious about their ascent to a social status beyond the reach of their parents and beyond the means of thousands of their contemporaries who were impoverished or excluded because of their race. Those so aware had a sense of guilt that alerted them to social injustice and informed their criticisms of the status quo.

Some of their discontent grew out of conditions at the institutions they attended. The number and the size of colleges and universities had grown to meet the demand for higher education, but enrollments had increased faster than had the supply of qualified instructors. Classrooms bulged with students, especially at state-supported universities that could not turn away the high school graduates demanding to get in. Privately endowed institutions felt a comparable pressure for admissions and a comparable tightness in the market for new faculty. The sheer number of undergraduates, compared with the relative paucity of faculty, made teaching ordinarily impersonal and remote. Undergraduates complained about the unavailability of professors, the self-preoccupation of graduate students who graded their papers and exams, and the apparent irrelevance of the curriculum to current issues and later life. Those complaints were partly valid. Some professors were unavailable either because they had no interest in undergraduate education or because they gave so much of their time to their own research. Graduate students and younger faculty were hard put to complete their own work so as to gain professional advancement. Some courses were banal, and few faculties could convincingly explain the educational purposes of required courses or curricula originally designed twenty or thirty years earlier.

American colleges and universities needed reform. The discontented leaders of the SDS intended to make the case for it while they also criticized the racism and militarism of the larger society. They linked their causes. As they contended, many universities and their faculties undertook classified research for defense agencies in order to acquire income but at the predictable risk of losing the freedom of information and communication so vital to an intellectual environment. Further, as students at northern colleges could not help observing, the enrollment of blacks and of other minorities was so low as to demonstrate an active bias against them on the part of offices of admission and those senior administrators to whom they were responsible, including trustees.

The total indictment gained essential strength because it also served a general student need apart from education. Colleges and universities were proximate targets. They were closer, more susceptible to student influence and more vulnerable to attack than were large national institutions like the Pentagon or the Department of Justice. Residential colleges, moreover, exercised an authority that gave their students a common and frustrating sense of dependency. Most colleges in the early 1960s still acted *in loco parentis,* with parietal rules governing student dress and conduct. The student who resented a parent's conventional codes about those matters also objected to similar campus rules. But as with education, so with parietals; students normally had no vote. Student government elections almost everywhere consisted primarily of popularity contests—the winners powerless to alter conditions they disliked. Undergraduates who gave their summers to registering disfranchised black voters in the South returned to northern colleges to recognize themselves as totally disfranchised there.

In a summary analysis of the student movement, a leader at Berkeley recalled three kinds of influence that motivated his companions. One derived from family tensions, another from internal "problems resulting directly from being a student," and the third from external experience, "primarily from involvement in the civil rights movement" but also from recognition of the desolation of the poor. He might have added the sense that some students had of the needless and hideous prospect of nuclear war.

By 1962 the SDS had one paramount objective, a procedural one, to obtain a democratic mandate that would permit those affected to work out the problems they faced. That "participatory democracy" would involve the students themselves in a kind of town meeting of their college to make decisions, or at least recommendations, about courses and rules. Similarly, the poor in each urban ghetto, in some of which SDS leaders were already living and organizing, would develop a program to improve their lives. The people, instructed by the student spokesmen, would somehow end the power of the political elite to lead the nation into nuclear war.

The statement that the SDS issued at its 1962 national convention at Port Huron, Michigan, sounded a call to the colors of the student movement. It spelled out an "agenda for a generation . . . bred in at least modest comfort, housed now in universities, looking uncomfortably to the world we inherit." The impulse to activism, the Port Huron Statement contended, arose from "the permeating fact . . . of human degradation, symbolized by the Southern struggle against racial bigotry" and "the enclosing fact of the Cold War, symbolized by the presence of the Bomb." Four months before the Cuban missile crisis, the students observed "that we may be the last generation in the experiment with living." Holding their values as essential to human survival, they expressed their regard for people as "infinitely precious and possessed of unfilled capacities for reason, freedom, and love."

As a *"social system,"* the statement went on, "we seek the establishment of a democracy of individual participation," a system that would "replace power rooted in possession, privileges, or circumstance by power . . . rooted in love, reflectiveness, reason, and creativity." Then for many pages the statement protested poverty and unemployment, the accumulation of nuclear arms and the policy of deterrence, the American recourse to "gunboat" adventurism—in particular at the Bay of Pigs— in the face of the worldwide colonial revolution, and the role of the university in developing techniques of social engineering to preserve the status quo. So it appeared to the SDS, and of that appearance the organization composed its reality.

The SDS was not ready to give up on the university. On the contrary, in 1962 the movement saw the university as a "potential base and agency . . . for social change." A "new left . . . consisting of younger people" needed intellectual skills in order to assume "significant social roles throughout the country." That New Left had to "start controversy across the land" so as to reverse "national apathy" and "give form to . . . feelings of helplessness and indifference."

Paradoxically the students were to lead the nation to their goals. The Port Huron Statement made the students the new elite, though few students had yet acquired the skills that the statement deemed necessary for that role. Further, within the SDS, an elite few had fashioned the statement, which followed closely a draft prepared by Thomas E. Hayden, a founder and leader of the organization. A former editor of the student newspaper at Ann Arbor, Tom Hayden brought his sharp intelligence and dynamic personality to service in the New Left. Over the next decade he was at once to shape and to follow the contours of revolt. In 1962 he had constructed a reading list for the SDS that highlighted works by C. Wright Mills, who had made a theoretical case for participatory democracy and a personal statement of nonconformity on his conspicuous motorcycle. Mills believed that students, not the proletariat, would be in the vanguard of revolution. Like Mills, with whom they agreed, the leaders of the New Left postured a good deal. Many of them were personally more ambitious for power and fame than they readily admitted. A few confessed they were paranoid in their response to opposition or even criticism, much of it from the old left.

At Port Huron the SDS, by declining to bar Communists, leaned so far away from the anticommunism of the 1950s that it exposed itself to criticism from socialists like Michael Harrington, who knew from experience how the Communist party could first infiltrate and then take control of left-wing organizations. But at that time the SDS, still small, was not Communist or Marxist or doctrinaire. Both the SDS and its platform were still evolving. The student movement was only in the morning of its new age, half a decade from its noon. Ambitious, exuberant, self-confident, and self-righteous, the leaders of the movement were eager to enlist both liberals and socialists in their cause. In the retrospection of one of them, they sought "not to protest but to transform as well—to transform society, to transform ourselves."

More than they allowed, their goals reflected the best of the ideals John F. Kennedy had espoused. The young Turks were not wholly unlike Norman Mailer, who began one of his novels by having his protagonist go off on a double date with Kennedy. The SDS leaders did not share that fancy, but Hayden and others among them had been impressed by Kennedy's youthfulness and eloquence. Indeed, Kennedy was a potent symbol for the generation bred in modest comfort. More than they knew, he used in private the earthy vocabulary that the young were to bring to public discourse. More important, in his public life he was moving toward policies they commended—toward nuclear disarmament, toward federal programs to combat poverty and racism, though not toward participatory democracy as the SDS envisaged it; that would have violated Kennedy's sense of the politically practicable.

Kennedy had power; the students did not. Partly on that account, they did not trust him or other liberals of their parents' age. Indeed, the student left was soon to proclaim that it could trust no one over thirty. But through 1962 and for several years thereafter, the SDS was performing an essential service of the left in a democracy by pressing the liberals of the center to reassess the problems of the day and to speed their solution. Kennedy and others in the New Frontier needed to hear that message. The mounting national crises over race and the catastrophic possibility of nuclear war demanded constructive imagination that would transcend normal political expediencies. The president, as the SDS saw him, promised more than he intended to deliver. In their view, he supported genuine change only for political advantage and only when he was pushed. They were not entirely wrong. They were evangelical, and he was the rector of the established church. They were passionate; he was the embodiment of the cool.

4

Neither Peace nor Tranquillity

John F. Kennedy brought to the presidency, as he did to life, a shifting balance of vision and practicality. He needed both qualities to convert the near stalemates of the 1960 and 1962 elections into the mandate he hoped to gain in 1964. He also needed both if he was to join the heroes of his *Profiles in Courage* as a statesman notable for his attainments as well as his convictions. Eunice Shriver, Kennedy's sister, who had often served as his hostess in Washington before her marriage, once said that her brother's favorite president was Theodore Roosevelt. Certainly Kennedy shared Roosevelt's scorn for political dreamers and his taste for realizable ideals. Both men were susceptible to adopting as their own those political dreams that had become realizable because of the determination of supposedly impractical visionaries to make them so. Both men, shrewd politicians, knew how to ride with their times as well as how to shape them. Kennedy's motives, like those of most men, were mixed. During the year after the missile crisis he acted now because of principles in which he believed, now to pursue political advantage, now because events pushed him; ordinarily on all those counts. Taken together, they moved him from the cautious and sometimes faltering performance of the early months of his incumbency to bolder and more enduring achievements.

A calculated circumspection continued to characterize the president's policies on civil rights, where, in the words of Martin Luther King, Jr., Kennedy was "committed but . . . feeling his way." Eager to hold the support of southern Democrats and to avoid alienating white voters in the North, Kennedy deliberately waited until November 30,

1962, after the congressional elections, before issuing the order he had so long postponed to stop segregation in federally supported housing. He then made that order prospective but not retroactive, applicable only to housing financed by direct federal loans or grants, and, as it worked out, enforced only sporadically. The order had little effect. "Negroes," the *Pittsburgh Courier* wrote, "are getting weary of tokenism hailed as victories."

That remark could also have characterized Kennedy's civil rights message to Congress in February 1963. He called for legislation to help southern blacks to register to vote, to offer assistance for school desegregation, and to empower the Civil Rights Commission to "serve as a national . . . clearing house providing information . . . to any requesting agency." He said: "We are committed to achieving some equality of opportunity . . . because it is right." But the administration delayed sending specific proposals for legislation to the Hill. For its part, and against the wishes of the White House, the Civil Rights Commission at the end of March 1963 issued an interim report deploring the denial in Mississippi of the constitutional rights of blacks. It also urged the president to "explore" the authority he had said he lacked to withhold federal funds from the state until Mississippi complied with the law. Instead, Kennedy during the winter of 1963 continued to give priority to his tax bill. With southerners constituting a majority of Democrats on the Ways and Means Committee, White House specialists on relations with Congress warned the president to go slowly on civil rights if he wanted those southerners to support his revenue measure, about which they were in any case dubious.

1. BIRMINGHAM

The president was reckoning without sufficient allowance for the building impatience of civil rights leaders. No less than Kennedy did Martin Luther King, Jr., face a test of leadership as 1963 began. His personal reputation and the program of the Southern Christian Leadership Conference were suffering from the recent failures of the campaign for integration in Albany, Georgia, and generally throughout the South. Only 8 percent of black children there yet attended school with whites. The restlessness of many blacks, especially young blacks, over the lack of visible results drew them increasingly toward Elijah Muhammad's Black Muslims and other radical groups that scoffed at nonviolence as a technique and preached black separatism and hatred of whites. To sustain his influence, King needed a major victory, and to that end he had to force Kennedy to stop temporizing about civil rights.

It required special courage for King, at the invitation of his SCLC compatriot the Reverend Fred L. Shuttlesworth to lead a campaign of nonviolent demonstrations in Birmingham, Alabama. In that city, as the *New York Times* put it, "every channel of communication, every inch of middle ground has been fragmented by the emotional dynamite of racism." Birmingham had as its chief of police the notorious Eugene T. ("Bull") Connor, a vicious segregationist who could be relied upon to respond outrageously to any demonstration by blacks. And King risked Connor's wrath in order to provoke the chief to actions that would make Kennedy intercede.

On April 3, 1963, the day after a runoff election for mayor that Connor lost, King announced his plans for a boycott and demonstrations against white merchants—"a moral witness" to end racial discrimination in employment and public accommodations in Birmingham. During the next several days sit-ins at segregated luncheon counters resulted, as King had expected, in the arrests of participating blacks, which attracted the attention of national news media. While the boycott continued, Shuttlesworth on April 6 led a march on City Hall, where Connor arrested all those involved, as he did again on April 7, when his police intercepted a second march. The city then obtained an injunction from an Alabama court that forbade further racial demonstrations. On April 12, Good Friday, King announced his intention to violate that injunction, which he denounced as immoral. His act of civil disobedience, another march on City Hall, in which some fifty others joined, led Connor to order his arrest. Reporting the episode, television cameras depicted the growling police dogs with which Connor had supplied his men. That made grim fare for the evening news on Easter weekend.

Before the demonstrations had begun, Burke Marshall had urged King to postpone them. Otherwise the administration had kept out of Birmingham, a city superficially still orderly in spite of the widespread arrests. But when King was placed, incommunicado, in solitary confinement, both the president and the attorney general reassured Coretta King, who had telephoned in fear of her husband's safety. The conditions of King's imprisonment were then improved, but he had not yet convinced either the president or the white citizens of Birmingham of the righteousness of his purpose. He now tried to do so in a public letter replying to eight local clergymen who had asked him to abandon his "unwise and untimely" campaign.

The powerful logic and passionate eloquence of King's "Letter from the Birmingham Jail" made it an instant classic. He was no "outside agitator," King wrote, but a Christian and an American, bound therefore by duty to fight injustice anywhere. In Birmingham the white elite had resisted integration, broken their promises of amelioration, refused to negotiate with blacks. Those who counseled patience failed to understand that "wait" meant "never." Black Americans could no longer wait.

> When you have seen vicious mobs lynch your mothers and fathers at whim . . . when you see that vast majority of twenty million Negro brothers smothering in an air-tight cage of poverty in the midst of an affluent society . . . when you have to concoct an answer for a five-year-old son asking in agonizing pathos: "Daddy, why do white people treat colored people so mean?" . . . when you are humiliated day in and day out by nagging signs reading "white" and "colored"; when your first name becomes "nigger" and your middle name becomes "boy" . . . and your last name becomes "John," and when your wife and mother are never given the respected title "Mrs."; when you are forever fighting a degenerating sense of "nobodiness"—then you will understand why we find it difficult to wait.

Philosophers since Augustine and Aquinas, King continued, had recognized, as he did, the moral responsibility to disobey unjust laws like those imposing segregation. Disobedience through "nonviolent direct action" provided a channel without which "millions of Negroes, out of frustration and despair, will seek solace and security in black nationalist ideologies, a development that will lead . . . to a frightening racial nightmare." Registering disappointment in moderates (of whom the president and the attorney general were certainly two) for placing law and order above justice, King praised the heroes of the civil rights movement, among them James Meredith, who were "standing up for the best in the American dream and the most sacred values of our Judeo-Christian heritage."

King remained in prison a week. In that time young blacks in Birmingham reacted to continuing arrests of civil rights demonstrators by throwing rocks and bottles at the police. Once released on bond, King opened negotiations with the Senior Citizens Committee, a group of white businessmen and civic leaders established a year earlier to try to keep racial peace in the city. Those negotiations failed at just the time, on April 23, of the murder elsewhere in Alabama of William L. Moore, a black mail carrier who had set out on a "freedom walk" to Mississippi. As members of CORE and SNCC marched to complete Moore's mission, Alabama police arrested them. The state as well as the city of

Birmingham: Connor was brutal.

Birmingham was at the brink of racial violence when King opened the next phase of his campaign.

With hundreds of black adults in Birmingham's jail, King on May 2, 1963, mobilized more than a thousand black children to march for freedom through the city. Singing, laughing, praying, the children climbed without resistance into the vans that Bull Connor sent to carry them to jail. Critics of King's tactic, conservatives and radicals alike, chided him for exposing children to danger. He answered that children had a "sense of their own stake in freedom" and a right to influence their own futures. Connor thought otherwise. On May 3, as another thousand children gathered at the Sixteenth Street Baptist Church, he had the police block the entrance to the building, beat up the demonstrators who were able to emerge and the observers in the area, and turn loose dogs to attack the young people. When some adults threw bricks in retaliation, Connor ordered firemen to direct their punishing high-pressure hoses on the blacks, both young and old. The brutality of the police stunned millions of Americans who viewed it on evening television.

On May 4 the violence continued, as did the shock. Connor's police had arrested more than a thousand children and injured at least as many others. With the national mood now aroused, the president, "sick" about the violence, as he said, sent Burke Marshall and his deputy, Joseph Dolan, to Birmingham to mediate between the protesters and the white establishment. Hurt by the boycott and afraid of a bloodbath, the Senior Citizens Committee nevertheless rejected the terms for desegregation that SCLC proposed. The demonstrating continued, as did Connor's savagery. On May 7 fire hoses injured Reverend Shuttlesworth, who was trying to calm an angry crowd. "I waited a week to see Shuttlesworth get hit with a hose," Connor said. "I'm sorry I missed it. I wish they'd carried him away in a hearse."

That evening, after long negotiations, the Senior Citizens Committee approached agreement with SCLC. Three days later, on May 10, with an agreement at last in hand, King announced "that we have come today to the climax of a long struggle for justice, freedom and human dignity in . . . Birmingham." The city's establishment had conceded the "desegregation of lunch counters, rest rooms and drinking fountains" and had agreed to the "upgrading and hiring of Negroes on a nondiscriminatory basis throughout the industrial community." SCLC in return accepted a plan to make those changes in stages rather than at once and agreed to the release of the arrested demonstrators on bonds from the United Auto Workers, rather than unconditionally.

Connor and some other state and local officeholders immediately denounced the Senior Citizens Committee, King, and Kennedy. That night, following a rally of the Ku Klux Klan, bombs damaged the house of King's brother and the motel where SCLC had its headquarters. Infuriated, hundreds of blacks, most of them from the city's impoverished ghettos, rioted, attacked police and firemen, and vilified whites. They had never subscribed to doctrines of nonviolence, and they had long suffered oppression by the city's whites. "Let the whole fucking city burn," one rioter shouted. "I don't give a god-damn."

While King rushed back to Birmingham the next day to urge a return to nonviolence and the preservation of the racial accord, the president met in Washington with a group of his advisers. Robert Kennedy warned that Birmingham might blow up again. Governor George Wallace had claimed he could maintain law and order, but state police would predictably treat black rioters roughly. It was essential, the attorney general said, to make the blacks feel that the federal government was their friend; important also to honor King's plea for a statement from the president. Robert Kennedy was worried, as were the others, about the possibility of riots by blacks in cities throughout the South. Even Burke Marshall, notable for his imperturbability under stress, agreed that blacks in Birmingham would be "uncontrollable" if the agreement with the

Senior Citizens Committee broke down. The president was considering moving federal troops to positions close to that city. Marshall believed
that knowledge of that plan would have a calming effect. After consulting King, he reported that in the absence of further incidents of
white violence, King thought he could control his own people. The
president and the attorney general then decided to send enough troops
to the area to overwhelm the city if the need arose and to draft a statement for broadcast that would call for an end to the rioting and command support for black rights as delineated in the racial accord.

In making that statement, President Kennedy also announced that
he had ordered military units trained in riot control to the Birmingham
area, arranged to federalize the Alabama National Guard if it became
necessary, and sent Burke Marshall back to the city for further consultation with local citizens. Though Governor Wallace questioned the
constitutionality of the president's use of troops, the federal presence
in Birmingham helped King, SCLC, and the Senior Citizens Committee restore sufficient calm for the desegregation program to begin.

The crisis in Birmingham had lasting effects. King's victory encouraged blacks everywhere to press for similar gains. Dissatisfied with
gradualism, even the moderate civil rights organizations demanded
"freedom now." For more and more blacks, especially the black poor,
who had only begun to act in their own behalf, the events in Birmingham confirmed their distrust of the white police and their experience
with white intransigence. In the end, after all, violence had succeeded
nonviolence in pushing the white elite to agreement on desegregation
and in driving the federal government to intercede. As one Democratic
observer wrote Robert Kennedy on May 13, "The accelerated tempo of
Negro restiveness and the rivalry of some leaders for top billing cou-
pled with the resistance of segregationists may soon create the most
critical state of race relations since the Civil War." Black militancy
expressed itself in rent strikes that CORE organized in northern cities,
in the stepped-up voter registration campaign of SNCC in Louisiana
and Mississippi, in angry demonstrations for civil rights throughout the
old Confederacy. "There go my people," Martin Luther King, Jr., was
wont to remark, quoting Gandhi. "I must catch them, for I am their
leader."

The Kennedys, anxious about those developments, knew that they
could cope with King as a leader far more successfully than with his
radical rivals. They were aware, too, of growing white support for civil
rights. Like King, the president had to stay ahead of his army.
Throughout the spring of 1963 the attorney general met with groups

of business leaders, who were themselves increasingly worried about racial unrest, to urge them to desegregate their hiring. He and Marshall also prodded the executive departments to employ more blacks, particularly in post offices and other federal facilities in the South. As Marshall observed, the federal government had no better record in Birmingham than did private industry, and improvement would not be easy, for decades of inadequate education left local blacks without preparation for the jobs the government had to fill. The president, for his part, decided at last that the time had come to prepare a major civil rights measure for Congress. Although he still believed that a bill to guarantee fair employment practices would fail, he endorsed Marshall's proposal to draft legislation for the desegregation of public accommodations. In that form the bill, so he intended to argue, would provide a substitute for mob action.

The Kennedys also hoped that their activities would lessen the appeal of black separatists. Robert Kennedy had been reading the literature of black rage, the most publicized example of which was James Baldwin's *The Fire Next Time* (1963). The title derived from the text of an old spiritual: "God gave Noah the rainbow sign, / No more water, the fire next time!" Baldwin, a leading American novelist, described the humiliation and hatred of the black past, his own past, especially the "hatred for white men so deep that it . . . made all love, all trust, all joy impossible." He warned that blacks were ready to retaliate unless they received "total liberation, in the cities . . . before the law, and in the mind."

The attorney general asked Baldwin to bring together a group of prominent blacks familiar with the problems of northern ghettos to discuss useful programs for the federal government. On May 24, 1963, Kennedy met with that group in New York City. As Baldwin later said, Jerome Smith, a young CORE Freedom Rider, "set the tone of the meeting . . . when . . . he . . . stammered . . . and said that he was nauseated by the necessity of being in that room. I knew what he meant. It was not personal at all. . . . Bobby took it personally." Kennedy, who had spent the morning trying to persuade owners of hotel and motel chains to desegregate their facilities, was bound to take it personally. A proud man, fiercely loyal to his brother, proud of his courageous staff, he defended the administration's record in civil rights. But Jerome Smith went on. Would he fight for his country? Baldwin asked. "Never, never, never," Smith answered, shocking Kennedy. "This boy," recalled Lena Horne, the great blues singer, "just put it like it was. He communicated the pain . . . of being a Negro." The meeting, which went on for three hours, in the words of sociologist Kenneth Clark, "became . . . one of the most violent, emotional verbal assaults . . . I have ever witnessed." The attorney general agreed. "They seemed possessed," he said. ". . . It was impossible to make contact with any of them."

As the group left, Harry Belafonte, the popular singer, told Kennedy that he had "done more for civil rights than anyone else." Kennedy asked why Belafonte had not said that to the others. The singer replied that if he had sided with Kennedy, he would have "become suspect." Kennedy was despondent. "They don't know . . . what the facts are— they don't know what we've been doing," he told Arthur Schlesinger. ". . . It was all emotion, hysteria." But the participants felt that Kennedy had learned from the meeting. "The Attorney General and Mr. Burke Marshall," wrote Clarence Jones, a lawyer who had been there, "have been more vigorous in their prosecution of actions in behalf of civil rights than any previous Administration. Our complaint . . . is that this admittedly . . . vigorous activity is incommensurate with the enormity of the racial crisis confronting our country." So it was, and therefore what Clark called the "excruciating sense of impasse" and thus also "the jolt" that, in Schlesinger's view, brought Robert Kennedy "to grasp . . . the nature of black anguish."

As with the missile crisis, so with the racial crisis, Robert Kennedy had the sensitivities as well as the toughness that made him the indispensable adviser to his brother. Indeed, he had become more attuned to the America of his day and to the conflicts among its cultures than had the president. As Schlesinger later wrote, Bobby Kennedy was a romantic disguised as a realist, and as such he complemented his brother perfectly. With the racial crisis mounting, the harmony between the brothers, and their ability to learn from each other and from experience, determined their course. The administration's civil rights legislation might fail in Congress, the president decided, and he might lose popular support and the 1964 election because of it, but the time had come "when a man has to take a stand."

Kennedy had a chance to do so after Governor Wallace of Alabama had announced his intention of preventing black students from registering at the state's university in Tuscaloosa. Both the president and the attorney general tried unsuccessfully to persuade Wallace to yield. Determined to prevent another episode like that at Ole Miss, Kennedy was prepared to federalize the Alabama National Guard and to send in other troops as well if Wallace provoked trouble. For his part, Wallace was not ready to resist the president. He intended only to make a

Governor George Wallace at the University of Alabama: "Segregation forever."

show of seeming to resist. On June 11, 1963, Deputy Attorney General Nicholas Katzenbach faced Wallace, who stood blocking the doorway to the building where students registered. Katzenbach read a proclamation from the president ordering the governor to cease impeding a federal court ruling for the admission of two black students. Wallace replied with a proclamation of his own denouncing federal intrusion in the state's affairs. But the governor made no effort to prevent United States marshals from escorting the students to their dormitories. Kennedy then federalized the Alabama National Guard, and later in the day, at the request of the commander, Wallace allowed the students to enter the registration building. His defiance of federal authority had stopped with his rhetoric.

Kennedy used the episode as the occasion for a television address to the nation, a speech which Sorensen and several other of his advisers had considered politically dangerous. The president borrowed his spirited text from Martin Luther King, Jr.:

If an American, because his skin is dark, cannot eat lunch in a restaurant open to the public; if he cannot send his children to the best public school available; if he cannot vote for the public officials who represent him; if, in short, he cannot enjoy the full and free life which all of us want, then who among us would be content to . . . stand in his place?

Who among us would be content with the counsels of patience and delay? One hundred years of delay have passed since President Lincoln freed the slaves, yet their heirs . . . are not fully free. . . . And this nation . . . will not be fully free until all its citizens are free. . . . It is time to act in the Congress, in your state . . . above all, in all our daily lives.

It was already too late to contain the private fury of diehard southern segregationists. Only hours after Kennedy's speech, a gunman murdered Medgar Evers, a NAACP organizer in Mississippi. A week thereafter the president sent the administration's bill to the Hill, where the attorney general had the responsibility for seeing it through to enactment. Now a strong measure, the bill called for desegregating public accommodations, granted authority to the attorney general to initiate suits for school desegregation, and gave the federal executive power to withhold funds from programs and facilities in states where discrimination occurred. The "moral and constitutional crisis," as Kennedy had called it, he had put to the Congress and to the nation. Significant civil rights legislation took its appropriate place in the agenda he had been developing since 1961. It had come also to include disarmament.

2. THE PATH TO PEACE

In the months after the missile crisis, Kennedy increasingly felt the urgency of reducing the nuclear arms race and the accompanying chances for a nuclear war. Since Eisenhower's negotiations with Khrushchev in 1958, the most probable first step in that direction had been a bilateral agreement to suspend the testing of nuclear weapons. Such an agreement with the Soviet Union promised to reduce tensions between the superpowers, open a road toward détente, provide a basis that other nations might accept as a substitute for nuclear ambitions of their own, and terminate the dangerous pollution of the earth and its atmosphere that competitive nuclear testing was causing. A step forward in the process of arms reduction would also help Kennedy's candidacy, for peace and prosperity remained, as they had been during the 1950s, the most salient issues in American politics. The missile crisis had also raised Khrushchev's concern for avoiding nuclear war, while increasing Chinese hostility to the Soviet Union turned the Soviet leader toward détente with the United States. As his letter to Kennedy during the crisis had said, "We should like to continue the exchange of views on the prohibition of . . . thermonuclear weapons, general disarmament, and other problems relating to the relaxation of international tensions."

Soviet-American negotiations about nuclear testing had stumbled in the past over American suspicions, strong in the Pentagon and on Capitol Hill, that the Russians would cheat unless subject to continuing inspections and over Soviet suspicions that such American inspections would constitute continual espionage. Conscious of those obstacles, Kennedy hoped for a comprehensive test ban but also worked toward a limited test ban that would affect only the atmosphere and the oceans, where American instruments could monitor Soviet compliance. No instruments placed outside the Soviet Union could then sufficiently distinguish between seismic disturbances in that huge nation and underground testing there. In January 1963 the president ordered the Atomic Energy Commission to postpone its planned underground tests while American, Soviet, and British representatives explored terms for a treaty. Those talks failed because the Soviet Union was willing to permit only three inspections annually and the Americans insisted upon at least eight. The American tests then proceeded. In May, in the midst of the growing crisis over civil rights, Kennedy, for the first time, authorized American atmospheric tests. But strong support for an antinuclear resolution in the Senate stiffened his own resolve to sound out Khrushchev again, as he did through Norman Cousins, the editor of the *Saturday Review*. Khrushchev told Cousins that he had to placate his own Council of Ministers. The Americans, he said, could police nuclear testing from outside the Soviet Union, but he realized the Senate would reject a treaty based on that condition. "Very well," Khrushchev concluded, "let us accommodate the President."

Cousins's report encouraged Kennedy to keep trying. He had already directed Sorensen to draft an important speech on peace and disarmament. In spite of the distractions in Birmingham, he proposed, jointly with Harold Macmillan, new discussions about a test ban treaty. Khrushchev accepted their invitation early in June, just as Kennedy was reviewing his pending address on the subject while traveling through the West advocating civil rights. He delivered his speech at commencement at American University in Washington, D.C., on June 10, 1963, only a day before his televised appeal to the nation for action on civil rights. The American University address had equal significance.

"A peace for all time," Kennedy said, could not be a "*Pax Americana* enforced . . . by American weapons of war." Rather, a practical peace would have to be "based . . . on a gradual evolution in human institutions." Americans, he believed, would help "the leaders of the Soviet Union adopt a more enlightened attitude." To do so, "we must re-examine our own attitude." Both nations abhorred war. They had never been at war against each other. "Let each nation," he continued, "choose its own future so long as that choice does not interfere with the choice of others. . . . If we cannot now end our differences, at least we can help make the world safe for diversity. For . . . our most basic common link is the fact that we all inhabit this planet. We all breathe the same air. We all cherish our children's future. And we all are mortal." Kennedy then announced his decision not to resume nuclear testing in the atmosphere and to send an American delegation to a forthcoming meeting in Moscow about a test ban treaty. Those were his steps, he concluded, "not toward a strategy of annihilation but toward a strategy of peace."

Though Americans at the time paid less attention to Kennedy's address than they did to civil rights, Khrushchev called it "the best speech by any American President since Roosevelt." As Sorensen later wrote, "the outlook for some kind of test ban agreement turned from helpless to hopeful." But as with the tax bill and civil rights legislation, so with any test ban treaty that Kennedy could negotiate: Support on the Hill remained questionable. As the president realized, he had come a much longer way since his inauguration than had the Congress. He would need to cultivate Republicans as well as Democrats in both houses. For that purpose he would have to mobilize public opinion behind his policies. At the risk of offending civil rights leaders who wanted his attention in Washington, he undertook an exercise in public relations that he had been planning: a quick trip to Europe designed to reinforce his influence by reverberating the glamour of his reputation. He intended also to reassure the nation's allies about the negotiations scheduled for Moscow.

The trip was a triumphant tour. In West Berlin three-fourths of the population filled the streets to see the American president. He addressed the tumultuous crowds shortly after he had first seen the wall. Shaken by that barrier to freedom, he spoke about the many people "who really don't understand . . . the great issue between the free world and the communist world. . . . *Lass sie nach Berlin kommen*," he declaimed, chopping the air with his arm. "Let them come to Berlin, and . . . as a free man, I take pride in the words: '*Ich bin ein Berliner.*' " Of course, the crowd cheered wildly. That night Kennedy reached Dublin. In the next several days in Ireland he visited Cork, spoke before the Irish

"Ich bin ein Berliner."

Parliament, and stopped at Limerick, where he recited lines all Irish-men knew from "Mavoureen." In England next he saw Harold Mac-millan, who continued to be dubious about the multilateral force, as Kennedy had expected. Then he moved on to an audience with the pope in Rome. In Naples the crowds gathered again, and Kennedy rehearsed for them the themes of his journey: the significance for the freedom of Western Europe of "social justice and economic reform"; his own enthusiasm for the growing unity and strength of Western Europe; his recognition that "the age of interdependence is here." As Arthur Schlesinger observed, "In the summer of 1963, John F. Kennedy could have carried every county in Europe." But not yet in the United States.

The president returned to the unfinished business of revenue legis-

W. Averell Harriman: A wise old hand.

lation, civil rights, and the test ban negotiations for which he had appointed a mission with Undersecretary of State Averell Harriman as its head. A wise old hand in Soviet affairs, by this time also one of Kennedy's most trusted advisers, Harriman, whom Khrushchev respected, was to work with his British counterpart, Lord Hailsham (Quintin Hogg), also an experienced statesman but during the negotiations always the junior partner. Harriman called the president daily. Almost every evening Kennedy discussed the talk with Secretaries Rusk and McNamara and several of their subordinates. As one of them recalled, the president "showed a devouring interest. . . . He'd delve into the subject with gusto and in considerable detail. . . . He set the tone of the outgoing instructions very personally and . . . in his own words." Confident "that the Soviets wanted a test ban agreement," Kennedy told Harriman to wait for them to "accept what we want."

In defining that goal, the president had to adjust his terms to meet the minimum demands of the Joint Chiefs of Staff, who otherwise could have caused trouble when the treaty reached the Senate. As discussion went on, the hawks and the doves remained in the positions they had taken during the missile crisis. "The President," Bundy reported to Harriman, ". . . talked to each of the Joint Chiefs . . . individually. . . . General [Air Force] [Curtis] LeMay was solidly opposed to the test ban

treaty while Marine Corps Commandant General Shoup saw in the
. . . treaty a major turning point." General Maxwell Taylor, as always
more militant than Kennedy, stood close enough to LeMay to insist on
safeguards for the American nuclear program that made impossible
the hopes of some of the president's scientific advisers for a comprehensive test ban.

The Soviet Union, still wary of on-site inspections, in any case would
probably have rejected a comprehensive ban satisfactory to the Senate,
and Taylor did endorse the terms of the limited test ban on which
Harriman, Hailsham and Gromyko agreed, under the close supervision of their principals. The treaty provided for the abandonment of
tests of nuclear weapons in the atmosphere, in outer space, and under
the oceans. It permitted other nations to accede to it, though France
and China—potentially important nuclear powers—did not do so. The
president arranged for six senators, two of them Republicans, to initial
the treaty in a bipartisan spirit that he continued to cultivate.

That effort succeeded. The Senate approved the treaty by the necessary two-thirds vote in spite of the opposition of the influential atomic
scientist Edward Teller and of several former chairmen of the Joint
Chiefs of Staff. The president and his closest advisers considered the
treaty an important step toward ending the cold war. "For the first time
in many years," Kennedy told the nation in a televised address, "the
path of peace may lie open."

3. Social Justice

Negotiation of the test ban treaty took place while leaders of the civil
rights movement were organizing a march on Washington, the largest
peaceful demonstration they had ever planned. The initiative came from
A. Philip Randolph, the creative head of the Brotherhood of Sleeping
Car Porters, who had threatened a similar march in 1941 in order to
persuade Franklin D. Roosevelt to end discrimination in defense
employment and in the armed services. Randolph began late in 1962
to collaborate with Bayard Rustin, a young man, dedicated and courageous, who had come early in his life to advocate Gandhian tactics.
Both men, socialists in their fundamental convictions and concerned
primarily with a "program for economic justice," roused little support
from moderate civil rights groups until they redefined their mission as
a "March on Washington for Jobs and Freedom." Even then the president was leery, worried about possible violence in Washington and,

March for jobs and freedom: They had a dream.

even more, about turning Congress against his civil rights bill. But Randolph, supported by Martin Luther King, Jr., and James Farmer, reminded Kennedy that "the Negroes are already in the streets." It was preferable, he argued, to have them directed by responsible organizations rather than radicals. The president agreed at least to "keep in touch."

The moderates took charge of plans for the rally that won approval of the NAACP, the Urban League and dozens of labor and civic groups. The president then also endorsed it. On August 28, 1963, almost a quarter of a million people, about a third of them white, gathered in Washington in the heat. They listened and accompanied the radical folk singers Bob Dylan, Joan Baez, and the trio of Peter, Paul, and Mary, as well as the gospel singer Mahalia Jackson. And they heard speech after speech extolling civil rights for American blacks. In the culminating address Martin Luther King, Jr., described his transcendent dream:

I have a dream that one day . . . the sons of former slaves and the sons of former slaveowners will . . . sit down together at the table of brotherhood. . . . I have a dream that one day . . . little black boys and black girls will be able to join with little white boys and white girls as sisters and brothers.

I have a dream today. . . .

When we let freedom ring . . . we will speed up that day when all God's children, black men and white men, Jews and Gentiles, Protestants and Catholics, will be able to join hands and sing in the words of that old Negro spiritual, "Free at last! Thank God almighty, we are free at last!"

King's vision moved millions of Americans. In that way, along with the temperate march itself, it lifted public support for Kennedy's civil rights bill. Hundreds of white southerners nevertheless remained determined to fight integration, and hundreds of black militants agreed with Malcolm X, who dismissed the rally as the "Farce in Washington." Those passions would someday explode. For the short term the leaders of the march, like the leaders of civil disobedience in Birmingham, had shoved Kennedy in the direction he had to go and assisted him in making his case as well as in making up his mind. The president, moving with the time, was moving much faster than he had thought possible six months earlier.

The momentum carried beyond the reconvening of Congress after the Labor Day recess. Kennedy had continued to give tax reduction priority over civil rights because he feared that if he succeeded in getting the House to vote favorably on civil rights, southerners would retaliate by defeating the revenue bill. Now, with tax reform eliminated from the administration's program, Wilbur Mills accepted the political logic of tax reduction for economic stimulation in 1964 and saw the necessary legislation through his previously resistant Ways and Means Committee. With that hurdle cleared, the bill had good prospects for success on the floor of the House if Kennedy, deferring to Mills and other conservative Democrats, could keep the projected budget for the next fiscal year, 1964–1965, close to $101 billion, a level he was willing to accept. While still nurturing the tax bill, the administration could concentrate on civil rights.

For almost two months the civil rights bill had been languishing in a subcommittee of the House Judiciary Committee. The president had persuaded the committee's chairman, veteran Brooklyn Democrat Emanuel Celler, to strengthen bipartisan support. But Robert Kennedy had started awkwardly with his testimony before the full Judiciary Committee in June. Because he neglected to obtain proper briefing about the Republican members, he had not known that John V. Lindsay of New York, with some twenty others in his party, had introduced a public accommodations bill weeks before the administration did. Lindsay, a bright, liberal, and handsome young man with the credentials and ambition for higher office, resented the attorney general's ignorance and his needlessly abrupt response to a civil question about the Republican proposal. During the congressional recess Burke Marshall compensated for that gaucherie by his private discussions about civil rights with the senior Republican on the subcommittee, William M. McCulloch of Ohio. The sponsor of a moderate civil rights bill of his own, McCulloch proved ready to cooperate with the administration, provided that Marshall could guarantee that the Senate would not soften the measure and that the president would give the Republicans full credit for their help. McCulloch also later told the president that the bill would meet defeat if a provision to forbid discrimination in employment were added to it. Kennedy, for his part, after the rally in Washington warned A. Philip Randolph and other civil rights leaders with whom he met that their advocacy of an equal employment opportunity section would jeopardize the whole measure.

The administration's expedient moderation riled civil rights activists, who wanted a stronger bill, as did the "real liberals" (the phrase, intended pejoratively, was the Kennedys'). Once again irreconcilable segregationists inadvertently accelerated the pace of reform. Governor Wallace of Alabama sent state troopers and guardsmen to four cities, one of them Birmingham, to prevent public schools there from opening on an integrated basis. The federal courts in Alabama issued an injunction prohibiting the troopers from obstructing court orders, and the president federalized the Alabama Guard and withdrew guardsmen from the schools, which black children then entered. A few days later, September 15, 1963, a bomb went off at a Sixteenth Street Baptist Church in Birmingham. The explosion killed four girls and wounded twenty other children. When blacks in the city then rioted, Birmingham police, using guns and tanks, killed two more children. Burke Marshall thought the city was on "the verge of a real racial war." The president, who agreed, hoped the civil rights bill would provide "a breathing spell" unless black radicals prevented it. SNCC, he believed, had "an investment in violence." Eager to keep the federal government out of Birmingham, he tried to calm the city by sending to it two personal mediators. They proved indecisive and ineffectual, and the president's own conversations with some white hard-liners yielded no better results. Nevertheless, the city gradually settled down.

Meanwhile, the "real liberals" in Congress assisted by Chairman Manny Celler, defied the administration and strengthened the civil rights bill. McCulloch called the revised measure "a pail of garbage." The president, just as angry, knew he needed McCulloch to "deliver sixty Republicans" in the House. He needed also to woo the Republican leader in the House, Charles Halleck of Indiana, a self-styled "gut fighter," who was under pressure from fellow Republicans to keep the bill as narrow as possible. Halleck conveyed their feelings to a meeting on October 8, 1963, with Democratic Speaker of the House John McCormack and Deputy Attorney General Nicholas Katzenbach. They agreed to soften the measure. The Republicans, Halleck promised, would offer half the necessary amendments, but only if Democrats—"not . . . Southerners, but . . . liberal Democrats"—introduced the rest.

Robert Kennedy accepted those terms. He testified before the Judiciary Committee in behalf of the changes on which he and McCulloch had agreed. "What I want," he told the press, "is a bill, not an issue."

"There is no reason," said the head of the Washington NAACP, "for this kind of sellout." The president, James Farmer complained, thought he could "back out on civil rights." Kennedy in turn attacked the "real liberals" for sponsoring legislation that could not pass. For their part, the liberals went right on rounding up support.

At that juncture, on October 23, 1963, the president met with the leadership of the House, Democrats and Republicans, to bring them together. Like many other conservatives, Halleck had come to believe that legislation was necessary. "Hell," he told a colleague, "I didn't do it for political advantage. The colored vote in my district didn't amount to a bottle of pee." McCulloch, who was of the same spirit, helped the cause by recruiting John Lindsay. The administration in return accepted most of the proposals McCulloch and Lindsay made. They did not much differ from the provisions the president privately preferred. Vice President Johnson thought the Senate would soften even those terms. "This fight," Kennedy responded, "is going to go on. In about three years we're going to have another bill."

The bill they had in October 1963 had teeth in it, though fewer than the liberals had proposed. The section on voting rights prohibited exclusion on the basis of race in national elections, but not in state and local contests. The section on public accommodations empowered the Justice Department to act, but only to assist individuals who brought suit to desegregate public facilities. The section on desegregation of public schools applied only to de jure, not de facto, conditions, and therefore only to the South, not to the North. The new draft, as the president had suggested himself, established an Equal Employment Opportunity Commission but limited its authority to investigation only. To keep the Judiciary Committee from reporting out the stronger version of the bill, the administration needed seventeen votes. Kennedy could count on nine or ten Democrats on the committee. Halleck delivered nine Republicans, more than enough to hold the bill to the terms satisfactory to the president and McCulloch. As Robert Kennedy said publicly, without Halleck and McCulloch "the possibility of civil rights legislation . . . would have been remote."

Though the Judiciary Committee approved it, the civil rights bill had yet to reach the full house. It had first to clear the Rules Committee, whose chairman, Judge Howard Smith, opposed it. Many Republicans, moreover, berated McCulloch and Halleck for letting Kennedy avoid defeat. With the tax bill also still before the Congress, the president made a series of speeches to promote his program. As he traveled through the country, he tried to unite the squabbling factions of his party. In Philadelphia black Democrats boycotted the dinner for him, whereas in Tampa local whites were noticeably cool. Kennedy had hoped to see the controversial legislation passed before 1964. Now he knew the civil rights and tax bill would go over into the election year. Still, once he had become personally involved in the legislative process, the measures had begun to move along. He expected eventually to prevail.

Indeed, Kennedy was preparing to add to his objectives, which still included his 1961 proposals for federal aid to education and federal medical insurance. At the president's meeting with civil rights leaders after the August March on Washington, Roy Wilkins, the head of the NAACP, had told him that most blacks "want a change of climate that will affect their daily lives." They needed more than just equal employment opportunities, for poverty as well as discrimination weighed upon them. Blacks suffered from unemployment at a rate two and a half times that of whites. They needed training in industrial skills and in literacy. Only a crash program could help black teenagers, three-quarters of whom would not complete high school. Those young blacks were running out of hope, Wilkins said, and had lost all faith in whites and in the government. Kennedy in reply cited the experience of American Jews, who had taken responsibility for the education of their children. A parent with only a fourth-grade education, he was reminded, found it hard to educate a child in the sixth grade. The others at the meeting agreed: What impoverished blacks, especially adolescents, needed was "tangible, visible, massive help."

The administration had made a small start in that direction with several programs that were categorical—aimed at specific problems that inhered in the structure of American society or local economies. For one example, Mobilization for Youth, an experiment in a dozen cities, emphasized training and education to prepare young people, otherwise possible delinquents, for opportunities in employment. The Area Redevelopment Administration also used its limited budget for training but, beyond that, for loans to small businesses and for improving public facilities in depressed regions. The Manpower Development and Training Administration, too, was designed to "help people help themselves . . . off welfare." All those efforts assisted blacks and whites alike; but they lacked adequate funding, and they neglected most of the American poor.

Poverty in the United States was not primarily structural but endemic and therefore not subject to structural remedies. Of the 34 million poor in 1964, 5.4 million were over sixty-five years old; 5.7 million were preschool children; 2.8 million were the mothers of those children and almost all of them housebound. There were also hundreds of thousands of physically or emotionally disabled Americans who were needy but unable to work. Those millions of unemployable indigents had a special champion in Wilbur Cohen, a veteran of the New Deal who became an assistant secretary of health, education, and welfare (HEW) in the New Frontier. Cohen and the social workers whom he consulted persuaded the president and Congress, as a first step, in 1961 to revise and expand the program for Aid for Families with Dependent Children (AFDC). Previously that program had applied only to one-parent families. As revised, with the hope of keeping families together, it also applied to two-parent families whose heads of household were jobless and ineligible for unemployment benefits under Social Security. But half the states, most of them rural, refused to participate in the enlarged version of AFDC. In further legislation in 1962, the federal government assumed 75 percent, instead of the previous 50 percent, of the cost of rehabilitative social services for the needy, with the balance to be paid by the states. That increase was intended to induce the states to provide more generous services, but the term "service" proved so hard to define that by and large states were able to redefine what they were already doing so as to obtain federal financing without improving their programs for the poor. And Wilbur Cohen's intelligent advocacy of federal medical assistance for the poor made no new converts on the Hill. The limitations of federal remedies for endemic poverty continued therefore to fall short of improving the lot of the impoverished of all races.

The problems of poverty demanded broader treatment than Kennedy had devised by early 1963, as his recent reading of Michael Harrington's *Other America* indicated, and as Ken Galbraith continued to maintain. Galbraith had argued consistently that a tax cut would benefit the rich and the middle class without reaching the neediest Americans. At first Walter Heller did not entirely agree. The proposed new rates, he wrote Kennedy, would cut general employment to 4 percent and eliminate half of black unemployment above that figure. Though he believed in "an ethically and politically tolerable" distribution of income, Heller considered stimulation of economic growth the more important way to relieve poverty. By the spring of 1963 he was proposing other methods. Revised data on poverty, he wrote on May 1, 1963, were "distressing." He then recognized, like Galbraith, "that the tax cut . . . wasn't going to do much for low income groups." Consequently in June, encouraged by Ted Sorensen, Heller asked the Council of Economic Advisers to "consider what lines of action might make up a practical Kennedy antipoverty program in 1964." The CEA's expert on poverty, Robert Lampman, persuaded Heller by June 20, as he then wrote Kennedy two months before the March on Washington, that half of black unemployment "must be whittled away by particularized attacks on training, discrimination, motivation, health and so forth."

To develop the necessary policies, Heller needed the president's approval, but in June 1963 even Galbraith considered a "particularized attack" politically impossible. Kennedy's political advisers agreed, holding that the black vote had no place to go except to the president. But Heller kept the issue of black unemployment alive during the summer while the civil rights movement fortified his case. Meanwhile, Wilbur Cohen was continuing to press for combating endemic poverty. Robert Solow, one of Heller's influential senior advisers, had come wholly to agree. As Heller put it to the president in October 1963, the administration's dramatic program for civil rights made it both "equitable and politically attractive" to launch another program for all the "disadvantaged groups," the white poor not the least. The president was persuaded. "The time has come," he told Schlesinger, "to organize a national assault on the causes of poverty, a comprehensive program, across the board." It was to take its place on his "must" list for the Congress.

4. DIEM

During 1963, as before, the president, whatever his changing priorities, could never entirely escape the continual irritants of Vietnam.

Bundy had expressed Kennedy's attitude toward Vietnam in a memorandum he prepared for him on January 21, 1963, about matters for discussion with the National Security Council. "Another part of our military effort," he wrote, "is symbolized by Viet Nam. Here you may want to indicate merely that we are prepared to stick to it and are not a bit disheartened by incidental differences along the way . . . although it would be helpful if our officials on the spot would keep their understandable impatience out of the newspapers." Yet there was cause to be disheartened. During 1962 the Diem government had been devious about the strategic hamlet program it officially and only cosmetically adopted. Strategic hamlets, fortified villages surrounded by barbed wire, were intended in American doctrine to function like "oil spots," spreading replicas from secured areas to contested territory. Within them villagers were supposed to receive protection from the Vietcong and training in collective action for security. But Diem's brother, Ngo Dinh Nhu, tried to indoctrinate the inhabitants with his own curious and self-serving concepts of freedom and consistently located the villages with little regard to their vulnerability to Vietcong forces, which continually infiltrated them. In the judgment of the staff director of Kennedy's Special Group (Counterintelligence), the strategic hamlet program "became more of a sham than was realized. . . . You could not have all this visible apparatus of control outside and at the same time not be controlling anything inside."

Conditions were also discouraging outside the hamlets, where the American military was playing a growing role under the command of General Paul D. Harkins. McNamara at first considered Harkins "an imaginative officer" but later judged him "not worth a damn." Harkins continually squabbled with American diplomatic and intelligence officers in Saigon and continually sent Washington overly optimistic reports about the Army of South Vietnam (ARVN). The CIA, in contrast, warned that the war in Vietnam remained "a slowly escalating stalemate." Galbraith was even more pessimistic in a personal letter to the president: "We are increasingly replacing the French as the colonial military force and we will increasingly arouse the resentments associated therewith. Moreover, while I don't think the Russians are clever enough to fix it that way, we are surely playing their game. They couldn't be more pleased than to have us spend our billions in those distant jungles where it does us no good and them no harm."

Kennedy, too, worried about American entanglement in Vietnam. He told Averell Harriman that he "wished us to be prepared to seize upon any favorable moment to reduce our investment, recognizing that the moment might yet be some time away." But in January 1963 it certainly was far away, contrary to Bundy's seemingly confident memorandum. New trouble in Vietnam was soon to share with violence in Birmingham morning headlines and evening television reports in the United States.

The Dinhs were Catholics, a minority in South Vietnam, where the Buddhists constituted the largest religious group, one whose leaders often dissented from official policy, partly because they were uncomfortable with Western ways. Influenced by his brother, Thu and Thu's arrogant and ambitious wife, Diem on May 8, 1963, forbade the display of religious flags during the celebration of Buddha's birthday in Hue, the ancient capital of Vietnam. The resulting demonstration drew gunfire from local troops, who killed seven in the crowd. The next day, after a protest by some ten thousand Buddhists, their leaders demanded equal rights with Catholics, an end to government persecution of Buddhists, and compensation for the families of the dead and injured. Seemingly conciliatory at first, Diem delayed acting on those matters. A Buddhist hunger strike in Saigon on May 30 led to further killings of them. The American deputy chief of mission there, in charge while Ambassador Frederick Nolting was on leave, believed the situation required "dramatic action." Madame Nhu, in contrast, vilified the Buddhist leaders as Communists, though there was no evidence for that charge. While Diem dallied, Quang Duc, an aged Buddhist monk, poured gasoline over himself on a busy street in Saigon and sat silently while the flames he ignited burned him to death. During the summer demonstrations continued, with another suicide by fire about which Madame Nhu remarked: "All they have done is barbecue a bonze."

Civil disobedience in Vietnam, like civil disobedience in Alabama, presented the Kennedy administration with what the deputy chief of mission called "an ominous warning," symbolized by photographs of the suicides in American media. Since no one in the administration understood Vietnamese history and culture, the debate about policy reflected assumptions dating from the Truman and Eisenhower years about the extent of American interest in Southeast Asia. The governing contention held that prevention of Communist control in South Vietnam remained a necessary objective in the cold war. In that view, the loss of South Vietnam would ultimately lead to the collapse of American influence in the entire area, open the way for Soviet or Chinese domination there, and allow the Republicans a telling attack on the administration for the loss of an ally. The question of policy centered upon preventing those eventualities. The president, dismayed by religious persecution in Vietnam and annoyed by Madame Nhu's insensitivity, wanted Diem to dismiss Nhu and make concessions to the Buddhists. Ambassador Nolting predicted that Diem would resist American pressure to remove Nhu. Roger Hilsman, at the time an assistant secretary of state, leaned toward a coup d'état, which he considered probable in any event, as did Michael Forrestal, a member of Kennedy's National Security Council (NSC) staff with special responsibilities for Vietnam. But General Taylor thought the United States could work with Diem, as did General Harkins, still senior commander in the field.

Before Ambassador Nolting reached Washington, Kennedy, eager for stability in Vietnam, had decided to replace him with Henry Cabot Lodge, the Massachusetts Republican who had been Nixon's running mate in 1960. A Boston patrician with an interest in international affairs, Lodge, in 1952 Kennedy's defeated opponent for a seat in the Senate, was eager for his new post. As he arrived in Saigon to deal with Diem, American journalists there joked that "our old mandarin can lick your old mandarin." A contest was pending, for Lodge expected Diem to heed American counsel, but just before his arrival Diem had declared martial law and then ordered his palace troops to attack Buddhist pagodas nationwide and to arrest Buddhist monks and nuns.

The incident, as Lodge now learned, was entirely the doing of Nhu, not of the South Vietnamese Army. Several senior ARVN officers, as well as several civilian leaders, urged Americans in Saigon to force Diem to oust Nhu. Those pleas, cabled to the State Department, confirmed Hilsman's convictions, which were those also of Averell Harriman. On August 24, together with Forrestal, they drafted a telegram to Lodge telling him the "U.S. government cannot tolerate situation in which power lies in Nhu's hands." The draft instructed Lodge so to inform Diem and added: "We must face the possibility that Diem himself cannot be preserved." Lodge was also told to "tell key military leaders that U.S. would now find it impossible to support GVN [government of Vietnam] unless Diem also placated the Buddhists" and to make "detailed plans as to how we might bring about Diem's replacement if this should become necessary."

Seeking the president's permission to send that cable, Forrestal called him at his home in Hyannis. Kennedy suggested waiting over the weekend "to get it cleared." Secretary of Defense McNamara, McGeorge Bundy, and John McCone, head of the CIA, all were out of Washington. But Forrestal reached Secretary of State Rusk, who was in New York and approved the draft "if the President understood the implications." Undersecretary of Defense Roswell Gilpatric, though "somewhat unhappy," also cleared the draft, as did Richard Helms, the officer in charge at the CIA, who considered the matter a "political issue," as did Gilpatric. Though General Taylor was waiting to see the rest of the draft, Forrestal simply assumed that neither Taylor nor Bundy would object to it. On that assumption, he called the president to report that everyone was in agreement. Kennedy then ordered the cable sent.

When it arrived in Saigon on August 25, Lodge discussed it with senior officers in the American mission, all of whom believed Diem would refuse to dismiss Nhu. If Lodge nevertheless delivered the message, they feared Diem might act to block a coup. Lodge therefore cabled Washington to suggest "we go straight to generals with our demand, without informing Diem. Would tell him we preferred to have Diem without Nhus but . . . up to them to keep him." The State Department endorsed that plan. But before Lodge could see the generals, the Voice of America on August 26 broadcast a statement, also cleared by State, that blamed Nhu for the raids on the Buddhist pagodas. By alerting Diem to American views, that broadcast, in Lodge's opinion, "complicated our already difficult problem." Diem and Nhu reinforced the defenses at the palace. CIA personnel found key Vietnamese generals, some of whom had been plotting a coup, disturbed by the American breach of security, for they feared any attempt to overthrow the government would now involve heavy fighting.

Meanwhile, in Washington on August 26 Kennedy discovered angry confusion about the August 24 cable. McNamara, Taylor, and McCone were indignant that they had not been consulted. The president berated Forrestal for failing to do so. He also the next day met with former Ambassador Nolting, who doubted the Vietnamese generals had the courage for a coup d'état. The president had not canceled the instructions to Lodge because, as General Taylor put it, Washington could not change policy every day, but on August 28 Kennedy did ask for up-to-date advice from Lodge and Harkins in Saigon.

Sure that there was no turning back, Lodge replied that there was also "no possibility . . . the war could be won under a Diem administration." He urged "all-out effort to get generals to move promptly" and suspension of economic aid to Diem. Harkins recommended instead giving Diem an ultimatum to remove Nhu. Kennedy sent Lodge authorization both to have Harkins talk to the generals and to suspend economic aid. "Failure," the president added, "is more destructive than an appearance of indecision. . . . It will be better to change our minds than fail." By August 31 even Lodge admitted there was "neither the

Secretary McNamara, Generals Taylor and Hawkins: Inspecting the stalemate in Vietnam.

will nor the organization among the generals to accomplish anything." Diem remained in power, and so did Nhu.

Kennedy clearly intended to avoid another Bay of Pigs, but in 1963 in both Washington and Saigon, the confusion within the administration about policy in Vietnam resembled the confusion of 1961 about Cuba. In Saigon protests continued, now by high school students; Diem was stumbling in the war with Hanoi, but Kennedy ruled out American withdrawal, and his advisers were deeply divided about what to do next. Secretaries Rusk and McNamara and General Taylor argued that the United States "had been winning the war," while Hilsman and others in the State Department working on Vietnam believed that the corruption and inefficiency of the Diem government would surely lead to defeat. Harkins and Lodge differed with each other along just those lines. The president, as he recognized, could not make decisions on the basis of "such divergent views of the same facts." He needed a sound analysis of the war and of the Diem government, and for it he elected to rely on his senior military advisers McNamara and Taylor, whom he sent to Vietnam.

Neither man undertook that mission with an open mind. Max Taylor, "Kennedy's kind of general," as it was so often said, was an impressive professional soldier, candid, intelligent, articulate, who believed in flexible response, had written a persuasive book about it, and subscribed also to the related doctrine of counterinsurgency. He had therefore, particularly as chief of staff, an investment in the American presence in Vietnam and in a tough stance toward the Soviet Union, policies he did not question. He had been on the hawkish side during the Berlin and missile crises. Now he interpreted what he saw in Vietnam as evidence of the correctness of his beliefs. The ARVN was winning the war, he concluded, and would have it won by 1965 even with the withdrawal soon of a thousand American advisers. Robert McNamara did not disagree. McNamara had a growing reputation as a bright and talented manager with extraordinary ability to collect and interpret quantitative data. But he had no experience in politics and no expertness about Asia. To be sure, he joined Taylor in visiting every sector in South Vietnam where there was important fighting and in conferences with Diem. Indeed, McNamara scolded Diem about the unpopularity of his government and the offensiveness of Madame Nhu. But Diem gave little evidence of understanding that message and none of intending to act upon it. Nevertheless, McNamara, impressed by the large number of enemy the ARVN claimed to have killed, subscribed to Taylor's optimism about the course of the war. Their official report incorporated Taylor's estimate of victory in 1965 and his position about withdrawing a thousand American advisers before the end of 1963. A minority of the mission privately disagreed, especially William Sullivan, representing the State Department, who saw Diem as in political trouble so deep that American reinforcement would soon be needed.

The president accepted the analysis of Taylor and McNamara. Informing Lodge about their report, he directed him to give no encouragement to a coup against Diem but secretly to identify alternative leadership. Lodge had then just learned through a CIA agent in Saigon about plans of General Duong Van Minh, "Big" Minh, to lead a coup. So apprised, Kennedy sent the ambassador ambiguous instructions: "While we do not wish to stimulate a coup, we also do not wish to leave the impression that the United States would thwart a change in government" or deny assistance to a new regime capable of winning the war. The CIA was clearly implicated in the schemes of the dissident generals for a coup, which Harkins continued to oppose and Lodge to recommend. For its part, the White House wanted to avoid involvement in the plans and to "preserve security and deniability," but also to control American policy in Saigon—in the still-confused circumstances, two mutually exclusive goals. "We should not thwart a coup,"

Lodge cabled on October 25, 1963. ". . . It seems at least an even bet that the next government would not bungle . . . as much as the present one. . . . This is the only way in which the people of Vietnam can possibly get a change in government. . . . Certainly a succession of fights for control of the Government of Vietnam would interfere with the war effort . . . [but] the war effort has been interfered with already by this government." For the president, Bundy replied that "we would like to have the option of judging . . . any plan with poor prospect of success." The burden of proof, he later added, should be on the group planning the coup, for "we do not accept as a basis for U.S. policy that we have no power to delay or discourage a coup." But little ambiguity remained, for Bundy continued: "Once a coup under responsible leadership has begun . . . it is in the interest of the U.S. Government that it should succeed." In other words, the president was eager to place a bet so long as he could be sure he had winner.

There was also a related vexing and unsettled issue. During any successful coup, as CIA agents in Saigon realized, the conspirators might assassinate Diem and Nhu. In Washington John McCone refused to permit any member of the agency to condone such an action, but he also took care not to discuss the matter with the president or the attorney general. Similarly, the CIA had not revealed to the president its own earlier clumsy and unsuccessful schemes to assassinate Fidel Castro. The agency was again preserving Kennedy's deniability by leaving him uninformed, even though no American in Saigon had the means to control the Vietnamese plotters. Lodge, for his part, recognized the possibility of assassinations and, unbeknown to the president, on that account requested and received permission from the State Department if necessary to offer Diem and Nhu asylum.

The coup in Saigon began on November 1, 1963, with a CIA agent continually privy to its development. In their last conversation Diem asked Lodge what the attitude of the United States was. "I do not feel well-informed enough . . . to tell you," the ambassador replied, disingenuously. ". . . It is 4:30 A.M. in Washington and the U.S. Government cannot possibly have a view." He also offered Diem and Nhu safe-conduct. "I am trying to reestablish order," Diem answered. He failed. After hard fighting the rebellious forces took the palace early in the day of November 2. Diem surrendered. The leaders of the coup asked for an American airplane to take him and Nhu out of the country, but none was to be available for another day. Several hours after the surrender Diem and Nhu, who had fled to a Catholic church, were captured and killed by Big Minh's aide-de-camp, who committed suicide before revealing who had ordered the shooting.

General Taylor, who was with the president when they received word of the assassination, recalled that "Kennedy leaped to his feet and rushed from the room with . . . a look of shock and dismay." The killings, according to Michael Forrestal, shook the president's "confidence . . . in the kind of advice he was getting about South Vietnam." They should have. The contradictory counsels of Kennedy's advisers had muddied the making of American policy. The president, for his part, had failed to dispel the confusion, had trusted the military too much, and had operated, like most of his advisers, under the illusion that Washington could govern events in Saigon, a corollary of their confidence in the application of American power. As Galbraith had warned, American authority did not reach that far. The ambiguities in Kennedy's directions compromised matters further. During the missile crisis a year earlier the president had mastered the facts, understood the risks, and defined the tactics and goals of a successful policy. In the case of Vietnam in1963 he was only partially informed, partly for that reason he miscalculated the risks, and he never really controlled the tactics. Yet he had approved the coup, and any coup involved the risk of the assassination of Diem and Nhu. Further, American complicity in the coup made it harder than it had been for the United States to extricate itself from Vietnam, and the coup itself made it no easier for South Vietnam to win its war—Kennedy's primary objective. A month after Diem's death McNamara, again in Saigon, described the Minh government as "indecisive and drifting," the situation as "very disturbing." So things had been since Kennedy took office.

5. DALLAS

Several of the administration's senior officials were in Honolulu or on their way there to confer about Vietnam when the president left Washington for Texas on November 21, 1963. He was off on another "journey of reconciliation," as Sorensen later wrote, "to harmonize the warring factions of Texas Democrats, to dispel the myths of the right wing in one of its strongest citadels, and to broaden the base for his own reelection in 1964." San Antonio welcomed him enthusiastically. That evening in Houston he talked politics with Vice President Johnson. The next morning, November 22, in Fort Worth, he reminded his audience of the importance of its local industries as producers of essential materials for national defense. He then went on to Dallas, a seat of conservative strength. There, with the first lady next to him, the president sat in the rear of an open car in the motorcade moving through the city. Crowds lining the street cheered as they passed. Kennedy was waving back when, half an hour after noon, three shots were fired, apparently from a nearby building. One killed him.

The assassination of John F. Kennedy shook the nation and the world. So did the assassination, two days later, of Lee Harvey Oswald, the erratic, self-important radical who had shot Kennedy. The official commission under the chief justice appointed to explore the matter concluded that Oswald had acted alone, but the inquiry was so hasty that speculation about a conspiracy continued for decades, as it had in the case of Abraham Lincoln. Many believed Kennedy's assassination involved several people. Some attributed the supposed plot to Fidel Castro, others to the Kremlin, or to adherents of Diem, or to southern segregationists, or to the Mafia, or even to the CIA or FBI. But the immediate importance of the event was beyond speculation. Kennedy was dead, his presidency terminated, his promises unrealized. As it had for no one since Franklin Roosevelt, the nation sorrowed.

Americans mourned the loss of youth and promise, of the hopes Kennedy had symbolized, of the inspiration he had nourished. A twenty-two-year-old ensign in the United States Navy told his captain: "You can't understand what Kennedy meant to my generation." But his captain, just Kennedy's age, did understand, for his own contemporaries felt just the same way. Admiration for the courageous bearing of the Kennedy family, for Jacqueline Kennedy during her ordeal at the Dallas hospital and on the long flight back to Washington, for the children during the state funeral, admiration for their gallantry could not prevent the despondency that overtook millions of people, their sense of waste and deprivation.

There was an irony that Kennedy might have relished in his instant but fleeting apotheosis. The eulogists who praised his humanity included liberal critics who only yesterday had chastened him for his hesitation in fighting for social justice, for the delay of his program in Congress, for the administration's clumsiness in Vietnam. Kennedy had been essentially a man of politics, a moderate leaning gently to the left, a veteran of public office never unaware of the issues of the next election. He selected his objectives ordinarily as they became politically useful. When he became involved in issues, he pursued them with intelligence, practicality, and energy. His style contrasted with the spirit of civil rights advocates like James Farmer and Martin Luther King, Jr. They were men possessed, driven by their belief in the righteousness of their cause, commanded by their need to witness. Their passions compelled them to indict Kennedy's sense of limits, his instinct for the practicable. For his part, Kennedy was puzzled as well as repelled by the rigidity of impassioned segregationists like George Wallace. He despised the destructive extremism of Malcolm X and Bull Connor. Suspicious of moralism, Kennedy was a man without passion for causes, though not without convictions and commitments. He was a man so detached that he could see himself and see others with exceptional clarity. The resulting insights informed his wry wit. Because there was no false humility or self-conceit in Kennedy, he listened, read, and observed in order constantly to learn, and he could then accommodate to what he had learned. His intelligence and his method of using it, in the 1986 judgment of Burke Marshall, himself a thoughtful and astute man, made Kennedy the last president for whom it was fun to work.

Kennedy's failures occurred in situations in which he did not absorb enough pertinent data or fresh ideas to alter either his previous convictions or the policies he inherited. So it was in the case of the Bay of Pigs, after which he changed his advisers. So it was, too, in the case of Vietnam, but there was no way to know whether he would have repeated the pattern. He had some success in his practical approach to world affairs. Western Europe when he died was moving, albeit slowly, toward economic unity, though the burden of its defense remained heavier for the United States than Kennedy would have preferred. The Alliance for Progress was providing useful economic support to democratic regimes in Latin America, though political and social reform in that area still had major obstacles to overcome. Most important, Kennedy and Khrushchev, with the missile crisis behind them, had started their two nations toward disarmament and détente, the brightest hope that Kennedy bequeathed.

Other unfinished business of his administration constituted a domestic agenda for a decade: civil rights; the attack on poverty; Medicare; federal aid to education; management of the economy for full employment. Kennedy had not been committed to all those goals in January 1961, though he had suggested their importance during his campaign. His advisers, assisted by circumstance, spurred by the agitation of impassioned activists, led Kennedy to those ends that ultimately appealed to his intelligence and satisfied his sense of the practicable. His agenda indicated the distance he had traveled since his inauguration. That agenda was Kennedy's large legacy alike to his successors and to his grieving public. It was for good and sufficient reason that the nation mourned.

5

Continuations

"Eternal and ever-blessed God," so spoke the chaplain of the House of Representatives on November 27, 1963, "today we are praying especially for Thy grace and favor upon Lyndon B. Johnson, who now occupies the exalted office of the Presidency of the United States." The Congress was meeting in joint session to hear the new president deliver his first address. A tall and somber man, with conspicuous ears and nose offsetting his sleepy eyes, Johnson moved to the lectern, where the microphones before him carried his words to Americans everywhere. "All I have," he began, "I would have given gladly not to be standing here today." That sentence and the next caught the mood he shared with his people: "John Fitzgerald Kennedy lives on. . . . No words are sad enough to express our sense of loss. No words are strong enough to express our determination to continue the forward thrust of America that he began."

Johnson listed the "dreams" that he had inherited from Kennedy, dreams "of conquering space . . . of partnership across the Atlantic and the Pacific . . . of education for all of our children . . . of jobs for all who seek them . . . of care for our elderly . . . above all . . . of equal rights for all Americans whatever their race or color." Kennedy, Johnson recalled, had said at his inaugural in 1961: "Let us begin." Now, in 1963, Johnson said: "Let us continue." That was the challenge: "to continue on our course," with "the most immediate tasks . . . here on this Hill": "passage of the civil rights bill . . . early passage of the tax bill . . . action on . . . education bills . . . on the foreign aid bill." Congress could expect the full cooperation of the executive branch. With a knowing concession to those on his right, Johnson pledged "the expenditures of your Government will be administered with the utmost thrift and frugality." In his peroration he continued: "The need is here. The need is now. . . . Let us put an end to the teaching and preaching of hate and evil and violence. Let us turn away from the fanatics . . . the prophets of bitterness and bigotry. . . . Let us here highly resolve that John Fitzgerald Kennedy did not live—or die—in vain." The president concluded with "Those familiar and cherished words": "America, America, God shed his grace on thee. . . ."

1. LBJ

Though Johnson shared fully the nation's shock and grief, he responded to his new office, as Theodore Roosevelt had after McKinley's assassination, with an expansive sense of its possibilities. In the good, gray *New York Times* on the day after his speech, two eminent journalists, Tom Wicker and Anthony Lewis, praised the address, praised the commitment, the energy, the political skill of the speaker. They expressed a sense of relief and gratitude that a strong, determined, and experienced hand had succeeded to the presidency. Less than a week after the assassination, though grief for the fallen victim was by no means

President Lyndon B. Johnson: "Let us continue."

exhausted, there accompanied it, both in Washington and in the country at large, a growing confidence in the new chief.

The savants of the Potomac understood the age-old formula "The king is dead; long live the king." Indeed, a longtime aide to Johnson had counseled him about the appropriate tone and arrangements for his address to Congress. "Be natural," he advised. The Johnson family should be present in the gallery, as should a representative of the Kennedy family, preferably a brother-in-law, with Attorney General Robert Kennedy on the floor of the House with the rest of the cabinet. Johnson should also invite some of his old New Deal friends in order "to underscore the favorable factor of long experience in and around the Presidency." And he should avoid a disproportionate representation of Texans. Always alert to public relations, Johnson followed those suggestions. He cared deeply about the image he conveyed. So it was years later when former President Herbert Hoover died. Johnson walked into the press room and delivered a moving eulogy with tears flowing from his eyes. Immediately upon finishing it, he pointed to the television cameramen. "Goddam it," he said, "I told you not to focus on my belly-button. Focus on my eyes." Then he repeated his performance, tears and all, in ample time for the evening television news.

Contrivance was part of the Johnson manner, but Johnson was not the product of contrivance alone. As his first days in office revealed, he had the capacity for natural compassion and spontaneity, as well as for extremely hard work. During the unreality of the hours following Kennedy's death, Johnson, against the advice of the Secret Service, refused to return to Washington from Dallas before Jacqueline Kennedy was ready to do so. He wondered, he later wrote, "with what inadequate words I could try to console her." He saw to it that she used the private quarters on Air Force One while he, the president now, sat in the crowded forward stateroom. He did his best to remain in the background until after the state funeral. He saw himself as the caretaker of Kennedy's people as well as his policies, and he immediately asked the senior officials Kennedy had appointed to stay on. Most of them did.

Johnson knew he had to prove himself. During his first month in office he averaged, he said, "no more than four or five hours' sleep a night." Then and thereafter, in behalf of Kennedy's program and of his own, he constantly exerted the extraordinary force of his person. As he put it himself, "I pleaded. I reasoned. I argued. I urged. I warned." The Johnson technique, honed earlier in his career, often overwhelmed its victims. "He moved in close," according to one observer, "his face a scant millimeter from his target, his eyes widening and narrowing, his eyebrows rising and falling. From his pockets poured clippings, memos, statistics. Mimicry, humor, and the genius of analogy made the Treatment an almost hypnotic experience and rendered the target stunned and helpless" and alarmed. In the judgment of one of Johnson's sympathetic biographers, "people felt they had no private space left in Johnson's presence. . . . The exercise of large power, the bending of other people's will to his, was a frightening thing to observe." Johnson intended it to be. More than most men, he seemed to need constant, overt approval. He wanted men around him, as he admitted, "who were loyal enough to kiss his ass in Macy's window and say it smelled like a rose."

Lyndon Baines Johnson was born in 1908 near Johnson City in southwestern Texas. His father, a coarse man unsuccessful in his search for glory, proved wanting in farming, salesmanship, and politics. Johnson's mother brought a pious, genteel, and steely determination to her home. Deep in the heart of Texas, in the hill country along the Pedernales River, the Johnson family enjoyed a middling social status that the future president later romanticized as poverty. He was a bright boy, facile, egotistic, sensitive, eager for visible success, easily discouraged by failure. Prodded by his mother, he worked his way through Southwest Texas State Teachers College, the institution most convenient for a young man seeking higher education in the region. He then taught high school briefly but well before leaving for Washington as the secretary of a Texas Democratic congressman in whose office he began to learn about the sinews of power and influence.

In 1934 Johnson married Claudia Taylor, a young, superficially diffident, but unfailingly supportive Texas woman whose family called her Lady Bird. She immediately became an indispensable and devoted partner in Johnson's advancement, which she hastened by her support of his ambitions and by her gracefulness as his hostess. Captured by the excitement of the New Deal, Johnson returned to Texas in 1935 to manage the state's branch of the National Youth Administration, a federal agency created to provide work relief to young Americans needing it. He owed his appointment to the favor of Sam Rayburn, an admirer of both Johnsons and even then a leader of the Texas delegation to the House of Representatives. Assisted by friends he hired, Johnson discharged his responsibilities with speed and flair. His programs for highway improvements, playgrounds, and parks offered part-time employment to youthful Texans, including a fair share of Mexican-Americans and blacks, as did the work-study projects his office sponsored at high schools and colleges throughout the state. The experience afforded Johnson psychological reward and, more important, gave him the recognition he needed in 1937 to win a special election for a vacant seat in Congress. In the House on his own, he attended assiduously to the requests of his constituents, voted consistently for Democratic measures, cultivated young members of the White House inner circle, and viewed Franklin D. Roosevelt as a patron rather more than the president saw him as a disciple.

Johnson's House seat was safe, but he aspired to the Senate. In 1941 the death of Morris Sheppard, a Texas incumbent gave him the chance to campaign on a platform that supported most New Deal policies, Roosevelt, and the president's increasing commitments to national defense and aid to Great Britain, then besieged by the Nazis. That mixture of issues exactly suited Johnson's ardent patriotism as well as his calculated identification with his party. But the issues were lost in the carnival that the election became. The contest deteriorated as Johnson tried, at great expense, to outdo the cornball and demagogic tactics of W. Lee O'Daniel, his chief rival for the nomination, whose corrupt supporters eventually stole the primary for their folksy hero. After Pearl Harbor Johnson requested active duty in the navy. With the exception of one bombing mission on which he flew as an observer, he served primarily at large mahogany desks until the president ordered all congressmen either to resign their seats or return to their duties on the Hill. Johnson returned, bought a house in Washington, and won reelection with ease. Helped by insiders' tips, he also profited from real estate and other investments in Texas, especially the radio station Lady Bird purchased in Austin. In 1948 he undertook his second campaign for the Senate. Still considered a New Deal liberal, he had tacked conveniently to the right, particularly on questions related to labor, communism, and civil rights. After a close race in which both candidates and their supporters tried to purloin the election, Johnson won the primary by the tiny margin of eighty-seven votes. That victory assured success in the general election. "Landslide Lyndon"—so his colleagues greeted him—was on his way to the United States Senate, where his political career was to flower.

As a senator Johnson achieved two central purposes: to satisfy his Texas constituents, thereby assuring his regular reelection, and to establish himself as a leader of his party. To those ends he struck a middle position on the political spectrum, a stance that accorded with his flexible beliefs. He also became an artist at conciliation and compromise. With Lady Bird's help, he gained the friendship and confidence of influential colleagues, including the powerful conservative

Richard Russell of Georgia. Unlike the young Jack Kennedy who in eight years in the Senate remained a glamorous outsider, Johnson in his twelve years became the dominant insider. He won to his side promising Democratic newcomers, such as Hubert Humphrey of Minnesota, a steady liberal, and Robert Kerr of Oklahoma, a talented tactician. Johnson also continued to cultivate members of his party's establishment on the Potomac; Clark Clifford, Tommy Corcoran, Abe Fortas, James Rowe. All were former assistants to Roosevelt or current associates of Truman, and all were lawyers who in Republican years could prosper at the bar while they plotted the return of the Democrats.

Like those party brokers, Johnson avoided the doctrinaire. He thought of himself as a latter-day New Dealer, a practical idealist. Beyond that, he had no interest in ideology, no philosophy of politics. But he had already become expert about how things worked and about strategies for gaining and for using power. In the Senate he staked a shifting position, designed for personal success. He stayed just enough to the left of his southern colleagues to keep their trust while he also courted his more liberal northern brethren. And he protected the interests of the Texas oil industry. In 1952 he quietly won election as Democratic whip. After the defeat of several senior Democratic senators in Eisenhower's Republican sweep that fall, Johnson in 1953 became minority leader and in 1955, when the Democrats regained control of the Senate, the majority leader, a major office he seemed born to, his savoir faire and extraordinary energy undiminished even after a heart attack.

Johnson's achievements as majority leader made him the national figure he wanted to become. Recognizing Eisenhower's enormous popularity, he cooperated with the president on matters of foreign policy and national defense, which he considered in any case properly the province of the White House. He shared Ike's concern for frugality in federal expenditures. But he also retained his independence. Johnson helped dissuade Eisenhower from providing aerial support for the French in their doomed defense of Dien Bien Phu, the besieged fortress in Vietnam; he sparked the creation of the National Aeronautics and Space Administration (NASA); and he worked out the compromises between northern liberals and resistant southerners that made possible the Civil Rights Acts of 1957 and 1960, the first such acts since Reconstruction.

By 1960 Johnson had more influence in Washington than any other Democrat and a demonstrated capacity for leadership. He also had a hunger for the presidency. The preferred candidate of the South and of many conservative and moderate Democrats elsewhere, Johnson lost the nomination in 1960 partly because believing that the country was not ready for a Dixie candidate, he organized his campaign too late. Kennedy quickly asked Johnson to become his running mate probably because he respected his abilities and needed him on the ticket. For his part, Johnson did not long hesitate to accept. Sam Rayburn, his close adviser, quoting John ("Cactus Jack") Garner, described the vice presidency as "not worth a bucket of cold piss," but Rayburn, like Johnson, believed in the Democratic party. Both men disliked and distrusted Nixon. Both knew Kennedy needed strength in the South to win. Johnson was also tiring of his role as majority leader and flattered by Kennedy's invitation. He may have sensed, too, that Kennedy understood his genuine concern for the poor and the proscribed. Remembering his own youth, Johnson was sensitive to the needs of his rural neighbors and ever admiring of Franklin Roosevelt's accomplishments. More than Kennedy, he believed in the beneficence of big government and had a vaulting view of American possibilities. All those traits had built his commitment to reform beyond the limits of the prudential politics he had long practiced. By 1960, though he had absorbed much of the culture and manner of the "good ol' boys," Johnson was authentically democratic. He was a provincial, but as one of his intimates said, he had come to think like a provincial not from Texas but from Washington, D.C.

Johnson campaigned vigorously for Kennedy, but he was never comfortable on the New Frontier. He could not be content as a subordinate. He also resented the apparent disdain for all things southern among Kennedy's circle of friends. Without his former power in the Senate, he sustained his ego in gossip with his friends by flaunting his insider's information. Without influence on the president, he sulked about decisions he disapproved. Abroad he expressed his patriotism in exaggerated rhetoric. At home he became almost desperate to be heard. So it was in the fall of 1963, when in a prolonged, passionate, scolding telephone conversation he implored Ted Sorensen to urge Kennedy to convince the Republicans that support for the civil rights bill was a moral issue. But Kennedy had already defined civil rights as a moral issue, and Sorensen, who agreed with him, did not need Johnson's advice. Rather, Johnson apparently needed to make himself feel important, as he did also by recourse to the macho language of the ranch. His public vulgarity tended to confirm the suspicions of those who found him gauche and also vain, devious, emotional, and egocentric.

That assessment was partly valid, but it also underestimated the intelligence, social consciousness, and personal command of Lyndon

Johnson. Johnson entered the presidency with more experience in politics and in government than any of his predecessors since Franklin Roosevelt, whose memorable record he was determined to exceed. Johnson "may have been a son of a bitch," as one of his staff said, "but he was a colossal son of a bitch."

2. Two Victories

Johnson found it both easy and convenient to adopt Kennedy's program as his own. He had no doubts about the timeliness or significance of the objectives involved, for their origins dated from Franklin Roosevelt, as did Johnson's related perceptions of the proper role of the federal government. The Kennedy agenda, furthermore, especially as Johnson went about refining it to enlist congressional and public support, provided an appealing platform for the election in his own right that Johnson was resolved to win. Those qualities characterized the revenue and civil rights bills, already well along their way through the House and so closely identified with Kennedy that a penitent Congress might grant the late president in death what it had denied him in life.

After urging that outcome in his November 27 address, Johnson pursued it vigorously during the ensuing months. As one of his first steps, he asked Larry O'Brien, the head of the White House staff for congressional relations, to report on the organization of that office. O'Brien explained that his staff set up regular meetings with committee chairmen, corresponded with members of both houses, arranged to have members themselves announce "good news" about new federal contracts or grants for their districts, wrote weekly reports on the progress of legislation, kept all parts of the executive branch involved in issues of interest on the Hill, and through O'Brien himself "participated in all patronage decisions throughout government." An enlarged staff, O'Brien suggested, could accomplish even more than the "300 per cent increase in contact between members of Congress and the White House" that had already been achieved. The system was excellent, but Johnson did increase the staff and gradually bring in men of his own to supplement and succeed the Kennedy appointees who departed during the next year. He preserved the structure O'Brien had built, retained O'Brien, kept on with Kennedy's weekly breakfasts with congressional leaders, and continued, too, Kennedy's efforts at bipartisanship, so necessary if the administration's legislation was to pass. Johnson also talked intensely with individual congressmen whose votes he needed. Ordinarily they succumbed to the Johnson treatment.

Kennedy's senior advisers, also subjected to the force of Johnson's ways, adapted their manner of operation to the temperament and expectations of their new chief. Such was the case with Walter Heller. The tax bill that Heller had persuaded Kennedy to sponsor had made its way through the House before the assassination. Wilbur Mills had been the key, and he brought along many of his southern brethren. Mills had been converted by Heller's argument that the nation needed a temporary deficit to accelerate growth, to reduce unemployment, and later, with national income rising, to generate new revenues that would balance the budget. Mills was also comfortable with Kennedy's proposed budget deficit for fiscal year 1964–1965 of $101 or $102 billion. But Lyndon Johnson was not. Eager to placate business leaders who had considered Kennedy fiscally irresponsible, Johnson also wanted to make the revenue bill compatible to Harry Byrd, chairman of the Senate Finance Committee, and other conservative Democrats. In concert with the Republicans, they had the votes at least to delay the measure in the Senate, and they were demanding a reduction in government spending plans to accompany any reduction in taxes. In contrast, Heller was pressing his own, more expansionary case. The day after Kennedy's death he had written Johnson that without the tax cut, there would be an economic slowdown in the second half of 1964, a prediction that implied a political liability for the president. That very evening Johnson assured Heller that he was not a conservative, but only two days later he warned Heller that the revenue bill would fail in the Senate without a spending cut of $2 to $3 billion. Unless the proposed budget fell below $100 billion, Johnson said, "You won't pee one drop."

With no further choice in the matter, Heller incorporated Johnson's view in drafting a statement for the president to make to the AFL-CIO Executive Council. "The tax cut," he wrote, "is the most massive single attack we can make on the problem [of jobs]. We must be sure we don't lose a prompt $11 billion in tax lift in trying to gain another $1 billion . . . of spending. After the yeasty effect of the tax cut begins to work in the economy, there will be more dough for everyone." The combination of the tax reduction, which the Senate enacted at the end of January 1964, and of Johnson's proposed budget of $98 billion, a figure reached by McNamara's promise of efficiencies to limit the costs of defense, would provide a net fiscal stimulus, so Heller calculated, "greater than in any other peacetime year in history." That was the kind of economic forecast the president was delighted to receive.

It was also a forecast correct in both its economic and political aspects.

Coming as it did at a time of virtually no inflation, the tax cut by September 1965 had stimulated an increase in gross national product of twenty-five billion dollars. That growth in turn moved the federal budget into surplus and pushed unemployment down to the exceptionally low level of 4.5 percent. Indeed, the economy by the end of fiscal 1965 had achieved over the previous five years an average growth rate, without inflation, of 5.3 percent annually. Though later a rise in defense expenditures did provoke inflation and ultimately retard growth, the response of the economy to the tax cut by that time had wholly vindicated the Keynesian recommendations of the Council of Economic Advisers.

For Lyndon Johnson, the political gains from his handling of the revenue act were equally impressive. By appearing to champion fiscal responsibility, he won confidence both on the Hill and within the business community, which accepted him as it never had Kennedy. The revenue act itself eased the taxes of both the wealthy and the middle class, of both big business and smaller enterprise, and predictably enhanced Johnson's standing with those groups. Like Kennedy, Johnson had made no effort for tax reform. He was content to leave open the loopholes through which the rich avoided taxes, content to retain taxes that cut into the incomes of the working poor. But by endorsing the tax reduction that worked so well in 1964, Johnson made prosperity his issue and built an enlarged constituency for his election and for the rest of his program.

The impact of the revenue act had still other longer-range consequences. Pleased by the quality of the economic advice that Kennedy's appointees had supplied, Johnson replaced them as they departed with academic economists of similar views and notable ability. Heller, the last of the original three to leave, returned to the University of Minnesota in October 1964. Before then he and Tobin and Gordon had made their mark on national policy. They were dedicated professionals, aware, to be sure, of politics but concerned essentially with the performance of the economy rather than the manipulation of elections. Still, the political effects of the tax cut made an enduring impression on aspirants for high office. In the 1970s it therefore became common practice to seek stimulation of the economy for political gain, regardless of the economic consequences. The accompanying distortions of Keynesian theory and its applications reversed the substantial gains, doctrinal and practical, attributable to Heller and his colleagues. But in 1964, by accepting Heller's advice, Johnson had become his particular beneficiary.

Between December 1963 and February 1964 the momentum of Kennedy's bipartisan tactics carried the administration's civil rights bill through the House of Representatives. Manny Celler and Bill McCulloch together managed the debate, while Johnson prepared to throw the weight of the White House into the pending battle in the Senate. Only one amendment significantly altered the measure before the House voted. Judge Howard Smith, a powerful opponent of civil rights, attempted to make the bill unpalatable to the Congress by enlarging the definition of the kinds of discrimination forbidden in employment. As it stood, the bill prohibited discrimination on the basis of race, creed, color, or national origin. Smith moved to add the word "sex"—a change he described as a "chivalrous action." That change gave all women, for the first time in American history, equal rights to men's for all kinds of jobs, public or private, commercial or professional. Surprised by Smith's move, Celler opposed it, but five women members of the House flew to its support. As Representative Katharine St. George said just before the amendment was passed, "We are entitled to this little crumb of equality." Smith's amendment received little more congressional attention at the time. It predated the spirited movement for women's rights that began later in the decade. Kennedy had appointed a committee on the status of women, and its activities were beginning to feed a growing concern about the issue, but neither he nor Johnson had expected women's struggle for equal rights to rise as high as that for blacks—with similar social, economic, and political implications.

Johnson was never a bigot. He had come by 1964, as he wrote in his memoirs, "face to face with the deepseated discrimination against blacks" in his role as chairman of Kennedy's Committee on Equal Employment Opportunity. He understood that his beloved South had to purge itself of the demagoguery and the brutality of the extreme segregationists if it was to become an integral and prosperous part of the nation. He believed in the moral as well as the political imperative of equal opportunity for black Americans, and he was resolved to put his prestige as president behind Kennedy's civil rights bill. He was also eager to drive that bill rapidly through the Senate in order to tap national remorse over Kennedy's death. That done, he could move on to other issues bearing his personal stamp and thereby build a record on which he could run convincingly for election in his own right.

As Johnson told the press while the civil rights bill was under debate in the House, he did not expect the Senate seriously to weaken the measure, but he did expect a filibuster by southern senators. It required a two-thirds vote of the Senate to pass a cloture motion to stop a filibuster, more votes than the president thought his supporters could obtain. He proposed, therefore, to wear out the southerners by scheduling round-the-clock sessions, the tactic he had used in behalf of the civil rights bills of 1957 and 1960. But in those years the southerners had ended their filibuster only after securing major concessions. Robert Kennedy and his associates in the Justice Department told the president that they had promised McCulloch to protect the House's bill from compromise. They wanted, therefore, at an appropriate time to force a vote on cloture, as did Mike Mansfield of Montana, now Democratic majority leader, and Hubert Humphrey, whom Mansfield had designated floor leader for the bill. Johnson let them have their way. The Justice Department would handle the bill, he conceded, telling Mansfield to do nothing "that didn't have Bob's approval." That unusual deference, so Robert Kennedy suspected, was calculated. "If I worked out the strategy," he said, "then if he didn't obtain passage of the bill, he could always say he did what we suggested and didn't go off on his own."

Perhaps Kennedy was partly correct. Johnson did like to hedge his political bets, but the president also remained personally involved. He knew just as well as Mansfield that the Democrats could not carry a vote for cloture without heavy Republican support. That support depended upon the cooperation of the Republican minority leader, Everett Dirksen of Illinois. "The bill can't pass unless you get Ev Dirksen," Johnson told Hubert Humphrey. "You and I are going to get Ev. It's going to take time. . . . You've got to let him have a piece of the action. He's got to look good. . . . You drink with Dirksen! You talk with Dirksen! You listen to Dirksen!" Johnson knew his man. Dirksen sometimes seemed the posturing buffoon, egocentric, grandiloquent, immobile. In fact, he was a shrewd and experienced legislator, a member of the Senate's inner club, where Johnson had functioned for so many years. Dirksen was also a careful observer of public opinion, and public opinion was running more and more strongly for the civil rights bill. He would need careful handling, but Humphrey, also a member of the inner circle, was determined to succeed. Success in managing the civil rights bill would enhance Humphrey's already glowing liberal credentials and please Johnson, who would later in the year pick his own vice president, a position for which Humphrey yearned. The president could count on Humphrey to heed his advice, and he could also reach Dirksen himself. The Justice Department, as Johnson had said, would carry a major responsibility for the civil rights bill, but no more so than the White House.

Senator Russell of Georgia, the veteran leader of the southern opposition to the civil rights bill, began the filibuster against it early in March 1964. "We are preparing," he said, "for a battle to the last ditch—to the death." No less prepared, Humphrey had put together a bipartisan team to direct tactics in support of the bill. The team met regularly with cooperating representatives of the National Association for the Advancement of Colored People, the Americans for Democratic Action, and other lobbyists rich in wisdom about the Senate and its ways. Again and again they rejected the president's urging to "run the show around the clock" so as to exhaust the filibusterers. Instead, they worked with religious groups organized to put pressure on the Senate. Protestant, Catholic, and Jewish leaders arranged prayer vigils at the Lincoln Memorial and national campaigns to reach senators by mail and by visits from clerical and lay delegations. The president, though impatient with that procedure, enlisted Monsignor Joseph P. O'Brien, the vice chancellor of the New York Archdiocese, and made a "magnificent appearance before the Baptists" at their Christian Citizenship Seminar. "Cardinals, bishops, common preachers and rabbis," Richard Russell complained, had encouraged "thousands of good citizens to sign petitions supporting the bill." The capital city, Russell said, had not seen "such a gigantic and well-organized lobby since the . . . days of . . . Prohibition."

That "coercion by men of the cloth" also impressed Dirksen, whom Johnson and Humphrey were courting assiduously. The Republican leader realized his party could not afford to block the civil rights bill, which he had come to accept in principle as both just and necessary. He was nevertheless uncomfortable with some of the bill's language and some of its enforcement procedures. With the filibuster nearing the end of its third month, Humphrey and Mansfield went along with Dirksen's minor modifications of the measure. Those amendments stipulated that suits to enforce fair employment were to be initiated by the attorney general rather than the Civil Rights Commission, and then only in cases in which he found "a pattern of discrimination." Further, in cases relating to public accommodation, individuals with grievances had to seek local remedy before filing federal suit. Most important for the success of the bill in the Senate, Dirksen's revisions made it clear that the section of the measure on school desegregation applied only to the de jure segregation of the South, not to the de facto segregation so common in northern cities. The bill in general was obviously directed against conditions in the South. That form of regional discrimination had long infuriated Russell and other Dixie Democrats, who saw that racial prejudice and injustice were a national rather than a regional addiction.

But the southerners stood defeated. With Dirksen, the bill gained the support of Republican centrists, who provided enough votes to assure passage of the cloture motion that ended debate early in June. The bill itself, which the House later accepted without further change, passed the Senate seventy-three to twenty-seven. Only five Republicans from outside the South voted against it. One of them, Barry Goldwater of Arizona, a leading Republican candidate for the presidential nomination, argued that "to give genuine effect to the . . . bill will require the creation of a federal police force of mammoth proportions." He was wrong. "America grows, America changes," Dirksen said. "In the history of mankind there is an inexorable moral force that carries us forward."

Dirksen and McCulloch and their Republican allies deserved much credit for the Civil Rights Act, but so did Johnson and Humphrey and the Kennedys and their men in the Justice Department. The bill most of all reflected the impact on the nation's conscience, educated by the civil rights movement and its leaders, King and Farmer particularly. They had created an environment that made the act, as Dirksen said, quoting Victor Hugo, "an idea whose time has come." Lyndon Johnson had the good fortune to be president when that moment arrived. He helped hasten it, and he never objected to the growing journalistic habit of calling the Civil Rights Act of 1964 Johnson's act. Exaggerating his own role, he expected American blacks and their spokesmen to express their gratitude to him by preserving racial peace during the coming summer and by wholeheartedly supporting his election in the fall. Their debt to him, as he saw it, also derived from the "unconditional war on poverty" he had already declared.

3. ATTACK ON POVERTY

In the autumn of 1963 President Kennedy had begun to consider poverty as a central issue for his attention in 1964. He had asked the Council of Economic Advisers to begin a study of poverty and its remedies. That study had special importance for the council because the revenue act would ease taxes on the rich and the middle class but provide no help to the poor who paid no income tax. The most impoverished Americans, many of them children or disabled or aged, needed direct assistance. The council's studies revealed that need was growing. There had developed a "drastic slowdown in the rate at which the economy is taking people out of poverty." The CEA classified 20 percent of American families as poor—that is, as earning less than thirty-one hundred dollars a year. The proportion of poor families was much larger among four groups: blacks, the undereducated, families headed by a woman, and southern and rural families. Taken in combination, those factors could be devastating. So it was that among families headed by single black women with less than eight years of schooling, 94 percent were poor. Further, as the CEA observed, poverty bred poverty: "Poor parents cannot give their children the opportunities for better health and education needed to improve their lot." A "lack of motivation, hope, and incentive" acted as a subtle barrier to advancement.

To reverse that trend, Walter Heller drew up specific antipoverty proposals based upon suggestions from the executive departments. He presented them to Lyndon Johnson on November 23, 1963, the day after Johnson had become president. "That's my kind of program," Johnson said. ". . . Move full speed ahead."

"The attack on poverty program," as redefined in early December, called for "a major long-run effort to weld together a set of measures designed to prevent, remedy, and alleviate poverty in America." It left Aid to Families with Dependent Children as the responsibility of the Social Security Administration. It added to the categorical programs of the Kennedy administration a new element, one intended to break the cycle of poverty by using local development corporations. Both the federal government and the Ford Foundation had earlier experimented with such institutions on a small scale. Each of the corporations would assemble and coordinate various existing antipoverty projects. That concept was renamed community action. It appealed to President Johnson, who called for its application on a general rather than an experimental scale and made it the centerpiece of the message he sent to Congress in January 1964. The budget proposed for the existing antipoverty efforts came to five hundred million dollars, just as Kennedy had planned, with five hundred million dollars more for community action, an amount obtained by paring military appropriations. The total, one billion dollars, had a resounding resonance but represented only about 1 percent of the administration's overall budget. Further, community action offered no additional financial assistance to victims of endemic poverty. The scope of the problems of the poor exceeded by far those limited resources by which Johnson prepared to fight, as he put it, an "unlimited war on poverty."

Yet Johnson, who had allowed himself to believe his own fanciful claim that he had emerged from a youth of poverty, allowed himself also to believe that his recommendation to Congress had revolutionary dimensions. That confusion had a counterpart within the program itself. Community action, as yet undefined, could imply that existing local authorities would impose antipoverty policies on their constituents or that federal officials would do so. It might also mean that the poor themselves would generate policies of their own—rather in the manner in which SDS leaders were already trying to instruct residents of ghettos in Cleveland, Ohio, and Newark, New Jersey, and other cities. Indeed, community action remained an amorphous idea in many ways. The Community Action Program (CAP), according to one memo trying to explain it, was not a public works or housing or job-creating program, though all those goals were part of its purpose; nor was it a crash program, for its major value would "show up over the next decade, not the next year or two." But there was an immediate need for the programs CAP did not include: for new jobs, to which the Department of Labor gave top priority; for health services and educational innovations, which the Department of Health, Education, and Welfare stressed; and for direct subsidies to the helpless.

Continuing disagreement among the executive departments persuaded Johnson to create an independent executive agency, the Office of Economic Opportunity (OEO), to coordinate the attack on poverty and to direct programs outside the authority of any cabinet officer. The President appointed Sargent Shriver head of the new agency. Shriver, the husband of Kennedy's sister Eunice, had energized the Peace Corps, probably the most popular invention of the New Frontier. He turned now with equivalent zest to his new task. Charged with guiding the enabling legislation for the antipoverty program through Congress, he endeavored to satisfy the concerns of cabinet members influential on the Hill and of potentially helpful liberal interest groups. Almost as impatient for results as the president, Shriver made community action only one facet of a diffuse bill he fashioned. Johnson's insistence on fiscal prudence allowed the addition of specified objectives to the antipoverty program only if they required no new taxes or increases in the budget. As those additions grew in number so as to meet the demands of congressmen Shriver was trying to woo, the funds available for each purpose diminished. The process of gathering votes led also to the inclusion in the final legislation of distorting provisions. Among those was one providing for small loans to low-income businessmen and

Sargent Shriver and LBJ: Allies in the war against poverty.

farmers and another for the assignment of 40 percent of the Job Corps to conservation camps—facilities revered by those nostalgic for the New Deal's Civilian Conservation Corps but irrelevant for fostering skills useful in contemporary industries. Shriver testified in March 1964 that the antipoverty bill was now "new in the sweep of its attack" and so "prudently planned" that "it does not raise the national budget by a single dollar."

That fiscal restraint should have quieted conservative apprehensions, but the president took no chances with his bill. He saw to it that a conservative southerner, Representative Phil Landrum, introduced it in the House. At the insistence of others from Dixie, Johnson also agreed to discharge Shriver's designated deputy, Adam Yarmolinsky, an intelligent veteran of the Kennedy administration who had offended only by his identification with liberal causes. Wilbur Cohen in HEW recognized that the aged, the young, and the handicapped among the poor would always need welfare payments in order to subsist. Nevertheless, the content and the title of the measure, the economic opportunity bill, expressed the president's hazy hope that the programs included would provide exits from poverty by correcting deficiencies in

education and training or local pockets of economic underdevelop-
ment. Then and later Johnson oversold his poverty program. He made
it seem that his initiatives would end both poverty and welfare—objectives beyond the reach of his policies. But his hype convinced the bill's
supporters in Congress, who prevailed easily by votes of 226 to 185 in
the House and 61 to 34 in the Senate.

The legislation had yet to be tested, but by its enactment, Johnson
won a major victory in 1964. It added allure to his reputation as a
master of politics. The Economic Opportunity Act also fitted tidily into
his campaign package. Extrapolating on his record, Johnson in a commencement speech at the University of Michigan called the result the
"Great Society"—his New Deal, his New Frontier. The Great Society
as it stood in 1964 offered something to almost everyone: lower taxes
for the wealthy and the professionals; economic expansion for investors and workers; civil rights for blacks and other minorities; opportunity for the poor. The coalitions in Congress that Johnson had forged
in behalf of his goals foreshadowed the construction he had under way
of a "consensus" so broad that he could achieve election by an overwhelming majority. In part his achievements reflected the education of
the electorate during Kennedy's years in the White House. In part they
were based on national remorse over Kennedy's death. But Johnson
had built sturdily on his inheritance. Now, as a Texan, he expected the
support of the South in spite of the Civil Rights Act, while that statute
and the antipoverty act would also attract eastern liberals, whose favor
he pretended to scorn but privately valued. With the economy booming, Johnson also appealed to business leaders. Many of them recognized in him financial prudence, entrepreneurial instinct, and expertness
in public relations not unlike their own prescribed qualities for success.
In cultivating the managers of American business, Johnson departed
from previous liberal practice. His tactic and rhetoric for that consti-
uency resembled Eisenhower's rather than those of FDR in 1936 or
Harry Truman in 1948. Indeed, there stood outside the president's
intended fold only inveterate Republicans, adamant segregationists, and
a small but growing number of clerical and blue-collar workers disgruntled by the recent gains of the blacks and the poor. The diverse
elements in the coalition the president was shaping did not necessarily
agree about the desirable future of the nation. Their consensus, rather,
related to Johnson himself. Compleat politician that he was, he meant
his campaign to involve every friend, convert every skeptic, thwart every
foe.

4. BOBBY AND BARRY

Lyndon Johnson often seemed unreal, gross, larger than life. In his memoir he recalled that in 1964, while considering a national campaign, he had had doubts about the willingness of the country to accept his leadership, doubts also about his health, though it had been excellent since his heart attack nine years earlier. Actually he could have had no serious doubts. With a visible confidence that outmatched any hidden anxiety, he believed he could become the greatest of presidents. He wanted the job desperately. Every incumbent president eager for election had needed the loyalty of his staff. Johnson demanded it. His sensitivities about his southern background, his piques over the slights he had suffered from some of Kennedy's entourage, his personal and political vanity made him obsessive about loyalty. Other incumbent presidents had worked, as Kennedy had planned to, for a clear mandate for their policies. Johnson, seeking a victory larger even than Roosevelt's in 1936, engaged, as one of his advisers observed, in "a relentless pursuit of that last possible vote." As he went about it, the election of 1964 marked the high point of his career.

During the early months of 1964, once the period of transition had passed, Johnson made the executive branch of the government the province of his own people—of men who were willing and able to transfer their allegiance from Kennedy to him or of those, many of them with Texas backgrounds, who had long been his supporters. In the sphere of military and foreign policy, the senior Kennedy advisers, riveted to their responsibilities, had earned Johnson's confidence or soon did so. Secretary of State Dean Rusk, Secretary of Defense Robert McNamara, National Security Adviser McGeorge Bundy, and CIA Director John McCone remained in their important offices, and General Maxwell Taylor in July 1964 accepted the major post of ambassador to South Vietnam. But several of the cabinet departed, and except for Larry O'Brien and speech writer Richard Goodwin, Kennedy's special friends and counselors in the executive office also left. Their most influential successors included Bill Moyers, a young protégé of Johnson's who had many of Ted Sorensen's talents, and George E. Reedy, an experienced journalist who became press secretary. Those men, along with reinforcements Johnson recruited later and with his powerful personal friends like Abe Fortas and Clark Clifford, whom he consulted regularly, constituted as a group the equal of the Kennedy staff. They were doggedly faithful to the president and ardent in their service to him. During the spring of 1964 Adlai Stevenson, who was no man's man, felt the change that had occurred. On a visit to the White House he remarked: "The atmosphere, the people—well, they are Johnsonian, or Johnsonized."

Soon thereafter the Democratic party was Johnsonized, too. The president, confronting no serious challenge to his own nomination, was determined to accept no challenge to his choice of running mate. The threat, as he saw it, arose from Robert Kennedy. In their shock over President Kennedy's death, some of his most dedicated admirers, particularly those who had never respected his vice president, thought that it was somehow unfair that Johnson had inherited his office, his program, and much of his acclaim. They naturally met with each other at social occasions, sometimes in company with Jacqueline Kennedy, and exchanged their sorrows and disappointments, frequently in the form of gossip critical of Johnson. The president, convinced that they were conspiring against him, resented them deeply. He especially distrusted the attorney general, the central figure among the disgruntled New Frontiersmen and their candidate for nomination as vice president. As John F. Kennedy's closest and most influential adviser, the coauthor of many of his major decisions, Robert Kennedy, in the view of his entourage, deserved Johnson's endorsement for the office. John F. Kennedy, after all, had selected Johnson as his running mate; now reciprocity seemed appropriate to them, particularly because Robert Kennedy of all men best represented his brother's legacy. But Johnson could scarcely endure Robert Kennedy. "He never liked me," the president said, "and that's nothing compared to what I think of him." Indeed, Johnson more and more dismissed criticism of his policies or behavior as expressions of Kennedy's alleged plotting against him.

For his part, Robert Kennedy never declared his candidacy. He knew that Johnson did not want him, but he was unwilling to convenience the president, whom he despised, by removing himself, and he was resolved to remain in public life. Johnson thought Kennedy was campaigning. The president stopped it in July 1964 by announcing that he considered it "inadvisable . . . to recommend . . . any member of the cabinet" for Vice President. He had already told Kennedy about that decision, which incidentally eliminated several others unacceptable to him, and had told Kennedy also that political considerations required him to balance his ticket with a candidate from the Middle West. Later Johnson ventured the implausible explanation that he had had to keep the cabinet from campaigning in order to prevent a halt in the business of government. Kennedy knew better. Without recriminations, but with

Hubert H. Humphrey: He had a liberal record.

the president's punctilious public support, he resigned from the cabinet to become United States senator from New York. Johnson meanwhile conducted a charade that teased and humbled other aspirants for his favor. In the end, at the eleventh hour but to no one's surprise he picked Minnesota Senator Hubert H. Humphrey, whose ingratiating assurances of personal loyalty and unquestionably liberal record made him on all accounts an appropriate choice.

The Democratic platform had evolved with each of Johnson's triumphs on the Hill. With him as the candidate, the party had to run with statements of pride in Kennedy's record and his own and on the promises of the Great Society. As Johnson later put it, "We built the campaign strategy around a progressive program, the program that formed the framework of the Great Society . . . a program of action to clear up an agenda of social reform . . . and to begin the . . . agenda for tomorrow . . . to . . . commit the nation to . . . the War on Poverty, to provide greater educational opportunities . . . to offer medical care to the elderly, to conserve our water and air . . . to tackle . . . the housing shortage."

Those objectives, like the civil rights legislation already passed, lay to the left of the center of the American political spectrum of 1960. By 1964 they stood closer to the center because militant blacks and young white radicals were fashioning a New Left. The center also became more capacious as the dominant faction of the Republican party moved the GOP to the right. The Republican shift accompanied the party's choice as its presidential candidate of Senator Barry Goldwater of Arizona, then the most eligible and conspicuous spokesman of a resurgent and self-conscious conservatism. In part Goldwater owed his nomination to his personal qualities. He was a handsome, genial man, honest, decent, and courageous. Yet his deeply conservative convictions attracted some venomous sponsors, who saw him as an instrument for gaining power for themselves and for their ideas. In 1964 he faced little competition for the nomination. Republican liberals could not rally support for Governor Nelson Rockefeller of New York after his quick remarriage following a scandalous divorce. Too late they put forward Governor William Scranton of Pennsylvania, who entered the convention with few delegates and little recognition. Richard Nixon was temporarily disqualified by his reputation as a loser; he had lost his 1962 race for the governorship of California. That left Goldwater, whose backers believed, as other Republican regulars hoped, that a silent majority of disaffected Americans stood ready to jump behind a genuine conservative. Goldwater's men dominated the Republican Convention, where their aggressive tactics offended their rivals. So did Goldwater's acceptance speech with its assertion, ominous because of his ultraconservative leanings, that "extremism in the defense of liberty is no vice."

Goldwater's understanding of "liberty" or of "freedom" impelled that anxious reaction. In 1960 he had published a tract, *The Conscience of a Conservative*, that advanced the beliefs that he repeated and elaborated during the 1964 campaign. He directed his case against the "liberals"—Roosevelt and Truman Democrats and Eisenhower Republicans alike, whom true conservatives had to supplant. "The *legitimate* functions of government," he argued, were "actually conducive to freedom," whereas "the corrupting influence of power" had led to a dangerous aggrandizement of the American state. Though the framers of the Constitution had created "a system of restraints against the natural tendencies of government to expand," "liberal" policies had breached those barriers. Goldwater lamented the resulting "extent of government interference in the daily lives of individuals." The farmer, he complained in a litany reminiscent of Herbert Hoover, was told how much wheat he could grow; federal labor legislation left wage earners at the mercy of powerful union leaders; government regulations hampered businessmen; Social Security taxes compelled "millions of individuals to postpone until later years the enjoyment of wealth they might

otherwise enjoy today." That last contention distorted the purpose and the effect of old age insurance. But Goldwater believed what he wrote; he believed, too, that the first duty of public officials was "to divest themselves of the power they have been given."

Goldwater followed his paean to minimal federal government with a corollary reading of the Constitution that maximized states' rights. The Tenth Amendment, as he interpreted it, reserved to the states authority over both civil rights and education. The Supreme Court had erred in *Brown v. Board of Education* (1954). Though Goldwater said he agreed with the objective of the *Brown* decision, he held that the Court had abused its authority. Therefore, he supported "all effort by the States . . . to preserve their rightful powers over education." Indeed, Goldwater rejected the very concept of equality as the federal government had understood it. The laws of nature, for his purpose convenient constraints where the Constitution faltered, including the natural right of property, precluded the graduated income tax. "We are all equal in the eyes of God," Goldwater conceded, "but we are equal *in no other respect.*" So the income tax, like the Social Security tax and the integration of southern public schools, had to go, as did other instruments of "collectivization" and the welfare state. "Socialism-through-Welfarism" posed the greatest threat to freedom.

Except one, so Goldwater warned: the loss of the cold war to the Soviet Union, a rival "that possesses not only the will to dominate absolutely every square mile of the globe, but increasingly the capacity to do so . . . controlled by a ruthless despotism." Americans had been losing the cold war since the early 1950s, Goldwater wrote, because they had "waged" peace while the Soviet Union waged war. "A tolerable peace," he continued, "must *follow* victory over Communism." In his view the nuclear "balance of terror" was "not a balance at all, but an instrument of blackmail." The United States could prevent defeat only by developing superior power, enough to "defeat the enemy." To that end the American system of alliances in Europe and Asia was inadequate. Further, American economic aid had been counterproductive. The Constitution did not contemplate it, and in any case, it had flowed to nations already friendly and therefore presumably not worth courting or, worse, to nations admittedly neutral. As for negotiations with the Soviet Union, they could not succeed because Communists would agree only to terms advantageous to themselves.

"If our objective is victory," Goldwater concluded, "we must achieve superiority in all of the weapons—military, as well as political and economic" at whatever the necessary cost. He wrote:

> Our strategy must be primarily offensive. . . . We should encourage friendly peoples that have the means and the desire . . . to undertake offensive operations for the recovery of their homelands. For example . . . should the situation develop favorably, we should encourage the South Koreans and the South Vietnamese to join Free Chinese Forces in a combined effort to liberate the enslaved peoples of Asia. . . . We must—ourselves—be prepared to undertake military operations against vulnerable Communist regimes. . . . Assume . . . a major uprising in Eastern Europe . . . we ought to . . . be prepared . . . to move a highly mobile task force equipped with appropriate nuclear weapons. . . . The Kremlin should be put on notice . . . that resort to long-range bombers and missiles would prompt retaliation in kind.

Such a policy involved the risk of war, Goldwater admitted, "but any policy, short of surrender, does that. . . . War may be the price of freedom. . . . The risk of war . . . holds forth the promise of victory." And of annihilation, his critics feared.

On foreign policy as on domestic, Barry Goldwater was an ideologue. That was why his call for extremism on behalf of his conception of liberty frightened his opponents in 1964. That was why it was he, not Johnson, who seemed radical then. Goldwater's program threatened to overturn the prevailing American consensus and to destroy social arrangements that reflected three decades of political accommodation. Goldwater seemed out of step with the times. He alienated a large fraction of his party. His staff could not prevent his political gaffes. Consequently, many of Goldwater's critics failed to take his campaign seriously. They were wrong. Goldwater spoke in what was becoming the authentic voice of American conservatism, so much so that as late as 1988 support for Goldwater in 1964 remained a litmus test of the Republican right.

More pragmatic and less ideological than Goldwater, Governor George Wallace of Alabama ran an abbreviated campaign for the Democratic nomination that demonstrated the persisting strength of bigotry in American politics. As the champion of segregation Wallace had not hesitated to condemn the leaders of the civil rights movement and their sympathizers in Washington. In the spring of 1964 Wallace tested his popularity, so high among segregationists in the South, in Democratic primaries in Wisconsin, Indiana, and Maryland, states with large cities and substantial black minorities. He chose a propitious time. Tensions within communities of impoverished urban blacks and between those blacks and their white neighbors had been rising for several years. They began to explode in the summer of 1964, first in Harlem and in Rochester, New York, then in Philadelphia and several cities in New Jersey. The conditions underlying those episodes were the same: frustration, especially among young black males, over the scarcity of employment; the seeming irrelevance of public education; often the absence of family cohesion. In addition, there was the sensed hostility of whites, especially of the white police—all in all, the anomic degradation of poverty. Most victims of the rioting were other blacks. Like the rioters, they were confined to the ghettos, but neighboring whites perceived the riots as threats to themselves and as evidence of a black anger that they had long feared and reciprocated.

That had been the mood also in cities where George Wallace campaigned, attacking the federal government—president, Congress, and the courts. Wallace condemned the government for favoring blacks at the expense of hardworking whites, for encouraging illegal protests, for destroying law and order. He won about a third of the Democratic votes cast in the three northern states he canvassed. A breakdown of his support disclosed the power of the white "backlash"—in the words of one observer, "the fear that working-class Americans have of Negroes." On Milwaukee's south side, Italian-, Polish-, and Serbian-Americans chose Wallace; so did the steelworkers of Baltimore; he carried every precinct in Gary, Indiana, a tough middle western mill town. Those Democratic Wallace supporters were vulnerable to Goldwater's conservatism. But to his credit, Goldwater at the peak of the rioting made a private agreement with Johnson: He would not appeal to race during the campaign. For his part, the president persuaded most civil rights leaders to cancel or postpone demonstrations until the country had quieted down. Those conciliatory measures helped temporarily to cover the incipient turbulence of the cities with a patina of tranquillity.

Johnson meant to manage the Democratic Convention to the same effect, but civil rights activists in Mississippi had contrary intentions. Under the leadership of Robert Moses, a dedicated, educated, and courageous New Yorker, SNCC in Mississippi had been conducting a voter registration campaign for several years. Police there regularly arrested and beat up SNCC workers. Angry whites shot one of Moses's assistants and tried to terrorize blacks who attempted to register to vote. But SNCC persisted. In 1964 its political arm in the state, the Mississippi Freedom Democratic party (MFDP), challenged the regular lily-white Democratic organization. SNCC organizers had persuaded seventeen thousand blacks to take the risk at local courthouses of completing voting registration forms, but state officials allowed only sixteen hundred of them to register. In contrast, some eighty thousand blacks registered as members of the MFDP. The MFDP selected a delegation to represent its constituency at the Democratic National Convention and there to contest the seats of the state's segregationist regulars. Pursuant to Democratic party rules, the MFDP had been open to blacks and whites alike. It was committed to Johnson's election. The regulars excluded black voters, opposed civil rights, and selected a delegation that included many Goldwater supporters. But the president was intent on courting the favor of the white South. He opposed the MFDP challenge and instructed the FBI to arrange surveillance of the MFDP delegates.

He also ordered his supporters and those of Hubert Humphrey to block the MFDP in the credentials committee. The compromise he offered would have allowed MFDP delegates to participate orally in the convention but not to vote. A majority of them rejected it. A revised proposal allowed the MFDP two token votes and promised to ban segregated delegations in 1968. Bob Moses turned it down in spite of the efforts on its behalf of Bayard Rustin, Martin Luther King, and Hubert Humphrey, all of whom were eager to keep the Democratic party peacefully united. Fannie Lou Hamer, one of the MFDP delegates, put her case simply: "We didn't come all this way for no two seats!"

Following Johnson's bidding, the convention endorsed the final compromise proposal. Nevertheless, the regular Mississippi delegation walked out in protest against the party's civil rights plank. Several MFDP delegates attempted to take the vacated seats, but the administration's men threw them out. That treatment made radicals of many of its victims. As one of them wrote, "This kind of dictation is what Negroes in Mississippi face and have always faced, and it is precisely this that they are learning to stand up against."

But Johnson was exuberant. He saw the party as united, the convention as "a place of happy . . . crowds." In one sense, the MFDP delegates had helped him. In the view of most Americans, they represented the left. Consequently, Johnson's handling of them confirmed his stance at the center, about halfway between the extremes defined by Robert Moses at one end and Barry Goldwater at the other. "Right here," Johnson said, "is the reason I'm going to win this thing so big. You ask a voter who classifies himself as a liberal what he thinks I am and he says a liberal. You ask a voter who calls himself a conservative what he thinks I am and he says I'm a conservative. . . . They all think I'm on their side." And that, as the president later recalled, was "where the vast majority of the votes traditionally are."

They certainly were in 1964 as Goldwater continually played into Johnson's hand. Offering the electorate "a choice, not an echo," the Republican gave the president the peace issue by suggesting the use of tactical atomic weapons to hasten victory in Vietnam. American involvement there was rising, and Johnson had requested and received authority from Congress to increase it. But the president presented himself at once as a guardian against aggression and a champion of restraint. He condemned those "eager to enlarge the conflict." He said: "They call upon us to supply American boys to do the job that Asian boys should do. They ask us to take reckless action which might risk the lives of millions and engulf much of Asia." That rhetoric concealed the implications of the secret advice Johnson was receiving from his Joint Chiefs of Staff "to go north and drop bombs." Disingenuous as he was, the president stood out during the campaign as the candidate of thoughtful moderation.

So, too, on domestic issues, which in his candid way Goldwater fumbled. In the heart of the Tennessee Valley Goldwater attacked public power; in the squalor of Appalachia he criticized the antipoverty program; in Florida, the garden of the old, he opposed Democratic proposals for Medicare for the aged. Indeed, Medicare, in the judgment of one shrewd senator, was "the hottest domestic issue" in the campaign, the "most emotional topic" that "excites the most enthusiasm." Probably more important, though less remarked, the tax cut was working political magic. Consumer spending approached new highs, and the GNP broke records. Assisted by a strong campaign organization and generous spending, much of it on television advertising, Johnson stumped the whole country. And with commendable courage he faced down his enemies in the South. In New Orleans he told the story of a former Texas Democrat who realized the great future open to the South if only the region could surmount its racial conflicts. "Poor old Mississippi," that politician supposedly had said, "they haven't heard a Democratic speech in thirty years. All they ever hear at election time is 'Nigger, Nigger, Nigger.' " Not so in 1964 from Johnson. The nation heard instead about the promise of the Great Society.

Prosperity, peace, and progress overwhelmed Barry Goldwater. He carried only six states, his home turf of Arizona and five from the Deep South: Alabama, Georgia, Louisiana, Mississippi, and South Carolina. In exchange for those states, Johnson throughout the country carried almost unanimously the precincts populated by black voters. The popular vote satisfied the president's most extravagant dreams. He won the highest percentage of votes in all of American history to that date— 61 percent—more even than FDR had in 1936. In Johnson's wake the Democrats gained two seats in the Senate and thirty-seven in the House. For the first time since 1938 reform Democrats could overcome the coalition of convenience of Republicans and southern Democrats. Johnson had the clear mandate he had sought, a mandate, as he read it, for the Great Society.

6

The Great Society

The Great Society had diverse origins, some remote in the New Deal, in Franklin Roosevelt's 1944 economic bill of rights, and in Harry Truman's Fair Deal—some more immediate in the Kennedy agenda, which included the earlier heritage, and in Lyndon Johnson's personal antipathy to racism and poverty. The phrase itself came from the president's speech writer, Richard Goodwin, but Walter Lippmann, the Nestor of American journalism, had written about a "great society" during the 1930s and had taken the words from his British teacher and friend Graham Wallas. Johnson had little interest in those roots as such. His concern was with tangible results and with speed in achieving them. He realized that his mandate would effectively expire within two years, concurrently with the terms in office of members of Congress elected with him. Johnson had a capacious sense of the objectives of the Great Society. In his inaugural address in 1965 he stressed the war against poverty and the struggle for racial equality. But he also asked "not only how much, but how good; not only how to create wealth, but how to use it; not only how fast we are going, but where are we headed." He urged Congress to beautify America, to eliminate water and air pollution, to clean up the cities, provide education for the young and medical care for the aged. At the right time for its achievement, Johnson evoked the American dream.

In order to give precise definition to its parts, he turned to a method Kennedy had employed on a smaller scale: the appointment of task forces. The task forces of the years 1964 to 1966 ordinarily contained some members from within the federal government, at least one a member from the White House staff, and a majority of outsiders, mainly from universities. Johnson wanted to enlist the wisest and the best-informed Americans in the construction of the Great Society. He did not study their reports, which covered a prodigious range of issues, each at generous length. But he took their recommendations seriously and employed his formidable political skills to convert them into a cascade of legislation.

1. THE RIGHT TO VOTE

By and large the task forces built upon initiatives taken or contemplated during the Kennedy years, often in response to pressures originating outside government. Again in 1965, it was not the cogitation of any task force but black militancy that prompted the president to act on voting rights. In the afterglow of the election he enjoyed the political support of moderate black leaders like Bayard Rustin and Roy Wilkins of the NAACP. His staff was eager to give his opposition in the white South time to adjust to the changes already under way. He seemed, too, irritated by the earlier protests of the Mississippi Freedom Democrats and jealous of the acclaim for Martin Luther King, Jr. Most of all, Johnson underestimated the restiveness of King's army.

King had recently received the Nobel Prize for Peace. He stood near the pinnacle of his international reputation, but he was facing new troubles close to home. J. Edgar Hoover, the ruthless and reactionary director of the Federal Bureau of Investigation, was attacking King openly. While attorney general, Robert Kennedy had authorized an FBI tap on King's conversations to abet surveillance of Communists allegedly influencing the civil rights leader. Those conversations revealed no Communist influence, though at least one of King's advisers was personally suspect. But the bugs did disclose King's amorous dalliances. His affairs had little public significance during the 1960s, when private morality had yet to receive the close scrutiny of the media. But King's womanizing, like John F. Kennedy's, had it been revealed, would have damaged him. As it was, Hoover's irresponsible charges did hurt King. Hoover called King "the most notorious liar in the country" and implied that the Southern Christian Leadership Conference was "spearheaded by Communists and moral degenerates." Worried by the FBI's persecution, King also faced immediate pressure from the youthful members of the Student Nonviolent Coordinating Committee who were ready to use force as a means to gain the right to vote.

For some time SNCC leaders had been impatient with King and envious of his eminence. In 1963 John Lewis, the SNCC chairman, in the most strident speech of the March on Washington, had criticized the administration's civil rights bill and urged American blacks to join the "great social revolution sweeping our nation." Bob Moses during the ensuing year intended the mobilization of southern blacks to coerce the federal government into promoting stronger legislation for voting rights. The rejection of the Mississippi Freedom Democrats at the 1964 Democratic Convention spurred the growing radicalism within SNCC and attenuated the organization's ties with more moderate black groups and with white liberals. By 1965 SNCC and the NAACP were struggling against each other for control of the civil rights movement in Mississippi, while SNCC leaders, all of them young men, were simultaneously engaged in factional disputes. Moses had become SNCC's philosopher, the proponent of revolutionary ideas. Stokely Carmichael, more the agitator, was preaching his own brand of black Marxism and defending SNCC's associations with the National Lawyers Guild, allegedly a Communist organization. James Forman, influenced by the ideas of Malcolm X, advocated deliberate confrontations with segregationist southern police as the means to radicalize black students throughout the country. John Lewis, now to the right of the others, remained willing to cooperate with King and SCLC.

Pushed from the youthful left, King in 1965 was preparing to push the president. King and his staff wanted a strong voting rights law. They counted again on using nonviolent demonstrations to provoke violent racist retaliation that would move public opinion to support federal intervention and legislation. They chose Selma, Alabama, a notoriously racist city with a brutal sheriff, as the site for their campaign, which Lewis agreed to have SNCC join. Almost daily during January 1965 King led protest marchers to the courthouse in Selma, where the sheriff, James G. Clark, managed to control his anger. Major demonstrations in early February prompted Clark to arrest some fifteen hundred blacks, many of them students. Clark avoided official violence though aroused segregationists later in the month beat a local black minister and murdered a young black agitator. With national attention flagging, King on March 6, 1965, called for a march from Selma to Montgomery, the capital of Alabama, to present a petition of grievances to Governor George Wallace. But when Wallace issued an order prohibiting the march, an order President Johnson wanted King to obey, King returned to his home in Atlanta.

With the departure of "de Lawd," as they derisively called him, SNCC militants and their local supporters embarked anyway on the road to Montgomery. At the Pettus Bridge out of Selma, a hundred of Sheriff Clark's deputies awaited them. Another hundred state troopers under Major John Cloud also blocked their way. Cloud gave the marchers two minutes to turn around and go back to their church in Selma. But as the leaders of the march began to confer, Cloud ordered his troops forward, and Sheriff Clark's men joined the attack. They used tear gas, cattle prods, and night sticks indiscriminately, beating bystanders, including women and children, as well as the fleeing marchers, while television cameras recorded the savagery.

National outrage over the incident exceeded any previous response. Thousands of Americans, black and white, sent telegrams, signed petitions, or joined demonstrations demanding federal intercession. In Atlanta King promised to lead a second march from Selma to Montgomery on March 9 and to request a federal injunction to prevent Alabama authorities from blocking it. To King's surprise, the federal judge, pending further hearings, instead enjoined SCLC from marching. The president still opposed an illegal march. But SNCC and the angry victims of the first march, again the young especially, were resolved to carry on. King knew he needed Johnson's support for voting rights. But he also had to retain the lead in Selma or risk losing his influence throughout the South. In that pass, and because he and his aides feared attacks on his life, King asked the president to send a federal mediator to Selma and later privately accepted the compromise course the mediator proposed. In exchange for a promise that Alabama police would not hurt the marchers, King agreed to lead his followers to the Pettus Bridge, pray there, and then return.

Without informing other black leaders of the agreement, King called for a march to Montgomery. "There may be beating, jailings, tear gas," he said. "But I would rather die on the highways . . . than make a butchery of my conscience." Then he led fifteen hundred men and women to the bridge, where he stopped in front of Major Cloud's troops. Cloud ordered the march to cease but granted King's request to pray. He then departed from the scenario on which King had agreed and ordered his troopers to line both sides of the highway. King, with the road open, was embarrassed, but he followed the scenario and flabbergasted his followers by asking them to return to Selma. His unexplained retreat disheartened his supporters in the ranks and infuriated SNCC leaders. Except for Lewis, they withdrew from further participation in the march. That episode marked a crucial turning point in

Pettus Bridge, Selma: Television recorded the savagery.

the civil rights movement. Thereafter radical black activists, alienated from King, went their own way.

Segregationist violence bolstered King's reputation. SNCC militants were denouncing him when Selma thugs beat up three white Unitarian ministers who had come to join the march. One of the ministers, James J. Reeb of Boston, his skull fractured, died three days later. His death provoked a new wave of national outrage; a pilgrimage of concerned students, teachers, and clergymen to Selma; and thousands more telegrams to Washington calling for voting rights for blacks. Now King's moderation again stood in bold contrast with racist murder, and wanton rage lent an aura of patience and vision to Lyndon Johnson's stand for "law and order."

Johnson seized the moment magnificently. Of course, he recognized his political chance, but he also poured his convictions into the nationally televised address he delivered to Congress on March 15, 1965. "There is no constitutional issue here," the president then said. ". . . There is no moral issue. . . . There is only the struggle for human rights. . . . And should we defeat every enemy, and should we double our wealth and conquer the stars, and still be unequal on this issue, then we will have failed as a people and a nation." He continued: "The real hero of this struggle is the American Negro. His actions and protests, his courage . . . have awakened the conscience of this nation." For all the complexity of many aspects of civil rights, the president said, "about this there can be no argument. Every American citizen must have an equal right to vote." But the enactment of the voting rights bill would not end the battle. The events in Selma were part of "the effort of American Negroes to secure for themselves the full blessings of American life. This cause must be our cause too. It is not just Negroes, but all of us, who must overcome the crippling legacy of bigotry and injustice." Johnson closed with the words of the spiritual that had become the anthem of the civil rights movement: "And we shall overcome." Sincerity had informed his eloquence, which the Congress and the country cheered.

Johnson moved quickly. He urged the hesitant federal district judge to permit the march to Montgomery. He endorsed SCLC's plan for that march. On March 12 he had met with Governor Wallace at the White House and warned him that the federal government would protect the marchers if Alabama did not. Now Wallace saved face by wiring Johnson that the state could not afford to mobilize its National Guard units. Johnson then federalized the guard and also sent a contingent of military police and United States marshals to Alabama.

With protection guaranteed, King set off on March 21 with three hundred others on the road from Selma to Montgomery. There on March 25, before presenting the petition of grievances to Governor Wallace, King addressed the largest civil rights demonstration in southern history. "The battle is in our hands," he said. ". . . [W]e must come to see that the end we seek is a society at peace with itself, a society that can live with its conscience. . . . It will not be long . . . because the arm of the moral universe bends toward justice. . . . Our God is marching on." But that night Klansmen in Alabama shot and killed Viola Liuzzo, a civil rights volunteer from Detroit, and soon thereafter Stokely Carmichael told a black protest rally that "we're going to tear this country up." Nevertheless, at the time Selma seemed a triumph for King and for Johnson.

The president pressed his case on the Hill. Though the Democrats had larger majorities than in 1964, he again needed bipartisan support in the Senate to avoid a crippling filibuster. Again he turned to Everett Dirksen, whose cooperation assured the enactment in August of the administration's civil rights bill. The measure eliminated discriminatory literacy tests, provided federal officers to assist black voters in registering to vote, and established severe penalties for interference with any individual's right to the ballot. Further, whenever a county in any state failed to register 50 percent of its voting-age population, the Justice Department could suspend any test which that county applied to voters and, if necessary, use federal examiners to register those requesting the vote. Those tough provisions worked. Within a few years registration of black voters in the Deep South approached 50 percent and was rising, as it was elsewhere in the nation. Blacks began to win local elective offices, and southern politics entered a new era. Democratic candidates, eventually even George Wallace, came to court black support while a growing percentage of the white vote moved toward the GOP.

The Voting Rights Act of 1965 was one of Johnson's great achievements. It earned him the quick acclaim he savored. For his part, King had played an indispensable role. He had prepared the nation for the legislation, as he had for the Civil Rights Act of 1964, and he had quickened the president's pace. So, in their turn, had young blacks, including those in SNCC, hurried King along. Indeed, as Johnson had said in his March 15 speech, the courage of black Americans themselves had forced others to take account of their grievances. Without the hopes and the boldness, the frustrations and the ideals of anonymous thousands of blacks who were determined to win their full rights as Americans, the leaders of the civil rights movement would have had no flocks. But without those leaders, the gathering of their troops would have lacked in number and in spirit the force that prevailed in the stunning events of 1963, 1964, and 1965. So, too, without those leaders and the pressures they generated, Presidents Kennedy and Johnson would not have acted when they had, nor could they then have won the votes they needed on the Hill. But *mutatis mutandem*, the civil rights movement succeeded when it did and as it did in part because Kennedy and Johnson had the personal sympathies and essential convictions that their immediate predecessors and successors lacked. It was not just a matter of a ground swell of demand from the folk below or of powerful men shaping society from above. Rather, the flocks and the leaders needed each other and in creative reciprocity profoundly altered the conditions of American society, primarily conditions in the South.

The rest of the country also felt the impact of Johnson's executive order of September 1965, instituting the policy of affirmative action foreshadowed by the Civil Rights Act of 1964. The president's order required federal contractors and institutions receiving federal assistance to take special steps to employ more women and nonwhites. Over time that order had profound effects. Universities had to admit significant numbers of women, blacks, Hispanics, and Asians. Affirmative action opened the door for Americans of those groups to jobs previously denied them in the construction industry; to both clerical and executive positions in banking, finance, manufacturing, and retailing; to partnerships in major law firms and seats in corporate boardrooms. During the 1960s movement toward those ends remained slow, but Johnson's order started it.

The achievements of 1964 and 1965 were no less impressive or important for being incomplete. But incomplete they were, as racism North and South continued to contribute to the intractability of a social structure that still excluded millions of Americans from the privileges and expectations common to the middle class.

2. OEO

At the Howard University commencement in June 1965 Johnson promised to go far beyond the Civil Rights Acts. "We must seek," he declared, "not just freedom but opportunity. We seek . . . not just equality as a right and a theory but equality as a fact and equality as a result." He did not mean exactly what he said, for "equality as a fact," if it had been possible to achieve, would have offended most Americans and would have required radically redistributive legislation unpalatable to the president and the Congress. Johnson did mean a constantly expanding equality of opportunity through which poor Americans of all races would gradually achieve a decent standard of living. In the interval he also meant the federal government to assist those in need.

As he had said during his presidential campaign, Johnson believed in democratic government based on the "free enterprise system." He saw that system as a partnership among business, labor, and the state— a partnership more prosperous and more just than communism. Especially in a period of prosperity like the 1960s, democratic government, in Johnson's view, had to assist the poor. But like a large majority of his constituents, he rejected the notion of a continuing policy of supplementing the income of the poor, for he conceived of poverty as a transitory condition from which government could help the poor to escape. Like most middle-class Americans, Johnson subscribed to long-standing American attitudes toward the poor, as the historian James T. Patterson described them: "that many, if not most, of the destitute are undeserving; . . . that social insurance is preferable to welfare, which is wasteful and demoralizing; that wise public policy seeks to prevent poverty, not to provide income maintenance; and that work, not welfare, is the essense of the meaningful life."

Within that framework of ideas, the administration's attack on poverty moved on two fronts. One was officially under the direction of Sargent Shriver and his Office of Economic Opportunity; the other, less publicized but more effective, channeled various programs to provide cash and services directly to the poor. The OEO constantly stumbled over the confusion inherent in the legislation that created it. Troubles arose from the first with the regular executive departments, the Department of Agriculture for one, where established bureaucracies spent funds allocated to them in their usual ways, regardless of OEO preferences. So, too, in spite of OEO doubts, the Justice Department endorsed the propriety of one grant, by no means atypical, designated to save a miners' hospital in Kentucky from bankruptcy. "In actuality," as a member of Johnson's staff wrote the president, the grant would "be used to pay off the hospital's debt to the UMW [United Mine Workers] Welfare Fund, from which we receive absolutely no consideration." The ample fund could have waited; many other conditions could not. The OEO had difficulties, too, with John Gardner, secretary of health, education, and welfare, and with Willard Wirtz, secretary of labor, both of whom criticized the lack of coordination in its programs while they also persisted in preserving their independence from OEO officials. For their part, those officials were sometimes extravagant, as in the per capita expenses they allowed for employees in the Job Corps during that program's first year.

Though Shriver brought his élan to public and congressional relations, he was so busy with the programs he directed—VISTA, the Job Corps, CAP, the Peace Corps—that he lacked time for other duties. Some Johnson loyalists distrusted him simply because he was Robert Kennedy's brother-in-law. Their suspicions, as well as Johnson's public identification with the war on poverty, accounted in part for the continual dabbling of the White House staff in OEO affairs. The White House also intervened because of the self-serving but mounting criticisms of groups hostile to the OEO. The efforts of the agency to bypass the welfare bureaucracy predictably offended professional social workers. They perceived OEO officials as interfering amateurs running an essentially political and consequently ineffectual program. That was also the view of right-wing Democrats and Republicans and of the conservative press. They complained, ordinarily without cause, about sloppy accounting, administrative bungling, waste, and favoritism to blacks or "leftists." In a spirit and vocabulary reminiscent of attacks on the New Deal in the 1930s, Barry Goldwater derided the Job Corps for attempting to give young men whom it employed in conservation camps "sun tans and an appreciation for outdoor living." A like-minded journalist wrote: "The only solution to poverty is free enterprise and continued economic growth—those things which made America great."

Community Action Programs with their emphasis on maximum feasible participation (MFP) by the poor aroused the wrath of those antagonistic groups. Social workers, often maternalistic and moralistic in their outlook, believed they knew better than did the poor how to combat poverty. Local officials argued that radical demagogues would dominate the CAPs. Those officials had always wanted to distribute the loaves and fishes from Washington that were now flowing instead through OEO channels. For their part, the CAPs faced an enormous task for which maximum feasible participation was not necessarily an effective instrument. Indeed, their convictions to the contrary, SDS leaders working in the ghettos of Cleveland and Newark had found participatory democracy much less than efficient. As one critic later observed, some of the poor in any neighborhood were inarticulate and irresponsible; others were divided by race; still others objected to middle-class outsiders attempting to organize them. Those remarks could have been made also, of course, about the rich.

The difficulties inherent in MFP probably hurt the Community Action Programs less than did conventional politics. In 1965 OEO raised a storm by withholding funds from five major cities because their CAPs did not give the poor maximum feasible participation. Two West Coast mayors blamed the agency for "fostering class struggle." Another office holder commented: "You can't go to a street corner . . . and tell the poor to write you a poverty program. They won't know how." In June the Conference of Mayors urged OEO to work through city halls or established welfare agencies instead of CAPs. State governors agreed, as one of the president's staff reported after attending the governors' conference that year. He had not talked "to a single governor," he wrote, who approved of the way OEO was "being handled in Washington and at the state level. Our closest friends are very much upset."

They were upset because lawyers in the Community Action Programs undertook to educate the poor about the rights that federal legislation had given them. Once informed about those entitlements, the poor demanded them, often to the dismay of local politicians. Johnson was peeved. So was Congress, which amended the enabling legislation for OEO by eliminating the words "maximum feasible participation" and by confining the representation of the poor on CAP boards to one-third of the membership. Local elected officials and local community groups each were allotted another third. Congress also designated an increased proportion of antipoverty appropriations for popular purposes like Head Start, a preschool program for needy children, with proportionately less money allocated to supposedly threatening activities, like legal services for the poor. Further, the Model Cities Act of 1966, ignoring OEO, sent money directly to qualified city governments. Johnson called that process creative federalism. Those changes saved the Community Action Programs but in a reduced form. They also outraged the proponents of MFP but suited the president, who could not understand how Shriver had recruited so many "crooks, communists," and "kooks."

Though its reputation faded after 1965, OEO continued to operate, always on the cheap. From 1965 to 1970, after which it controlled no major program, the agency never received more than 1.5 percent of the total federal budget, or about one-third of 1 percent of the GNP. As the outstanding study of poverty in the United States later concluded, "If all the OEO money had gone directly to the poor as income . . . each person . . . would have received around $50 to $70 per year"— a pittance.

Yet some OEO programs worked, at least for a time. The training offered by the Job Corps resulted in small improvements in the employment of teenagers and young adults, particularly those from minority groups. The educational efforts of Head Start, according to a later study, "had a powerful, immediate impact on children," though the resulting gains in literacy often faded in the environment of incompetent and uncaring grammar schools. Community action, while fostering many useful neighborhood projects, also demonstrated that most of the poor were eager to find employment and to obtain more help to that end from both local and national government. Johnson's hyperbolic rhetoric had stimulated the expectations of the poor, whose local organizers took his words seriously. They believed, as did many of their constituents, that the poor had a right to jobs and to decent living conditions for themselves and their families.

So did Shriver, though he knew he was losing his influence. "The crisis of the city," he wrote in August 1966, "is the crisis of the poor. . . . Democracy based on full participation of the poor offers the only viable solution." Even in 1968 Shriver fought on. He presented to Johnson a plan, as he then wrote, "which can wipe out poverty . . . as we define it today within ten years from the time the resources . . . become avail-

Job Corps: Training for employment.

able. I realize that these resources are not now available, but . . . the War on Poverty is . . . making a beginning." But the president after 1966 steadily lost interest in OEO. The war in Vietnam absorbed his attention, and the poor seemed to him to be becoming carping and politically ungrateful for his efforts on their behalf. Nevertheless, the percentage of Americans who could be classified as poor continued to shrink, for OEO had never provided the principal means for alleviating poverty. Rather, the most telling improvements derived from the economic boom that followed the 1964 tax cut, just as the Council of Economic Advisers had predicted it would. By March 1966, with the economy further stimulated by federal expenditures for the war in Vietnam, unemployment had dropped to 3.7 percent, half the 1961 figure. Indeed, the CEA warned the president that some restraint was now required, for the economy was "moving . . . at breakneck speed." Its rising tide, then and for another year and more, lifted the working poor into new jobs, higher pay scales, and overtime with its increased remuneration. At least until mid-1967 the resulting losses to inflation struck most Americans, especially those who had found jobs, as relatively trivial compared with the gains in both jobs and income.

The growth of the economy had been crucial, but Great Society programs also helped the poor. An increase in Social Security coverage and benefits and in other transfer programs—programs whereby the federal government transferred income from some groups to others—accounted between 1965 and 1973* for an extraordinary decrease in the percentage of Americans living below the poverty line. The Social Security Administration placed an urban family of four below the poverty line if it had a three-thousand-dollar annual income in 1961 and forty-two hundred dollars in 1972. A more humane and realistic definition of deprivation would have almost doubled those figures and covered three times the number of families, especially families of the working poor. But as calculated, the Social Security standard did cover substantially all the poor without resources except for welfare. Those destitute Americans, 17 percent of the population in 1965, constituted only 13 percent in 1968 and 11 percent in 1973. When benefits rendered in kind—such as food stamps—as well as in cash were taken into account, by 1973 the destitute constituted only 6.5 percent, historically a dramatically low figure.

Americans designated as poor had also been aided by the policy to which Johnson gave a high priority in 1965; the long-pending Democratic bill to establish a system of medical care for men and women sixty-five years and older. With the recently elected Democratic majority behind it, that measure now also had the support of Wilbur Mills, who rapidly guided it in an expanded form through the House of Representatives. The Senate liberalized it further. As passed, the act covered most medical and hospital costs for the aged beyond a small annual deductible. It levied an additional payroll tax to raise the necessary funds for the program, which the Social Security Administration was to run. "No longer," the president said in signing the bill, "will older Americans be denied the healing miracle of modern medicine. No longer will illness crush and destroy . . . [their] savings."

Those words seemed justified in 1965. They applied to the working poor, who paid payroll taxes, as well as to the middle class. Indeed, they applied to all the poor, for the Medicare bill on its journey through Congress carried with it a major addition: Medicaid, a program for health care for those on welfare of all ages. It arose to assist the states in financing various aspects of existing Social Security grants. With little debate Congress committed the federal government to bear between

---

*Though Johnson left office in January 1969, transfer programs persisted through 1973. See Chapter 10.

50 and 80 percent of the costs of medical care to the indigent blind, disabled, and members of families with dependent children—the same groups covered by federal welfare before 1965—as well as to individuals with "insufficient financial needs." As with Medicare, so with Medicaid: In the ensuing years costs outran by far the calculations of the Congress, with increasing expenditures—within a decade some nine billion dollars—for medical care for the poor. The recipients had attendant gains in their real standard of living.

Other federal payments to the poor in goods and services also multiplied under the guardianship of the Great Society and in the wake of its momentum. The Kennedy administration had begun a modest program to provide food stamps to recipients of AFDC. By 1965 about six hundred thousand people received $36 million of those stamps; by 1975 more than seventeen million were receiving more than $4 billion of stamps. During those years public housing support rose from $236 million annually to $1.2 billion, largely because of legislation the Johnson administration sponsored. With Johnson's policies persisting, albeit at a diminished rate of growth, in 1974 total assistance to the average AFDC family in New York City came to about $6,000 a year, with 38 percent of that amount in cash.

In the same decade the number of American families on AFDC rose from 4.3 percent in 1965 to 6.1 percent in 1969 to 10.8 percent in 1974. That "explosive growth in the welfare rolls" did reduce poverty in the country. In 1965 cash payments alone carried a third of the poor across the poverty line; by 1972 those payments, together with in-kind benefits, raised 60 percent of the poor above that level. Expenditures to help the poor constituted 6.7 percent of the federal budget in 1965, 8.2 percent in 1969, and 11.2 percent in 1973. That amount was not trivial. Contrary to later conservative criticisms, "throwing money" at the problem did ameliorate poverty.

Nevertheless, the Great Society's war on poverty exposed persisting anomalies in American attitudes toward the indigent. Johnson's emphasis on economic opportunity reflected a national preference for interpreting poverty as an exceptional and transient condition rather than recognizing the enduring and endemic nature of the issue. The president believed that the poor deserved training for jobs and help in finding them, but he thought, as so many Americans did, that they should then work for a living. That work ethic overlooked the many poor who were too young or too old or too sick to work. Johnson and most of the Congress in 1967 supported a work-incentive program intended to substitute "workfare for welfare." They also tried to curtail the growth of welfare rolls by setting limits on available funds. Those limits fractured under the pressure of need. It was anomalous, too, from 1965 onward, that the administration backed local programs—such as MFP—that encouraged the poor to organize and even to agitate on their own behalf, while it also treated the poor paternalistically, as almost all caseworkers in AFDC did.

Most contemporary critics agreed that the antipoverty programs of the Great Society were often inefficient and always inadequate, but the Great Society did not create the "welfare mess." On the contrary, the nature and the scope of poverty constituted a major American social failure that the Great Society tried to correct. It was not AFDC, a program the Johnson administration enlarged, that caused the "tangle of pathology" described by Daniel Patrick Moynihan in his controversial 1965 report about the families of the poor, especially of the black poor. To be sure, a long experience of poverty had a devastating impact on family structure. But poverty was not the only cause of family instability. The traditional structure of the American family had been changing and continued to change among all social and ethnic groups, black and white, poor and rich.

Other critics of welfare, especially critics left of center, complained accurately that even poor families receiving maximum federal assistance were still deprived, still without the means to purchase the amenities normal in the lives of other Americans. Yet those families had an annual income in cash and kind almost 50 percent higher than a full-time worker could earn at the minimum wage. Measured by a standard of social decency, the minimum wage was too low, but the Johnson administration could not escape the prevailing American concern that welfare payments were providing disincentives to work. All in all, the Great Society transferred growing billions of dollars from the comfortable to the destitute. During Johnson's presidency the United States moved toward the company of other Western nations in the range and energy of its treatment of the poor.

3. AN EXTRAORDINARY RECORD

Eager to succeed where Kennedy had failed, Lyndon Johnson also had a major personal interest in providing education to the children of the poor. Public education had played a crucial part in his own life. The distinguished task force he appointed to explore the federal role in education reported that education lay at the heart of the Great Society. It was essential to assure literacy for all Americans, to develop their talents, and to create a sound community. The men to whom Johnson delegated responsibility for the education bill shared that view. Douglass Cater, a cerebral journalist who had become a member of the White House staff, was both a native southerner, intense in his loyalty to the president, and a graduate of Phillips Exeter Academy and Harvard College. Cater had urged Johnson to make education an issue in the 1964 campaign and had been preparing himself to manage the administration's education program on the Hill. Both he and Johnson admired the political savvy of Francis Keppel, the federal commissioner of education, a former dean of the Harvard School of Education, and a Kennedy appointee. Keppel had been exploring with Catholic leaders forms of federal assistance suitable to them. The resulting formula, neatly compatible with Johnson's major goals of 1965, related the amount of federal support for elementary and secondary schools to the incidence of poverty in the districts they served. It also allowed the use of federal funds to provide new educational services to private and parochial as well as public schools.

That approach removed the sticky religious issue on which Kennedy had tripped. Further, as Cater observed, by assuring blacks equal access to public schools in the South, the Civil Rights Act of 1964 had quieted congressional debate about segregation. After the Democratic sweep in the election, only the right-wing Republicans in Congress remained opposed to Johnson's proposals of January 1965 to meet "the special . . . needs of educationally deprived children." The bill for elementary and secondary schools carried an authorization of just over one billion dollars, far more than any previous legislation had contemplated, to be granted to local school districts to pay for new facilities or new staff in order to equalize educational opportunity for poor children. The measure moved rapidly to enactment. Johnson signed it, as he later wrote, "in the one-room schoolhouse near Stonewall, Texas, where my own education had begun," with his first teacher, "Miss Kate," Mrs. Kathryn Deadrich Loney, flown in from California "to sit by my side."

As it worked out, the Elementary and Secondary Education Act of 1965 improved the quality of education. "The legislation," Keppel later noted, "put the poor and the minorities on the educational agenda and kept them there." Yet it fell short of its sponsors' hopes largely because localities, which received and controlled the use of federal funds, did an inadequate job of raising the quality of teaching and motivation for learning. New equipment, new staff, and new programs for compensatory instruction in reading and mathematics ordinarily reached all

Johnson at Stonewall, Texas, where his education had begun.

children, not only or even primarily the children of the poor. Consequently, middle-class children, primarily children whose parents considered education important, often gained the most from federal assistance.

That was the case, too, for the whole range of the educational measures of the Great Society. They did help students from low-income families, for whom they subsidized college scholarships and work-study programs, but directly and indirectly they provided more assistance to colleges and universities and to middle-class students attending them. The Higher Education Act of 1965 made generous grants for libraries and for training librarians, for helping the development of financially shaky colleges, and especially for insuring loan programs available to all college students. Those provisons, along with subsidies for fellowships for graduate study, continually expanded under the National Defense Education Act, financed an explosion of enrollment during the late 1960s in colleges and graduate schools of arts and sciences. The beneficiaries were the thousands of now teenaged children of the baby boom of the 1940s and early 1950s, a cohort of young people whom American society needed to absorb and therefore to train. The contribution of the Higher Education Act to that process opened relatively few exits from poverty; but it did boost the aspirations and make possible the future professional careers of young Americans from blue-collar families, it gave important assistance to young men and women of the middle class, and it strengthened American institutions of higher learning. In all those ways the educational programs of the Great Society enhanced the nation's capacity for locating the talents and instilling the skills vital for the functioning of a modern industrial and bureaucratic society and for the state governing it.

Like the major episodes of domestic reform that preceded it—the Square Deal, the New Freedom, the New Deal—the Great Society reflected and advanced the hopes of American liberals. Those hopes were rooted in decency and compassion as well as in an eagerness to quell social unrest. All those elements underlay Johnson's attack on poverty. But his educational and medical programs helped the middle class as much as or more than they helped the poor. The number of middle-class Americans who benefited from Medicare far exceeded the poor who benefited from Medicaid. That fallout soon became apparent both to advocates of more direct aid of all kinds to the poor and to a majority of the middle class, who naturally wanted to retain the support, particularly the entitlements, that they had gained.

Other endeavors of the Great Society were undertaken to improve the quality of life of all Americans without regard to social class. The administration persuaded Congress to subsidize museums; to underwrite grants for theater and dance; to offer fellowships to artists, writers, musicians, and scholars under the National Endowment for the Arts and the National Endowment for the Humanities; and to support public radio and television broadcasting. American cultural activities had received no such boost from the federal government since the New Deal. The president also responded to the exigent needs of the environment, which had appropriately become a major public concern. The Great Society "is a place where the city of man serves not only the needs of the body . . . but the desire for beauty," Johnson had said. "That beauty is in danger," he added in a special message to Congress in February 1965. "The water we drink, the food we eat, the very air we breathe, are threatened with pollution. . . . We must act . . . for . . . once our natural splendor is destroyed, it can never be recaptured."

The Senate had already acted in 1963, led to do so by Edmund S. Muskie, the Maine Democrat outstanding in his dedication to protecting the environment. Muskie's bill for controlling water pollution had failed in the House of Representatives. Now only slightly altered, it had again cleared the Senate late in January 1965 by a thumping sixty-eight to eight margin. In the House the responsible committee rejected mandatory federal controls, which the president had recommended,

Edmund S. Muskie: Cham-
pion of pollution control.

but increased the authorizations in the bill for sewage treatment projects. At that juncture Johnson's influence helped Muskie convert the
members of the conference committee to accept a federal standard to
be determined by the agency the bill created, the Water Pollution Control Authority (WPCA). In signing the act, Johnson observed that additional measures would be needed in the years ahead. Muskie had already
begun to champion them, including the Clean Water Restoration Act
of 1966, which lifted federal support for municipal sewage treatment
facilities and added grants for "the management of pollution control
activities on a whole river, lake or other body of water." Through 1969
the administration, largely because of alternative priorities, especially
the war in Vietnam, asked for appropriations of less than half of the
funds Congress had authorized. But Johnson had at least supported
the start of the federal effort to clean up the nation's water, which
Eisenhower had opposed and Kennedy had slighted.

Building on preliminary legislation of 1963, Muskie had begun also
to study ways to reduce air pollution. As his subcommittee found, about
half of all air pollution was attributable to automotive exhaust. "The
automobile industry," the governor of California observed, was "in
interstate commerce and the Federal Government has jurisdiction." In

full agreement, Muskie in January 1965 introduced a bill directed particularly against automobile emissions, for which it defined federal standards. The bill also authorized grants to help states enforce those standards and to subsidize research on air pollution. But Johnson balked. In nurturing his consensus in 1964, he had cultivated Henry Ford II, the reigning monarch of the Ford Motor Company. The president in his message to Congress about preserving national beauty announced that before proceeding on the quality of air, he wanted to consult the leaders of the automobile industry. His skeptical audience knew that Detroit had never subordinated the pursuit of profits to any ecological consideration. Then Johnson simply stalled. But with the press critical of his unlikely waltz with Detroit, Johnson in April let Muskie go ahead. For their part, the leaders of the automobile industry preferred federal control to the varying and sometimes more rigid controls that the states were considering. At the industry's request, Muskie agreed to postponing the enforcement of federal standards for a year. His bill, another important beginning, then passed.

Meanwhile, Johnson had continued Kennedy's program of adding to the number and the size of national parks and recreation areas. Moved in part by the special enthusiasm of the first lady, he also took a first step toward controlling outdoor advertising. The measure he sponsored withheld a fraction of federal highway funds from states that did not exclude billboards from noncommercial areas. Never a strong partisan of the environmental movement, Johnson by and large just rode its waves. As one of his biographers wrote, "he loved to add environmental protection, along with beautification, to his array of Great Society achievements."

That was the case, too, in the president's relation to the burgeoning consumer movement with its persisting goals of protecting Americans against false advertising and shoddy goods and of protecting the health and safety of industrial workers. Responding to public anxiety, the administration initiated regulatory legislation, including, for several examples, the Fair Packaging and Labeling Act and the Automobile Safety Act, both passed in 1966, and the landmark Occupational Health and Safety Act of 1968. The last of these measures created as its agency of enforcement the Occupational Safety and Health Administration (OSHA). Like the new agencies established to enforce environmental legislation, OSHA was licensed to penetrate the operations of private industry. Affected corporations, predictably, soon trumpeted their protests.

Johnson rejoiced. His Great Society had assailed the nation's major domestic problems: poverty; health; education; environment. From 1964 through 1966 he had shepherded more significant legislation through Congress than had any other president during a comparable period of time. Yet much remained to be done. Johnson continually spoke of his achievements as beginnings, first steps. He was ever aware of the need for further action and more money to complete the promises of his exuberant rhetoric. Yet he also knew that the beginnings in themselves lent a luster to his White House years. In his happiest moods he glowed in the reflected glory.

4. Grandiosity

Even as it seemed triumphant in 1965, the Great Society was reaching its peak. Destructive riots had begun to rock American cities. The war in Vietnam was becoming the president's overriding concern. In the fall of 1966 Republican gains in Congress restored the power of the conservative coalition that had blocked reform throughout Kennedy's administration, indeed since 1939. By the next year critics to the right and critics to the left of Johnson were protesting either the intrusiveness or the incompleteness of reform. Similar criticisms had accompanied every previous episode in the development of the liberal state. As before, so again, those criticisms were not without substance.

Microeconomic regulation of all kinds was now in place as part of the Great Society. Whether designed to protect the environment or to promote industrial safety, regulation always depended upon the probity, expertness, and judiciousness of public regulators, and invariably some of them were wanting. That was also true of some of the chiefs and braves in private corporate bureaucracies. Indeed, their fallibility had created the need for public supervision. Then and later, however, mixed capitalism—private enterprise subject to public regulation— proved a mixed blessing, especially when knaves or fools were granted supervisory authority. Consequently, some Americans advocated restoring a theoretically free market, and others called for stricter regulation, even socialism. Selecting a middle course, as he did, Johnson exposed both flanks. He and his associates followed the pragmatic course of modern American liberalism, which was no less prudent or more relevant for being conventional and nonsystemic.

Keynesian macroeconomic policy in theory supplied the umbrella under which American mixed capitalism was supposed to work. But the Johnson administration always seemed extravagant to fiscal conservatives—those who believed that the federal budget should be balanced by reductions in domestic spending. Critics on the left called for more spending to help the poor and for redistributive taxation to finance it. Especially after 1966, there was something to be said for both those views.

The Council of Economic Advisers, the wise men of Keynesian policy, began in 1967 to warn the president that total spending, domestic and military, was creating deficits that would bring on serious inflation unless taxes were raised. That problem did not inhere in Keynesian theory or practice. Rather, military spending on the Vietnam War had created it. Domestic spending on antipoverty measures was growing but remained insufficient. Redistributive taxation at a moderate rate could have reduced the shortfall. Both personal and political factors prevented that course. By 1967 Johnson lacked the votes in Congress for tax reform. He had never had any enthusiasm for it anyway. Indeed, he lacked the votes even for a tax increase. And he had no intention of curtailing the war in Vietnam to contain military expenditures.

Without Lyndon Johnson, social reform in the 1960s might not have traveled as far as it did. But government under Johnson suffered from his personality. Obsessed about his place in history, he was in a rush, almost a frenzy, to build his record before the mandate of his victory in 1964 had run out. He believed he had no choice, and he was probably correct. But by hurrying legislation along, he risked imprecision and ambiguity in the resulting statutes. Vulnerable to criticism, protective of his reputation, he never understood that the media would exercise their independent judgment of him, so he scolded news reporters he considered unfair, tried to rig the news, and soon alienated many of the journalists he was trying to woo. The press was often unfair to Johnson, as the columnist Stewart Alsop admitted. But Johnson, Alsop continued, was a "proud, cruel . . . insecure . . . and bitterly driven man." Partly to compensate for his insecurity, partly out of lifelong habit, Johnson indulged in excesses of speech that promised more than anyone could deliver and boasted more than anyone could believe. No president could abolish poverty, but Johnson claimed he could and later that he almost had.

Johnson appointed capable subordinates. The men he brought to the White House were also usually his kind of men. He felt comfortable with many of them from the South, especially from Texas. Others were experienced analysts of politics or veterans of liberal political organizations. As a group they were the equal of Kennedy's men, and two of his young aides, Joseph Califano and Harry McPherson, were not afraid to talk back to the president. But ordinarily Johnson reined his men in.

He did also with the women he brought to Washington—more women than any of his predecessors had appointed. At times he had to be tough, as in the case of Secretary Gardner, who submitted spending requests he had not studied. "Next year," Johnson said, "budget him a [Seeing Eye] dog." More often the president reacted with jealousy to initiatives other than his own. He was, one of his advisers wrote, "an elemental activist." "Don't ever let me catch you playing President," he warned his staff members. Suspicious even of the loyal Bill Moyers, Johnson brought on their eventual estrangement.

Moyers was no exception. Johnson felt threatened by publicity he did not inspire himself. He jumbled the jurisdictions of his subordinates so that he could cut off the authority of those who exceeded his skittish tolerance. Obsessed with secrecy, he limited the access of his staff to newspaper and television reporters. So resolved was he to make all the news himself that a published leak of a pending appointment could provoke him to cancel that appointment, as in the case of Lloyd Cutler, an able Washington lawyer to whom he had planned to give a major post. He bruised his assistants by lavishing praise and gifts on them one day and berating them or ostracizing them the next.

So, too, with his cabinet, as Johnson admitted: "I was determined to turn those lordly men into good soldiers . . . to make them more dependent on me than I was on them." Through his control over the budget and over liaison with Congress he increased the dominance of the White House over the executive departments. He ordered the cabinet officers to send reports of their task forces only to him. He took perverse pleasure in dangling a major appointment before an eager aspirant so long that the candidate, like Hubert Humphrey, had to beg for the job. As he told one cabinet wife, with obvious pride, all her counterparts and their husbands were afraid of him.

Johnson's grandiosity complicated government. He tried to make the White House the sole arbiter of departmental rivalries for funds and authority. Bureaucratic confusion, always there, persisted and even grew. His own aides dared not decide an issue without his approval, but Johnson, despite his energy, could not do everything. As a consequence, some of his programs went askew. Standards for clean air, clear water, and urban development had to be promulgated; but the proliferation of regulatory agencies generated conflicting orders, and the hodgepodge of authority magnified those conflicts. "The government," in the recollection of one senior Johnson aide, "simply got into too many nooks and crannies of American life." The disarray bothered the specialists brought to Washington almost as much as the corporate managers subject to their regulation. Both groups became dubious about the capacity of the federal government to use its power constructively. Concurrently, as developments in the cities revealed, many black Americans and poor Americans came to doubt the sincerity of Johnson's purpose.

Government of any kind had always been vulnerable to the idiosyncrasies of rulers and managers. Further, much of the blame that critics placed on the liberal state properly belonged to the national security state, which had grown up alongside it. Fostered after 1963 by Johnson, the national security state with its military priorities had been predatory for two decades before he became president. So, too, some of the most impressive and most controversial developments of government during the 1960s originated not with the president or Congress but with Supreme Court decisions about individual rights and freedom.

All in all, the credits the Great Society earned overbalanced its debts, at least through 1966, when the costs of American foreign policy had begun to reduce domestic striving. Until then Johnson's record and his rhetoric had lifted American faith in affirmative government. Twenty years later the achievements of the social activism of the 1960s remained memorable. As the *New York Times* observed in 1985, in 1965 90 percent of black adults in the Deep South were not registered to vote, and nationwide, at all levels of government, there were only a few hundred black officials; half of all Americans over sixty-five years old had no medical insurance, and a third of them lived in poverty; only a third of all children from three to five years old attended nursery school or kindergarten. The Great Society initiated policies that by 1985 had had profound consequences: Blacks now voted at about the same rate as whites, and nearly six thousand blacks held public offices; almost every elderly citizen had medical insurance, and the aged were no poorer than Americans as a whole; a large majority of small children attended preschool programs.

The Great Society had its failings. So did Lyndon Johnson, especially in his foreign and military policies. But the Great Society also worked social and political wonders. "Where would this country be if it had not been for the Great Society," one of Johnson's senior advisers asked himself in 1985. "How many kids would not have been able to go to college? How many more people would have died . . . for lack of proper health care? . . . What would our air be like? Our water? . . . We as a country would be much worse off." That answer provided an appropriate eulogy for Lyndon Johnson at his very best.

7

The Politics of the Warren Court

Neither Lyndon Johnson nor his associates ever developed a political theory of the Great Society. Johnson had no interest in the theoretical, no more than John F. Kennedy, though Kennedy would probably have agreed with those of his advisers who described him as a liberal pragmatist. Indeed, no recent American president had thought much about the theoretical foundations or implications of his policies. To be sure, all presidents had operated within the general boundaries of what they accepted as democratic principles. Yet none could have put forth a persuasive and systematic exposition of his application of those principles.

Nevertheless, discernible compatibility existed between the intentions of the Great Society and the political theory inherent in the decisions of the Supreme Court during the fifteen years beginning in 1954. Those were the years in which Earl Warren presided as chief justice of the United States—the years of the Warren Court, in the nomenclature of judicial history. President Eisenhower had appointed Warren chief justice to pay off an obligation incurred in 1952. At the Republican National Convention that year Warren had moved the California delegation into Ike's column at a propitious time. A favorite son candidate, Warren was then governor of California and had been the GOP nominee for vice president in 1948. Like most other Republicans, Eisenhower considered him a moderate. Warren was a fiscal moderate, but he possessed other qualities that Eisenhower failed to take into account: a determined independence of mind and a commitment, as one of his biographers put it, to "ethical imperatives."

"Warren," that biographer wrote, "held a set of values that he believed represented moral truths about decent, civilized life. It was inconceivable to Warren that these values should not be embodied in constitutional principles. . . . Indeed Warren felt bound, as a judge, to consider ethical imperatives in his adjudication." Warren's pursuit of moral ends often guided his perceptions about legal principles. Contrary to Ike's expectations, Warren proved to be rather more a liberal politician with a program than a master of constitutional law. That characteristic made him something of a maverick in the opinion of adverse academic experts.

Though the membership of the Warren Court changed gradually as one associate justice or another left the bench, the years in which Warren presided were characterized by a continuity of decisions. Both admirers and critics of the Warren Court remarked on that continuity, as well as exceptions to it, in their analyses of the jurisprudence in the Court's opinions. While Warren himself wrote only a few of the Court's majority opinions, his leadership encouraged his brethren to reach conclusions notable for their judicial activism.

1. PREFERRED FREEDOMS

The thinking of the Warren Court reflected the influence of the doctrine of preferred freedoms. That doctrine was first formulated in 1938 by Harlan F. Stone, whom Franklin Roosevelt had appointed chief justice. In a footnote to his decision in an otherwise unexceptional case, *United States v. Carolene Products Co.* (1938), Stone suggested that the judiciary had a special responsibility in reviewing legislation that might impair civil rights or civil liberties. Stone had long subscribed to the principle of judicial restraint in instances of economic regulation by the states or federal government. In other words, he was disposed in such cases to permit the will of legislatures to prevail. That had been the strong preference, too, of Associate Justice Oliver Wendell Holmes, Jr., and Louis D. Brandeis, giants of American jurisprudence in Stone's youth. He remained within their spirit when he wrote the *Carolene* footnote. "The presumption of constitutionality," he observed, might have "narrower scope for operation . . . when legislation appears on its face to be within a specific prohibition of the Constitution, such as those of the first ten amendments, which are deemed equally specific when held to be embraced within the Fourteenth."

In its last clause that sentence raised a constitutional issue of major significance then and later. One of Stone's colleagues, Associate Jus-

HUGO L. BLACK

WILLIAM O. DOUGLAS

Earl Warren

Associate Justice

Associate Justice

TOM C. CLARK

JOHN M. HARLAN

CHIEF JUSTICE *of the* UNITED STATES SUPREME COURT

Associate Justice

Associate Justice

WILLIAM J. BRENNAN

POTTER STEWART

BYRON R. WHITE

ARTHUR J. GOLDBERG

Associate Justice

Associate Justice

Associate Justice

Associate Justice

© 1963

The Warren Court.

tice Hugo Black, in 1938 had articulated the principle of incorporation—the principle, in other words, that the Fourteenth Amendment
to the Constitution applies to the states the restrictions on the authority
of the federal government which are set forth in the Bill of Rights.
Black, also a Roosevelt appointee, had wisely made the principle of
incorporation a major objective of his judicial argumentation. After
1954 Black seemed to have prevailed; the principle of incorporation

was clearly established in the jurisprudence of the Supreme Court.

Stone in his footnote called for "more exacting judicial scrutiny" in particular of those substantive rights he wanted the courts to protect alike from federal and from state incursions. Close judicial oversight was also necessary, in his view, of statutes "directed at particular religions . . . or national . . . or racial minorities." The Court had to ascertain whether prejudice against those minorities curtailed the operation of "those political processes which can ordinarily be expected to bring about repeal of undesirable legislation." Keeping democratic processes open under all circumstances required judicial vigilance, he believed, as in time did the Warren Court.

Stone's observations did not persuade his brethren quickly to modify their continuing practice of judicial restraint, even in the sensitive circumstances he identified. The Supreme Court from 1938 to 1954 moved only partially and tentatively toward the determinations Stone's language implied. But after the appointment of Earl Warren the doctrine of preferred freedoms became appropriately a major pillar of the Court's evolving jurisprudence.

It probably would have done so in any event, but Warren hastened the development. He did so because so many of the issues of his time raised major moral questions that he wanted answered according to his own decent criteria. "Is it *right?*" he was prone to ask lawyers arguing a case before the court. "Is it good?" He was prepared, as one of his severest critics wrote, to "cut through legal technicalities," to pierce "through procedure to substance." Stone's footnote lent itself to that approach. Warren's moralism, and his leadership of the court in that direction, did produce decisions of outstanding democratic value. But those decisions often stirred political controversy, and they skirted legal technicalities, which, so his conservative critic also wrote, were "the stuff of law." Consequently, the decisions of the Warren Court, however noble, were sometimes vulnerable—susceptible to dissents that portended eventual judicial correction. But in the time in which they were handed down, those decisions carried weighty social and political significance.

2. FROM BROWN TO GREEN

Earl Warren assumed his seat on the Court in time to preside over the rehearing and decision in *Brown v. Board of Education* (1954) and four related cases. He also wrote the momentous decision of the unanimous Court, which held that separate schools for black children were inherently unequal and, as such, violations of the equal protection clause of the Fourteenth Amendment. That ruling overturned the Court's earlier decision in *Plessy v. Ferguson* (1896), which had permitted segregated facilities so long as those for blacks were presumably equal to those for whites, an institutional fiction throughout the South. Warren's opinion in *Brown* incorporated much of the argument of the NAACP lawyers who had pleaded the case. With them, he cited some unnecessary sociological evidence. But also with them, he rested his opinion on the commanding, commonsensical meaning of "equal protection of the laws" and its significance for public education.

"Education," the chief justice wrote, "is perhaps the most important function of state and local governments. . . . It is required in the performance of our most basic public responsibilities. . . . It is a right which must be made available to all on equal terms." He asked then if "the segregation of children in public schools solely on the basis of race . . . deprives the children of equal educational opportunities," and he answered: "We believe it does." Segregation, he continued, connoted inferiority, which in turn "had retarded educational and mental development of Negro children." Accordingly, in the field of public education, "the doctrine of 'separate but equal' has no place."

Though the Court had been moving toward that conclusion for a decade, the decision in *Brown* stunned the South. As white southerners realized at once, it threatened the whole legal apparatus of apartheid that had kept the races socially segregated for more than half a century. Almost immediately, condemnations of Earl Warren became standard fare in southern political oratory, along with angry reassertions in new dress of the antebellum doctrine of nullification and states' rights. As one corollary to that assertion, southern politicians urged their willing constituents to defy the court. The Southern Manifesto of 1956, signed by 101 members of Congress, expressed the outrage of the region. It declared the *Brown* decision "a clear abuse of judicial power," a substitution of "personal judicial and social ideas for the established law of the land." But that contention, with its accompanying demands for the impeachment of Earl Warren, expressed a futile commitment to a doomed way of life.

Those reactions neglected aspects of the *Brown* decision that made it less coercive than at first it seemed. The Court had condemned segregation in education, but it had not defined an acceptable standard for desegregated schooling, nor had it established a timetable for that eventuality. On the contrary, the Court invited the litigants in *Brown* to reappear to speak to the question of implementing the decision. After hearing their arguments, the Court in *Brown* II (1955), again unanimously and again speaking through the chief justice, set no date for the desegregation of public schools. It ruled instead that the admission of black children on a nondiscriminatory basis should begin "with all deliberate speed." Desegregation, *Brown* II explained, had to await local solutions of "problems related to administration," including the condition of school buildings, the transportation of pupils, and the revision of boundaries for school districts.

Obviously, "all deliberate speed" gave the South time to adjust to *Brown* I. The justices had intended to do just that in order to mitigate racial tensions in the region. They served the same end by assigning to federal district judges the supervision of desegregation. As informed southerners realized, almost all those local federal judges were southerners themselves and sympathetic to educational conditions as they existed. Warren's opinion in *Brown* II said that "the vitality of . . . constitutional principles cannot be allowed to yield simply because of disagreement with them." Yet the decision permitted massive resistance to develop. As one southern newspaper observed, the decision was "pretty much what the Southern attorneys in general had asked for." The measure of their victory appeared in the slow pace of change. As late as 1964, a decade after *Brown* I, only 2.3 percent of southern black children attended desegregated schools.

In a sense, the Court waited for ten years for the other branches of the federal government to catch up to its forward egalitarian position. The election of John F. Kennedy abetted that movement. Though Kennedy appointed many segregationist judges to federal courts in the South, the Civil Rights Division of his Justice Department gave important assistance to activists testing southern resistance to desegregation. The gradual conversion of the Kennedys and of Lyndon Johnson to strong support for civil rights brought the executive departments into step with the Court. And Kennedy and Johnson spurred Congress to join the march with the civil rights legislation of 1964 and 1965.

Meanwhile, the Supreme Court had continued to point the way. By overriding the separate but equal doctrine in *Brown* I, it had begun dismantling the legal basis for segregation. From the late 1950s forward the Court advanced in counterpoint with the civil rights movement. Civil rights demonstrators invited arrest by violating local statutes or ordinances prohibiting blacks from using segregated public facilities. With those arrests, NAACP lawyers appealed the question of the constitutionality of those laws from state jurisdictions to the federal courts. Continuing that process, civil rights lawyers carried adverse rulings from federal district courts to United States courts of appeal and, when necessary, on to the Supreme Court. Before 1960 the Supreme Court struck down laws segregating municipal parks, swimming pools, golf courses, transportation lines and terminals, and other such facilities.

Southern diehards tried to use local ordinances and state laws against disturbances of the peace as barriers to civil rights protests. In response, the Supreme Court expanded its reading of the Fourteenth Amendment to protect the right to demonstrate peacefully. In *Garner v. Louisiana* (1961), another unanimous decision, Warren held that blacks sitting quietly at a luncheon counter could not be charged with "violent, boisterous, or disruptive acts" or with behaving in a manner "as to unreasonably disturb or alarm the public." There was no evidence to support those convictions, and that violated the due process clause of the Fourteenth Amendment.

In *Edwards v. South Carolina* (1963), the Court ruled with only one dissent in a case involving the arrest of student demonstrators who, disregarding a police order to disperse, remained on the grounds of the statehouse where they sang patriotic and religious songs and listened to a sermon. The South Carolina statute under review defined as a criminal offense speech that "stirred people to anger, invited public dispute, or brought about a condition of unrest." Associate Justice Potter Stewart, an Eisenhower appointee and often one of the more conservative members of the Court, wrote the opinion. "In arresting, convicting, and punishing" the demonstrators, Stewart held, "South Carolina infringed the . . . constitutionally protected rights of free speech, free assembly, and freedom to petition for redress of . . . grievances." The Fourteenth Amendment, he continued later in his opinion, "does not permit a State to make criminal the peaceful expression of unpopular views." That strong conclusion did not in itself compel integration, but it did call into question southern recourse to disturbance of the peace laws as a device to prevent civil rights protests.

Southern businesses had persisted in apartheid behind the protection of local ordinances requiring segregation of such private facilities as restaurants, hotels, and department stores. The demonstration against those practices in Birmingham in 1963, of course, soon involved the Kennedy administration. In *Shuttlesworth v. Birmingham* (1963), one of five similar cases, the Supreme Court held that laws requiring segregation could not be enforced. Neither could local statutes referring to trespassing, disorderly conduct, or disturbances of the peace when they were used to prevent integration of facilities serving the general public. Such state action violated the equal protection clause of the Fourteenth Amendment.

The Court carried the application of that clause further the next year. In *McLaughlin v. Florida* (1964), it declared invalid a statute on "Adultery and Fornication" that forbade cohabitation between blacks and whites. That decision cut to the core of southern racism. In his concurrence Justice Stewart again spoke eloquently to the central issue: "I cannot conceive of a valid legislative purpose under our Constitution for a state law which makes the color of a person's skin the test of whether his conduct is a criminal offense." That was very much the spirit of the Civil Rights Act of 1964. A week after the *McLaughlin* opinion, the Supreme Court unanimously validated that act as an appropriate exercise of federal authority over interstate commerce.

The Court continued on its egalitarian track in *United States v. Mississippi* (1965). Following the logic of the able solicitor general of the United States Archibald Cox, Justice Black for the Court found unconstitutional the "long-standing, carefully prepared, and faithfully observed plan to bar Negroes from voting." As Black put it, "The Fifteenth Amendment protects the right to vote regardless of race against any denial or abridgement." Later that year the Voting Rights Act of 1965 assured federal enforcement of that straightforward interpretation of the language of the Constitution.

By that time the Court had evinced a revived concern for the desegregation of southern schools. While the civil rights bill of 1964 was still being debated, the Court ruled in a case of particular interest to the Kennedy and Johnson administrations. It related to Prince Edward County, a rural Virginia county that in 1959 had been ordered to desegregate its schools immediately. Instead, in one of the maneuvers by which southern countries evaded *Brown* II, Prince Edward closed its public school system. White children thereafter attended private schools, which were supported by contributions from individuals and accredited by the county. The county also provided a tax credit for the contributions. Black children by and large received no education at all. Prince Edward was just the kind of affront that Warren had said in *Brown* II the Court could not allow. But until 1963 the Supreme Court with few exceptions had ducked cases on the implementation of *Brown* II until the temper of the executive branch and of the public made it more propitious to get tough.

The issue came to a head in *Griffin v. Prince Edward County* (1964), in which Justice Black ruled for the majority that black children in the county had been denied due process of law. Virginia, he held, could not permit public schools to close in one county while they remained open elsewhere in the state, nor could private schools be maintained by public funds when public schools were closed. The opinion empowered the federal district court to enjoin tuition grants and tax credits to those supporting private schools. It also authorized the district court to order Prince Edward officials to reopen and fund racially desegregated public schools.

Those were broad rulings. Obviously "all deliberate speed" did not mean indefinite delay. That message acquired immediate force because of the role assigned the district court. Two associate justices considered that role excessive, as did many members of the bar in the South. The decision gave to the district court the kind of authority normally vested in a local school board, an institution elected by local people or appointed by their local representatives. Southern resistance to desegregation of public schools had left the Supreme Court little choice. It had to discipline Prince Edward County or surrender its own egalitarian principle and constitutional role. In that dilemma the Warren Court, always an activist court, made the lower federal courts powerfully intrusive. Through the district courts it extended federal authority into local affairs, as *Brown* II had portended. To those affected, that authority, once exercised, seemed alien. Since a district court was not answerable to local preferences, its decisions seemed arbitrary to the communities affected. The decision in *Griffin*, long deferred and arguably necessary, was pungent in the vectors it drew.

The Civil Rights Act of 1964 gave added impact to that decision. Besides forbidding discrimination in public accommodations, that act authorized the Justice Department to bring suit "for the orderly achievement of desegregation in public education." Since NAACP lawyers had already begun to challenge segregation in public schools in southern cities, government lawyers focused on rural areas, where resistance to desegregation was strongest. As one observer commented, those initiatives of the Justice Department "tended to deepen and solidify the Executive's commitment to equality." In keeping with the Civil Rights Act, the Department of Health, Education, and Welfare (HEW) issued guidelines for desegregation. Relatively mild at first, those standards became exacting by 1966. Southern school districts that failed to meet them faced the prospect of a cutoff of federal educational aid, which in 1965 had reached a considerable amount. Further, the courts began to incorporate HEW standards in desegregation decrees. The United States Court of Appeals for the Fifth Circuit—

Alabama, Florida, Georgia, Louisiana, Mississippi, and Texas—explicitly recommended that "courts in this circuit should give great weight to . . . HEW guidelines." Enjoined to do so by those courts, resistant southern school officials faced contempt of court charges that could result in large fines or imprisonment. The resulting process brought the number of black children in the South who were attending desegregated schools from 2.3 percent in 1964 to 12.5 percent in 1966.

The figure still remained appallingly low, especially at a time when black self-consciousness and militancy were rising all over the nation. In the absence of a federal statute mandating the integration of public schools, the continuing southern evasion of the Supreme Court's intentions still depended largely on the permissiveness of the judiciary. But the judges on the Court of Appeals for the Fifth Circuit, in particular Judges Elbert Tuttle and John Minor Wisdom, rendered decisions in 1965 and 1966 that sped desegregation throughout the South. School authorities, they believed, had an "affirmative constitutional duty to furnish equal educational opportunities to all public school children." As Judge Wisdom put it in one of his decisions, "The only adequate redress for a previously overt system-wide policy of segregation . . . is a system-wide policy of integration." Wisdom and his fellow judges on the Fifth Circuit measured integration by results and ordered it on a comprehensive basis. Their decrees affected the assignment to schools of both students and teachers. Those decrees also ordered bus transportation necessary for their goals. With that sweep, judicial intervention in local education assured the ultimate elimination of segregation in the South.

The Supreme Court followed the Fifth Circuit. A case involving New Kent, a rural Virginia county, tested "freedom of choice," a common means by which southern school districts evaded *Brown* II. In theory the system did not discriminate against blacks, for in theory they could choose to attend the school they preferred. But in practice whites never chose black schools, and most blacks were too intimidated to choose white schools. In New Kent, as elsewhere in the South, segregation persisted in counties where the system obtained, with 85 percent of black children remaining in black schools. In *Green v. School Board* of New Kent County (1968), the Supreme Court at last rejected not just the theory but the results of freedom of choice. "The burden," the Court ruled, "is on a school board to provide a plan that promises realistically to work *now*. . . . A dual system is intolerable." The district court was to "assess the effectiveness" of a plan and to retain jurisdiction "until it is clear that . . . segregation has been completely removed."

That requirement spelled the imminent end to southern evasive tactics. Never had it been clearer than *Green* made it that law was policy. The decision left the district courts with little room for maneuver. Now they would have to demand results or expect to be overruled by a United States court of appeals or eventually by the Supreme Court itself. In 1954 *Brown* I had warned the South that segregation faced a serious challenge from the federal judiciary. By 1964, with the *Griffin* case and the Civil Rights Act, the whole federal government had mobilized to end apartheid in the region. In 1968, with *Green*, the Court closed the last loophole. *Green* portended still more: the recourse to forced busing of children to achieve racial balance within a school system. Further, by examining results—the actual racial statistics for schools within a system—*Green* opened the way for the judiciary to attack de facto school segregation in the North and to do so with the same vigor and intensiveness that had offended so many voters in the South. *Green* made palpable the intent implicit in *Griffin*.

Each stage in these developments echoed in national politics. The Goldwater campaign in 1964 rejected the reasoning of the Warren Court in *Brown* I and its successor cases. Goldwater also condemned the Democrats for their complicity in the attack on segregation in the South. As he expected to, he ran best in that section. In 1968 the Republicans again made an issue of the Court. By that time, indeed even by 1964, the Warren Court had made enemies North and South by its interpretations of the Constitution on issues unrelated to segregation. Not surprisingly, hostile responses to those interpretations occurred most

viscerally among those Americans who were most inimical to *Brown* I and II, *Griffin*, and *Green.*

3. RESPECTING AN ESTABLISHMENT OF RELIGION

The First Amendment to the Constitution forbids Congress to make laws prohibiting the "free exercise" of belief or "respecting an establishment of religion." Those preferred freedoms, in Chief Justice Stone's formula, made it necessary for the Supreme Court to scrutinize with special care the rights of religious as well as racial minorities. Before Earl Warren became chief, the Court struck down state laws that restricted the unusual and often annoying practices of Jehovah's Witnesses. Those decisions protected the sect's freedom of belief. The question of the establishment of a religion was less clear, for the Court had allowed the use of public money to pay the fares of parochial school pupils.

The question of establishment reached the Warren Court in *Engel v. Vitale* (1962). Acting under state law, the board of education of New Hyde Park, New York, had directed the recitation of a nondenominational prayer composed by the State Board of Regents. The prayer was to be said daily by each class in the presence of a teacher. Pupils who so desired were to be excused from the exercise. Nevertheless, the parents of ten pupils objected, contending that the official prayer violated the religious beliefs or practices of them and their children. New York, they maintained, was establishing a religion. In arguments before the Supreme Court, attorneys for several Jewish groups supported the parents, while attorneys for twenty-two states supported New York. Speaking for the Court, Justice Hugo Black ruled that "the constitutional prohibition against laws respecting an establishment of religion must at least mean that . . . it is no part of the business of government to compose official prayers for any group of Americans to recite as a part of a religious program carried on by government." Black's opinion reviewed part of the history of the establishment issue in England and in the American colonies, as well as in the drafting of the First Amendment. States could not require the recitation of official prayers, he concluded, "even if the prayer is denominationally neutral and pupils . . . may remain silent or be excused."

Only Associate Justice Potter Stewart dissented. "I cannot see," he wrote, "How an 'official religion' is established by letting those who want to say a prayer say it." He questioned the relevance of the history Black had reviewed. The history of American religious traditions, Stewart proposed, militated to a contrary conclusion. Both the Supreme Court and the houses of Congress opened their sessions with prayers. The president on assuming his office invoked the protection of God, whose name was also used in the Pledge of Allegiance and on American coins. Only ten years earlier an opinion of the Supreme Court had said: "We are a religious people whose institutions presuppose a Supreme Being." Consequently, Stewart could not agree that New York had established a religion. As he put it, the state had recognized and followed "the deeply entrenched and highly cherished spiritual traditions of our Nation."

Whatever the strength of Stewart's reasoning, conservative religious leaders, particularly in the South, attacked Black's opinion on other grounds. The Supreme Court, they asserted, was promoting atheism, agnosticism, and secularism. The House of Representatives held hearings on a proposed amendment to the Constitution to permit prayer in public schools. A relay of clergymen testified in its support, as did Governor George Wallace of Alabama. Predictably, southern bigots like Wallace associated the Warren Court, a liberal court that was furthering desegregation, with atheistic communism. "They put the Negroes in the schools," said Representative George W. Andrews of Alabama. "Now they have driven God out." It came as no surprise to men like Wallace and Andrews that President Kennedy called on Americans to support the Court's decisions, "even though we may not agree with them." In the *Engel* case, the president added, Americans had "a very easy remedy. And that is, to pray themselves."

The storm over *Engel* broke out briefly again after the Supreme Court decided *School District of Abington Township v. Schempp* (1963) and a companion case. Again only Stewart dissented from the opinion, which built upon the precedent of *Engel*. No state, the Court ruled, could require the recitation of passages from the Bible or of the Lord's Prayer even if individual students could be excused. Most lawyers accepted the Court's position, as did most authorities on the Constitution and most religious leaders. But that was not the political issue. By innuendo at least, Goldwater in 1964 wooed the votes of fundamentalist Protestants, advocates of both prayer and Bible readings in public schools. Along with various evangelical sects, fundamentalists continued thereafter to urge their cause, to condemn the Supreme Court for irreligion, and to organize for political influence. Representing the view of only a minority of Americans, they nevertheless held their opinions devoutly. In ruffling fundamentalist feelings, the Court, though inadvertently, had given its political enemies inexhaustible ammunition.

So, too, though not immediately, did the Court's decision about birth control. That decision also provoked broad disagreement among the justices themselves about constitutional theory. A Connecticut statute forbade the dissemination of information about birth control and the prescription of contraceptive devices. Enacted in the nineteenth century to mollify Roman Catholic opinion in the state, the law, though constantly violated, was rarely enforced. Advocates of family planning and of free speech were nevertheless eager to challenge it and similar statutes in other states. Opportunity for a challenge came following the arrest and conviction of the executive director of the Planned Parenthood League of Connecticut and the league's medical director, who had prescribed a contraceptive pessary for a married woman.

Associate Justice William O. Douglas, noted for his latitudinarian reading of the Constitution, wrote the majority opinion in *Griswold v. Connecticut* (1965), which found the controversial law unconstitutional. Citing earlier cases, Douglas argued that a state could not "consistently with the spirit of the First Amendment, constrict the spectrum of available knowledge." The right of freedom of speech included "freedom of inquiry, freedom of thought, and freedom to teach." That conclusion would have been enough.

But Douglas went on. "In other words," he held, the First Amendment has "a penumbra where privacy is protected from government intrusion." Citing further cases, he suggested "that specific guarantees in the Bill of Rights have penumbras formed by emanations from those guarantees that help give them life and substance." Various of those guarantees created "zones of privacy." Here he referred to the First, Fourth, Fifth, and Ninth amendments before concluding that the "right of privacy" was a "legitimate one" that the Connecticut birth control statute violated. A man much divorced, Douglas ended with unintentional irony: "We deal with a right of privacy older than the Bill of Rights. . . . Marriage is a coming together for better or for worse . . . and intimate to the degree of being sacred. It is an association that promotes a way of life . . . a harmony of living."

By 1965 the time was ripe for recognition of a right of privacy, as many law professors were saying. The late Justice Louis D. Brandeis had long since argued that the Fourth Amendment protected privacy. Certainly, too, marriage was a private institution. Further, Douglas followed precedent in endowing the Bill of Rights with a penumbra. But the phrase "penumbras formed by emanations" confounded exegesis. It suggested at the least some considerable multiplication of rights guaranteed by the Constitution, a prospect about which many proponents of judicial restraint were uneasy. Associate Justice Arthur J. Goldberg, an appointee of President Kennedy, went even further than Douglas. In a concurring opinion in which Chief Justice Earl Warren and Associate Justice William Brennan joined, Goldberg called explicitly "for the creation of a whole body of extra-constitutional rights." Those rights, he contended, would conform with the spirit of the Ninth Amendment and the due process clause of the Fourteenth. With those rights affirmed, Goldberg continued, the Court would be able to strike down all legislation violating "fundamental principles of liberty and justice" rooted in the "tradition and conscience of our people." That was the kind of mandate that exactly suited the moralism of Earl Warren.

Douglas and Goldberg went beyond the limits of interpretation acceptable to four of their colleagues. Justices John M. Harlan and Byron R. White concurred in the conclusion that the Connecticut birth control statute was unconstitutional, but each did so in his own way, simply by finding it in conflict with the due process clause of the Fourteenth Amendment. Justice Hugo Black and Justice Potter Stewart dissented. Stewart observed that Douglas had cited six amendments to the Constitution without saying "which of these Amendments . . . is infringed" by the Connecticut law. Though "an uncommonly silly law," the statute was not on that account unconstitutional. For his part, Goldberg, as Stewart saw it, had turned "somersaults with history." It was not the function of the Supreme Court, Stewart wrote, "to decide cases on the basis of community standards." He reminded his brethren of an earlier decision holding "that courts do not substitute their social and economic beliefs for the judgment of legislative bodies, who we elected to pass laws."

While agreeing with Stewart, Hugo Black delivered an attack of his own on the reasoning of Douglas and Goldberg. The Constitution, he noted, mentioned no "right of privacy." Privacy was a "broad, abstract and ambiguous concept" that could "easily be interpreted as a constitutional ban" against practices not specified in either the First or Fourth Amendment. "I get nowhere in this case," Black wrote, "by talk about a constitutional 'right of privacy,' as an emanation from one or more constitutional provisions. I like my privacy as well as the next one, but I am nevertheless compelled to admit that government has a right to invade it unless prohibited by some specific constitutional provision." Even Harlan and White, Black continued, reached too far. As he saw it, like Goldberg, they claimed "for this Court and the federal judiciary power to invalidate any legislative act which the judges find irrational, unreasonable or offensive." They supposed, Black argued, a "natural justice" or a "natural law . . . philosophy." That concept allowed judges to decide what was or was not constitutional "on the basis of their own appraisal of what laws are wise"—a question properly for legislative bodies. "Subjecting federal and state laws," Black held, "to such an unrestrained and unrestrainable judicial control . . . would . . . jeopardize the separation of governmental powers that the framers set up and at the same time threaten to take away much of the power of States to govern themselves which the Constitution plainly intended them to have."

Both *Griswold*'s result and the content of the opinions delivered about it raised political as well as constitutional issues. Though most Americans practiced birth control and believed in family planning, there were others, some Catholics, some evangelicals, who considered sexual intercourse sinful for any purpose other than procreation. To them, *Griswold* seemed as obnoxious as did *Engel*. It was to seem more so a decade later, after the Court, expanding the doctrine of privacy, banned state laws forbidding abortion. The opinions of Douglas and Goldberg, pointing in that direction, shared a view of the Court's authority that carried beyond the range of *Engel* or *Brown*. It was a view that permeated other decisions of 1964 and 1965 about the rights of individuals accused of crimes and about the representative nature of state senates. For Americans vexed by those and related decisions, *Griswold* portended judicial intercession into all aspects of daily life. They might not have understood the jurisprudence of the justices, but voters offended by *Brown*, *Griffin*, *Engel*, or *Griswold* knew what kind of society they liked, and believed that the Court was denying it to them, and they were eager to retaliate through political action.

Many conservative commentators on constitutional law were also disturbed. The Douglas and Goldberg opinions in *Griswold* met severe criticism from legal scholars like Alexander Bickel, who believed that principled decisions required close legal reasoning comprehending a knowledge of the Constitution, judicial precedent, and history relevant to both. Those critics believed that *Griswold* asserted a judicial authority that exceeded the implications of Stone's assignments for "exacting judicial scrutiny." Indeed, the question of the Court's appropriate authority was becoming as controversial, and concurrently as politicized, as the results of the Court's decisions.

4. "ONE PERSON, ONE VOTE"

The activism and assertiveness of the Warren Court accompanied and encompassed its commitment to majoritarian democracy. In *Gomillion v. Lightfoot* (1960), the Court ruled on an Alabama statute of 1957 that had drawn the boundary lines of the city of Tuskegee so as to alter its shape from a square to an "uncouth twenty-eight-sided figure." That shape excluded from the franchise almost all of the city's two hundred black voters. In the spirit of Stone's footnote, the justices unanimously struck down the statute. Legislative acts, they held, "generally lawful may become unlawful when done to accomplish an unlawful end." The gerrymander in Alabama had deprived the affected black voters of participation in the political process. Without denying that result, the state of Alabama had questioned the Court's jurisdiction, but the Court had acted under the Fifteenth Amendment. Associate Justice Charles E. Whittaker in a concurring opinion held that the issue also fell within the meaning of the equal protection clause of the Fourteenth Amendment.

Whittaker's view had a bearing on the apportionment of electoral districts, historically a prerogative of the states. In most states rural areas were overrepresented. For a century and more, rural population had been falling and urban population rising, but characteristically the geographic definitions of electoral districts placed many more voters in the average urban district than in the average rural. Consequently, rural areas, especially but not exclusively in the South, dominated state legislatures, whose members, eager to retain the offices they held, persistently and successfully resisted efforts at redistricting. Yet as late as 1946 the Supreme Court, though not without dissent, had ruled that reapportionment was a political question outside the range of adjudication.

A reexamination of that question lay at the center of the Court's decision in *Baker v. Carr* (1962). The state of Tennessee, required by its constitution to reapportion legislative districts every ten years, had not done so since 1901. As decennial census figures indicated, only redistricting could correct the increasing imbalance of population among the state's counties. A suit to force that action had the support of the United States Department of Justice. Speaking for the Court, Justice William J. Brennan held that the constitutionality of the Tennessee districting related to judicial standards familiar under the equal protection clause of the Fourteenth Amendment. On that basis he remanded—that is, returned the case for decision—to the federal district court in Tennessee. Brennan's opinion, in other words, made reapportionment an appropriate matter for adjudication. In a concurring opinion Justice Tom Clark said he "would not consider intervention by this Court into so delicate a field if there were any other relief available to the people of Tennessee." Justice Stewart, in a separate concurrence, held that the Supreme Court was deciding only that the district court had jurisdiction over the "subject matter" and that the "appellants have standing"—that is, the right to have their case heard.

Even those narrow grounds provoked the dissenting opinion of Justice Felix Frankfurter, whom Justice Harlan joined. In Frankfurter's view, the Court was casting aside an impressive body of precedent. "Disregard of inherent limits in the effective exercise of the Court's 'judicial power,' " Frankfurter warned, ". . . presages the futility of judicial intervention in the essentially political conflict of forces by which the relation between population and representation has time out of mind been and now is determined." The Court's authority, he argued, ultimately rested on "sustained public confidence in its moral sanction." That confidence depended upon the "Court's complete detachment . . . from political entanglements." It was not for the judiciary but for the electorate to remedy malapportionment: "In a democratic society like ours, relief must come through an aroused popular conscience that sears the conscience of the people's representatives." The issue, he concluded, was beyond the reach of the federal judiciary.

Among legal scholars who shared Frankfurter's conviction, the decision in Baker v. Carr raised a lasting storm. Yet the Supreme Court had disposed of issues no less political in Brown I, in which Frankfurter had been influential in forging unanimity, and in other cases bearing on segregation. By 1962, of course, those cases were under political attack, as Engel was about to be. Further, Brown II had provided no clear guidelines to the district courts, a failing that Baker repeated, as Frankfurter indirectly observed. The judiciary was clearly enmeshed in conflicts of political forces. Perhaps especially on that account, Frankfurter was so intense in opposing another political foray.

But Frankfurter, whose failing health soon forced him to resign, had not influenced other justices on the matter of apportionment. The decision in Baker opened the way for citizens in thirty-nine states to seek judicial remedy for various instances of malapportionment. Their cases quickly reached the Supreme Court on appeal. In Gray v. Sanders (1963) the Court ruled against Georgia's notoriously imbalanced county unit system of voting as it affected primaries for the nomination

of both United States senators and statewide officers. In the majority opinion Douglas offended his critics by his typically loose use of history. "The conception of political equality," he wrote, "from the Declaration of Independence, to Lincoln's Gettysburg Address, to the Fifteenth, Seventeenth, and Nineteenth Amendments can mean only one thing, one person, one vote." An informed schoolboy would have known better, but the simplism in Douglas's reading of the past did not alter the facts of the case. The Georgia system had a rural bias worse even than Tennessee's.

The ruling in *Gray* built toward the Court's decision in *Reynolds v. Sims* (1964), in which Chief Justice Warren, speaking for the majority, made "one person, one vote" the general rule for apportioning all state representative bodies, including upper houses in state legislatures. In a companion case Warren made it clear that the Court would reject plans that did not conform to that rule. In his opinion in *Reynolds* the chief justice observed that "the right to vote freely for the candidate of one's choice is the essence of a democratic society, . . . the bedrock of our political system." Overweighting the votes of those residing in rural districts diluted that right and therefore violated the due process clause of the Fourteenth Amendment.

That reasoning did not convince Justice Harlan, who stood alone in dissenting. The Fourteenth Amendment, as he understood its history and meaning, did not apply at all to the right to vote. The majority decision gave federal district courts "blanket authority . . . to supervise apportionment of State legislatures." It was difficult, Harlan wrote, "to imagine a more intolerable and inappropriate interference by the judiciary with the independent legislatures of the States." But so it had been with school districts since *Brown* II. Harlan, of course, realized as much. As he put it, he opposed the "current mistaken view of the Constitution. . . . This view, in a nutshell, is that every social ill in this country can find its cure in some constitutional 'principle,' and that this Court should 'take the lead' in promoting reform when other branches of government fail to act." The Constitution, he continued, was "not a panacea for every blot upon the public welfare." The Court did not "serve its high purpose when it exceeds its authority, even to satisfy justified impatience with the slow workings of the political process."

Harlan's admonition, like Frankfurter's earlier caution, deserved reflection. The Constitution, as both justices noted, provided a form of representation that gave weight to geography, among other considerations. It explicitly guaranteed a "republican," not a "democratic," form of government. Indeed, some members of Congress proposed a constitutional amendment to permit the election of upper houses of state legislatures on a basis other than population. After all, the United States Senate represented such a case.

But in asserting its authority over apportionment, the Court imposed a more democratic order. Taken together, its decisions forced the states toward a majoritarian system of government. As several constitutional authorities later observed, those decisions proved to be a major success story for the Warren Court. Harlan and Frankfurter believed the Court incurred grave political risks in assuming the lead in reform. But to Warren and his supporters, the results of the rulings made those risks necessary. That was true, as they saw it, for desegregation, for reapportionment, for privacy, and for the rights of the accused, which the Court's decisions were vigorously expanding.

5. FROM MALLORY TO MIRANDA

In 1957 the Supreme Court reviewed the conviction of Andrew Mallory, a mentally retarded black man who had raped a white woman in Washington, D.C. He had confessed to that crime after the police held him without arraignment for some seven and a half hours, during which they used intimidating techniques. In *Mallory v. United States* (1957), the Court, speaking through Justice Frankfurter, invalidated the conviction because the police had violated the federal criminal code, which called for "arraignment without delay." The District police and their champions in Congress, many of them from the South, at once objected to the decision for complicating law enforcement.

That angry response was to recur with each succeeding decision in which the Court enlarged its definition of the rights of the accused under the Fourth through the Eighth amendments, all of which applied to aspects of criminal or civil prosecutions. The Kennedy administration was urging improvement and standardization of criminal justice throughout the country, an objective also of the Johnson Justice Department. Doubtless the Court would have moved as it did anyway, but as the judiciary and the executive moved together, both became targets of self-proclaimed defenders of law and order, police forces not the least. Those critics had a receptive audience among Americans, of whom many found urban life increasingly vulnerable to crime in the streets, to muggings, rapes, and murders that no city could wholly prevent. Prevention was becoming especially difficult in a time of growing drug use, teenage violence, and racial tensions. The resulting public awareness of crime exposed the Supreme Court to charges of coddling criminals; in fact, it was protecting the rights of all Americans from violation by ignorant or overzealous police. In so doing, the Court was ruling against the kind of dangerous police procedures that characterized totalitarian governments, fascist and Communist alike.

So it was in *Mapp v. Ohio* (1961), a case involving a search and arrest without a warrant. Police in Cleveland, Ohio, forcibly entered the home of Dollree Mapp over her protest. They were looking for policy paraphernalia—evidence of illegal gambling—but found none. Instead, they came upon some obscene material, and for possessing it, Mapp was arrested and convicted. In a six to three decision, the Supreme Court threw out the conviction because it violated the Fourth Amendment. That amendment, Justice Clark ruled for the majority, meant that "conviction by means of unlawful seizure and enforced confessions . . . should find no sanction in the jurisdiction of the courts." Half the states had already excluded from trials evidence illegally seized. Now local police forces in all states would have to obtain warrants from judges before undertaking searches. "Nothing can destroy a government more quickly," Clark wrote, "than its failure to observe its own laws, or worse, its disregard for the charter of its own existence."

The Sixth Amendment to that charter stipulated that in all criminal prosecutions "the accused shall . . . have the Assistance of Counsel for his defence." In a dissent in 1942 Justice Black had invoked that guarantee in arguing that no one charged with a crime should be deprived of counsel because of poverty. The court reconsidered that issue in *Gideon v. Wainwright* (1965), a case that received wide publicity. Clarence E. Gideon, an indigent, stood convicted of breaking and entering a poolroom in Florida and of stealing some wine, cigarettes, and petty cash. He had asked for a lawyer, but the trial judge had denied him one. After conviction, Gideon composed his own petition to the Supreme Court for review, as many other prisoners had. In accepting Gideon's eloquent petition, the Court assigned to him an experienced and accomplished attorney, Abe Fortas, who undertook the task without a fee—as was customary under the circumstances.

In his plea Fortas urged the justices to keep in mind "what happens to . . . poor, miserable, indigent people when they are arrested and . . . brought into the jail and . . . questioned and . . . brought in . . . strange and awesome circumstances before a magistrate" and then forced to defend themselves. Fortas argued in a vein designed to please Justices Black and Harlan, both opposed to intervention by federal courts in state criminal proceedings. In Gideon's case, Fortas contended, the Supreme Court should intervene, for the Sixth Amendment was obviously involved. In a unanimous decision the Court agreed. Justice Black wrote the opinion. Guarantee of counsel, he ruled, was a fundamental right, essential to a fair trial, spelled out in the Bill of Rights, and made "obligatory upon the States by the Fourteenth Amendment." Gideon's conviction was therefore reversed.

In arguing against that reversal, the attorney for the state of Florida had warned that it would open the prison gates to criminals who had been tried without counsel. In states that had not provided counsel, the decision had that effect. During the next three years, in Florida alone, more than six thousand of the state's eight thousand inmates filed for reconsideration of their cases. Some twenty-five hundred received new trials, and some thirteen hundred were released. But thirty-seven states had made provision for counsel for the indigent before *Gideon*. The decision, as one constitutional historian said, conformed to the American sense of fair play. In 1964 Congress passed the Criminal Justice Act, which provided defense attorneys for poor defendants in federal jurisdictions and at government expense.

The law and order issued revived, however, over the Court's decision in *Escobedo v. Illinois* (1964). Danny Escobedo, a young Chicago laborer of Mexican descent, had been arrested for shooting and killing his brother-in-law. Under interrogation at the police station, he asked to see his lawyer, who was in the building. Declining that request, the police proceeded to harass Escobedo until they extracted a confession. After Escobedo's conviction, his lawyer appealed his case, ultimately to the Supreme Court. By a margin of only five to four, the Court invalidated the conviction. Joined by Chief Justice Warren and Justices Black, Brennan, and Douglas, Justice Goldberg wrote the opinion. The police, he held, had employed "a process of interrogation that lends itself to eliciting incriminating statements." In violation of the Sixth Amendment they had denied Escobedo "an opportunity to consult with his lawyer" and had not "effectively warned him of his absolute . . . right to remain silent." Then Goldberg went on: "A system of law enforcement which comes to depend on the confession, will in the long run be less reliable than a system which depends on extrinsic evidence . . . secured through skillful investigation. If the exercise of constitutional rights will thwart the effectiveness of a system of law enforcement, then there is something wrong with the system."

Those sentences, indeed the opinion in general, met with three acid dissents. Justice Harlan believed the decision "unjustifiably fetters perfectly legitimate methods of law enforcement." Justice Stewart argued that the majority had moved the beginning of judicial proceedings from the trial to the arrest stage. In so doing, it had converted "a routine police investigation of an unsolved murder into a distorted analogue of a judicial trial." It had thereby frustrated "the vital interests of society in preserving . . . functions of honest . . . police investigations." Justice White, joined by Justice Clark, claimed that the majority was inventing a new constitutional right. Soon, he predicted, the Court would exclude all convictions from evidence.

Police officers applauded those dissents. They complained that the Court had removed their most effective means of obtaining confessions. The Court, so one of them said, was "hampering the administration of criminal justice, while 'vicious beasts' were loose in the streets." That belief, widely held, intensified adverse public reactions to decisions about racial and religious issues. It helped foster proposals to limit the Court's jurisdiction or at least the effect of its decisions. The American Bar Association, the National Association of Attorneys General, and the International Association of Chiefs of Police published statements criticizing the Court's expansion of its authority. That view was common among members of the bar and of the bench, including Judge Learned Hand of the United States Court of Appeals for the Second Circuit, a jurist of immense reputation.

Escobedo raised the storm against the Court to gale force. Congress increased the salaries of all federal judges except for those on the Supreme Court. At the 1964 Republican National Convention former President Eisenhower, still a national hero, urged the delegates "not to be guilty of maudlin sympathy for the criminal who, roaming the street with switchblade knife and illegal firearms seeking a prey . . . counts upon the compassion of our society and the . . . weakness of too many courts to forgive his offense." Barry Goldwater used that theme in his campaign. The Court, he contended, was fostering a breakdown of law and order. "No wonder," Goldwater said, "that our law enforcement officers have been demoralized and rendered ineffective in their jobs." Striking a note the Republicans continued to play, he expressed his worry about "who is the President for the next four . . . years thinking of . . . the make-up of the Supreme Court."

Undeterred, the Court continued along the line of decisions begun with *Mallory* and *Mapp*. Justice Stewart, so often a dissenter, wrote the majority opinion in *Stanford v. Texas* (1965), which denied to the states the use of a general search warrant. Also in 1965, the Court, invoking the Sixth Amendment, reaffirmed the right of a witness to confront and cross-examine his accusers. Those rulings rested on strong historical and constitutional precedents that the states were violating. In the absence of corrective legislation, the burden of upholding the constitution lay on the Court. On that account the American Law Institute devised a Model Code of Pre-Arraignment Procedures. It was less restrictive on the police than Justice White had predicted the Court would become, and it won the endorsement of an impressive number of legal scholars and judges, several of whom had spoken out against any expansion of the *Escobedo* ruling.

That decision had produced confusions about criminal procedure that needed clarification. With both the states and the Congress delaying in that task, Chief Justice Warren assumed it in the opinion he wrote for the majority in *Miranda v. Arizona* (1966). Ernesto Miranda, a poor Mexican laborer with a record of burglary and sexual offenses, was arrested and convicted of rape. The conviction depended upon evidence that included a confession obtained after a police interrogation in an isolated room and in the absence of an attorney. Miranda had no apparent knowledge of his constitutional rights. In his and four companion cases, the Supreme Court, again by a majority of only five to four, reversed the decision of the states' trial courts. The majority ruled that the prosecution could not use any statement "stemming from custodial interrogation of the defendant unless it demonstrates the use of procedural safeguards effective to secure the privilege against self-incrimination."

Warren's lengthy opinion then spelled out those safeguards. Prior to any questioning, Warren wrote in a sentence that was to become famous,

"Of Course, I Believe In The People's Rights — But For The Right People"

— from *The Herblock Gallery* (Simon + Schuster, 1968)

an accused "person must be warned that he has a right to remain silent, that any statement he does make may be used in evidence against him, and that he has a right to the presence of an attorney, either retained or appointed." A defendant might "voluntarily, knowingly, and intelligently" waive these rights, but at any stage in the process he could reassert them. Warren cited historical precedents for the Court's ruling, one of them from a thirteenth-century commentary on the Old Testament Book of Judges, ordinarily not a source for American jurisprudence. "There is no doubt," he asserted, "that the Fifth Amendment privilege is available . . . to protect persons in all settings . . . from being compelled to incriminate themselves."

The opinion was typical of the chief justice. To specify police procedure as he did, he had extended the reach of the Court beyond precedent. His argument for doing so rested more on the strength of his convictions than on judicial craftsmanship. His purpose was clear. As he said in an oral aside, when the police neglected fairness, they became "a menace to society." Those who then most often suffered were the uneducated, the poor, the black and Hispanic who did not know their rights or how to find out about them. They needed protection from the police, which Warren felt morally as well as legally obliged to provide. In that sense, *Miranda*, like *Escobedo* and *Gideon*, was distinctly egalitarian.

The chief's opinion occasioned three strong dissents, in two of which Justice Stewart joined. Unpersuaded by Warren's excursion into history, Justice White called the majority ruling "a departure from a long line of precedents." He went on; "The obvious under-pinning of the Court's decision is a deep-seated distrust of all confessions." The decision was making "new law" and "new public policy" that would "impede the conviction of murderers and rapists." Justice Clark, upset by Warren's criticism of the police, condemned the chief's "strict constitutional specific" as a hindrance to law enforcement. Justice Harlan objected that the decision hastily imposed new rules at a time when serious considerations of "long-range and lasting reforms" were under way by the American Bar Association, the American Law Institute, and the President's Commission on Law Enforcement. The *Miranda* rules, Harlan argued, would "impair, if they will not eventually serve wholly to frustrate, an instrument of law enforcement that has long and quite reasonably been thought worth the price paid for it. . . . The Court is taking a real risk with society's welfare in imposing its new regime on the country."

Amplified by those dissents, the uproar that followed the *Miranda* decision refreshed the hostility to the Warren Court. Democratic Senator John L. McClellan of Arkansas, a fervid enemy of the Court since *Brown* I, attacked *Miranda*. "This 5–4 decision," he said, "is of such adverse significance to law enforcement that it . . . demands . . . legislation . . . to alleviate the damage it will do to society." Senator Samuel J. Ervin of North Carolina, also a conservative Democrat but a respectable legal scholar, called for a constitutional amendment to allow any confession as evidence so long as it was voluntary. "Enough has been done," he said, "for those who murder and rape and riot! It is time to do something for those who do not wish to be murdered or raped or robbed."

Protests against *Miranda* mounted in spite of evidence that the decision was far less crippling than its detractors claimed. In a separate case the Supreme Court held that *Miranda* did not apply retroactively. In a second trial Ernesto Miranda was again convicted, now without recourse to a confession. United States Attorney General Ramsey Clark, the son of Justice Clark, from the first defended the decision so disturbing to his father. Several studies concluded that *Miranda* did not significantly damage law enforcement even though the rate of confessions dropped. And for its part, the Supreme Court became somewhat less restrictive about police procedures. Over Warren's dissent, it allowed the use of undercover agents to obtain narcotics convictions. It also permitted informers to provide evidence from self-incriminating statements that the accused had made to them. And it allowed bugging where police had prior judicial approval. Police, the Court held, could enter a home without a warrant "in hot pursuit" of a suspect. Those rulings notwithstanding, by 1968, an election year, the controversial decisions from *Mallory* through *Miranda* had entangled the Court in a political thicket from which it could not escape.

6. LAW AND ORDER

Early in Earl Warren's term as chief justice, soon after the most vicious congressional witch-hunts for alleged subversives, the Supreme Court handed down several decisions that limited the conditions under which the state and federal governments could discharge or penalize "leftists." Those decisions accorded with the continuing efforts of the Warren Court to protect the freedoms of belief and of expression guaranteed by the First Amendment. But those decisions upset President Eisenhower. They protected "Commies," he said. The appointment of

Warren, Eisenhower believed, was "the biggest damn fool mistake I made." The innocence of Ike's understanding of the Constitution was not uncommon. By 1968 many Americans were eager to get rid of the chief justice.

Under any circumstances the Court's decisions about police procedures would have contributed to that mood. As it was, by 1968 the issue of law enforcement had taken on meaning far beyond the rights of accused persons. Several developments had brought unusual discord and unusual violence to American society. From 1964 onward, opposition to the Vietnam War and social and racial unrest in the cities had continually disrupted the surface serenity normal in American life. The unrest and the violence, moreover, commonly involved angry confrontations about values and behavior between the youth of the country and their parents' generation. The Supreme Court was responsible for none of those developments, nor did the Court speak directly to the central questions they raised. What little of relevance the Court did say was on the whole ambiguous. Yet that little said enough to permit the Court's opponents, as they had for more than a decade, to link the issue of law and order to the disruptions caused by other questions agitating and dividing the American people, particularly race, poverty, and war.

The Court took care to avoid having to rule on the legality of the war in Vietnam, a war Congress never declared. Citing the First Amendment, it did rule that a state legislature had to seat a properly elected representative despite his opposition to the war and the draft. But it also held that the public burning of draft cards was not an act of "symbolic speech." It required protesters to abide by regular judicial processes in seeking permits to hold parades. Nevertheless, conservative critics of *Escobedo* and *Miranda* looked upon demonstrations against the war in Vietnam as just another kind of violation of law and order. And they held the Warren Court responsible.

So, too, with the race riots that swept American cities in the late 1960s. The Court never condoned them. But it had provided crucial support for the civil rights movement. Opponents of that movement, especially white racists north and south, saw the Court as a friend to blacks and an enemy of the police. Americans of that temperament associated disorder in general with the Court's decisions and associated it, too, with the youth movements of the 1960s. Some leaders of those protest movements boasted of their radical and disruptive goals. Those goals, as conservatives interpreted them, were inseparable from the drug culture and promiscuous sex of outré young rebels. Here, too, complicity visited the Warren Court because of its newly permissive decisions about the definition of obscene literature and film and about restrictions on their circulation. Courtbashers liked to think of obscenity as a characteristic primarily of lewd and sinful radicals.

Exaggerated and distorted in the climate of 1968, the Court's reputation for coddling criminals made it particularly vulnerable. Members of Congress returning to Washington that January reported that among their constituents "anger over riots and crimes overshadowed all other domestic issues." That punitive mood contrasted directly with the report of the President's Commission on Law Enforcement. The commission's majority had pointed out that the criminal justice system was not "designed to eliminate the conditions in which crime breeds." Its report concluded: "Warring on poverty . . . is warring on crime. A civil rights law is a law against crime. . . . A community's most enduring protection against crime is to right the wrongs . . . that tempt men to harm their neighbors." That had been a premise of the Great Society, and that was Earl Warren's belief. But many, probably most Americans disagreed. By 1968 they had come to reject explanations of the relationship between poverty and crime. They dismissed the commission's report as a permissive liberal litany. Their responsive representatives on the Hill passed the Omnibus Crime Control Act. Title II of the statute attempted to modify the *Miranda* decision by making confessions admissible in evidence if they were voluntary. It also allowed police to hold a suspect six hours before arraignment. President Johnson reluctantly signed the measure. He would otherwise have risked the political consequences of a veto.

It was, as it turned out, too late for Johnson or for the Court to avoid further political retaliation. In June 1968 Earl Warren, feeling his age, resigned as chief justice, effective at the pleasure of the president. Johnson nominated his close adviser Associate Justice Abe Fortas to succeed as chief, and for the place Fortas would vacate as associate justice, he named an old friend from Texas, Judge Homer Thornberry. Fortas, a lifelong defender of civil liberties and an advocate of judicial activism, had pleaded the *Gideon* case and joined the majority in *Miranda.* His nomination at once ran into a roadblock constructed by the Republicans with some help from antiadministration Democrats. "With the Court in adjournment," one Republican senator said, "and the American people about to pick a new administration which may considerably re-orient the philosophy of our national government, it would be a major mistake to presume to fill such an important role."

That was emphatically the opinion of Senator Strom Thurmond, the political leader of the Dixiecrat South. Still unreconciled to *Brown* I, Thurmond was outraged by the potential effects of the *Green* decision. The Republicans had to have his support if they were to carry the white southern votes that governor Wallace was courting in his third-party campaign against desegregation and for law and order. Richard Nixon secured Thurmond's support by promising to appoint federal judges satisfactory to the senator. Such judges would not be judicial activists. Further, Nixon and the GOP made the issue of law and order, with its racial overtones, a centerpiece of their campaign. Meanwhile, the Senate held up the nominations of Fortas and Thornberry. The era of the Warren Court had just about reached its end.

7. CODA

As the Supreme Court had been through most of its history, the Warren Court was of its time. Both the spirit and the results of its decisions resonated in harmony with the New Frontier and the Great Society. It was an activist Court in a period of activist government. It was activist in order to effect egalitarian and democratic ends, as that government endeavored to effect similar ends. Even more than that government, the Warren Court was committed to the protection of the rights of individuals, especially to freedom of belief and expression. Like all law, the law handed down by the Warren Court was policy, policy that complemented the programs of the Great Society. And the majority opinions of the Warren Court framed a political theory consonant with those democratic goals.

As the Great Society was flawed, so was the Warren Court. Qualities of haste in drafting legislation and of sloppiness in administration damaged the functioning of the Great Society. Similar qualities characterized the majority opinions of the Warren Court. Those opinions lacked the judicial craftsmanship to protect them from future modification, as the dissents from them suggested. That vulnerability played into the hands of conservatives determined to see the decisions overturned. And that political threat endangered the democratic results of the Warren Court's rulings.

A leading advocate of judicial restraint, Alexander Bickel, later complained about the "powerful strain of populism in the rhetoric by which the Court supported its one-man, one-vote doctrine." There was, too, Bickel went on, a powerful strain of populism in Lyndon Johnson. "It was utterly inevitable," Bickel wrote, with the presidency in mind, "that such a populist fixation should tend toward the concentration of power in that single institution which had the most immediate link to the largest constituency." A natural consequence, in Bickel's words, was a presidency "making war . . . being secret . . . needing no excuse for aggregating power to itself."

But the Warren Court had taken power unto itself for reasons not in the least majoritarian. "The whole *point* of an independent judiciary," as Laurence H. Tribe later put it, in the liberal spirit of Earl Warren, "is to be 'antidemocratic,' to preserve from transient majorities those human rights and other principles to which our legal and political system is committed." Johnson, in contrast, was frankly majoritarian. He had gained an exalted station, so he believed, from the electoral mandate of 1964. Even earlier, on ascending to the presidency, he had taken power unto himself to draw the country more deeply into the Vietnam War, and he continued to do so. In using their power as they did, both Warren and Johnson excited the wrath of their opponents. Only in that sense was Bickel's equation correct. Toward the end of their days the chief justice and the president alike had come to the edge of political retribution.

8

"The Greatest Power . . ."

When he became president, Lyndon Johnson was a master of domestic affairs. About foreign policy, he was neither experienced nor confident. At first he leaned on Kennedy appointees in making decisions about foreign and military matters. Johnson also invariably presented his ventures abroad as extensions of major decisions earlier made by his predecessors, not by Kennedy alone but also by Eisenhower and Truman. In a large sense Johnson's claim was correct. Continuity did characterize his foreign and military policies, as it had Kennedy's. Just as Kennedy accepted the premises of the cold war that had governed official doctrine since the late 1940s, so did Johnson. Just as Kennedy retained the prevailing American strategy of containment of Soviet and Chinese expansion, so did Johnson. To that end, again like Kennedy, Johnson in his tactics relied on responses short of nuclear confrontation.

Of course, Johnson was not Kennedy. As vice president Johnson continually had been more of a hawk than Kennedy, and Johnson as president turned to Kennedy's more hawkish counselors. For personal as well as political reasons, he also turned away from Robert Kennedy, whose partisans ordinarily accepted Kennedy's views as those his brother would have had. Since Robert Kennedy and his circle were usually among Johnson's critics, they discerned discontinuities where the president thought otherwise. Though no one could know exactly what John F. Kennedy had intended, by their own lights Johnson's critics were also correct, for Johnson brought to the White House a new and different background, temperament, and manner of deciding and pursuing policy. Those differences gave his administration a distinctive stamp. For good or ill, it no longer mattered what John F. Kennedy would have done. Johnson's decisions about foreign affairs, now the drivetrain of national policy, had to stand or fall on their own merits.

1. PANAMA

Especially during his novitiate, Johnson interpreted anti-American stirrings abroad as both tests of his personal strength and challenges to national interests. So it was six weeks after he took office, when long-festering tensions in Panama erupted briefly into violence. In 1962 President Robert Chiari of Panama had negotiated an agreement with President Kennedy that regulated the number of sites and the manner of display of the flags of the two nations within the area of the Panama Canal Zone. That zone consisted of the strip of territory on both sides of the Panama Canal in which the United States had secured special rights by the Treaty of 1903 imposed upon the Panamanians by Theodore Roosevelt. American rule in the zone had rankled Panamanians ever since. Though American authority there had been reduced gradually, it still symbolized Yankee colonialism, which Latin Americans generally detested. The American presence in the zone generated social as well as political grievances. In contrast with the largely destitute Panamanians surrounding them. American military and civilian personnel lived in circumstances of relative splendor. Like Yankee rule, Yankee affluence and the "shameless arrogance" accompanying it accounted for growing hostility toward the United States.

For twenty years and more, Panamanians had toppled any government that seemed to truckle to the Colossus of the North. Kennedy nevertheless had been tough with Chiari, as the Panamanians realized. On January 7, 1964, a group of chauvinistic American students roiled tempers by hoisting the Stars and Stripes at their high school in the zone in violation of the 1962 agreement. Two days later a protest march of Panamanian students, some of them looting and scuffling on the way, entered the Canal Zone and moved toward the school, where they intended to raise their own flag. After Canal Zone police had forced them back into Panamanian territory, crowds of Panamanians rioted for several days in Panama City and Colón, the cities at the Pacific and Atlantic terminals of the canal. On the advice of the senior American military commander in the area, Johnson ordered American troops there to supplement the small force of Canal Zone police. Before the rioting

American students in the Canal Zone: Symbol of Yankee imperialism.

ended on January 12, Panamanian snipers had killed four American soldiers and wounded others, and American troops had killed some twenty Panamanians.

The pattern of the incident—the nature of the social tensions underlying it, the unthinking actions of the youths who provoked it, the escalation of the violence after the intrusion of the police and the army—at once resembled and foreshadowed similar incidents of disorder within the United States during the decade of the 1960s. But in 1964 in Panama, as elsewhere both at home and abroad later, Johnson saw in the episode the threat of international communism. The commanding general in Panama informed him on January 10 that Castro-trained organizers had seized control of the situation, and Johnson later repeated that contention. There were doubtless some Communists in Panama, and the Panamanian government had not exerted itself to maintain order. Yet from the outset President Chiari made it perfectly clear that he and his people were not radical revolutionaries but frustrated nationalists.

On January 9, 1964, after the first American use of force, Chiari broke diplomatic relations with the United States. In so informing the State Department, the Panamanian ambassador to Washington protested against the "acts of ruthless aggression . . . by the armed forces of the United States . . . against the territorial integrity of the Republic." The only acceptable remedy, the ambassador said, would be a complete change of the treaty of 1903—an overt American recognition of Panamanian sovereignty in the Canal Zone. Chiari made the same point when Johnson telephoned him that day. Since he had talked to President Kennedy, Chiari said, "not a thing has been done to alleviate the situation." Johnson concluded that "Chiari was going to try to exact a new treaty from me by force."

Refusing to discuss the treaty until Chiari restored order and resumed diplomatic relations. Johnson revealed no comprehension of the pressure on the Panamanian chief of state, who had to stand for reelection in May 1964. Communism had nothing to do with the matter. In April Chiari took the issue to the Council of the Organization of American States (OAS), a step useful at least to appease his constituency. He then also agreed to negotiate, as did Johnson, but it was June, a month after the Panamanian election, before Panama formally resumed diplomatic relations and both governments officially expressed the hope that continuing discussions about the 1903 treaty would lead to a mutually satisfactory agreement. Though they did not during Johnson's term in office, Johnson believed that he had passed his "first test in Latin America." He knew, he maintained, that "Castro had not abandoned his plans for testing the United States and its new President."

Johnson's delusion about the actual developments in Panama derived in part from his own feelings of personal insecurity, in part from his reliance on the truculent senior military people in the area, who suspected Communist influence behind every disturbance. Johnson relied equally on his fellow Texan Thomas Mann, his new appointee as assistant secretary of state for Latin American affairs. Scornful of Latins, Mann had zealous regard for American commercial interests and an unshakable faith that he could buy anything he wanted south of the Rio Grande. The president might instead have listened to Senate

Majority Leader Mike Mansfield, whose opinion he solicited and then ignored. As Mansfield realized, the fundamental American interest in Panama was "untroubled . . . water passage through Central America." Pressure for social change "just short of violent revolution" in Panama arose from inside the area and long predated Castro. The United States, therefore, should not blame Castro "too much," should not quibble with the Panamanians, should avoid costly and offensive military operations, and should reduce the number of American personnel in the Canal Zone. That prescription had merit for trouble anywhere in Latin America, indeed throughout the world where the peoples of emerging nations were jealous of their national independence and honor and resentful of American wealth and interference.

But Johnson took only the advice with which he agreed. He took the advice on Panama that suited his macho temperament and his persistent conviction that Communist leaders were determined to embarrass him. Even so, his response fell short of more aggressive steps available to him. Consequently, he persuaded himself that he had acted with restraint. The Panamanians disagreed, as did most foreign observers. As the United States Information Agency reported on January 13, 1964, "On Panama we are taking a shellacking." At least temporarily Johnson's course hurt his reputation and his country's. More important, it displayed injurious traits of mind and personality.

2. THE DOMINICAN REPUBLIC

The leading sponsors of the Alliance for Progress considered Johnson's appointment of Thomas Mann a challenge to the goals they had set. They had expected American economic assistance to promote democratic reform, indeed in the course of a decade to work a "peaceful revolution" in Latin American social structure. Mann's influence, they believed, would feed Johnson's own inclination to support authoritarian regimes that were safely anti-Communist and anti-Castro, regimes with which American businessmen preferred to deal. So it was in Peru, where the United States suspended aid to a democratic government in an attempt to force it to submit to terms offered it by an American oil company. So it was also in Johnson's quick recognition of a reactionary military coup in Brazil. And so it was notably in the Dominican Republic.

Until 1961 the Dominican Republic had suffered for three decades under the dictatorial rule of Generalissimo Rafael Trujillo, who was assassinated during a coup that year. After almost another year of unrest the United States promised to support a settlement that assured free elections in December 1962. Those elections resulted in the choice as president of Juan Bosch, a social democrat, a poet, and an intellectual. Though an eloquent spokesman for civil rights and social reform, Bosch was also regrettably unrealistic and ineffectual. In September 1963 a military junta deposed him. Bosch fled to Puerto Rico. The junta in its turn fell in April 1965 to another coup engineered by a mélange of forces: some former associates of Trujillo; some disaffected army officers; some supporters of Bosch. That coalition crumbled almost at once when General Elías Wessin y Wessin, who opposed the return of Bosch, led an attack against the "constitutionalists," the deposed president's political allies who held a shaky control of the accoutrements of authority. From April 25 through April 27, 1965, fighting in the streets of the capital city frightened foreigners residing there, including American nationals.

The American ambassador to the Dominican Republic, W. Tapley Bennett, Jr., shared that fright as well as the confusion inherent in the unstable Dominican political situation. Perhaps because he wanted Wessin to prevail, he made no effort to negotiate a settlement between the Dominican factions. His calls to Washington revealed his patently hysterical belief that the constitutionalists had fallen to the domination of Communists. That contention accorded with President Johnson's a priori conviction that Castro "had his eye on the Dominican Republic." When Bennett cabled on April 28, 1965, that the time had come to rescue endangered Americans, Johnson sent in two hundred marines. He did so with the support of his senior civilian and military advisers but without consulting the Organization of American States. He also took over himself the day-by-day direction of policy toward the Dominican Republic. With Bennett exhorting him, on May 2 the president dispatched some fourteen thousand troops—ultimately twenty-two thousand in all—in an effort, so he told the American people, to restore order and "to prevent another Communist state in this hemisphere."

During the several days before he acted, Johnson had ample time to ask the OAS to address both the exigent question of the safety of foreigners in the Dominican Republic and the larger question of Communist influence there. The size and emotionalism of the OAS, he and his advisers believed, would have prevented it from acting quickly and decisively. Privately Johnson said that the organization "couldn't pour piss out of a boot if the instructions were written on the heel." Yet after the fact, eager to legitimize his unilateral intercession, he welcomed the cooperation of the OAS in dealing with the Dominicans.

Johnson's policy needed justification. Though he consulted the factions in the Dominican Republic, he had intervened in violation of Dominican sovereignty, and he followed his intervention by trying to arrange for a new government on his own terms. He and his senior agents, among others McGeorge Bundy and Abe Fortas, rejected the idea of another military junta, but Johnson also rejected Juan Bosch and his supporters. To be sure, Bosch refused to sign a statement alleging that there were Communists among his followers and asking American troops to occupy his country. But Bosch and his faction were reaching for a compromise solution, whereas Johnson wanted to impose a settlement on the Dominican Republic.

With American troops maintaining order, Ellsworth Bunker, United States ambassador to the Organization of American States, building on Bundy's earlier effort, brought the several Dominican parties to agreement. Announced in mid-June, the agreement called for a general amnesty, free elections, and a provisional government until the elections could be held. Bunker's negotiations led a month later to the selection of Bosch's former foreign minister as provisional president. A year thereafter Joaquín Balaguer, a moderate, was elected president by a large majority of Dominican voters. Those voters, Johnson later wrote, had demonstrated their ability to discharge their democratic responsibilities. That vindicated his decision, he believed, to intercede "to protect the security of the United States and its neighbors."

But the outcome of American intervention in the Dominican Republic did not in itself confirm Johnson's belief or justify his methods. Even if, as he argued, he had had to use the marines to evacuate endangered Americans, the larger forces he then employed were, as Undersecretary of State George Ball later wrote, "wildly disproportionate" to the size of the problem. The Dominican Republic had not been about to fall to Castro. President Rómulo Betancourt of Venezuela, a dedicated democrat who had an excellent intelligence operation in the Dominican Republic, was confident "that the United States could work with the non-Communist leaders . . . and swiftly isolate the few Communists." But Johnson did not consult Betancourt. He listened only to what he wanted to hear from the FBI and the CIA. Among his advisers, only Jack Hood Vaughn, his new assistant secretary of state for Latin American affairs, once "bravely challenged the President and then left the room with an angry exchange when the President rejected his views."

As in the case of Panama, Johnson overreacted to developments in the Dominican Republic and overrode Latin American sensitivities. He attributed the outrage of his critics to their innocence or to the machinations of his supposed enemies. The episode revealed disturbing qualities in his way of assessing American security and in his manner of governing. As Adlai Stevenson later said to Arthur Schlesinger, Jr., "When I consider what the administration did in the Dominican Republic, I begin to wonder if we know what we are doing in Vietnam."

3. Tonkin Gulf

When Lyndon Johnson assumed the presidency, the problem of American involvement in Vietnam seemed to him and his confidants "no bigger than a man's fist." That illusion mirrored Johnson's hopes. It was domestic reform, not embroilment in Southeast Asia, for which his career had prepared him and on which he wanted to concentrate. But the war in Vietnam demanded attention. Eisenhower had committed the United States to the preservation of the independence of South Vietnam. He did so, as he saw it, to contain Soviet and Chinese influence in Southeast Asia. Kennedy had increased that commitment, most seriously by the complicity of his administration in the overthrow of the Diem government, a venture Johnson had opposed. Nevertheless, like Kennedy before him, Johnson, eager for election in his own right, believed he could not afford politically to "lose" Vietnam. Temperamentally he could not countenance the idea of becoming the first modern president to lose a war. Further, he shared the assumptions about world politics and about Southeast Asia that underlay the policies of his predecessors. Basically, all in the White House, the Pentagon, and the State Department spoke with one voice. It resonated in the National Security Action memorandum that Johnson issued four days after Kennedy's death: "The President expects that all senior officers of the government will move emphatically to insure the full unity of support for established U.S. policy in South Vietnam."

That policy called for a concentration of effort—political, economic, and military—to help the government leaders of South Vietnam (GVN) "win their contest against the externally directed and supported Communist conspiracy." As they had for some time, the National Liberation Front, or Vietcong—the antigovernment guerrillas in South Vietnam—were continuing to gain ground, especially in the delta of the Mekong River and in the vicinity of Saigon. The Vietcong were

VIETNAM, 1966

□ Major U.S. bases

0   200 Miles

0   200 Kilometers

Communists, just as Washington had long contended, and they were operating under the direction of and receiving important support from North Vietnam's Communist government. Like that government, however, they were also nationalists, determined to reunite their country. Ho Chi Minh's regime in Hanoi, expecting Saigon soon to obtain increased American aid, was investigating means for expanding the jungle route—the Ho Chi Minh Trail—along which, partly through Laos, North Vietnam sent supplies and reinforcements to the Vietcong. Work to improve that network began in 1964 and steadily converted a tortuous path into a highway of sorts, suitable for trucks and defended against air attacks, a route well able to carry the troops and equipment that moved along it. North Vietnam, again as Washington contended, procured much of that equipment from China and from the Soviet Union. Those former allies were rapidly drifting apart. Suspicious of Khrushchev after the resolution of the missile crisis, Ho in 1963 was tilting toward China, but hesitantly. Over the centuries China and

Vietnam had often been enemies, and the Soviet Union had the capacity China lacked to supply Hanoi with modern weapons. After Khrushchev lost power in October 1964, Ho counted more and more on Soviet assistance, but he kept his lines open to Beijing, partly to avoid offending China, partly because China sent North Vietnam thousands of industrial and agricultural workers, partly to use China as a potential threat to American ambitions. All in all, by 1964 the Soviet Union, China, and North Vietnam were arrayed against the preservation of an independent South Vietnam, the fundamental American objective.

Johnson's administration had to face essential questions involving the attainability of that objective and its increasing costs. In December 1963 conditions in South Vietnam were still deteriorating. General Duong Van Minh, "Big Minh," who had succeeded Diem, had neither the will nor the ability to govern. His subordinates were as corrupt and ineffective as their predecessors. Desertion from the army was growing. Indeed, the army was doing its best not to fight. The strategic hamlet program, unpopular in the countryside, was collapsing. Uncertain about what to do, Johnson sent Robert McNamara to report from the scene. "I am optimistic as to the progress that can be made in the coming year," McNamara announced in Saigon on December 19, 1963. He was indeed hopeful, but privately he told Johnson that "current trends, unless reversed in the next two or three months, will lead to neutralization at best or more likely to a Communist-controlled state." The Minh government was "drifting" while the "country team," the collection of American officials in Vietnam, lacking leadership, suffered from the persisting antagonism between General Hawkins and Ambassador Lodge. The United States, McNamara concluded, should prepare "for more forceful moves if the situation does not show early signs of improvement."

To put it another way, McNamara was arguing that the United States had to increase its activities and responsibilities in South Vietnam in order to compensate for the deterioration of the government there. Not he or Johnson or anyone else in authority questioned the validity of American policy. The case for that policy still rested on the hoary domino theory that Eisenhower had advanced a decade earlier. Recast in a secret memorandum of January 1964 from the Joint Chiefs of Staff to McNamara, the theory held that the collapse of South Vietnam would lead inexorably to the collapse also of Laos and Cambodia. That genuine probability, the theory held, would in turn call into question the American commitment to protect other nations in Asia and in Africa and South America. That was a dubious proposition; American resources, spared from Vietnam, would be available for deployment elsewhere. But the conflict in Vietnam, in McNamara's words, was regarded "in the rest of the world" as a "test-case of U.S. capacity to help a nation meet a Communist 'war of liberation.' " Consequently, "purely in terms of foreign policy" the stakes were high, and they were "increased by domestic factors."

In 1964, an election year, Johnson needed no reminder about those stakes. A major setback in Vietnam, he believed, would permit the Republicans to accuse him of softness toward communism. But he also wanted to avoid a war that would threaten his domestic goals and might, if China interceded, become a political disaster, as the Korean War had for Harry Truman. Consequently, during 1964, in the pattern set by Eisenhower and Kennedy, Johnson tried to arrest the deterioration in South Vietnam by taking a series of steps short of war. Each step was intended to buttress the anti-Communist position while leaving it as much as possible to the South Vietnamese to "win their own fight." Each step necessarily increased American involvement.

In January 1964 the Minh government, which Johnson had hoped to stabilize, fell to a coup engineered by General Nguyen Khanh. Dispatched again to Saigon, McNamara found the Khanh government "highly responsive to U.S. advice" but not yet either popular or in control. He recommended broad American support "to make it emphatically clear that we are prepared to furnish assistance . . . for as long as it takes" to subdue the Vietcong and that "we . . . are opposed to further coups." The assistance was to help the GVN to increase its armed forces, to improve its paramilitary operations, and to continue covert attacks on North Vietnam. The United States should also prepare for larger "retaliatory actions" against North Vietnam should they become desirable.

Johnson followed that advice but on a scale smaller than the Joint Chiefs had proposed. Concurrently he tried to bolster the American mission in Saigon, and through it the GVN, by putting men of his own choice into positions of authority. When Lodge resigned as ambassador, McGeorge Bundy, Dean Rusk, and Robert Kennedy all offered to replace him, but Johnson chose General Maxwell Taylor. Taylor, who had helped forge the American commitment to Vietnam, was eager to sustain it. Impatient with the convoluted politics of Saigon, he offended Vietnamese leaders by admonishing them to snap to. Since the ARVN was loath to fight, he believed the Americans would do better to take charge themselves of the military effort. So did General William C. Westmoreland, the management-minded West Pointer whom Johnson selected to replace General Hawkins as commander of the United States advisory group. So, too, after years of frustration did Secretary of State Rusk, who would have shaken the South Vietnamese leaders "by the scruff of the neck and insist [ed] that they put aside all bickering."

But American exhortations for efficiency moved none of the factions competing for power in Saigon. South Vietnam, a country beset by political rivalries and religious division, had no tradition of democracy or official probity. As unreliable as Diem and Minh before him, Khanh presided precariously over a loose coalition of ambitious and squabbling officers and their civilian agents. He and his associates habitually told the Americans whatever the Americans wanted to hear, but the facade of government in South Vietnam could not hide the bankruptcy of indigenous leadership. Neither in 1964 nor later did there exist a viable party or political leader that was genuinely democratic, or popular, or effectual. Each successive malodorous caudillo knew that he could safely ignore American demands for efficiency and reform. As long as the Johnson administration was riven to its policy of preserving an anti-Communist South Vietnam, it had to support the reigning head of state.

In March 1964 Johnson still resisted "overt militarization" in Viet-

Council of war: William Bundy, Dean Rusk, LBJ, Robert McNamara, Maxwell Taylor.

nam. "Planning for action against the North," he cabled the embassy in Saigon, remained "on a contingency basis." But the president's preferred civilian advisers were already pushing him toward Americanization of the conflict. Johnson had forced the resignation of Roger Hilsman, the devoted Kennedy man who had favored the overthrow of Diem. Hilsman was replaced as assistant secretary of state for Far Eastern affairs by William Bundy, an older brother of McGeorge Bundy, a former assistant secretary of defense, and a supporter of direct American military initiatives. The head of the State Department's Policy Planning Office, Walt W. Rostow, had long had bellicose views, especially about the desirability of American bombing of North Vietnam. The two Bundys, Rostow, Taylor and Westmoreland, Rusk, and McNamara held the president's attention partly because he respected them, primarily because by and large their counsel fitted his own preferences, adjusted always to his political sensibilities. As in the case of Latin America, so in the case of Southeast Asia, Johnson was never the innocent captive of his advisers. On the contrary, he selected his advisers and sifted their recommendations. He was always in charge.

The president set the pace of American escalation in Vietnam. Cautious at this point, he consulted Mike Mansfield and Richard Russell, leading senators and two of his closest congressional advisers. Though they warned him against getting caught in a morass in Asia, Johnson continued to endorse the covert military activities of American advisers in South Vietnam. He worried about undertaking open ventures without congressional support. So did his senior subordinates, including William Bundy and Walt Rostow, who separately drafted similar texts of a congressional resolution giving the president virtually unlimited authority to use the armed forces to assist South Vietnam in preserving its independence. There was precedent for that resolution in one that Congress had passed in 1955 to give Eisenhower similar authority during a crisis over Quemoy and Matsu, China's offshore islands. Ike had then had strong bipartisan support, and Johnson would need it, too, if a resolution were to receive congressional approval without a prolonged and possibly embarrassing debate. While the Pentagon was preparing a detailed scheme for bombing North Vietnam, Johnson decided in June 1964 to defer going to Congress. He did not want to appear belligerent during the campaign, and as yet he lacked dramatic evidence to persuade Congress and the American people of the need to damage North Vietnam.

In August continuing clandestine operations against North Vietnam provoked two incidents that gave the president his opening. American naval vessels were operating in the Gulf of Tonkin—which lay just southeast of Hanoi—charting the coast and the positions along it of North Vietnamese radar and radio facilities, prime targets for quick ARVN attacks or future American bombings. An American destroyer, the USS *Maddox*, on such a mission on August 1, 1964, was attacked by several North Vietnamese torpedo boats, on which it then fired. The *Maddox*, untouched by the torpedoes launched toward it, hit two of the boats and sank a third. Since the *Maddox* suffered no casualties, the president in public made little of the engagement. But on the hot line to Moscow, in his first use of that instrument, he sent a message to Khrushchev telling him that he hoped the North Vietnamese would not molest American ships in international waters. In a note to Hanoi, also a first, he warned that "grave consequences" would result from such an action. Johnson also ordered the *Maddox*, as well as another destroyer and covering aircraft, to return to the Tonkin Gulf and to "attack any force that attacks them."

That response skirted many issues. Though the United States defined international waters as beginning beyond a three-mile distance from the shore, North Vietnam, like most Communist-bloc nations, considered its territorial waters to extend twelve miles. By that standard the *Maddox* had entered North Vietnamese territory prior to the attack before returning to international waters. More important, the *Maddox*'s cooperation with South Vietnamese commandos gave Hanoi reason to view the destroyer as engaged in a hostile and provocative act. Nevertheless, the senior United States naval commander in the Pacific instructed the *Maddox* to "assert the right of freedom of the seas."

Back on patrol in the Tonkin Gulf on the night of August 4, 1964, the *Maddox* met rough seas and thunderstorms, which characteristically impaired the operation of the ship's radar and sonar gear. An intercepted radio message gave the captain the "impression" that North Vietnamese patrol boats were again about to attack, an impression that the erratic radar and sonar reception seemed to confirm. The ship thereafter began to maneuver evasively and opened fire in all directions, as did the destroyer accompanying it. According to the still-unreliable radar and sonar, the *Maddox*, during the ensuing hours, evaded twenty-two enemy torpedoes and sank two or three enemy ships. But there had been no "actual visual sightings." As the ship's captain soon realized, his men had been counting ghosts—squeaks and blips from an agitated sea, not weapons or vessels. The "entire action," he radioed his superiors, "leaves many doubts."

Sharing those doubts, Secretary of Defense McNamara wanted to be "damned sure what happened," but Dean Rusk, spoiling for a fight, believed the time had come for the United States to retaliate against North Vietnam, and so did the president. Typically Johnson felt he was "being tested," that he had to guard against criticism from Goldwater Republicans and so "must not allow them to accuse him of vacillating." Before receiving sufficient clarification about what had actually happened to the *Maddox*, the president ordered the bombing of five North Vietnamese military targets that the Joint Chiefs had long since selected. "We are not going to take it lying down," Johnson said in private. "We are going to destroy their cities." In a television address to the American people he announced that "repeated acts of violence against the armed forces of the United States must be met . . . with positive reply. That reply is being given as I speak." The next day, August 5, he sent to the Hill the joint resolution granting him the authority he wanted to conduct war in Vietnam. On August 6 the Senate passed the resolution with only two dissenting votes; the House approved it unanimously.

On the basis of information he had neglected to confirm, and in a precipitant rush, the president in August completed the scenario William Bundy had proposed in March. Polls indicated that 85 percent of the American people stood behind him. But like the Congress, the people had not been told the whole story. Few understood the full implications of the administration's actions. The two dissenters in the Senate were lonesome in their perceptions. Wayne Morse of Oregon, for many years a political maverick, did not believe that the attack on the *Maddox* had been unprovoked. Ernest Gruening of Alaska, an independent liberal, held that "all Vietnam is not worth the life of a single American boy." But many of those who disagreed with him argued, with Richard Russell, that the "national honor" was at stake.

Most congressmen preferred not to oppose the president during an apparent crisis, and Democrats were eager to support him in an election year. The resolution's floor manager, Senator William Fulbright, though chairman of the Foreign Relations Committee, was, like all his colleagues, misinformed about the *Maddox*. To his later regret, Fulbright called the resolution "moderate" and "calculated to prevent the spread of war." Privately he reassured fellow senators who were dubious about granting the president such large powers.

Nevertheless several congressmen took care to say, as one analyst put it, that the "resolution did not constitute a declaration of war, did not abdicate Congressional responsibility for determining national . . . commitments, and did not give the President carte blanche to involve the nation in a major Asian war." Still, the Congress accepted capa-

cious wording. The resolution as passed gave the president the authority to take all measures necessary to repel attack against American forces,
to "prevent further aggression," and to determine when "peace and
security" had returned to Southeast Asia. That language, Johnson
thereafter maintained, was tantamount to a declaration of war. He used
it that way.

But in August 1964, not yet ready to move to a war footing, Johnson
had been approaching North Vietnam through a Canadian interme-
diary with a proposal to end the fighting. If Hanoi would agree to end
support for the Vietcong, the United States in return would at last formally recognize North Vietnam's government and furnish it with substantial economic aid. Otherwise the United States would soon
commence aerial and naval attacks. The offer merely restated and
dressed up the familiar American purpose, for it presumed the independence of South Vietnam, which North Vietnam was resolved to
prevent. Within a week of the retaliatory air strikes of August, the North
Vietnamese prime minister declined any deal that did not assure both
total American withdrawal from Vietnam and Vietcong participation
in a neutral, coalition government in South Vietnam. Ho Chi Minh
had maintained that position for a decade, and Hanoi was to hold it
steadfastly for a decade more. Neither side would yield to the other.

Hanoi's stance risked Johnson's threat, and behind that threat lay
plans of the State and Defense departments for aerial warfare against
North Vietnam. Those plans also directly involved far more American
forces than those already engaged in open or covert South Vietnamese
operations. But Johnson was campaigning as the candidate of peace
and freedom. It was his opponent, Barry Goldwater, criticizing the
president for indecisiveness, who called for heavy bombing of North
Vietnam. Johnson soon replied. In spite of his threat to Hanoi, in spite
of the plans for aerial warfare, he condemned those "eager to enlarge
the conflict." He said: "They call upon us to supply American boys to
do the job that Asian boys should do. They ask us to take reckless
action which might risk the lives of millions and engulf much of Asia."
He wanted his way without those actions, but he knew how tenuous
was that hope. Knowingly, then, he contributed to his administration's
growing record of deceit.

4. Escalation

In part Johnson was deceiving himself. Because, as he later said, he
hated the war in Vietnam, he still hesitated to accept the full implica-

tions of his policy. While he was campaigning in September, a Pentagon study concluded that "the situation in South Vietnam" was "deteriorating with Viet Cong incidents increasing . . . and . . . becoming . . . more successful." To reverse that trend and boost morale in South Vietnam, the president ordered anew the naval patrols in the Gulf of Tonkin that he had temporarily suspended. Then he canceled them again within a week. The Vietcong on November 1, in a surprise attack on an air base near Bien Hoa, killed five American advisers there, but Johnson, in spite of Taylor's urgings, decided not to retaliate. Indeed, he held back in late December even after a Vietcong victory over ARVN forces in a major battle in Binh Gia.

The president was apparently waiting for the completion of a review of American options that he had assigned on the day before the election to a working group headed by William Bundy. Preparation of that report and discussions about it among Johnson's principal advisers disclosed broad but not total agreement on the desirability of a larger American military effort in Vietnam. Only Undersecretary of State George Ball warned against any escalation. It would serve, he said, to provoke a counterescalation. The intelligence services supported his further argument that Hanoi would not yield to bombing, but Ball alone called for "an immediate political solution" and predicted that the global credibility of the United States would lose "by an erosion of confidence in our judgment." Johnson and the others, as they had before and would again, suffered Ball's opinions about Vietnam without really taking them in, just as Ball offered those opinions without really expecting to prevail.

At the other extreme from Ball, Walt Rostow contended that the growth of industry in North Vietnam made that country more vulnerable to strategic bombing than were underdeveloped areas elsewhere in Southeast Asia. But Rostow proposed much more than bombing. He recommended the "introduction of massive forces," ground as well as air forces, aimed at Hanoi and also at China "should the Chinese . . . enter the game." By raising the stakes, he expected to bring Hanoi and Beijing to heel. If they held out, he called on the president, who in that event would have had a huge war on his hands, to exercise "determination and staying power." Rostow wrote with characteristic temerity and characteristic certitude: "The real margin of influence on the outcome . . . flows from the fact that at this stage of history we are the greatest power in the world—if we behave like it."

Many of the president's counselors, albeit with less exuberance than Rostow, shared his fundamental belief, as did most Americans at the time. It was a belief grounded on old and dangerous illusions about American power and American innocence. The United States was presumed to have the strength to defeat any enemy or combination of enemies. In fact, the military buildup since 1961 had given the country a huge arsenal. The land-based nuclear missile force had been expanded to one thousand modern Minutemen, and the submarine-based Polaris force was a growing reality. More relevant to Vietnam, general-purpose forces, organized for swift use and equipped with modern weapons, had grown prodigiously. Combat-ready army divisions had been increased from eleven to sixteen; special forces from three to seven groups; tactical aircraft squadrons from sixteen to thirty-eight; army helicopters from fifty-five hundred to eight thousand. The marines had added to their previous strength a fourth division and a fourth air wing. McNamara and the Joint Chiefs, seemingly eager to test some of that new power in actual combat, had also created STRIKECOM, a major new command group designed to "provide the President with tailored responses for any level of warfare." As the military saw it, the United States was invincible.

The secretary of defense, like the president's other advisers, also presumed that American foreign policy was motivated by unselfish ideals. That kind of thinking permitted the president and his advisers to conclude that the United States was entitled to punish North Vietnam, a Communist state, in order to sustain freedom in South Vietnam, where in fact, there was little freedom, religious or political, and the government lacked popular support. Some measure of punishment inhered in the recommendations Johnson received from those senior civilian advisers—Rusk, McNamara, the Bundys—who stood between George Ball and Walt Rostow. In November 1964 they counseled him to bomb military targets in North Vietnam on a "steady, deliberate," and progressively more serious tempo—a "slow squeeze"—intended to improve the morale and effectiveness of the government in Saigon and to retaliate against Hanoi's rejection of American terms. The Joint Chiefs believed it would be necessary also to use infantry to protect American installations. For the while Johnson approved only continuing operations in Laos to interdict Vietcong supplies and retaliatory bombing in the event of a "spectacular enemy action." He was still wavering, unwilling to appear to retreat, yet anxious to damp public and congressional apprehensions about Vietnam. Privately the president was considering a modified version of Rostow's plan. Bombing in itself would never win the war, he cabled Maxwell Taylor in December. Rather, victory would require "appropriate military strength on the ground on the scene . . . and I . . . am ready to substantially increase the number of Americans in Vietnam if it is necessary."

To resolve the issue, Johnson, on the advice of Taylor, sent McGeorge Bundy to Vietnam. As had Kennedy earlier, so Johnson now revealed his cast of mind by his choice of envoy. Bundy went to Saigon already in favor of bombing North Vietnam—the "slow squeeze." Exposure to the political mess in Saigon hardened his conviction. On February 7, 1965, the Vietcong attacked Pleiku, a major base of the ARVN and its American advisers. In that action eight Americans died and more than a hundred were wounded. The Vietcong suffered few casualties. Bundy immediately cabled Johnson that the Vietcong's "energy and persistence are astonishing." The "grim" situation, he added, demanded "a generalized pattern of reprisal" to offset the "outrages in the South" without seeming to attempt a conquest of the North. Continuous bombing of North Vietnam would involve "significant U.S. air losses" and higher American casualties, but the cost was cheap compared with the "cost of defeat," and the bombing would result in "a sharp . . . increase in optimism in the South."

With the losses at Pleiku Johnson had "had enough." Though Mike Mansfield and Vice President Humphrey dissented (Humphrey was banished to the "doghouse" for a year), the president gave orders for Operation Flaming Dart, sorties by airplanes from the carrier USS *Ranger* to bomb military targets in North Vietnam. Flaming Dart II soon followed, to be succeeded in March 1965 by Rolling Thunder, the sustained and increasing bombing of North Vietnam. By the end of that month hundreds of American planes were involved, and thousands of bombs, many of them napalm bombs, which set off devastating fires. On many evenings by that time the president devoted hours in the White House basement to picking targets. He had brought the country into a major air war in Vietnam, and he was in command of it.

In order to protect the airfield at Da Nang, a large base for American bombers, General Westmoreland asked for two battalions of marines. General Taylor warned the White House that the step would open the way to a major buildup of American forces. American soldiers, he predicted, would fail, as had the French, to adapt to jungle fighting and to "distinguish between a Vietcong and a friendly Vietnamese farmer." Undeterred, Johnson in March sent in the marines and less than a month later authorized another two battalions as well as eighteen to twenty thousand more troops for logistical support. At that time he also approved "a change of mission" for the marines "to permit their more active use." With that permission, Westmoreland ordered the marines' employment in search and destroy missions against the Vietcong. American boys had now begun to fight a land war in Asia.

As his advisers had suggested he should, the president tried to excuse the escalations and their implications. The State Department instructed American diplomats to describe North Vietnam as an aggressor state that the United States was helping resist. That interpretation preached only to the converted. Even before 1956, when the United States had encouraged Diem to refuse to permit the elections prescribed by the Geneva accords of 1954, Hanoi had considered itself engaged in a civil war to unify the nation. To that end, Ho moved to his affiliations with the Soviet Union and China. The treaty of 1954 establishing the Southeast Asia Treaty Organization (SEATO), which the State Department cited as authorizing American policy in Vietnam, did not mandate the American presence there. France criticized that presence, and Britain sent no troops, though both were SEATO signatories.

At home the administration during the spring of 1965 tried to forestall criticism by withholding or distorting information about developments in Vietnam. The president treated the deployment of marines at Da Nang as a temporary expedient and denied any change in strategy after he had given Westmoreland latitude in using them. Up to a point his dissimulation worked. Almost all the American people remained supportive, as did Congress, but Johnson began to lose the credibility he needed when journalists in Vietnam reported home about the activities of American soldiers. Among the admittedly dubious at that stage of the war, wholly apart from radical dissenters, were the seasoned newspaper columnists James Reston and Walter Lippmann and a group of influential senators—no longer just Mansfield and Russell but also Republicans George Aiken, John Sherman Cooper, and Jacob Javits and Democrats Frank Church, George McGovern, and J. William Fulbright. Johnson kept Church in line by threatening to deny his state of Idaho a dam, but he never forgave Fulbright for his mounting criticisms on the Senate floor. Then and later the president put no stock in any suggestion of his critics for a compromise solution. Compromise, as Johnson came to realize, was no part of Ho's intention.

But the Johnson treatment—the alternation of kindness and cruelty—was not working at all in Vietnam. While McGeorge Bundy had been in Saigon, Aleksei Kosygin, the Soviet prime minister, had been in Hanoi on a mission to persuade the North Vietnamese to give up Chinese for exclusively Soviet sustenance and to move, if possible, toward a compromise with the Saigon government. Operation Flaming Dart undercut Kosygin. Though he would probably have failed anyhow, thereafter he and his Soviet superior, Communist party chief Leonid Brezhnev, became increasingly the captives of Ho Chi Minh, as for his part Johnson was the hostage of the Saigon regime. Neither superpower, once its grandeur was engaged, was willing to risk the loss of face that the collapse of its client would presumably entail. Both clients exploited their resulting leverage.

Unable to instill stability or efficiency in Saigon, Johnson attempted to sway Ho with the kind of offer that worked so well on Capitol Hill. In a televised speech on April 7, 1965, the president said the United States would not withdraw from Vietnam "either openly or under the cloak of a meaningless agreement," but he urged the North Vietnamese to join in "unconditional discussion." He also promised, if peace resulted, to finance the development of the Mekong River on a scale comparable with the Tennessee Valley Authority. Johnson doubtless had a fantasy of converting the Mekong area into a thriving industrial and agricultural region served by cheap hydroelectric power, a model for all Asia. "Old Ho can't turn me down," he told Bill Moyers. But Ho's prime minister declined any discussions until the American bombing ended and, as before, until the United States accepted a coalition government in Saigon. In May the president announced a "pause" in the bombing and asked the North Vietnamese for an "equally constructive" response, but like Johnson, they would negotiate only on their own basis and only from strength.

As they had planned to, the North Vietnamese increased the flow of men and supplies to the Vietcong, whose pending offensive, so General Westmoreland informed Washington early in June, threatened to destroy the ARVN. Westmoreland again called for additional American forces. Less than a week later another of Saigon's tottering civilian coalitions fell to another military coup. Now General Nguyen Van Thieu, as head of state, and Colonel Nguyen Cao Ky, as prime minister, assumed office. Though a shrewd and tough politician, Thieu was arguably the greediest of the successors to Diem; Ky, an admirer of Adolf Hitler, was perhaps the most flamboyant. Attired ordinarily in a tight jacket, tapered trousers, and pointed shoes, Ky looked as if Hollywood had cast him, as one American said, in the "role of a sax player in a . . . Manila night club." The government of that obnoxious brace, "absolutely the bottom of the barrel" in Williams Bundy's assessment, was to survive and profit when Johnson acceded to Westmoreland's request for heavy reinforcements.

First, the president again undertook a long review of policy during July 1965. Rusk repeated his familiar refrain about Vietnam: "The

Johnson with Thieu and Ky: "Bottom of the barrel."

integrity of the U.S. commitment is the principal pillar of peace throughout the world." The Joint Chiefs supported Westmoreland's proposal with an accompanying recommendation for calling up the National Guard and other reserve units. That mobilization would have put the nation on a full war footing. McNamara's chief adviser on Vietnam, Assistant Secretary of Defense John McNaughton, had already questioned such an action. The American purpose, he wrote, was no more than 10 percent to permit the people of South Vietnam "to enjoy a . . . freer way of life," no more than 20 percent to keep South Vietnam from China, but 70 percent "to avoid a humiliating U.S. defeat." That analysis interpreted Johnson's policy shrewdly. American involvement in Vietnam—initiated by Eisenhower to contain China and the Soviet Union, continued by Kennedy partly because of his fear of the domestic repercussions of withdrawal—had become, aside from those continuing purposes, largely an exercise in protecting American credibility.

Secretary McNamara now saw no way to bring North Vietnam to negotiate, and thus no way to avoid humiliation, except by acceding substantially to the Joint Chiefs "even though casualties will increase and the war will continue for some time." He believed the North Vietnamese were about to move from guerrilla to conventional warfare, and he therefore called for doubling the number of American troops in Vietnam to some two hundred thousand men in all. McNamara also favored increased bombing of Hanoi and the harbor city of Haiphong. Now McGeorge Bundy disagreed, predicting continual guerrilla warfare, for which American troops were ill prepared. McNamara's proposal, Bundy wrote, was "a slippery slope toward U.S. responsibility and corresponding fecklessness on the Vietnamese side." That was the opinion of the CIA and, predictably, of George Ball, who urged the president at the least to "limit our liabilities in South Vietnam." So did Johnson's friend Clark Clifford.

It fell to William Bundy to define a middle way, one to defer the unrestricted bombing of Hanoi and the full buildup of ground forces while testing the military efficacy of a contingent of twenty-five thousand more men, Westmoreland's minimum suggestion. That solution obviated the need to call up the reserves, which would alarm Congress and the public. Indeed, the middle way had been Johnson's preference all along. It permitted him to instruct McNamara to plan new expenditures of only three to four hundred million dollars. Though the Defense Department expected that the probable figure for the balance of the year would approach two billion dollars, Johnson on the basis of his unrealistically lower estimate would avoid asking Congress for the formidable, larger sum. Had he done otherwise, he might have impeded the enactment of Medicare. Further, by letting the press know that a call-up was under consideration, Johnson in rejecting it gave the appearance of moderation without sacrificing anything he actually intended to do. That appearance would reassure the Chinese government as well as the American people. Before the end of July the president had brought all his advisers except Ball to accept his course. That outcome typified government under Johnson. The essence of the consensus he constantly said he sought, the product of his process of "reasoning together," was the endorsement of decisions he had already begun to reach.

In fact, the decision of July 1965, like the earlier decisions that resulted in Rolling Thunder and the landing of marines at Da Nang, constituted just another, though a weighty, step in the policy that the administration had been following since before the Tonkin Gulf Resolution. The war had become an American war. As one veteran Pentagon analyst later wrote, the incrementalism in 1965 "did not follow from illusion about victory around each corner; it followed from the strategy of progressive pressure and the progressive failure of strategy." The authorization of forty-four battalions also sent Johnson down the slippery slope McGeorge Bundy had forecast. By the end of 1965 there were 184,000 American soldiers in Vietnam. That number continued to rise: some 385,000 by the end of 1966; more than 485,000 by the end of 1967; more than 536,000 by the end of 1968. So it was, too, with Rolling Thunder. By the end of 1968 Americans had dropped 3.2 million tons of bombs in Vietnam, more than they had used during all of World War II.

5. Brutalization

During the summer and fall of 1965 the Americanized war in Vietnam fell into enduring patterns. General Westmoreland used the troops he received to protect American supply and air bases and to undertake search and destroy missions against the enemy. American forces also joined the ARVN in the pacification program in rural areas. That program was designed to protect villagers in South Vietnam from attack by the Vietcong while assisting their economic development. Within limits those tactics seemed at first to work. United States marines secured and expanded the area around the growing base at Da Nang, and an American army division defeated the enemy in a major engagement nearby. In that battle three hundred Americans died, but the Vietcong lost two thousand men.

That ratio persuaded Westmoreland that he would win if he had enough soldiers. But body counts were unreliable measures of progress, especially as time went on and ARVN commanders, eager to please the Americans, regularly exaggerated the figures they reported. So did American officers, who, like their counterparts in other wars, overestimated the impact of their victories. In any case, body counts begged the question, for the measure of victory in Vietnam departed from conventional standards. The president and his senior civilian advisers accepted instead the definition of John McNaughton: "The word 'win' . . . means that we succeed in demonstrating to the VC that they cannot win." That demonstration would, of course, have to convince the North Vietnamese, too. Since the North Vietnamese were prepared to fight indefinitely and had ample manpower to risk, Westmoreland's favorable "kill ratio" did not deter them. They would fight a long war of attrition, but the American public was bound eventually to tire of increasing casualties.

So, too, the conquest of enemy territory, a conventional gauge of progress toward military victory, had little significance in Vietnam. When they retreated, the Vietcong merely melted into the local population until they could regroup and attack again. In July 1965 McNamara and Westmoreland had expected Hanoi to begin to fight a conventional war, but the North Vietnamese did not oblige. After a debate of their own about strategy, they held largely to guerrilla tactics, at which, with continued reinforcements from the North, the Vietcong excelled. Those tactics undercut the pacification program, for American soldiers "liberating" a village, even with the help of the ARVN, were unable to differentiate between friend and enemy. Liberation often entailed the forceful confinement of villagers behind barbed wire or their removal to barbed-wire barricades far from their homes. After one evacuation, as an American major put it with the logic peculiar to the military mind, "It became necessary to destroy the town in order to save it." Millions of villagers chose to escape liberation by fleeing to the overcrowded cities, where they were able to subsist only as day laborers or mendicants, wards of American largess. That strategy of "liberation" had the predictable effect of alienating those it purported to free.

The strategy of bombing North Vietnam proved equally anomalous. President Johnson continued to control the selection of targets. He agreed with McNamara that the United States "should avoid bombing which runs a high risk of escalation into war with the Soviets or Chinese and which is likely to appall allies and friends"—those friends being the American public. The administration depicted the air strikes as "surgical" in their concentration on military objectives, as somehow remote from North Vietnamese civilians. In fact, there were many civilian casualties. People lived or worked close to military targets, and bombing was an inexact exercise. Bomber crews, threatened by flak and interceptors, often had to release their deadly loads far from designated targets. But even if Johnson had allowed the bombing of northern cities without stint or let, the United States could not have destroyed the military industry of North Vietnam. Much of it was located in the Soviet Union and China, and most of the rest consisted of small-scale facilities easily rebuilt or moved underground by Hanoi's large, patriotic, and disciplined labor force. Indeed, senior American officers, supported by Walt Rostow, proved entirely wrong in assuring the president that they could cripple North Vietnam if he permitted the bombing of refineries and storage depots for petroleum, oil, and lubricants (POL). During the summer of 1966, with Johnson's consent, extensive POL air strikes cut out some 70 percent of North Vietnam's original storage capacity but left "undiminished" the flow of men and supplies to the South as the "resourceful" North Vietnamese switched "to small, dispersed sites, almost impossible to bomb."

Attacks on the supply trails did damage North Vietnamese camps, motor vehicles, and field hospitals, but matériel and reinforcements for the Vietcong kept coming on foot or bicycles, hidden by the jungle. Since the jungle also provided secluded staging areas for groups of Vietcong, American tacticians utilized chemical defoliants and napalm to strip and destroy the trees and other growth. The resulting conversion of thousands of verdant acres into wastelands despoiled Vietnam without deterring the Vietcong. So, too, the North Vietnamese, angered by civilian casualties, met American attacks on their cities with crippling gunfire and high morale. Wholly apart from the loss in American pilots and crews killed or captured, the toll in American aircraft damaged or downed exceeded by far the value of the targets destroyed. But above all, no arithmetic of death or damage could persuade the government of North Vietnam that it was going to lose the war.

The burden of the war fell heavily on the Vietnamese people, North and South, bombed or displaced, killed or maimed in their villages and cities and in battle. The Americanization of the war also profoundly altered the economy and social order of South Vietnam. Catering to the Americans or stealing from them became the dominating industries. Senior officers of the ARVN excelled at both functions, as did many of their subordinates. United States army jeeps and motorscooters, small arms and ammunition, food, clothing, and accessories—shipped to South Vietnam for American or ARVN troops—were always available for a price in black markets in Saigon and other cities, as were television sets and refrigerators imported by those favored with the appropriate licenses. Services for American soldiers throve: hotels, nightclubs, tailor shops, massage parlors, bordellos, and processing and vending establishments for all kinds of narcotics. Americans were shoving so much money into Vietnam that it overflowed normal commercial channels and poured into the hands of those shrewd or powerful enough to get it. The Vietnamese were not peculiarly sinful or corruptible. The presence of so many American soldiers and so much American money had been the same during World War II in Chungking, Trinidad, Naples, and elsewhere. But very few beneficiaries of American extravagance had ever done as well for themselves as did General Nguyen Van Thieu, who accumulated millions in gold.

The burden of the war also fell on the American soldiers, sailors, marines, and airmen who fought it. They were as brave, as confident,

The burden of war fell on the Vietnamese people.

and as well equipped as Americans had ever been. The armed services saw to it that the men at the front, as well as those behind the lines, received many of the comforts of home—cigarettes, beer, Coca-Cola, toilet paper, hot meals on holidays, in all by 1967 an average of a hundred pounds of supplies for each man each day. Much of that freight consisted of the most advanced nonnuclear weaponry and attendant spare parts and communications gear. Many young soldiers, especially in the early years of the war, believed in the American cause and in themselves. "My generation," one of them recalled, "came of age totally post-World War II. We were the savior democracy . . . and I was bred to believe that . . . you served your country." War proved to be a "total cultural shock." Sloshing through the rice paddies, "you didn't think politics. . . . The reality was survival, keeping warm, keeping dry, getting your mail." A marine remembered seeing "the John Wayne flicks. We were invincible. So . . . every one went in with the attitude . . . 'we're going to wipe them out.' . . . Until they saw the realities. . . . The first guy I saw hit, I was just shaking. . . . The whole John Wayne thing went out the window." Another said he and his buddies marched in carrying, "along with our packs and rifles, the implicit conviction that the Vietcong could be quickly beaten. We kept the packs and rifles; the conviction, we lost."

Like soldiers in all wars, the Americans in Vietnam experienced a constant mix of fear and nostalgia. But "the soldiers in Vietnam," one major general said, "were the best I'd ever seen on any battlefield. . . . They did their job. . . . Everybody's afraid, but to do your job you have to put your fear down. If you're not afraid in combat, you're either a fool or a liar." As ever, fear generated anger, and anger, hate. All wars brutalized their combatants. To Americans, all the Vietnamese, ARVN or enemy, looked alike, spoke the same language, might be tomorrow's sniper, might arrange the next day's ambush. Mixed with fear and hate and anger, that uncertainty on occasion provoked the cruelties associated with the war, most vividly in civilian minds at home with the American massacre of a hundred peasants at the village of My Lai. The enemy often behaved no better. But My Lai and other episodes almost as ghastly, while understandable, were outrageous and inexcusable. The atrocities in Vietnam made it impossible to believe in American innocence any longer. And the terror and horror of the war were continually the shocking subject of evening television news.

As the enemy kept fighting, as casualties mounted, the experience of war eroded the American sense of mission and of invincibility. Military policy rotated men home after a year in Vietnam. Those on combat patrol and those flying sorties counted the passing days, many of them rife with the possibility of death or disfigurement. The North Vietnamese and the Vietcong were a tough, tenacious foe, stealthy, brave, quick to kill, by no means immune from brutality of their own. Particularly as the war wore on, the resulting terror and loneliness, the unrelieved anxiety led most Americans to seek escape, often in alcohol when it was at hand or often in marijuana or heroin, which were nearly always available. By 1967 and 1968 most American soldiers could not continue to believe that the United States was winning the endless, grinding war.

6. PENUMBRAS OF WAR

There were no glimmerings of peace. Late in 1965 Henry Cabot Lodge, as militant as ever, returned to Saigon as American ambassador, and so, for a brief visit, did Robert McNamara, the self-assured secretary of defense. The American buildup was reaching the end of its first phase, but concurrently the enemy had increased its forces almost 50 percent. Westmoreland had asked to begin a second phase with another 154,000 men. With rare public candor, McNamara admitted to the press that "it will be a long war." To the president he reported the dramatic increase in "infiltration from the North" and the willingness of the enemy forces "to stand and fight." In spite of American naval and air attacks, they could also support their growing armies at the probable level of operation. Just to hold its own, the United States would need the additional troops; the alternative was "to go now for a compromise solution."

In either case, McNamara recommended a "three- or four-week pause in the bombing." The administration, he argued, "must lay a foundation in the minds of the American public and in world opinion for such an enlarged phase of the war and . . . we should give NVN [North Vietnamese] a face-saving chance to stop the aggression." After another round of consultations the president, admittedly puzzled, took McNamara's advice. He intended no compromise. Without changing his objective, he hoped the bombing pause would persuade the North Vietnamese to bargain, but Hanoi was just as stubborn as Washington. In the event, however useful for public relations, the pause could only delay further escalation.

Johnson made the most of the bombing pause, which began on Christmas Day 1965. He sent senior American envoys to vouch for his sincerity to the leaders of forty nations. He informed North Vietnam through the American Embassy in Burma that he might extend the pause if Hanoi made "a serious contribution toward peace." But the pause was no standstill. American ground forces began two major offensives during the week after Christmas. Rejecting the pause as a "trick," the government in Hanoi demanded permanent and unconditional cessation of the bombing as a condition of any settlement. In January Johnson ordered the bombing to resume. He and those around him remained self-deluded. "Thieu and Ky are men of high leadership," Humphrey reported in February 1966, after a visit to Saigon. "Vietnam," Johnson said, was "part of a larger struggle" for the safety of the free world.

So the familiar pattern persisted during 1966 and 1967. Westmoreland and the Joint Chiefs asked for more troops and for the lifting of restrictions on strategic bombing. Johnson granted some but never all of each request. The administration authorized various "peace offensives," one accompanied by another bombing halt, none making any real concessions to North Vietnam, which, conceding nothing in return, met every escalation with increased infiltration.

During the continuing impasse the administration's preoccupation with Vietnam, as George Kennan said, limited resources available for the nation's other global obligations. Had China been less self-absorbed or the Soviet Union less wary of the Chinese, the war in Vietnam might have proved more embarrassing to American foreign policy than it did. As it was, the American presence in the Mediterranean and the Middle East was marginal, and in Europe the NATO nations grew more and more anxious about the capability of the United States to provide enough support in case of a conventional war. That anxiety derived partly from Charles de Gaulle's independently nationalistic policies. Nursing his resentment of the United States, pursuing as ever the grandeur he attached to France, de Gaulle continued on his separate way. He recognized China. He criticized the American war in Vietnam. More important, in 1966 he announced the withdrawal, long imminent, of all French forces from the military command of NATO and the termination of permission for NATO or American bases in France. Aware of de Gaulle's fierce independence, Johnson with becoming equanimity accepted the general's terms as nonnegotiable. He also looked to Great Britain and Germany to maintain the strength of the Western alliance. Great Britain could not afford the cost of the responsibility, but West Germany picked up some of the expenses of keeping American troops in Europe, expenses Congress was reluctant any longer to defray on top of those for the war in Vietnam.

British Prime Minister Harold Wilson, the leader of the Labour party, which won control of Parliament in 1965, had serious reservations about the Vietnam War. It offended the sensitivities, political and ethical, of his party's left, and it ran counter to the purpose of the Geneva agreement of 1954, which he respected as much as did the Tories who had negotiated it. A donnish, pipe-smoking, seemingly deliberative man, Wilson was uncomfortable with Lyndon Johnson, to whom he never gave the warm and firm support that Macmillan had given Kennedy. In 1965 Wilson urged the president not to bomb "oil targets near Hanoi and Haiphong." He cabled: "The possible military benefits . . . do not . . . outweigh the political disadvantages. . . . If this action is taken we

President Johnson and Prime Minister Harold Wilson: The war offended Wilson's sensibilities.

shall have to dissociate ourselves from it," though not openly from American policy in general. In 1967, while Aleksei Kosygin was visiting London, Wilson made a major effort to arrange a bombing pause in Vietnam as a prelude to negotiations intended to arrange a reciprocal cessation of the augmentation of forces there. Kosygin appeared to agree, and the Johnson administration seemed at first to encourage the plan; but at the eleventh hour, blaming North Vietnam, the State Department abruptly cut off discussions. Thereafter Wilson and Johnson preserved only a semblance of the "special relationship." Their mutual alienation, like de Gaulle's dissociation, reflecting in part European dissatisfaction with the Vietnam War, weakened NATO, the most critical of all American alliances.

Under the circumstances, it was prudent—and natural—for Johnson, as he intended to in any event, to continue Kennedy's efforts to ease relations with the Soviet Union. It was also prudent for the Soviet Union to reciprocate. Apart from Soviet concerns about China, internal tensions in the Politburo had accompanied the fall of Khrushchev and later the ascendancy of Brezhnev over Kosygin. With each world power eager to avoid needlessly disturbing the other, the two reached a few mutually beneficial agreements. In 1966 both signed a United Nations treaty internationalizing and demilitarizing space. The following year President Johnson, on the hot line to Kosygin, discouraged possible Soviet interference in the Six-Day War between Israel and its Arab neighbors. In 1968 the United States and the Soviet Union concluded a treaty, signed by fifty other nations but not by France or China, on the nonproliferation of nuclear weapons.

Nevertheless, the nuclear arms race continued, echoed by the rivalry in Vietnam, with the Soviet Union moving forward with its antiballistic missile (ABM) program. For his part, Johnson could not persuade Congress to spend the money necessary for an American ABM program equivalent to the Russians'. Johnson's hope for a treaty limiting both offensive and defensive nuclear arms foundered in 1968, when Soviet troops entered Czechoslovakia in force to put down a flourishing democratic movement there. The thaw in the cold war, such as it was, left the two superpowers still on guard against each other, on guard also against China, and armed with growing arsenals more than sufficient to blow up the world.

For Johnson, as McGeorge Bundy later wrote, the use of a nuclear bomb in Vietnam "was quite literally unthinkable." The president took pains, too, to avoid risking war with China. But his administration escalated its rhetoric about the Chinese. Secretary of State Dean Rusk continually exaggerated the danger from China. So did Vice President Humphrey, who held that "the threat to world peace is militant, aggressive Asian communism." The United States, he said, was fighting in Vietnam for "the future of our country." That was nonsense. China could not directly damage the United States, and the war in Vietnam had small deterrent effect on China. The United States had been containing China successfully for a decade from a ring of powerful offshore bases in Japan, Taiwan, Okinawa, and the Philippines.

By 1968, 40 percent of the nation's combat-ready divisions, half of the tactical air power, and a third of the naval strength were at war in Vietnam. Johnson had therefore become cautious even with rhetoric. In January of that year the North Koreans captured the USS *Pueblo*, an American gunboat and spy ship. The South Koreans urged the United States to retaliate, but the president, while reinforcing the American position in South Korea, otherwise confined his response to diplomatic measures. The incident, in the view of a senior Pentagon civilian, "revealed the poignant truth that the country's military, but even more its psychological, resources had been stretched . . . thin by . . . the Vietnam involvement."

Troublesome in its impact on American foreign relations, the Vietnam War and its costs gravely compromised the programs of the Great Society and their potential effectiveness. The war became an obsession for the president that consumed his emotional energy and warped his political perceptions and priorities. He did not ask for full funding of the environmental legislation Congress passed. His budget for social programs continued to rise slowly, but much of the butter had begun to melt into the guns even before the Council of Economic Advisers began to warn Johnson in 1966 that federal spending, enlarged by military appropriations, was creating deficits that were overstimulating the economy and spurring inflation. Not until 1967 did Johnson ask Congress for a surtax, bound to be unpopular, to lift revenues and reduce the rising deficit. By that time the Republicans had made substantial gains in the 1966 off year elections, and with their help, southern Democrats on the House Ways and Means Committee, led by Wilbur Mills, could block the president's proposal. By 1968, when the surtax was belatedly enacted, inflation had become a national problem, soon to be pushed higher by worldwide increases in commodity prices.

The underfunding of reform not only slowed social progress but also increasingly reduced confidence, especially among the poor, about the administration's actual intentions. Johnson's rhetoric had lifted expectations that, particularly among poor blacks, foundered on frustrations attributable partly to the slow pace of change. The president's failure to face the budgetary implications of the war, his refusal to admit, until too late, the need for new taxes, his effort through that delay to avoid a test of the nation's willingness to sacrifice for the war, skewered macroeconomic policy. Keynesian principles called for tax increases by 1966. When the country instead paid for the war indirectly through inflation, which was most costly for the poor and the middle class, those adversely affected often incorrectly blamed the Keynesians for a condition that the Keynesian CEA had tried unsuccessfully to persuade the president to forestall.

Early and late, Congress voted for appropriations that the administration demonstrated as necessary for the men fighting in Vietnam. The soldiers could not be penalized for serving their country. But not all the funds requested were really needed to support the troops. Each of the armed services attempted, as usual, to maximize its appropriations and its share of total authorizations. Each counted upon help on the Hill from industries eager for contracts to manufacture the arms and the hardware of war. Each of those industries in turn had factories or other facilities in election districts where congressional incumbents usually saw in military contracts more jobs and favors for their constituents. The war in Vietnam did not create the interrelationship of public and private bureaucracies that Eisenhower had called the military-industrial complex, but it extended that network's influence in Washington. Even McNamara's careful budgeting could not prevent the excesses, the waste, the technological follies, and sometimes the chicanery of military procurement.

Because the war in Vietnam underscored the need for controlling the defense establishment, some critics of the war blamed the establishment for American policy in Vietnam. Those who did so miscalculated. Johnson acted as he did because of convictions: the conviction that otherwise he would lose politically; more important, the conviction shared by his close friends and advisers that the safety of the world was at stake unless the United States stood firmly in Vietnam, otherwise the nation would lose its credibility. That was the honest opinion, for two major examples, of Abe Fortas, probably the president's most intimate political friend, and of Walt Rostow, who in 1966 succeeded McGeorge Bundy as the president's national security adviser. Like so many members of their generation, Johnson most significantly, they were hostages of memories of World War II. They misread the lesson of history. By appeasing Hitler, they recalled, the British and French had encouraged Nazi aggression. Now, they argued, any accommodation with Ho Chi Minh would invite the spread of totalitarian communism first in Asia and then throughout the world. "No more Munichs," they repeated again and again. That metaphor vastly understated the dangers Hitler had posed and overstated the strength and ambition of Ho and his allies. Nevertheless, it fed Johnson's comforting delusion that American involvement in Vietnam was preventing a third world war.

So the war went on. Its costs mounted, especially in the devastation of the cities and villages and forests of Vietnam, in the deaths of thousands of Vietnamese, in the maimings and killings of hundreds of Americans. Much of that horror flowed graphically through television to the homes of the American people. Worst of all from the president's angle of vision, his escalations in Vietnam failed to achieve his purpose. No wonder Johnson hated the war. He could not see how to avoid it, he could not end it, and he believed it was destroying his beloved Great Society. Further, increasingly after 1965 the war and its waste were exciting corrosive dissent within the United States.

9

Polarization

On August 6, 1965, Lyndon Johnson celebrated his signing of the Voting Rights Act. "Today is a triumph for freedom," he said to a national television audience, "as huge as any victory that's ever been won on any battlefield." The leaders of the major civil rights organizations who attended the signing ceremony agreed with Johnson. Several of them, deeply moved by the Great Society programs, called him the greatest president American blacks had ever had. Martin Luther King, Jr., discomforted though he was by the escalation of the war in Vietnam, believed that Johnson had "amazing sensitivity to the difficult problems that Negro Americans face." King had just told the president that more federal legislation was needed to combat de facto segregation in housing, schooling, and employment in the North. The rising cost of the Vietnam War made Johnson less amenable to that counsel than he yet admitted or than King yet realized. Nevertheless, King's alert was timely.

1. WATTS

Less than a week later, on the evening of August 11, with Los Angeles simmering in a heat wave, a highway patrolman arrested a young black man for speeding. Called to the scene to control a gathering crowd, one police officer hit an innocent black observer with his billy club, and another dragged a young black woman into the street. After the police had departed, the crowd threw rocks at passing automobiles, attacked some white motorists, and set several cars on fire. The next day city officials rebuffed efforts by community spokesmen to mediate between the police and the residents of the area, a part of Watts, the ghetto of Los Angeles. In less than two days, in the absence of any police response, crowds elsewhere in Watts began looting, fire-bombing, and otherwise destroying property "in order to drive white 'exploiters' out of the ghetto." The National Guard, whose help the police chief requested, and the police themselves retaliated with firearms. Before the six-day riot subsided, thirty-four blacks were killed, nine were injured, and thirty-five million dollars of property was damaged.

Martin Luther King, Jr., had been fearing that something like Watts might occur in some northern city. Desolate about the riot, he flew to Los Angeles to implore his fellow blacks to turn away from looting and burning. In the rubble of Watts, young black men heckled him. "We won," one group exulted. How could they say that, King asked, with so many blacks dead and their community destroyed? "We won," an unemployed youth replied, "because we made the whole world pay attention to us." The rioting, as King understood, was the desperate cry of one "so fed up with the powerlessness of his cave existence that he asserts that he would rather be dead than ignored."

King also understood that the rioting, however provoked, however therapeutic, was illegal and counterproductive. As he had expected, many white Americans responded to the episode by blaming only the ghetto blacks. The Los Angeles police chief dismissed the rioters as criminals and "monkeys," the mayor insisted that the city had no racial prejudice, and the president denounced urban violence. As a liberal white lawyer later said wistfully about Watts, "Everything seemed to collapse. The days of 'We Shall Overcome' were over."

Though the race riot in Watts came to symbolize the beginning of three summers of recurrent explosions of black frustrations in northern American cities, there had been recent earlier episodes of racial violence, most dramatically in Birmingham in 1963, as well as in Jacksonville, Harlem, Jersey City, and Milwaukee in 1964. Ghettos in other cities, in Newark, New Jersey, for one example, were uglier and more oppressive than Watts, which had some treelined streets and middle-class houses. Indeed, the Urban League considered the condition of blacks in Los Angeles unmatched in any other major American city. But in Los Angeles, as elsewhere, most ghetto residents dwelt in slums, confined not by laws but by prejudice operating through economic and political institutions dominated by whites. Urban political machines, providing only token recognition for blacks, allocated to the ghettos inadequate and inequitable funds for education, housing, sanitation, and police protection. White landlords, their properties filled with blacks who were excluded from other areas by unwritten real estate agreements, charged exorbitant rents for substandard flats. White store-keepers gouged black customers, who lacked automobiles to drive to shopping centers outside their neighborhoods. That immobility also kept blacks from reaching jobs in the outer cities and suburbs to which manufacturing was moving. Discrimination in employment reduced the availability of jobs for blacks. Poor prospects as well as poor schools contributed to the high incidence of dropouts among black students, of whom strikingly few completed high school. Throughout the ghetto, residents continually feared the spreading crime that flourished in the absence of law enforcement and on the traffic in numbers, prostitution, and drugs.

In the North among the majority of urban blacks, recognizably an underclass, hope withered as the tinsel of a prosperous society remained tantalizingly beyond reach. Against those conditions, civil disobedience seemed irrelevant, partly because there were no obvious laws against which to demonstrate. Segregation and discrimination were rooted instead in caste and class. So rage grew, and rage produced the riots.

2. BLACK POWER

Black rage also fractured the civil rights movement. The angry militants of the northern cities had kindred spirits among southern black separatists, who were scornful of the tactics of civil disobedience and of the rate of social change. Those separatists took some of their emerging doctrines from the Lost-Found Nation of Islam—the Black Muslims, and their leader, Elijah Muhammad. Elijah, who rejected Christianity as a white faith that deluded black men and women, had carried his gospel of black solidarity to the disadvantaged of the ghettos. His disciples adopted his prescription for abstinence from drugs and liquor and promiscuous sex, as well as for hard work and self-education. Muslim leaders, particularly Elijah's fiery lieutenant Malcolm X, also called for hostility toward whites. Malcolm urged blacks to separate from white society into "a land of our *own*, where we can ... lift up our moral standards." To achieve that end, he argued, blacks needed a "bloody" revolution. Malcolm broke with Elijah in 1964 and turned toward integrationist solutions before his assassination in 1965.

*Martin Luther King, Jr., and Malcolm X: They delivered
different sermons.*

But his earlier preachings and autobiography influenced young blacks,
North and South, who identified with his message of black nationalism
and black pride.

Two of the most prominent young militants, Stokely Carmichael of
SNCC and Floyd McKissick of CORE, were committed to radical separatism. Each was working, at times in harness with the other, to take
over his own organization, to achieve national primacy in the civil rights
movement, and to convert that movement to a strategy of class action

and violent confrontation. In formulating their radical doctrines, both Carmichael and McKissick drew heavily on Malcolm X. Carmichael, a native of Trinidad who received his collegiate education at Howard University, had never believed in the philosophy of nonviolence, though as an inveterate opportunist he subscribed to the tactic of nonviolence in the struggle for voting rights in Alabama and Mississippi. A tough, cynical, fearless man, he had concluded after the defeat of the Mississippi Freedom party at the Democratic convention of 1964 that black people could not rely on white allies. He found a supporting text in Frantz Fanon's *Wretched of the Earth*, which exerted a major influence on American black radicals. Fanon, also a West Indian, married aspects of Marxist ideology to an exhortative black separatism in his angry indictment of European and American treatment of "colonized peoples," especially black people in Africa and in the United States. Rejecting both compromise and nonviolence, he exalted the therapeutic value for blacks of violence as a "cleansing force" that would expunge fear and restore self-respect.

Fanon's manifesto, originally directed against French rule in Algeria, gave a revolutionary twist to the platform of Carmichael, McKissick, and their youthful adherents both in the South and increasingly in the ghettos. In the spring of 1966 Carmichael and his faction gained control of SNCC, as had McKissick and his associates in CORE, which then expelled whites from its ranks. The two leaders, eager to challenge less radical civil rights organizations, soon found a ripe occasion to do so. It arose in June, when James Meredith, the hero of the integration of the University of Mississippi in 1962, began a personal march from Memphis to Jackson to inspire Mississippi blacks to exercise their rights to vote. On the second day of that march a white assailant fired a shotgun at Meredith, who was wounded all over his body. Civil rights organizations then sent representatives to Memphis to consider how to continue Meredith's cause. McKissick and Carmichael, aggressive in their new authority, constituted the left at that meeting, offset on the right by the older and more prudent Roy Wilkins of the NAACP and Whitney Young of the Urban League, as well as by Martin Luther King, Jr.

The meeting came at a difficult time for King. He and his associates in SCLC had joined a nonviolent campaign against segregation and poverty in Chicago, where his personal participation was important. He had also recently spoken out for the first time, in spite of the advice of his closest friends, against the war in Vietnam. As a committed champion of peace he felt he had to do so, particularly since the war, as even the president acknowledged, was limiting the availability of funds to fight poverty. But Johnson, resentful of any opposition, stepped up FBI surveillance of King and terminated King's access to the White House. That hostility was bound to hamper SCLC's campaign in Chicago, as was also the diversion of King's personal energies to the Meredith March.

Yet King had no choice. He could not turn away form Meredith's cause at a time when the civil rights movement was splintering. At the meeting in Memphis the NAACP and the Urban League wanted to bring whites into a nonviolent demonstration to raise support for the Johnson administration's 1966 civil rights bill, which banned discrimination in the rental or sale of housing. With McKissick's backing, Stokely Carmichael rejected that possibility and demanded instead a manifesto condemning Johnson's policies as inadequate. He also insisted on arranging to protect the Meredith march with a group of armed blacks and on minimizing the role of whites. Deliberately to offend Wilkins and Young, Carmichael, as he later admitted, "started acting crazy . . . started cursing real bad." Disgusted, Wilkins and Young withdrew. Their departure, as Carmichael had intended, prevented King from holding a center position, where he might have been most influential. King had sat silently through Carmichael's diatribe in the hope that he could keep Carmichael and McKissick from leaving. Now he found himself yoked to them in the Meredith March, which they had successfully skewed to the left.

As the march got under way, King agreed to focus its efforts on voter registration. While he was briefly in Chicago to confer with his staff there, police in Greenwood, Mississippi, arrested Carmichael for trespassing and held him for several hours. Upon his release, he addressed an audience of marchers and local blacks. "Every courthouse in Mississippi," he said, "should be burnt down tomorrow so we can get rid of the dirt." Then, using in public a phrase he had previously employed only in private, he shouted: "We want black power." The crowd responded, chanting: "We want black power."

That demand continued to punctuate rallies even after King returned. Over his protest, Carmichael and McKissick made "black power" their slogan for the balance of the march. Though the SCLC contingent continued to call instead for "freedom now," King had lost ground to the radicals. As he put it sadly to one rally, "I'm sick and tired of violence. I'm tired of the war in Vietnam. . . . I'm tired of shooting. I'm tired of hatred. I'm tired of evil."

Though King wired President Johnson to request protection for the march, the state patrol that the president said would provide it instead used tear gas against the demonstrators. The marchers reached their destination in Jackson anyhow, but they had made relatively little impact on public opinion. Though King tried to reassure white supporters of civil rights whom Carmichael had offended, King had concluded he could no longer cooperate with SNCC. The NAACP, for its part, had decided it could no longer work with King. "Because Stokely Carmichael chose the March as an arena for a debate over black power," King said, "we didn't get to emphasize the evils of Mississippi and the need for the 1966 Civil Rights Act." Instead, Carmichael had made himself a national figure and black power a national issue. In the process, he and his allies irreparably damaged the civil rights movement.

3. Chicago

"Black power" then and later had many connotations. It signified black pride, an apt and necessary attitude. It reflected an identification of American blacks with blacks in Africa and elsewhere, a historic association like those cherished by other ethnic groups. It also often expressed a separatist black nationalism that most American blacks did not want. In its most extreme usage, "black power" communicated a vindictive hostility to whites. "The Negro," Carmichael had said during the Meredith March, "is going to take what he deserves from the white man." He soon thereafter threatened the press with language like "offing the pigs" and "killing the honkies." He intended, he said, to "smash everything Western civilization has created." H. Rap Brown, who succeeded Carmichael as head of SNCC, called Lyndon Johnson a "honky cracker" and urged blacks to "get some guns" and shoot "that honky to death." He predicted that angry blacks would "burn America down." Those were the sentiments that had animated rioting in Watts, that stirred unrest in urban ghettos, and that frightened whites and spurred their retaliation.

Those were also the sentiments that King and SCLC in 1966 were trying to channel into nonviolent demonstrations in the campaign to desegregate Chicago. After the Watts riot in 1965, King had led some thirty thousand people to Chicago's City Hall in a march to protest racism. Early in 1966 he leased an apartment for his family in a black neighborhood known locally as Slumdale. The wretched condition of the flat underlined the importance of housing, which served as one major theme in the mobilization of Chicago blacks. Desegregated public schools and the appointment of blacks to the police board were among other local goals. To that effort King recruited leaders of several street gangs. They needed power, they said, and he agreed, but he told them that power in Chicago meant getting the country's most notorious political machine to go their way.

That machine answered to Mayor Richard Daley, the last of the traditional political bosses, who ran the city with a tight hand. He had bribed enough blacks with political office and favors to exert a large influence in Chicago's slums, where most of the city's eight hundred thousand blacks lived in conditions of poverty and squalor. Because of Daley's strength, a victory in Chicago would do for King in the North what Birmingham had done for him in the South. But Daley was a shrewd and tough antagonist. He was a friend and supporter of the president's. His black lieutenants organized diversionary community actions of their own, and he announced a city program, a phantom as it turned out, to clean up the slums by the end of 1967. The business community stood behind Daley, not least because the issues in Chicago, as SCLC leaders realized, were as much the function of social class as of race. King insisted that "we're not interested in a campaign against Mayor Daley. We're fighting the system." But Daley represented the system—a loose collectivity of political and economic interests—which would stand or fall with him in command. King intended it to fall. As he said boldly and explicitly, "The slum is little more than a domestic colony which leaves its inhabitants dominated politically, exploited economically . . . segregated and humiliated at every turn." The basic "problem is economic"; the solution, "to organize this total community into units of political and economic power."

SCLC was itself disorganized. Rivalries among the men in King's entourage, inadequate financing, and wasteful spending crippled the campaign in Chicago. So did the continuing lack of cooperation from the Black Muslims, from CORE, and from Daley's loyal black constituents. Conscious of the growing militancy among blacks, King wanted to keep that mood free of violence. Daley failed to understand King's warning that unless gains were "made in a hurry through responsible civil rights organizations, it will open the door to militant groups." But a major rally of July 10, 1966, drew only half the crowd King had expected. To his demand that real estate brokers list properties without discrimination, Daley replied that Chicago was already doing its best to alleviate conditions in the slums.

Two days later, on July 12, 1966, a hot day in the city, black youngsters were splashing in an illegally opened fire hydrant when two police officers turned it off. A young black opened it again, the police arrested him and seven others, rumors spread that they had been beaten, and black teenagers, joined by some adults, for several hours broke windows and threw rocks and fire bombs. King tried but failed to restore calm. The next day the violence began again, with some random gunfire that the press exaggerated as "guerrilla warfare." Still, in the language of an official national report, "[b]efore the police and 4,200 National Guardsmen managed to restore order, scores of civilians and police had been injured. There were 533 arrests, including 155 juveniles. Three Negroes were killed by stray bullets, among them a 13-year-old boy and a 14-year-old pregnant girl." The riot resulted in less damage than had the riot in Watts, but in Chicago, as elsewhere, "the long-standing grievances of the Negro community needed only minor incidents to trigger violence." King was disconsolate. "A lot of people," he said, "have lost faith in the establishment. They've lost faith in the democratic process. They've lost faith in nonviolence."

Though King rejected black power, he had developed no alternative new strategy of his own. At least one of his aides believed SCLC was failing in Chicago because it had not forced an open confrontation with Daley. There might have been more serious trouble. When several hundred blacks marched into a white neighborhood in a demonstration for open housing, hostile residents threw bottles and rocks at them while the police stood by. Daley then urged white community leaders to preserve law and order. "Ignore the marchers," he told them, "and they'll go away." SCLC in its turn threatened a protest march into Cicero, a notoriously tough white district. The Chicago Realty Board then agreed to endorse open occupancy of private housing, and the city promised to construct scatter-site public housing instead of the high-rise buildings that tenants so disliked.

Those were limited concessions little honored thereafter, but King accepted them. Without remaining leverage in Chicago, he called off further demonstrations there. The agreement he had obtained, he claimed, was "the most significant program ever conceived." But many blacks felt "sold out." In fact, Daley had won the battle, though the war had shifted to the tumultuous streets of other American cities.

4. CITIES ON FIRE

Less than a week after calm returned to Chicago in July, rioting went on for four nights in another black ghetto, the Hough section of

Cleveland, Ohio. Black extremists did not instigate the disorder there, but they did exploit it. All in all, according to the later *Report of the National Advisory Commission on Civil Disorders*, forty-three instances of urban turmoil occurred during the summer of 1966, most of them set off by minor episodes, all of them "fueled by antagonism between the Negro population and the police." All of them also took place in cities where blacks had long suffered from discrimination in employment, education, and housing, as well as from underrepresentation in local government and on local police forces. And in all of them, too, blacks felt the oppression and alienation inherent in their poverty.

Those conditions and the failure to remedy them underlay the resumed sweep of rioting through the summer of 1967. In Tampa, Florida, on June 11 and in Cincinnati, Ohio, on the next day, with temperatures over ninety degrees, small incidents involving police and local blacks quickly inflamed long-simmering grievances. Blacks constituted 20 percent of Tampa's population, but no one of them served on the city council or school board or in a high post in the police department. Most blacks left school before eighth grade. Sixty percent of housing available to blacks was substandard. So, too, in Cincinnati, blacks were almost without political representation, one of every eight black men was unemployed, two of every five black families lived below the poverty line. Young black militants believed that nonviolent protests were futile. The disturbances in Cincinnati followed the usual pattern of urban violence with Molotov cocktails setting off fires, crowds stoning cars, random gunshots wounding innocents, "all hell" breaking loose, according to the chief of police, before the National Guard arrived to help restore order.

In Atlanta, Georgia, on June 17, "the same type of minor police arrest that had initiated the Cincinnati riot took place." The endemic inequalities were also similar. In Atlanta "the economic and educational gap between the black and white populations may . . . have been increasing." Blacks were confined to several ghetto areas, where housing was dismal, schools were badly overcrowded, "garbage sometimes was not picked up for two weeks . . . littered streets and . . . empty lots were breeding grounds for rats," and nearby parks lacked swimming pools and recreational equipment. SCLC was strong in Atlanta, but so was SNCC, whose leaders were eager to make trouble. Stokely Carmichael urged blacks "to take to the streets and force the police department to work until they fall in their tracks." He seemed to have his way for a day until the city government reduced tensions by beginning to equip the playgrounds and by establishing a Negro Youth Patrol.

Those gestures and the promise of more substantial change permitted moderate black leaders to prevail. But Atlanta had had a close call.

In Newark, New Jersey, on June 20, residents of the black ghetto crowded a meeting of the city's planning board "to denounce the city's intent to turn over 150 acres . . . as a site for the state's new medical and dental college." The city had serious problems. It had reached its borrowing limit. Property taxes were soaring, as were welfare costs. Whites who could afford to were moving into neighboring suburbs. In the Central Ward, the heart of the ghetto, blacks were left with crowded schools, dismal housing, a police department they perceived as hostile, a high crime rate, and rising unemployment. A large segment of the black population had become militant, primarily because of the city's failure to improve conditions, secondarily in response to social activists from SDS and other groups involved in the federal antipoverty program. The militants packed the planning board meeting.

A week later, led by local members of CORE, militants disrupted a meeting of the board of education. On July 12 still another police incident led to looting and rock throwing, which resumed the next evening. Shouts of "Black power" accompanied a barrage of rocks that held one police station under siege. Heavy looting, some shooting, and some fire bombing in the downtown area persuaded the governor to call in the National Guard. During the next afternoon stray police gunfire wounded a black child and an aged civil rights leader. Black snipers retaliated. In the confusion, the director of police later said, "Guardsmen were firing upon police and police were firing back at them. . . . I really don't believe there was as much sniping as we thought." Nevertheless, the frightened police and guardsmen continued their shooting and random killing. Before the city settled down on July 17, the riot had resulted in ten million dollars in damages and in twenty-three deaths—one white detective, one white fireman, and twenty-one blacks, six of whom were women and two children.

Rioting continued intermittently elsewhere in New Jersey before jumping north and west to reach a culmination from July 22 through July 27, 1967, in Detroit. There the hostility between the black community and the police department contributed to the "high stress and tension" of the Twelfth Street area, the heart of the city's ghetto, where the density of population was double the average for the whole city. Detroit, like Newark, was deeply in debt. The city had inferior schools for blacks, inadequate garbage service in slum neighborhoods, a declining economy with more than a quarter of young black men unemployed, and a high crime rate. Polls had revealed a deep dissat-

Detroit: A city saturated with fear.

isfaction among blacks residing in the ghetto. They had little political representation and little hope for a better life. About a third of the inhabitants of the slums owned weapons.

In the heat of a late July Saturday the ghetto blew up, ignited initially by a police raid on a drinking club. As looting increased, a "spirit of nihilism" took hold. Destruction became an end in itself, an outlet for years of accumulated grievances. Fire started by a Molotov cocktail engulfed one block of houses, then several blocks, then an area of some three square miles. On Sunday afternoon Mayor Jerome Cavanagh called for the National Guard and imposed a curfew. Governor George Romney declared a state of emergency. But the looting continued in spite of the gunfire of police and guardsmen.

On Monday the governor and mayor requested federal assistance, President Johnson authorized the dispatch of a task force of paratroops to a base near Detroit, and that afternoon and evening its commander and Cyrus Vance, the president's representative, toured the city. Since they saw no looting or sniping, and since the fires seemed to be coming under control, they decided to delay sending in federal troops. But Monday night, when sniping resumed, they concluded troops were needed. The president then authorized their employment and federalized the Michigan National Guard. His tense statement to the nation about the necessity for law and order said nothing about the seeds of ghetto anger and revenge. In Detroit the guardsmen, inexperienced and excited, again and again opened fire on the basis of suspicion or rumor, as, for their part, did the snipers, too. The city had become "saturated with fear. The National Guardsmen were afraid, the residents were afraid, and the police were afraid." The commanding general ordered the troops to unload their weapons; but some never received the order, and gunfire continued into Tuesday evening. In one instance that night guardsmen, looking for snipers, poured hundreds of bullets into a house where the bewildered residents, all black, had committed no crime. In another, police volleys killed three young blacks in the Algiers Motel though no one had fired from inside that building.

When at last the rioting ended on Thursday and Friday, twenty-seven people had been charged with sniping, but charges against twenty-four of them were soon dismissed. One man pleaded guilty; only two cases went to trial. The damage from the riot, which early estimates put at five hundred million dollars, actually amounted to some forty million dollars. Forty-three people were killed during the riot; thirty-three blacks and ten whites. Seventeen were looters, two of them white. After examination most of the deaths appeared to be accidental. The police and the guardsmen together were responsible for at least twenty-seven of the killings; the rioters, for no more than three.

The devastation in Detroit placed still another major mark on the path of urban violence and destruction that had begun before Watts. Television had carried pictures of Detroit to the whole country, pictures of a city in flames, flames that silhouetted the figure of an angry black man whose implicit message was "Burn, baby, burn!" The fear that suffused Detroit, as it had Newark and Chicago and Los Angeles, touched Americans far away. It affected whites who were afraid of blacks and blacks who were afraid of whites. From the resulting hostile attitudes, neither white nor black had anything to gain.

5. THE BLACK PANTHERS

With Detroit the worst of the urban rioting was over, but a legacy of hatred remained. It was a legacy ripe for exploitation by extremists, by white reactionaries and black revolutionaries alike. It terrified much of white America in its expression in the Black Panther party, an overtly revolutionary, paramilitary organization. In the autumn of 1966 two young ghetto militants, Huey P. Newton and Bobby Seale, had formed that party in Oakland, California, though other militant groups had used the same name earlier in San Francisco and New York. Newton and Seale, self-proclaimed minister of defense and chairman respectively, had absorbed the texts of Frantz Fanon and Malcolm X and applied their message to the mood of the ghetto. "We want freedom," Newton's program began. "We want power. . . . We want full employment. . . . We want an end to robbery by capitalists. . . . We want all black men to be exempt from military service. We want . . . an end to POLICE BRUTALITY. . . . We want land, bread, housing, education, clothing, justice."

The Black Panthers, the two leaders decided, had to establish disciplined armed patrols for "policing the police." Those patrols drew attention to the organization, which recruited only from the ghetto. As Seale put it, he sought "brothers off the block—brothers who had been . . . robbing banks . . . pimping . . . peddling dope . . . brothers who had been fighting pigs—because . . . once you organize those brothers . . . you get niggers . . . you get revolutionaries who are too much." Recruits received training in the use of firearms, agreed to abjure alcohol and drugs, and dressed in a uniform of black trousers, a light blue shirt, a black leather jacket, a black beret, black shoes, and dark sunglasses. They also learned the constitutional rights of all suspects so that they could assist any black who was arrested.

The increasing visibility of the Panthers and the resulting trepidation among whites provoked the Oakland representatives in the California legislature to introduce a bill barring the carrying of firearms in any public place. On the day in which the bill was to be debated, thirty armed Panthers marched into the California statehouse, where TV cameramen recorded their arrival on the floor of the assembly. Seale and five other Panthers were arrested and sentenced to jail for "the willful disruption of a State . . . legislative body." The incident gave the Panthers instant celebrity nationwide. It also persuaded the California police to increase their surveillance of the party. In October 1967 Oakland police stopped a car Huey Newton was driving. As Newton left the automobile, shooting broke out, killing two officers and wounding Newton. Newton claimed self-defense; but details of the incident remained murky, and he was charged with murder and held without bail.

With Seale and Newton in prison, Eldridge Cleaver took over the leadership of the Panthers. While in prison for rape in the early 1960s, Cleaver had become a Black Muslim minister, then a disciple of Malcolm X, and also an avid reader of Marx, Camus, and Fanon. A fluent writer, he published articles in *Esquire* and *Ramparts*, a magazine of the left. He received parole late in 1966 to become a senior editor of *Ramparts*. Soon thereafter he began to serve as the ideologist for the

Huey Newton.

Bobby Seale.

Black Panthers. In that role and later as the party's leader, Cleaver held that American blacks had to be prepared to fight their way out from under white colonialism. He called for the overthrow of the American state and for the establishment of a socialist society, both to be accomplished with the help of sympathetic whites. Early in 1968 Cleaver and Seale brought Stokely Carmichael into the Panthers, and later also H. Rap Brown and James Forman. But the SNCC leaders soon clashed with Cleaver. In less than a year personal feuding drove the two groups apart. Meanwhile, police harassment of the Panthers intensified while national membership in the party grew, partly under the spur of Cleaver's "Free Huey" propaganda.

By 1968, with Cleaver planning to run for the presidency of the United States, the Black Panthers had become the foremost symbol of black radicalism and the foremost object of white fear. Cleaver's collection of essays *Soul On Ice* (1968) was providing texts from which radicals of both races could draw confirmation for their revolutionary views. Those essays, written over the previous decade, equated the domestic role of the police with the role of the armed forces in Vietnam. Cleaver interpreted both as instruments of "those in power." He wrote: "Blacks . . . all over America could now see the Viet Cong's point: both were on the receiving end of what the armed forces were dishing out." The police, he held, were the "armed guardians of the social order." That social order protected the private property of the large corporations within the United States and imposed their will on black and yellow peoples everywhere. Consequently, the "lasting salvation" of the black American required at once the socialization of property and freedom for the nations of Africa, Asia, and Latin America. Merging the issue of social class with the issue of race, Cleaver related both to "the black man's interest in . . . a free and independent Vietnam."

That conclusion seemed to many blue-collar and middle-class white Americans to be as threatening as they had found the Panther's militancy and the urban riots. In that view, the Panther leadership, informed by Cleaver's ideology and drawing support from the alienated within the ghetto, pointed to the possibility of a major social eruption. For those who were alarmed, as for the police, the path of prevention lay in repressing the Panthers. For more thoughtful Americans, vigorous social reform offered a preferred alternative.

6. BACKLASH

Radicals like Cleaver were not alone in seeing the connections between racism and poverty and between those conditions and the Vietnam War. Martin Luther King, Jr., had been talking in those terms before 1964. Eager to combat black radicalism and to prevent urban violence, King after the Chicago riot began to organize what he hoped would become a national campaign against poverty. He understood that poverty among blacks and in American cities was only a part of the poverty, rural as well as urban, white as well as black, that persisted throughout the country. Federal legislation to provide decent, guaranteed annual incomes to all needy families became one of King's major objectives, as it was also for white reformers like Adam Walinsky and Mayor John Lindsay of New York. Others committed to reform, Robert Kennedy for one, urged "a massive effort to create new jobs," a goal King also supported. The troubles of the cities called, too, as King argued, for federal legislation and executive action to reduce the cost of housing by restricting the power of the building trades unions and for federal efforts to end de facto segregation in northern public schools.

Those were the conclusions that the National Advisory Commission on Civil Disorders later spelled out as essential ingredients of a remedial social program. As the commission noted, the legislation of the Great Society had required of both local agencies and federal departments "a level of skill, a sense of urgency and a capacity for judgment" never previously encouraged. Beyond the necessary improvements in

public service, the nation also faced the "difficult challenge" of training and finding jobs for five hundred thousand "hard-core" unemployed residing in the central cities. By 1970 the country would need
two million new jobs, half of them in the public sector. Factors of both
class and race, the commission also reported, had burdened the education of black children in the cities. Apart from new efforts to integrate northern public schools, schools in the ghettos required major
educational improvements, especially in teaching the disadvantaged
skills in reading and arithmetic. The increased costs of an adequate
educational program would have to fall on the federal government.
The commission also recommended expanding the welfare program to
include all Americans in need, lifting the assistance provided to reach
the "minimum necessary for a decent level of existence," and undertaking new ventures to encourage welfare recipients to seek employment. "After . . . three decades of fragmented and . . . under-funded
federal housing programs," the report continued, "decent housing
remains a chronic problem for the disadvantaged urban household."
Two-thirds of all ghetto housing was substandard. The supply of new
housing had to be "expanded on a massive basis" and subjected to a
comprehensive and enforceable open housing law.

Those proposals, implicitly critical of the achievements of the Great
Society, went beyond the tolerances of the consensual liberalism of
Lyndon Johnson and most of his supporters. The president had no
stomach for a volume of spending that would have required genuinely
redistributive taxation. That taxation would have fallen on the middle
class as well as the wealthy. He had no interest in battling with the
conservative unions in the building trades or with working-class whites,
Democrats most of them, in northern neighborhoods opposed to integrated schooling. Johnson had cultivated consensus politics, policies
attractive insofar as possible to men and women of every class and
color. But that kind of reform was no longer enough. The liberal agenda
had to expand, just as King and Robert Kennedy maintained. The agenda
as it had developed through 1963 could not assure the creation of a
just society. Calculated incrementalism in the course of reform was
now too slow to meet the deferred expectations of the underclass. Indeed,
the old formula of moderate reform at home mixed with the cold war
abroad had ceased to work after the escalation in Vietnam first froze
and then reduced the persistent underfunding of the Great Society.

Even if Lyndon Johnson had advocated all the remedial measures
requiring increased federal expenditures, he could not have reconciled
their cost with the size of the military budget. Nor could he have brought

social peace to the country without ending the Vietnam War. As it was, his obsession with Vietnam kept him from recommending any costly reform. Indeed, by the end of 1966 he had stopped talking much about the Great Society. Later he refused to accept the report of the Commission on Civil Disorders. But he was not peculiarly to blame. The impact of black power and of the urban riots denied the prospect of reform any real chance.

White backlash to those developments engulfed cities and suburbs alike. At the extreme, the National States Rights party preached racial hatred and proposed the deportation of all blacks and other nonwhite peoples. The suburban middle class had always insulated itself from blacks and other minorities. Similarly, ethnic neighborhoods in northern cities, especially but not exclusively those consisting of blue-collar workers and their families, organized to keep blacks out of their residential turfs and their public schools. Scornful of black pride and black nationalism, they rallied to Polish pride or to Serb or Croatian or Greek or Italian or Irish or Jewish pride. The backlash affected Congress, where most members had had enough of reform. Everett Dirksen opposed the housing provisions in the administration's civil rights bill as "a package of mischief." He stood aside while southern Democrats conducted a filibuster that killed the measure. Though without the concurrence of the Senate, the House had already responded to urban disorder with a bill making rioting a federal crime. Congress also voted to deny antipoverty funds to persons who incited or participated in riots or other civil disturbances. As the *New Republic* then observed, "Riots are nasty, and every effort must be made to control them when they occur. But what sense is there . . . to insist that vocational education or youth employment benefits be withheld from participants in a riot . . . that they shall remain—they of all people!—untrained, unemployed, on the streets."

But violence and the preaching of violence had had predictable effects. The riots and the revolutionary doctrines of the radicals bore no relationship to civil disobedience. Those who had practiced civil disobedience broke the law with the expectation of being arrested. Arrest was the anticipated result of their witnessing, part of their self-consciously moral act. Rioters and revolutionaries broke the law with the intention of defying the state or of destroying it. But the state had the means to protect itself. Revolution, even riot, could be validated only by success, and the great majority of Americans were resolved to prevent that success. Neither the alienated nor the radicals had a chance to prevail. There was need for reform, but also, as always in times of racial and class tensions, for order in the process of resolving conflicts. When protest became massive, as one perceptive conservative critic wrote, "when it is not civil, when it borders on violence or threatens it, when it is coercive . . . in its immediate impact, when its impact is not of inconvenience but of terror, then it is unacceptable."

Without recognition of the accompanying need for reform, the Republicans seized the hot issue of law and order after the riots of 1966. They attributed both riots and radicalism to the "soft" social programs of the Democrats. In November 1966 the GOP gained forty-seven seats in the House of Representatives and three in the Senate, enough to restore the conservative coalition that the Johnson landslide of 1964 had only temporarily overcome. "I view this election as a repudiation of the President's domestic policies," said Gerald Ford, the Republican leader in the House. ". . . Congress will write the laws, not the executive branch." Appropriations for the antipoverty program fell in 1967, and the administration's housing measure again stalled. It passed in 1968 only after Congress had added a section making it a crime to cross state lines in order to incite a riot. Riding the backlash of 1966 by campaigning against the Watts riot and campus disorders at Berkeley, Ronald Reagan, who stood where Goldwater had, won office that year as governor of California. Politics there reflected the national mood. Black radicalism and urban turmoil, by no means yet spent, were pushing the American political center to the right. More and more of the Johnson electoral coalition were moving that way. Left of the center there remained only the radicals and a diminishing number of committed liberals clustered around King and Kennedy. Increasingly those two men and their adherents were aware that the financial means and the moral energy essential for further reform were vanishing in the expense and futility of the Vietnam War.

7. The New Left

During 1966 the antiwar movement in the United States steadily grew, moving, as it did so, along two separate tracks. One was still largely invisible within the federal government. The other had increasing visibility primarily on the campuses of American colleges. The latter had begun earlier and had drawn, as it continued to draw, upon the spirit and ranks of the civil rights movement. Indeed, in 1966 the outspoken opposition to the war of Stokely Carmichael and of Martin Luther King, Jr., marked the informal merging respectively of the radical and liberal wings of the civil rights movement with their antiwar equivalents.

Unrest on American college campuses expressed student concern with a number of issues, of which the Vietnam War was not initially paramount. That unrest involved students and faculty, of whom a majority were never radical. So it was that the disturbances of 1964 at the University of California at Berkeley began as a student protest against an arbitrary order of the administration restricting the access of student organizations to desirable space for making speeches, recruiting members, and raising funds. The protest had links to national issues. Among the organizations involved were local chapters of CORE and SNCC, and the leading student spokesman of the protest had participated in the Freedom Summer of 1964. A later, less disruptive protest at Yale University, a bastion of conventionality, began over the dismissal of a popular assistant professor whose scholarship had failed to meet his department's criteria for promotion. A leading member of the faculty in that incident and his close associate, the university chaplain, both were veterans of civil rights agitation in the South. Like the undergraduates, they interpreted the dismissal of an outstanding teacher as a violation of student interests. Soon thereafter they found a new cause in opposition to the Vietnam War.

So had the Students for a Democratic Society. Its Economic Research and Action Program (ERAP), after ebullient beginnings in Newark and Cleveland, had begun to falter. Tom Hayden had expected ERAP to mobilize the urban poor. But ERAP efforts in various city slums, while effective in teaching the poor about their rights, had made few converts for the SDS or its political goals. Turning back to recruitment on college campuses, SDS leaders realized that antiwar activities would attract students. Late in 1964 the SDS started planning a march against the Vietnam War. The reprisal bombing that Johnson ordered in February 1965 prompted guarded cooperation in that march by other national organizations identified with movements for nuclear disarmament and peace. The antiwar impulse at that time largely reflected moral repulsion against the bombing and killing of helpless and innocent people. At teach-ins on campuses throughout the country, student and faculty speakers also expressed doubts about the integrity and representativeness of the government of South Vietnam and about the existence of any essential American interest in Southeast Asia.

By April 1965 Senators Ernest Gruening, Wayne Morse, Frank Church, and George McGovern all had openly opposed the war. Those senators and the national peace organizations were restless in harness with the SDS because it had issued statements praising Ho Chi Minh. Nevertheless, the coalition temporarily held together, and some fifteen thousand marchers appeared at the Washington Monument in April. They heard Gruening criticize the Communist regime in Beijing and also urge a cessation of bombing against North Vietnam. A welfare worker described the American poor as the real victims of the war. A folk singer rendered Bob Dylan's "The Times They Are a-Changing." And the head of the SDS condemned American capitalism.

That mixture of moods and views was to continue to characterize the movement against the war. Many groups were involved, some of them radical, some not. Most of them naturally romanticized their cause. Of the April march, one participant wrote: "It was unbearably moving to watch the sea of banners . . . move out . . . toward the Capitol as Joan Baez . . . and others sang 'We Shall Overcome.' Still more poignant was the perception . . . that . . . there was nowhere to go but forward . . . that our movement was irresistibly strong."

The march gave the SDS the chance to assume leadership of the antiwar movement. SDS membership grew from twenty-five hundred in December 1964 to ten thousand in October 1965. But with that growth, SDS national headquarters lost touch with the increasing number of local chapters. And then and later the SDS suffered from ideological disagreements that reduced its potential effectiveness. It was not "just a peace group," as one of its spokesmen said. It cared also about poverty, civil rights, and university reform, and some of its members continued to emphasize participatory democracy as a major objective. Further, as the SDS grew, personal rivalries at the national level resulted in administrative confusion and in uncertainty about priorities. By 1966 those conditions had permitted the more radical elements in the SDS to control the national office as well as some local affiliates.

Apart from the SDS, much of the New Left, which included organizations like SNCC and CORE, subscribed to an ideology that changed over time but always retained a considerable antiwar emphasis. The war in Vietnam, so the standard argument went, was the product of liberal corporatism. By corporatism the New Left meant the cluster of institutions, political and economic, that corporate capitalism had allegedly generated to dominate the state, the United States in particular. Corporatism appealed both to middle-class professionals and to blue-collar workers with a surfeit of distracting consumer goods that advertising identified with a fulfilling life. Liberals, in that construct, exercised some political authority, as John F. Kennedy and Lyndon

Johnson did, to promote cosmetic reforms. But those reforms did not alter the structural inequalities of corporate capitalism. Indeed, liberal corporatism preserved a surplus of labor, as among the unemployed in the ghettos, so as to keep wages down and corporate profits high. Further, so the theory held, corporatism had to rely on the production of military goods to assure its profits. Corporate capitalism had turned imperialistic so that war would provide an expanding market for its goods. Thus Vietnam, a war for which corporations supplied napalm and various defoliants, as well as conventional weapons. And thus the persisting cold war, for which continuing preparedness guaranteed a growing market.

By and large that case outfitted Marxist-Leninist theory, especially as it applied to imperialism, in the garb of current issues. New Left politics allowed space for Old Left groups, for Stalinists, Trotskyites, and Maoists. They shared opposition to the Vietnam War and admiration for Ho Chi Minh. The internal contradiction between the theoretically participatory SDS and the dictatorial Ho rarely bothered the faithful. But the New Left departed from the Old Left in significant ways. The Old Left of the 1930s had embraced the Communist party and its authoritarian control over ideology and program. The New Left recognized no single authority. The Old Left accepted industrialism with its high technology as part of a necessary stage in the march toward an idealized Communist state. An oppressed proletariat was to lead that march. The New Left, in contrast, worried about the depersonalization of technology. And the New Left believed that "a new working class"—teachers, lawyers, and professionals—was the spiritual victim of corporatism. Universities, in that view, were training students for those professional roles, and disenchanted students would lead the revolt against the state. They would begin appropriately by resisting the war and the draft.

New Left views about the oppressiveness of American society and about the Vietnam War found influential expression in much of the music of the counterculture. In 1965 Bob Dylan changed the beat of his singing to rock and roll—"folk rock" in the phrase of the day—and infused his lyrics with political as well as cultural radicalism. His "Highway 61" and "Desolation Row" carried obvious antiwar and anti-American connotations. Following in his tracks, rock performers during the latter half of the 1960s glorified peace and revolution as well as drugs and sex. The counterculture, never a single movement, had a variety of expressions and a variety of adherents. For many of its devotees, by the late 1960s lysergic acid diethylamide (LSD) and Methedrine (speed)—both psychologically dangerous hallucinogens—had become popular drugs. The Haight-Ashbury section of San Francisco became the most celebrated center of hippie bands and hippie habits. Yet there were also genuine mystics in the counterculture who did not depend upon either drugs or geography for their experience. And many of the alienated among American youth embraced the counterculture for other reasons—because of its exuberance, the freedom it symbolized, the love and community it offered. Those positive qualities drew less notice from antagonistic Americans than did the free sex, bad trips, and outlandish behavior that they associated with cultural rebels. The counterculture had only an occasional and incidental relationship to the New Left. But conservative critics—"straight" in their antipathy to political radicalism and hippie manners—identified both as parts of a sinister, anarchical threat.

While rejecting the norms of the middle class, the New Left and the counterculture by and large retained conventional attitudes toward the role of women, just as the civil rights and peace movements had. Hundreds of women joined demonstrations against nuclear war or for desegregation, worked in the Mississippi Freedom Summer, or participated in ERAP efforts to organize the poor in Newark or Cleveland. Almost invariably those women found themselves excluded from positions of leadership that radical young men, no less than conservatives, considered a strictly male prerogative. When Marilyn Salzman Webb addressed an antiwar rally, men there shouted: "Take her off the stage and fuck her." As many women soon realized, inequality derived as much from sex as from race. The movement for women's liberation drew great strength from that realization. It prompted young women experienced in agitating for the rights of others to begin to organize and agitate for their own rights.

In doing so, they discovered that their objectives were compatible with those of a growing number of older women who had long suffered from discrimination in employment in the professions as well as in the marketplace. By the late 1960s employment for middle-class women was becoming as normal as it had been for many years for women in blue-collar families. Most elite colleges nevertheless either excluded women or segregated them. The most prestigious law schools, business schools, and medical schools discouraged women applicants and admitted few of them. The major corporations rarely hired women executives. Justification for those practices rested in the common assumption of mid-century American culture that women, biologically and emotionally, were both fitted for and contented with domestic

Betty Friedan: No longer living a lie.

preoccupations—with caring for their husbands, their children, and their housekeeping. In fact, millions of women were not contented. They resented the male conviction that they were or should be, a constant theme of commercial advertising. They resented, too, receiving less remuneration for the jobs they held than did men in equivalent positions.

Both the injustice of discrimination and the pretense of female contentment were exposed by Betty Friedan in her powerful book *The Feminine Mystique* (1963). As she recalled, writing about her title:

> *The Feminine Mystique* . . . kept us passive and apart, and kept us from seeing our real problems and possibilities. . . . We didn't admit it to each other if we felt there should be more to life than peanut-butter sandwiches with the kids. . . . I needed a name for whatever it was that kept us from using our rights, that made us feel guilty about anything we did *not* as our husband's wives . . . but as people ourselves. . . . I and every other woman I knew had been living a lie. . . . If women were really *people* . . . then all the things that kept them from being full people in our society would have to be changed.

The Johnson administration, cool to that message, made little effort to enforce the prohibition against sexual discrimination in Title VII of the 1964 Civil Rights Act. To secure their rights, women activists, middle-aged as well as young, in 1966 formed the National Organization for Women (NOW). Through propaganda, demonstrations, and legal and political action, both NOW and more militant women's organizations made women's liberation a major issue in reform politics. Militant feminists identified men as the enemy. The cruelty and indignity of male dominance supplied the themes for Robin Morgan in her angry anthology *Sisterhood Is Powerful* (1970). Contributors to that anthology demanded equal rights for women in marriage and the family, in higher education and medicine, and before the law. As Morgan put it in her introduction, "It isn't until you begin to fight in your own cause that you . . . become really committed to winning, and . . . become a genuine ally of other people struggling for their freedom." By 1967 committed women were a major force in the movements for their liberation and against the Vietnam War.

The political and cultural rebellions, distinctive though they were, shared some common interests, for two examples in community and in ecology and at least one common intellectual source: the philosophy of Herbert Marcuse. Marcuse was an émigré German existentialist scholar who in his late years completed his journey through the academy by accepting an appointment at the University of California at San Diego. An enormously learned man of mild countenance and bearing, European in training and in outlook, something of a poseur, Marcuse basked in the adulation he evoked from the American young. In *Eros and Civilization* (1955), a tract on Freudian theory, he presented the history of civilization as the history of repression. The "pleasure principle," he wrote, yielded to the "reality principle," which taught the utility of obedience to external authority, whether to conventional notions about sexuality or to the dictates of the bourgeois state. Labor then became dissociated with satisfaction. As the "scientific rationality of Western civilization began to bear its full fruit," it prevented the realization of human potentialities. But "the struggle for existence," as Marcuse saw it, could instead "proceed on new grounds and with new objectives . . . into a struggle against any constraint on the free play of human faculties." Then work would yield pleasure.

Moving on in *One Dimensional Man* (1964), Marcuse translated his earlier hypotheses into an indictment of the contemporary United States. He found it a society of absurdity in which magic merged with science, life with death, joy with misery. It was for him a repressive society where technological rationality under centralized authority had obliterated "the romantic space of imagination." He looked for remedy to the outcast, to the exploited nonwhite races, to the unemployed and unemployable. Their opposition to conditions as they had become, he argued, was revolutionary "even if their consciousness was not." That opposition became, therefore, an "elementary force." In its turn, that force, so Marcuse later contended, could result in a new freedom if a youthful elite—an elite free of bourgeois morality and bourgeois politics—led it in the appropriate direction. "The New Society,'" he wrote, "will be one where the hatred of the young bursts into laughter and song, mixing the barricade and . . . love play," mixing hedonism and revolution. Marcuse's worshipful followers, whether identified with the New Left or with the counterculture, set out joyously to create that utopia.

8. Confrontations

Dissent was generating its own orthodoxy. In November 1965 some thirty thousand people joined in Washington, D.C., in the largest demonstration against the Vietnam War to that date. Liberals as well as radicals participated in that occasion, but the two groups soon parted. Two leaders of the SDS, Tom Hayden and Staughton Lynd, visited Hanoi late in December 1965 during a temporary bombing pause then prevailing. They described that visit in their laudatory book *The Other Side* (1966). The authors identified North Vietnam "rice-roots democracy"—the "constant dialogue" of Communist guerrillas—with colonial American town meetings. They praised Hanoi for creating a "socialism of the heart," which they found expressed in "the freedom to weep practiced by everyone—from guerrillas to generals."

There was indeed a passionate patriotism in North Vietnam, and the Communist party there did encourage participation in political demonstrations in villages. But later even Hayden admitted that he "didn't see the whole truth." As he then put it, "I presumed because the Vietnamese were superhuman under the American bombing that they were superhuman in fact. That didn't turn out to be the case. There was a significant element of Stalinism in the Vietnamese Communist Party." So there was, but at the time and during the next several years Hayden and others on the New Left were lionizing Ho Chi Minh. Their glorification of Ho, often along with Mao Zedong and Che Guevara, naturally infuriated the president and his supporters. It also dismayed those opponents of the war who recognized North Vietnam as the oppressive state that it actually was. Opposition to the policy of the United States government after all, did not require support of the government of North Vietnam or of its Soviet and Chinese sponsors.

The intolerance of the New Left met the perversity of the Defense Department in November 1966 at Harvard University. Antiwar students there surrounded and stopped a limousine in which Secretary Robert McNamara was leaving a conference he had attended. Stepping out of the car, McNamara agreed to answer a few questions. "Don't listen to him," a student shouted. "He's killing the people of Vietnam! He doesn't even have the right to speak!" The crowd nevertheless did listen, but McNamara, so he said, did not know how many civilian casualties there had been in Vietnam. He did tell the students he was tougher than they were. Neither statement dignified his office. After twenty-seven hundred students signed an apology to McNamara, the SDS published a rejoinder. "An architect of a controversial American policy," it asserted, not without justice, "has a duty to confront criticism of that policy in public, especially when the Johnson Administration has continuously evaded the criticism."

"We are . . . involved," the broadside continued, ". . . in an effort really to confront establishment people. . . . We are organizing students . . . against the draft by which the government continues its war in Vietnam." By that time there were on college campuses some forty chapters of the movement to resist the draft. Without conscription, as the SDS maintained, the government could not have raised the forces needed in Vietnam. But conscription policy had other liabilities. It granted deferments from service to university students making progress toward the degrees for which they were enrolled. Since those deferments applied to candidates for professional degrees as well as to undergraduates, college students could plan to move on directly after earning their baccalaureates to candidacies for advanced degrees in law or medicine or business. In effect, middle-class students whose families could afford higher education, or who could qualify for private or federal scholarships to pursue their education, could avoid military service. The poor, particularly the poor who received submarginal schooling in their childhood, had no such escape. Consequently, there were a disproportionate number of black men in the army.

The issue of the draft therefore involved questions of class and race as well as questions about the Vietnam War. But reform of conscription could eliminate the social issues, as it later did. Students on the left, while by no means opposed to reform, addressed primarily the ques-

Conscription raised questions about class, race, and peace.

tion of the war itself. They gained countless new recruits during the summer of 1967, when the government ended deferments for students after their first four years of college. Military service thus became a probability for undergraduates who had been counting upon deferment while at professional schools, presumably for long enough to allow the war to end. They then discovered a crucial personal stake, as did many of their parents, in what for most of them had previously seemed a remote war. In the observation of a young Harvard socialist, "Now everyone, up to and including the Young Republicans, was against the war. . . . There's nothing wrong with that, even if it was only the change in the draft laws which impelled so many students to give Vietnam a thought. And it was nice . . . to see oneself suddenly part of a general consensus against . . . a lousy war."

On the left, intellectuals committed to opposition to the war were calling for open defiance of the government. Some of them retained part of their income taxes as a protest against the war. On October 12, 1967, more than a hundred signed "A Call to Resist Illegitimate

Authority," which declared the Vietnam War illegal and immoral. But few of those signers endorsed the conscious resort to guerrilla tactics recommended by some former advocates of nonviolence. In mid-October several thousand militants of that mind clashed with police in Oakland, California, while trying to close an army induction center there. Intellectuals and militants alike turned next to the March on the Pentagon of October 21, 1967.

Organized by the National Mobilization Committee to End the War in Vietnam (Mobe), a coalition of pacifist and radical groups, that raucous happening drew some hundred thousand people to Washington, D.C. Prominent among them were the eminent linguist Noam Chomsky, the poet Robert Lowell, the radical critic Dwight Macdonald, and the self-absorbed novelist Normal Mailer. Joining them were representatives of the lunatic fringe of the antiwar movement, including Abbie Hoffman and Jerry Rubin. Flamboyant masters of self-promotion, Hoffman and Rubin were eager always to supply the stuff of media coverage. They mixed absurdity with violence in their leadership of the Youth International party, the Yippies, avowedly revolutionaries but diverted often by hallucinatory drugs.

At the Pentagon, Hoffman tried to levitate the building. Others in the crowd urinated on it. Many waved Vietcong flags. Some men scaled the Pentagon's outer walls; young women shoved flowers into the barrels of the rifles of the tense military police or blew them kisses. Mailer caught the spirit of the confrontation in his entertaining account *Armies of the Night* (1968): "The demonstrators, all too conscious of what they consider the profound turpitude of the American military might in Asia, are prepared . . . for any conceivable brutality here. On their side, the troops have listened for years to small-town legends about the venality, criminality, filth, corruption, perversion, addiction, and unbridled appetites of . . . hippies . . . linked with . . . the Reds! . . . Each side is coming face to face with its own conception of the devil." That night the devils in police uniforms arrested hundreds of demonstrators and needlessly mauled many of them, particularly women, while others of the protesters remained on the steps of the Pentagon until morning. The war went on, but as Mailer wrote of the demonstrators, "who was to say that the sins of America were not by their witnessing a tithe remitted?"

The outpouring of so many Americans against the war, so the leaders of the Mobe concluded, had revealed "the political drama that's going on in this country." The Mobe began to plan another confrontation, legal and nonviolent, to take place in Chicago while the Democratic National Convention met there in 1968. The prospectus for that event envisaged a "loose counterconvention" that would contrast with the "authoritarian convention of the Democrats." But the Yippies considered that kind of theater much too tame. They intended, for their part, to bring guerrilla warfare to the streets of Chicago so as to provoke the authorities there to retaliation and thus to show the world the brutal nature of the American state. Black radicals, in contrast, had little interest in either the Democrats or any demonstration in Chicago.

The New Left had begun to splinter, with the disciples of nonviolence unable to restrain the apostles of force, who were themselves not united. At the National Conference for New Politics (NCNP), the blacks who attended had intimidated the whites. The black delegations met in their own closed caucus, guarded against white intruders by black toughs with shaved heads. The whites surrendered without opposition to the blacks' demands for control of the conference. Disenchanted by that kind of interracial coalition, many whites soon left the organization. Thereafter militant blacks went their own way, with their leaders quarreling over doctrine and command, while radical whites continued along their parallel and equally fractious course.

Still, all of them agreed with the opening sentence of a statement issued by the Mobe: "Election year 1968 will be a fateful one for American democracy but the deeper crisis is the failure of democracy and representative government to work." That was a sentence validated by the crisis of the cities and the crisis of Vietnam. It was also a sentence to which liberals as well as radicals could subscribe.

9. FUNGUS

"Vietnam was a fungus," so wrote Jack Valenti, one of Johnson's trusted aides, "slowly spreading its suffocating crust. . . . No matter what we turned our hands and minds to, there was Vietnam, its contagion infecting everything that it touched, and it seemed to touch everything." By the end of 1965 the "escalating stalemate" in Vietnam had begun to worry even Robert McNamara. Returning from Saigon, he informed the president that "the war will be a long one." With the rising infiltration of troops from North Vietnam, the increase in American forces then contemplated would probably result as early as 1967 only in a "military standoff." There was no sure victory ahead. In January 1966 McNamara's closest adviser proposed redefining the national commitment so as not to rule out a coalition government in Saigon including the Vietcong—a government neutral or even anti-American. The president allowed no such heresy. So escalation continued, casualties rose, as did costs, and the fungus spread further, with dissent from Johnson's policy growing both outside the government and within it.

As 1966 began, so did nationally televised hearings of the Senate Foreign Relations Committee. J. William Fulbright, the Arkansas Democrat who chaired that committee, had concluded that the president had used him disingenuously as the chief sponsor of the Tonkin Gulf Resolution. Fulbright believed that in escalating the war in Vietnam, Johnson had exceeded the authority of that resolution and of his office. Testifying before Fulbright's committee, General Taylor and Secretary of State Rusk restated the administration's familiar case. The United States, so Rusk asserted, was fighting in Vietnam to stop the forceful expansion of Communist power throughout the world. George Kennan, the author of the doctrine of containment, disagreed, Preoccupation with Vietnam, he told the committee, was stretching American power too far, stripping other, more important strategic areas of sufficient deterrent force. Fulbright concurred in that appraisal. In lectures he delivered at the Johns Hopkins University in April, he said the United States was losing its perspective about the limits of its power. In their "arrogance of power," Americans were "not living up to our . . . promise as a civilized example to the world."

In a similar vein, Walter Lippmann had written that Johnson had "never defined our national purpose except in the vaguest, most ambiguous generalities." Unless the United States changed its policy, Lippmann predicted, the war would further divide the American people. Like Kennan a realist, and like Fulbright a moralist, Lippmann was, as they were, essentially a conservative man, uneasy with the turmoil of the cities and the demonstrations, respectful of the constitution and its restrictions on executive authority, habituated to civility, and, on the latter accounts, scornful of Lyndon Johnson. For his part, the president dismissed Fulbright, Kennan, and Lippmann as "yellow," as "nervous Nellies." He condemned Fulbright as disloyal; he excoriated Lippmann for aiding the enemy.

During 1966 more and more men of substance and station spoke out against the war. Hurt and angered by their disaffection, Johnson would brook no opposition where he could locate and eliminate it. Apart from half a dozen senators from whom he withdrew favor, he had little to worry about on the Hill. But his intolerance of criticism and his fulminations against Robert Kennedy, on whom he blamed all his problems, and his ugly manner persuaded some of his ablest counselors to leave government. George Ball resigned from the State Department. The White House staff lost several of its standouts, especially among those concerned with national security. McGeorge Bundy departed in February, 1966; Jack Valenti, in May; Bill Moyers, in December. "I thought I could make him more like me," Moyers told a friend who knew the president, "but I've found in the last several months that I'm becoming more like him; so I got out."

Their replacements fed the president's biases. John Roche, a political scientist from Brandeis University, newly appointed as a liaison to liberals, shared Johnson's dislike of the Kennedy camp. So, too, whereas Bundy had scrupulously informed the president about the full range of senior opinions about matters of national security, Walt Rostow, his successor, gave a tendentious cast to his hawkish advice. From 1966 onward Rostow, as Townsend Hoopes wrote, "possessed great weight on Vietnam policy because he was both physically close and intellectually reassuring to the President. . . . It was a position of great temptation for a dedicated partisan whose mind automatically filtered out evidence that did not support his own established beliefs. . . . He was altogether too much the compulsive advocate. . . . He shaped the evidence. . . . Rostow was no deliberate villain; he was a fanatic in sheep's clothing." He was also just the type of adviser Johnson wanted. Increasingly isolated from criticism by his own choice, the president was secure only in the company of yes-men.

McNamara, his doubts about the war growing, nevertheless tried to accommodate to Johnson's temperament. The secretary of defense did not want to leave the president exposed only to the superhawks—to Rostow, Rusk, and the Joint Chiefs. Consequently, as one of his subordinates said, McNamara, "could argue the case for moderation . . . privately, selectively, and intermittently," but only cautiously. Still, argue he did, with ascending intensity. A special study commissioned by the Defense Department found "no measurable direct effect" from strategic bombing of North Vietnam, except in boosting patriotism in that country. After a trip to South Vietnam in October 1966, McNamara reported to the president that in spite of heavy losses, the enemy showed no signs of "an impending break in . . . morale. . . . Pacification is a bad disappointment. . . . The VC political infrastructure thrives in most of the country. . . . Full security exists nowhere. . . . Nor has . . . ROLLING THUNDER . . . either significantly effected infiltration or cracked . . . morale." McNamara therefore recommended stabilizing both the level of American ground forces in Vietnam and the bombing program against the North, while also "taking steps to increase the credibility of our peace gestures in the minds of the enemy." He concluded that probably neither military operations nor peace negotiations could end the war in the next two years. The Joint Chiefs, disputing that report, called for a "sharp knock" against North Vietnam through intensified bombing of target areas previously spared in Hanoi and Haiphong. McNamara rejected their advice in a memo to the president in November. It argued also for reducing their requested troop allotments. He had begun to question the judgment of the military. So did the CIA in reporting in January 1967 that the casualties in the air war against North Vietnam had been some 80 percent civilian, contrary to the claims of the air force.

Through 1967 doubts about the Vietnam War affected more and more senior civilians at the Pentagon, as well as in the CIA, though for the most part they persisted in their public optimism. John McNaughton, for many months McNamara's preferred adviser, told the secretary that throughout the country, the feeling was growing that "the Establishment is out of its mind . . . trying to impose some U.S. image on distant people we cannot understand." The president, caught between McNamara and the Joint Chiefs, grumbled about the military's recommendations. But he authorized bombing attacks on power plants and ammunitions dumps in Hanoi and Haiphong. For political reasons, he balked at Westmoreland's request for two hundred thousand more troops, for that step would have required calling up the reserves and triggered a bitter debate in Congress. "When we add divisions can't the enemy add divisions?" Johnson asked Westmoreland in April. "If so, where does it all end?" The Joint Chiefs replied by advising the extension of the war into Cambodia and Laos to attempt to stop infiltration from North Vietnam. Walt Rostow in May 1967 urged carrying the ground attack into North Vietnam.

McNamara and his senior aides evaluated those proposals. The "primary costs" of bombing, they noted, were American lives, on the average one pilot for every forty sorties. There was also the nasty "picture of the world's greatest superpower killing or seriously injuring 1,000 non-combatants a week." The "most important risk" was "likely Soviet, Chinese and North Vietnamese reaction." Intensified bombing would probably lead only to intensified Soviet and Chinese efforts to supply North Vietnam. The mining of Haiphong Harbor could challenge Soviet prestige and might force either a naval confrontation or Soviet retaliation elsewhere in the world. Ground action against North Vietnam would probably bring China into both the ground and the air war.

Rejecting those costs as too high, McNamara's evaluation recommended limiting any reinforcement of troops and de-escalating the bombing. The time had come, it also maintained, "to eliminate the ambiguities from our objectives . . . in Vietnam. . . . Our commitment is only to see that the people of South Vietnam are permitted to determine their own future. . . . This commitment ceases if the country ceases to help itself." On that assumption, as McNamara must have realized, the war would already have ended. His memo went on in that spirit to contemplate a cease-fire and non-Communist political settlement in South Vietnam. Though no such settlement was possible, the rest of the analysis provided a hardheaded assessment of conditions in Vietnam, an analysis pointing toward compromise rather than further escalation of the war.

As McNamara observed, one drawback to the latter course would arise from its "impact on the reputation of the United States and its President." That prospect alarmed Johnson. So did the attitudes of the Joint Chiefs, who denounced McNamara's analysis. But the president had small room to maneuver. He would not call up the reserves for fear of a national debate about the war at a time when major antiwar demonstrations were clearly occurring. He could not risk drawing China into the war. But he would not compromise his long-standing objectives. So he appeased the Joint Chiefs by authorizing an increase of troops of only about a third of Westmoreland's request. In the ensuing months Johnson also approved more of the targets which the Joint Chiefs had requested for bombing but, as so often before, without discernible effect.

Johnson went as far as he did in large part to satisfy the hawks on the Senate Preparedness Subcommittee. That committee was the preserve of senators influential with their Democratic colleagues and notorious for their unquestioning agreement with the military. Now spurred by the Joint Chiefs, the chairman of the committee, the obstinate but powerful John C. Stennis of Mississippi, set out in August 1967 to hold hearings designed to destroy McNamara. With invariable deference, Stennis and his colleagues listened to a parade of senior officers urge the expansion of the war in Vietnam on the ground, on the sea, and especially in the air. Then McNamara testified to the contrary, with impressive facts and figures at his hand. The committee scoffed. Civilian interference in military matters, its report concluded, had hampered the conduct of the war. "What is needed now," that report held, "is the hard decision to do whatever is necessary, take the risks that have been to be taken, and apply the force that is required to see the job through."

The president knew better than to unleash the generals, but the hearings confirmed his growing disenchantment with McNamara. The secretary of defense had moved too far toward dissent. In October 1967, at a luncheon with Johnson and other senior advisers, McNamara, weary and depressed, characterized the administration's strategy in Vietnam as "dangerous, costly, and unsatisfactory." His memo supporting that view drew rebuttals from the military, from the secretary of state, and from Johnson's influential advisers Abe Fortas and Clark Clifford. Johnson decided McNamara had to go. Without previously informing him, late in November the president announced McNamara's appointment as the new head of the World Bank. It was the "only job," Johnson said, that McNamara wanted, but privately the president expressed his pique. McNamara, he claimed, was close to nervous collapse. The fault was Bobby Kennedy's: "Every day Bobby would call up McNamara, telling him the war was terrible and immoral, and that he had to leave." It was, Johnson believed, part of an invidious and pervasive Kennedy plot to do him in. Some on the White House staff thought the president's behavior had become paranoid.

There was no plot, but by October 1967, Kennedy was leading Johnson in public opinion polls on political appeal. With McNamara and with thousands of other Americans, Kennedy had also become openly critical of the conduct of the war. Johnson worried about the senatorial hawks, but they were out of touch with much of the country. Almost half of the public—46 percent—considered the war a "mistake," though few yet favored an American withdrawal; only 44 percent still supported the war. Among comfortable middle-class Americans, men and women who were neither students nor radicals, there was a growing understanding of the war's adverse effects at home.

At a farewell luncheon McNamara revealed the anguish he shared with many of them. "His voice broke," one of those present recalled, "and there were tears in his eyes as he spoke of the futility, the crushing futility, of the air war." Robert Kennedy felt the same way. He also understood the mood of the radicals, both black and white, and the distress of the disenchanted middle class. "The people are terribly disturbed across this country," Kennedy said on national television. ". . . There is general dissatisfaction . . . with our society . . . I am dissatisfied with our country." As he soon added there had to be an outlet for "the unhappiness and the uneasiness within the United States."

10

The Politics of Discord

The polarization of American society strained the country's political system. The two major parties, for decades central to the functioning of that system, had operated as institutions to reconcile conflicts among their contending factions. But by 1967 contention exceeded conventional boundaries. Radical Americans, black and white, stood outside the parties. They were preaching revolution, not reconciliation. Further, about many of the issues of the time reconciliation had become at best difficult and unlikely. Yet disruptive demonstrations, whatever their therapeutic value as outlets for political emotions, antagonized most Americans. They were habituated to expressing their political views, if they expressed them at all, within the political system—at the polls and through the major parties. They had done so in 1964 in the coalition of groups—"the consensus"—that gave Lyndon Johnson his huge victory. The president expected them to do so again. But by 1967, under the impact of the war, the urban crisis, and the related onrush of protest and dissent, the once victorious coalition had dissolved.

1. ENTER GENE MCCARTHY

The Johnson consensus, at its peak in 1964 and 1965, had never consisted primarily of liberals, though it became fashionable to describe it as if it had. Rather, it encompassed the broad center of American politics, with some conservatives—habitual Republicans and sturdy business and professional men and women—preferring Johnson, though he was a Democrat, to his reactionary opponent. Johnson also counted on the regular Democrats. Those regulars included many southern voters who stood at the political center or to its right, as well as the urban machines and their constituents, many of them leery of any social reforms except those to their own clear advantage. Beyond those groups Johnson had a mixed constituency: almost all the blacks who voted; almost all the very poor, of whom relatively few voted in 1964 or any other year; and the union leaders and blue-collar workers whom they claimed to influence.

Finally, the Johnson coalition included bona fide liberals, many of them academicians, authors, lawyers, journalists, who gave thought and energy to social reform within the existing political and economic systems, and other men and women who leaned that way. Never as influential as they aspired to be, liberals had always been a minority even within the Democratic party. Some of them belonged to the Americans for Democratic Action (ADA), the national organization that liked to think it spoke for all liberals, though in fact, it constituted a minority within their minority. Liberals, furthermore, had always in some measure disagreed with one another, as they had during the Kennedy administration when the president used the word "liberal" as a pejorative term for those on his left.

By 1967 disagreements among liberals were driving them into warring factions. One group, riven to conventional cold war attitudes, continued to support President Johnson. With him, they viewed the Vietnam War as the current and crucial battle in the continuing contest between the forces of freedom, as represented by the United States and its allies, and the forces of darkness, as represented by North Vietnam, the Soviet Union, and China. From that belief it followed that the Vietnam War had a legitimate claim to the highest national priority. That conclusion linked the Johnson loyalists to those like-minded blue-collar and machine Democrats who also resented the urban riots and opposed extending poverty programs and integrating northern schools and neighborhoods. Indeed, the Johnson faction, now centrists bending right, expected the unions, the urban machines, and the South to stand with it to control the Democratic party.

The liberals who opposed the Vietnam War regarded it, as did the radicals, as both a source and a symbol of other pressing national problems. Those antiwar liberals lamented the negative impact of the war on the availability of funds for social improvements. So minded, many of them, again like the radicals, supported redistributive taxation; increased federal expenditures for welfare, education, and job programs; and integration of northern public schools. Indeed, they shared the sense of urgency of the young rebels, though not their passion, rhetoric, or style. For the antiwar liberals of 1967, unlike the radicals, were not anti-American. Neither were they admirers of Ho or Mao or Castro. Rather, the antiwar liberals continued to have faith in the American economic and political system and in their own ability to reform it from within.

Like liberals in previous eras, they found it difficult, often impossible, to work with the radicals whose ideological certitudes and confrontational tactics they rejected. So did most of the American middle class, whose growing antipathy to the war gave the antiwar liberals an opportunity to recruit a substantial centrist cohort. But neither the liberals themselves nor their potential allies in the center were prepared to have the United States suddenly run from Vietnam. Instead, various leaders of liberal dissent put forward a number of different scenarios. Each of them contemplated a reduction or cessation of bombing, a drawback of American troops toward enclaves relatively easy to protect and later to evacuate, and a concurrent opening of negotiations with North Vietnam for a settlement based on some kind of coalition government in Saigon.

The Johnson administration contended that no such scenario would either satisfy North Vietnam or sustain the American commitment to a free and independent South Vietnam, and the military situation in Vietnam made the enclave solution unrealistic. Nevertheless, whatever the weaknesses in the liberal scenario, it called at least for a beginning of de-escalation of the war. The other options were either the continuation, probably the further escalation of the war, or precipitous American abandonment of the area. Further, the options available to a liberal effort for reform within the system were either the continuation in office of the Johnson administration with the violent opposition it provoked or the election of one of the Republican aspirants to the presidency, all of whom were as hawkish as Johnson.

By the time of the departure of Robert McNamara from the Defense Department, antiwar liberals had become convinced that they had to prevent the renomination of Lyndon Johnson. But Robert Kennedy, their obvious candidate, still hung back. He knew how improbable it was to defeat a sitting president. He also realized that if he tried, Johnson and thousands of other Americans would attribute his attempt to personal animosity and ambition. Partly to change Kennedy's mind, partly to smoke out some other candidate, partly to provide an avenue for constructive dissent, J. K. Galbraith, then the national chairman of the ADA, addressed antiwar meetings throughout the country during the summer of 1967. Allard Lowenstein, the ADA vice-chairman, led a "dump Johnson" movement on college campuses and among Democratic politicians. Factions of reform Democrats in New York, California, and several midwestern states also moved to oppose the president. In September the *New Republic* came out against Johnson. Its talented editor, Gilbert Harrison, used the journal, after Kennedy refused to run, to put pressure on Senator Eugene McCarthy of Minnesota to enter the race. So did the senator's daughter, at that time an undergraduate at Radcliffe College, where many young women, like many of their male counterparts at Harvard, were passionately antiwar.

McCarthy yielded. "There is growing evidence," he said on announcing his candidacy on November 30, 1967, "of a deepening moral crisis in America—discontent, frustration and a disposition to take extra legal . . . actions to manifest protest. I am hopeful that this challenge . . . may alleviate . . . this sense of political helplessness and restore to many people a belief in the processes of American . . . government." It was necessary, he added soon thereafter, to give youthful demonstrators "entrance back into the political process," to offer an alternative to radicalism. To that end he attacked the administration's position on Vietnam, particularly its refusal to move to negotiate. Instead, he proposed a cessation of bombing, an immediate cease-fire, and a negotiated settlement giving the National Liberation Front, the Vietcong, a place in a coalition government.

Johnson was furious, incensed equally by the March on the Pentagon and by McCarthy's candidacy. He countered with a propaganda blitz claiming great progress in the war. Unable to appear in public without provoking a disturbance, the president toured military installations to display his confidence to a captive audience and an increasingly unfriendly press. He also convened the wise men, a group of elder statesmen, who listened to the State Department's roseate reports about Vietnam and then dutifully endorsed the administration's course. But neither Johnson nor most prominent Democrats took McCarthy seriously.

Eugene McCarthy was indeed a most unlikely candidate. In his youth a novice in a Benedictine monastery, he had an enduring interest in Thomistic theology and in modern poetry, which he wrote with considerable skill. Perhaps because of his notorious boredom with the business of the Senate, perhaps because of his brilliant speech placing Adlai Stevenson before the Democratic Convention of 1960, the Kennedys called McCarthy the "wrong Catholic." He had little interest in organization. He treated his staff with arrogance. Unpredictable as a campaigner, he could put an audience to sleep one day but the next day stir a sympathetic gathering to frenzied applause. He appealed primarily to the young and to the educated middle class, who responded enthusiastically to the two issues he stressed: the need to end the war and the need to reform the processes of Democratic politics by opening them to full participation by the people. The latter objective was essential to his candidacy, which could prosper only through open primaries. For in states where the Democratic organizations controlled the conventions that selected delegates, those delegations were sure to be for Johnson.

Never gregarious, often petulant, McCarthy nevertheless had a personal charm. He brought wit, precision, and originality to his discourse. He seemed genuinely to enjoy the company of young people. With women, he could assume a gentle, attentive, responsive manner. Those qualities, along with his platform, attracted to his cause several useful constituencies: college students, who supplied much of the energy required for canvassing; suburban matrons, who were less remarked but more important in staffing offices for fund raising and local planning; and aspirant liberal politicians, women included, who saw in the McCarthy movement a chance to leapfrog to prominence over the patient servants of the party. But those assets seemed wholly inadequate during the first two months of McCarthy's campaign. With the New Hampshire primary approaching, his green staff and amateur volunteers faced the veteran state organization. Johnson was not officially on the New Hampshire Democratic ballot, but the regulars were promoting a campaign to have voters write in the president's name. They were confident in the knowledge that every voter knew who Johnson was, while most could not yet identify McCarthy.

Then, surprisingly, at the end of January 1968 events in Vietnam, as they had so often before, altered the political calculus within the United States.

2. Tet

On January 31, 1968, Vietcong commandos stormed the American Embassy in Saigon, where they killed five American soldiers before they were repulsed. They damaged much of the rest of the city, including Westmoreland's headquarters, attacked the presidential palace, and temporarily grabbed the major radio station. Fighting in the streets

Saigon: Murder made an indelible impression.

continued throughout the day. That evening television news in the United States carried shocking pictures of the bloody combat in Saigon. The Vietcong achievement astonished Americans. It seemed wholly to contradict official optimism about the war. The next day General Nguyen Ngoc Loan, chief of the South Vietnam national police, extended his right arm and fired his revolver into the head of a Vietcong captive. That brutal assassination, depicted on television as well as in American newspapers, made an indelible impression of the brutality of the leaders of South Vietnam. Westmoreland claimed that the Vietcong had failed. Atrocities accompanied the warfare of both sides. But the pictures of Loan as an executioner and of the enemy within the American compound in Saigon made a permanent impact on the consciousness of many Americans. Within weeks public support of the president's conduct of the war had fallen from 40 to 26 percent, with about half of those critical of Johnson convinced that he had not employed sufficient force in Vietnam.

The Vietcong attacks in Saigon were part of a major enemy offensive planned months earlier to take place during Tet, the lunar new year, a Vietnamese national holiday. General Vo Nguyen Giap, the North Vietnamese strategist who shaped the campaign, intended it to cost enough enemy lives to diminish the American will to fight. In that he succeeded. He also expected to rend the enemy alliance by demonstrating American vulnerability to the South Vietnamese. But the alliance held. Giap was prepared, if necessary, to lose ten of his men for every one his forces killed. "Even at those odds," Ho Chi Minh had warned the Americans years earlier, "you will lose and I will win."

The Tet campaign began in September 1967 with North Vietnamese attacks on American positions in the highlands of central Vietnam near the demilitarized zone between the North and the South. Giap's troops, supplied with modern Soviet weapons, hit American bases in that region of mountains and jungles, and Westmoreland retaliated with some of the heaviest bombing of the war. Undeterred by his losses, Giap in December and January concentrated some thirty-five thousand men against Khe Sanh, a major American forward base. To reinforce that position, Westmoreland sent in six thousand marines with strong artillery support. He also organized Operation Niagara, an uninterrupted torrent of bombings. Recalling the French disaster at Dien Bien Phu, the precipitating occasion of the French withdrawal from Vietnam, Westmoreland announced: "We are not, repeat not, going to be defeated at Khe Sanh."

Though Khe Sanh was not really analogous to Dien Bien Phu, President Johnson, too, made it the object of his particular attention. Giap had expected that American response. His advance against Khe Sanh was a feint, to be sure an expensive feint, designed to pull American forces away from the cities that the Vietcong was then to attack during Tet. At Khe Sanh Giap tolerated dreadful casualties, up to 90 percent of some units. But the feint worked. Westmoreland in late December transferred many of his troops to the northern region, where he expected the enemy offensive to focus. Saigon was left to the protection of the South Vietnamese, in effect to no protection at all. Then, with the Tet holiday, with punishing combat under way at Khe Sanh, the Vietcong who had already infiltrated the major cities in South Vietnam, began their assault in Saigon. Other Vietcong and North Vietnamese units attacked cities in the central highlands. Still others overran the region of the Mekong Delta, where they just about destroyed the vulnerable towns and villages supposedly secured by the American pacification program.

The Tet offensive opened weeks of grim fighting. Combat continued around Saigon until February 20. Until February 24 American marines, assisted by ARVN troops, faced rough resistance, door to door and street by street, in retaking Hue, the cultural capital of Vietnam, where the enemy had murdered several hundred civilians and buried them in a common grave. That atrocity had its near equivalent in the American bombing that leveled the ancient city. Around Khe Sanh, where American bombing and enemy shelling inflicted heavy casualties on both sides, fighting went on through March. By the end of February the kill ratio for Tet favored the Americans and ARVN by close to ten to one, as Giap had predicted.

The enemy, as Westmoreland said, had "suffered a military defeat." But while he claimed victory, he also admitted his need for additional troops. The Joint Chiefs put the figure just above two hundred thousand men, half of them for Vietnam, half for the American strategic reserve or for service elsewhere in Asia or Europe. That requirement underlay the Joint Chiefs' repeated recommendation for calling up the reserves. Their assessment, so Clark Clifford, the new secretary of defense, recalled, was "somber . . . to the point where it was really shocking." Johnson, stunned, ordered Clifford to review the whole situation in Vietnam.

The Tet offensive decimated the Vietcong and cost the North Vietnamese too much to qualify as a victory for them, although most American commentators at the time interpreted it that way. Still, its political cost within the United States constituted a defeat for Lyndon Johnson and his policies. Tet made a travesty of his public optimism about the war. The United States obviously was not in control in Vietnam. The nation was not winning the war. Tet awakened even the conservative press. "The American people," wrote the *Wall Street Journal,* "should be getting ready to accept . . . the prospect that the whole Vietnam effort may be doomed." *Newsweek* and NBC News came out for de-escalation. The Gallup poll early in March reported its sampling of public opinion as 41 percent hawks and 42 percent doves, the rest undecided. Under the impact of Tet, doubters in the Pentagon revealed their previously private opinions to each other. Paul Nitze, never a dove, now worried about the ability of the country to discharge its commitments around the world. He warned against "the unsoundness of continuing to reinforce weakness." Half a dozen other senior civilians expressed similar views.

The American people reacted with dismay to Tet, to the ensuing response of the media, and to the revelation on March 10, 1968 that the Joint Chiefs had requested two hundred thousand more men. On March 12 Eugene McCarthy drew 42 percent of the vote in the Democratic primary in New Hampshire. He had expected no more than 30 percent. Though 49 percent of the voters wrote in Lyndon Johnson's name, McCarthy won more delegates than did the president. Johnson had lost to a senator who had been almost unknown a month earlier. The returns were less a victory for McCarthy than a defeat for Johnson. The vote for McCarthy included as many hawks as doves. In New Hampshire, as elsewhere, many Americans wanted a president who would win the Vietnam War quickly at whatever cost. They were as anti-Johnson as were the advocates of peace at any price or the proponents of a controlled de-escalation. The New Hampshire vote expressed all kinds of disenchantment with a president who had been unable to win the war or quiet the cities. But McCarthy's corps of anti-war volunteers, "clean for Gene," were elated by the taste of blood. They moved on exuberantly for the April 2 primary in Wisconsin, where Johnson's name was officially on the ballot.

By establishing McCarthy as a serious national candidate, the New Hampshire Democrats forced Robert Kennedy to make the decision he had been trying to avoid. "We've got to get out of Vietnam," he had told one journalist privately. "We've got to get out of that war. It's destroying the country." Kennedy admitted he had been wrong in seeing victory ahead in 1962 and 1963. Now openly condemning the bombing and the Saigon regime, he called for a settlement giving "the Vietcong a chance to participate in the political life of the country." Nevertheless, he still resisted the advice of his wife, his sisters, and most of his friends who were urging him to run. Then Johnson spurned the report of his own Commission on Civil Disorders and predictably turned down Kennedy's suggestion to have a commission of distinguished outsiders review policy in Vietnam. "He's not going to do anything about the war," Kennedy concluded, "and he's not going to do anything about the cities, either."

Kennedy did not want to miss his big chance or to lose his constituency to McCarthy. He also believed that he was a stronger candidate than McCarthy and would be a much stronger president. With the vain hope of working in guarded concord with McCarthy, Kennedy declared his candidacy on March 16, 1968. His statement attacked the war, deplored conditions in the cities, and solicited the largest possible vote for McCarthy in Wisconsin. The president had always believed that Kennedy was planning to sabotage his administration. He saw Kennedy's candidacy as confirmation of that belief. And he knew that Kennedy's announcement underscored the administration's political decline. Late in March one of Johnson's scouts informed the president that he had no chance to win the primary in Wisconsin. "Everyone," another wrote him, "has turned into a dove." So it had begun to seem even in the Department of Defense.

3. EXIT LYNDON JOHNSON?

In February 1968, shortly before he took office as secretary of defense, Clark Clifford received a thoughtful letter from Townsend Hoopes, the eloquent and concerned undersecretary of the air force. "The idea of a U.S. military victory in Vietnam," Hoopes wrote, "is a dangerous illusion primarily because both the Soviets and the Chicoms [Chinese Communists] have the capacity to preclude it. . . . If events in Vietnam are ever to take a turn toward settlement, definite de-escalation is a prerequisite. . . . The most promising approach to negotiations and . . . settlement continues to involve a cessation of the U.S. bombing against North Vietnam." But the Joint Chiefs, committed as they were to a military solution in Vietnam, had requested an expansion of the bombing as well as the two hundred thousand troops they said they needed. As Clifford then discovered, the difference between Hoopes and the Joint Chiefs marked the boundaries of the debate about policy in Vietnam that the president on February 28 directed him to evaluate.

Johnson had appointed Clifford to succeed McNamara on the confident assumption that Clifford, in contrast with his predecessor, would be comfortably hawkish. Clifford had always been so before. But the president apparently forgot that Clifford, though a trusted adviser, had always also been too intelligent and too independent to accept the received wisdom about any major political issue. Clifford listened for a week to the members of the task force Johnson had named to assist him in reviewing the war in Vietnam. Several of them were adamant hard-liners. They argued that enemy losses in the Tet offensive presented new opportunities for an American victory if Westmoreland received the necessary support. Most of the others disagreed. The enemy, they observed, still held most of the countryside; Tet had shaken public opinion at home; the involvement in Vietnam was already eroding American positions in the rest of the world. Those positions would crumble if China or the Soviet Union were drawn directly into the Vietnam War by another escalation.

The hawks framed the report that the task force submitted to Johnson, a report that granted substantially everything the military had asked for. Though Clifford submitted it, he was privately worried. The military had not convinced him of its case, and the proposed escalation invited serious domestic difficulties. So he said to the president on March 8. Without either agreeing or disagreeing with the recommendation of the task force, Clifford expressed doubts about both the ground strategy and the bombing operation in Vietnam. Johnson was not pleased. For him, support for the war had become a matter of personal loyalty. Now Clifford, like McNamara, was becoming an apostate.

Then, on March 12, the New Hampshire primary shocked the president. Robert Kennedy's announcement on March 16 enraged him. "Let's get one thing clear," Johnson told his senior advisers that day. "I am not going to stop the bombing. . . . I am not interested in further discussion. . . . I'm not going to stop it." By that date the *New York Times, Time* magazine, and Senators Fulbright and Church, appalled by the size of Westmoreland's request for more soldiers, were condemning both the possibility of reinforcements and the bombing. The president continued his tantrum in public. "We are going to win," he told one audience. "Today we are the Number One Nation," he told another. "And we are going to stay the Number One Nation."

That bombast covered Johnson's private insecurity. With his encouragement, Dean Acheson, the most prestigious of all cold warriors, had been discussing Vietnam with responsible officials in the State Department, the CIA, and the Pentagon. On March 15 he had told the president that the JCS was misleading him. Clifford, who knew in general what Acheson had concluded, suggested to the president a meeting with the Wise Men—the Senior Advisory Group on Vietnam, of which Acheson was one. The president agreed. Several days before that meeting, he also relieved Westmoreland of command, put General Creighton Abrams in his place, and accepted a suggestion of Harry McPherson, his loyal aide and favorite speech writer, to test with the State Department the idea of a cessation of bombing north of the twentieth parallel. Bombing south of that latitude would spare North Vietnam but permit efforts to interdict supplies. In return, Hanoi would be expected not to attack any major South Vietnamese cities.

Johnson, then, had begun to draw back from another escalation before the Wise Men met on March 25 and 26, 1968. Most of them believed, with Acheson, that American policy had reached a dead end. The United States, they reported to the president, could not defeat North Vietnam without recourse to unlimited resources, but the majority of Americans no longer supported the war. The group recommended no precise alteration in policy, but to Johnson's surprise, they clearly counseled de-escalation and negotiation. Two days later, at a conference about a speech for the president on which McPherson was working, Clifford in a "brilliant and utterly courageous performance" attacked the militant text Johnson had called for. McPherson, at Clifford's suggestion, then submitted to the president both a hawkish draft and an alternative "peace speech" with the proposal for a bombing halt north of the twentieth parallel.

Johnson selected the "peace speech" as the basis for his televised address to the country on March 31, 1968. "I am taking the first step," he then told his astonished audience, "to de-escalate the conflict . . . unilaterally and at once. . . . I have ordered our aircraft . . . to make no attacks on North Vietnam, except in the area . . . where the continuing enemy buildup directly threatens allied forward positions. . . . I call upon President Ho Chi Minh to respond positively . . . to this new step toward peace." The United States, Johnson also said, "will never accept a fake solution . . . and call it peace," but he expected peace to come "because America lent her sons to help secure it."

The president had still another surprise to announce. "There is division in the American house now," he said in his peroration. ". . . And holding the trust that is mine, as President of all the people, I cannot disregard the peril to the . . . prospect for peace. . . . I do not believe that I should devote an hour or a day of my time to any personal partisan course. . . Accordingly, I shall not seek, and I will not accept, the nomination of my party for another term as your President."

Johnson had been thinking about that course for a long time. His wife had worried about his health since his heart attack years earlier. He had accomplished just about all he expected to achieve domestically. Indeed, he was involved in a prolonged struggle to persuade Congress to enact a 10 percent surtax on personal incomes in order to raise some of the revenue required by the war. That tax, in itself inadequate, came too late to stem the inflation, a function of defense spending, that was overheating the economy, irritating consumers, and weakening the dollar abroad. Johnson's political opponents, many Democrats as well as Republicans, were spoiling, as he knew, to punish him with a major personal defeat, as they later did in blocking his nomination of his friend Abe Fortas as chief justice of the United States.

The polls showed how unpopular the president had become. He confronted a bruising fight for renomination, a fight that would further divide the Democrats and enhance Republican chances. Indeed, he faced imminent defeat in Wisconsin. But Johnson had survived rough political battles, and Johnson loved power. It would not have been in character for him to drop out because of the rivalry of McCarthy and Kennedy or because of the possibility of the loss of a few primaries. He would still have controlled the party in a majority of states. Rather, Johnson withdrew in part for just the reasons he cited: to help reunite the nation, to help move the war toward a negotiated settlement.

Probably in larger part he withdrew because the war, and the bitter opposition to it, had drained his spirit. He had always had doubts, usually unexpressed, about the war in Vietnam. He had always rejected at least some part of the requests the military made. He had always found the war a torment and feared its consequences for his domestic programs. In dealing with Vietnam, he had, therefore, always especially needed praise and reassurance. Now the statesmen he most respected had told him he had erred. That must have cut him as much as the hostile mood of the majority of Americans whose adoration he so desperately sought. Weary, wounded, old beyond his sixty years, Johnson had sufficient reason to abjure a contest for reelection.

But by no means did the president renounce the politics of the election year. He was as determined as ever not to lose the war in Vietnam.

LBJ: The war had drained his spirit.

He was convinced that antiwar protesters were poisoning the country, that "we are defeating ourselves." For six months he heeded the advice of Rusk and Rostow, the still-influential hawks, who urged heavy bombing of enemy positions south of the demilitarized zone (DMZ). With General Taylor and General Earle Wheeler, chairman of the Joint Chiefs, they still pursued a military victory, though within the constraints of Johnson's speech of March 31. For his part, the president, eager to sustain the strongest military position possible, still wanted negotiations somehow to assure a free and independent South Vietnam. Since Hanoi would not consider that eventuality, and since Hanoi demanded a total end of the bombing as a condition for a cease-fire, negotiations began but immediately faltered. The war went on, and the issue of the war therefore remained central to Democratic politics.

The president still controlled the apparatus of the party—the national and state organizations, the committees responsible for managing the convention. He insisted on a platform devoted to his record, his Great Society, his policy in Southeast Asia. He also insisted on a candidate of his own selection, a candidate dedicated to that record. Predictably he turned to his obsequious vice president. So after March 31, just as the war went on, so did the race for the nomination. Johnson was able to forgo that race only because he meant nevertheless to prevail through his substitute. He was tired; but he still enjoyed the power of his office, and he was avid to use it to defeat Robert Kennedy, "that grand-standing little runt," who dared oppose him. Johnson was wounded, but he was as vindictive and as dangerous as he had ever been.

4. MEMPHIS

With Johnson's withdrawal and Hubert Humphrey's decision to delay the official announcement of his candidacy until a more propitious time, McCarthy and Kennedy faced off against each other. The first test of their comparative strength came in the Indiana primary on May 7. Both continued to condemn the adminstration's conduct of the war, but McCarthy also attacked Kennedy as a ruthless opportunist, a Johnny-come-lately in the contest for the nomination. Kennedy, avoiding open criticism of McCarthy, set out, as he put it, "to heal the deep divisions that exist between races, between age groups and on the war." Standing as the candidate of reconciliation, he also appealed, as McCarthy never had, to the poor and the powerless, the men and women who had remained apart from national politics largely because the major parties had made no effort to involve them.

Those Americans—the impoverished, the excluded, the despairing of all races—were the designated beneficiaries of the Poor People's Campaign that Martin Luther King, Jr., had made his top priority for 1968. Though he had yet to endorse Kennedy, King was planning "to get behind Bobby." On April 4, 1968, he went to Memphis to lead a demonstration for the striking garbage workers there. That evening, standing on the balcony of his hotel room, he was assassinated by a rifle shot fired by a racist ex-convict. Later one of King's lieutenants tried without success to reinvigorate the Poor People's Campaign. But on April 4, with the first reports of King's death, riots broke out in Washington, D.C., and in more than a hundred other cities. King had preached nonviolence, but the rioters, in an ironic catharsis, burned the ghettos in which they lived to vent their grief over his death and their fury at his white assassin.

In the Ebenezer Baptist Church in Atlanta on April 7, the dignitaries of white politics joined with sorrowing blacks at the services for Martin Luther King, Jr. The vice president attended, as did Republicans Richard Nixon and Nelson Rockefeller and as did Kennedy and McCarthy. Later that day Kennedy met with King's closest friends. "White America," so King's successor in SCLC said of Kennedy, "does have someone in it who cares." Another black leader thought: "Maybe Bobby Kennedy would come up with some answers for the country."

In the largest sense, King had had the answers: cessation of the Vietnam War: interracial harmony; financial support and employment for the poor. The epitome of the liberal spirit, he had been the most dynamic of the men and women resolved to preserve the essentials of the American system by reforming that system from within, by redistributing its wealth, by purging its inequalities. And he had known that he could succeed only by proceeding peacefully, without violence and without hatred. As a political as well as a moral force, King had been the greatest black American of his time. Now he was gone. "Martin Luther King," Robert Kennedy had said when first he heard about the assassination, "dedicated his life to love and to justice for his fellow human beings, and he died because of that effort. . . . For those of you who are black . . . you can be filled with bitterness, with hatred, with a desire for revenge. . . . Or we can make an effort, as Martin Luther King did, to understand . . . with compassion and love. . . . I had a member of my family killed. . . . But we have to make an effort in the United States, we have to make an effort to understand."

5. LOS ANGELES

Late in April, while Kennedy and McCarthy were campaigning hard in Indiana, Hubert Humphrey officially announced his candidacy. The vice president entered no primaries, but he had the support of the Democratic city machines, Mayor Daley's Chicago organization particularly. He could also count upon centrist and hawkish Democrats, including the leaders of organized labor and of the party in the South—in all, most of those who had long provided the bulk of Democratic campaign funds. As Johnson's puppet Humphrey had continually lashed out against opponents of the Vietnam War. Late in April the fighting was still heavy, the memory of King's assassination and of the ensuing riots still fresh, when the vice president declared. He stood, he then said with perverse insensitivity, for "the politics of happiness . . . the politics of joy."

For their parts, McCarthy and Kennedy were addressing the issues dividing the country. Both advocated a total end to the bombing in Vietnam as well as the inclusion in the peace negotiations of representatives of the National Liberation Front—conditions Johnson and Humphrey opposed. Both peace candidates also proposed new ventures in urban reform. McCarthy wanted to build new communities at the periphery of the cities so that ghetto blacks could move out to the sites of most jobs. Kennedy, convinced that the ghettos would not be eliminated in the near future, believed government should cooperate with private enterprise to rebuild the inner cities, locate new industry in them, and train the residents for the resulting opportunities for employment. Those differences between the two men were easily reconcilable, but their contrasting views of the presidency were not. McCarthy criticized John F. Kennedy and Lyndon Johnson for personalizing and aggrandizing their office to the detriment of the other branches of the federal government. He suggested limiting presidents to one six-year term. Robert Kennedy, as his knowledgeable biographer put it, thought that "only an activist President and an affirmative national government . . . could pull together a divided people in a stormy time."

Those issues were less divisive than were the temperaments and personalities of the two candidates. Kennedy kept repeating his desire for harmony with McCarthy, whose cooperation he would need if he were to win the nomination. But McCarthy and many of his supporters continued to resent Kennedy's entrance into the race. Uncomfortable in the company of the underprivileged, especially with minority groups,

McCarthy had little appeal for black or Hispanic Americans. His following was essentially white, middle-class, and suburban.

Kennedy, his sympathies and perceptions growing, as they had been for years, had extraordinary rapport with Americans of color who had long suffered from social and economic discrimination. By 1967 the example of black power had encouraged movements for brown power and red power. Kennedy related to them all. His sympathy for their plight earned him the admiration of Puerto Ricans in New York City. He supported Cesar Chavez in his heroic effort to organize Mexican-American agricultural workers in California. Kennedy investigated destitution on Indian reservations in Oklahoma and upstate New York. Even his critics recognized the authenticity of his compassion. As Gore Vidal, one of those critics wrote, "He had a real affinity for the hurt people of the world, the blacks, the poor, the misunderstood young."

Yet, as another observer put it, Kennedy could also "do the miraculous: attract the support of . . . working class white people." Kennedy even faced the law and order issue squarely. He talked "honestly and openly. . . . He respected . . . himself too much to utter the usual lies and evasions." So on the stump, after urging social justice, he "was blunt in warning his black supporters that lawlessness and violence were intolerable." He had been attorney general of the United States,

Robert F. Kennedy with Cesar Chavez: Extraordinary rapport.

he reminded his listeners, and he demanded law and order—law and order not just for themselves but as necessary in "a single, shared nation."

The results of the Democratic primaries revealed both the strength of the antiwar candidates and the preference of the voters for Kennedy. In May Kennedy led in Indiana with 42 percent of the vote to McCarthy's 27 percent, and only 31 percent for the organization's stand-in candidate. In the District of Columbia Kennedy polled 62.5 percent to Humphrey's 37.5. In Nebraska Kennedy received 52 percent of the votes. Late in May, in Oregon, a state of mostly white middle-class voters, McCarthy won with 45 percent to Kennedy's 39. They moved then to California, where McCarthy at times seemed lackadaisical or churlish. The audience for their televised debate much preferred Kennedy's performance. So on June 3 did the voters, who went 46 percent to Kennedy, 42 to McCarthy, the balance to Humphrey's stand-in.

That night the Kennedy camp calculated that Humphrey had more than 900 convention delegates from states without primaries, while Kennedy had more than 500 and McCarthy more than 200, with some 870 still undecided. Kennedy was outdistancing McCarthy, but he had to convert his rival's following and to woo the undecided delegates. At his victory address to the crowd gathered in the ballroom of his Los Angeles hotel, Kennedy congratulated McCarthy for "breaking the political logjam," asked McCarthy's people to join him, and exhorted his fans: "On to Chicago and let's win there." He had a fair chance to do so. But as he was departing through the adjoining hallway, a fanatic Arab nationalist shot and killed him.

While Kennedy's casket lay in St. Patrick's Cathedral in New York City, huge crowds filed past in mourning. Chicago Mayor Richard Daley cried, and in a rear pew Tom Hayden wept. In death Kennedy had brought together those representatives of American political extremes, just as he might have done in life. After the service the train carrying the casket, the Kennedy family, and close friends passed grieving Americans, black and white, waiting alongside the tracks on the way to Washington. Kennedy had been the last liberal who could reach both races as well as both generations. In April, King; in June, Kennedy—the two most understanding, the two most magnetic, the two most needed Americans were gone. Robert Kennedy, so one of his associates recalled after thirty years, was "the last major leader who allowed us to at least imagine we could realize the ideals of American politics."

6. CHICAGO

Kennedy's death gave a quick burst to McCarthy's candidacy. Public opinion polls revealed McCarthy's rising popularity. In the New York primary in mid-June he won a majority of the delegates. But McCarthy sank into a listless detachment. His speeches became flat. He left the direction of tactics so important for the organization of his national campaign to the direction of his squabbling lieutenants. He made little effort to gain the support of the Kennedy loyalists, of whom some turned to Humphrey and others, in a holding operation, to Senator George McGovern of South Dakota, a liberal, antiwar Democrat. As the convention approached, McCarthy seemed not really to want the nomination, though his supporters remained fervent.

He worried about the army of his student volunteers, who were eager to join him in Chicago. McCarthy instructed his local offices to keep those young people away, and he had his staff consult Chicago officials about how to insulate those who came from trouble. For there was bound to be trouble. The Mobe was organizing antiwar demonstrations for which Mayor Daley had little tolerance, and the Yippies, intent on proving the repressiveness of the American state, were planning disruptive provocations to rile the Chicago police.

Lyndon Johnson dominated the convention even though he dared not attend it for fear of hostile responses to his presence. With Daley as his agent on the scene, the president arranged to seat the large antiwar New York and California delegations at the rear of the hall, well separated from each other. Nearer the rostrum reliable delegations would respond to signals Daley sent to Carl Albert, the majority leader of the House of Representatives, who was to chair the convention. The president's men also controlled the crucial committees on rules, on credentials, and on the platform. They could turn back almost any challenge by the McCarthy camp to the legitimacy of Humphrey delegations from contested states. They could see to it, though not without a battle with the McCarthy forces, that the platform praised the president's policy in Vietnam.

Humphrey had no voice about those matters. Indeed, he had no influence on Johnson, who had been mocking him in private for weeks. Sullen and mean in his exile, the president appeared determined to display his power over the party and his disdain for his chosen successor. Emasculated by his ambition, Humphrey glumly accepted his humiliation. Though he would like to have moderated the platform on

Vietnam, he yielded to the president's preference. He did nothing to curb Daley's bullying tactics on the floor. Worst of all, he made no effort to persuade Daley to restrain the Chicago police, who bloodied the downtown streets at the very time Humphrey was waiting to receive the prize that his disgrace permitted him to collect.

In Chicago during the last week of August 1968 Humphrey's "politics of joy" exploded in the disarray of the Democratic Convention. Television reached millions of Americans with an alarming counterpoint depicting now the turbulence among the delegates and now the brutality of the city police. On August 27, a Tuesday, there began and ended a movement manqué to draft Senator Edward Kennedy, the youngest of the Kennedy brothers. It depended on the unlikely cooperation of Richard Daley and Eugene McCarthy. Daley saw no way in which a draft could succeed; McCarthy was predictably cool to the idea. Kennedy, still feeling the shock of his brother's death, was not ready to run. That night proceedings centered on the party's rules, though the New York delegation whooped it up for Kennedy, and the police fought with the Yippies in downtown Lincoln Park.

The Yippies had found the violence they sought in that park, where local ordinances forbade both demonstrations and sleeping on the grass. There were skirmishes with the police Sunday, Monday, and Tuesday of convention week. Tuesday night the Yippies and some members of the Mobe, as well as many young bystanders, retreated from Lincoln Park to Grant Park, just outside the Hilton Hotel, where McCarthy and Humphrey had their separate headquarters. The police had given Grant Park a temporary immunity from the restrictive ordinances. But the Yippies did not want immunity. The leaders of the Mobe, also eager to make a splash on television, announced that on Wednesday they would march through the streets of Chicago to the site of the convention, though they had been denied a permit to do so. They were timing their demonstration to follow the debate at the convention about the plank on Vietnam and to coincide with the nominating speeches.

Street theater would compete with the drama on the convention floor, and street theater had put on revolutionary garb. The Yippies, taunting the police, had been shouting: "Fuck pigs, oink, oink!" The police, charging, had shouted in return: "Kill the Commies! Get the bastards!" Twice arrested and twice released, Tom Hayden of the SDS and the Mobe had adopted a series of disguises. He had condemned the Yippies for their "media gamesmanship," but in addressing demonstrators in Grant Park, he said: "Now that the pig is on the collective back of all of us, we are going to find a way to go underground." That sounded dangerously radical to the police. Hayden was playing at being Che Guevara. On a high that week, he had refused to condemn the recent Soviet invasion of Czechoslovakia. In Chicago he acted at times like a furtive juvenile. Jerry Rubin was worse. I. F. Stone, the eminent socialist journalist, mourned the behavior of radical youth in and around Lincoln and Grant parks. "In revulsion against the war," he wrote, "the best of a generation was being lost—some . . . to drugs, some . . . to almost hysterical frenzy and alienation." As for the police, as one British journalist wrote, their reaction "was worthy of any Wehrmacht Einsatz Kommando in Poland."

On Wednesday afternoon, August 28, the convention rejected a peace plank on Vietnam by a margin of five hundred votes. Johnson had the endorsement he had demanded: "We strongly support . . . the initiative of President Johnson which brought North Vietnam to the peace table." The bombing would stop only when that action "would not endanger the lives of our troops." Disgusted by that phraseology, the

Daley's troops in Chicago: The Democrats were finished.

New York and California delegations began to sing "We Shall Overcome," but the president's loyalists turned down their mikes. Outside the hall news of Johnson's victory soon reached the mob of people in Grant Park or walking along the neighboring streets. Some were students from the McCarthy movement. Others were from the Mobe, or were Yippies, or were just observers. Early that evening a few bumped the police. The National Guard let go with tear gas, which soon penetrated the ground floor of the Hilton.

About an hour later on Michigan Avenue, the Mobe march, approaching the hotel, confronted a thick line of policemen. Some of the marchers were shouting: "Peace now, peace now," then: "Fuck you, LBJ, Fuck you, LBJ." A wedge of cops pushed through the crowd, with policemen clubbing the demonstrators and dragging them into paddy wagons. The crowd scattered. Then came more tear gas, another police charge. The violence continued for another half hour with police seizing the demonstrators and the demonstrators sometimes resisting, sometimes yelling, "Sieg heil. Sieg heil." and, conscious of the TV cameras, shouting, "The whole world is watching. The whole world is watching."

Certainly the American people were watching, appalled by what they saw. Theodore H. White, in Chicago in his role as reverent chronicler of presidential campaigns, wrote himself a note: "The Democrats are finished." The police had been taunted and ridiculed, but they had overreacted. The country saw Daley's cops batter defenseless young Americans, most of them children of the white middle class. McCarthy, observing the scene from his hotel window, seemed at first detached, then outraged, but unwilling to go down to try to calm the crowd. The people in Grant Park, he implied, had become captives of the agitators: "If I go down, I claim them, and they're not mine."

Humphrey managed to see nothing of the violence. Instead, he turned to television focusing on the speeches putting his name before the delegates. As the speeches proceeded, and then the balloting, Daley appeared continually on camera, looking like an angry bullfrog as he signaled his instructions to the chair. Through it all, TV interrupted with shots of the turmoil that had filled the streets. A quarter before midnight Humphrey had the nomination, but a nomination drenched in bile. On Thursday Humphrey chose as his running mate Senator Edmund Muskie of Maine, best known as a champion of clean water and clean air. In his acceptance speech that night Humphrey expressed his pride in Lyndon Johnson. That comment erased his closing message: "Put aside recrimination and disunion. Turn away from violence and hatred."

Daley's henchmen paid no heed. At the convention, guards punched a CBS reporter for questioning the suppression of dissent. When Senator Abraham Ribicoff of Connecticut at the podium courageously condemned Daley's "Gestapo tactics," Daley shook his fist and shouted obscenities. A Colorado delegate described Chicago as a police state. The city seemed to be exactly that. Downtown, before dawn on Friday, the police outside the Hilton complained that they were being hit by cans thrown from the windows of the hotel. They claimed the cans came from the fifteenth floor, where some of the McCarthy workers had gathered. There was no evidence to support that claim. Nevertheless, without a warrant and without cause, the police charged the hotel, took elevators to the fifteenth floor, beat the young men and women who were there with billies, and muscled them toward the lobby.

Summoned by his staff, McCarthy arrived only after the police had left in order to escape the television crews on their way to the hotel. The senator remained to help steady his wounded warriors. But Humphrey's staff would not awake the candidate to report the police attack. In a sense Humphrey slept through the whole convention, indeed the entire preceding campaign. He had won no primary. Rarely, if ever, had he seemed alert to the passions surging through and beyond the politics of 1968.

For Jerry Rubin and the Yippies, Chicago was a triumph. "We wanted exactly what happened," he later wrote. ". . . We wanted to create a situation in which the . . . Daley administration and the federal government . . . would self-destruct." Rubin even secretly agreed with the government when it indicted him along with Hayden and four others—in the end without a conviction—for conspiring to riot in Chicago.

The unindicted conspirators were Lyndon Johnson and his agent Richard Daley. The mayor need not have feared the radicals as he did. Had he been generous in issuing permits for demonstrations, had he permitted young out-of-towners to sleep on the grass, had he sustained discipline among the police, he could have managed the week without bloodshed. The National Commission on Violence concluded that the police response to the provocations of the crowd had been "unrestrained and indiscriminate." The events in the city had been a "police riot." Daley raised police salaries. The mayor hated the radicals, their beliefs, their manner, their dress, and so did his policemen. So, too, did the president, who had wanted for months, as he had said, "to get

them in the balls." And so did most of the American people. A national
poll reported that only 19 percent thought the police had used "too
much force." In public Hubert Humphrey also maintained that Daley
had done nothing wrong. But in private he was desolate. Too late, after
the convention was over, Humphrey realized the damage he had suffered. "Chicago," he wrote, "was a catastrophe."

7. Nixon Redux

Chicago was a boon for the rival presidential campaigns of George
Wallace and Richard Nixon, both of whom were making a major issue
of law and order. Wallace had been pushing toward the presidency
since his strong showing in several Democratic primaries in 1964. He
based his independent national campaign on the same strategy that
had guided him in Alabama. As he had put it in 1958, "I'm not going
to be out-niggered again." Nor was he. In 1968 he campaigned unabashedly as a racist. As a southerner and a racist he blamed the civil
rights movement for the disorder in southern cities during the Kennedy administration, and he blamed black radicals and their white allies
for the urban violence of the Johnson years. He condemned the federal
government for encouraging those disruptions. In the custom of southern racists, he maintained that the president and the Supreme Court
especially had exceeded their constitutional authority in order to impose
integrationist policies on unwilling whites.

Those arguments found a receptive audience in blue-collar neighborhoods in northern cities. "By the fall of 1968," Wallace had predicted accurately, "the people of Cleveland and Chicago and Gary and
St. Louis will be so goddamned sick and tired of Federal interference
in their local schools, they'll be ready to vote for Wallace. . . . Law and
order. Crime in the Streets. People are going to be fed up with the sissy
attitude of Lyndon Johnson. . . . They're fed up with . . . [the] Supreme
Court . . . a no account outfit. . . . Housing? . . . That'll be an issue . . .
any time the Federal government lays down the law . . . fixing the terms
. . . on which they can sell their own homes."

The Wallace organization, to the amazement of most political pundits, succeeded in placing his new party, the American Independence
party, on the ballot in all fifty states. Wallace climbed in the polls from
9 percent in May 1968 to 16 percent in June, and in September, just
after the Democratic Convention, to 21 percent. He was cutting into
the Republican vote in the South and the Democratic labor vote in the

North. If his support continued to grow at its prevailing rate, he would have 30 percent in November, enough to throw the decision into the electoral college. That was his objective, for then he would be in a position to demand the concessions he wanted. Meanwhile, a dangerous candidate, he denounced the "overeducated, ivory-tower folks with pointed heads" and the "sissy britches" running Washington. As he attacked them, he continued to cultivate the hatreds with which his chosen constituency was bursting.

With Wallace on the right wing of American politics and the antiwar Democrats on the left, Richard M. Nixon commanded the center. Nixon had staged a remarkable comeback. Defeated in an ill-conceived race for governor in California in 1962, he had seemed then at the end of his political career. But he had moved to New York City as a partner in an established and prosperous law firm, made more money than he had ever had before, and in 1964 campaigned vigorously for Barry Goldwater. In 1966 he spoke in behalf of Republican congressional candidates all over the country and received much of the credit for the party's resurgence that year. Thereafter the odds-on favorite for the Republican nomination in 1968, Nixon put together a skilled personal organization to assure his capture of that prize. They were fortified with ample funds and experienced in the techniques of commercial advertising. They packaged their man as the "new Nixon," a seasoned veteran of world politics, calm, confident, and, of course, available. Even veteran reporters believed that hype, especially after Nixon, utilizing television with calculated effectiveness, carried the New Hampshire primary with more votes than his Republican opponents and the Democrats combined. Even more than McCarthy, Nixon was the beneficiary of Tet. More primary victories followed.

Nixon had no strong rival for the Republican nomination. Governor Nelson Rockefeller of New York, the leading Republican moderate, at first helped finance the campaign of George Romney, the former Michigan governor who proved to be politically inept. After Romney withdrew, Rockefeller poured millions into his own campaign, but the Republican right wing detested him. Always more shadow than substance, Rockefeller, like his brothers, had bought ideas from eminent intellectuals and publicity from journalists in awe of wealth. Now, in 1968, he represented, most of all, his own raw ambition to stop Nixon, in the end by a futile alliance of convenience with the Republican right. Governor Ronald Reagan of California emerged as the favorite of that right wing; but his organization was in disarray, and the shattering defeat of Goldwater had soured the reputation of Reagan's reaction-

Nixon and Agnew: Candidates for Middle America.

aries. Nixon had prudently recruited for his staff several of Goldwater's former advisers and after the New Hampshire primary made the promises necessary to bring the leading southern Republicans into his fold. Months before the Republicans gathered in Miami early in August 1968, Nixon had wrapped up the nomination. He selected as his running mate Governor Spiro T. Agnew of Maryland. A declared enemy of radicals, Agnew came to rival George Wallace in the folksy vitriol of his oratory. He was to be the hatchet man in the Republican campaign.

Nixon had already established the tenor of that campaign. He had shrewdly avoided taking a position on Vietnam. In March, when he had felt pressed to speak on that issue, he had canceled a planned address so as not to conflict with the president, who chose the same date, March 31, to announce his partial bombing halt as a step toward peace. Thereafter Nixon held that he should say nothing that might damage negotiations with North Vietnam. In the autumn he found it convenient to imply that he had a secret plan for Vietnam, though he had no genuine plan at all except to prevent an American defeat. That was what he meant when he promised the Republican Convention "an honorable end to the Vietnamese War." And that was just the outcome most voters wanted.

The time had come, Nixon also said in his acceptance speech, "for an era of negotiation" with the Communist nations, but that theme receded during his campaign. Instead, Nixon stressed domestic issues, including law and order. In part he was talking about a war against crime, with the Supreme Court's decision in *Miranda* one of his targets. In at least equal part he was telling a genteel audience just what George Wallace was saying to his fellow red-necks. For Nixon, as for Wallace, "law and order" in large degree was an anagram for "race." So conceived, law and order provided the foundation for the strategy by which Nixon expected to carry the border states of the South, as well as Florida and Texas. He conceded the Deep South to Wallace. But with the near southern states, the West, and several northern industrial states, he could attain the electoral votes he needed for victory. He cultivated the South by prómising to appoint to the federal courts, the Supreme Court especially, judges committed to strict construction of the Constitution. They would lead a retreat from the liberal interpretations of the Warren Court, particularly on civil rights but also on the rights of individuals accused of crimes. In contrast with the evolving doctrine of the Supreme Court, Nixon opposed the compulsory busing of children in order to achieve racial balance in public schools. In the same vein he said he would not withhold federal funds from school districts that were tardy in meeting federal standards for desegregation.

Those assurances, like his criticisms of *Miranda*, comforted not just the white South but also the northern suburbs. Nixon made a continual appeal to the latter constituency. "I say it's time," he asserted, "to quit pouring billions of dollars into programs that have failed." In contrast with the Great Society, he would turn to private enterprise to reconstruct the country. "Black capitalism"—federal loans to black entrepreneurs—would supplant Democratic handouts. The objectives of the new leadership that Nixon promised—restoration of international respect, restoration of a stable economy—met the yearnings of the middle class. In his set text he spoke of "a new voice . . . being heard across America." He said: "It is different from the old voices, the voices of hatred, the voices of dissension, the voices of riot and revolution." The new voices were those of "the forgotten Americans, those who did not indulge in violence, those who did not break the law, people who pay their taxes and go to work, people who send their children to school, who go to their churches, people who are not haters, people who love this country." Those were Nixon's people—"laborers . . . and managers," he said, "white and black." Primarily they were middle-class people, tired of the war but loath to see it lost, burdened by taxes, resentful of federal programs that interfered with their lives. They were people offended by college kids who did not behave and by ghetto blacks who lacked gratitude for federal assistance.

The Middle Americans to whom Nixon appealed were mostly regular Republicans, some of whom had voted for Johnson in 1964 and come to regret it. Nixon had no need for the votes of regular Democrats so long as Wallace attracted enough of them to keep Humphrey from winning the industrial states of the North and so long as Wallace attracted too few to defeat the Republican strategy in the South. But the Wallace candidacy was not predictable. In October the AFL-CIO financed a strong operation to turn the labor vote from Wallace back to the Democrats. For his part, Wallace chose as his running mate General Curtis LeMay, former chief of staff of the air force. A rigid authoritarian, LeMay was the supreme advocate of nuclear weaponry. The United States, he had said, seemingly recommending the prospect, could "bomb the North Vietnamese back to the Stone Age." The thought of nuclear war scared marginal voters away from Wallace and LeMay. Humphrey ridiculed the ticket as "the bombsy twins." Wallace's poor judgment, his awkwardness on TV, and his vulnerability to the unions' attacks hurt his campaign. Through October the polls registered his steady decline. Nixon had a real race on his hands after all.

8. VERDICT

Wallace's decline coincided with Humphrey's resurgence. During September Humphrey had stumbled, his campaign underfinanced, his message unpersuasive. Ringing the changes on traditional Democratic themes, he had evoked FDR, Harry Truman, and Jack Kennedy. But they were not the salient symbols in 1968. Humphrey promised jobs, peace, harmony, but he ran in the shadow of Chicago and as the surrogate of Lyndon Johnson. Eugene McCarthy would not endorse him. Protesters at Democratic rallies shouted, "Peace now" and "Dump the Hump." Then two developments turned the campaign around. The

AFL-CIO drive for Democratic votes began to take hold. And Humphrey decided to declare his personal independence from Johnson. He did so in a televised speech at Salt Lake City on September 30. "As President," Humphrey said, "I would stop the bombing of North Vietnam as an acceptable risk for peace because I believe it could lead to success in the negotiations and thereby shorten the war. . . . If the government of North Vietnam were to show bad faith, I would reserve the right to resume the bombing. . . . I would take the risk that the South Vietnamese . . . are now ready to assume . . . their self-defense; I would move . . . towards de-Americanization of the war."

The speech did not satisfy the North Vietnamese demand for an unconditional bombing halt, but it took one step more toward peace than Johnson had. Humphrey thereafter stood as his own man. The hecklers at the hustings disappeared. Sizable contributions flowed to the Democratic National Committee. Most of McCarthy's supporters endorsed Humphrey, as did the Americans for Democratic Action. In contrast with his rivals, Humphrey had become plausibly the candidate of peace. During the last third of October the polls showed him closing in on Nixon.

Concurrently opportunities arose for a cease-fire in Vietnam, which might have tipped the balance to the Democrats. Negotiations with the North Vietnamese in Paris had been stalled over several related issues. The United States would not agree to stop the still-heavy bombing near the DMZ without assurances of the safety of American troops in the cities of South Vietnam. Hanoi held out for an unconditional bombing halt. Hanoi also declined the American demand for the South Vietnamese government to join the negotiations, while Washington in turn opposed seating the National Liberation Front. But the Soviet Union, increasingly worried by the enmity of the Chinese, was weighing the advantage of rapprochement with the United States. Pressed by Moscow, Hanoi responded cautiously to American overtures in Paris. "Step by step," as Lyndon Johnson recalled, "hour by hour, argument by argument, we worked out a new arrangement with the North Vietnamese." On October 28 President Thieu gave it his assent. Future negotiations would include both the South Vietnamese government and the NLF. All bombing would stop, with the United States reserving the right of reconnaissance flights over North Vietnam and, in the event of an attack on South Vietnamese cities, of retaliation. On October 31, a Thursday—the election was the next Tuesday—Johnson informed Humphrey, Nixon and Wallace. On national television that evening the president announced the total halt in American bombing, effective the next day, and expressed his belief that it would lead to a peaceful settlement of the war.

If the arrangement had held, Humphrey might have won the election, but Thieu had spoken only for himself. At the insistence of Vice President Ky and the National Assembly, on November 1 he stated that his government would not participate in talks with the enemy. The next day eleven South Vietnamese senators declared their support of Richard Nixon. It was mid-January before the South Vietnamese joined the negotiations at Paris. Infuriated, Johnson instinctively blamed the Republicans for sabotaging peace. Anna Chan Chennault, the Asian wife of the late American general and cochair of Republican Women for Nixon, had used Nixon's name at his instigation, to recruit opposition in Saigon to Johnson's "arrangement" while its terms were leaking during the week before the president's announcement. As if to excuse his interference, Nixon later wrote that he found it "difficult to accept" Johnson's timing: "Announcing the halt so close to the election was utterly callous if politically calculated, and utterly naive if sincere." Johnson also faulted Humphrey's Salt Lake City speech for making "the leaders in Saigon . . . nervous and distrustful of the . . . entire Democratic party." But it was Johnson himself who had accepted the vainglorious Ky and feckless Thieu as the agents of American policy in South Vietnam. And characteristically, so he boasted, Johnson remained "convinced that if I had run again I would have been elected."

Humphrey lost, though his late surge helped his count. Nixon received 43.4 percent of the popular vote, Humphrey 42.7 percent, Wallace 13.5 percent. In the electoral college Nixon ran well ahead with 302 votes to Humphrey's 191. Nevertheless, the Democrats held both houses of Congress. Those mixed results obscured the magnitude of Humphrey's defeat. As Theodore White observed, "The election of 1968 was . . . a negative landslide." Between them Nixon and Wallace polled just under 57 percent of the popular vote, "undeniably a swing to the right."

The Johnson coalition of 1964 splintered in 1968. Humphrey carried even less of the old South than Johnson had. Four million voters there cast their ballots for Wallace. In the North Humphrey carried only one-third of the white vote. The "hard hats," the blue-collar workers of the north-central states, gave Wallace strong support—overall more than 10 percent of the total turnout in Ohio, Michigan, Indiana, and Illinois. Wallace did even better in the mountain states of Nevada and Idaho. The conservative tide in those regions lifted Republican prospects for the future. So did the renaissance of the GOP in the suburbs west of the Appalachians. Though most blacks remained Democratic, in 1968 many of them stayed home, as did some antiwar liberals, but the Republicans did not need those constituencies to remain in power. If they could hold the vote that Nixon drew and add the vote for Wallace, they could win presidential elections for years to come. In that respect, after thirty-four years of Democratic primacy, the Republicans in 1968 became potentially the dominant American political party.

As Nixon had understood, the voters had not repudiated all the programs of the Great Society. He intended to continue, though in modified form, those Democratic policies that he considered socially useful and politically attractive. That was part of his strategy to convert the Wallace vote, which he meant to solicit also by delivering on his promise to the South about civil rights.

The election of 1968 did register a national rejection of the Johnson administration and of the apparent results of liberal policies. Since most voters could not differentiate those appearances from the policies themselves, the liberals lost as much as Johnson did. In the liberal agenda, Keynesian fiscal policy had provided the key to full employment. But in Johnson's practice, full employment turned into inflation because the president, to the dismay of his Keynesian advisers, delayed too long in requesting and obtaining increased taxation to finance the Vietnam War. The liberal agenda included the fight against poverty, which Johnson expanded, but it never attacked the endemic nature of the problem and never received the federal funds necessary for its success. The liberal agenda focused on civil rights, a cause Johnson nurtured for the South. But when civil rights became an urgent issue in the North, Johnson drew back, solicitous of traditional Democratic constituencies, penurious in his priority for the Vietnam War. After the riots in the cities Johnson ignored the recommendations for appropriate remedies that his own commission of investigation proposed. On all those counts, Robert Kennedy had found Johnson wrong. So did those Democrats, most of them liberals, who by 1967 had come to oppose the Vietnam War. More than they realized at the time, they, too, were rejected in 1968. The country, as Theodore Roosevelt had once put it, was no longer "in an heroic mood."

Johnson was not entirely to blame. The millions of baby boomers would have come of age in the late 1960s no matter what the federal government had done. Tension between the generations would therefore have developed on an unprecedented scale and would have racked the colleges and universities, enclaves of the young. Hostility between the races marked the whole American past, as did conflicts of interest between social classes. Johnson could not have erased them. But the intensity of the divisions between Americans, the virulence of their disagreements, owed much to Lyndon Johnson's policies in Vietnam. So did the election of Richard Nixon. With that election the Vietnam War became Nixon's war, and the discord among Americans became Nixon's to alleviate.

11

R N

As president Richard Nixon was a paradox. He was serious, intelligent, inventive, and sometimes bold. He had several senior advisers of extraordinary talent. His major decisions exerted powerful influences on his times. Yet he was also isolated, phobic, wrathful, and continually dishonest—"the most dishonest individual," Barry Goldwater later wrote, "I have ever met in my life . . . Nixon lied to his wife, his family, his friends . . . his own political party, the American people, and the world." Prevarication, secretiveness, and suspiciousness filled Nixon's days. He was sane, and he was responsible; but his were the characteristics of a disturbed personality.

Nixon anchored his personal stability in his unyielding defense of what he called the square virtues. At the time of his election he felt that his values—those also of most other citizens—were under siege. Uncomfortable with people of color, he scorned black power, brown power, red power. He feared that feminism would shred the American family and that drugs would destroy American youth. "I was ready to take a stand on these social and cultural issues," he recalled. ". . . in some cases—such as opposing the legalization of marijuana and provision of federal funds for abortion, and in identifying myself with unabashed patriotism—I knew I would be standing against the prevailing social and cultural winds."

The square virtues, Nixon believed, helped sustain the established order. He had to be a bulwark of that order, or it would crumble. "I had watched the sixties from outside the arena of leadership," he later wrote. "I saw the mass demonstrations . . . become a cultural fad. And the new sensitivities to social inequities . . . spawned an intolerance for the rights and opinions of those who disagreed. . . . I had no patience with mindless rioters and professional malcontents, and I was appalled by the response of most of the nation's political and academic leaders to them." Convinced that a radical, international conspiracy lay behind the campus disorders and urban riots, Nixon resolved to suppress challenges to his authority, if necessary by covert means. In the conduct of foreign policy, the object of so much controversy during the Johnson years, he was determined to operate free from the interference of politics or the press. Hence his preoccupation with secrecy and with the prevention of leaks.

1. BREAKFAST

Nixon's siege mentality permeated his first major act as president: In March 1969 he ordered the bombing of Cambodia, a neutral country, and he did so without consulting Congress or informing the public. As he explained his decision in his memoirs, he and his national security adviser, Henry Kissinger, "had wondered whether a new President and a serious new peace overture would produce a breakthrough that would end the Vietnam war." He had made no overture when the "North Vietnamese gave us the answer in February when they launched a small-scale but savage offensive in South Vietnam." In fact, the North Vietnamese may have been preparing for new attacks by stepping up the provision of arms and other supplies along their routes to the South, but no "savage offensive" had started. Rather, Nixon, contemplating one of his own, considered the North Vietnamese activity "a deliberate test, clearly designed to take the measure of me and my administration at the outset."

Nixon was much given to discerning challenges to himself. Further, he frequently identified himself with the nation, as he had admitted in *Six Crises* (1962), an autobiographical volume he wrote about "moments of tension and drama . . . closest to me." Each of those crises, he said, constituted "an acute personal problem," but each also "involved far broader consequences." He then went on: "The bigger the problem, the broader its consequences, the less does an individual think of himself." So the "natural symptoms of stress . . . do not become self-destructive." In handling crisis, a man "learns not to worry when his muscles tense up, his breathing becomes faster, his nerves tingle, his

Nixon and Kissinger: Riven to secrecy and deceit.

stomach churns, his temper becomes short." Those were "natural and healthy signs" that he was ready for battle.

In that pattern, so he said, when Nixon conveniently identified a "test" from North Vietnam in 1969, his immediate instinct was to retaliate. For some months, General Creighton Abrams, in command of American forces in Vietnam, had been recommending B-52 bombing runs against North Vietnamese supply lines running through Cambodia. In an advisory cable, Abrams drew Washington's attention to photoreconnaissance information that allegedly located the enemy's Central Office for South Vietnam (COSVN) headquarters in Cambodia. Requesting permission to attack, Abrams assured his reporting senior, General Earle Wheeler, that the targets he had identified were situated where it was unlikely that Cambodian nationals would be hurt by the bombing. Nixon discussed Abrams's request with his closest military advisers and had it studied, too, by the National Security Council. That study went on for five weeks in February and early March 1969, during part of which Nixon was abroad, visiting heads of government in Europe.

In that time, Nixon later asserted, the "Communist offensive intensified." Fighting in Vietnam was indeed severe, with hundreds of American casualties every week. But the larger intensification occurred in Washington in the president's deliberations about Abrams's proposal. By his own account, Nixon was reluctant to resume the bombing of North Vietnam, for to have done so would have provoked adverse reactions from opponents of the war in Congress, in the press, and among the public. Nixon wanted no recurrence of the agitation that had chased Lyndon Johnson from office. In March he decided therefore to endorse Abrams's scheme. On March 17, 1969, American bombers from Guam and other Pacific bases hit areas in Cambodia designated as North Vietnamese sanctuaries. On the president's orders, they did so in secrecy in an operation with the code name Breakfast, and they continued to bomb Cambodia secretly for fourteen months, under the code name Menu, with each major episode of bombing designated by the name of other meals. Through it all, on orders from "highest authority" (the president), the pilots and those directing their flights falsified all relevant records so that they seemed to report only sorties within Vietnam. The Cambodian venture was known only by those immediately involved in it and by others whom the president chose to consult or inform, including just two senators, Richard Russell and John Stennis, senior members of the hawkish Armed Services Committee.

Nixon had urgent reasons for secrecy. Apart from his determination to deceive the public in order to prevent protests, he had also to deceive Congress so as to prevent debate about the constitutionality of the bombing. That bombing was a clear act of war against a neutral nation. The Constitution said categorically that only Congress could declare war. Nixon and his advisers later maintained that the sanctuaries in Cambodia were in effect part of North Vietnam and that in any case the government of Cambodia had invited the United States to attack. Those were specious arguments. Cambodia was not North Vietnam. Though Cambodian leader Prince Norodom Sihanouk did not protest, his government was not reconciled to American violations of its neutrality. Even if the Cambodian government had sought the bombing, the constitutional issue would have remained. Nixon acted without proper authority, and by sustaining effective secrecy, he avoided accountability to Congress or to the people.

Further, it developed that there was no COSVN-HQ, Abrams's alleged objective, though Nixon persisted in claiming there was. Indeed, the bombing did not significantly retard North Vietnamese deliveries of supplies to the South. It did kill hundreds of Cambodians and destroy dozens of their villages. Without producing any substantial gain for the United States, Operation Menu expanded and intensified the war in Southeast Asia in 1969.

Operation Breakfast also revealed Nixon's resolve not to lose the war in Vietnam or at least not to appear to do so. To that end he did not hesitate to escalate the war. In those respects he was just like his immediate predecessors, Kennedy and Johnson. They, too, had been less than candid with the American people. Nixon simply outdid them in his capacity for brutality in Vietnam and for the manipulation of the truth.

Along with Henry Kissinger, Nixon was also ruthless in trying to protect the secrecy he cherished. On March 26, 1969, soon after Operation Breakfast, William Beecher, the *New York Times* Pentagon correspondent, reported that Abrams had asked for the bombing of North Vietnamese sanctuaries in Cambodia. On May 9 Beecher reported further that the bombing had occurred as a signal to Hanoi that "while pressing for peace in Paris," the Nixon administration was "willing to take military risks" in order to demonstrate that it was "different [from] and tougher" than its predecessor. Those accurate accounts went largely unnoticed except by Nixon and Kissinger, who moved to stop the leak that had informed Beecher. Kissinger asked J. Edgar Hoover, the director of the FBI, to make a "major effort" to find the culprit. Hoover soon replied that Kennedy people in the Pentagon talked too much, but he pointed specifically to Morton Halperin, one of Kissinger's own staff, as the source for Beecher's stories. "Dr. Kissinger," Hoover wrote in a memo about the matter, ". . . hoped I would follow it up . . . and they will destroy whoever did this if we can find him." The FBI then placed a wiretap on Halperin's home telephone and soon also on the telephones of several others. The Halperin wiretap remained even after he had resigned his position. The United States District Court in the District of Columbia later ruled that Nixon and his attorney general, in authorizing the wiretap, had violated Halperin's rights under the Fourth Amendment. The same court found Kissinger not liable because of his "lack of oversight authority" though FBI memorandums showed that he had indeed ordered the continuing surveillance of Halperin.

Though it was 1973 before the facts about Operation Breakfast and about the Halperin wiretap became public, President Nixon during his first five months in office twice violated the Constitution. He also skirted the law on campaign financing. Eager to accumulate funds for his personal reelection campaign in 1972, Nixon as early as February 1969 enlisted a close friend, Bebe Rebozo, to "contact J. Paul Getty," one of the richest men in the world, "regarding major contributions." The president wanted to keep the money for his personal use. That was the purport of a memo from one of his two most trusted advisers to the other: "Bebe would like advice from you . . . as to how this can legally and technically be handled. The funds should go to some operating entity other than the National Committee so that we can retain full control of their use." Nixon in this instance intended to operate on the edge of the law. He was proceeding in his characteristically surreptitious way. Another president might have asked Getty for the funds for the Republican party while also moving openly to put a man of his own choice in charge as national chairman. But Nixon seemed to prefer functioning in the shadows.

As he moved, in his view from crisis to crisis, Nixon continued to cover his tracks. In April 1969, less than a month after Operation Breakfast, North Korean jets shot down an American reconnaissance plane, an EC-121. "I reacted in the same way and with the same instincts," Nixon recalled. ". . . We were being tested, and therefore force must be met with force." Dismissing arguments for restraint, he considered two options. One involved "a military strike against a North Korean airfield." A second involved sending combat planes to escort further EC-121 flights. Nixon announced to the press that he would pursue the latter course. But he also, secretly, ordered Operation Lunch, "a second round of bombing of North Vietnamese sanctuaries in Cambodia." He considered that oblique tactic less risky than direct action against North Korea but still "an effective way to impress the communist leaders of both North Korea and North Vietnam with our resolve." The Russians and the Chinese, he believed, would also get that message. As Kissinger put it, they would say: "This guy is becoming irrational—we'd better settle with him." But it was never clear that Operation Lunch conveyed a message to anyone but its immediate victims. And like Breakfast, Lunch also failed to intercept the flow of supplies from North Vietnam.

Nixon had meant to seem insane. As he put it himself, he was operating on "the madman theory. . . . We'll just slip the word to them that, 'for God's sakes, you know Nixon is obsessed about communists. We can't restrain him when he's angry—and he has his hand on the nuclear button.'" If the Communists thought he was unpredictable, he believed, they would hesitate to cross him. And when they did cross him, he could behave like a madman so as to reinforce the image he was cultivating. That reasoning, he seemed to think, excused his tantrums, including his passion for punitive bombing when he did not have his way.

As Kissinger wrote, Nixon had an "antipathy to personal negotiation," so the president delegated that function to him. Kissinger thought delegation saved the president's time and kept him from having to compromise. But Nixon's antipathy to negotiation also suited his own temperament. Nixon had no patience with the delicacy or the pace that negotiations demanded. He preferred to act under the stimulus of crisis. Crisis provided the exhilaration that he "would not for the world have missed." Crisis could "be agony," he wrote. "But it is the exquisite agony."

2. ISOLATION

Richard Nixon embodied the American success story. Born in 1913, he was the child of parents who struggled for respectability, in their case in Yorba Linda and Whittier, California. There the boy Nixon, serious and fastidious, dreamed of escaping through travel from his shabby and crowded home. He worked hard in his father's lemon grove and later in his grocery store, and he dutifully attended Quaker meeting. He thought his mother was a saint. Even in his youth he displayed confidence in performing for a group of people, in playing the piano or reciting poetry. But in private he was diffident, reserved, remote. In high school he threw his small body into football, at which he was clumsy but persistent. He excelled in debating and amateur theatricals. His solid academic record earned him a scholarship to Harvard, but one that covered only tuition, and his family could not afford the expenses of travel, room, and board. If he was disappointed, he did not then reveal it, but in later years he nurtured an outsider's resentment of the Ivy League.

To Whittier College, which he attended, Nixon brought uncommon enthusiasm. There, in the pattern of his high school years, he stood out for his skill in debate, his academic success, and his awkward perseverance at football. He went on to law school at Duke University, where

Nixon in the South Pacific: "A solitary type."

penury and hard work continued to mark his life. Third in his class and president of the Student Bar Association, he nevertheless could find no starting position in corporate law in New York. He returned to Whittier to practice. One of his ablest professors at Duke considered Nixon much too good for the role of hometown lawyer. Also of that mind, Nixon in 1941 moved on to the Office of Price Administration, possibly the most beleaguered agency in wartime Washington. The head of his section, a leading liberal lawyer, remembered Nixon as "a

nice-looking boy . . . intelligent . . . obviously a person we could use."
But Nixon disliked the routine and the bureaucracy. Further, apart
from his bride of 1940, Patricia Ryan, he had no intimates. Like her,
he felt out of place in the urbane world of Washington. In 1942, then
twenty-nine years old, he enlisted as an officer in the navy.

The United States Navy helped prepare Nixon for politics. He served
at shore facilities in the South Pacific, where he won the cooperation
of the enlisted men under his command. He also won the respect of
his peers and superiors. With them, in surviving the boredom of their
lot, he learned to play profitable poker and to join his fellows in a
regular drink. He practiced the camaraderie of men engaged in a common task, but he made no permanent friends. As one officer later said,
Nixon "was a solitary type, a loner. . . . He was afraid of becoming
involved with anyone . . . because he would have to reveal something
of himself."

After the war ended, in September 1945 the Republican party in the
Whittier district offered Nixon the nomination to run against the Democratic incumbent, Jerry Voorhis, a liberal with an impressive record
of support for civil liberties. That was exactly the opportunity Nixon
wanted. Implying that Voorhis had Communist leanings, Nixon won
his place in the House of Representatives in 1946, retained it in 1948,
and won a seat in the Senate in 1954 in another nasty campaign against
another liberal Democrat, Helen Gahagan Douglas. He went on to
successful campaigns for the vice presidency under Eisenhower in 1952
and 1956. He lost his race against John F. Kennedy in 1960 but won
his second campaign for the presidency in 1968. Nixon by that time
had established himself as the dominant politician in the country. Had
he lived, John F. Kennedy might have done as well. As it was, Richard
Nixon forged a career in politics that no one of his contemporaries
could match. Whatever the deficiencies of his tactics, his success said
much about the American people, who in large number kept voting for
him, and that success said much about Nixon, who kept running and
usually winning. He could not have won had he not struck responsive
chords with the electorate. He would have been put off by his defeats—
in 1960 nationally, in 1962 for the governorship of California—had he
not been determined, resilient, and tough.

Nixon genuinely represented his successive constituencies and con-
sciously spoke to their moods. In his early campaigns his cramped gen-
tility mirrored the circumstances of most of his neighbors. His escape
from that condition to respectable prosperity then fitted the mold of
many Californians. In 1952 the Democrats had attacked Nixon for

accepting illegal campaign contributions. Eisenhower moved to dump him from the ticket, but Nixon turned the tables with a mawkish national television address that identified him, as he intended it to, with an average American—a concerned father of small children who had no special assets except a beloved dog, Checkers; a devoted husband who could afford to dress his wife only in a plain wool coat. Nixon seemed always to feel sorry for himself. But then and later he stood for his country and against those who knocked it, especially against Communists who were trying to subvert it. That was a telling message in the 1940s and early 1950s, a message Nixon put across with his successful exposure of Alger Hiss. His detractors could not expunge the outcome of that triumph, for whatever Nixon's excesses, it was Hiss, not Nixon, who stood convicted of perjury. Radicals, those who threatened the middle-class way of life that his constituents enjoyed, remained the targets of Nixon's campaigns. In 1968 and the ensuing years students in revolt and blacks in protest simply replaced the alleged subversives he had vilified for twenty years. His was always the same bumper sticker: "America: Love It or Leave It."

In pitching his early campaigns to paint his opponents as dangerous radicals, Nixon relied continually on innuendo and deceit, on tricky statistics and almost transparent hypocrisy. Those tactics naturally infuriated their victims. Consequently, those victims and their sympathizers tended to underestimate Nixon's skill in other aspects of campaigning. A formidable partisan, he was invariably informed about major issues. His speeches, delivered with a debater's facility, carried conviction and force. He surrounded himself with experts on public relations. From the first he appreciated the potentialities of television. After his damaging televised debates with Kennedy in 1960 he adjusted his style and became adept at the medium, the most effective way to reach the general public. As president he saw to it that he had maximum access to prime network time, though he privately overrated the persuasiveness of his appearances.

Hypersensitive to criticism, Nixon felt persecuted by the media, the television networks, the national magazines, and the national newspapers, especially the *New York Times* and the *Washington Post*. He identified them with an eastern establishment, conspiring, so he believed, to drive him from office, as it supposedly had driven Lyndon Johnson. Like Johnson, he meant by the "establishment" the men and institutions he associated with northeastern power and status—particularly "liberals" of both parties who had connections with Harvard, Yale, and other Ivy League colleges and had gone on to positions of authority at

organizations like the Ford Foundation, the Council on Foreign Relations, Time Inc., the Brookings Institution, and the Foreign Service of
the State Department. Indeed, the conception, shaky at best, of an
antagonistic, liberal eastern establishment became the bogeyman of
most American conservatives. Here again, though Nixon's suspicions
were irrational, his instincts were sound politically. The folk shared his
jealousy and resentment of those he defined as a privileged elite. That
elite was patrician, at least in manner. Nixon and his natural allies
were arrivistes. So aware, Nixon preened in 1969 when British Prime
Minister Harold Wilson called him a gentleman. Hidden from Wilson,
as from most others, were Nixon's personal and social insecurities. So
unsure of himself was the president that on state occasions he had
trumpets announce his entrance and, until he surrendered to the ridi-
cule of the press, in 1970 ordered the White House police to dress in
opéra-bouffe uniforms which one TV commentator appropriately
described as "Bismarck style."

In selecting both his personal friends and his official staff, Nixon
turned largely to other arrivistes, men whose suspicions and jealousies

Nixon, Abplanalp, and Rebozo: Ostentatiously successful.

matched his own. Apart from his family, his only intimates were two self-made and ostentatiously successful multimillionaire businessmen, Robert Abplanalp and Bebe Rebozo. Both of them had large estates in southern Florida where Nixon could enjoy his favorite pastime, solitary swimming. They also helped him acquire a similar property of his own on Miami's Key Biscayne. With Rebozo Nixon found "understanding mental relaxation." As one observer of their friendship wrote, "Nixon has always found it effortless to be with Rebozo. Bebe makes no requests or demands. He is a bartender of some accomplishments. Above all . . . Rebozo is completely loyal to Richard Nixon. And he does not gossip. . . . On Florida trips, Nixon and Rebozo would go cruising on Bebe's boat or simply sit by the water, drinks in hand, Nixon talking and Rebozo passively listening."

H. R. Haldeman and John Ehrlichman, the staff members closest to the president, were young Californians who had played major roles in Nixon's election campaigns. Haldeman, a product of UCLA, had been working for the J. Walter Thompson advertising firm when he first volunteered to assist Nixon in 1956. In 1960 he recruited Ehrlichman, whom he had known in their college days, as one of Nixon's advance men. Haldeman at that time explained to his friend that he was not to intrude upon the candidate. Nixon, he said, "should never be engaged in unnecessary conversation under any circumstances."

In the White House Haldeman as chief of staff and Ehrlichman as the president's counsel regularly had to converse with their chief, but in that role they were almost alone. With Haldeman overseeing political matters and Ehrlichman domestic issues, some forty other staff members ordinarily reported through them about those questions, as did the cabinet, largely an undistinguished group. Now and then others were allowed to see the president, but only infrequently, and he conducted much of his business in writing even with Haldeman and Ehrlichman. As Nixon's senior foreign policy adviser Henry Kissinger also had regular meetings with the president. With Nixon's knowledge, Kissinger organized the National Security Council and its operations so that Secretary of State William Rogers and Secretary of Defense Melvin Laird had minimal access to the president. Rogers was too lazy or too unconcerned much to resist. Laird did try to break through Kissinger's barrier, but he had indifferent success. Laird also failed to cut Kissinger's direct line of communication to the Joint Chiefs of Staff. Determined to keep foreign affairs as his own preserve, Nixon gave Kissinger less rein than Kissinger liked to admit, but the two men did have to spend considerable time together in order to determine and to advance the president's policies.

All in all, Nixon centralized authority in the White House beyond any precedent, though he did not on that basis create an efficient administration. On the contrary, both the president and his two domestic watchdogs were more concerned with politics than with government. Nixon did seem obsessed by orderliness, as did Haldeman and Ehrlichman. The president again and again announced reorganizations of agencies, functions, and lines of authority. But the organization of the White House created major bottlenecks to the flow of ideas and the implementation of policy. Interior Secretary Walter Hickel complained that he could not reach the president to discuss environmental issues. Nixon's cavalier treatment of the cabinet resulted in bureaucratic confusion and duplication. Treasury Secretary David Kennedy insisted on tight money after Nixon had decided against it. Centralization as Nixon imposed it served best to protect his privacy. He could retain his equanimity, preserve his ability to think objectively and thoroughly—so he believed—only in the absence of distractions. He wanted no television in the Oval Office or in his small sanctuary in the Executive Office Building where he often worked.

He worked hard, usually twelve hours a day with few interruptions. But he communed largely with himself. He wanted to have no complaints, to engage in no taxing conversations. He did not even read newspapers and magazines but instead had his staff prepare synopses of probable interest to him. Those he sometimes annotated and returned with written comments, many of them describing the media as the "enemy," others calling for action to improve public relations.

Often Nixon seemed unable to differentiate the trivial from the significant. He wasted time on memorandums, for several examples, about the red wines to be served at the White House dinners, about his prowess at bowling, about the design of his phone service, about his dental appointments. In one instance, he described in detail the end tables he wanted for the right side of his bed. That memo was for action by the first lady, whom he chose to address through an aide. Richard Nixon was more insulated both from life and from the government than any other president had ever been.

In the words of Tom Wicker of the *New York Times*, Nixon was "reserved and inward . . . driven . . . by deep inner compulsions toward power and personal vindication, painfully conscious of slights and failures, a man who has imposed upon himself a self-control so rigid as to be all but visible." Other presidents, gregarious men like the Roose-velts, Eisenhower, and Kennedy, had had friends to whom they talked about their hopes and plans, friends with whom they joked, with whom they shared their zeal for living. It was not high office but personal temperament that contained Nixon. By his own choice he had no one to relieve his most difficult hours, no one to question his ideas, no one to help him laugh at his foibles. He had absolutely no humor at all. His ambition would have been better served, his intelligence honed; his politics made more subtle had he had even a few honest, bright, irreverent, and forthcoming friends.

3. SOUTHERN STRATEGIES

Richard Nixon subscribed to the argument of one of the aides in his 1968 campaign, Kevin Phillips, who expected a new conservative majority soon to dominate American politics. As Phillips made his case in his book *The Emerging Republican Majority* (1969), that new force would consist of white residents of the South and the western Sunbelt, whose population was growing rapidly, along with the Roman Catholic working class and the suburban middle class fed up with rebellious and promiscuous youth and with "permissive" liberal intellectuals. To those fed-up groups Nixon appealed in 1968 with his stress on law and order and its overtones of racism.

It was the same constituency—the "silent majority" or "forgotten Americans" in Nixon's phrases—that the president cultivated with his domestic policies. Those policies also accorded with his convictions, the convictions of a conservative centrist uncomfortable with much of the purpose of the Great Society. Attorney General John Mitchell, for-merly Nixon's New York law partner and 1968 campaign manager, told reporters "to watch what we do instead of what we say." That was good advice. Nixon revealed his domestic priorities by his early efforts to prove tough on crime, reluctant about school desegregation, and resolved to bring the Supreme Court toward agreement with his views. Several days after he took office he instructed Mitchell and Ehrlich-man to "get going with announcement in 48 hours of *some* action" on an anticrime bill for the District of Columbia. Within a fortnight Nixon reminded Ehrlichman that "I am for strong legislation" requiring prison sentences for convictions in crimes in which a gun was used. In March the president told his counsel to "get a . . . statement from RN to net-works . . . coming down hard" against sex and violence on TV.

The attitude behind those orders characterized the administration's proposed bill for the District of Columbia court reorganization. The District was then still without self-government, and that measure empowered judges to send criminal suspects to jail for sixty days before trial. That "preventive detention" blatantly violated due process of law as the federal courts had defined it. So, too, another provision of the bill, disregarding the Fourth Amendment, allowed police to break into a residence without a warrant. One administration spokesman called the bill an "exercise" in "symbolic leadership." Another said it "reflected the rhetoric of the 1968 campaign," for it would "suggest a tough law-and-order demeanor" even though it would not assist the police in combating crime. It was a "sort of law-and-order window dressing" to ease the anxieties Americans felt about crime in the streets. As such it was designed to embarrass Democrats, who were expected to vote against it. But the Democrats declined to oblige, and Congress passed the bill with the unexpressed certainty that the federal courts would disallow its unconstitutional provisions, as they did.

Meanwhile, the administration had moved to enhance its standing with the white South. In his inaugural address Nixon said he would ask for no further civil rights legislation. "The laws," he said, "have caught up with our consciences." As it worked out, the administration actually favored a retreat. It made a tepid gesture toward support of "black capitalism" but its true intentions emerged on the Hill, where the attorney general testified against renewal of the Voting Rights Act of 1965. Congress renewed the act anyway. For his part, Nixon had turned his attention to the desegregation of southern schools. Ever since his years at Duke, he had prided himself on his understanding of the South. As he now saw it, the decision of the Supreme Court in *Green*, calling for faster desegregation, imposed too precipitant a schedule on the region. He had campaigned on the promise that he would not cut off federal funds to schools opposing integration through the use of "busing and the like." As he told Ehrlichman in May 1969, he was "not opposed" to legislation denying federal funds for busing. But Robert Finch, Nixon's longtime political associate and now his secretary of health, education, and welfare, initially stood behind the people in his department who advocated cutting off funds to segregated southern schools. In contrast, Attorney General Mitchell proposed to limit enforcement activities to the courts. Under pressure from the White House, Finch retreated. The Justice Department then, in July, joined the state of Mississippi in arguing against the integration of its school districts. Finch now agreed, holding that integration would "produce chaos, confusion and a catastrophic educational setback to the . . . children, black and white" who would be affected. Nevertheless the Supreme Court, in line with its decision in *Green,* ordered the Mississippi districts integrated "at once."

When the Justice Department had sided with Mississippi, sixty-five lawyers in the Civil Rights Division signed a letter of protest to the attorney general. Like so many of their colleagues in HEW, they believed in desegregation and in vigorous enforcement of the law. The president considered "the bureaucracy" subversive, guilty of deliberate sabotage of his efforts to set policy for the federal government. Clearly he wanted to twist the law to conform to his own political preference. But the decision about Mississippi left him no choice, as he said, but to "carry out the mandate of the Court and . . . enforce the law."

Early in 1970 Nixon appointed a cabinet-level committee under Vice President Spiro Agnew to devise means to help the South desegregate. When Agnew ducked that responsibility, leadership of the committee fell to Secretary of Labor George Shultz. A strong man of intelligence and integrity, Shultz had originated the "Philadelphia plan," under which construction unions working on federal contracts had to accept quotas for black apprentices. Now he set up advisory committees of prominent citizens of both races to assist desegregation in seven states of the Deep South. Those committees met with Shultz and Nixon, who persuaded them to take their mission seriously. The resulting efforts proved successful. In the fall of 1970 southern school districts complied with *Green* without serious trouble, and within four years the number of black children in totally black schools in the area, 68 percent in 1968, had declined to 8 percent. The president deserved some of the credit for that improvement, but the Court had pushed him into his role, which Shultz had then shaped.

The Court continued to push the administration. In *Swann v. Charlotte-Mecklenburg Board of Education* (1971), with Nixon's appointee as chief presiding, it upheld a decision of the district court in the Charlotte area that ordered mandatory busing of some 13,300 children. "Desegregation plans," the Supreme Court ruled, "cannot be limited to the walk-in school." Bus transportation had to become "an integral part of the public education system," available to "achieve the greatest possible degree of actual desegregation." The ruling was not entirely unambiguous. It did not require desegregation in every school in a district. It recognized that busing might be excessive "when the time or distance of travel is so great as to . . . risk the health of the children or significantly impinge on the educational process." Those reservations, leaving room for some discretion on the part of district courts, also encouraged Nixon and Mitchell to make only a minimum effort for enforcement.

The president's strategy for desegregation, as one aide put it, was to assure compliance in a few key districts. But only "a few," Nixon told him. ". . . Don't make big statements about a massive Federal program for forcing integration in all districts. . . . Do what the law requires— no more and as low profile as possible."

By opposing busing, Nixon intended to appeal not only to southern whites but also to millions of northern urban voters who considered busing a threat to their children. The president agreed with them. Busing, he believed, was "a new evil . . . disrupting communities and imposing hardship on children—both black and white." HEW and Justice, as he saw it, continued to go beyond the necessary in enforcing the Court's opinions. "I want you personally to jump" on those departments, Nixon wrote Ehrlichman in 1971, ". . . and tell them to *knock off this crap.* I hold them . . . accountable to keep their left wingers in step with my express policy—Do what the law requires and not *one bit* more." By standing fast against busing in areas where segregation was de facto rather than de jure, especially areas in northern cities, Nixon gained support for reelection. Even an observer sympathetic to his policies on civil rights conceded that Nixon's "judgment was heavily influenced by his immediate political interests." But he was also moved by his personal beliefs. Replying to a memo about making a national holiday of Martin Luther King's birthday, Nixon wrote, underlining both words: *"No never!"*

As Nixon realized from the first, his policies on crime and on civil rights could prevail only if he could change the membership of the Supreme Court. In that way he could curtail the Court's judicial activism and perhaps also bring it to modify *Miranda* and *Green,* decisions he particularly disliked. On assuming office, Nixon was able to name a successor to Earl Warren whose resignation remained effective at the president's pleasure. With Warren's agreement to remain active through the June 1969 session of the Court, Nixon began looking for a "top-flight legal mind," a man "young enough to serve at least ten years," and preferably one with experience both as a practicing lawyer and as a judge on a court of appeals. He wanted a chief justice with the ability to bring the Court together but also one who shared his own preference for judicial restraint—his own "view that the Court should interpret the Constitution rather than amend it by judicial fiat." Several early prospects withdrew their names from consideration for personal reasons or proved unsatisfactory to the southern senators whom the president consulted, as he had promised to. Nixon then turned to Judge Warren E. Burger of the United States Court of Appeals for the District of Columbia. "I knew Burger to be philosophically a moderate conservative," Nixon recalled, "and personally an impressive man."

That was a fair assessment. Burger, then sixty-one years old, had served on the bench for twelve years. He had earned a reputation as a spokesman for those who believed the Warren Court had gone too far. He was known, too, for his work for the American Bar Association on standards for the administration of criminal justice. He first attracted Nixon's attention in 1967 because of his views about *Miranda*. As a result of that decision and its immediate predecessors, Burger believed, it had become "often very difficult to convict even those who are plainly guilty." Consequently, the balance between the "needs of society" and the protection of individual rights had tipped away from "ordered liberty." As Burger put it in an opinion he wrote only weeks before Nixon selected him, "The seeming anxiety of judges to protect every accused person from every consequence of his voluntary utterances has given rise to . . . rules . . . which even the most alert and sophisticated lawyers . . . are taxed to follow. . . . We are well on our way to forbidding *any* utterance of an accused to be used against him unless it is made in open court." No mere sloganeer, Burger stood close to the positions earlier assumed by Associate Justices Stewart, Harlan, and White. He was, as one critic said at the time, "a law-and-order man, but . . . an enlightened law-and-order man."

That was enough for Richard Nixon. He nominated Burger on May 21, 1969, and the Senate, after a speedy and noncontroversial hearing, confirmed him almost unanimously. He succeeded Earl Warren on June 24. During Nixon's remaining years in office Burger led the Court to some easing of its rulings about the rights of the accused, but *Miranda* was not overturned.

Burger had yet to be confirmed when Abe Fortas, a committed judicial activist, resigned from the Court. A man of vaulting intelligence and equivalent arrogance, Fortas had never wholly believed that the rules of conduct appropriate for others were necessarily binding on him. As an associate justice he had continued to serve as an intimate, largely uncritical adviser to Johnson. That was not an unprecedented role for a member of the Supreme Court, but it was also not a discreet one. Further, before joining the Court, Fortas had agreed to accept a retainer from the family foundation of the financier Louis Wolfson, who soon thereafter had been convicted of violating the securities laws.

In May 1969 *Life* magazine broke the story, which the Justice Department was then investigating. Fortas had returned the only fee he ever received, but as the Justice Department discovered, he had agreed in writing, in return for assuming vaguely defined responsibilities to the foundation, to accept twenty thousand dollars a year for life with the money to go to his wife after his death. That, too, had been indiscreet and seemingly greedy. To be sure, Fortas had given up a rich law practice to join the Court, but his wife, herself a distinguished lawyer, continued to earn handsomely, and the foundation's honorarium seemed superfluous except as a trifle to maintain such amenities as the Fortas Rolls-Royce. As Fortas contended, "there had been no wrongdoing on my part"—nothing illegal, nothing immoral. But the appearance of suspicious wheeling and dealing was enough for Senator Strom Thurmond and several like-minded colleagues, who demanded Fortas's resignation. After a week's delay, with controversy mounting, Fortas gave in. Agitation of the issue, he wrote the chief justice, was "likely to continue and adversely affect the work and position of the Court . . . In the circumstances . . . it is . . . my duty . . . to resign."

Nixon used the appointment of a new associate justice as an opportunity to gratify the South. To succeed Fortas, he nominated Judge Clement F. Haynsworth of the United States Court of Appeals for the Fourth Circuit—a southern circuit. A native southerner and judicial conservative, Haynsworth while on the bench had sided with segregationists in two cases. In another case he had decided for the textile industry in a dispute with labor. Still, he was a competent, if not a distinguished, selection. But civil rights and labor leaders opposed his nomination, and many Democrats resented the Republican treatment of Fortas in 1968. Further, it developed that Haynsworth had failed to disqualify himself from ruling in a case in which he was accused of having a conflict of interests. Though the validity of that accusation was shaky, in the wake of the controversy over Fortas even the aura of inpropriety hurt Haynsworth. Those factors persuaded seventeen Republican senators to join the Democrats in rejecting Haynsworth's nomination.

That vote should have alerted Nixon to the inadequacies of the Justice Department's screening of judicial candidates; it should also have moved him to find a new, impeccable, albeit conservative, choice. But Nixon reacted with anger rather than reason. Further, as one White House aide remarked, "the President really *believes* in the Southern strategy—more than he believes in anything else." Deliberately seeking a southern jurist to the right of Haynsworth, Nixon expressed his

"FITS YOU LIKE A GLOVE!"

defiance of the Senate by sending up the name of Judge G. Harrold Carswell of the United States Court of Appeals of the Fifth Circuit. Another conservative, Carswell, as it became clear during the next several months, lacked the qualifications for the Supreme Court. In 1948, while campaigning for a seat in the Georgia legislature, he had said: "I am a Southerner by ancestry, birth, training, inclination, belief and practice. I believe the segregation of the races is proper. . . . I yield to no man . . . in the firm, vigorous belief in . . . white supremacy, and I shall always be so governed." In 1970 Carswell expressed shock when he was reminded of what he had said. But he was disingenuous. Eight years after his racist statement he had been involved in transferring a

Tallahassee golf course from municipal to private ownership so as to evade a Supreme Court decision desegregating municipal facilities. He misrepresented his part in that transaction at the Senate hearing on his confirmation. The Senate also learned that an astonishing 60 percent of the rulings Carswell had made while he was a district judge had been reversed on appeal to a higher jurisdiction. That ratio of reversals suggested sheer incompetence. As the dean of the Yale Law School said, Carswell had "more slender credentials than any nominee for the Supreme Court put forth in this century." Two hundred former clerks to Supreme Court justices signed a public letter urging the Senate to turn down Carswell. Almost half of Carswell's colleagues on the Fifth Judicial Circuit declined to sign an endorsement of him. In trying to defend him, Senator Roman Hruska, a Nixon loyalist, put forth a novel theory: "Even if Carswell were mediocre, there are a lot of mediocre judges and people and lawyers. They are entitled to a little representation, aren't they?" A more plausible theory held that Nixon's "choice of Carswell was vengeance," to make the Senate sorry it had not accepted Haynsworth and to "downgrade the Supreme Court and implement the Southern strategy."

In behalf of Carswell Nixon asserted his exaggerated view of presidential power. "What is essentially at issue in this nomination," he wrote, "is the Constitutional responsibility of the President to appoint members of the Court—and whether this responsibility can be frustrated by those who wish to substitute their own philosophy or . . . judgment for that of the one person entrusted by the Constitution with the power of appointment." That statement ignored the constitutional requirement of the "advice and consent" of the Senate. Fulfilling its role, the Senate rejected Carswell by a vote of fifty-one to forty-five.

Now furious, Nixon indulged in one of his calculated fits of expedient nastiness. "Judges Carswell and Haynsworth," he told the press, "have endured with admirable dignity vicious assaults on their intelligence . . . and their character . . . but when all the hypocrisy is stripped away, the real issue was their philosophy of strict construction of the Constitution—a philosophy that I share—and the fact that they had the misfortune of being born in the South. . . . I understand the bitter feeling of millions of Americans who live in the South about the act of regional discrimination that took place in the Senate yesterday." Though, as he saw it, the Senate had usurped his authority, the two nominations had served one of Nixon's purposes: Thousands of white southerners were satisfied.

Nixon also sought political advantage as well as revenge for the defeat

of Carswell through a Republican attack on Associate Justice William
O. Douglas, whose activist opinions had long offended conservatives.
Gerald R. Ford, the minority leader in the House of Representatives,
had undertaken an investigation of Douglas's connections with the Albert
Parvin Foundation, a charitable organization with alleged connections
to gamblers. With the rejection of Carswell, Ford started a movement
to impeach Douglas. Urging Ford on, Nixon promised to "supply relevant information to the legislative branch," which in the end included
hundreds of documents, some from the FBI and CIA. But Douglas, as
a House committee concluded, was guilty of no impeachable offense.
Douglas had been planning to resign from the Court, but the investigation persuaded him to stay on.

For his part, Nixon, after his tantrum had ended, demonstrated that
he could satisfy objections to judicial activism without selecting incompetent candidates for the Court. He now nominated Judge Harry A.
Blackmun of the United States Court of Appeals for the Eighth Circuit—a midwestern circuit. An old friend of Chief Justice Burger's and
a fellow Minnesotan, Blackmun was a graduate of Harvard College
and Harvard Law School, a quiet man and a meticulous judge. He
described himself as having been "brought up in the Frankfurter tradition," the tradition of judicial restraint. The Senate quickly confirmed him.

In 1971 Associate Justices Hugo Black and John M. Harlan, both in
failing health, resigned. One of the great jurists of the twentieth century, Black had much influenced the Court, particularly in his advocacy of the doctrine of incorporation. Harlan had brought unusual
precision of thought and language to his luminous dissents. Nixon's
first response to filling the vacancies those resignations created was
again vindictive. He displayed contempt for the Court and for the Senate by submitting to the American Bar Association (ABA) for its review
the names of six patently second-rate candidates. Later he reduced
that list to two. The association would endorse neither. As Senator
Edward Kennedy observed, "Surely the compilation and submission of
this list will rank as one of the greatest insults to the Supreme Court in
its history."

The president, his political theater completed, then named two fully
qualified candidates, both jurisprudential conservatives, Lewis Powell
and William Rehnquist. A Virginian then sixty-four years old, Powell
was an eminent lawyer and past president of the ABA. Rehnquist, an
Arizonan, only forty-seven years old, was head of the Justice Department's Office of Legal Council, in Nixon's phrase: "the President's

lawyer's lawyer." He had a deserved reputation as a brilliant legalist. In describing his nominees on national television, Nixon stressed law and order. "As a judicial conservative," the president said, "I believe some Court decisions have gone too far in weakening the peace forces as against the criminal forces in our society. . . . I believe we can strengthen the hand of the peace forces without compromising . . . the rights of individuals accused of crimes. . . . It is with these criteria in mind that I have selected the two men."

Without mentioning the matter, Nixon had also furthered his southern strategy. Senator Harry Byrd of Virginia had been on the list sent to the ABA. Powell was a southerner, and though not a segregationist, once on the Court he soon expressed misgivings about *Swann.* The four Nixon appointees did tilt the Supreme Court to the right, but the controverted decisions in *Escobedo* and *Miranda* were narrowed, not overruled. So, too, with the Court's position on busing. The Nixon appointees were on the bench but divided when the Court ordered busing in Denver, Colorado, to end de facto segregation there. But later, to Nixon's gratification, the Court declined to include suburban schools with Detroit's largely black schools as constituting an area subject to busing as a means to end de facto segregation.

As time went by, Powell's decisions and dissents revealed the large legal talent of his reputation; Blackmun, also a first-rate intelligence, sided often with the liberals or activists, particularly in cases involving civil rights; Burger waffled but stayed close to the center; only Rehnquist proved to be a conservative stalwart. Nevertheless, Nixon could take countervailing compensation from the success of his nominations in promoting his political popularity in the South.

4. FAP

While the issues of law and order and of race had provided the Republicans with major mileage in their 1968 campaign, Nixon had profited, too, from the growing doubts among the "silent majority" about the Great Society's war on poverty. As an intelligent conservative he recognized the need for continuing federal efforts to assist the poor. Indeed, expenditures for that purpose continued at about their previous levels for the first two years of Nixon's term. But Nixon, without abandoning the poor, intended to get rid of Great Society programs he considered unsuccessful. Model Cities was one example. "I want you to phase out those programs," he wrote Secretary of Labor Shultz, "which have failed in meeting their objectives and to eliminate the overstaff-ing, overlapping and inefficiency." Shultz moved toward those goals in part by shrinking the Job Corps.

In establishing his own policy toward poverty, Nixon at first opposed an "increase in *any* . . . program until more evidence is in." He viewed the bureaucracy in HEW as too liberal and too influential. Indeed, he made a point of keeping HEW Secretary Finch uninformed about his plans. The president especially distrusted black leaders, who, as he saw it, were both unreasonably demanding and too close to the Democrats. On those accounts he was hostile even to Whitney Young of the rela-tively conservative Urban League. Reluctantly Nixon agreed to an audience for Ralph Abernathy, who had succeeded Martin Luther King, Jr. as head of the Poor People's March. Their meeting turned into a shouting match. Abernathy denounced it on national TV as "the most . . . fruitless of all meetings we have held in Washington." Comment-ing to Haldeman and Ehrlichman, Nixon wrote: "This shows that my judgment about *not* meeting such people is right—*No more of this!*"

The president's hostility to black activists accorded with the identical attitude of most blue-collar Americans. Consequently, the political as well as the social aspects of poverty policy recommended changing the perceived emphasis of the Great Society. That was the conviction of Daniel Patrick Moynihan, the most influential of Nixon's early advis-ers about poverty. Pat Moynihan had served as an assistant secretary of labor in both the Kennedy and Johnson administrations. In that role he wrote a controversial analysis of the history and current status of family life among American blacks. His work offended civil rights leaders, who read it as racist. But Moynihan, whatever his errors about history, was not a racist. Neither was he as liberal as Nixon thought or as conservative as his critics contended. Rather, Moynihan, an able social scientist, belonged within the useful and humane tradition of progressive American Catholic social thinkers, though unlike most of them, he aspired to political influence and office.

Moynihan's natural sympathies ran with those of Roman Catholic workingmen and women, and his genuine concern for the stability of the nuclear family reflected normal and commendable Catholic val-ues. Indeed, most adult Americans considered the family a natural and indispensable social unit. Moynihan opened himself to criticism, how-ever, in focusing on instability among black families, for by the time he wrote, instability was spreading among all American families regardless of their national origins, races, or religions. Moynihan was vulnerable, too, for linking family instability with poverty to the degree

Nixon and Moynihan: Shared convictions about welfare.

that he did. Middle-class and wealthy families in the United States were also experiencing unprecedented stress by the late 1960s. It was not so much that Moynihan erred. Rather, by examining primarily impoverished blacks, his analysis spoke to their problems specifically even though those problems affected Americans generally.

Moynihan's analysis also had political potentialities, which he exploited unabashedly in forging his relationship with the president. Nixon later recalled that their "shared conviction that the current welfare system had to be totally reformed helped to establish the rapport I immediately felt with him." He made Moynihan head of his Urban Affairs Council, a shadow for domestic policy of the National Security Council, and counterweighed Moynihan's presence in the White House by appointing Arthur Burns, a conservative economist, as counselor to the president. But Burns resented Ehrlichman's status and struck Nixon as too much the pedagogue. Moynihan, in contrast, was content to work through Ehrlichman and adroit at playing to the president's biases, which were often also his own.

Concerned about the growth of welfare rolls, Nixon was aware, too, of increasing criticisms of the costs of welfare programs. The increase actually arose in large part from the rising awareness of the poor about their entitlement to welfare and from their insistence upon their rights. Those changes reflected the success of the Office of Economic Opportunity in educating the needy. Eager to abolish OEO, Nixon knew he could not terminate the federal government's responsibility to the poor. In a shrewd memorandum, Moynihan linked his own proposal for welfare reform to the president's political and social leanings. The urban working class, so Moynihan wrote, had not taken to the streets or broken the law but was now angry, unable to see what it was getting from the government. It was all too aware of what the government provided to impoverished minorities. The time had therefore come to stop defining social problems in a way that separated blacks and Hispanics from the rest of society. To that end the government had to move away from a "service strategy" to an "income strategy." Service-dispensing people—teachers, planners, OEO welfare workers—were preoccupied with blacks, Moynihan contended. Consequently, the service strategy tended to exclude whites. In the same way, upper-class intellectuals, increasingly radical in their social views, were contemptuous of the working class. By implication, an income strategy could correct those and other inequities inherent in the attitudes and programs of the Great Society.

The income strategy that Moynihan championed had originated with Milton Friedman, who had been Barry Goldwater's economic adviser in 1964. Two decades earlier Friedman had suggested replacing welfare with a negative income tax—that is, with direct payment of cash to individuals whose incomes fell below the minimum liable for the federal income tax. That plan would aid the poor without requiring a welfare bureaucracy. Friedman intended the negative income tax to eliminate all other support for the indigent and to provide only for subsistence. During the Johnson years some liberal welfare experts came to favor a relatively generous guaranteed annual income. Several of them in HEW modified Friedman's plan to include the working poor who had children to raise. The scheme in that form guaranteed a level of payments to supplement income without penalizing those who earned some of what they needed. Both Pat Moynihan and Robert Finch embraced that proposal which they named the family security system (FSS). Though Nixon had campaigned against a negative income tax, Moynihan, supported by Finch and Ehrlichman but opposed by Burns, brought the president to endorse FSS. George Shultz refined the administration's recommendation by improving its inducements to work and earn. It was then also renamed, now the family assistance plan (FAP).

FAP promised to correct obvious flaws in the existing system of aid to families with dependent children (AFDC). Under that system payments varied from state to state. In all but six states, payments fell below the federal definition of poverty. Indeed, the average national AFDC stipend for a family of four reached only about halfway to the poverty line. But other federal programs—especially old age pensions, unemployment compensation, and Medicaid—made up much of the difference. One study of AFDC recipients in New York City showed that the average family there on AFDC received the equivalent annually of $6,088, of which less than 40 percent was in cash. That total income, cash plus kind, was more than an individual could earn by working full-time at the minimum wage. Conservatives contended that welfare was destroying the work ethic, which they considered essential to a healthy society. Their argument ignored the inability of the great majority of welfare recipients—children, the aged, single mothers with infants, the infirm—to hold a job. But their argument reached Nixon, who cherished the work ethic, so vital in his personal creed. As he wrote Ehrlichman, "I like the idea of working off welfare checks."

Moynihan's income strategy appealed to the president because in part it substituted workfare for welfare. Nixon also subscribed to Moynihan's questionable belief that the "tangle of pathology" in poor families had spread because AFDC ordinarily excluded two-parent households. As one consequence, so the theory held, men—especially black men—left home so that their women could collect welfare. In their absence, children suffered emotionally from growing up without a male parent. In contrast, FAP would provide payments to needy two-parent families. Further, by basing payments wholly on calculations of income, FAP would remove the social workers who administered the Great Society programs. As Moynihan saw it, poor black and Hispanic families especially would benefit from less observation, evaluation, and interference by the welfare bureaucracy. He said as much in advocating "benign neglect," a phrase his critics misinterpreted. But the main case for FAP flowed from Friedman's plan, improved to provide a decent as well as a guaranteed annual income. FAP promised in principle to do more in treating the problem of poverty than had any previous proposal. Indeed, informed liberals, J. K. Galbraith for one, had praised Friedman's original idea as truly important.

Nixon decided to support FAP in the spring of 1969, though he waited until August to take the plan to Capitol Hill. He realized that it was "almost revolutionary domestic legislation" that would require him to forge an alliance with liberal Democrats, a chancy tactic.

Expecting his opposition to come primarily from the right, Nixon presented FAP in conservative rhetoric that emphasized the workfare provisions. But the left proved to be as negative as the right. Some liberals, uneasy with workfare, also attacked the income floor the plan provided—sixteen hundred dollars a year—as too low. Many conservatives considered it too high. Most Democrats hung back from cooperation with Nixon, while some Republicans balked at the president's daring. During the hearings of the House Ways and Means Committee, moderately liberal groups praised FAP but also recommended changes. For one, George Meany, head of the American Federation of Labor, urged paying individuals in work-training programs at local prevailing wages, a standard that would have increased costs beyond political tolerance. On the right, the Chamber of Commerce rejected FAP as a step toward a guaranteed income, which, of course, it was. On the left, the National Welfare Rights Organization, condemning FAP as "anti-poor and anti-black," called for a guaranteed annual income of fifty-five hundred dollars—a figure that would have put half the population under the plan and cost some seventy-one billion dollars for 1970—an impossible target. But the most telling political liability of FAP arose from the absence of any organized and powerful group working in its behalf. Further, in the perceptive assessment of James T. Patterson; "Americans generally seemed cool to the idea of a national floor under income. . . . Few middle-class Americans wanted to spend very much time or money on a largely 'undeserving poor.' "

Nevertheless, with Chairman Wilbur Mills converted to FAP, the House Ways and Means Committee voted favorably in March 1970, and the House followed in April. But the Senate balked. Republican conservatives there joined with Democratic liberals to defeat the measure in 1970 and again in 1971. Much less willing than Johnson had been to twist congressional arms, Nixon was also less adept at building support for the policies he favored. Even if he had been more skillful, he probably could not have budged the conservatives. And by the time FAP reached the Senate, liberal Democrats, whom Nixon blamed for the defeat of his proposal, had come so deeply to resent his military adventurism in Asia that they had no stomach for cooperation with him on any issue.

The administration did salvage part of its program. Congress in 1972 approved a plan for a guaranteed annual income for the elderly, the blind, and the disabled—a victory for principle. Further, when Nixon first introduced FAP to the nation in August 1969, he had also urged revenue sharing. That scheme constituted much of what the administration later called the New Federalism. The president considered the federal government "muscle bound" and local government too weak. He wanted to "start power and resources flowing back from Washington to the states and communities." Revenue sharing, as proposed in 1969, involved the distribution of federal funds to state and local governments in the form of broad grants rather than as grants for categorical—closely defined—purposes. That change would relieve the growing fiscal problems of industrial states like New York and Michigan. Its advocates intended revenue sharing primarily to give local governments new latitude in spending federal money. Revenue sharing might in that way add to the funds states had available for social purposes. As support for FAP declined, Nixon moved toward that emphasis, partly in order to raise federal spending so as to stimulate the economy.

In 1971, without consulting the cabinet, the president urged Congress to transfer ten billion dollars from categorical programs to block grants for education, urban development, transportation, job training, and law enforcement. After long debate Congress in 1972 appropriated thirty billion dollars for distribution to states and localities over five years. Those general grants allowed local governments to exercise a considerable choice in using the funds made available to them, and the role of the federal bureaucracy was correspondingly reduced, as Nixon had intended.

In other ways, revenue sharing had mixed results. Some states increased their expenditures for the impoverished. But with the decrease in categorical grants designated to help the poor and the minorities, federal funds sent to the states often went to other purposes. Further, most state and local governments had difficulty attracting men and women of outstanding ability. Consequently, the movement of responsibility from the federal bureaucracy to local bureaucracies resulted in no improvement in government, though the movement of funds did spare the states some increases in their taxes. Perhaps the chief beneficiaries of the New Federalism were those who found satisfaction not in the effects but in the adoption of their ideas.

Meanwhile, FAP had perished. To be sure, there had been problems with it as the Nixon administration presented it. It did not adequately cover poor individuals or poor families without children. It provided too little money for training welfare recipients for desirable jobs and too little for day care for the children of welfare mothers. Still, Moynihan was correct in describing FAP as an "extraordinary, discontinuous, forward movement in social policy," and Nixon was innovative and constructive in adopting the plan as his own. Had Congress acted favorably, FAP would have provided a basis on which the country could soon have completed an equitable and economical floor under poverty. But FAP conflicted with the American work ethic. It also suffered from a major political flaw. At a time of deep division about social issues, FAP attracted too little support from moderates to overcome the hostility of those to their left and right. Both liberals and conservatives contributed to the defeat of FAP. Liberals believed at the time that they had won an important battle. In fact, they had forgone an extraordinary chance to reduce poverty in the United States. Nixon, too, doomed FAP, though inadvertently. His conservative arguments for it won few converts on the right while raising enduring suspicions on the left. More important, before the votes on FAP Nixon's policies in Vietnam and the deviousness of their pursuit had alienated the Democrats whose help he needed. Once again the war in Vietnam had damaged the prospects of the American poor.

12

Incursion

Before his election Nixon had recognized the need to resolve two dominating and intertwined issues: the war in Vietnam and the divisiveness of domestic protest against that war. Those were the primary issues that had undone Lyndon Johnson, the issues that created the climate in which Nixon's campaign had flourished. During that campaign Nixon had attacked the Democratic leadership for its inability to make peace in Vietnam. He had, he suggested, his own secret plan to end the war. The major theme of his inaugural address was peace, and anticipating that theme, he had earlier promised "to bring the American people together again." As he knew, the latter objective depended upon the former.

1. VIETNAMIZATION

Nixon never contemplated ending the war except on his own terms. In an article he wrote in 1964, he had warned that the fate of Asia hinged on American aims in Vietnam—his reiteration of the domino theory. "All that is needed," he wrote, ". . . is the will to win—the courage to use our power." No more than had Lyndon Johnson would Nixon consider defeat. "I won't make it hard for the North Vietnamese if they genuinely want a settlement," he told the Republican congressional leaders, "but I will not be the first President of the United States to lose a war." He believed that "to abandon South Vietnam to the Communists would cost us inestimably in our search for a stable, structured, and lasting peace." So he remained tied to Johnson's concern about the credibility of American commitments. Indeed, credibility was essential for Nixon's intention to preserve the balance of international political and military power among the United States, the Soviet Union, and China.

Nixon also knew that he had to prepare public opinion "for the fact that total military victory was no longer possible," a task Johnson had undertaken in beginning negotiations. Nixon wanted "to end the war as quickly as was honorably possible." So had Johnson, but Nixon's sense of what was honorable precluded his agreement to the only terms North Vietnam had ever been willing to accept. Until he could sway Hanoi, prudence required the avoidance of another round of angry protests at home. That objective, as Nixon admitted, accounted for the secrecy of Operation Menu.

It also helped to explain Nixon's choice of Henry Kissinger to head the National Security Council, for Kissinger shared both the president's beliefs about the war in Vietnam and his penchant for secrecy. Like Nixon, Kissinger had risen from obscurity to prominence. Arriving in the United States as an immigrant—his parents were fleeing nazism—Kissinger had served in the army during World War II, then entered Harvard, where he became a brilliant undergraduate and graduate student and later a professor of government. His doctoral dissertation on Metternich revealed his sensitivity to the nuances of power politics. The author also of a thoughtful book about nuclear policy, Kissinger consulted on national security for both the Kennedy and Johnson administrations. Equally important in his career, Kissinger served as a foreign policy adviser to Nelson Rockefeller, whose influential friends he cultivated. As obsessed with power as was Nixon, Kissinger had insinuated himself into Nixon's good graces during the 1968 campaign by delivering secret information about Johnson's plans for peace overtures to Hanoi. Gregarious where his chief was isolated, comfortable with the journalists the president distrusted, Kissinger brought a rare ebullience to the Nixon administration. At the same time he had a taste for intrigue and an impatience with opposition that exactly fitted the temper of the Nixon White House. Obsequious toward the president, domineering with his subordinates, dangerously jealous of his rivals, Kissinger contributed his deep learning, his diplomatic finesse, and his delight in deception to the service of Nixon's foreign policy.

After his nomination Nixon had hinted that to end the conflict in Vietnam, he might follow the example of Eisenhower and the Korean

War. Ike had threatened to use an atomic bomb. But a similar threat in 1969 might have had to be followed out, and both Nixon and Kissinger dreaded "the domestic and international uproar that would have accompanied" even the use of tactical nuclear weapons. Nixon contemplated alternatively still another escalation of aerial warfare, perhaps now accompanied by the bombing of irrigation dikes in North Vietnam. All in all, he doubted he "could hold the country together" while American casualties mounted before victory was possible. Operation Menu failed to satisfy the president's objective. That goal, as Kissinger phrased it, required the prevention of "a change in the political structure of South Vietnam brought about by force."

To that end Nixon adopted several tactics. For one, he undertook to de-Americanize the war. After a visit to the front Secretary of Defense Melvin Laird in March 1969 repeated his recommendation for Vietnamization—the training and equipping of South Vietnamese soldiers to replace American forces. Except for aircrews needed to shield South Vietnam, as Laird saw it, the Americans could then gradually withdraw. Taking Laird's advice in spite of Kissinger's doubts, Nixon told the American people in a speech on May 14, 1969, that the time was coming "when the South Vietnamese . . . will be able to take over some of the fighting." In July, while in Guam on a trip to Asia, the president announced the Nixon doctrine. Henceforth, he said, nations receiving American military and economic assistance would have to supply their own troops. That was "not a formula for getting America out of Asia, but one that provided the only sound basis for America's staying in and continuing to play a responsible role." In effect, Nixon was reverting, step by step, to Johnson's illusory promise that American boys would not fight an Asian war. That had clearly become the desire of most Americans. Moving toward Vietnamization, the president during the summer and fall of 1969 ordered the withdrawal of sixty thousand men. He told Thieu and General Abrams that the rate of withdrawals would depend upon the level of enemy activity and the progress of peace talks. The United States, he assured Thieu, would remain "steadfast." But as Nixon realized, Thieu "knew that the first American withdrawals would begin an irreversible process, the conclusion of which would be the departure of all Americans from Vietnam."

While calming public opinion, those withdrawals, Nixon believed, would also "demonstrate to Hanoi that we were serious in seeking a diplomatic settlement." In the view of some analysts, the president was separating military from political issues. But Kissinger believed that a continuing American military presence in Vietnam was essential for the political settlement of the war, and Nixon was removing only ground forces. American aerial strength, much of it on Pacific bases or aircraft carriers, remained readily available. Indeed, Kissinger repeatedly proposed the punitive bombing of North Vietnam as a means to convert Hanoi to American peace terms. Nixon had offered Hanoi a peace plan that provided only for mutual troop reductions and a United Nations-supervised election in South Vietnam. As it had before, Hanoi rejected these conditions.

With Kissinger, Nixon then turned to an "elaborate orchestration" of diplomatic pressures. Through the Soviet Union, the president offered to have Kissinger begin secret talks in Paris with the North Vietnamese, talks from which the South Vietnamese (and incidentally the American State Department) would be excluded. Nixon also had Kissinger tell Soviet Ambassador Dobrynin that a settlement in South Vietnam was crucial for all other issues in Soviet-American relations. Eager for an agreement on nuclear disarmament, Kissinger was less comfortable than was Nixon with that linkage, but he followed his instructions. For its part, the Soviet Union may have been weary of supporting Hanoi, but considerations of prestige tied it to its client. Moscow either could not or would not influence Hanoi. In replying to Kissinger, Dobrynin said simply that the Soviet Union was eager to improve relations with the United States regardless of Vietnam.

Impatient with the lack of progress and distressed by continuing American casualties, Nixon in July 1969 sent Ho a secret ultimatum warning that unless some "breakthrough" occurred before November, the United States would adopt "measures of great consequence and force." The North Vietnamese answered by agreeing to secret talks between Kissinger and their chief negotiator Xuan Thuy. Ho died early in September, but his successors did not retreat from his demands for total withdrawal of American forces and South Vietnamese determination of its own government without foreign influence. Later in September Nixon had Kissinger tell Dobrynin that "as far as Vietnam is concerned, the train has just left the station and is now headed down the track." Unruffled by the implied threat, Dobrynin said: "I hope it's an airplane rather than a train, because an airplane can still change its course in flight." Nixon's "elaborate orchestration" had reached stalemate.

Preparing to act, the president spoke to the mood of the country. "I understand," he told the press, "that there . . . continues to be opposition to the war in Vietnam on the campuses, and also in the nation. . . . Under no circumstances will I be affected whatever by it." As he later recalled, "[because I was] faced with the prospect of demonstrations at home that I could not prevent, my only alternative was to try to make it clear to the enemy that the protests would have no effect on my decisions. Otherwise my ultimatum would appear empty."

As Nixon saw it, much in the manner of Lyndon Johnson, the Vietnam Moratorium in Washington on October 15, 1969, a major antiwar demonstration, gave aid to the enemy. The Moratorium, accompanied by teach-ins at many universities and peaceful marches in various cities, reflected the growing sentiment for ending the war. The organizers of the Moratorium, few of them radicals, had participated in the McCarthy or Kennedy presidential campaign. They had support from two dozen senators, including some Republicans, and from millions of middle-class Americans. That mattered little to Nixon, who viewed them all as his enemies and therefore the nation's. He felt challenged by hostile forces, the media especially. "The pent-up fury" of the antiwar movement, he later wrote, "the controversy over Judge Clement Haynsworth, the debate over welfare reform . . . the vocal impatience of some civil rights leaders—all prominently in the news—created the impression of an administration under siege." Nevertheless, his "primary concern" was "that these publicized efforts aimed at forcing an end to the war" would destroy the "credibility of my ultimatum to Hanoi."

Using the Moratorium for his own purpose, North Vietnam Premier Pham Van Dong reinforced the president's worry. Over Radio Hanoi Dong expressed his confidence that the solidarity of "peace-loving" Americans with the people of North Vietnam would lead to total victory over "American aggression." That propagandistic statement should have surprised no one. But Nixon interpreted the broadcast as interference in American domestic affairs. He had Vice President Agnew demand that the leaders of the Moratorium repudiate Dong's support. He also blamed the Moratorium for destroying the possibility of peace in 1969, a possibility that had been at best only a fantasy. And in a note to himself, Nixon wrote: "Don't get rattled—don't waver—don't retract."

One after another, the president took on the enemies he perceived: international communism, antiwar agitators, and the media. In a private session with Dobrynin he scolded the Soviet Union for its "intransigence" about Vietnam and other issues. "You may believe the American domestic situation is unmanageable," Nixon said. ". . . I do not propose to argue . . . I want you to understand that the Soviet Union is going to be stuck with me for the next three years. . . . If the Soviet Union will not help us get peace, then we will pursue our own methods

NATIONAL COLLEGE AND HIGH SCHOOL MORATORIUM
in Commemoration of Kent State, Jackson State and Augusta
& Demanding Total, Immediate Withdrawal from Southeast Asia

STUDENT MOBILIZATION COMMITTEE TO END THE WAR IN SOUTHEAST ASIA/ 1029 Vermont Avenue, NW, 8th Floor/ Washington, D.C., 20005/ (202) 628-5893

Moratorium.

for bringing the war to an end. . . . The humiliation of a defeat is absolutely unacceptable. . . . I recognize that the Soviet leaders are tough. . . . But so are we." Kissinger considered Nixon's diatribe extraordinary. In its own way it was.

Next, in November 1969 the president moved to cut off the antiwar movement by appealing on national television to his preferred constituency. The United States, he said, would continue to fight until the

"Communists" agreed to a "fair and honorable peace" or until the South Vietnamese could "defend themselves on their own . . . whichever came first." The pace of troop withdrawals would remain "linked to the . . . level of enemy activity, and developments on the negotiating front," regardless of antiwar demonstrations. "And so tonight—" Nixon went on, "to you, the great silent majority of my fellow Americans—I ask for your support. . . . North Vietnam cannot defeat . . . the United States. Only Americans can do that."

That speech, Nixon later maintained, altered the course of history, for the "silent majority" responded with an outpouring of support, some fifty thousand telegrams and thirty-thousand letters. The enemy, he asserted, "could no longer count on dissent." But the outpouring was tainted, for the White House staff had organized it, and its impact on Congress was less unequivocal than the president believed. In the House of Representatives 300 members and in the Senate 58 expressed support of Nixon's Vietnam policy. But some 135 representatives and 42 senators did not. A national poll showed 68 percent of Americans approving the president's overall performance, his highest rating to that date. But in the immediate aftermath of a major presidential speech, Americans usually approved before a more critical reaction set in. The Congress and the country remained divided, a condition Nixon acknowledged by attributing it to the media.

Right after his speech he had, typically, dined alone in the Lincoln Sitting Room at the White House. The rest of his family listened to TV commentaries, almost all of them negative about the president's course and intentions. Infuriated by what he considered the distortions in those "instant" analyses, Nixon had Agnew rush to attack. In Des Moines on November 13 the vice president denounced the "small group of men . . . perhaps no more than a dozen anchormen, commentators and executive producers" who decided about the "commentary that is to reach the public." Agnew's speech drew blood. The head of the Columbia Broadcasting System called it an "unprecedented attempt . . . to intimidate a news medium which depends for its existence upon government licenses." It was just that, and in some measure it succeeded. The next round of antiwar demonstrations received far less television coverage than its predecessors had.

But a year after his election Nixon had succeeded neither in making peace nor in healing the country. The Soviet Union had not brought North Vietnam to heel. Negotiation with Hanoi remained stalled. Most leading independent journalists persisted in print and on the airwaves to criticize the war in Vietnam. Antiwar sentiment had not declined. On the contrary, as the war continued, protests grew, deriving a new virulence from the administration's overt hostility.

2. Diaspora on the Left

During 1969 and 1970 the antiwar movement flowered, becoming more diffuse, attracting more middle-class Americans on its right wing. Similar growth occurred on college campuses in part because of the imminence of conscription. But other issues—particularly a concern about racial injustice and a rising awareness of feminist goals and ecological problems—also fed student discontent. That discontent, moreover, frequently became indistinguishable from the spreading counterculture, which involved behavioral as well as political issues. The Nixon administration hoped that troop withdrawals and, ultimately, reform of the conscription system would quiet the universities and the country, but those remedies operated too slowly and too narrowly to still dissent. The president and his most trusted advisers always underestimated the antiwar sentiment of thousands of patriotic and law-abiding Americans and overestimated the number and influence of radical agitators. Consequently, they tended to identify all dissent with disloyalty, just as Lyndon Johnson had and just as Nixon had in the early stages of his political career.

Without question, there were some violent and dangerous fanatics on the political left, but as Johnson's intelligence services had concluded, they were not the agents of hostile foreign governments. Nevertheless, Nixon turned again to the FBI, the CIA, and the Defense Intelligence Agency to investigate. A summary of their findings in June 1969 reported that some New Left leaders and some black militants had traveled to foreign countries, as the American press had observed. Yet there was no "ironclad" proof that China or Cuba was "funding campus disorders." Playing it safe, the report noted that "this is not to say that it could not be concluded from the evidence that such funding is taking place." That surmise was enough for Nixon. "1. Keep after this," he instructed Ehrlichman. "2. Give Huston (or some one of his toughness and brains) job of developing hard evidence on this. 3. Pass information to Karl Mundt and McClellan."

The president apparently intended to lead Senators Karl Mundt and John McClellan, both itchy about supposed subversives, into a new congressional witch-hunt. But history did not repeat itself. Tom Charles

Huston, a White House staffer and Nixon's preferred agent, sent back to the president only a recommendation to have the Internal Revenue Service look into the activities of tax-exempt left-wing organizations. "1. Good," Nixon commented. "2. But I want *action*. Have Huston follow up hard on this thing." Nothing came of that directive. There also emerged no evidence of foreign agents in the New Left or even of misuse of tax exemptions by left-leaning organizations.

Nevertheless, Nixon's suspicions persisted, whetted especially by violence on the campuses, which caught the attention of media, as always alert for the sensational. The violence also obscured the divisions that weakened the left. At American colleges during the two years before May 1969 there were 25 bombings, 46 cases of arson, 207 buildings occupied, and more than 6,000 arrests. Concurrently, however, the swollen enrollment of the Students for a Democratic Society was splintering into mutually hostile groups, with some on the far left openly Marxist-Leninist in their orientation, some Maoist, and one—the Weathermen—committed to enlisting the working class in revolution through immediate terrorism. In Chicago in October 1969 the police arrested almost 300 Weathermen who were trashing businesses in the Loop. Other Weathermen bombed major corporate buildings in New York, and one group blew itself up while trying to manufacture a bomb. The Weathermen were by then fading away, however, imprisoned after arrest, lost in a shrinking underground, or weary of their own counterproductive rage. Police informers and police action also contributed to the decline of the Black Panthers, who were increasingly feared and rejected by the people in the ghettos. Huey Newton admitted the Panthers had lost their following. Rivalries among their leaders were also tearing them apart. Eldridge Cleaver fled into exile to escape both a jail sentence and the hired guns of his Panther opponents. Like the Weathermen, by 1970 the Panthers were becoming insignificant as agents of revolution.

The trial of the Chicago Eight in September and October 1969 had presented the nation not with a drama of revolution but with a sick comedy. The eight defendants were charged with crossing state lines for the purpose of inciting riots during the Democratic Convention in 1968. One of them, the Panther leader Bobby Seale, incurred six counts of contempt of court because of his verbal attacks on Judge Julius Hoffman, who refused to let him act as his own defense council. The other defendants also reviled Judge Hoffman at televised daily press conferences outside the courtroom. When the judge ordered them to cease, a courtroom brawl resulted, followed by more contempt charges.

The Chicago Eight, without Bobby Seale: The trial was a farce.

The television audience perhaps expected outrageous behavior from Abbie Hoffman and Jerry Rubin, the accused Yippie leaders, but David Dellinger and Tom Hayden also succumbed to the temptation to play to the cameras.

For their parts, the judge and prosecuting attorney came across as heavies, with Judge Hoffman continually departing from proper judicial behavior in his antipathy for the defendants, and the prosecutor seemingly obsessed with irrelevant questions about homosexuality. The trial was such a farce that no verdict could have survived appeal. Worse, it disgraced the federal judicial system. When, in 1970, Bobby Seale was indicted in New Haven, Connecticut, for murder, Yale President Kingman Brewster, a lawyer himself, said he was sad to be "skeptical of the ability of black revolutionaries to achieve a fair trial anywhere in the United States." Though Seale was acquitted, Brewster's doubt rested on ample grounds, for the Chicago trial had exposed biases on the official right that threatened the prospect of justice as much as did the excesses of the lunatic left.

President Nixon feared that anarchy stalked American campuses.

The episodes that most disturbed him reflected the explosive hostility of black students who, like the Panthers, were moved by a separatist ideology. Exhibiting their own African-American identity, many of them adopted ghetto rhetoric, Muslim names, and African styles in hair and dress. They also demanded separate black curricula and recreational facilities. As they pressed their demands, they often drew sympathy and support from white antiwar students and organizations. So it was at San Francisco State College, where agitating blacks found allies in Asian- and Hispanic-American students and in the SDS. A student strike in 1968 had erupted into a riot when police on the campus clashed with a crowd of undergraduates. Castigated by Governor Ronald Reagan for his earlier concessions to students, the president of the college resigned. His successor, the semanticist S. I. Hayakawa, an articulate conservative, condemned the striking students, who continued to strike and intermittently to riot. After police arrested 453 students in January 1969, Hayakawa prevailed, sustained by public opinion in California, where middle-class sympathy for militant students had evaporated.

So, too, at Cornell, concessions by the university's president failed to quell a black student uprising during which armed agitators took over an administration building in December 1968 and, in spite of further concessions, continued their protests, on occasion with guns in

Radicals at Cornell: Violence and threats of violence.

their hands. Some faculty members and many white students joined in the giddy charade of revolution, of "brain-washing by fear and by liberal guilt." The violence and threats of violence, and the administration's unwillingness to stand up against them, prompted the resignations of several distinguished scholars. In the end, Cornell's president also had to step down.

Episodes like those at San Francisco State and Cornell persuaded some observers, as Arthur Burns wrote Nixon, that radical students and faculties were determined to destroy the universities, which only the state could protect. But the state, when it was summoned, appeared in the form of the police, whose presence on campus radicalized moderate students, exactly as the extremists had hoped it would. So it had been at Columbia in 1968, and so it was again at Harvard in 1969. The trouble at Harvard in many ways typified the crisis in the academy. The faculty there was divided, with very few radicals, largely from junior ranks; with a large number of liberals who wanted to negotiate a settlement; and with a majority of conservatives, most of whom supported the unfortunate recourse to the police.

The students were divided, too. Radical blacks, pressing for financial assistance to the local black community and for a black studies program, were only loosely allied with supportive white students. The latter were determined primarily to gain some voice in academic policy and to abolish the Reserve Officers Training Corps (ROTC), the academic correlative of the military and the war. Only a minority of the white students were radical, some in the SDS, some in rival organizations of the old Marxist left, like the Young People's Socialist League.

At Harvard, as elsewhere, adherents of the Old Left, faculty and students alike, scorned both the SDS and the transient protesters, who, except in their dress and manner, became radicalized only for the duration of the campus crisis. Eager to preserve the university as a center of intellectual activity, most faculty members in all political groupings objected to the posturing and destructiveness of the New Left. Marxist historian Eugene Genovese of Rutgers University dismissed the student rebels as "pseudo-revolutionary middle class totalitarians." That was the view, too, of Harvard sociologist Barrington Moore, at once a leading Marxist and a committed scholar worried about the fragility of the university. Many of the scholars who opposed the Vietnam War—some socialists, some liberals—also criticized the authoritarianism of student leaders and the adolescent conformism of their followers. Among conservative academicians, universally appalled by campus violence, no one attacked the New Left more directly than did George Kennan. The campus, he held, had no place for politics but only for preserving and advancing learning. The "seat of evil in this world," he continued, lay "not in social and political institutions, and not even, as a rule, in the inequities of statesmen, but simply in the weakness and imperfection of the human soul."

Student rebels also had their faculty defenders, who saw them as more learned and more interesting than their peers. Kenneth Keniston, then a Yale psychologist whose research focused on college-age Americans, considered "the radicalism of a minority of today's college students a largely appropriate, reasonable and measured response to blatant injustices." Kenniston found that the typical student activists had grown up in comfortable and liberal homes. They accepted the professed values of their parents but perceived the performance of their fathers especially as at variance with those values. Their rebellion, in that analysis, had less to do with the conditions at their colleges than with their rejection of authority. Yet as critics of the radicals contended, those findings did not excuse the trashing of the universities. There was no excuse at all for those faculty members, presumably adult, who joined in dumping card catalogs at the University of Pittsburgh library or destroying files in the office of the Harvard College dean. That kind of wanton behavior disgusted most students and faculty.

Partly on that account, during 1970 youthful rebellion against authority was beginning to express itself less in hard political action than in softer countercultural life-styles. For that change of focus, Theodore Roszak produced an influential text. His *Making of a Counter Culture* (1969) inveighed against the "technology." By that term, Roszak meant "that social form in which industrial society reaches the peak of its organizational structure"—a social form characterized by "efficiency, rationality, and necessity." Within that system the "paternalism of expertise" repressed the natural instincts of youth. Consequently, in a "generational revolt," young Americans would remodel their inherited culture. The New Jerusalem of the young would begin not with class or party or race but "at the non-intellective level of personality." For—so Roszak argued—"building the good society is not primarily a social, but a psychic task."

Charles A. Reich, an unlikely new cultist from an establishment background, provided a variant and simplified alternative to Roszak's tract. A professor of law at Yale, Reich based his book *The Greening of America* (1970) on a diffuse existentialism. He advanced a loose theory of American culture that rejected older values for the behavioral preferences he had in common with the alienated young. In his formula-

tion, Americans had passed through two stages. The first of these, Consciousness I, "expressed the realities of the new nation." It "focused on self . . . accepting much self-repression as the essential concomitant of effort, and allowing itself to be cut off from the larger community of man, and from nature." Those in Consciousness I still believed "that success is determined by character, morality, hard work and self-denial." That belief, Reich asserted, was "drastically at variance with reality."

A second stage, Consciousness II, emerged as "a response to the realities of organization and technology." It rested on the belief that "richness, the satisfactions, the joy of life are to be found in power, success, status . . . rewards, excellence, and the rational . . . mind." Consciousness II wanted no part of mystery or magic. It expressed itself in the corporate state of the 1950s and later years in which "technology, organization and administration" were out of control, "running for their own sake . . . for . . . non-human ends." The American corporate state bound business and government together in a relentless "but essentially mindless" system.

A new stage, Consciousness III, had come into being about 1967 as a reaction to its predecessors and to "the threat . . . posed by everything from neon ugliness and boring jobs to the Vietnam War and the shadow of nuclear holocaust." The revolt had begun among young Americans. "What happens is simply this," Reich wrote. "In a brief span of months, a student, seemingly conventional, changes his haircut, his clothes, his habits, his interests, his political attitudes . . . his whole way of life." Youth was discovering itself as a generation. Consciousness III materialized "the moment the individual frees himself from automatic acceptance of the imperatives of society."

Consciousness III started with the expression of self. It was not political. Liberals, Reich maintained, envisaged a massive reorganization of politics and law, but the resulting reforms would prove as illusory as the New Deal had. The New Left preached class struggle, which Reich considered "a hopeless head-on fight against a machine." Indeed, the New Left, Reich observed, failed to see that bureaucratic socialism or communism produced the same evils as capitalism. In contrast, Consciousness III people were "notably unaggressive, nonviolent, uninterested in the political game." Their issues were cultural: "unrestricted use of drugs, an end to laws regulating private sexual behavior, the right to wear hair and clothing styles of their own choosing, communal living arrangements." The revolution took palpable form in bell bottoms, beads, beards, pot, and sex. "The new consciousness," Reich preached, "was sweeping all before it." For validation he pointed to the 1969 Woodstock Music and Art Fair, in Bethel, New York, that largest of happenings, which had attracted thousands of young Americans to its euphoric "love-in," a rock festival of communal joy. But it was on a parochial note that Reich clinched his case: "When, in the fall of 1969, the courtyard of the Yale Law School, that Gothic citadel of the elite, became for a few weeks the site of a commune . . . who could . . . doubt that the clearing wind was coming?"

There were many doubters. Blue-collar and clerical workers especially viewed the cultural revolution as a distasteful aberration of the spoiled rich. It also proved to be a vehicle for upward mobility. For every young man or woman who dropped out of college in order to join a commune in Vermont or New Mexico, there were eager replacements among the ambitious children of the ethnics eager for traditional success. Most of the dropouts, for their part, soon wearied of their pottery wheels or jewelry shops and returned to the mainstream. While they were gone, their hirsute styles became for a time the rage among some of the affluent middle-aged who had earlier thought it chic to entertain black radicals at their soirees. The fads spawned by the new consciousness spread, too, among the vulnerable in high schools who had always tried to emulate college ways.

But even in 1970, when the new consciousness was rising, it posed no present danger to the state and small potential threat to the academy. On the contrary, it was diverting the energies of the rebellion among the young away from political activism, depleting the ranks of the radicals. By 1970 the "confident rage" of 1967 and 1968 was subsiding. After the antiwar demonstrations of November 1969, widespread but peaceful, a respite set in even in activism for peace. A coalition of convenience no longer held the New Left together. The civil rights movement, dispersed in the North, was playing itself out in a quest for Afro-American studies at the colleges. The SDS was dissolving in factional controversy. The Black Panthers and the Weathermen were destroying themselves. The children of the new consciousness were substituting pot for politics and rock for revolt. Only an enveloping aversion to the war in Vietnam any longer connected those fragmented parts.

3. PITIFUL GIANT?

Misreading those developments, President Nixon identified opposition to the Vietnam War in general with the revolutionary teachings of the Weathermen. "There is a feeling of International anarchy in the air," he wrote an aide in March 1970, "and it *began* in the United States." Episodes of protest on college campuses, Nixon held, though often responses to local issues, persuaded the nation's enemies that Americans were divided (as, of course, they were). Early in 1970 a Gallup poll showed that two-thirds of the nation approved of the president's handling of Vietnam, but North Vietnam's negotiator in Paris told Kissinger that he believed the antiwar movement had grown in recent months. Senator Fulbright and the Democratic party, he added, opposed the war, as did "the people and the press of the United States."

That assertion was a good negotiating ploy. Nixon interpreted it as a conviction that in his view contributed to Hanoi's rigidity about terms for peace. So did Vietnamization, for as long as it continued, North Vietnam had only to await the day when all the Americans were gone.

Nixon was caught in the trap that had bedeviled American policy for so long. He would not lose the war, but he could not end it until he brought Hanoi to his terms. He could not do so while North Vietnam counted upon dissent and war fatigue in the United States, as well as on Soviet and Chinese supplies. Yet without further troop withdrawals, dissent would grow. March and April 1970, as Henry Kissinger later recalled, were months of "great tension." His talks with the North Vietnamese were "maddeningly ambiguous." The president was "getting testy," irritated by the delay, furious that the Senate had rejected Carswell as well as Haynsworth, eager to dispatch his troubles with a triumphant blow.

Nixon found his occasion for action through developments in Cambodia. The North Vietnamese, besides moving supplies through that country, had been training Cambodian Communists, the Khmer Rouge, as armed guerrillas. Their presence kept the country on the edge of civil war. In January 1970 Prince Sihanouk, the neutralist Cambodian head of state, departed for France for treatment at an obesity clinic. He left the prime minister, General Lon Nol, and the deputy prime minister in charge. They stirred up young Cambodians against their ancient enemy the Vietnamese, with the result that Cambodian mobs attacked the North Vietnamese Embassy and killed innocent Vietnamese residents in and near Phnom Penh, the nation's capital. In March 1970 Lon Nol deposed Sihanouk, who left France first for Moscow and then for Beijing. There Sihanouk enlisted the Cambodian Communists, his former enemies, in an attempt to restore his rule. Gangs of Khmer Rouge and gangs of Lon Nol's supporters brought chaos to Cambodia as they fought each other. The North Vietnamese and the Vietcong in Cambodia assisted the Khmer Rouge; the South Vietnamese penetrated the border to help Lon Nol.

Official American policy at first seemed restrained. On March 25 Secretary of State Rogers told the press that the United States would respect "the neutrality, sovereignty and independence" of Cambodia. Events there, he said, "will not cause the war to be widened in any way." But Rogers was not privy to the plans of the White House, where Nixon was contemplating intervention. Determined to prevent Cambodia from going "down the drain," the president on March 25 told Kissinger to "get a plan to aid the new government." The White House sent secret orders to the American mission in Saigon to provide arms to Lon Nol and to fly to Phnom Penh Cambodian soldiers whom the United States had trained. General Abrams and Ambassador Bunker in Saigon and the Joint Chiefs in Washington favored still-stronger measures. Rogers and Laird urged caution, with Laird worried especially about public opinion. Indeed, on the Hill Senators Frank Church, a Democrat, and John Sherman Cooper, a Republican, were drafting legislation forbidding American forces from entering Cambodia. Intending to mount just such an operation, Nixon on April 20 tried to obscure his plans by announcing further troop withdrawals on national television. "We finally have in sight," he said, "the just peace we are seeking."

In a memo for Kissinger on April 22, the president remarked that "we need a bold move in Cambodia to show that we stand with Lon Nol." Secretary of Defense Laird suggested a South Vietnamese attack on Parrot's Beak, a small Cambodian frontier area that poked like a nose into South Vietnam. But Nixon, rejecting that "pusillanimous little nitpicker," decided on "the big play" even though he expected it to cause "a hell of an uproar at home." Devious as ever, the president prodded Abrams to recommend the employment of American forces. Abrams responded by calling for attacks both on Parrot's Beak and Fishhook, another border region where North Vietnamese troops found sanctuary. Alternatively Abrams suggested an area farther north that, so he claimed, harbored the elusive COSVN, the supposed target that the secret bombing of 1969 had never found. On April 23 a leak to the *New York Times* reported the American arming of Cambodian troops. Nixon, according to Kissinger, "flew into a monumental rage." During the next several days, urged on by Kissinger and the Joint Chiefs, the president moved to his decision of April 26. Accepting then Abrams's earlier recommendations, he resolved to "go for broke."

Nixon had consulted neither the Congress nor Lon Nol. Proceeding in secret, he violated Cambodian sovereignty, as he had in 1969 with Operation Menu, and broadened the war without congressional authorization. He was prepared to rebut his critics by reference to an opinion he had had Assistant Attorney General William Rehnquist provide. It asserted that the Constitution allowed the president "to engage U.S. forces in limited conflict," a questionable finding. Later Kissinger advanced the fallacious excuse that strategically "Cambodia could not be considered a country separate from Vietnam." But strategic considerations notwithstanding, Cambodia was a separate country, so recognized in international law and by the United States. Further,

Cambodia was a country with which the United States was officially at peace. In ordering the invasion of Cambodia by American forces, Nixon exceeded his constitutional authority. Arguably Kennedy and Johnson had already done so in Southeast Asia, but their transgressions did not excuse Nixon's.

Foreseeing the domestic consequences of his action, Nixon, during the days before he took it, performed the rituals he practiced to sustain his spirits. Over one weekend he retreated to Camp David, where he spent much of his time alone. One evening he watched the motion picture *Patton*, in which George C. Scott portrays the indomitable general, a figure with whom Nixon identified. Another evening at the White House Bebe Rebozo joined Nixon in drinking enough to slur their speech. "The President," Rebozo told Kissinger on the phone that night, "wants you to know . . . if this doesn't work, Henry, it's your ass."

South Vietnam announced the attack on Parrot's Beak on April 29, 1970. With rumors about American involvement circulating in Washington, antiwar senators immediately demanded American disavowal of the operation. On the evening of April 30 Nixon addressed the nation on TV. The new, joint American-Vietnamese attack on Fishhook, he said, was not an invasion of Cambodia, for once the North Vietnamese had been expelled, the Americans would depart. His purpose was not to expand the war into Cambodia but to end it in Vietnam by making possible Vietnamization and, with it, peace. But Nixon's "incursion" looked just like an invasion, and it did take the war into Cambodia.

Doubtless so aware, Nixon stressed the underlying reason for his action. "We live in an age of anarchy both abroad and at home," he said. "We see mindless attacks on . . . great universities and . . . small nations." Consequently, he continued, "If, when the chips are down, the world's most powerful nation, the United States of America, acts like a pitiful, helpless giant, the forces of totalitarianism and anarchy will threaten free nations and free institutions around the world." Diplomacy alone could not sustain American credibility, for the war in Vietnam provided a test of the nation's "will and character." He then said: "We will not be humbled. We will not be defeated."

The speech linked the war in Vietnam to campus unrest and linked both to American credibility. It pitted that credibility against international totalitarianism. Characteristically, the president had created a crisis. As Kissinger later wrote, the speech was delusionary—"vintage Nixon." There was more to come. At a briefing at the Pentagon the next day Nixon urged officials there to "blow the hell" out of the sanctuaries in Cambodia. Then, speaking informally to some civilian employees, the president said: "You see those bums, you know, blowing up the campuses . . . the boys that are on the college campuses . . . are the luckiest people in the world . . . and here they are . . . storming around about this issue. . . . Get rid of the war, there will be another one. Then out there we have kids who are just doing their duty. . . . They stand tall and they are proud." He told his own staff: "Don't worry about divisiveness. Having drawn the sword . . . stick it in hard."

Divisiveness certainly greeted the incursion, the president's speech, and reports of his tantrum at the Pentagon. A majority of Americans, so the polls showed, approved of Nixon's leadership. Other millions joined a nationwide protest against the invasion of Cambodia. The protest involved mostly adult middle-class citizens. Eminent professional men and women spoke out against the invasion. The *New York Times* and *Washington Post* criticized Nixon, and the *Wall Street Journal* deplored "deeper entanglement" in Southeast Asia. Two hundred and fifty employees of the State Department signed a petition opposing the president's action. Secretary of the Interior Walter Hickel also protested the decision, as well as the president's failure to consult or even to inform the cabinet and his general inaccessibility. On college campuses, where protest had been abating, the invasion of Cambodia produced a storm of demonstrations. As one parent wrote Nixon, most participants were neither radicals nor "bums." Thirty-seven college presidents urged Nixon to end the war. An hour after Nixon's speech a professor at one eastern campus met a sobbing undergraduate. "I feel so helpless," she told him. Frustration like hers rather than revolutionary zeal provoked the students, some of whom lashed out at university targets, often ROTC buildings, in their distress over national policy.

In Ohio Republican Governor James Rhodes, aping the president, condemned campus demonstrators as "worse than the Brown Shirts and the Communist element" and threatened to "eradicate" them. After a protest rally at Kent State University, he ordered national guardsmen to that campus. There, on May 4, 1970, confused by the movements of participants in a peaceful demonstration, guardsmen fired a volley into a crowd of students, hit fifteen and killed four, of whom two were just observers. In a similar episode two innocent students were killed at Jackson State University in Mississippi. Those episodes shocked most Americans.

But referring to Kent State, Nixon said smugly that it "should remind us all . . . that when dissent turns to violence it invites tragedy." Vice President Agnew called the killings "predictable and avoidable" and

Kent State shocked most Americans.

condemned "elitists" who interpreted the Bill of Rights as a protection for "criminals in our society." Like the killings themselves, those comments fueled the continuing protests, which closed hundreds of campuses across the country. A peaceful student demonstration in downtown Manhattan drew the attack of a group of construction workers who battered the students with their fists and tools. That reaction of those "hard hats" struck Nixon as "very meaningful." It also revealed the social disintegration of the nation.

Apparently troubled by the furies he had evoked, the president modified his conduct. American troops, he said, would leave Cambodia within the next three to seven weeks. He had little choice, for the Cooper-Church resolution, then moving through the Senate, demanded withdrawal of those forces. Briefly the president also softened his attitude toward protesting students. During the night of May 8, Nixon was unable to sleep. Near four o'clock in the morning, accompanied only by his valet, he walked out spontaneously to the "groups of young people gathering on the Ellipse" near the Washington Monument. He wanted, so he later wrote, "to lift them out of the miserable intellectual wasteland in which they . . . wander aimlessly around." His goals in Vietnam, he told several students, "were the same as theirs—to stop the killing and end the war." When the young people seemed dubious, Nixon said that he "hoped that their hatred of the war . . . would not turn into a bitter hatred of our whole system, our country, and everything it stood for." He continued: "Most of you think I'm an SOB, but . . . I understand how you feel." Still lacking a favorable response, Nixon "tried to move the conversation into areas where I could draw them out." He talked about travel, about surfing, about football, about arms control and clean air and clean water. Then he shook hands with a "bearded fellow," stepped into his car, and drove away. Later that day he told a reporter: "I doubt that I got over."

The Cambodian incursion was no more successful. American troops invading Fishhook could not find the COSVN of their commander's imagination. They did destroy some North Vietnamese supplies, but the Soviet Union and China quickly provided new materials, which the North Vietnamese sent down the Ho Chi Minh Trail. At the most the operation relieved enemy pressure near Saigon long enough to allow American withdrawals in that region, as well as from Cambodia later in June. The marauding Vietnamese forces remained, despised by the Cambodians, whose civil war, intensified by American involvement, continued for years.

4. Getting Tough

Before the end of June 1970, Nixon's mood had hardened again. He ordered Haldeman to restrict the availability of White House news to the *New York Times* and *Washington Post* and to help their competitors. He also ordered reductions in grants and contracts to universities whose faculties or administrations had criticized his policies in Vietnam. On June 5 the president called a meeting of his senior intelligence chiefs: Richard Helms of the CIA, Vice Admiral Noel Gayler of the National Security Agency, Lieutenant General Donald Bennett of the Defense Intelligence Agency, and J. Edgar Hoover of the FBI. He asked all of them to work with Tom Huston, his staff member in charge of domestic spying. When next they met, Huston told the others that the president had decided "everything is valid, everything is possible" in rooting out domestic threats. Huston was to oversee a secret team, the Interagency Group on Domestic Intelligence and Internal Security, made up of operatives from the four agencies and others, like the Internal Revenue Service, concerned with law enforcement. That team would have presidential authority to commit crimes against possible subversives. It could surreptitiously tap phones, open mail, and break into the homes and offices of suspects. "The discussions were open and frank . . ." Huston wrote Haldeman. "All were delighted that an opportunity was finally at hand to address themselves jointly to the serious internal security threat that exists." To Huston's surprise, however, Hoover balked. The plan intruded upon the FBI's turf. Hoover also considered it too risky, too liable to discovery by the press, bound to get the president into trouble. In July Nixon approved the Huston plan, but Hoover's opposition led him to reverse his decision.

The president remained convinced that the Weathermen and Black Panthers and other radicals were fomenting revolution and that the Huston plan was as justifiable as Lincoln's suspension of habeas corpus during the Civil War. Sustained by that attitude on the part of the president, his subordinates later employed the illegal acts that the Huston plan had contemplated in order to spy on Americans identified as "targets of intelligence interest." Rarely radicals, those Americans were critics of administration policy in the media, at the universities, and among Democrats.

During the several months prior to the elections of 1970, open opposition to the Vietnam War abated except in the colleges and on the part of antiwar Democrats in the Senate. A special commission under William Scranton, which Nixon had appointed to study campus protest, reported that the Cambodian invasion had radicalized student opinion. Nothing was more important, the report held, than an end to the war in Vietnam. Otherwise there might occur another explosion of student violence that would jeopardize the nation. Students regarded Nixon as dangerous, the report continued, and the government as repressive of women and blacks. In a memorandum for the president, Pat Moynihan called the report political "blackmail, carried out by an elite group, that is contemptuous of democratic processes, or rather the outcome of those processes." The report, in Moynihan's opinion, described only a loud minority, perhaps 10 percent of Americans, few of them working people. "In a larger political sense," he advised Nixon, "it is your task to restore order and civility to the nation."

That conclusion coincided with the most influential political analysis of 1970, *The Real Majority*, a book by two Democrats. Richard Scammon, who had been Kennedy's director of the Census Bureau, and Ben Wattenberg, a speech writer for Johnson, intended their work to persuade the Democrats of the importance of the "social issue." The average voter, they wrote, was a forty-seven-year-old housewife from Dayton, Ohio, married to a machinist and worried about black radicals, urban crime, the collegiate counterculture, and the erosion of old values. In order to win the election, the Democrats needed to appeal to middle-class, middle-aged, middle-of-the-road Americans like her, not to minority constituencies made up of the poor, the black, and the young. That counsel in effect described the strategy Nixon had been pursuing since 1968. Naturally it struck him as appropriate for 1970 and 1972. The Republicans, he believed, "should pre-empt the Social Issue in order to get the Democrats on the defensive. We should aim . . . primarily at disaffected Democrats, at blue-collar workers and at working-class white ethnics."

To that end Vice President Agnew stumped the country. "The great question for all of us," he said in an early speech, ". . . is becoming clearer and clearer. Will America be led by a President elected by a majority of the American people, or will we be intimidated . . . by a disruptive, radical, and militant minority—the pampered prodigies of the radical liberals in the United States Senate?" Nixon picked up the theme as the campaign progressed. His staff allowed some demonstrators into his meetings so that he could then attack their rock throwing and shouted obscenities. He blamed their boorish behavior on the "creeping permissiveness" of the courts, the legislatures, and the universities. "All over this country today," the president said in one address, "we see a rising tide of terrorism, of crime, and on the campuses . . . we have seen those who . . . engage in violence. . . . It's time to draw the line and say we're not going to stand for that! . . . It's time for the great silent majority of Americans to stand up and be counted."

With antiwar sentiment still strong in the Senate, Nixon also tried to neutralize the peace issue. In a major TV address in October, he offered Hanoi a "standstill cease-fire" during which negotiators would work out a settlement. Though leading senatorial doves applauded the offer, it contained nothing new. Nixon had made any mutual withdrawal that followed the cease-fire conditional upon principles he had earlier delineated. Those principles called for the total departure of North Vietnamese forces, a prospect Hanoi would still not accept unless and until a coalition government including the Vietcong replaced Thieu's regime in Saigon. The North Vietnamese rejected the cease-fire, but the speech eased controversy about the war for the duration of the fall campaign.

In November the Republicans gained two seats in the Senate, lost nine in the House, and also lost eleven governorships. That was an inconclusive but acceptable result in an off year election. Determined to win grandly in 1972, Nixon recognized the continuing political utility of the social issue and the potential political significance of ending the war. He also resolved to take advantage of "flexing the political muscle that goes with being the party in the White House." So he intended to keep pressure on his staff "to get organized, to get tough . . . to come up with the kind of imaginative dirty-tricks that our Democratic opponents used against us . . . in previous campaigns." But the greatest advantage of incumbency did not depend upon dirty tricks. It lay in the president's ability to seize the imagination of the country by the magnitude of his achievements. In fashioning his foreign policies, Nixon had the opportunity to do exactly that.

13

The Glorious Burden

Reflecting on his presidency, Richard Nixon spoke in his diary of the enormous responsibility it imposed, accompanied "by the greatest opportunity an individual could have." That combination made the office a "glorious burden." The description particularly fitted Nixon's approach to foreign policy. He intended his new departures to move the country toward an acceptable settlement of the Vietnam War. Apart from Vietnam, in both geopolitical ideas and diplomacy, Nixon redirected the posture of the United States toward much of the rest of the world. Working intimately with Henry Kissinger, the president made the White House the vital and often secret center of their planning. Kissinger was more articulate than the president about the conceptions underlying their purpose, and more active in the negotiations that advanced their goals. But the "glorious burden" itself was Nixon's, and it was he who formulated the strategies they pursued.

1. A STRUCTURE OF PEACE

In his inaugural address Nixon called for an "era of negotiation" to succeed in "era of confrontation"; the result would be "a structure of peace." A close observer of the world scene, Nixon believed in the uninhibited use of national power to achieve a world peace based upon a balance of power—a multipartite equilibrium in which the offsetting strength of several powers would continue to sustain international stability. Describing that system in a speech in 1971, Nixon said there were five great economic powers in the world: the United States, the Soviet Union, Western Europe, Japan, and Communist China. "These are the five," he continued, "that will determine the economic future and, because economic power will be the key to other kinds of power, the future of the world in other ways in the last third of this century." He expanded upon that theme in 1972: "The only time in the history of the world that we have had any extended period of peace is when there has been a balance of power. It is when one nation becomes infinitely more powerful in relation to its potential competitors that the danger of war arises. . . . I think it will be a safer world and a better world if we have a stronger, healthy United States, Europe, Soviet Union, China, Japan, each balancing the other, not playing one against the other, an even balance."

Though powerful economically, neither Japan nor Western Europe had the military strength to defend itself without the assistance of the United States. Consequently, the major players in Nixon's proposed equilibrium were only three, and China, unlike the United States and the Soviet Union, had not the nuclear arsenal or status of a super-power. Nevertheless, the relationships of the three strongest nations to each other were developing toward a stage ripe for Nixon's purpose. Recognizing that condition, he made the establishment of a tripartite equilibrium with the Soviet Union and China the chief objective, along with the termination of the Vietnamese War, of the diplomacy of his first term.

To that end Nixon based his diplomacy on realism, as he understood that word. In order to further American interests, he was prepared to negotiate with all governments, Communist as well as democratic. Nixon did not expect the Soviet Union to give up its faith in the historical inevitability of communism or its hope for speeding up the flow of history in the nations of the developing world. He believed that international communism remained a dangerous enemy. Consequently, he was excessively suspicious about Soviet conduct and needlessly tough toward Soviet challenges to the United States as he discerned them. Only that toughness, so he believed, would make foreign policy credible as well as realistic. But realism also required mutual concessions on matters of mutual interest. In order to increase the possibility of those concessions and to extend the range of negotiations, Nixon linked issues of national interest to each other.

Linkage provided the basis for Nixon's approach to the Soviet Union. Above all, he wanted the Soviets to pressure Hanoi for an end to the Vietnam War. He was ready in exchange to offer American concessions on other matters. But he knew that negotiations with Moscow were bound to be difficult, as they had always been. The key to softening Soviet attitudes, he believed, the key to détente, lay in normalizing American relations with China. In itself a desirable end, that goal could also further his hopes for world peace, for the end of the Vietnam War, and for the domestic political assets attached to those achievements. But most immediately the road to Moscow ran through Beijing.

2. THE CHINA CARD

Since the 1949 Communist Revolution in China and China's later role in the Korean War, the United States had refused to recognize the government of the People's Republic, had opposed its admission to the United Nations, and had persisted in the pretense that the government of Chiang Kai-shek in Taiwan constituted the real China. The Kennedy and Johnson administrations had preserved that fiction, and the related obsession with a Sino-Soviet threat, to which no one had given more credence than had Nixon. But Nixon, so long a hard-liner, now saw China in a new light. For both Chinese and Americans, he later wrote, movement toward rapprochement was "based on . . . mutually advantageous interests." In 1967 he had mused about "pulling China back into the world community," though without conceding China a sphere of influence in Asia. "We must not forget China," he said during his 1968 campaign. ". . . We must always seek opportunities to talk with her." But first, he told the press in 1969, changes would have to occur on the Chinese side.

To encourage those changes, Nixon instructed a dubious Kissinger to open secret channels of communication to the Chinese and to let them know that the administration was "exploring possibilities of rapprochement." While doing so, Kissinger had the National Security Council begin several studies of Chinese-American relations. Those studies soon resulted in a partial relaxation of trade controls and travel restrictions that had applied to China. But Nixon kept the important approaches to the Chinese secret even within the administration. Only close secrecy, he believed, could prevent leaks that might otherwise arouse opposition to his demarche. And only secrecy would permit the president to exercise exclusive control over Chinese policy.

Nixon took crucial first steps himself. In Paris in March 1969 he told President Charles de Gaulle that he intended to open a dialogue with the Chinese government, which France had long since recognized. He also enlisted President Nicolae Ceauşescu of Romania to serve as a secret channel to the Chinese, a role President Yahya Khan of Pakistan had already assumed. Through those intermediaries, Nixon signaled to the Chinese his opposition to any attempt to isolate them through an Asian alliance that the Soviet Union was then proposing.

The Chinese had been anxious about Moscow's plans since the Soviet invasion of Czechoslovakia in the summer of 1968. At that time Brezhnev promulgated his doctrine asserting the Soviet Union's right to intervene in another "socialist" state in order to preserve "true socialism" from counterrevolutionary threats. That doctrine worried both China and the Eastern European countries, particularly Romania and Yugoslavia, then deviating from Soviet practices. Privately the Chinese assured those two nations of their support. Troubled also by the buildup of Soviet forces along their contested northern border, where there had been intermittent fighting for several years, the Chinese in March 1969 precipitated an engagement that initiated six months of border incidents. Chinese propaganda during that period condemned the Soviet Union for expansionist aggression. For its part, the Soviet Union, while reinforcing the border area, hinted at the possibility of a preemptive nuclear strike against Chinese nuclear facilities. But in the late summer of 1969 the Soviet leadership also appealed for Communist unity. Tensions then receded, though mutual suspicions remained.

In the last months of 1969 continued American signals to China, some public, some secret, and persisting Chinese trepidation about the Soviet Union meshed in an official Chinese-American agreement to resume long-suspended conversations in Warsaw. There in 1970 the American delegate expressed his government's intention to reduce its military presence in Taiwan. The Chinese, for their part, agreed to an American proposal to send a presidential envoy to Beijing.

That tenuous rapport almost vanished when Mao Zedong condemned Nixon's incursion into Cambodia. Volatile as ever, Nixon told Kissinger to order every available American warship to the Taiwan Strait. Kissinger wisely did not relay that instruction to the Joint Chiefs. He did not know it, but sharp policy differences had developed among Chinese leaders. Mao and Zhou Enlai favored turning toward the United States, which Mao's designated successor, Lin Biao, strongly opposed. Zhou did not prevail within the Central Committee of the Chinese Communist party until September, 1970.

Mao then invited Edgar Snow, an American journalist sympathetic to the Chinese, to visit Beijing. When they met, he told Snow that he would be glad to receive Nixon "either as a tourist or as President." He intended Snow's visit to send a major signal to Washington, but Nixon and Kissinger failed to understand it. As Kissinger later wrote, the Chinese "overestimated our subtlety, for . . . our crude Occidental minds completely missed the point." But Nixon had sent his own clear signal in October by telling *Time* magazine that "if there is anything I want to do before I die, it is to go to China." He also asked Agba Muhammad Yahya Khan to let the Chinese know that he believed a rapprochement "essential" and was prepared to send an envoy to Beijing. Further, through Ceauşescu of Romania Nixon informed Beijing that he considered Taiwan a problem to be settled by the Chinese themselves.

Replying through Khan, Mao and Zhou told Nixon in December 1970 that they would welcome a special envoy to discuss the withdrawal of American forces from "Chinese territories called Taiwan." A month later Nixon received Zhou's explicit invitation for a visit of his own. The South Vietnamese invasion of Laos temporarily stopped communication, but friendly, reciprocal signals resumed in April 1971. The United States then lifted part of the embargo against Chinese goods, and China invited the American Ping-Pong team to the table tennis championship matches in Beijing. In doing so, Zhou said that a new page had turned in the relations between the two peoples. Privately the Chinese leaders were contemplating also inviting several Democrats to Beijing. Disturbed about that possibility when he learned of it unofficially, Nixon moved to protect the political benefit he wanted for himself. He told Kissinger, as the latter put it, "to discourage any temptation for Peking to deal with his political opponents," a caveat delivered through Pakistan.

Nixon next made Kissinger his secret envoy, though secrecy had imposed burdens of its own. Nixon's signals to China had already been confused by anti-Chinese speeches of Secretary of State Rogers and Vice President Agnew. Now Rogers objected to having Kissinger undertake a mission to Vietnam and Pakistan. The secretary of state could not know—and was not to be told—that the mission was a cover for the visit to Beijing. The cover included arrangements for Kissinger, while in Islamabad, to develop a stomachache that would require him to spend a few secluded days recuperating in an official rest house in the mountains. During that period he would fly to Beijing and return. President Yahya Khan, Kissinger later recalled, "was enthralled by the cops-and-robbers atmosphere of the enterprise." According to plan, on July 9, 1971, Kissinger and a few assistants boarded a Pakistan airplane for their flight across the Himalayas. They arrived about noon at the Beijing airport.

That afternoon Kissinger had the first of several meetings with Zhou Enlai, whose dignity and urbanity immediately captured his respect. Their discussions involved the difficult issues of Taiwan and Vietnam. Speaking for nations that had been enemies for three decades, both men talked with a "frankness," as Kissinger put it, "rarely achieved among allies." Their common perception of the danger of the Soviet Union fostered their relationship. Also effective was Kissinger's promise to Zhou "to inform Peking in detail of any understanding affecting Chinese interests that we might consider with the Soviets." Kissinger supported that promise by giving Zhou top secret American satellite photos of Soviet military deployments along the Chinese border. He also now made firm the earlier American indication that the United States would withdraw its forces from Taiwan.

For his part, Zhou agreed within limits to abet American policy in Vietnam. He was also willing to have Nixon visit Moscow before Beijing, but Kissinger said the summits would occur in the order in which they were planned. They settled on the spring of 1972 for Nixon's trip, a date that suited the president's timing for its domestic political impact. They agreed, too, to communicate further through a new secret chan-

Kissinger at the Great Wall, 1971: Walk to Eureka.

nel in Paris. Along that route Kissinger subsequently fulfilled his promise to inform the Chinese about American negotiations with the Russians. On July 11, back in Pakistan, Kissinger cabled Nixon the code word "Eureka," which indicated the success of his mission.

On national television on July 15, 1971, the president announced "a major development in our efforts to build a lasting peace." He had sent Kissinger to China; now he was accepting an invitation from the People's Republic to visit himself the following May in order "to seek the normalization of relations between the two countries." That action, Nixon continued, "will not be at the expense of our old friends. It is not directed against any other nation. . . . All nations will gain from a reduction of tensions . . . between the United States and . . . China."

Coming as a complete surprise, the announcement had the extraordinary impact Nixon had intended. Some of it was negative. The NATO countries naturally resented an American failure to consult or inform them about the reversal of policy toward China. Informed himself only after Kissinger's return, Secretary of State Rogers tried to placate the Europeans and particularly Japan, where the "Nixon shokku" embarrassed Prime Minister Eisaku Sato, long a friend of the United States. The administration eased that shock by announcing the scheduled return to Japan of Okinawa and the Ryukyu Islands, territories taken over after World War II. The response in Taiwan, predictably more negative, remained heated even though the United States did not renounce the mutual defense agreement between the two countries.

But on the whole, Nixon had ample grounds for gratification. The news of his impending visit to Beijing troubled the North Vietnamese, who recognized it for what it was, a step by China away from its support, already diminishing in shipments of arms. Nixon also rejoiced in the dramatic, positive effect of his announcement on public opinion in the United States. Though some conservatives growled, leading senators in both parties supported his mission and recognized his need for continued secrecy in dealing with China. Most significantly, the United States gained leverage with the Soviet Union. Right after Nixon spoke on TV, one of Kissinger's aides handed a copy of his remarks to the Soviet chargé in Washington along with a note chiding the Soviet Union for delaying a summit meeting. The note, as Kissinger described it, also "reaffirmed our willingness to place relations with the Soviet Union on a new basis." It warned of "serious results" should American hopes be disappointed. Nixon's public assurances to the contrary, Kissinger admitted, "the bargaining positions between Washington and Moscow had changed." To speed the way to détente, Nixon had played the China card successfully.

3. Accommodation or Confrontation?

Eager to enlist Soviet cooperation in ending the Vietnam War, Nixon knew he had to bargain to achieve that end. The Soviet leaders, Nixon realized, wanted particularly to resume strategic arms limitation talks (SALT), which Johnson had suspended after the Soviet invasion of Czechoslovakia. The Russian leaders also wanted to increase trade with the United States, to obtain access to advanced American technology, and to receive American credits for the purchase of grain, of which they grew far too little for their people. But the Russians resisted Nixon's efforts to link those questions to Vietnam, largely because they had less influence with Hanoi than Nixon assumed. Attributing the Soviet stance to stubbornness, the president also persisted, as he had for so long, in seeing a malign Soviet influence in every crisis he identified. Determined in each case to prove that he was tough, he blocked the path to accommodation again and again. Had the Russians been less eager than they were to advance their own purposes, Nixon would have wasted the opportunities he had to ease the cold war.

As it was, in his first meeting with Soviet Ambassador Anatoly Dobrynin, Nixon held back from the idea of a summit but suggested that serious talks about other issues proceed between Dobrynin and Kissinger, not the State Department. As in the case of China, that secret channel spawned some confusion, especially when Kissinger made independent decisions about strategic arms without consulting the official American SALT negotiators. But early in 1969 Nixon had deferred considering SALT until he obtained congressional approval of an antiballistic missile (ABM) program to offset the Soviet buildup of those weapons. Later that year, with the United States also testing multiple, independently targetable reentry vehicles (MIRVs), the Soviet Union in turn delayed negotiations. By that time other questions were disturbing Soviet-American relations, as they continued to do for several years.

Mutual suspicions rose on several fronts. In the summer of 1969 Nixon, on his second presidential trip to Europe, went to Romania. That restless Soviet satellite welcomed him, the first American head of state ever to visit. His presence in itself expressed both American and Romanian opposition to the Brezhnev doctrine. The visit also stirred hopes among the peoples of Eastern Europe for improved political and economic relations with the United States. From Brezhnev's point of view, Nixon was intruding on Soviet turf. Reciprocally, Brezhnev was cultivating détente with Western Europe. His chance came later in 1969, when Willy Brandt, the leader of the Social Democratic party in

West Germany, became chancellor of that nation. Brandt looked to early recognition of East Germany and of the boundaries in effect since the end of World War II. He began the negotiations that resulted in a 1970 West German-Soviet nonaggression pact. Uneasy about Brandt, Nixon and Kissinger wanted to prevent any Western European arrangements with Moscow that excluded the United States. Therein, as Kissinger later said, lay one motive for moving to an American détente with Russia first.

American mistrust of Soviet policy in the Middle East militated to the contrary. During the Kennedy and Johnson administrations the United States had regularly supplied Israel with arms for defense against its Arab enemies. Washington had almost no relations with the Arab states. In 1967, during the Six-Day War, the Israelis had crushed Egyptian and Syrian forces supplied by the Soviet Union. Israel then occupied areas along the Suez Canal, on the west bank of the Jordan River, and on the Golan Heights along the Syrian border. The humiliated Arab states welcomed Soviet help in rearming for revenge. Nixon believed the Soviet Union wanted to control the whole region. Though he exaggerated Soviet intentions, he also worked for peace. Through Secretary of State Rogers, he informed Jordan and Egypt that he wanted a new relationship to find a compromise settlement in the area. He also delayed endorsing an Israeli request for fighter airplanes and a loan. After an abortive Soviet-American effort to quiet the region, Israeli and Egyptian forces engaged in several skirmishes along their frontiers. Rogers in December 1969 then called on Israel to return the occupied Arab lands in exchange for Arab promises to respect Israel's independence.

Israel rejected that proposal, as did Arab extremists. Defining the Soviet position at that juncture, Aleksei Kosygin, the Soviet premier, wrote Nixon that "if Israel continues its adventurism, to bomb the territory of the . . . Arab states, the Soviet Union will be forced to see to it that the Arab states have means . . . with . . . which a due rebuff . . . could be made." He intended to provide the Arabs with an adequate air defense. In similar messages to France and Great Britain, Kosygin urged the four powers to compel Israel to stop fighting and to withdraw from the occupied territories in accordance with a UN resolution. But Kissinger called Kosygin's letter "the first Soviet threat to the administration." Actually neither the United States nor the four powers acting collectively had the means to compel Israel to follow any peaceful course, nor could the Soviet Union control the Arab countries. The limits of superpower influence in the Middle East recalled similar limits in Vietnam. Yet Kissinger blamed the Soviet Union for fomenting trouble. In focusing on great power equilibrium, he constantly underestimated the local nature of regional conflicts arising from deep historical and religious antagonisms, like the rivalries between Israel and its neighbors.

Though Nixon thought alike, his response to Kosygin, as he said, was more "low-keyed." He continued to resist the requests of Golda Meir, the Israeli prime minister, for Phantom jets—technically advanced American airplanes. "One of the main problems I faced," Nixon later recalled, ". . . was the unyielding and shortsighted pro-Israel attitude prevalent in large and influential segments of the American Jewish community, Congress, the media, and in intellectual . . . circles." Johnson had felt the same way. Their critics, as Nixon said, tended to confuse "not being pro-Israel" with anti-Semitism. He was equally annoyed that congressmen dovish about Vietnam were hawkish about Israel. "We will oppose a cut-and-run policy either in Vietnam . . . or anywhere else in the world," the president wrote Kissinger. "This is the kind of friend that Israel needs. . . . Mrs. Meir . . . must trust RN completely. He does not want to see Israel go down the drain. . . . On the other hand, he must carry with him not just the Jewish community . . . but . . . the 60 per cent of the American people who are in . . . the silent majority, and who must be depended upon in the event that we have to take a strong stand against Soviet expansionism in the Mideast. . . . We are going to stand up in Vietnam . . . and in the Mideast, but it is a question of all or none."

So persuaded, a number of Jewish Americans, many of them formerly liberals, were moving toward the Republican party and conservatism. Once strong for civil rights, they had also become disenchanted by black militancy and offended by its frequent association with Muslim names and symbols. They were uneasy about the possibility that affirmative action for blacks and Hispanics would result in lost opportunities for their fellow American Jews. Indeed, the Jewish new conservatives, including their intellectual leaders, were hawks about Vietnam as well as Israel, bourgeois in values and in manner, and by 1970 part of the silent majority to which Nixon appealed. In the Mideast, as always and everywhere, he never overlooked the domestic implications of his foreign policy.

Nevertheless, it was primarily suspicions of Moscow that brought the president, with Kissinger, to blame the Soviet Union for the next Mideast crisis. In September 1970 the Palestine Liberation Organization (PLO), nationalistic Arabs under Israeli occupation on the west bank and in adjoining parts of Jordan, threatened a civil war against King Hussein, the moderate Jordanian ruler friendly to the United States. Kissinger believed the Soviet Union was pushing the Syrians, who in turn were behind the Palestinians. Convinced, as was Golda Meir, that the Russians were fomenting a Palestinian insurrection, Nixon told the press that the United States might have to intervene if Syrian tanks invaded Jordan. The Soviet Union replied in a note assuring Nixon that it had no intention of intruding in Jordan. The note also urged the United States to keep out. When Syrian tanks did invade Jordan, Nixon told Kissinger, who had sent a stern note to Moscow, that the Soviet Union was "testing us." He also had Kissinger inform the Israelis that the United States would support their air strikes against Syria should they become necessary, he alerted twenty thousand American troops, and he sent additional naval forces to the eastern Mediterranean. A day later Hussein's troops drove the Syrians into retreat.

The United States, as Nixon concluded, had influenced events in the Middle East. The Soviet Union had not. But neither had the United States influenced the Soviet Union, which had been only marginally involved in the episode. Yet Nixon and Kissinger believed they had triumphed in a superpower confrontation. That was a self-serving delusion.

It was a delusion reinforced by developments in Cuba. Driving toward nuclear parity with the United States, the Soviet Union tested American interpretation of the missile crisis agreement of 1962. In August 1970 Moscow assured the administration that it was adhering to the ban on Soviet nuclear weapons in Cuba in exchange for the American promise not to invade that island. But the Jordanian crisis was not yet over when on September 18, 1970, reconnaissance photography over Cuba, in Kissinger's words, "confirmed the construction of a probable submarine . . . base" in Cienfuegos Bay. A new base for nuclear-powered Soviet submarines seemed to violate the 1962 understanding because those submarines ordinarily carried nuclear weapons. Nixon, with the 1962 confrontation in mind, put off any public protest until he could negotiate from "a position of unyielding strength." He had Kissinger look into possible actions to irritate Castro and to position American missiles in Turkey.

Unlike Kissinger, the State Department urged caution. Nixon proceeded that way in spite of a leak that reached the press about the Cienfuegos construction. Without mentioning that report, Ambassador Dobrynin told Kissinger on September 28, 1970, that the Soviet leaders were eager for a summit. Kissinger replied that Nixon agreed in principle. He added that the United States would take a grave view if the building at Cienfuegos continued. Dobrynin in October presented a note reaffirming the 1962 understanding. In a response drafted by Kissinger and the Joint Chiefs, Nixon said that the United States for its part "understands that the U.S.S.R. will not establish . . . or permit the establishment of any facility in Cuba that can be employed to support or repair Soviet naval ships . . . armed with nuclear-capable, surface-to-surface missiles." The Soviets news agency then issued a statement that no such submarine base existed, and Nixon considered the matter closed. It had never reached the crisis proportions that Nixon and Kissinger attached to it.

They also believed that the Soviet Union would gain a new foothold in the Western Hemisphere with the election of a radical president in Chile. That prospect arose in September 1970, when Salvador Allende, an avowed Marxist, won a plurality in the presidential contest in Chile. Since Allende had no majority, the Chilean Parliament in October was to decide the election, with Allende the probable victor over the next two candidates. The American ambassador believed that Allende's election would constitute a "grievous defeat" for the United States. Though Allende and his opponents were proceeding according to the provisions of the Chilean constitution, Kissinger was alarmed, and Nixon characteristically considered the situation a test of his resolve.

Against the advice of the State Department, the CIA authorized covert expenditures for propaganda against Allende. Nixon also told the head of the CIA that he wanted "a major effort" to prevent Allende's election. While the CIA could not do much, its agents did supply several submachine guns to a small military faction that bungled a bizarre attempt to kidnap a senior Chilean general. Allende was duly elected and inaugurated. The Nixon administration then worked to sabotage his regime because, as Kissinger later admitted, it did not see why the United States had "to let a country go Marxist just because its people are irresponsible." There spoke the voice of tyranny. The Soviet Union and Cuba had supported Allende, just as the United States had supported his opponents, but it was the people of Chile and their elected representatives who put Allende in office. In a military coup that American attitudes encouraged, he was overthrown several years later. It had taken a perverse imagination, one bent on finding Communist confrontations where none existed, to interpret Allende's victory as a Communist-inspired crisis for the United States.

4. ROLLER COASTER

During the winter and spring of 1971 Nixon compounded his problems by his conduct of the war in Vietnam. After the Cambodian incursion Congress had passed legislation barring American forces from entering either Cambodia or Laos. But in January 1971, with the North Vietnamese moving supplies into Laos for further shipment south, Nixon expected a spring offensive. He therefore ordered a "major military operation" to cut the Ho Chi Minh Trail in Laos. Extensive American air support assisted ARVN infantry in the invasion, which began in February. It soon collapsed. Saigon furnished only half the troops that American strategists had considered necessary. Those green soldiers, led by timid officers, fought badly. Only after American bombers had destroyed their objective, the town of Tchepone, did the ARVN soldiers reach it. By mid-March they were in full retreat.

The operation damaged opinion of the administration within the United States. Nixon had again attacked a neutral nation, without congressional authorization, and over the protest of its head of government. Vietnamization had not created a South Vietnamese Army with the morale to fight. The disarray of their retreat reached American television audiences in pictures of ARVN soldiers desperately grabbing the skids of American helicopters carrying wounded from the front. The rout frightened the Saigon government while a prospect of future defeats after more American withdrawals fed anti-Americanism in young men subject to military service. Demonstrations against the United States and incidents of hostility toward GIs diminished the already sagging spirits of American troops. Early in April Nixon reported on national TV "that Vietnamization has succeeded." Public opinion polls spoke to the contrary. Confidence in the president sank to 50 percent, his lowest rating to that time, and support for his conduct of the war to 34 percent.

Nixon further excited antiwar passions by his leniency toward Lieutenant William Calley, Jr., the commander of an infantry company that in 1968 had massacred hundreds of Vietnamese civilians while taking the village of My Lai. Not until 1970 did news of that barbaric episode reach the United States; in March 1971 a court-martial sentenced Calley to life in prison. Both sides in the Vietnam War had committed untold atrocities, but the slaughter at My Lai was especially wanton. Many Americans nevertheless considered Calley a scapegoat who did not deserve punishment. Nixon contended that public outrage over My Lai was part of an attack on the war itself. In April, with

Calley's conviction under appeal in the federal courts, the president ordered Calley released from prison and confined to his own quarters. He then announced that he would personally review Calley's case before any sentence could be carried out. That hint of a forthcoming pardon understandably angered the prosecutor. "The greatest tragedy of all," he wrote Nixon, "will be if political expediency dictates the compromise of such a fundamental moral principle as the inherent lawlessness of the murder of innocent persons."

The invasion of Laos and the indulgence for Calley stirred renewed protests. On April 18, 1971, the Vietnam Veterans Against the War demonstrated in Washington as a witness to the atrocities they had themselves committed. Early the next week the Mayday Tribe, an organization of young radicals, began another demonstration with the unlikely purpose of stopping the government unless the government stopped the war. Convinced that Hanoi had encouraged "hard-core agitators," Nixon had the CIA assist the District of Columbia police, who jailed thousands of protesters without proper charges. Now the president had been lawless, for the CIA was not authorized to engage in that kind of activity. Such severe repression exceeded by far any danger of disruption of the government by a relatively small demonstration.

The president at that time was exceptionally skittish. In the spring preceding an election year, the economy was not robust, his foreign policy initiatives had not yet succeeded, antiwar protests had resumed, and he was losing ground in the polls. Then, to his dismay, on June 13, 1971, the *New York Times* began to publish segments of a top secret study, "The History of U.S. Decision-Making Process in Vietnam." Commissioned by Robert McNamara when he had begun to have doubts about American policy, the Pentagon Papers, as they became known, revealed a depressing record of mistaken assumptions, prevarications, and flawed judgments. They had led the Eisenhower, Kennedy, and Johnson administrations into the morass in Vietnam. The Pentagon Papers were history, but Nixon, already vulnerable to criticism, feared that their publication would shake confidence in his conduct of the war. Kissinger reinforced that concern.

Contending that publication would impair national security, expose state secrets, and impede the termination of the war, the Justice Department obtained an injunction ordering the *Times* to cease publishing the papers. The *Times* at once appealed. While that case moved toward the Supreme Court, other newspapers, among them the *Washington Post*, the *Boston Globe*, and the *St. Louis Post-Dispatch*, began publishing the material and were also enjoined. On June 30, 1971, the Supreme Court, in *New York Times v. United States*, ruled against the government; Chief Justice Burger and Justices Blackmun and Harlan dissented. In the majority opinion, with which there were several concurrences, Justice Black rejected the contention of the executive branch that the courts could "make laws enjoining publication of current news" in the name of "national security." The injunctions against the newspapers, he continued, constituted "prior restraint." They amounted to "a flagrant, indefensible" violation of the First Amendment. That amendment "gave the free press the protection it must have to fulfill its essential role in our democracy. . . . The press was protected so that it would bare the secrets of government and inform the people . . . and prominent among the responsibilities of a free press is the duty to prevent any part of the government from deceiving the people and sending them off to distant lands to die of foreign . . . shot and shell. In my view, far from deserving condemnation of their courageous reporting, the New York Times . . . and other newspapers should be commended for serving the purpose that the Founding Fathers saw so clearly."

The decision angered Nixon. He had already ordered proceedings against Daniel Ellsberg, the former Defense Department official from whom the *Times* had received the Pentagon Papers. The president and his closest advisers suspected that Ellsberg was part of an antiwar con-

Daniel Ellsberg: He made Nixon furious.

spiracy. "In the aftermath of the Pentagon Papers leak," Nixon later recollected, "and all the . . . renewed criticism of the war it produced . . . I was furious and frustrated. . . . I wanted someone to light a fire under the FBI. . . . If a conspiracy existed, I wanted . . . the full resources of the government brought to bear in order to find out." The Democrats were trying to discredit him, Nixon believed. He "wanted ammunition against the antiwar critics." Most of all, he was determined to prevent further leaks, if necessary "surreptitiously." Leaks, as he saw it, would threaten negotiations with China, about SALT, and about ending the war.

Accordingly, on July 17, 1971, John Ehrlichman assigned Egil Krogh, a personal friend and subordinate with investigative experience, to take charge of Nixon's "leak project." That was a task for the "Plumbers," who included David Young, a former assistant to Kissinger; E. Howard Hunt, formerly of the CIA; and G. Gordon Liddy, formerly with the FBI. Maintaining that there had been an outbreak of leaks, Nixon "tried to motivate Krogh in the strongest terms." He succeeded. On Labor Day the Plumbers organized a break-in at the office of Ellsberg's psychiatrist, where they expected to find evidence about Ellsberg's motives and associates. There was no such evidence. But the Plumbers had broken the law. As Nixon came to realize, the crime was "at least in part an outgrowth" of his "sense of urgency" about discrediting Ellsberg. That sense derived from his recognition that the winter and spring of 1971, beginning with the invasion of Laos and ending with the Pentagon Papers, marked the "lowest point" of his first term in the White House. But he had no intention of surrendering his "glorious burden." To preserve his office, he had encouraged a reckless disregard of the law. He argued, with some justification, that Kennedy and Johnson had been equally guilty of wiretapping and black-bag jobs. But he had exceeded every precedent. He was, of course, also capable of constructive action. His office allowed its incumbent to shift the political scenery, and Nixon, assisted by Kissinger, was about to do just that—to bring to fruition plans that would carry him rapidly from his temporary low to a giddy new high.

5. SALT

That reversal commenced with progress in the SALT negotiations. Since 1969 SALT had stumbled partly because of differences between the president's stated and actual aims. Nixon had said boldly that the

United States would seek only a sufficiency, no longer a superiority, in nuclear weapons. That announcement seemed to accept parity with the Soviet Union, a condition toward which Moscow had been striving since the missile crisis in 1962. A treaty embodying a recognition of parity would enhance Brezhnev's status and possibly relieve the Soviet Union of the mounting cost of the arms race. But Nixon, in all important details supported by Kissinger, was not in fact prepared to surrender nuclear superiority. He would agree to equitable limitations in ABMs, which were defensive weapons. He was willing, too, to limit the number of each country's ICBMs. But he intended to maintain overall American nuclear superiority in offensive weapons by sustaining the large American lead in submarine-launched ballistic missiles (SLBMs), in missile-carrying aircraft, and in the number of ICBMs equipped with MIRVs.

When SALT meetings began late in 1969, the Soviet Union expressly favored mutual deterrence and its continuation through arms limitations. But the Russians wanted to limit all systems for delivering nuclear weapons, a proposal that the United States declined to consider. Aware of the Soviet desire to move toward an agreement, Kissinger deliberately delayed by encumbering American proposals for limits in MIRVs and SLBMs with predictably unacceptable conditions, including demands for on-site inspections. Nixon and Kissinger were also pondering an American defensive redeployment that would have used ABMs to protect ICBM launching areas. Theoretically that change would have precluded a first strike against the United States. But the Senate in 1970 made it clear to the administration that it would not go along with the plan. Consequently, the administration moved closer to the Soviet position on defensive missiles. Each side would have an ABM system only to defend its capital city. In March 1971 the Soviet Union formally proposed a draft ABM treaty to that end, but the United States held out for a simultaneous limitation on offensive arms.

For some months prior to that time, talks had been proceeding through two different channels, officially between the arms negotiating teams, unofficially and secretly between Kissinger and Dobrynin. In May 1971 the Soviet team informally suggested the possibility of an ABM agreement accompanied by an "understanding" about ICBMs. That solution resembled the content of the secret talks in which Kissinger had told Dobrynin that the United States preferred a partial to a comprehensive limitation on offensive missiles. Nixon, suspecting a leak by someone on Kissinger's staff, feared the official American delegation might get the credit for success that he wanted for himself. He had

Kissinger warn Dobrynin that "sooner or later the President's tenacity and my control of the bureaucratic machinery would get matters to where we wanted them." Thereafter the Soviet Union knew which talks really mattered. And Dobrynin, as Kissinger insisted he should, quickly accepted terms similar to those the official Soviet team had suggested. On May 20, 1971, Nixon, the public credit exclusively his own, announced a breakthrough. The United States and the Soviet Union, he said, would couple restrictions on the building of ABMs with certain limitations on offensive strategic weapons, though "intensive negotiations . . . will be required to translate this understanding into a concrete agreement."

Nixon was orchestrating the SALT negotiations to fit his political calendar. He genuinely wanted some agreement to control arms, though arms control in itself interested him less than did a general settlement of outstanding Soviet-American issues. Because Brezhnev also genuinely wanted an agreement, Kissinger was able to manage the timing as he did. The president's statement about a breakthrough preceded by just two months Kissinger's return from China and Nixon's dramatic announcement of his own forthcoming trip. That development in turn strengthened the American position on SALT.

So did concurrent discussions about the status of Berlin. The four powers occupying that city had begun conversations in March 1970. Those talks accompanied the relaxation of European East-West tensions initiated by West Germany and reciprocated by the Soviet Union. As with SALT, so with Berlin. In 1971 the critical exchanges occurred between Kissinger, who linked the two issues, and Dobrynin. Late in August the principals arrived at the terms that constituted the quadripartite agreement on Berlin signed the next month by the United States, the Soviet Union, Great Britain, and France. The agreement gave both sides their major objectives. To the satisfaction of the Western countries, it recognized the economic and cultural ties between Berlin and West Germany, and it acknowledged the continuing role of the four powers in governing the city. To the satisfaction of the Soviet Union, the agreement prohibited West Germany from attempting to incorporate Berlin or any part of that city, and it accepted East German control of East Berlin. The peaceful resolution of the Berlin crisis in 1961 and later the Western acceptance of the Berlin wall had reduced the danger of a Soviet-American clash over the city. Now the 1971 pact ended the arguments about Berlin and prepared the way for further easing of cultural and economic relations between the NATO countries and those in the Soviet bloc.

More immediately, once the terms of the Berlin agreement had been settled, with the SALT negotiations also proceeding and Nixon's visit to China arranged, the president had a clear road to Moscow. The Soviet Union had postponed a summit before Kissinger went to Beijing, but Brezhnev after that journey agreed to a mutually convenient time. In another surprise announcement, in October 1971, the president informed the American people that a Moscow summit would take place the following May, three months after his trip to China. Exultant, Nixon knew he had assumed center stage as the dominant figure in world as well as American politics. He expected the two summits to keep him there during 1972. In the four months since the publication of the Pentagon Papers, he had recovered all his lost ground, and more.

6. BEIJING

Nixon's improving prospects did not temper his distrust of the Soviet Union or his tendency to exaggerate its influence. So it was that, with Kissinger, he misconstrued the significance of the treaty of friendship concluded in August 1971 between the Soviet Union and India. Discussions about that treaty, under way for almost a year, culminated when they did because the signatories saw a need to offset the news of the previous month of the American opening to China and the role Pakistan had played in that development. Further, Kissinger had just informed the Indians that they could expect no American support in the event of Chinese involvement in their long-standing territorial disputes with Pakistan. Indian Prime Minister Indira Gandhi had to turn elsewhere, as she then did. But in September Soviet Foreign Minister Gromyko and Secretary of State Rogers agreed to urge India and Pakistan to settle their differences peacefully. Kissinger nevertheless contended that Moscow, in negotiating the treaty with India, was seeking to "humiliate China and to punish Pakistan" and in this way deliberately opening the door "to war on the subcontinent." Nixon concurred. As he confided to a group of business executives, he considered the Indian people repulsive. He also attributed the admiration of Indian culture within the United States to the whims of the liberal establishment. And he frankly distrusted Indira Gandhi. Consequently, as he had told Kissinger in July, he wanted "to tilt toward Pakistan." It suited his prejudices to see India as a coconspirator with the Soviet Union against American interests.

Hostility between the Hindus of India and the Muslims of Pakistan had flourished for centuries. After World War II, when Great Britain granted independence to the subcontinent, religious and ethnic rivalries in the area accounted for its division into three parts, with India positioned between West Pakistan and East Pakistan, a Bengali region ruled from Muslim Islamabad. The Bengalis thereafter sought independence from West Pakistan, a goal the Indians recognized as in their own interest. During 1971 West Pakistan imposed martial law to control resistance to its rule in East Pakistan, tensions increased, and thousands of Bengalis fled to India to escape repression. It required no Soviet involvement to inflame that situation.

War began in December 1971, when West Pakistan bombed nearby Indian territory and sent tanks into Kashmir, a border area under Indian administration. The Indians retaliated by moving into East Pakistan. In Washington the State Department, supported by the CIA, viewed the independence of East Pakistan as inevitable and saw little risk of Soviet or Chinese intervention. The United States, the State Department recommended, should "keep calm . . . and let the inevitable happen." But Nixon and Kissinger decided "to discourage both Indian aggression and Soviet adventurism." The president wrote Brezhnev that Indian military forces were trying to dismember Pakistan. The spirit necessary for the summit, Nixon went on, required "the most urgent action to end the conflict." Ignoring the implied threat, the Soviet Union proposed to Washington an immediate cease-fire based on the recognition of the independence of East Pakistan. But Nixon interpreted that condition as "hard line." An American failure to help Pakistan, he believed, would lead Iran, a valued ally, and other countries "within the reach of Soviet influence" to question "the dependability of American support." Kissinger agreed. "We can't allow a friend of ours and China's," he told the president, "to get screwed in a conflict with a friend of Russia's."

In that frame of mind, Nixon indirectly warned the Soviet Union that the United States would not stand by if India attacked West Pakistan. Though there was no sign of such an attack, Nixon also, without consulting the Joint Chiefs, ordered the USS *Enterprise*, an aircraft carrier, and an accompanying task force to steam from Vietnam to the Bay of Bengal. "Our objective," Kissinger boasted, "was to scare off an attack on West Pakistan" and "to have forces in place in case the Soviet Union pressured China." But as the chief of naval operations later concluded, Nixon probably wanted to demonstrate to China that the United States was a power in the region. Only after assurances from Moscow that India had no aggressive designs, and after word from Beijing that China, too, wanted only a cease-fire, did Nixon and Kissinger relax.

With the great powers in accord, the war quickly ended. India offered and Pakistan accepted a cease-fire. East Pakistan soon thereafter became the independent state of Bangladesh. There had been no attack on West Pakistan; there had been no danger of Soviet interference. Yet Nixon and Kissinger believed, characteristically, that they had again prevented Soviet expansion in the third world. At the most, they had played up to the Chinese before the pending summit in Beijing.

Preparations for that meeting had been under way for several months. In Beijing again in October 1971, Kissinger had worked out terms for the joint communiqué that Nixon and Mao were to sign after their meeting. Kissinger also instructed the Chinese about the kind of reception for the president that Haldeman considered appropriate for American TV audiences. While he was so engaged, the United Nations voted to seat the People's Republic of China in place of Taiwan. The United States had sponsored dual representation instead, but Kissinger's presence in Beijing suggested flexibility in the American stance. The vote removed an issue that might otherwise have continued to trouble Sino-American relations. For their part, Mao and Zhou consolidated their power by arranging the death in an airplane crash of Lin Biao, the last important opponent of rapprochement with the United States. Mao had also provided ideological justification for the summit by proclaiming the tactical need for collaboration with a less threatening enemy, the United States, against a more dangerous one, the Soviet Union. A week before Nixon's departure for Beijing, the United States further eased trade restrictions on China.

At the end of February 1971 Nixon spent a week in China. "The

"It's going to be a long week . . ."

enormous ability, drive, and discipline of the Chinese people" impressed him, as did both Mao and Zhou. He found Mao alert, compatible, and wise, and Zhou brilliant and dynamic. They were brought together, the president told Mao, by a "recognition of a new situation in the world" in which a nation's "internal political philosophy" was no longer important. They looked instead to a nation's policy toward the rest of the world and to the danger of Soviet aggression. They had "common interests which transcend" the "great differences" in their political systems. "So let us," Nixon continued, ". . . start a long march together . . . on different roads to the same goal. . . . There is no reason for us to be enemies."

The United States, the president told Zhou privately, had to preserve a nuclear balance with the Soviet Union and to sustain its military power in Europe and the Pacific. To do otherwise would not be in China's interest. The Soviet Union, he went on, wanted the United States tied down in Vietnam because the Soviets wanted to influence Hanoi. So long as the North Vietnamese kept fighting, Zhou maintained, China could "do nothing but continue to support them." He was more interested in the question of Taiwan. In Nixon's recollection, the "Chinese were . . . determined . . . to assert their unequivocal claim" to that island, but he was equally "committed to Taiwan's right to exist as an independent nation." On that basis they agreed to disagree, but Zhou, alerted to Nixon's concern about the American right wing, softened the language he had drafted for the joint communiqué.

That communiqué, issued from Shanghai, openly stated the differences between the two nations, with particular reference to Vietnam, Korea, Japan, and Taiwan. But their agreements were just as significant. The Chinese accepted the principle of peaceful coexistence, which they had previously opposed. In return the United States, while committed to the independence of Taiwan, stated as its ultimate objective the withdrawal of all its forces there. Meanwhile, the United States would gradually reduce its military presence "as the tension in the area diminishes." That timetable, as Hanoi realized anxiously, gave the Chinese an incentive for easing the stress arising out of the war in Vietnam. The most important section in the communiqué, in Nixon's view, provided that neither the United States nor China would "seek hegemony" in the Asia-Pacific region and that both opposed efforts by any other power to do so. In his triangular diplomacy Nixon here obviously tilted toward China as an ally against the Soviet Union.

Nixon's mission had accomplished his major purposes. It demonstrated to the Chinese the advantages of cooperation with the United

States. It showed the president's willingness to confront the Soviet Union if that country intruded in Asia, a point he thought his policy in Vietnam also made. And the official Chinese-American rapport bothered the Soviet leaders, who, Nixon believed, would therefore be more malleable when their turn for a summit arrived.

Nixon hoped that history would remember him most of all for his opening to China. Not least, his visit was a triumph of public relations, a boon for his reelection campaign. Evening television in the United States depicted the president greeting Mao, attending state banquets with Mao and Zhou, riding through Tiananmen Square, inspecting the Great Wall. He gloried in the publicity, but he thought the press led it fade too soon. "It is very much in our interest," Nixon wrote Haldeman on March 13, 1972, ". . . to keep the China story alive. . . . I would like for you to put somebody to work on seeing what can be done to follow up on the China visit so that the press does not succeed in its obvious effort to bury it." Haldeman was also to have Kissinger, in a pending television address, stress "the following. . . . RN goes into such meetings better prepared than anyone who has ever held this office. . . . He has . . . exceptional knowledge of world problems. . . . He never gives an inch on principle. . . . He always keeps an eye on the main goal." Richard Nixon was determined to spread through the land his high opinion of RN.

7. Moscow

It was the toughness on which Nixon prided himself that he displayed in his response to the North Vietnamese offensive of March 1972. Planned a year and more earlier, that broad-scale attack also served as Hanoi's counter to more recent developments, especially the American overtures to China and the Soviet Union. The Chinese, in Hanoi's view, had been duplicitous in receiving Nixon. Mao had earlier advised the North Vietnamese to reach agreement with the United States by acceding to Thieu's continuing presidency. Moscow, too, had urged compromise. Nixon, for his part, made public Kissinger's secret discussions with the North Vietnamese and characterized his proposal for a cease-fire in place as a reasonable basis for peace. Defying those pressures, the North Vietnamese advanced across the demilitarized zone while Vietcong guerrillas intensified operations around Saigon. The offensive underscored their unchanged intention to unite all Vietnam under their rule.

Nixon and Brezhnev: Eager for agreement.

As Nixon saw it, both his political future and the credibility of American foreign policy were at stake. He ordered heavy retaliation by B-52 bombers and from aircraft carriers in the area. The B-52s flew more than five thousand sorties while the fighting went on. The president also instructed the Joint Chiefs to revive plans for smashing Hanoi and mining the harbor at Haiphong. He had told Brezhnev in January that he would cancel the summit if the Russians supported North Vietnamese ventures "designed to humiliate" the United States. Now Nixon had Kissinger tell Dobrynin that Moscow had either planned the North Vietnamese offensive or allowed it to go forward. In an amicable reply Dobrynin made no promises; but he said Hanoi would be "responsive" at the next session of secret talks with Kissinger, and he suggested Kissinger visit Moscow secretly to complete plans for the summit.

In approving that trip, Nixon directed Kissinger "to make Vietnam the first order of business and to refuse to discuss anything that the Soviets wanted . . . until they specifically committed themselves to help end the war." But concerned more about détente, Kissinger pursued his own priorities. The Soviet Union had reacted calmly to American bombing damage to four of their ships in Haiphong Harbor. Brezhnev seemed eager for the summit at almost any price. Kissinger therefore discussed arms control at some length before Brezhnev, just before their sessions were to end, said that North Vietnam and China had initiated the March offensive in order to prevent the Moscow summit. Hanoi, Brezhnev added, was using Soviet arms hoarded from previous years.

Ignoring Nixon's instructions, Kissinger suggested that if the Russians could arrange for fruitful negotiations, the United States would concede to the North Vietnamese demand for a settlement of political as well as military issues. He was ready to discuss an electoral commission including some Communist members to choose a successor to Thieu. After Kissinger had departed, Brezhnev sent a senior Soviet official to Hanoi, but the North Vietnamese continued to insist on the removal of Thieu as a condition for peace. Nixon, accusing them of "naked and unprovoked aggression," refused to stop the bombing. "I intend to cancel the Summit," he wrote Kissinger on May 2, 1972, "unless the situation . . . improves by May 15." There had been no improvement by May 8, when Nixon decided to mine all entrances to North Vietnamese ports and to strike at military targets in North Vietnam. The United States would continue to do so, he announced, until Hanoi met his two terms for peace: the return of all American prisoners of war and an internationally supervised cease-fire. He would let the Vietnamese themselves negotiate political issues. Meanwhile, so Nixon wrote Kissinger, "We must punish the enemy." The official Soviet news agency denounced Nixon, and Dobrynin protested the bombing. But Brezhnev did not cancel the summit, and neither, his private threats to the contrary, did Nixon. Both men had too much at stake to postpone their meeting.

On May 22, 1972, Nixon, accompanied by Kissinger, reached Moscow for four days of intense discussions with Brezhnev and other Soviet leaders about the major issues in Soviet-American relations. Brezhnev was at once blunt and warm, as Nixon saw him, shrewd but inelegant, craving respect as an equal, emotional about American policy in China and Vietnam, eager for agreement about important matters. Nixon was equally eager. With little reference to the expert negotiations of the American arms control team, Nixon completed SALT I on terms that suited his political objectives. The major part of the SALT I agreement consisted of the 1972 ABM treaty. It limited each signatory to two ABMs to protect their national capitals but did not limit antisatellite weapons, which the State Department negotiators would have tried to include.

The second part of SALT I was an interim agreement on offensive strategic weapons. It fixed the number of ICBMs and SLBMs for five years, or until further negotiations could effect a more comprehensive plan. But it set the number of those weapons so high that the Soviet Union could complete the building it had planned. Related agreements reduced the risk of accidental war and enhanced the verification of compliance by improving the hot line between Washington and Moscow and by obliging each principal not to interfere with the other's spy satellites.

Nixon gave up little that he actually had in order to achieve those terms. The Senate, as he knew, was averse to expanding the ABM program. The limitations on offensive weapons did not curb strategic aircraft or air-launched cruise missiles, in which the United States had a considerable advantage. SALT I also left out MIRVs, in which competition between the two powers soon accelerated, with the United States in the lead. Nevertheless, the JCS, predictably, objected to the concessions Nixon made. But the price was worth paying, for SALT I was the first successful effort at strategic arms control since the onset of the cold war. It promised further progress. It revived the deferred hopes for nuclear disarmament that had motivated Kennedy and Khrushchev to restrict nuclear testing. It reduced the arms race in ABMs and reduced the possibility of nuclear war. As Nixon said, SALT I also contributed to making "permanent the concept of deterrence through mutual terror." Each side in the ABM treaty "was leaving its population and territory hostage for a strategic missile attack. Each . . . therefore had an ultimate interest in preventing a war."

Both Nixon and Brezhnev could rejoice over the summit. SALT I made a powerful impression on American public opinion. It redounded to Nixon's credit. For his part, Brezhnev took particular satisfaction in the American acceptance of nuclear parity implicit in the SALT agreement and in other benefits he received. As he promised he would, Nixon recommended that Congress give the Soviet Union status as a most favored nation for purposes of trade. He also arranged a credit for Soviet purchases of American grain of at least $200 million in the first year and $750 million over three years. The linkage of trade to SALT appeared to have a double payoff, partly in arms control, partly in opening a new market coveted by American farmers. But the Russians had bargained skillfully. They, too, wanted arms control, and they needed grain. Indeed, they bought so much that in 1973 grain prices rose sharply in the United States. As Kissinger later wrote, "the Soviets beat us at our own game."

The spirit of the summit infused still another agreement to which Brezhnev attached significance, the agreement on "The Basic Principles of Relations" between the two nations. In the nuclear age, that pact said, there was no alternative to peaceful coexistence. The signatories would therefore "do their utmost to avoid military confrontations and to prevent the outbreak of nuclear war." Both countries recognized that the "security interests" of each were "based on the principle of equity and the renunciation of the use or threat of force." Nixon saw little importance in that declaration of good intentions except as a "guide for future action." Brezhnev took it as avowing a "fundamental improvement in U.S.-Soviet relations."

In keeping with the content and tone of the basic agreement, Brezhnev talked with Nixon for two hours about Vietnam. He asked whether Nixon would like to have Soviet President Nikolai Podgorny visit Hanoi in the interest of peace. Replying affirmatively, Nixon also agreed to suspend bombing during Podgorny's stay. Clearly Podgorny would try to placate Hanoi's anger about the summit, as Kissinger observed, but his visit might also serve to restrain the North Vietnamese. As it worked out, once again they would not yield to Russian influence, though they realized that détente was bound to reduce the support the Russians had been providing. Nixon's triangular diplomacy, as he had intended, was isolating Hanoi.

The Moscow summit, so Kissinger told the president, had been "one of the great diplomatic coups of all time." Indeed, Nixon had gone well beyond his predecessors in easing relations with the Soviet Union. That thawing of the cold war disturbed right-wing Republicans, but they had too few votes to prevent the Senate's approval of SALT I. Nixon had made dazzling use of his foreign policy. The summits had brought a new stability to the relationships among the three strongest powers on earth. As Nixon said, they had worked "toward a more peaceful world." In spite of the persisting war in Vietnam, Nixon had made the issue of peace his own. And in so doing, he had virtually assured his reelection.

14

The Politics of Connivance

Like almost every other president, Richard Nixon began to run for his second term in office as soon as he commenced his first. He had other interests, of course. The family assistance plan, the opening to China, détente with the Soviet Union were policies eminently worthy in themselves. But Nixon kept in mind their implications for domestic politics. "Richard Nixon," John Ehrlichman wrote, "was a full-time politician, and he never let us forget it. At home and abroad, every day of the week and whatever the occasion, he (and we) looked after the politics." That priority gained urgency after the 1970 congressional election with the founding of the Committee to Re-elect the President (CREEP) and again in the first half of 1971, when Nixon felt his presidency had reached its lowest point. In the ventures he then undertook at home and abroad, he aimed directly at gaining ground for his national campaign in 1972.

1. Timely Conversions

In economics, Nixon had prejudices rather than principles—prejudices against an unbalanced budget and against government controls. He also had a sharp awareness of the political consequences of adverse economic conditions. Eisenhower's refusal to stimulate the economy in 1960 had accentuated and prolonged a recession that, so Nixon believed, contributed to the Democratic victory that year. In 1968 rising inflation had hurt the Democrats. In that campaign Nixon, asserting his belief in a free market, had attacked Johnson's reliance on wage and price guidelines to retard inflation. As president, according to the first chairman of his Council of Economic Advisers, Nixon "was predisposed toward using the market to make most economic decisions" but too pragmatic to be "confined by any ideology."

Nixon's approach to ecological questions reflected the motives that characterized his economic pragmatism. He considered Senator Edmund S. Muskie one of the most formidable candidates the Democrats could nominate for president in 1972. Muskie had identified himself with clean air, clean water, and consumer safety. Eager to capture those issues for himself, Nixon supported legislation that improved the effectiveness of the ecological programs initiated under Johnson. The president seemed genuinely to believe in those objectives. But apart from that belief and his rivalry with Muskie, he also wanted big business on his side in 1972, and he trusted private enterprise more than he trusted federal bureaucrats. For those reasons he opposed the automobile safety standards proposed by his own Department of Transportation. In 1971 Henry Ford II told John Ehrlichman that the installation of air bags as passive restraints in passenger cars, which the department had mandated for 1972, was impractical. So informed, Nixon wrote Ehrlichman: "Let's not go crazy on this." In the same note, the president ruled out a department requirement for the installation of flashers and buzzers to warn drivers that their seat belts were not fastened.

As with safety, so with ecology, Nixon was suspicious of a 1971 program of the Environmental Protection Agency (EPA) to develop an unconventional internal-combustion engine in order to meet automobile emission standards mandated for 1975. "This whole program," Nixon wrote Ehrlichman, "smells like an upcoming boondoggle—with mediocre men in government . . . making major decisions. *Ride herd* to get the ribbon clerks out and a few experts in." The CEA questioned whether the benefits of pollution control were worth the costs of attaining them. Nixon agreed. "We have gone overboard on the environment," he told Ehrlichman in August 1971, "and are going to reap the whirlwind for our excesses—get me a plan for cooling off the excesses." In the same spirit, the president later commended the head of the EPA for jolting consumers into the realization that the cost of environmental protection would be "very high" and the laws regulating the quality of air were "very impractical."

Principle soon yielded to politics in the making of macroeconomic policy. At the start of Nixon's first term his economic advisers, with his support, attempted to sustain a slow rate of growth while trying to reduce inflation. During 1968 inflation had run at 4.7 percent, twice the average annual rate for the period 1956 to 1967, with unemployment at 3.3 percent, a record low since 1953. But scheduled federal outlays during 1969 and 1970 would foster further inflation if the new administration did not cut expenditures. Nixon set out to do so, while he also hoped to reduce inflation by tightening interest rates. Yet the president, pressed by leading Democrats, called for income tax reductions through increased personal exemptions for low-income families. The Democrats, their political motives obvious, in December 1969 enacted a revenue measure that gave those exemptions to all taxpayers. The resulting loss in federal revenue was to lead to an inflationary deficit, a condition aggravated by the president's unwillingness to run the political risks necessary to pare the budget for 1970 and 1971. Consequently, during 1970 inflation persisted and unemployment grew, developments damaging for Republicans facing election that fall.

Before that time some of Nixon's economic advisers had come to believe that inflation arose from circumstances that monetary and fiscal policies could not in themselves affect. Two senior Treasury officials argued that prices were rising largely in response to cost-push pressures exacted by collective bargaining agreements that increased wages and also costs. Arthur Burns, Nixon's conservative chairman of the Federal Reserve Board, attributed the "worldwide inflationary trend" to public insistence upon expenditures for humanitarian and ecological programs. Inflation was indeed a worldwide problem but, Burns to the contrary, a function primarily of rising prices for commodities, food and fuel especially, for which demand was outstripping supply, as it continued to do for much of the decade.

Public anxiety about American inflation forced Nixon to address the issue. The CEA, he announced in June 1970, would thereafter release "periodic inflation alerts" about significant increases in wages and prices. But these alerts, he maintained, did not constitute a return to the Johnson guidelines. Repeating his opposition to government controls, which some private economists were then recommending, Nixon added: "I will not take the nation down the road of wage and price controls, however politically expedient that may seem." But veteran Nixon watchers knew that he often did exactly what he said he wouldn't do.

He soon took himself down the road to Keynesian economics, which he had previously rejected. Almost three decades earlier American Keynesians had worked out the concept of a full employment budget. That idea complemented Keynes's argument for running a budgetary deficit in order to stimulate the economy in years of unemployment.

With full employment, further stimulation—either increased spending at constant tax schedules or constant spending at reduced tax schedules—would become inflationary. So in years of full employment, expenditures should be held to anticipated revenues in order to balance the budget. Nixon had always subscribed to the Republican doctrine of a balanced budget whatever the economic conditions. In April 1970, eager to retain his economic options, he reversed his position. "At times," the president then told the nation, "the economic situation . . . calls for . . . a budget deficit. There is one basic guideline . . . we should never violate. . . . Expenditures should never be allowed to outrun the revenues that the tax system would produce at reasonably full employment." One startled Republican said: "I'm going to have to burn up a lot of old speeches denouncing deficit spending." Nixon replied: "I'm in the same boat."

In the last quarter of 1970 a mild recession set in. Disturbed by the success of labor unions in recent contract negotiations, corporate executives criticized the administration for allowing wage and price increases. Many of them also urged the adoption of some kind of federal controls. Nixon instead called upon both union and management to exercise restraint. But he worried. In June he had made George Shultz director of the Office of Management and Budget (OMB). By November Shultz and the CEA believed that the Federal Reserve was not increasing the money supply fast enough to combat the recession. Nixon, too, was losing confidence in Arthur Burns, who seemed too easily influenced by businessmen and too accessible to the press. But the president could neither dismiss Burns nor prevent his frequent public statements. In December, in a surprise move, Nixon appointed John Connally his new secretary of the treasury. He intended to offset Burns's influence and to designate, as he put it, a "spokesman who would be the authoritative source" on the administration's economic policy. Nixon had long admired Connally, a conservative Texas Democrat and friend of Lyndon Johnson's who had served three terms as governor of his state. Connally was articulate, as Nixon saw him, and understood power, qualifications important for his new post.

But Connally was no magician, and Nixon continued to thrash. Adverse economic news, so said the CEA, was damping business confidence. "This bears out my point on psychological recession," the president wrote Ehrlichman. "I want an imaginative plan . . . to put a more positive line out. . . . This is *not* something to be left to 'those P.R. people.' This is a *substantive* problem and I want it treated that way by all concerned." A few months later, in March 1971, Nixon called for study of a fiscal stimulus to consumer spending, then "disappointing." In April he issued instructions to have the CEA encourage innovations in products for civilian use. "The time may come," he wrote, "when we should have something like a tax credit for intangible capital formation." In May, responding to criticism from the *Wall Street Journal*, the president floated another idea: "We need symbolic support of *new* private initiatives at the very least. Our domestic experts . . . seem as obsessed with *government* enterprise as L.B.J. was."

Those remarks provided a useless obbligato to worsening economic news. Wholesale prices for industrial commodities continued to advance during the first half of 1971. That sign of pending increases in consumer prices was accompanied by further inflationary wage settlements, to the dismay of Arthur Burns and of Connally's senior subordinates. By July 1971 Connally was supporting the imposition of wage and price controls. "If we don't propose a responsible new program," he told the president, "Congress will have an irresponsible one on your desk within a month." Early in August Connally and Shultz, who was still dubious, prepared a comprehensive plan. Nixon had expected "something bold" from Connally, but even so, he "was not prepared for the actions he proposed . . . total war on all economic fronts, including across-the-board wage and price controls." The president, for so long an opponent of "government interference in the free market," was now converted.

Nixon intended to time the announcement of the plan for maximum impact on the election, though delay raised the possibility of leaks that would induce corporations to raise prices before they were forbidden to do so. As it developed, a crisis in international money markets, long pending, came to a head in mid-August and forced the administration to act quickly. Ever since the second Eisenhower administration, the Western European nations, and later Japan, had been accumulating dollars as a result of their favorable balance of payments with the United States. The Kennedy administration had wrestled with the problem of Eurodollars without success, and the problem had grown during the Johnson years, when industrial production, distorted by procurements for the Vietnam War, provided too few goods at too high prices for sales abroad adequate to balance imports. From 1969 to 1971 American exports, as compared with imports, continued to fall, and holders of dollars began to sell the currency heavily.

Throughout the whole period the United States continued freely to convert dollars to gold at the fixed rate of thirty-five dollars an ounce. The future of that policy depended increasingly on the willingness of nations holding dollars to refrain from requesting conversion. Otherwise the flow of gold out of the United States would reduce American banking reserves with adverse consequences for the volume of domestic money and credit. In June 1971 the head of the CEA warned the president that the United States was dangerously vulnerable. In July he advised Nixon to sever the dollar from gold, a step that would lead to the depreciation of the dollar. Nixon designated Connally to consult the experts "and give me a recommendation for action—I incline to move on the problem and not just wait for it to hit us again—e.g. in the fall of 1972."

It hit them in the second week of August 1971. With the dollar under heavy selling pressure on international markets, the Bank of England asked the United States to guarantee the convertibility of Britain's dollar holdings, about three billion dollars. Paul A. Volcker, undersecretary of the treasury and earlier a strong supporter of convertibility, recognized, as he told Connally, that "a major crisis in the world's monetary exchange system" demanded action. Connally persuaded Nixon to treat the domestic and the international problems together, as one package. That tactic brought the doubters into agreement on price controls. "I would have continued to oppose controls if the plan had been to impose them in isolation," George Shultz recalled. "But as part of an overall change in economic policy, I was able to accept them. It was absolutely necessary to close the gold window. The old exchange rate policy was basically bankrupt."

On August 15, 1971, the president announced his "New Economic Policy." He was, he later wrote, philosophically against wage-price controls, but "the objective reality of the economic situation," and of national politics, forced him to impose them. The new policies included for their international effects the suspension of the convertibility of the dollar and a 10 percent surcharge on imports; and for their domestic effect, a ninety-day freeze on prices and wages and a 10 percent investment tax credit, as well as acceleration from 1973 to 1972 of the increased personal exemption on income taxes.

In some respects those policies produced temporary gains. For several months the rates of inflation and unemployment declined, though they rose again when controls were relaxed, and they soared in 1973 and 1974, when controls ended. Nixon himself concluded that recourse to controls "in the long run . . . was wrong." But he was gratified by the "overwhelmingly favorable" public reaction to his announcement. His decision, he remained convinced, "was politically necessary and immensely popular in the short run." The decision was certainly expedient. Herbert Stein of the CEA wrote a spoof that put it well: "On the 15th day of the 8th month the President came down from the mountain and spoke to the people on all the networks, saying: I bring you a Comprehensive . . . Program . . . thou shall enjoy in 1972 what the Democrats promised thee for 1973."

The sudden end of the convertibility of the dollar into gold stunned the nation's allies. The Japanese complained about a second "Nixon shokku," as upsetting as the announcement of his planned trip to China. Countries holding dollars lost severely as the depreciated dollar dropped in international markets. Those markets remained unsettled for many months while the shift continued from the dollar to sounder currencies, particularly the Swiss franc, the West German mark, and the Japanese yen. Those predictable developments, costly for American prestige, underscored the decline of the country's economic domination, which had been going on for more than a decade. Nixon had not caused that decline. But with the United States still in 1971 the leading nation in world monetary affairs, he had acted irresponsibly by failing even to seek an international agreement on flexible exchange rates. The Europeans resented his unilateral course as much as its disruptive effects. That was a high price for the domestic political lift the president obtained. But Nixon did not see it that way. When David Rockefeller, the head of the Chase Bank in New York, recommended several changes to restore stability in international currency markets, Nixon wrote Connally: "I totally disagree. . . . He wants to go back to a patched up old system— like all International bankers. It's right for them and totally wrong for the country." As that statement revealed, a touch of populism complemented Nixon's political expediency.

The quest for political advantage shaped the administration's other economic policies during 1971. Johnson had stepped up federal spending in 1964 to help his election campaign, but no previous president had attempted to stimulate the economy for political gain as thoroughly as Nixon did. The investment tax credit and the increased personal income tax exemption had that effect. Nixon and his advisers also turned to monetary policy—to increases in the supply of money and the easier credit they would generate—as one instrument of their purpose. In November 1971 Herbert Stein wrote Nixon that "an increase in the rate of monetary growth would provide the economy with useful additional stimulus." George Shultz agreed. In December, blaming Arthur Burns, Shultz wrote that he was "increasingly alarmed by the lack of growth in money supply." Nixon at once told Connally to lean on Burns. Connally did so, but in February 1972 Stein again warned the president that "prodding will continue to be needed on both the fiscal and the monetary fronts." Whether in response to that prodding or because Burns believed an expansionary policy was really necessary, the Federal Reserve accelerated the growth of the money supply in 1972 with a stimulative result.

A similar impact followed an increase in transfer payments—federal outlays for Social Security, veterans' benefits, and other such expenditures that transferred funds collected from taxes on all Americans to those Americans entitled by law to special payments. According to one reliable calculation, about seventy-five million Americans, "almost all of them of voting age, benefited directly from the increased cash flow from the government before the 1972 election." Late in 1971 Nixon had proposed a 5 percent increase in Social Security benefits for 1972. Apart from pleasing those voters who received Social Security, that boost, preceding later tax collections at it did, was to raise federal spending in 1972 with a resulting spur to the economy. No less politically minded than Nixon, several Democratic presidential aspirants in Congress suggested lifting Social Security payments by 15 percent, then 20 percent, then 25 percent, with a 20 percent increase finally enacted and signed by the president in September 1972. The first checks incorporating that extra money—eight billion dollars in all—went out to recipients in October, just before the election. Payments of veterans' benefits followed a similar pattern in 1972, as did federal grants to state and local governments.

So, too, Nixon urged the quick spending of funds Congress had authorized. "Federal purchases," Stein informed him in March 1972, "rose less than we assumed." The president, underlining that sentence, directed the OMB to ride herd on the cabinet, to "get them off their duffs." As one observer put it, "For a short time the President's conservative economic advisers, even Shultz and Stein, joined the euphoric rush toward stimulation." During the calendar year 1972, federal spending rose almost 11 percent. As Melvin Laird recalled, "Every effort was made to create an economic boom for the 1972 election. The Defense Department, for example, bought a two-year supply of toilet paper. We ordered enough trucks . . . for the next several years."

The strategy worked so well that by late summer the president's economic advisers were again worried primarily about inflation, as they should have been. But for 1972 the Nixon campaign, in the conclusion of the leading analyst of the question, "enjoyed a booming economy, with a particularly sharp upturn in the fall. . . . The exquisite political precision of this economic course must have been partly the result of sheer good luck. . . . Much of the . . . acceleration was, however, the result of deliberate planning and the mobilization of policy instruments producing acceleration in real disposable income growth." Consequently, Nixon could stand in 1972, as he had resolved to, as the candidate of prosperity.

2. SOCIAL ISSUES

Especially after 1970, Nixon cultivated both his southern strategy and the social issues he considered salient for Middle Americans in all sections of the country. So it was that early in 1972 he invited Congress to undercut the rulings of the Supreme Court about the use of busing to integrate public schools. "The Congress," he said on national television, "has both the Constitutional authority and a special capacity to debate and define new methods for implementing Constitutional principles." A constitutional amendment would take too long to ratify, but a statute imposing a moratorium on busing would serve the president's purpose. "What we need now," he said, "is not just speaking out against busing, we need action to stop it."

The Supreme Court gave Nixon a chance also to repeat his views about crime. In *Furman v. Georgia* (1972) the Court ruled on the death penalty. In the United States as well as the rest of the Western world criminologists had long since questioned the utility of the death penalty as a deterrent to homicides and other major felonies. Most states gave judges and juries broad discretion in deciding whether to condemn murderers to execution or to long prison sentences. American juries were imposing the death penalty in only about 10 percent of the murder cases they decided, and doing so disproportionately to blacks. A majority of the Supreme Court, all of them veterans of the Warren years, found the Georgia law under consideration to be unconstitutional. Justices Brennan and Marshall deemed the death penalty, as Georgia allowed it, in itself "cruel and unusual punishment" forbidden by the Fourth Amendment. The rest of the majority—Justices Douglas, Stewart, and White—declared the Georgia law unconstitutional because it permitted juries and judges to apply the death penalty in an arbitrary and capricious manner that made the sentence "cruel and unusual." The Nixon appointees dissented, arguing for upholding the law. Like the president, many of his silent majority at once associated the *Furman* decision with *Miranda* as another instance of the Supreme Court's coddling of criminals.

That was a skewed reading of the decision. The Court had indeed wiped out almost all existing state laws on the death penalty, but its ruling allowed the states—as thirty-seven of them did—to enact new legislation giving precise definition to the particular crimes for which the death penalty could be applied and to extenuating circumstances requiring modification of that punishment. In the trenchant analysis of Alexander Bickel, a leading constitutional authority, the Court was exercising the "passive virtues," mediating between the "ultimates of legitimation and invalidation." Nixon, less subtle in his response, followed Haldeman's recommendation for public relations in an election year. He proposed that Congress enact legislation for federal jurisdictions that would mandate the death penalty for kidnapping, hijacking airplanes, bombing, killing police, and "Big Time" dope peddling.

Nixon also opposed the growing feminist movement. Increasingly

political in their orientation, women activists were organizing to achieve goals for which federal action was necessary. On the feminist left, lesbians, joined by homosexuals, were abandoning the anonymity they had sought for so long in favor of a militant assertion of their rights to equal treatment under the law. At the feminist center the National Organization for Women (NOW) pressed for affirmative action for equal opportunities for women in employment and education and for equal pay with men in equivalent jobs. Those and other, related objectives informed the effort to obtain congressional approval for an equal rights amendment (ERA) to the Constitution, an amendment to assert equal rights regardless of sex. The ERA aroused the ire of much of Middle America. Traditionalists claimed that the amendment would lead to the conscription of women, to unisex toilets, to legalized abortion and the destruction of the family.

Though the Republican party had given lip service to the ERA since the 1920s, Nixon catered to those resisting the amendment. As he told Ehrlichman, he considered the appointment of women to federal offices of little political importance. It would be a "monstrosity," he said, to demand equal athletic facilities for women in colleges receiving federal grants. By 1972 feminists had publicized their demand for legalized abortion, one aspect of their belief that women had the right to control their own bodies. Siding with the "right to life" opponents of abortion, Nixon announced his stand for "the sanctity of human life— including the life of the yet unborn."

The president also vetoed a measure sponsored by the Democrats in Congress to provide a national system of day-care centers. In the feminist view of marriage, to which some men were subscribing, husband and wife had equal rights to a career. Feminists believed that spouses also had equal obligations to housekeeping and the family. With more and more women entering the work force, the availability of safe, clean, and affordable child care became an important issue for them and their husbands. Poor women especially needed federal assistance to finance day care. But many Middle Americans, particularly blue-collar Roman Catholics and conservative Protestants, found sexual equality as offensive as racial equality. They retained the conventional view of marriage that confined women to the home, the kitchen, and the nursery. Speaking to that prejudice, Nixon vetoed the day-care bill. He opposed legislation, he said, that would commit "the vast moral authority of the national government to communal approaches to child rearing, over against the family centered approach." By instinct and conviction, he was in harmony with his preferred constituency.

Even if Nixon had been less attuned to the politics of the social issues, the Democrats, as they went about reforming their party and selecting their candidate, were pushing Middle America to him. Democratic party reform grew out of the candidacy of Eugene McCarthy in 1968. In most states McCarthy and his antiwar supporters had encountered obstacles to their quest for delegates to the national convention. Through control of the state committees, the Johnson-Humphrey forces had also controlled the selection process except in the few states with presidential primaries. The McCarthy delegates who did get to Chicago were determined to reform the party's nominating procedures. They managed to get their resolution advancing that purpose through the rules committee and then the convention itself. It called for the appointment of a commission to study the nominating process and report back to the Democratic National Committee. The passions of the convention had moved many basically moderate Democrats to favor party reform, which the study commission soon endorsed.

The recommended changes in party rules, as the national committee adopted them, democratized the selection process by making it more participatory and less subject to the control of state organizations. In 1972 that system worked to the disadvantage of the traditional party stalwarts—organized labor and its leaders, city machines and their bosses, courthouse politicos in the South. The revised rules also operated to the advantage of advocates of the "New Politics"—antiwar Democrats, left-leaning civil rights groups, feminists, advocates for the poor, and other reformers. Further, the National Women's Political Caucus had obtained from the national committee an interpretation of the rules that specified numerical standards for representation within state delegations of women, youth, and racial minorities. That feminist victory tilted the contests for delegates away from orthodox Democrats. The reform Democrats, beneficiaries of all the changes, were taking positions on the social issues diametrically opposite to those on which the president was building his platform.

Nixon recognized the relationship between both social and personal issues to the strengths of the aspirants to the Democratic nomination. As a Catholic and a liberal Senator Edward Kennedy of Massachusetts, the younger brother of John and Robert Kennedy, had originally seemed a likely nominee. He lost his chance in 1969 in an accident at Chappaquiddick Island. There, apparently intoxicated, Kennedy drove his car off a bridge between the island and Martha's Vineyard. His companion, a young woman, drowned. After several futile attempts to save her, he swam to safety, but disoriented, frightened, and badly advised, he failed promptly to report the accident to the police. His delay, his confusion, and his attempt to cover up his role cast doubt on his reliability in an emergency and therefore on his qualifications for the presidency in a nuclear age. Leaving nothing to chance, the White House nevertheless sent one Anthony Ulasewicz, a former policeman, whom John Ehrlichman had interviewed, to check into Kennedy's personal life. Ulasewicz was paid secretly by Herbert Kalmbach, Nixon's personal lawyer, with funds left over from the 1968 campaign. Charles Colson, a senior White House staffer, encouraged a conservative Catholic to run against Kennedy in the senatorial race in 1970 and to keep the Chappaquiddick episode in the awareness of the electorate.

With Kennedy virtually eliminated, Senator Edmund Muskie of Maine, also a Catholic, became the early Democratic front-runner. In comparison with most of his rivals, Muskie, though critical of Nixon's policies in Vietnam, seemed a moderate. He had campaigned with dignity and effect as the party's vice presidential nominee in 1968. In the spring of 1971 Haldeman advised Nixon to counter Muskie's strength by associating himself with issues important to Catholics, including federal aid to parochial schools and opposition to legalized abortion. The president annotated that memorandum with a "Done." "Keep the heat on Big Ed," Haldeman also wrote, so that he would be scarred if nominated. "Correct," Nixon commented. The purpose, as Patrick Buchanan of the White House staff said, was to try to force Muskie, who was avoiding divisive issues, to address them and thereby split the Democratic party.

Haldeman worried about Muskie's "becoming increasingly acceptable in the South" because most southerners considered him a moderate on race and foreign policy. One remedy, Haldeman suggested, lay in publicizing Muskie's votes against Haynsworth and Carswell and his opposition to the Cambodian incursion. Another, more effective force arose from the candidacy of Governor Wallace of Alabama, whose vicious views about race were certain to cost Muskie support in southern primaries.

The White House had a strategy for handling Wallace. He could help Nixon by attacking northern Democrats on the question of busing, but if he were to run on an independent ticket, as he had in 1968, he would attract the same voters the president was wooing. In 1970, with Wallace involved in a primary for renomination as governor, the White House secretly contributed four hundred thousand dollars to his opponent's campaign. Again Kalmbach handled the transaction. Nevertheless, Wallace won. In 1971 the Committee to Re-elect the President spent freely to keep Wallace's independent party off the ballot in California. It failed. But in 1972 Wallace was useful to Nixon because of his candidacy in Democratic primaries. Though the Alabama governor had little chance of achieving nomination, his campaign forced Muskie and other moderate Democratic hopefuls to take positions on racial issues that contrasted with Nixon's calculated concessions to southern preferences.

Those moderates might otherwise have tried to remain ambiguous about race in order to distinguish themselves from candidates on the Democratic left, particularly Mayor John V. Lindsay of New York City and Senator George McGovern of South Dakota. As it was, with those two at one of the party's extremes and Wallace at the other, and with Muskie and Hubert Humphrey skirmishing near the center, the Democrats were heading for a series of crippling donnybrooks in the primaries.

3. DIRTY TRICKS

Neither Nixon nor John Mitchell, who had resigned as attorney general in order to run CREEP, could leave well enough alone. The president was so intent on winning a huge personal victory, and Mitchell so wedded to that purpose, that during 1972 neither trusted obvious Republican strength and Democratic weakness. Their subordinates at CREEP and in the White House were determined to heed the president's injunction of 1970, to "come up with . . . dirty tricks" to discombobulate the Democrats. To that end they needed large sums of money for which they would not have to account. Kalmbach's surplus from 1968 was not enough. To raise the rest, the Nixon camp relied upon the finance committee of CREEP, of which Maurice Stans, Nixon's first secretary of commerce, was chairman.

The Federal Election Campaign Act, which Nixon signed in February 1972, imposed an imminent deadline on CREEP's financial arm. The measure did not take effect until April 7, 1972. Thereafter it required disclosure of large contributions. Stans and his staff urged both corporate and private donors to pay up in time to avoid disclosure, "which we naturally want to avoid." They expected substantial gifts, at least a hundred thousand dollars from small corporations, 1 percent of profits from large businesses, 0.5 percent of net worth from wealthy Californians. Those were the sources of funds for all of Nixon's previous campaigns.

It was natural and traditional for corporate executives to contribute to presidential campaigns, particularly to Republicans, whom they ordinarily favored, and to probable victors, whose usefulness would be immediate. Corporate gifts were intended to provide insurance of a kind against onerous federal regulation and expensive new taxes. The buying and selling of influence were as old as politics, and the mushrooming costs of national campaigning, especially for television, made the trading of favors more urgent than ever. Nevertheless, some corporate executives considered CREEP's demands extortionate. Those demands were big enough to force many contributors to draw corporate funds from foreign affiliates and to launder money they removed from balances they should not have touched without accountability to their stockholders. American Airlines, for one flagrant example, contributed millions to the Nixon campaign, probably with the expectation of preferred treatment from federal authorities. Robert L. Vesco, an accused Wall Street swindler, gave $200,000 in $100 bills, which were handed to a CREEP agent in a black attaché case. Indeed, many of the contributions received before April 7, 1972, were in cash, which was kept in a secret fund of $1,770,000 in Stans's desk for distribution, with no accountability, to the political arm of CREEP. That money paid for the dirty tricks the president had ordered.

Mitchell, Stans, and their associates took care to keep the president uninformed about their shadowy activities. That protected his deniability. But even in episodes of corporate fund raising in which Nixon's policies were suspect, he later maintained that his motives were pure. So it was in the case of the International Telephone and Telegraph Company, a corporate conglomerate that had pursued Nixon's objective by conspiring to overthrow the Allende regime in Chile. ITT promised to put up several hundred thousand dollars to defray the costs of the Republican National Convention if that event were to occur in San Diego. After the convention was scheduled instead for Miami, an ITT employee, one Dita Beard, suggested that the corporation's "noble commitment" would stand in exchange for a favorable antitrust ruling. Nixon had the suit against ITT dropped. Later Beard repudiated as a forgery the memorandum containing her suggestion, but only after a CREEP operator, disguised in a cheap wig, had met with her privately in her hospital room in Denver. Nixon in his memoir contended that the antitrust suit against ITT violated his policy of sparing American conglomerates from prosecution so that they could compete internationally. On that account, so he said, he had ordered the action against ITT squashed.

In that explanation, coincidence rather than conspiracy explained a quid pro quo for corporate giving. So, too, in the case of the three major dairy corporations that among them contributed more than half a million dollars to various campaigns, four hundred thousand to Nixon's and the rest to seven Democrats. The dairy corporations originally promised Kalmbach two million dollars for Nixon. Their representatives subsequently informed the president that they were unhappy with the decision of the secretary of agriculture to support the price of milk at only 80 percent of parity in 1971 and 1972. That very day Nixon raised the support level to 85 percent, as Kalmbach told the dairymen. They then arranged for much of their total gift, though far less than they had at first pledged. When those transactions became public, Nixon denied any relationship between the contributions and his increase in the support price. He had acted, he claimed, to combat the depressed state of the dairy industry, and in order to obtain political credit for his decision before the Democrats in Congress could legislate to the same end. Unlikely. All in all, CREEP carried the practice of squeezing money from corporations to an unprecedented length. It collected some twenty million dollars before the April deadline, and it disbursed more than five million dollars in payments for campaign activities before those expenditures also had to be disclosed.

The president's men spent their funds to widen the divisions within the Democratic party and to weaken the candidacy of Edmund Muskie. In order to hassle Muskie and other Democrats, H. R. Haldeman approved the hiring of Donald H. Segretti, a graduate of the University of Southern California who had worked in the Nixon gubernatorial campaign in 1962. Eager for cash to pay for the sweet and easy life he enjoyed, Segretti had no scruples about political shenanigans. He hired agents to sabotage Muskie in the states with primaries. In New Hampshire they fed derogatory stories to the *Manchester Union Leader*, the state's widely circulated reactionary newspaper. Late in February 1972 that paper published an anti-Muskie editorial accusing the senator of supporting blacks while demeaning French-Canadians, an important minority group in northern New England. The editorial was based upon a spurious letter to the editor that claimed Muskie had referred to French-Canadians as "Canucks," an insulting term. Though no one could prove it at the time, one of Segretti's men had forged the letter. The editorial cost Muskie votes and reputation. The *Union Leader* the next day reprinted a magazine story claiming that Muskie's wife drank too much and used off color language. Incensed, Muskie while on the stump attacked the paper's irresponsible publisher as a "gutless coward." Then, his anger and frustration rising, Muskie broke into sobs.

The episode, in the observation of political reporters, "shattered the calm, cool . . . image that was basic to Muskie's voter appeal."

Muskie's campaign never recuperated. In New Hampshire he won 46 percent of the vote in the Democratic primary to 37 percent for George McGovern, but as the party's front-runner, canvassing a state that was a neighbor of his own, Muskie had been expected to win by a much larger margin. In the next primary, in Florida, where the liberal and antiwar McGovern chose not to run, Muskie faced the strength of George Wallace, who was stressing his opposition to busing. As they had in New Hampshire, dirty tricks damaged Muskie's effort. In a typical instance, posters broadcast the message "Help Muskie in Busing More Children Now." G. Gordon Liddy, a CREEP operative, hired spies to infiltrate the Muskie entourage, as well as those of Humphrey and McGovern, and to report about strategy through a line of command that ultimately reached Haldeman in the White House. The Florida vote effectively removed Muskie from the race. Wallace won the state with 41 percent, with Humphrey a weak second and Muskie fourth. Wallace might have done just as well without CREEP's interference. But the White House took credit for the result. "Our primary objective," boasted Patrick Buchanan, Nixon's most conservative speech writer, "to prevent Senator Muskie from sweeping the early primaries . . . and uniting the Democratic Party . . . has been achieved."

Muskie contributed to that achievement. He seemed not to understand that the party had changed the rules of the game. His calculated blandness misfired in a year in which his liberal opponents identified with the passions aroused by the issues of race and the Vietnam War. Wallace's right-wing exploitation of race gave the Alabaman the lead in the South and might have provided him with crucial influence at the convention. But on May 15 Wallace was shot in an assassination attempt. Paralyzed permanently, he had to withdraw from the race. By that time Nixon had concluded, correctly, that a Democratic candidate on the left would prove easiest for him to defeat.

Apart from Muskie, Hubert Humphrey seemed best to suit the Democratic center, most likely to command black support, most popular with the orthodox party leaders, and probably most dangerous to Nixon in a national campaign. In announcing his candidacy, Humphrey, borrowing from John F. Kennedy, had promised to get the country moving again. If he had won in 1968, he also said, he would have extricated the nation from the Vietnam War. But in an incautious statement to Pat Moynihan in 1970, Humphrey had "wholeheartedly" supported the president's "course . . . in foreign affairs." Nixon was ready to use that information if he needed it, but the need never arose. In the Wisconsin primary Humphrey ran as a "me, too" and lost in his neighboring state. George McGovern, who won a big victory in the analysis of the White House, had "really played the populism theme" in Wisconsin. He then went on to victories in Massachusetts and Nebraska. "To me," Nixon recalled, "his steady climb was as welcome . . . as it was almost unbelievable." In small measure, that climb was abetted by directions from a savvy White House aide to "lay off" McGovern because of his vulnerability in a national campaign against the president.

4. McGovern

McGovern's success was wholly believable in the context of the Democratic party in 1972. He had been chairman of the Democratic Commission on Party Structure and Delegate Selection. A proponent of the new rules, he recognized the lift they gave to the reform factions, and he based his candidacy on the support of those groups. The antiwar movement embraced McGovern, whose long record of opposition to American involvement in Vietnam expressed his deep convictions. Feminists also brought their political zeal to McGovern's campaign.

George McGovern: Educated, intelligent, decent.

To be sure, the antiwar activists were far weaker than they had been in 1968, and the feminists were not yet as strong as they were to become, but in the primary contests of 1972, particularly under the new party rules, the fervor of those factions, and their eagerness to organize and to get out the vote, made McGovern a much tougher candidate than his orthodox rivals initially realized.

The son of a Methodist minister, George McGovern was an educated, intelligent, thoroughly decent man. He had earned a doctor's degree in American history at Northwestern University with a dissertation that recited the brutality of the Rockefellers in suppressing a striking miners' union in the West. He left teaching to enter politics partly because of personal ambition but also because he believed in political action to make government the benefactor of needy people. A dedicated democrat and man of peace, an idealist in a cynical calling, McGovern was also in some ways naive. He had more confidence in the power of goodness than circumstances warranted. He placed more faith in his closest advisers than their talents deserved. He had little personal skill in organization and little learning about some of the issues he discussed almost offhandedly. In the jargon of the day, McGovern was a "beautiful man," a total contrast with Nixon. Nevertheless, Nixon was correct: McGovern was the most beatable candidate in serious contention to head the Democratic ticket.

In the crucial June Democratic primary in California, where the large delegation would go entirely to the winner, McGovern began his stumping with a twenty-point lead in the polls, but Humphrey closed in and lost by only a small margin. He then argued that the California delegation should be apportioned according to the percentage of votes each candidate received. That proposal to change the rules angered the McGovern supporters. At the national convention they treated Humphrey rudely, and they mocked Mayor Richard Daley, whom they were punishing for his behavior four years earlier. The McGovern managers made a hash of the proceedings. They allowed their people to appear unruly on television. They failed to hold to a timetable that would schedule major events for prime time. McGovern made his acceptance speech well after midnight in the eastern time zone. The networks, exhibiting no bias in favor of the Democrats, made all they could of the outré dress and hairstyles of the McGovern supporters. "There is too much hair," one veteran politician said, "and not enough cigars at this convention."

The resulting image hurt McGovern, as did his own disdain for the powers in the orthodox wing of the party. Nixon was delighted, as he wrote, that the representatives of the "new politics" seemed to consist of "women, blacks, homosexuals, welfare mothers, migrant farm workers." McGovern also damaged himself seriously by his haste in selecting Senator Thomas Eagleton of Missouri as his running mate. He and his advisers had failed to discover, and Eagleton had not disclosed, that he had twice voluntarily received shock treatment for depression. Episodes of depression need not have disqualified Eagleton, but most Americans thought they did when information about them became public. Ill advised, McGovern then waffled, first supporting Eagleton "1000 percent," then dumping him and replacing him with Sargent Shriver.

The Democratic party suffered most severely from the divisive effects of McGovern's controversial position on the issues. He was in favor of legalizing both abortion and marijuana. He proposed a thirty-billion-dollar reduction in defense spending, withdrawal of support from the Thieu government in Vietnam, amnesty for deserters in the Vietnam War, and the return of all American troops in exchange for the release of American prisoners of war, if necessary before that release. Misinterpreting an analysis prepared for him about a guaranteed annual income to combat poverty, McGovern also came out for granting a thousand dollars annually to every person in the country, as well as for redistributive taxation. McGovern's positions promised important improvements in American life, but they hurt him politically. A reduction in defense spending, accompanied by redistributive taxation, would have brought the United States closer to the equitable society that McGovern envisaged. So, too, the right of women to abortion on demand militated toward sexual equality. And the nation had no business loitering in South Vietnam to prop up a venal regime. Indeed, the left-leaning Americans for Democratic Action endorsed McGovern, but as its historian observed, the ADA "demonstrated little concern for middle-class anxiety over busing, law and order, or affirmative action." Characteristically, Mayor Daley deplored McGovern's stand on Vietnam, as George Shultz told Nixon, who instructed Shultz to "keep in close touch" with Daley. The AFL-CIO refused to endorse McGovern, and orthodox Democrats in Philadelphia, New York, and other large cities resolved, like Daley, to sit on their hands during the national campaign. Blue-collar workers, conservative Catholics, southerners, Middle Americans in general drifted to Nixon, exactly as he had hoped they would.

The McGovern campaign contributed more toward the president's reelection than did any other political development in 1972. "The most exciting aspect . . . for me," Nixon recalled, "was that McGovern's perverse treatment of the traditional Democratic power blocs . . . made possible the creation of a New Republican Majority as an electoral force in American politics." The peace issue might have compensated in part for that effect had not Nixon so modified the draft that antiwar sentiment even in the colleges was diminishing. Draftees no longer had to serve in Vietnam unless they wanted to. Indeed, troop withdrawals from Vietnam had made the draft virtually unnecessary. And Nixon and Kissinger, glowing over their triumphs in Beijing and Moscow, were pursuing another dramatic goal in their secret negotiations with Hanoi.

The signs had pointed to an easy Republican victory after McGovern won the California primary in early June. But with the president's political plans so·close to fruition, in the early hours of June 17, 1972, burglars hired by CREEP agents were caught breaking into the headquarters of the Democratic National Committee at the Watergate, a complex of apartments and offices in Washington, D.C. Now the imaginative dirty tricks that Nixon had called for had transgressed the law just when dirty tricks were quite unnecessary for realizing his purpose.

5. WATERGATE

According to his own account, Nixon had no prior knowledge of the break-in at Watergate. One of its purposes was to tap the telephone of Larry O'Brien, the head of the Democratic National Committee, whom Nixon considered a dangerous enemy. Indeed, an earlier CREEP break-in at the same place had put a tap on O'Brien's telephone, but that tap did not function. And perhaps Nixon wanted to learn what O'Brien was saying about him and some of his relationships with wealthy donors, particularly Howard Hughes. But the president claimed that his first news of the break-in came while he was in Key Biscayne. He was so furious, according to Charles Colson, that he threw an ashtray across the room. A political assistant to the president, Colson also said that Nixon "thought it was the dumbest thing he had ever heard of and was just outraged that anyone even remotely connected with the campaign organization would have . . . anything to do with something like Watergate." Perhaps Nixon was surprised and outraged. Even so, his closest friends and advisers had had a lot to do with the break-in, as the nation was to learn.

" HE SAYS HE'S FROM THE PHONE COMPANY... "

The origins of Watergate lay in CREEP and with the Nixon men who staffed it and worked with it. Both H. R. Haldeman and John Mitchell served on the committee that decided how to spend the secret funds raised by Maurice Stans and Herbert Kalmbach. Haldeman had installed as deputy director of CREEP one of his former assistants, Jeb Magruder, to supervise the collection of political information. Haldeman had also made John Dean, the president's counsel, responsible for overall campaign intelligence. Dean had recruited G. Gordon Liddy, the toughest of the Plumbers, to work with Magruder, and Liddy had brought with him his friend, E. Howard Hunt. In January 1972, in the office of Attorney General Mitchell, with Dean and Magruder present, Liddy had proposed a fantastic scheme to harass the Democrats with kidnappings, hijackings, and wiretaps. Mitchell rejected it as too complicated and expensive. But late in March Mitchell approved a revised and reduced plan for wiretapping the Democratic National Committee. Liddy received more than ten thousand dollars in cash for that purpose. After a first attempt had failed, the police intercepted the second attempt. The men they caught included James McCord, the head of security for CREEP, and three Cubans as well as an American associated with them. The Cubans were carrying thirteen new hundred-dollar bills, all from CREEP funds, as it developed, and had in their hotel room a notebook referring to Howard Hunt.

The potential fallout from those arrests was enormous. If McCord and Hunt revealed all they knew, their stories would implicate, among others, Charles Colson, John Dean, H. R. Haldeman, John Ehrlichman, John Mitchell, and ultimately the president, for their roles, direct and indirect, in the succession of dirty tricks, many of them illegal. Also bound to be aired were the earlier Huston memo and the creation of the Plumbers, the break-in at the office of Daniel Ellsberg's psychiatrist, and the bugging of Ellsberg's telephone. The news of the arrests and of McCord's connection with CREEP prompted the White House staff to destroy files that might incriminate the president's men. On June 18, the day after the break-in, the president's devoted press secretary, who knew no better, called the event a "third-rate burglary." John Mitchell, who knew the truth, lied in behalf of CREEP. "McCord and the four men arrested," he said, ". . . were not operating either in our behalf or with our consent." The cover-up had begun.

Whatever Nixon knew about Watergate then, between June 21 and June 22, 1972, he learned from Haldeman and others how many of the arrows leading to Watergate pointed back to the White House. He might have condemned the operation, chastised CREEP for a dumb mistake, and expunged the episode from the campaign. But his reaction was cynical. Lawrence O'Brien had filed a civil suit against the perpetrators. Irritated, Nixon chose to view "political bugging," as he called it, as a normal part of the game. He decided to "play it tough." On June 23 he discussed the FBI's investigation of the break-in with Haldeman.

"And you think the thing to do is get them to stop," Haldeman asked.

"Right, fine," the president replied.

"They say," Haldeman went on, "the only way to do that is from White House instructions . . . and it's got to be Helms and . . . Walters. . . . And the proposal would be that Ehrlichman and I call them in, and say. . . ."

"All right, fine," Nixon agreed, ". . . we've protected Helms from one hell of a lot of things."

So Richard Helms, the head of the CIA, and General Vernon Walters, his deputy, received White House instructions to tell the FBI that its investigation of Watergate, if pursued, would lead to a breach of security about matters of concern to the national interest. In agreeing to that scheme, the president joined the cover-up, a conspiracy with his closest associates to obstruct justice by trying to hide facts about the break-in, in itself a federal crime. But for six weeks the American public knew very little about Watergate, except that the break-in had happened, and for months thereafter, only gradually did the public learn more.

From late June 1972 through late September the cover-up continued in a series of stratagems to which Nixon, Haldeman, Ehrlichman, and Dean were privy. General Walters, at first going along with White House orders to head off the FBI, had changed his mind. Involving the CIA, he told Dean, would "transform . . . a medium-sized explosion into a multi-megaton explosion and simply was not worth the risk." With the FBI investigation proceeding, the White House tried to reduce its exposure. At Nixon's behest, John Mitchell resigned as head of CREEP with the excuse that his wife was ill. The president appointed Clark MacGregor to take Mitchell's place. A former congressman from Minnesota and a devout Republican, MacGregor knew nothing about Watergate or the White House involvement. He believed in the president and his assurances of innocence. Consequently, MacGregor, with a clear conscience, again and again denied charges of White House complicity, as did Ron Ziegler, the president's equally naive press secretary.

Mitchell continued to cooperate with Dean to raise a smoke screen between Watergate and the public. They used Maurice Stans and Herbert Kalmbach to provide more than two hundred thousand dollars, some of it newly raised, to the Watergate defendants, including Gordon Liddy and Howard Hunt, both of whom had been identified as accessories to the crime. The money, spent in part to pay the cost of defense before the grand jury then handling their cases, also bought the silence of Liddy and Hunt, who demanded large bribes. Magruder and Mitchell, for their parts, resorted to perjury, which they rehearsed with Dean, to protect themselves from prosecution.

The cover-up benefited from the cooperation of two Nixon appointees who held offices of central importance for law enforcement. After the death of J. Edgar Hoover, Nixon had nominated L. Patrick Gray as head of the FBI. Acting in that post pending Senate confirmation, Gray, a Nixon loyalist, obeyed instructions from Ehrlichman and Dean to destroy incriminating papers removed from the safe that Howard Hunt had used at the White House. Gray also permitted Dean to sit in at the interviews that the FBI conducted with Watergate suspects, and Dean regularly reported to Nixon about the data the FBI was collecting. The chief of the Criminal Division of the Justice Department, Henry Petersen, another Nixon loyalist, kept Dean and Nixon up-to-date about the testimony, supposedly secret, received by the grand jury. Petersen and his staff confined their investigation of the break-in so narrowly that they asked for indictments only against the five burglars, Liddy, and Hunt. On September 25, 1972, after the grand jury had handed down those indictments, United States District Judge John Sirica, who was presiding, scolded the Justice Department for its failure to ask obvious questions about the role of CREEP. "I don't think we should sit up here like nincompoops," Sirica said. "The function of a trial is to search for the truth."

Sirica scheduled the trial of those indicted for November 15, after the election, and the president was able to prevent an early effort in Congress to search for the truth. Texas Democrat Wright Patman, chairman of the House Committee on Banking and Currency, announced a plan to conduct hearings to determine whether CREEP had violated any banking or election laws. But Nixon, Haldeman, and Dean dreaded the possibility of Stans's being interrogated by Patman. The president therefore told Dean to have Gerald Ford, the House minority leader, get the Republicans on Patman's committee to "raise hell about those hearings." Ford did so. Dean also had Henry Petersen write Patman that the hearings would jeopardize the case against the Watergate defendants. Joined by some southern Democrats, the Republicans on the committee then voted against giving Patman the power of subpoena that he needed in order to hold hearings.

Through September, perjury and obfuscation kept the Watergate scandal from reaching the White House. Dean, who orchestrated the cover-up during the grand jury inquiry, had earned the president's gratitude. "The way . . . you've handled it," Nixon said on September 14, ". . . has been very skillful." The attorney working for the Democratic National Committee, Edward Bennett Williams, had aroused the president's wrath. He would regret his role, Nixon said, "because afterwards . . . that is the guy we've got to ruin. . . . We are going to fix the son of a bitch." And also fix the *Washington Post* for its probing of Watergate. The *Post* owned television stations with licenses that would be up for renewal. The Internal Revenue Service would make trouble for all the president's enemies. "This . . . is war," Nixon said. ". . . They are asking for it and they are going to get it."

Nixon had reason to hate the *Washington Post.* Two of the paper's

Woodward and Bernstein: They painted the landscape of scandal.

reporters, Carl Bernstein and Robert Woodward, both young, ambitious, and relentless, had been investigating the Watergate affair. Supported by their unflinching editor, Benjamin Bradley, Bernstein and Woodward were tracing the flow of CREEP campaign funds through banks in Miami and Mexico to the Watergate burglars. At the beginning of August the *Post* had published their first accounts, which MacGregor and Ziegler denied. But the reporters pressed on, aided by information from a secret White House source, never identified but known to them as Deep Throat, the name also of a pornographic movie. Revealing the shallowness of the FBI and grand jury investigations, they learned about Kalmbach and Segretti and the dirty tricks. They discovered connections between senior officials at CREEP, including Mitchell and Stans, and Nixon's White House staff. Their reports stirred the *New York Times* and other journals to compete in their coverage of Watergate. The resulting stories added to the landscape of scandal that Woodward and Bernstein continued to paint.

Their reports handed the Democrats a new issue. McGovern and O'Brien berated CREEP for its money-raising techniques and its dirty campaign tricks, and charged the White House with equal blame. The Nixon spokesmen, incredulous, were furious. Senator Robert Dole, chairman of the Republican National Committee, described the *Post* and McGovern as partners in innuendo. MacGregor said McGovern was resorting to the "politics of desperation." Ziegler denied that anyone at the White House had any association with the Watergate case. Privately Nixon called the revelations about Segretti "the last burp of the Eastern establishment." The denials for the while outweighed the charges. As the campaign moved into October, most Americans appeared uninterested in Watergate. A poll showed that half the respondents had never heard of the break-in. Other polls gave the president a commanding lead.

Confident of victory, Nixon declared that the White House had had no part in Watergate. He also hoped that with his reelection, the cover-up would succeed. His other political planning had satisfied his high expectations. Under the tight control of his people, the Republican National Convention had gone entirely to his schedule. He was renominated by acclaim. His campaign organization impressed Theodore H. White, that connoisseur of presidential elections, as "one of the most spectacularly efficient exercises in political technology of the entire postwar era." And by October Nixon thought that he might soon add the coup de grace—peace in Vietnam.

6. "Peace Is at Hand"

The Democrats in the Senate, as the president's political advisers saw it, had been trying for several years "to transfer the war label" to the Nixon administration. To that end, Democratic Majority Leader Mike Mansfield in February 1972 sponsored an amendment to the military appropriations bill calling for American withdrawal from Vietnam within six months. The Democratic Policy Committee endorsed that amendment with the argument that Congress was reasserting its rights in foreign policy and with the clear implication that it would not have condoned Lyndon Johnson's escalations had it known all the facts about Vietnam. The nomination of McGovern underscored those contentions with their firm basis in truth.

Resolved to have his way in Vietnam, Nixon was equally determined to frustrate every Democratic tactic. In May 1972, when he intensified the bombing of North Vietnam and ordered the mining of Haiphong Harbor, he also altered his terms for peace in Vietnam. Without reference to his earlier demands for mutual troop withdrawals, he said that American forces would leave Vietnam within four months of a cease-fire and the release of American prisoners of war. Further, he decoupled military and political issues by leaving any internal Vietnamese political solution to be settled "between the Vietnamese themselves."

The opportunity inherent in that new formulation did not at first attract Hanoi. But Nixon's successful trip to Moscow, like his earlier visit to China, marked American progress toward reducing the streams of supply on which North Vietnam relied. In July, moreover, the Democrats in the Senate passed their amendment, which now mandated the total withdrawal of American troops upon release of all POWs. As Kissinger ruefully said, Hanoi had only to wait until "Congress voted us out of the war." With Nixon's lead in the campaign becoming increasingly apparent to the North Vietnamese, they recalculated their tactics. They knew they would have to continue to deal with him. They also knew that the American presence in South Vietnam would continue to shrink. And without substantial Chinese and Soviet help, they could not expect to win a striking victory in the field, though Vietcong guerrilla operations could continue. Under those circumstances, they concluded that they should modify their demands before Nixon won reelection and stiffened his terms. Patient as ever, the North Vietnamese could afford to propose reasonable conditions that did not preclude the continuation of their long effort to control all Vietnam.

Early in August Kissinger first discerned a hint in the proposals of Le Duc Tho, the North Vietnamese negotiator in their private talks in Paris, that Hanoi would no longer insist on Thieu's resignation as a precondition of peace. During September American intelligence reports indicated that North Vietnamese cadres and the Vietcong were stepping up efforts to occupy as much territory as possible, probably to hold those areas in the event that a standstill cease-fire accepted a "leopard spot" pattern. On October 8, 1972, Tho at last "advanced a very realistic and very simple proposal": The United States and North Vietnam between themselves would work out the military questions, including a cease-fire, American troop withdrawal, and prisoner exchanges; political matters would fall to the warring groups in Vietnam; they would create an interim council consisting of representatives of the Thieu regime, North Vietnam, and the Vietcong. Meanwhile, the armies of North Vietnam and South Vietnam would remain spotted about in the places they occupied.

Those proposals, as Kissinger realized, portended a North Vietnamese triumph. They assured only the departure of the Americans. There was no guarantee that a "council of national reconciliation" would ever meet or deliberate. Fighting would continue, with the North Vietnamese operating from stronger positions. But Kissinger accepted the presence of the North Vietnamese forces in the South in return for Hanoi's agreement in effect not to resupply them. He felt he had no choice. Ten years of war had not expelled the North Vietnamese, as he said, and "we could not make it a condition for a final settlement. We had long passed that threshold." In an oblique way, George McGovern in a speech of October 9 assumed a similar stance. He promised, if elected, to remove all American troops and to end all aid to Saigon. He expected Hanoi to respond, he said, by releasing all POWs.

Nixon, like Kissinger, considered the new North Vietnamese terms a useful basis for further negotiations. The president wanted an exchange of prisoners to include South Vietnamese civilians in captivity. He also stipulated that replacements of war matériel should benefit neither side. Nixon was optimistic. On October 13 he reduced the scheduled bombing of North Vietnam and cabled Paris that he accepted the basic draft for a cease-fire "except for some technical issues," which Kissinger was to discuss with Le Duc Tho within the week. The North Vietnamese complained in their reply that the president was reopening questions they considered settled. Nixon then told Kissinger to review no terms "that we felt were less than acceptable." Expecting a landslide at the polls, he felt he could be firm. No settlement in Vietnam would help him politically, he thought, but "if Thieu . . . or the North Vietnamese blew it," that would hurt.

Thieu "blew it." By October 21 the North Vietnamese had accepted all of Nixon's conditions on "questions of arms replacement and . . . release of . . . POWs." The president cabled Hanoi that "the agreement could now be considered complete." He also wrote Thieu that "we have no reasonable alternative but to accept this agreement." He had already accelerated deliveries of two billion dollars of military equipment to Thieu's government, so much that South Vietnam acquired the fourth largest air force in the world. But in Saigon Kissinger found Thieu adamant. The United States, Thieu insisted, was collaborating with China and the Soviet Union against him. He rejected the agreement with Hanoi and demanded the withdrawal of North Vietnamese troops from the area south of the demilitarized zone. Thieu was trying to protect his own interests, but Kissinger cabled Nixon that Thieu's position verged on the insane. The president then told Kissinger to push the South Vietnamese as far as possible. He also wrote Thieu that if he persisted in opposition, his course "would have the most serious effects upon my ability to continue to provide support for you." But on

October 23 Thieu would still not yield, and Kissinger, aggrieved, returned to the United States.

Now Nixon backed off. He reasoned that if he abandoned Thieu, South Vietnam would fall to the Communists, whereas North Vietnam would make new concessions after he had won a clear mandate in the election. On October 24, in a speech to the National Assembly, Thieu denounced the draft agreement between the United States and North Vietnam. Two days later North Vietnam broadcast a summary of the draft and accused Washington of trying to sabotage it. In an effort to reassure Hanoi and discipline Saigon, Kissinger held his first televised press conference. "We believe," he said, "that peace is at hand. We believe that an agreement is within sight." Nixon, furious, felt that Kissinger's statement had impeded American bargaining with Hanoi. He was also disturbed that McGovern would claim the Republicans were trying to manipulate the election. Kissinger later admitted his statement had the latter effect even though Nixon repudiated it. "We are not going to allow an election deadline," the president said, ". . . to force us into an agreement which would be only a temporary truce."

Even if Thieu had accepted the agreement, it could not have improved Nixon's victory at the polls. On election day, November 7, 1972, the president crushed McGovern. He won 45.9 million votes—60.8 percent of those cast—to McGovern's 28.4 million. He carried every state but Massachusetts and the District of Columbia, and he swept the electoral college by a larger margin than Johnson had in 1964. But his was a personal rather than a party landslide. The Democrats, gaining one seat in the Senate while losing twelve in the House, retained majorities on the Hill. The president had so closely directed his reelection campaign that he neglected other Republican candidates. His cherished Middle Americans, splitting their tickets, had voted for Democrats locally. Most successful Democratic candidates had anticipated that result by distancing themselves from McGovern and assuming positions on civil rights, women's rights, and taxation distinctly to his right.

Nixon's personal triumph was not without substantial costs. To achieve it, he had oversold détente, overstimulated the economy, employed tactics that further divided the American people, whom he had promised to bring together, and broken the law that he had sworn to uphold. On those accounts, the second term he so coveted could not become the "new era" that he was so confident "was about to begin."

15

Double Trouble

At each stage in Richard Nixon's career, political pundits had wondered: Had he changed? Did the old Tricky Dick still prevail or was there a new Nixon, reasoned, mellowed and steeled by experience? With his reelection, as the president saw it, the American people had voted to let Nixon be Nixon. The victorious Nixon knew what he wanted. Indeed, some six weeks before the election, he spelled out plans for his second term to two of his subordinates. Caspar Weinberger, then head of the Office of Management and Budget, was to get to work on "austere budget levels for fiscal 1973," while John Ehrlichman was to prepare a "wholesale restaffing . . . of the Executive Branch." Concurrently Nixon would punish his enemies in the "traditional Eastern liberal Establishment" and also his enemies abroad.

1. Rewards and Punishments

The morning after the election, in a sullen mood, the president—as Henry Kissinger recalled—thanked the White House staff "in a perfunctory manner" for its help, quickly departed, and left Haldeman to tell staff members that each man was to submit his resignation immediately. The president, Haldeman added, would "announce his personal decisions for the new term within a month." An hour later Haldeman gave the identical message to the cabinet. Kissinger, though he had received assurances about his own continuing role, was appalled by "the frenzied, almost maniacal sense of urgency about this political butchery." Within weeks the most independent of the cabinet members were forced out, among them Secretary of Defense Melvin Laird, Secretary of Commerce Peter Peterson, and Secretary of Housing and Urban Development George Romney. Nixon made Kissinger secretary of state, effective in September, in place of William Rogers, who wanted to resign. Kissinger was to continue, too, as national security adviser. The president moved Elliot Richardson from HEW to Defense, and Caspar Weinberger to HEW, where his deep conservative instincts would brake that department's inclinations toward liberalism. Richardson, for his part, had the independence of mind to stand up to the senior military on budgetary matters and also the personal ambition to defer to the president on matters of policy, as he always had.

Nixon also moved to reorganize and "repopulate" the executive branch. There was much to be said for reorganization. The federal bureaucracy had become swollen and cumbersome. Long before Nixon's presidency bureaucratic inertia had often impeded innovative approaches to national problems, and bureaucratic resistance to change had often retarded policies the White House originated. But there were many able and dedicated career men and women in the federal service; most of them performed with energy and a genuine concern for the public interest. They regularly provided expert counsel to their politically appointed superiors. Nixon constantly griped because most of the bureaucracy had been appointed by Democrats and in his view were Democrats themselves. Some of the advice the bureaucrats rendered during his first term angered the president. He considered it sabotage when senior staff in HEW urged Secretary Finch to support integration of southern public schools and later when employees at the State Department expressed their disapproval of the invasion of Cambodia.

Nixon and Haldeman regarded the bureaucracy as a "bunch of bastards." So Nixon struck back. He intended reorganization to establish his personal control over the bureaucracy, to put his own people in senior positions in every agency. Before election day one of Haldeman's assistants had prepared a list of two hundred candidates, all carefully screened, for presidential appointment to important posts. But Nixon delayed acting on most of those offices until the list could be revised to take account of geographic and ethnic considerations.

Meanwhile, in January 1973, Weinberger and Shultz, recently made secretary of the treasury after Connally went home to Texas, submitted a budget for fiscal 1974. It included substantial cuts in defense and severe economies in all social welfare programs, some of which were designated for termination. Shultz considered those programs indefensible "except on political grounds," but much of the press viewed the excisions as evidence of the president's conservative leanings. Nixon meant to turn to the right. If Congress voted funds for programs listed for termination, he announced, he would impound the money. And he did so with six billion dollars appropriated for protecting the environment. "The Constitutional right for the President . . . to impound funds," he asserted in January 1973, ". . . that is, not to spend money . . . that right is absolutely clear." That was a fallacious claim. Because of inefficiencies in procurement or lack of adequate planning, other presidents on occasion had been unable to spend moneys Congress had appropriated, but Nixon was now declaring a right to withhold spending if he disapproved of a policy Congress was financing. That contention ran counter to the constitutional obligation of the president to enforce the law. Going still further, Nixon instructed his new director of the Office of Economic Opportunity to liquidate the agency. But Congress had created the office, and only Congress could abolish it.

In attempting to centralize control over the bureaucracy, in cutting back on domestic programs, in impounding appropriations, Nixon was taking on traditionally influential interests that he had long deemed his foes. "I had thrown down a gauntlet," he later boasted, "to Congress, the bureaucracy, the media, and the Washington establishment and challenged them to engage in epic battle." He intended to demonstrate the power of his office and of his mandate, precisely as he had to the government of North Vietnam.

2. LINEBACKER TWO

Upon his reelection Nixon's "first priority" was "to end the war in Vietnam." In aiming for that goal, he was unusually withdrawn, "difficult to reach" even for Henry Kissinger. Their relationship had begun to sour when Kissinger received favorable publicity after his first return from China. Now Kissinger sensed "an emerging competitiveness" in the president, and as they "headed into the troubled waters of a new negotiation, a steady course was not aided by the latent disaffection between the helmsman and his principal navigator."

Nixon expressed his disaffection by directing Kissinger to submit to North Vietnam the sixty-nine amendments that Thieu had demanded to the October draft agreement. Though he considered those amendments "preposterous," Kissinger blew up when Le Duc Tho suspended negotiations in mid-December 1972. The Communists, Kissinger told the president, were "just a bunch of shits. Tawdry, filthy shits." He recommended either intensifying the bombing in order to force Hanoi to talk seriously or waiting until January to resume negotiations on a tough note. Nixon needed no urging to step up the bombing. He gave orders for Linebacker Two—major attacks beginning on December 18 on more than thirty designated targets in or near Hanoi and Haiphong. "I don't want any more of this crap about the fact that we couldn't hit this target or that one," the president told the chairman of the Joint Chiefs. "This is your chance to use military power effectively to win the war."

During the next eleven days, excluding Christmas, American bombers flew some three thousand sorties and dropped some forty thousand tons of bombs on the afflicted area. That "Stone Age barbarism," as the *New York Times* called it, killed hundreds of civilians. It also cost the United States twenty-six aircraft and ninety-three airmen killed or captured. On December 26 the North Vietnamese indicated they would reopen negotiations as soon as the bombing ended. On December 30 Nixon stopped it. Talks began again on January 5, 1973. Three days later Kissinger and Le Duc Tho agreed to a cease-fire on terms essentially the same, except for some changed phraseology, as those they had arranged the previous October.

Nixon then told Thieu that he had decided to sign the accord. If Thieu refused to agree, "the result will be . . . an immediate termination of U.S. economic and military assistance." The president also promised to continue to recognize Thieu's government "as the only legal government of South Vietnam" and to "react strongly in the event the agreement is violated." Thieu had to go along. On January 18 Washington and Hanoi announced the imminent end of the fighting. Nixon was inaugurated for his second term on January 20. Lyndon Johnson died on January 22. The next day the United States, South Vietnam, and North Vietnam signed the cease-fire, to take effect January 27. The American war in Vietnam was over.

The December bombing had brought Hanoi back to the negotiations in time for their completion before the end of Nixon's first term, but the cease-fire could have been achieved in October if Nixon had forced Thieu's hand then instead of waiting until January. Nixon had intended the December bombing to help persuade Thieu that the United States would continue to protect the independence of South Vietnam. The conditions of the cease-fire and of American politics argued to the contrary. The North Vietnamese and the Vietcong remained in control of the areas they occupied in South Vietnam pending a political settlement by the impotent Council of National Reconciliation. As Hanoi knew, there was to be no political settlement. For a time the Thieu government, with its enormous stock of military equipment, would remain in office in Saigon. But in the countryside the "leopard spots" would gradually expand until the North Vietnamese and Vietcong had completed their conquest in South Vietnam, merely postponed by the cease-fire. That delay had become acceptable to Hanoi after the Chinese and Russians could no longer be relied upon for their support.

By January 1973 the American military presence in South Vietnam had become negligible. Nixon had withdrawn all but a token ground force. The bombers, whether from aircraft carriers or from bases else-where in Asia, remained the threat Nixon had shown them to be. But with the cease-fire that threat also receded. As the North Vietnamese realized, the American public had lost its stomach for renewed fighting in Vietnam, and the Congress, where the Democrats had the votes, was not about to condone it. Nixon and Kissinger persuaded themselves that the assurances to Thieu had a basis in reality. With his new man-date, they argued, the president could have retaliated against the North Vietnamese had domestic circumstances not changed before it became necessary. But Thieu himself had known better. He had kicked and screamed as he had in October because he recognized that once the Yanks departed, they would not likely return. The Congress in June 1973 denied the president funds to retaliate against the beastly Khmer Rouge then overrunning Cambodia as agents of North Vietnam. There would be no funds later for the South Vietnamese.

Public disenchantment with the Vietnam War took lamentable shape in the shabby treatment accorded returning veterans. The cease-fire brought home most prisoners of war, but even they found themselves somehow blamed for a war they had fought under orders. As brave as the veterans of other wars, they had endured the same dangers and fatigue, felt the same fright and nostalgia. Congress enacted no gen-erous GI Bill for the Vietnam veterans. There were few public parades. The American people displayed little sympathy for the victims of the war, Vietnamese or American. "The pain and the loneliness," one POW said, "were shallow compared to finding yourself stripped of all entitle-ment to reputation, love, or honor at home." A people who treated their returning soldiers as Americans treated the veterans of Vietnam would not tolerate a resumption of that war.

But Nixon and Kissinger could not admit that their promises to Thieu were empty. They could not admit that the cruel December bombing had brought no real improvement over the October terms. They could not admit that Linebacker Two—like Menu, like Fishhook—accomplished nothing worthwhile. As Averell Harriman said, he could have settled with Hanoi late in 1968, had Nixon let him, on very much the Nixon basis of 1973. Had Harriman concluded negotiations in 1968, Thieu would probably have had to surrender his office then. At enormous cost, Nixon bought him a few more years, a favor of no lasting importance.

Nixon could not admit that he had needlessly prolonged the war; to do so would be admitting that the United States had lost the war. At the end South Vietnamese independence was less secure than it had been at the beginning. And the face of communism in Hanoi was just as ugly in 1973 as it had been in 1954. Nixon, like Johnson, had considered the war a test of American credibility. They had dragged out the war in an effort to demonstrate that the United States stood by its client states. But the war had the opposite effect. The inability of the strongest power in the world to subdue the nationalistic spirit of a resolute people reduced American credibility. Along the way the war helped destroy the reputation of the United States as an exceptionally decent and humane nation. The armed services learned that they could not win a war without broad public support.

But Nixon could not admit even that. He believed, as did Kissinger, that power would always prevail in the affairs of men, that those who wielded power could behave with deceit and with criminality. He believed that power and those who used it were not accountable—not accountable to the people, not accountable to the law. Lyndon Johnson had tripped over that belief, and in January 1973 Richard Nixon was about to have to test its validity again.

3. A GROWING CANCER

On January 8, 1973, the trial of the indicted Watergate burglars opened, with United States District Court Chief Judge John J. Sirica presiding. To the pleasure of the White House, the Justice Department's chief prosecutor, Earl Silbert, indicated in his opening statement that he intended to treat the episode entirely as the machination of Gordon Liddy, who had been in charge of the break-in. Silbert admitted he could not account for most of the money CREEP had handed over to Liddy. But Woodward and Bernstein of the *Washington Post* had published evidence pointing to the involvement of senior CREEP officers and some of the White House staff. Those two report-

Judge John Sirica: He believed in the American dream.

ers and Seymour Hersh of the *New York Times* were ferreting out still more information. For his part, Judge Sirica had warned Silbert that the jury would have to know the purpose of the political espionage and who had started the burglars on their course. When one of the four Cubans—all of whom had pleaded guilty—told the judge that he had received the hundred-dollar bills in his possession in the mail in a blank envelope, Sirica replied: "Well . . . I don't believe you." Sirica remained incredulous after the jury on January 30 had returned a verdict of guilty against all the defendants. As the United States Code of law permitted him to, the judge put off sentencing until March 23 in order to give the defendants, all of whom had refused to testify, a chance to cooperate with the court in exchange for mitigation of their punishments.

Sirica could not know that one of the defendants, Howard Hunt, had already begun to weaken. Just before the trial Hunt's wife had been killed in an airplane accident. She had ten thousand dollars in cash in her purse—hush money she was delivering to the Watergate burglars. Desolate over her death and worried about his children, Hunt went to his friend Charles Colson, a senior White House staffer, to try to arrange a promise of clemency from the president. Unable to extract that promise, Colson began warning Nixon that he might have to get rid of Dean and Mitchell because of their vulnerability in the Watergate case. Haldeman and Ehrlichman were expressing similar views about Colson. All the president's men were uneasy, uneasy as was the president himself. "We began," Nixon later wrote, "to act on unspoken assumptions . . . and . . . fears."

Judge Sirica was concerned only for the truth in his determination to bring out the facts about Watergate. A lifelong Republican, Sirica had voted for Nixon. He did not suspect that the president was involved in the cover-up. But Sirica had the qualities of character and the commitment to the law that Nixon lacked. Sirica represented the Horatio Alger story come true. He had struggled for his success and in that process had come to value hard work, honesty, and common decency. He believed in the American dream and in American institutions, particularly the Constitution. Known as Maximum John because of his proclivity for handing down tough sentences, Sirica, though only one of hundreds of United States district judges, was a dangerous antagonist for any criminal conspirator, even the president.

Sirica was not alone. In January 1973 Senator Mike Mansfield, the Democratic majority leader, decided that Watergate and the other campaign dirty tricks exposed by the *Washington Post* called for investigation by a select Senate committee. He chose as chairman of that committee Senator Samuel Ervin, Jr., of North Carolina. Sam Ervin had considerable judicial experience, a thoroughly conservative record, and a strict view of constitutional interpretation. His well-deserved reputation for personal integrity was paired with the avuncular manner of a southern county judge. A unanimous Democratic caucus approved Mansfield's decision, and in February the Senate established the committee. It was to have power to subpoena relevant witnesses and records, and it received a generous budget for staff. Besides Ervin, three other Democrats and three Republicans were appointed to the committee by their parties' leadership. Without exception, they held the respect of their colleagues. Indeed, Republican Senators Howard Baker of Tennessee and Lowell Weicker of Connecticut proved no less zealous in investigating Watergate than did Ervin himself. They also benefited from the diligence of their chief counsel, Samuel Dash, and his staff. They all became celebrities of a sort when Ervin began televised hearings in May 1973.

In February the prospect of those hearings and the publicity they would generate worried the president's men more than did Judge Sirica's pending Watergate sentencings. Haldeman, Ehrlichman, and Dean agreed that "it was going to take an all-out effort by the White House to deal with the Senate inquiry." They decided, with the president's concurrence, that the White House should "take a public posture of full cooperation, but privately . . . make it as difficult as possible to get information and witnesses." Yet they were carelessly overconfident about another potentially damaging hearing that they could not prevent when the president persisted in his nomination of L. Patrick Gray to head the FBI. Before confirming Gray, the Senate Judiciary Committee was to interrogate him, beginning in March, and Gray had participated in the Watergate cover-up.

Nixon thought he could use assertions of executive privilege to protect Gray and stymie Ervin. On March 12, 1973, he announced his right to claim executive privilege to prevent the testimony of all current and former White House aides. That was a dubious assertion. And Gray, to Nixon's disgust, allowed the hearings "to become a disaster." He even implicated John Dean in Watergate-related activities. Worse, Gray had interviewed Kalmbach about dirty tricks, and Kalmbach had admitted his part in hiring Segretti. Gray gave a memorandum about that interview to the Senate committee, which made it public. Thoughtlessly, as Woodward and Bernstein said, Gray had "undermined the basic claim of White House innocence" and "helped establish the credibility of the *Washington Post.*" Nevertheless, on March 16 Nixon again insisted to the press that no one in the White House had been involved in Watergate. The next day he suggested privately that Dean prepare a statement saying that his investigation had turned up no evidence against any of the White House men against whom accusations had been made. Dean was simply to omit his personal knowledge, and Mitchell's, about the bugging.

But Dean did not write that statement, and on March 18, Howard Hunt, faced with the prospect of a harsh sentence unless he opened up to Judge Sirica, demanded $130,000 for his continued silence. Otherwise, Hunt warned Dean, he would talk about the "seamy things" he had done. He had done a lot: In disguise he had visited Dita Beard of ITT; he had forged cables contrived to implicate John F. Kennedy in the assassination of Diem; he knew about the persecution of Ellsberg and CREEP's role in Watergate. On March 20 Dean reported Hunt's threat to Ehrlichman. On March 21 Dean met with Nixon. "We have a cancer . . . close to the Presidency, that's growing," Dean said. ". . . We're being checkmated . . . people are going to start perjuring themselves very quickly that have not had to perjure themselves to protect other people." Dean listed the president's men who had known about Watergate and the cover-up: Mitchell, Haldeman, Ehrlichman, Colson, Liddy, Kalmbach, Magruder. Nixon asked about payments to the Cuban defendants for attorneys' fees and for their silence and guilty pleas. "Bob is involved in that; John is involved," Dean replied, referring to Haldeman and Ehrlichman. "I'm involved in that; Mitchell is involved. . . . And that's an obstruction of justice."

Hunt and McCord, the non-Cuban Watergate burglars, had been pressing for commutations of their pending sentences. Now Hunt had begun to blackmail the White House, and Dean feared the blackmailing would spread and require a million dollars within a couple of years. "Don't you agree that you'd better get the Hunt thing?" Nixon said. "I mean, that's worth it, at the moment. . . . You've got no choice with Hunt. . . . We've got to figure out where to turn it off at the lowest cost we can, but at whatever cost it takes." With that statement, as the president knew, the "question of who authorized the break in had been overtaken by . . . the far more serious problem of the cover-up." And he had now embraced more closely the conspiracy to obstruct justice.

Hunt received his money, pleaded guilty, and kept silent, but James McCord had already decided to talk. On March 20 he appeared unexpectedly in Judge Sirica's office with a letter containing much of what the judge had suspected. McCord wrote that there had been "political pressure applied" to the Watergate defendants to plead guilty and remain silent, that "perjury occurred during the trial," and that "others involved in . . . Watergate were not identified." He asked to talk to Judge Sirica because he could not "feel confident in talking with an FBI agent . . . or . . . other government representatives."

In court on March 27 for the provisional sentencing of the other Watergate defendants—Liddy received six to twenty years in jail; Hunt got thirty-five—the judge read aloud McCord's letter and postponed his sentencing. The chief counsel of the Ervin committee met with McCord later that day. Within the week members of that committee had started to leak to the press about what they had learned. Meanwhile, the prosecutor reconvened the grand jury for "further testimony about who had authorized the break-in." Early in April, Jeb Magruder and John Dean, on the advice of their lawyers, began meeting with the prosecutor to trade their information about Watergate for favorable treatment. The Watergate affair, as one columnist wrote, had become "a political bomb that could blow the Nixon Administration apart."

At the White House, Nixon, Haldeman, and Ehrlichman spent hours daily trying to devise an effective plan for damage control. The president seemed indecisive, in Ehrlichman's phrase, "catatonic," now eager to try one "scenario"—in the special vocabulary the conspirators used—now abandoning it to seize on another, equally fictitious. He could not afford to "let it all hang out"—to tell the whole truth—for that would reveal his role. But he realized he could not successfully "stonewall," for the prosecution and the Ervin committee were learning more every day. So was the grand jury. Indeed, Assistant Attorney General Henry

John Ehrlichman and H. R. Haldeman: They acted with Nixon's approval.

Petersen, the chief government prosecutor, indiscreetly reported to the president regularly about the confidential testimony the grand jury heard. In doing so, Petersen was violating the Federal Code, as he should have known. In April Nixon decided to adopt what Haldeman called a "modified hang-out." He would try to satisfy the prosecutor and the public by releasing as much information as he dared without revealing the extent of White House participation in the cover-up.

The plan also called for offering a scapegoat, someone other than the president's intimates on whom the blame could fall. On April 5, Nixon withdrew the nomination of L. Patrick Gray. But he needed a more important victim, and no one wanted to "fall on the sword." Nixon thought Mitchell might sacrifice himself, but Mitchell wanted to set up Haldeman. Then the president considered having Dean resign, but Dean would go only if he took Haldeman and Ehrlichman with him. Meanwhile, Dean was singing to the prosecutors. Attorney General Richard Kleindienst, tears in his eyes, warned Nixon that Dean had described the roles of Haldeman and Ehrlichman. Henry Petersen told the president that his two top aides should resign.

By late April, as Nixon realized, his standing in the polls was plummeting, the economy was in serious trouble, and the White House staff was distracted. Haldeman and Ehrlichman, he reluctantly decided, had to go. But they had talked with their lawyers, and now they, too, resisted. On April 24, 1973, Nixon confronted them. Ehrlichman was "uneasy and restless." He said: "Now let me . . . just spin something out for you, probably a far out point." If Dean told all, it was possible the president "might be faced with a resolution of impeachment." Nixon had begun to grasp that possibility himself. On April 28, as he recalled, Ehrlichman spelled it out over the telephone: "He said that all the illegal acts ultimately derived from me, whether directly or indirectly. . . . He also implied . . . that I should resign." The next day Nixon told Ehrlichman and Haldeman to resign. It was, he said, "the hardest decision I had ever made." Ehrlichman, bitter, replied: "I have no choice but to accept it. . . . But I still feel I have done nothing that was without your implied or direct approval." That afternoon Kleindienst also resigned, unable to face the unavoidable task of prosecuting John Mitchell, his friend and former boss.

The cancer in the presidency was spreading, but Nixon continued his evasive tactics. On television to the nation on April 30 he announced that there had been major developments in the Watergate case. He also announced the resignations of Haldeman and Ehrlichman—"two of the finest public servants it has been my privilege to know"—and of Dean and Kleindienst, as if he'd known nothing about the errands those four had done for him. Nixon went on to say that he was appointing Elliot Richardson attorney general and Leonard Garment counsel to the president to study Watergate and report to him.

Within the next two weeks Nixon had also appointed General Alexander Haig, who had been Kissinger's chief deputy, to replace Haldeman as chief of the White House staff. To his new appointees and to others he soon added, the president denied that he had had any role in Watergate, and they all, at least at first, believed him. They all tried to help him execute the duties of his office. Haig was forceful, partisan, ambitious, and shrewd. But he and his assistants, new to their responsibilities, had too much to learn to carry on the vendetta against the bureaucracy that had so appealed to Haldeman. Further, with the Ervin committee hearings about to begin on television, and with leaks and counterleaks flooding Washington, Watergate would not go away. The new men were soon as distracted by further developments in the case as Haldeman and Ehrlichman had earlier been. And Nixon, surrounded now by relative strangers to whom he had lied, missed the bond of complicity and the depth of loyalty of his two closest associates.

The sacrifice of Haldeman and Ehrlichman was futile. On May 17

Archibald Cox and Elliot Richardson: Cox recruited a remarkable staff.

the Ervin committee hearings opened. Soon McCord was telling the senators and a national television audience that Mitchell and Dean had known about Watergate. Magruder and Mitchell had authorized the break-in. Dean gave the key to his safe-deposit box to Judge Sirica, who turned over the classified documents he found to the federal prosecutor. Dean had also begun to leak his forthcoming testimony in order to sweeten the plea bargaining his lawyers were undertaking. The story of the Nixon administration's dirty tricks was becoming a matter of public knowledge.

The Senate Judiciary Committee had no confidence that any federal official was sufficiently disinterested to investigate Watergate. Consequently, the committee made it a condition of its confirmation of Elliot Richardson as attorney general that he appoint a special prosecutor. Richardson tried two lawyers, who declined. He turned then to his former law professor Archibald Cox, who agreed to serve only after Richardson had accepted his prescriptions for protecting his independence in investigating crimes related to Watergate and the 1972 presidential election generally. Richardson also promised the Judiciary Committee that he would not remove or interfere with Cox. The solicitor general of the United States during the Kennedy and part of the

Johnson administrations, Cox was a distinguished law professor at Harvard and an expert on the Constitution. He had been a champion of civil rights and civil liberties—a man notable for his high intelligence, exceptional judgment, and incomparable Yankee integrity. The Judiciary Committee, gratified, immediately approved Richardson's appointment and applauded his choice of Cox, who set about recruiting a remarkable staff.

Nixon, who feared Cox, made still another effort to camouflage his part in Watergate. Again he denied any role in the case and "any awareness of or participation in the cover-up." But now he admitted that he had approved the Huston plan and various wiretaps on Ellsberg and others. The admissions shocked the American public; the denial failed to persuade almost half of them. Early in June new leaks about Dean's pending testimony suggested Nixon had discussed paying the Watergate defendants for their cooperation. In the contest for credibility, Dean was at least matching the president. For sufficient reason, Nixon, as he recalled, "felt discouraged, drained, and pressured."

4. CAMOUFLAGE

Nevertheless, just as his foreign policy had enhanced his campaign for reelection in 1972, so the president hoped that his second summit meeting with Leonid Brezhnev in mid-June, 1973, would restore his popular standing. He needed a success, and détente needed strengthening. The Democrats were blaming Russian purchases of American grain, financed by credits the administration had granted, for the rising price of bread and other foods. Senators in both parties objected to a Soviet exit tax on emigrants. That tax was said to reimburse the government for the higher education it had provided to emigrants, but in effect it blocked the emigration of thousands of Jews and dozens of dissident intellectuals. Democratic Senator Henry Jackson of Washington led the effort, in which seventy-two other senators joined, to make repeal of the exit tax a condition for allowing the Soviet Union most favored nation status. A fervid hawk, Jackson opposed détente. He was also cultivating the Jewish vote in his unceasing quest for the presidency. As Kissinger put it, "conservatives who hated Communists and liberals who hated Nixon" were equally uneasy about the president's approach to Brezhnev.

The summit sessions in Washington and San Clemente would have proved difficult even if Nixon had had no "domestic differences"—his

'We're Declarin' A Short Intermission For That Nixon-Brezhnev Act!'

euphemism for Brezhnev in alluding to Watergate. Soviet and American rivalry was obvious in the Middle East, Soviet anxieties were rising over American support for China, Soviet hopes for mutual force reductions in Europe were receiving scant encouragement in Washington, and SALT negotiations were faltering. In Moscow in May, Kissinger had found the Russians unyielding toward a new American proposal for an interim freeze on the testing and land-based deployment of MIRVs. Since the United States had a lead of at least three years in both testing and deployment, the proposal, as Kissinger later admitted, "neatly shut the Soviets out . . . without significantly curtailing any program of our own." At the Washington summit the Russians predictably rejected it. The United States then turned down a Soviet counterproposal to ban the testing and deployment of all new strategic systems. Stymied, the two leaders promised only to make "serious efforts" to work out a permanent agreement on strategic arms limitations by the end of 1974.

Though the summit produced minor arrangements for expanding scientific and cultural exchanges, the major issues remained unsettled. There was no meeting of the minds about China. On the Middle East, Brezhnev urged a joint Soviet-American guarantee of the independence of Israel in return for Israeli surrender of the gains of the 1967 war. Those terms favored the Soviet Union's Arab allies, who, as Brezhnev warned, might otherwise resume their attacks on Israel. But the United States, though for many years the main protector of Israel, could not make policy for the Israelis, and Nixon declined the Soviet offer. He also misinterpreted Brezhnev's warning as a threat. Brezhnev was, in fact, trying to prevent a Middle Eastern war, while Nixon, for his part, intended to start courting the Arabs and underestimated the explosiveness of the situation.

Nixon and Brezhnev did sign a showy but cosmetic pact that expressed the spirit of détente. It stated that the objective of the policies of both men was "to remove the danger of nuclear war and the use of nuclear weapons." But they established no mechanism to advance that purpose. The agreement itself stopped short of a mutual pledge against a first use of nuclear weapons because the United States would not rule out that possibility in the event of a Soviet attack with conventional weapons against a NATO country. Brezhnev nevertheless attached considerable significance to the understanding. In 1973 Kissinger did, too, though he dismissed it later as "a bland set of principles."

Its significance lay in papering over the failure of the summit to produce any agreement of substance. Especially in the face of Kissinger's earlier announcement of the "Year of Europe," the NATO nations resented the recurrence of superpower negotiations that excluded them. And the fruitlessness of the negotiations left Nixon without the camouflage he needed to hide from continuing revelations about Watergate.

Soon after Brezhnev went home, John Dean on June 25, 1973, read the Ervin committee a 245-page statement about the break-in and cover-up that described in detail the roles of Haldeman, Ehrlichman, and Nixon. Even Judge Sirica was skeptical at that time about Dean's allegations. Operating independently of the judge, Ervin on occasion surprised him. So it was in mid-July, when, as Sirica recalled, "suddenly ... there appeared a way to test Dean's veracity. . . . Alexander Butterworth . . . a former deputy assistant to the president . . . revealed to the Senate committee that the president had an extensive tape-recording system operating in his offices." That system, installed in 1971, would also produce a test of Nixon's veracity.

5. THE TAPES

Nixon was not the first president to use a tape recorder. Franklin Roosevelt had recorded a few conversations. Kennedy had made tapes or dictabelts of more than one hundred conferences or telephone calls. Johnson had made many more, though still selectively. Nixon's taping system, in place at both the White House and the Executive Office Building, was sound-activated, so it recorded everything that was said in both the president's offices, though with such poor fidelity that it was sometimes difficult to identify the person speaking or his exact words. Nixon had probably begun taping for several reasons. He had a sense of history and understood the value the tapes would have for his presidential records. He intended to write his own account of his administration, for which the tapes would provide an extraordinary source. While he remained in office, the recordings would permit him to check his memory or the accuracy of anyone of whom he became suspicious. Very few of his staff knew about the taping system. Nixon became so accustomed to it that he talked as freely as if it had not been there. But he never expected its existence to be revealed. Once it had been, he contemplated destroying the tapes, but to have done so would have created an indelible impression of guilt in the public mind and would have constituted a flagrant obstruction of justice. Accordingly Nixon decided to cover the tapes with a broad claim of executive privilege in order to keep them from the courts and from the Congress.

On July 23, 1973, in a letter to Senator Ervin, Nixon invoked executive privilege to support his refusal to supply the tapes the Senate committee had requested. The committee at once voted to subpoena five of the taped conversations, along with related documents, to which John Dean had referred in his testimony. For his part, Archibald Cox asked the president for nine tapes, was refused, put the matter to the grand jury, and received its approval to petition Judge Sirica for a subpoena to have the president show why he should not produce the tapes. The judge, agreeing, served a subpoena duces tecum—an order to give the court the material in question—on the president. It was the first such subpoena since Chief Justice John Marshall had served one on Thomas Jefferson in 1807 to obtain documents relevant to the trial for treason of Aaron Burr. As it had worked out in 1807, Jefferson delivered the controversial letters on his own, without reference to the sub-poena and without forcing the court to hold him in contempt. Sirica had no commanding precedent for his action.

But now the burden lay on Nixon to show "why he should be an exception," as Sirica put it, "to the usual rule of law" that entitled a grand jury to the best evidence it could get. Sirica's subpoena, as Cox and Sirica knew, forced "a real test of the limits" of executive privilege. On August 7, 1973, in Sirica's court, Cox argued the case against the president's specially selected attorney, Charles Alan Wright, a law pro-fessor at the University of Texas and an authority on constitutional interpretation. Wright, speaking first, said no court had ever held a president "in contempt for refusing to produce information, either to the courts or to Congress." The courts, he contended, had no power to rule on the president's use of executive privilege, for the Constitution made the judiciary and the executive branches equal. It did not make the judiciary superior. Consequently, to compel the president to turn over the tapes would represent "a serious threat to the nature of the presidency as it was created by the Constitution." To do so would also deprive future presidents of candid advice. Further, Wright held, it was impossible to separate those parts of the tapes dealing with "sensitive issues of national security" from the parts relating to Watergate. So even if the tapes revealed criminal activity, the courts had no authority to demand that the president deliver them. For Wright, the president was sovereign.

Cox took a contrary view. "There is no exception for the President," he said, "from the guiding principle that the public, in pursuit of jus-tice, has a right to every man's evidence. Even the highest executive officials are subject to the rule of law, which it is . . . the province and duty of the courts to declare." An interest in confidentiality did not override the need to investigate criminal activity. Further, Cox held, in this case the president had already compromised secrecy by permitting Haldeman to listen to the tapes before testifying to the Ervin commit-tee that Dean had erred in his account. "Not even a President," Cox said, "can be allowed to select some accounts of a conversation for public disclosure and then to frustrate further grand jury inquiries." Since 1789 the courts had often issued orders requiring executive offi-cials to comply with the Constitution and laws as judicially interpreted. The president was not immune to the judicial process, and a "sub-poena is a judicial command. . . . Compliance is a legal duty." For Cox, the law was sovereign.

Sirica agreed. On August 29, 1973, he ordered Nixon to produce the tapes "for my private inspection." The president, he reasoned, was "entitled to some protection of his privacy and the nation was entitled to some protection from unnecessary publication of national secrets. But . . . no privilege existed for matters of a criminal nature." Nixon, refusing to comply with the order, appealed in September to the United States Court of Appeals for the District of Columbia. So did Cox, who wanted the tapes delivered directly to him rather than to Judge Sirica.

The court of appeals attempted to settle the issue without directly confronting the president. On September 13, in a unanimous memorandum, it urged the president and the special prosecutor to reach a compromise on the tapes. But three days of meetings between Cox and Nixon's lawyers failed to produce an agreement. On October 12, 1973, the court of appeals upheld Sirica's ruling. Nixon had already said that only a "definitive" decision by the Supreme Court would persuade him to give up the tapes. But by October 12 the tapes were just one of his urgent problems.

The administration was in serious trouble. The Ervin committee hearings had informed millions of Americans about the dirty tricks. A majority considered the president wrong in refusing to supply the tapes to the committee. Nixon had dominated television during 1972 with his trips abroad and his well-financed campaign. Now the medium was exposing him as it had exposed Bull Connor and his police dogs in Birmingham, Thieu and his villains in Saigon. It made them instant celebrities, instantly despised. In a reverse twist the hearings cast Nixon, off camera, in the role of the heavy. The resulting demoralization penetrated the administration. Secretary of Agriculture Earl Butz publicly blamed the White House freeze on prices in 1972 for the inflation Americans were suffering a year later. Secretary of Labor Peter Brennan told the press that Nixon had erred in ordering secret taps on telephones. Mel Laird, back in government as a member of the president's staff but unable to get Nixon to discuss Watergate with him, predicted to the press that Nixon would dislike him increasingly as time went on. The president considered talk of that kind a breach of loyalty. But he had been demoralized, too, wasting time in self-pitying monologues to Al Haig, fleeing Washington for Camp David or Key Biscayne or San Clemente.

Then, in September, a crisis that had been pending for several months galvanized the president's anxieties. He had learned that Vice President Agnew, under investigation by a grand jury, had accepted payoffs from contractors he had favored while serving first as executive for Baltimore County and then as governor of Maryland. Agnew had denied those charges. He counted on his right-wing constituency to protect him. For five years he had titillated the far right with attacks on the media and the eastern establishment that Nixon's speech writers prepared for him. Addicted to alliteration, the vice president took pride in his reputation as the pugnacious purveyor of pungent prose. His lawyers moved to stop the grand jury proceedings against him on the ground that a vice president could not be indicted unless he was first impeached and removed from office. Blaming the Justice Department for persecuting him, Agnew had said on September 30: "I'm a big trophy. I will not resign. . . . I intend to stay and fight."

Nixon feared that the impeachment of Agnew, by alienating the Republican right, would weaken his own position. But Agnew had been bluffing. On October 16 he resigned in exchange for the agreement of the Justice Department to let him plead nolo contendere to only one charge of income tax evasion. As part of that bargain, he received a sentence of just three years of supervised probation and a fine of ten thousand dollars. He had admitted his guilt and copped a plea, just like the cheap crook he was. Nixon had then to select a new vice president for confirmation by Congress. The choice of John Connally or Nelson Rockefeller, the men he considered best qualified, would have disturbed conservative Republicans. To satisfy them and to assure a friendly Democratic reception for his nominee, Nixon picked Gerald Ford, the minority leader in the House of Representatives. Ford was a popular, affable moderate-to-conservative Republican with long years of service to his party on the Hill. Honest and competent, Ford was a graduate of the University of Michigan, where he had been a football star, and of the Yale Law School. Despite that background, he was a man lacking any executive experience and totally uninformed about foreign affairs.

Nixon announced his choice of Ford on October 12, 1973, the day the court of appeals rendered its decision upholding Judge Sirica's ruling. Only six days earlier Syria and Egypt had attacked Israel. On October 10 the Soviet Union had started to airlift supplies to the aggressors. That airlift, the State Department then announced, "put a new face" on the conflict. On October 12, a day crowded with important news, Nixon endorsed Kissinger's proposal to begin an American airlift to Israel, as that country had requested. Now war in the Middle East involved both superpowers. But preoccupied as he was with the problem of the tapes, Nixon left the war primarily to Kissinger.

6. SATURDAY NIGHT MASSACRE

As ever, Nixon tried to use the tension in American foreign policy to influence his domestic antagonists, but primarily he relied on a new strategy to keep the contents of the tapes from Archibald Cox. He detested Cox and his eastern patrician background, his Kennedy connections, his prosecutorial doggedness. On October 15 Haig informed Attorney General Richardson that the president had decided to give Judge Sirica not the tapes but summaries of them authenticated by Democratic Senator John Stennis of Mississippi, a senatorial baron and conservative supporter of Nixon. Then, Haig said, the president would fire Cox. In the latter event, Richardson replied, he himself would have to resign, for he had appointed Cox and guaranteed his independence as a condition of his own confirmation by the Senate. But Richardson agreed to put the Stennis plan to Cox, as he did two days later. On October 18 Cox rejected the proposal. The only satisfactory verifiers of the tapes, he said, would have to be "special masters" of the court, and if later a case came to trial, the tapes themselves would have to be produced. Charles Wright then tried, but failed, to persuade Cox to drop the subpoena. "This would mean," Cox told him, "that my ability to secure evidence bearing upon criminal wrong-doing by high White House officials would be left to the discretion of the White House counsel."

While Cox was preparing his reply, Nixon revised his strategy so as to outflank him. He proposed to Senators Ervin and Baker that he give the Senate committee summaries of the tapes authenticated by Stennis. That prospect appealed to the institutional pride of the senators, whose request for a subpoena Sirica had declined. Uninformed about White House pressure on Cox, they agreed to the plan.

On the evening of October 19 Nixon issued a statement about his intentions. The aftermath of Watergate, he said, had placed "a strain . . . on the American people." What mattered "in this critical hour" in the Middle East was the government's "ability to act—and to act in a way that enables us to control events." After describing his plan to give summaries of the tapes to the Ervin committee, Nixon said he considered it necessary to order Cox "to make no further attempts by judicial process to obtain tapes . . . or memoranda of Presidential conversations." Cox announced at once that he would not obey because the president was "refusing to comply with the Court decrees."

October 20 was a beautiful Indian summer day in Washington. Cox broke into it with a televised press conference. He was, he told a national audience, "not out to get the President of the United States." But he would continue to "go about my duties on the terms on which I assumed them." He questioned whether anyone but the attorney general, who had appointed him, could give him instructions. Cox, Nixon told his counselors, had defied him and undercut his stature with the Russians. He had to be fired. In so informing Richardson, Nixon urged him not to resign just when Moscow needed to be shown that the president controlled the government. But Richardson, holding a different "perception of national interest," did resign. Al Haig then told William Ruckelshaus, next in command at the Justice Department, to fire Cox. "Your Commander-in-Chief," Haig said, with characteristic pomposity, "has given you an order." Ruckelshaus refused to follow it. Haig turned next to Solicitor General Robert Bork. As Bork later said, someone had to carry out the president's order, and the Justice Department could not afford to lose its entire staff. Richardson agreed. So Bork discharged Cox. Nixon made Bork acting attorney general. He also closed the Office of the Special Prosecutor and directed the FBI to take charge of it.

That evening the White House announcement of those developments set off what Haig described as a national "firestorm." A deluge of telegrams reached Congress, most of them condemning Nixon, almost all calling for his impeachment. Senator Edward Kennedy called the firing of Cox "a reckless act of desperation." Congress and the courts, he said, had to protect the rule of law. His Republican colleague from Massachusetts, Senator Edward Brooke, agreed that the House should think about impeachment. Drivers passing the White House honked the horns of their cars for impeachment. Within a few days the deans of seventeen law schools—among them Columbia, Harvard, Stanford, and Yale—petitioned Congress to "consider the necessity of impeachment." The *New York Times* called on Nixon to resign; the *Washington Post* favored impeachment; *Time* magazine described the White House as "pervaded by an atmosphere of immorality." Eighty-four members of the House of Representatives introduced resolutions for impeachment; ninety-eight, for legislation to establish a new office of special prosecutor.

The fire storm singed the White House. To the surprise of Judge Sirica, Nixon agreed to comply with the subpoena "in all respects." In so telling the court, Charles Wright added that it would require some time to put the materials together. The president's lawyers, Wright said, had hoped the Stennis plan would "end a constitutional crisis," but "the events of the weekend . . . have made it very apparent . . . that this did not adequately satisfy the spirit of the court of appeals ruling. . . . The president does not defy the law, and . . . he will comply in full."

Sirica was relieved, but a week later he learned from Fred Buzhardt, another White House lawyer, that two of the requested tapes did not exist. Soon thereafter Buzhardt reported that a subpoenaed dictabelt was missing and that still another tape contained an inexplicable eighteen-minute gap. Those disclosures provoked renewed calls for Nixon's resignation. What remained of his credibility was fast fading, and the issue of the tapes would not go away. It became a chief concern of Leon Jaworski, the sober, orderly, prestigious Texas attorney whom Nixon appointed to succeed Cox. Nixon had reopened the Office of the Special Prosecutor in an effort to quiet the furor over the Saturday night massacre.

7. THE YOM KIPPUR WAR

In interpreting the war in the Middle East as a crisis in Soviet-American relations, Nixon attempted to persuade the public of the indispensability of a powerful presidency and of his indispensability in that office. Kissinger recognized that at the least the war exposed Soviet-American rivalry in the region. "Detente," as he wrote, "was . . . a relationship between adversaries; it did not pretend friendship." Both the United States and the Soviet Union tried to use the war to enlarge their influence, while each protested its devotion to cooperation with the other. Actually in the Middle East, as in Southeast Asia, the superpowers controlled their clients less than those clients manipulated them.

The war began with Arab attacks that surprised both Israel and the United States. They occurred on Yom Kippur, the Day of Atonement, for Jews the holiest day of the year. Not yet fully mobilized, the Israelis fell back as the Egyptians crossed the Suez Canal into the Sinai Peninsula while the Syrians moved into the Golan Heights. Both invaded areas had fallen to the Israelis during the 1967 war, and Israel had annexed them in spite of a UN resolution urging restoration of the earlier boundaries. The Soviet Union, informed by the Syrians of the impending attack, had evacuated most of its civilian nationals the day before Yom Kippur, an action that made the invasion less than a total surprise. Indeed, the Russians had been warning Washington for months about the danger of Arab revenge. As Kissinger saw it, while Moscow did not encourage the war, it made no effort to prevent it. Neither did the United States.

On October 8, 1973, Brezhnev informed Washington that he was in touch with the Arab states about a cease-fire, as Kissinger had asked him to be. Both the Soviet Union and the United States had moved naval units to the eastern Mediterranean; both favored a UN resolution calling for a cease-fire. But both were also stalling. The Soviet Union knew the Syrians and Egyptians would resist a cease-fire as long as their troops were advancing. The United States knew Israel would resist until it had regained its losses. In order to retain its influence in the area, the Soviet Union airlifted supplies to the Arabs. For the same reason, the United States supplied the Israelis, especially with aircraft and ammunition, though only after some bureaucratic delay in the Department of Defense.

Kissinger was committed, as was Nixon, to preserving Israeli independence, but both were eager also to cultivate Egypt. Israel was adept at squeezing the United States, at that time its exclusive military supplier. Israeli intransigence, Kissinger realized, preserved Israel's "dignity in a one-sided relationship." But Nixon and Kissinger had passed beyond patience with the repeated demands of Golda Meir, the Israeli premier, and with her constant lobbying in Congress, with the media, and with the American Jewish community. She remained wholly in character in her approach to the war. Anwar el-Sadat, the Egyptian president, was turning away from the Soviet Union toward the United States. Distrustful of communism, he wanted to sever Egypt's Soviet connection. He knew his country needed peace and economic development to break out of its dreadful poverty. He was attempting, therefore, to establish a relationship in which the United States, as Kissinger put it, "would be not only formally but also psychologically the mediator," treating "Egypt's claims on a par with Israel's." The goal coincided with Kissinger's. But first Sadat sought to convince Israel to treat Egypt with respect. Thus the invasion, but also his intention not to widen the war.

Once the American airlift had begun to operate, the Israelis, in a successful counterattack, on October 15 won a major tank battle against the Egyptians and raced toward the Suez Canal. Sadat then let Kissinger know that he would not object to a cease-fire. Hedging his bets, Sadat also organized an oil embargo by the Arab states. At that juncture Soviet President Kosygin left for Cairo to see Sadat, and Nixon, though focusing on Watergate, on October 17 met with the Arab leaders in Washington. He was, he told Kissinger, "keenly aware of the stakes"—oil and the American strategic position. But primarily Nixon considered the crisis a Soviet-American confrontation, "bigger than the Middle East," which the United States could not afford to lose.

Nixon misinterpreted the situation. Kosygin went to Cairo to persuade Sadat of the necessity of a cease-fire. Sadat agreed on October 18. Brezhnev immediately sent a message to Washington urging a cease-fire. But Kissinger let the Israelis go on with their advance in the Sinai, partly because the United States lacked the influence to stop it, partly because it enhanced his negotiations with the Soviet Union, which continued in Moscow. On October 22 the UN Security Council adopted a cease-fire resolution, jointly sponsored by the United States and the Soviet Union. From the first that outcome had been as much a Soviet as an American objective.

When Israel nevertheless continued to advance, Sadat asked both the United States and the Soviet Union to supply troops to enforce the truce. Brezhnev warned Israel of the "gravest consequences" if the attacks did not stop. But Kissinger was determined to keep Soviet troops out of Egypt. He therefore opposed Brezhnev's proposal of October 24 for a joint operation, and he viewed as a threat Brezhnev's accompanying statement that the Soviet Union might otherwise have to act alone.

At the most Brezhnev was trying to preserve Soviet prestige in the Middle East. To be sure, he had mobilized Soviet airborne forces and moved Soviet ships into Cypriot waters, but he had taken those actions two weeks earlier. Nevertheless, Kissinger called a meeting of the senior members of the National Security Council on the evening of October 24. That group then issued a general military alert that included the Strategic Air Command and American strategic nuclear forces, as well as other American units around the world. Those at the meeting also drafted a letter for Nixon to send Brezhnev. Unilateral Soviet action, the letter said, "would produce incalculable consequences." Beyond that needless nuclear threat, the letter suggested sending to the Middle East a UN supervisory force including Soviet and American observers.

Newspaper reports of the nuclear alert made that maneuver a challenge to Soviet status, but Brezhnev, ignoring it, agreed to Nixon's proposal, as did Sadat. The Security Council in another resolution demanded that the belligerents return to the line of battle of October 22. On October 26 the United States canceled the nuclear alert, and the Soviet Union relaxed its earlier mobilization. But the war continued in the form of intermittent skirmishes, and the Israelis did not fall back to the October 22 line. Brezhnev naturally complained to Kissinger, who finally persuaded the Israelis to deal directly with the Egyptians. Kissinger's real achievement emerged in his continuing role as the outside negotiator working for a more stable relationship between Israel and the Arab states.

At a press conference on October 26 Nixon said he had participated in the meeting of October 24 that issued the global nuclear alert and drafted the letter to Brezhnev. The president also described the ensuing crisis as the worst since the confrontation over the Cuban missiles in 1962. That was nonsense. Brezhnev had risen above the nuclear alert, which nevertheless served its probable purpose, the increase of American influence in the Middle East. But a nuclear alert constituted a very risky device to achieve that limited end. If Nixon had ordered it, he displayed an inadequate sense of American responsibility for a possible nuclear disaster. And his exaggeration of Brezhnev's challenge suggested that his irresponsibility derived from panic about his falling reputation after the Saturday night Massacre. But Nixon may have been asleep in the White House during the meeting of October 24. In that event his public statement two days later was just another convenient lie in the chain of lies that followed Watergate. And in that event, in the president's absence, Kissinger, Haig, and the others at the meeting vastly exceeded their proper authority and did so with scant regard for the possible consequences of their action. Either way the nuclear alert suggested that Nixon, obsessed as he was by Watergate, was no longer fit to hold the presidency.

American policy during the Yom Kippur War also had other unfortunate consequences. It strained relations with the NATO countries. Even before the war, the Europeans had been persistently more critical of Israel than had the United States. In 1973 they refused to assist the American airlift of supplies to Israel, and they resented the American interpretation of the war as an East-West confrontation. The British, with their traditional concern for Arab friendship and their admiration of Arab culture, had predicted that American disdain for the Arabs was bound to breed reprisals. Worse, American support for Israel during the Yom Kippur War precipitated the decision of October 20, 1973, by the Organization of Petroleum Exporting Countries (OPEC) to place an embargo on oil shipments. That embargo hurt Western Europe and Japan, both without domestic oil resources, more than it did the United States. European irritation with Israel and solicitude for Arab feelings preceded the embargo as well as followed it, and European objections to Kissinger's unilateral diplomacy in the Middle East contributed to the difficulties of organizing cooperation among oil-consuming states to offset the strength of OPEC.

Reduction of Arab oil production, as well as the OPEC embargo, did have a deleterious impact on the American economy. With only 6 percent of the world's population, the United States had been using a third of the world's oil, of which it imported 60 percent of its supply, largely from the Middle East. The shortages resulting from the embargo sent the price of gasoline spiraling. Accustomed to inexpensive gasoline for the automobiles so central to their life-styles, Americans complained about the need to wait their turn at gasoline stations that often ran out of fuel before they could finish serving the long queues of impatient patrons.

The rising price of oil, therefore of energy, lifted the already troublesome rate of inflation. Apart from the Yom Kippur War, the administration's devaluation of the dollar, the currency ordinarily paid for oil, had made it necessary for the oil-producing states to raise their prices so as to sustain the value of their product. Neither Saudi Arabia, the world's major oil producer, nor Iran was then hostile to the United States, though neither wanted to receive the regional opprobrium that would have been invited by a failure to join the embargo. After the war Saudi Arabia became a leading spokesman for Arab political aims but, like Iran, eager also for increased revenues from oil. Those countries joined in the OPEC decision of late December 1973 to raise the price of oil again, now up to $11.65 a barrel, or 387 percent of the price just before the Yom Kippur War. By that action OPEC extracted extortionate profits, just as had modern Western industrial cartels on many previous occasions. But OPEC had the distinction of being the first effective cartel of developing states. Its strength served as another reminder, shocking to most Americans, of the limits of their national power.

OPEC had already demonstrated its political muscle in November by guaranteeing to the Western European nations and to Japan oil supplies in amounts equivalent to prewar levels as a reward for their disassociation from American policy in the Middle East. By that time Nixon was eager to persuade OPEC to lift the embargo entirely, an objective sure to increase his popularity, then still diminishing. He also proclaimed Project Independence, which looked forward to the eventual development of American sources for energy other than oil. He called, too, for a program of energy conservation. That proposal loitered in Congress partly because of Nixon's loss of influence there, partly because his recommendations did not affect the largest American oil companies, which were exploiting the energy shortage to their own advantage. In contrast, American diplomacy made slow gains in the Middle East. Nixon assured Sadat, whom Kissinger was courting,

THE ULTIMATE WEAPON

that the United States stood behind the terms of the UN cease-fire resolutions. Kissinger undertook his shuttle diplomacy to mediate between Israel and both Egypt and Syria. In January 1974 Israel and Egypt agreed to disengage their military forces. In March OPEC lifted the embargo against the United States.

Yet the Middle East was not stable. The Soviet Union, its influence with the Arab states reduced, turned instead to Arab radicals, especially the Algerians and the Palestine Liberation Organization. The rift between the United States and the NATO countries persisted. The price of oil remained high, and OPEC remained able to increase it. The resulting burden on American consumers and their growing irritation added to Nixon's political problems.

So did the adverse response of uncritical friends of Israel to Kissinger's handling of Middle Eastern issues. Though the administration continued to make Israeli independence the cornerstone of American policy in the Middle East, its critics believed it had deliberately delayed supplying Israel during the war. They objected, too, to rapprochement with Egypt. Though that stance was unfair, the war had destroyed Israel's aura of invincibility. Israel's future independence, as the administration understood but its critics did not, depended not on auras or conquests but on Arab recognition and acceptance. Those who disagreed, some of them Jewish, joined Americans who were critical of détente in a political alliance that the Yom Kippur War hardened. That alliance included intellectuals like Irving Kristol, Richard Pipes, and Norman Podhoretz, who formulated and promulgated the doctrines of a neoconservatism that gradually attracted new adherents from those disaffected by the cultural and political state of the nation.

The new conservatism resembled the old. Without deviating significantly from Barry Goldwater's platform of 1964, neoconservatives addressed domestic and international issues in the context of a decade of change. They differed from Nixon, though only marginally, on economic and social policies. Nixon was attempting to reduce the double-digit inflation of 1973 and 1974 by cutting federal expenditures and increasing interest rates. But those devices had little impact on the rising worldwide prices of energy and food. Instead, Nixon's program overcompensated for the fiscal and monetary stimulation he had arranged for 1972. During 1973 and 1974 the economy moved toward recession, with the GNP declining, productivity falling, and unemployment climbing toward 9 percent. That "stagflation"—a combination of stagnation and inflation, which persisted for the rest of the decade—constituted a political liability for the party in the White House. Neoconservatives attributed stagflation to the federal government's interference in the economy. They argued that the market would operate to rectify the situation if the government balanced the budget and ceased regulating business activities. And they remained critical of Keynesian principles, which Nixon had publicly accepted in his earlier support of a full employment budget.

On the social issues, neoconservatives believed the Nixon administration had given more support to affirmative action in employment and education than that policy deserved. They also deplored, as did Nixon, the decision of the Supreme Court on abortion in the landmark case *Roe v. Wade* (1973). Speaking for the Court, Justice Blackmun—a Nixon appointee—drew dissents from Justices Rehnquist and White in an opinion denying the constitutionality of a Texas statute restricting legal abortion. Citing the Ninth and Fourteenth amendments, Blackmun held that the "right of privacy . . . is broad enough to encompass a woman's decision whether or not to terminate her pregnancy." But that right, he continued, was not absolute. It had to be qualified "against important state interests" in protecting the fetus as a woman approached the end of her term. On the basis of his examination of medical history, of philosophy, and of Anglo-American common law, Blackmun concluded that the state could regulate maternal health after the end of the first trimester of a pregnancy, for example, by defining the qualifications of those authorized to perform an abortion. After the second trimester the state could go so far as to prohibit abortion. In spite of those reservations, the decision represented a major victory for the women's movement and for Planned Parenthood of America. It was a defeat for the National Right to Life Committee, an organization that the neoconservatives were cultivating.

Most emphatically, neoconservatives demanded a tough stance against the Soviet Union and its allies. They called for an increase in defense spending, which Nixon was reducing. Neoconservatism in foreign policy and on social and economic issues pushed both parties toward the right—the Democrats away from liberalism; the Republicans away from Nixon. Nixon was losing the party's conservative wing at a time he needed its loyalty in order to survive intensifying investigation of his conduct in office.

16

The Rule of Law

During the last months of 1973 Nixon's problems grew. Neither he nor his White House aides could explain omissions in some of the tapes delivered to Judge Sirica. Congress overrode his veto of the War Powers Act, an act intended to limit a president's power to go to war on his own. At best ambiguous, that measure gave the president explicit authority to go to war in specified circumstances, such as an attack upon the United States, but it also required termination of hostilities within ninety days unless Congress authorized their continuation. Designed as a reprisal for presidential initiative during the Vietnam War, the act had provoked Nixon's opposition. The failure of his veto to prevail reflected his declining prestige. More serious was a vote of the House of Representatives in February 1974 to authorize its Judiciary Committee to determine whether the president should be impeached.

1. EXPLETIVE DELETED

Attempting to restore his reputation, Nixon in November had headed south for a series of speeches before friendly audiences. At that time congressional investigations were disclosing irregularities in his income tax returns. In order to qualify for an income tax deduction for 1969, Nixon's lawyers had backdated his signing of the deed of gift of his prepresidential papers to the National Archives. Later they had failed to declare taxable improvements the government had made to his properties at San Clemente and Key Biscayne. Nixon asserted he had had no knowledge of those matters, but his attorneys claimed to have gone over his tax returns with him line by line. The president, it developed, owed four hundred thousand dollars in back taxes and interest. Asked about his taxes during a television interview while on his southern trip, Nixon replied: "In all of my years in public life, I have never profited . . . from public service. . . . I have never obstructed justice. . . . I am not a crook." He said he would pay his back taxes, but his returns had revealed that he had made only minimal gifts to charity while his personal worth had tripled. To many Americans, he seemed both crooked and mean, and a tax chiseler, too.

In mid-November the disheartened senior attorneys on his staff, Leonard Garment and Fred Buzhardt, suggested to Haig that Nixon resign. But again and again Nixon said that he would not resign. The pressure on him kept growing. In special elections in two congressional districts in February 1974 Democrats won traditionally Republican seats. Leon Jaworski, the new special prosecutor, was proving to be no less determined than Cox to get at the truth about Watergate. On March 1, 1974, the grand jury that had been hearing evidence about Watergate returned indictments against seven members of the White House and CREEP staffs. Among those indicted were Mitchell, Haldeman, and Ehrlichman, all charged with obstruction of justice and conspiracy to impede the Watergate investigation. "There had never been such wholesale proceedings against the top men in the administration of an American President," Judge Sirica later wrote. "Those closest to Richard Nixon were the ones most involved."

Since the grand jury was no longer considering evidence in those cases, Jaworski saw a diminished need for secrecy. At the instigation of Jaworski's office, the grand jury asked Judge Sirica to turn over to the House Judiciary Committee the tapes and other materials it had gathered, as well as a sealed report listing the major facts it had discovered that tied the president directly to the Watergate cover-up. Surprisingly the White House lawyers did not object. The defendants did, but Sirica overruled their objections. In preparing for their trial, Jaworski asked the judge to subpoena sixty-four more tapes to be delivered by May 2, 1974. For its part, the Judiciary Committee subpoenaed forty-two tapes. Both the court and the committee were closing in on the president.

The Judiciary Committee had been working quietly. Both its chairman, Peter Rodino, and its general counsel, John Doar, planned to complete preliminary investigations before the committee directly addressed the question of impeachment. Rodino, a Democrat, represented an Italian-American and black district in Newark, New Jersey, notorious for its poverty and crime. He was a respected veteran of twenty-five years in the House of Representatives, a combat soldier during World War II, and a consistent supporter of Nixon's military and foreign policies. A true believer in constitutional procedures, Rodino had been shocked by the Saturday Night Massacre. The Judiciary Committee of thirty-eight members included some liberal Democrats, but Republicans and southern Democrats together made up a majority. It was a not a liberal stronghold. As its chief counsel John Doar won the committee's confidence while he directed its investigative staff and helped Rodino set a timetable. Once a Republican, Doar had become an ardent advocate of civil rights before serving in the Justice Department under Robert Kennedy. There his personal courage matched his high legal ability. In March and April 1974 he and his staff were accumulating what became forty volumes of material on the issues of impeachment. The evidence that the grand jury delivered in March contributed to that collection, but Doar knew he also needed the tapes for which the committee issued the subponeas.

The president's legal team was now headed by James St. Clair, an experienced trial lawyer from Boston. Buzhardt was assigned to manage the tapes, and Garment to assist the others. They realized that Nixon could not defy the subpoenas from Sirica and from the Judiciary Committee without causing another public outcry. Consequently, they recommended an alternative tactic, which Nixon adopted. On April 30, 1974, the president published more than thirteen hundred pages of transcripts of the subpoenaed tapes. His lawyers had suggested including every word recorded, but in the interest of public relations, Nixon substituted "expletive deleted" for the profanity that frequently punctuated the taped conversations. The night before publication the president on national television said that the transcripts "include all the relevant portions of the subpoenaed conversations . . . the rough as well as the smooth. . . . The President has nothing to hide."

That was a bald lie, for Nixon had excized important sections of the tapes. A careful reading of the transcripts suggested that they did not report all that the president and his counselors had told each other. Judge Sirica, who had listened in private to some of the tapes, knew but could not say how unreliable the transcripts were. As he later wrote, for one example on March 23, 1973, the tapes—but not the transcripts—recorded Nixon's directions to his aides for protecting the secrecy surrounding the cover-up. His aides, the president had ordered, were

Response to the transcripts of Nixon's tapes.

to tell those testifying before the grand jury to say nothing. "I don't give a shit what happens," Nixon had said. "I want you all to stonewall it, let them plead the Fifth Amendment, cover-up or anything else." The transcripts included none of that conversation and, of course, not the "expletive deleted" in Nixon's remark.

Even as they stood, the transcripts stunned the country. "Expletive deleted" became a national joke. The vulgarity of the president's discourse, however, was not funny. Hugh Scott, the Republican minority leader in the Senate, called the transcripts "disgusting." John Rhodes, his counterpart in the House, said Nixon should consider resigning. The transcripts, in spite of the censorship, revealed that Nixon and Dean had discussed possible payments to Hunt and disclosed Kalmbach's payments for dirty tricks. They showed, too, as *The New Yorker* put it, the "double-dealing, the President's uncertainty . . . the cold, cynical view of the men" around Nixon. Within two weeks of the release of the transcripts, a Harris poll found that a majority of respondents who had an opinion favored Nixon's impeachment and removal from office.

More dangerous for the president were the decisions of the special prosecutor and the Judiciary Committee that the transcripts were unacceptable as substitutes for the subpoenaed tapes. In Judge Sirica's court, James St. Clair argued for Nixon that since the tapes recorded the president's conversations, and since the president was not indicted in the cover-up, the tapes were inadmissible hearsay. Jaworski asked the judge for permission to disclose in his reply some evidence from the grand jury investigation that had not been included in the indictment. Sirica suggested Jaworski first submit that evidence in private. In the presence of the judge and the White House attorneys, Jaworski then revealed for the first time that the grand jury had named Nixon as an unindicted coconspirator in the Watergate cover-up. The jury had not indicted the president because of its uncertainty about constitutional issues, especially as they related to the impeachment proceedings. Now St. Clair, dropping the hearsay argument, claimed that Jaworski, as an employee of the executive branch, had no standing to sue the president. But Sirica ruled that the subpoena should be enforced. Jaworski, he later commented, deserved "a lot of credit for the way he handled the case. The strategy of having the grand jury issue a report on the president, of asking that it be sent to the House committee, of encouraging the grand jury to name the president as an unindicted coconspirator, and then playing that card when it counted most, all these were the mark of a careful and experienced lawyer."

Immediately after the judge's ruling, Jaworski, as the law permitted him to do, asked for a direct review of the case by the Supreme Court. In spite of White House opposition, that Court agreed to hear argument in July. Sirica thought Nixon was doomed. But there was no certainty about what the Supreme Court would decide or how Nixon would respond. And Nixon intended to try again to show that his virtuosity in foreign policy made him indispensable in the White House.

2. THE HAWKS TAKE OVER

To that end the president attempted to capitalize on Kissinger's progress in Middle Eastern diplomacy by making a ceremonial trip to that area from June 12 through June 21, 1974, to be followed by a summit with Brezhnev in Moscow. In Cairo, to his satisfaction, Nixon received a "tumultuous welcome" from Egyptian crowds, as well as warm greetings from Anwar el-Sadat, who was eager to affirm his new friendship with the United States. In Saudi Arabia Nixon met King Faisal, who proved willing to discuss the impact of high oil prices, then pushing inflation in the United States up to 20 percent for 1974. In Damascus Nixon and Syrian President Hafez el-Assad announced the resumption of diplomatic relations between their countries. After a stop in Israel, Nixon ended his trip in Jordan, where King Hussein toasted his "journey for peace."

The president succeeded in capturing much of prime time on American television news. The camera showed Nixon and Sadat watching a belly dancer and Nixon and King Faisal kissing each other. Those transient impressions quickly faded, while Nixon's admonition to Israel rang on. "Continuous war in this area," the president told the Israeli parliament, "is not a solution for Israel's survival." In private he made it clear to the Israeli prime minister that he expected Israel to maintain "the momentum of peace negotiations" begun by Kissinger. Those intelligent and constructive messages won the applause of Nixon's Arab hosts but refreshed the opposition of perfervid pro-Israel Americans who had objected to the administration's course during the Yom Kippur War.

Some of those so minded remained allied with the opponents of détente on the political right. The president could no longer discipline even his own appointees. Within the administration, Secretary of Defense James Schlesinger, abetted by Admiral Elmo R. Zumwalt, head of the Joint Chiefs, sabotaged negotiations for Salt II. Those negotiations were faltering anyway because neither the United States nor the Soviet Union had put forward terms acceptable to the other. Nixon resented Schlesinger's hard line but dared not denounce it for fear of losing further conservative support in Congress. The Russians realized that Watergate was diminishing Nixon's stature. The two sides reached no agreement of significance while Nixon was in Moscow. "If detente unravels in America," Nixon had warned Brezhnev, "the hawks will take over." Before the 1974 summit, they had done so.

3. "To Say What the Law Is"

The president returned from Moscow on July 3, 1974, five days before the Supreme Court was to hear arguments in the case of *United States of America v. Richard M. Nixon.* That case was to test the constitutionality of the president's claim of executive privilege as the basis for his refusal to deliver the tapes to Judge Sirica. Chief Justice Burger and three of his colleagues—Justices Blackmun, Powell, and Rehnquist—were Nixon appointees. They were not of a single mind, though none of them subscribed to the judicial activism of Justices Douglas, Brennan, and Marshall. Justice Rehnquist, a devotee of judicial restraint, anchored the conservative end of the bench, with Justice White his nearest neighbor. Like the chief justice, Justice Stewart was a moderate. The Burger Court, a disappointment to Nixon, had overturned no major decision of the Warren Court, and in several cases it had irritated the president.

Nevertheless, in suggesting that he would abide only by a unanimous decision of the Supreme Court on the question of his tapes, Nixon probably counted on the support of one or two of his appointees. But the Court had been unanimous in its opinion on a related issue. Its decision in *United States v. United States District Court* (1972) found considerations of national security no excuse for the government's warrantless use of electronic surveillance. The president's power did not transcend the provisions of the Fourth Amendment. For the Court, Justice Powell noted that the case pertained to electronic surveillance without a warrant only against allegedly subversive domestic organizations, not against foreign governments. He also recognized that since 1946 presidents and attorneys general had frequently resorted to such surveillance. But that practice, Powell ruled, threatened the "cherished privacy of law-abiding citizens." The Fourth Amendment, he held, shielded "private speech from unreasonable surveillance," and the protection of that amendment became "the more necessary when the targets of official surveillance may be those suspected of unorthodoxy in their political beliefs." Without a prior judicial warrant, therefore, the executive could not legally engage in wiretapping, even in instances of national security. "We cannot accept the government's argument," Powell wrote, "that internal security matters are too subtle and complex for judicial evaluation. . . . Nor do we believe that prior judicial approval will fracture the secrecy essential to official intelligence gathering."

That ruling spoke directly to the snooping so rife in the Nixon administration. By July 1974 that snooping was a matter of public knowledge through exposure in congressional hearings and the litigation of those spied upon. The decision also challenged the president's contention that considerations of national security gave him latitude that the Constitution otherwise prohibited.

Nixon's claim to absolute executive privilege received a full hearing by the Supreme Court on July 8, 1974. In his opening argument, Jaworski asserted his right as special prosecutor to sue for the tapes. He also, he said, recognized the right of executive privilege, but the "public purpose" of executive privilege was only to protect "governmental deliberations." That purpose precluded application of executive privilege "to shield alleged criminality." Since the grand jury had named the president as an unindicted coconspirator in a criminal case, evidence from the White House "should not be confined" to what the president chose to make available. In response, St. Clair, arguing for Nixon, held that the tapes were subject to executive privilege because they contained conversations between the president and his close advisers. As the chief law enforcement officer in the country, only the president, so St. Clair maintained, could decide which material the prosecution needed. "This President," he said, "ought not to have any less power than any other President ought to have. . . . The framers of the Constitution had in mind a strong Presidency."

The chief justice then asked a question. He may have had in mind Justice Powell's decision in *United States v. United States District Court.* Why, Burger inquired, could Judge Sirica not screen the tapes and withhold any irrelevant or sensitive material? St. Clair had anticipated that question by asserting that the constitutional separation of powers precluded judicial review of a president's claim to executive privilege. If not absolute, St. Clair said, executive privilege at the least prevailed over Judge Sirica's subpoena. But Jaworski, quoting the great John Marshall, had observed that it was up to the Court "to say what the law is." The answer was expected within a fortnight.

Sooner, on July 19, 1974, John Doar presented his analysis of the case for the impeachment of Richard Nixon to the House Judiciary Committee. Doar had been preparing for months, as had his able colleague Albert Jenner, the committee's minority counsel, and their assiduous staff. In addressing the committee, Doar described the "Byzantine Empire" that was the White House and accused Nixon of "a pattern of conduct designed not to take care that the laws be faithfully executed, but to impede their faithful execution, in his political interest and on his behalf." Reasonable men, Doar said, would find the president guilty of "enormous crimes."

Supported by Jenner, Doar also submitted several sets of articles of impeachment, one of which his staff had drafted. It called for the impeachment of the president for the Watergate cover-up, for a "pattern of massive and persistent abuse of power for political purposes involving unlawful and un-Constitutional invasions of the rights and privacy of individual citizens," for failure to comply with the committee's subpoenas, for the use of the Internal Revenue Service for political purposes, and for income tax fraud in backdating the deed of gift of his vice presidential papers. The committee's debate over those articles was to begin on July 24, on national television. Meanwhile, St.

'I AM THE LAW!'

Clair refused to say whether Nixon would obey the Supreme Court's forthcoming decision about the tapes. With Washington in a state of near hysteria, seven Republicans on the Judiciary Committee, meeting privately, were reaching agreement that Nixon had committed offenses, though not all those of which he had been accused, serious enough to require impeachment.

On July 24 Chief Justice Burger read the unamimous opinion of the Supreme Court, Justice Rehnquist abstaining, in the *United States v.*

Nixon. Speaking first to the contention of Nixon's lawyers that the district court lacked jurisdiction because the dispute lay within the executive branch, between the president and the special prosecutor, Burger held that the special prosecutor had "standing to bring this action," which was itself justiciable. A subpoena for documents might be quashed, Burger continued, only if "their production would be 'unreasonable and oppressive.' " In this instance it was not. The chief justice then rejected the argument for an absolute executive privilege. "Many decisions of this Court," he said, "have unequivocally affirmed the holding of *Marbury v. Madison* . . . (1803) that 'it is emphatically the province and duty of the judicial department to say what the law is.' " Neither "the doctrine of the separation of powers," Burger went on, "nor the need for confidentiality of high-level communications, without more, can sustain an absolute, unqualified Presidential privilege of immunity from judicial process under all circumstances."

The president's need for candor from his advisers called for "great deference from the courts," but the "legitimate needs of the judicial process" here outweighed presidential privilege, for that privilege had to be viewed "in light of our historic commitment to the rule of law." Further, the president's interest in confidentiality of communications would "not be violated by disclosure of a limited number of conversations preliminarily shown to have some bearing on the pending criminal case." The district court bore responsibility for protecting against the release of any irrelevant material, but the subpoena was appropriate. As John Marshall had said, in no case involving a subpoena duces tecum would a court proceed against the president as an ordinary individual, but that statement, Burger concluded, could not be interpreted "to mean in any sense that a President is above the law."

The opinion required Nixon to deliver the subpoenaed tapes to Judge Sirica. A refusal would have provided ground for still another article of impeachment. For some hours Nixon hesitated. But that evening he released an announcement saying he had instructed his lawyers to comply with the Supreme Court's ruling.

4. High Crimes and Misdemeanors

Less than an hour later Chairman Rodino called to order the meeting of the Judiciary Committee to consider the impeachment of the president. The thirty-eight members of the committee, all of them conscious of television, spoke one by one in order of seniority, each for fifteen minutes. They had before them a revised version of the first article of impeachment, tempered to fit the preference of the seven Republicans, who had found the language of the staff's draft too strong. As that article stood after another cosmetic change, it cited as cause for impeachment Nixon's "violation of his constitutional oath faithfully to execute the office of President" and his obstruction of the administration of justice, with explicit reference to the Watergate break-in.

One of the first speakers, Robert Kastenmeier, a Wisconsin Democrat, quoted the late Louis D. Brandeis, the distinguished lawyer and Supreme Court justice: "In a government of laws, the existence of government will be imperiled if it fails to observe the law scrupulously. . . . If government becomes a law breaker, it breeds contempt for the law. . . . It invites anarchy." Kastenmeier voted for impeachment. Later Tom Railsback of Illinois, a senior and respected legislator, became the first of the Republicans to vote that way. "I have agonized over this particular inquiry," he said. ". . . We are considering a man, Richard Nixon, who has twice been in my district campaigning for me, that I regard as a friend . . . who has done wonderful things for this country." But Railsback also discussed the questionable things Nixon had done. They related, he said, "to what I would call abuse of power. I cannot think of any area where a conservative or a moderate or a liberal should be more concerned about the state of our government." Young Americans, Railsback said, expected the committee "to get to the truth." He would vote for impeachment.

Most of the Republicans on the committee disagreed, particularly Charles Wiggins of California, who, on the next morning, gave a spirited defense of Nixon. The statements of members continued through that next day and on to the evening of July 27. Rodino then put the question. Twenty-seven members—all of the Democrats, including the southerners, and seven Republicans—voted in favor of Article I; eleven members, all Republican, voted against. On July 29, by a vote of twenty-eight to ten, the committee adopted Article II, which charged Nixon with engaging repeatedly in conduct violating the constitutional rights of citizens, as in his recourse to illegal wiretaps and his misuse of the FBI, the IRS, and the CIA. A third article, adopted July 30, charged him with violating the Constitution by failing to produce materials subpoenaed by the Judiciary Committee—a charge accurate in its facts but uncertain in its legality since the Supreme Court had ruled only on a judicial, not a congressional, subpoena.

Those three articles defined, in the language of the Constitution, the "high crimes and misdemeanors" leading the Judiciary Committee to recommend that the House impeach President Nixon. As the Constitution stipulates, the House has "the sole power of impeachment" and the Senate "the sole power to try all impeachments," with no person to be convicted "without the concurrence of two thirds of the members present." On July 29 the White House had announced that the president would not resign if he were impeached. Apparently he intended to fight it out in the Senate, for by July 30 only a third of the members of the House, at the most, were still supporting him. For that matter, according to one White House leak on July 30, "It isn't down the chute yet in the Senate, but it's damn close."

The men around Nixon knew that the end was near. There were no heroes among them. Indeed, St. Clair had received a deserved scolding from Judge Sirica for failing to listen to the tapes personally. None of the president's staff or lawyers had made a genuine effort to penetrate Nixon's pattern of lies. None had tried to get at the truth. But Buzhardt could not escape the truth after July 24, when he listened, at Nixon's suggestion, to the tape for June 23, 1972. That tape recorded Nixon's assent to having the CIA stop the FBI investigation of Watergate. It was then obvious that Nixon was doomed.

As Haig saw it, and Kissinger agreed, Nixon ought to resign. If he did not, House debate about impeachment and then the Senate trial could drag on for weeks, even months. During that period a defensive president, discredited at home, would be unable to meet any crisis in foreign affairs or to resolve urgent domestic problems like inflation. The nation could not afford so crippled a chief executive. But Nixon, huddled with his family and Bebe Rebozo, seemed defiant. And Gerald Ford, who knew from Haig that the tapes were catastrophic, appropriately refused to intercede.

Haig therefore mustered the Republican congressional leaders to push Nixon to resign. Once informed about the content of the tapes, they realized Nixon had to go. His departure before the November elections was essential to minimize the party's predictable losses. Representative Wiggins, who had been Nixon's outstanding defender in the House, on August 2, 1974, found the transcript of the crucial tape "devastating." He immediately favored Nixon's resignation. For the same reason so did House Minority Leader John Rhodes, Republican National Chairman George Bush, and Senator Barry Goldwater, who described himself as "mad as hell" about Nixon's lies. On August 5, when the tapes were made public, Nixon admitted he had withheld evidence from the House Judiciary Committee. The secretary of defense, guarding against another of Nixon's madman responses, warned all military commanders to accept no orders from the White House without his accompanying signature. But on August 6 Nixon told the cabinet he would not resign.

Within hours he saw that he had no choice. Almost all his support in the House had dropped away. Impeachment had become a certainty. He could count on no more than twenty votes in the Senate, too few to prevent conviction. His family wanted him to battle on, but on August 7 three senior Republicans—Goldwater, Rhodes, and Hugh Scott—warned him that he was down to fifteen votes in the Senate. Goldwater added that he was leaning toward conviction himself. Only then, bitterly, did Nixon decide to resign. On evening television on August 8, 1974, showing no remorse, he said that it had become evident that "I no longer have a strong enough political base in the Congress to justify continuing" in office. The nation needed, Nixon went on, "a full-time President and a full-time Congress," so he would resign. He did so, effective at noon the next day.

But Nixon did not exit without a typical Nixon farewell. On television again, he took leave of the White House staff. "Sure we have done some things wrong ..." he said, "and the top man takes the responsibility." But it was the top man's underlings who were going to

Richard Nixon departing: "Sure we have done some things wrong."

prison. Then another lie: ". . . no man . . . came into this Administration and left it with more of the world's goods than when he came in."
Then bathos: "My father" was "a great man"; "my mother" was "a
saint." And as for himself: "I'm not educated, but I do read books."
Then there departed Richard Nixon, a bright man of considerable
achievements, who lacked the character for public office. At noon on
August 9, 1974, Gerald Ford became president of the United States.

5. Two Kinds of Justice

When Richard Nixon resigned, Herbert Kalmbach and John Dean
were in jail, and Mitchell, Haldeman, and Ehrlichman were about to
stand trial, as the prosecutor put it, for their parts in the "massive,
covert, secret operation" to cover-up those guilty of the Watergate break-
in. The jury found Mitchell guilty on five counts, Haldeman on five
counts, Ehrlichman on four. In February 1975 "Maximum John" Sirica sentenced them to terms in prison of not less than thirty months
and not more than eight years, which he later reduced to one to four
years. "The ceremony of sentencing," wrote Anthony Lewis in the *New
York Times*, ". . . celebrated the relearning of an old piece of wisdom.
Those who manage the delicate institutions of government have a special responsibility to represent the law."

But Richard Nixon went free. Special Prosecutor Jaworski thought
he should. Jaworski believed that several years would have to pass before
Nixon could receive a fair trail in any court. Jaworski was reluctant,
too, to proceed against a former president of the United States. But he
had struck no bargain to get Nixon to resign. Gerald Ford, for his part,
thought that any trial of Nixon would retard the healing which the
country needed so badly. So thirty days after taking office, Ford granted
Nixon a "full, free and absolute pardon" for all crimes he had committed against the United States during his presidency.

There were two standards of justice. One led to the punishment of
the men who had followed Nixon's instructions, expressed or implied.
The other let the major felon remain untried, unconvicted, and therefore eligible for the generous pension and other perquisites of former
presidents. Petty thieves incarcerated for minor offenses might have
concluded that the greater the crime, the less the accountability.

For there was no doubt about the guilt Nixon shared with his subordinates. The record was clear. And justice did not wholly fail. Officers of twenty major corporations were found guilty of having made

illegal contributions to Nixon's 1972 campaign, though none of them received much punishment. Vice President Agnew, two cabinet members, and a dozen of the White House staff were among those who pleaded guilty or were convicted of Watergate-related crimes.

At least in part the system had worked. To be sure, two resolute reporters for the *Washington Post*, one intrepid federal judge, two dogged special prosecutors, and two assiduous congressional committees had helped make the system work. Those important variables could not be counted on for the future. But as Sam Ervin said, "One of the great advantages of the three separate branches of government is that it is difficult to corrupt all three at the same time." Nevertheless, the nation had to remain on guard to prevent the excesses of power with which Nixon had used his office, as in considerable measure had his two predecessors.

Much also remained incomplete in the best of the initiatives they had undertaken. But presidential power, swollen by the responsibilities of the White House for foreign policy in the nuclear age, had become corrupt. And constant public stress had exhausted the country. The resolution of the Watergate scandal terminated fifteen years of social and political discord—racial conflict over civil rights, nuclear confrontation with the Soviet Union, war in Vietnam, angry protest against that war, three devastating assassinations, riots in the cities, violence on the campuses, crisis over the Constitution. With the resignation of Richard Nixon, most Americans felt a sense of weary relief. The confidence of the New Frontier and the bright promise of the Great Society had faded; the liberal spirit was spent.

Epilogue: Retreat and Revival

Between the inauguration of John F. Kennedy and the resignation of Richard M. Nixon, much of the political debate in the United States arose over questions of whether and how to use the federal government. The state of the nation in 1960, its social and economic inadequacies and inequities, argued that neither state and local government nor private enterprise had the scope or purpose necessary for a prosperous and free society. Kennedy came to recognize the need for a stimulative federal revenue policy to invigorate the economy. His New Frontier also included federal support for local and higher education and federal legislation to prohibit racial, religious, and sexual discrimination in employment and in access to social facilities. A wave of public and congressional approval of those objectives permitted their achievement in the wake of Kennedy's death. That approval also attended Lyndon Johnson's equally necessary use of the federal government. Johnson's Great Society took steps to combat poverty, to guarantee the right to vote, to provide medical care for the aged and the needy, and to protect the natural environment. Nixon during his first administration continued those policies. For a time he supported environmental legislation, used federal authority to influence the economy, and approved expenditures to relieve poverty while he also proposed an income maintenance plan as the means to that end. In those and other ways, the presidents and the congresses they dealt with utilized the state to improve the national condition.

But the state could also serve undemocratic purposes. On that account, the Constitution, while it provided capacious power for the executive and legislative branches of government, in the Bill of Rights also forbade those branches to abridge the personal freedom of Americans. Therefore the decisions of the Warren Court protecting those freedoms. Yet in growing degree, Kennedy, Johnson, and Nixon successively employed the large power of the presidency in ways that made the state a threat to Americans. The Kennedy administration, for one example, permitted the illegal wiretap on Martin Luther King, Jr. Johnson bugged his political opponents, the Mississippi Freedom Democrats and the Goldwater Republicans alike. Nixon encouraged and committed wholesale violations of federal law and of the Constitution.

All three presidents stretched the power of their office in foreign policy to and sometimes beyond constitutional limits. Misled by his military and intelligence advisers, Kennedy went forward with an invasion of Cuba that could have escalated into a major war if he had not had wiser second thoughts just in time. Congress authorized neither that invasion nor Kennedy's increasing involvement of American forces in Vietnam. There again he relied mistakenly on military counsel. Fortunately Kennedy chose other advisers during the missile crisis with the Soviet Union. Even so, with Khrushchev in that confrontation he took the world close to nuclear catastrophe without consultation beyond a circle of intimates. Johnson expanded on those questionable precedents in his posture toward Panama, his invasion of the Dominican Republic, his escalations in Vietnam. Nixon went still farther in Southeast Asia and in his madman gestures elsewhere. All three presidents engaged the nation in protracted military adventures that required the conscription of American citizens and the loss of many of their lives. Deceit accompanied those presidential activities, and recourse to deceit damaged the credibility of the presidency.

Congress retaliated by trying to curb presidential authority. But the United States, the most powerful nation in the world, could not escape responsibilities in world affairs. The Constitution gave the president the leading role in foreign policy and made him commander in chief of the armed forces. Consequently Congress could fashion only a superficial measure of control. The War Powers Act of 1974 included terms that would have forced Johnson to seek congressional approval of the Vietnam War more openly and directly than he ever did. But almost until the end of that war Congress had appropriated funds for its pursuit. Further, the War Powers Act recognized that in some circumstances the president had to move before he could consult the Congress. So it had been during the missile crisis, and so it would be in the event of an attack, particularly a nuclear attack, on the United States. So the legislation authorized the president to act on his own under those conditions.

The unavoidable ambiguities in decisions to make war, as well as repeated assertions of presidential authority prevented the War Powers Act from working as its authors hoped it would. Even Gerald Ford, a chief executive without a mandate, informed rather than consulted Congress when in 1975 he struck back maladroitly against Cambodia for seizing an American merchant ship. That reprisal was applauded on the Hill. Before the decade ended, President Jimmy Carter, again without consultation, ordered a military foray—in the end a fiasco—into the Iranian desert to try to rescue American hostages held in Teheran. During the 1980s President Ronald Reagan, without prior congressional consent, ordered an invasion of Grenada and an American military presence in Lebanon. His successor, George Bush, violating both a treaty and international law, brazenly invaded Panama to the predictable criticism of the Organization of American States and the United Nations. In 1990 Bush again neglected to consult Congress when he ordered more than four hundred thousand Americans troops to Saudi Arabia. Bush later asserted his right to resort to force in order to liberate Kuwait from Iraq, in accordance with a UN Security Council resolution he had sponsored. Presented with a fait accompli, Congress then approved the use of force. The War Powers Act did succeed in keeping presidents from engaging in extended military operations like those in Vietnam, but the act did not constrain the emergency power of the commander in chief or prevent contorted presidential interpretations of that power.

After the fact, Congress could expose illegal or capricious practices of executive agencies. It did so in 1975 and 1976 in hearings about the FBI and CIA. Both were guilty of frequent, flagrant abuses. The CIA had undertaken covert actions against properly constituted foreign governments and plotted assassinations of foreign heads of state. The FBI had planted warantless bugs and employed agents provocateurs to incite radical groups to illegal acts. But the United States had to have intelligence agencies. Congressional efforts to curb their behavior and to require them to report to oversight committees on the Hill provided only a partial remedy for past practices. So it was that the CIA conspired with President Reagan's national security staff in defiance of the law. The two agencies secretly and illegally arranged to transfer moneys obtained from Iran to antigovernment forces in Nicaragua. No statute could substitute for a president's own vigilance and sense of constitutional propriety.

Congress succeeded in curbing the presidency in internal affairs. The Budget and Impoundment Control Act of 1974 established procedures to prevent the kinds of impoundments that Nixon had considered his prerogative. But the veto power of the president, of course, remained a formidable block to any spending he opposed, as Gerald Ford often demonstrated. The Federal Election Campaign Act of 1974 instituted partial federal financing for presidential campaigns, but its provisions did not affect the spending of political action groups. Those lobbies for special interests poured money into the treasuries of candidates for national as well as local offices. Indeed, political contributions reached increasingly worrisome levels. So did the huge expenditures, much of them of public money, by national candidates for television advertising. That advertising, more even than in the past, was often deliberately misleading and sometimes scurrilous.

It was primarily in domestic social and economic policies that the programs of the federal government had been most salubrious during the Kennedy and Johnson period. Peaceful protests had educated Americans, as well as their presidents, in the need for federal action in the cause of social justice. Unequivocal but peaceful protest also alerted the country to the concerns of young Americans about the possibility of nuclear war. Civil rights leaders and their fellows on the campuses enriched and enlivened political discourse in the United States and pointed the way toward democratic possibilities and away from military adventurism.

But the New Frontier and the Great Society failed to address the endemic nature of American poverty. And Kennedy and Johnson, stymied by the influence of special interests on the Hill, would not propose truly redistributive taxation. Further, the Vietnam War absorbed federal energies and funds necessary for continued social reform. The expectations of the dispossessed remained unfulfilled. The consequent riots in the streets and violence at the universities might have occurred solely because of the growing tensions over race and class. As it happened, they were provoked also by the war itself. The war preoccupied both those who waged it and those who despised it. The resulting discord, no longer wholly peaceful, molded the politics of 1968. Its reverberations persisted for at least twenty years. Nixon did not have to invent his "silent majority," his Middle Americans. They were waiting for him.

Yet the conflicts of the 1960s also yielded important social improvements. The Civil Rights Act of 1964 and the affirmative action programs it spawned created new opportunities for Americans previously excluded from prestigious callings. Major colleges and universities—during the 1950s largely the preserve of white males—had admitted substantial numbers of women and minority candidates by the end of the 1970s. Within another decade medicine, law, and business management came to reflect that desirable diversity. The Voting Rights Act of 1965 similarly changed American politics. In 1984 a black man, Jesse Jackson, an outspoken social reformer, was a serious contender for the Democratic presidential nomination, and the party chose a woman, Geraldine Ferraro, for its vice presidential slot.

Yet in addressing the social issues as he did in 1972, Nixon spoke to the conviction of his Middle American constituents that politics was a zero-sum game. As they saw it, they suffered an equivalent social or economic loss for every gain that accrued to blacks, Hispanics, or the poor. That sour conclusion received psychological reinforcement from the problems of the rest of the decade. The reforms of the 1960s had not created those problems, but the problems impeded further reform. The late 1970s were years of energy shortages and galloping inflation, of worrisome unemployment, of troubled détente, of declining American power and prestige abroad. Under those conditions, politics proved loath to examine persisting inequities and injustices in American life.

The momentum of reform slackened also because of the fragmentation of social protest. Of the once militant groups, only the feminists and the environmentalists sustained their causes. Black protest for equal rights and against poverty either shrank or flowed into the political mainstream. There black and Hispanic candidates won more and more offices but ordinarily on conventional platforms. Like their white ethnic counterparts, each American group of color, each minority tended to turn inward. Their pride expressed itself in celebrations of past achievements as well as demands for an equitable share of the perquisites of contemporary society. That particularism had damaging political effects. Divided from one another, the outsiders in American life, the poor and the proscribed, lacked the political strength to force the leaders of the Democratic party to heed their needs. Many Republicans, as they always had, and some Democrats, too, attributed to the victims of prejudice and exploitation the primary blame for their troubles.

Retreat from the constructive use of the federal government began with Nixon's plans for his second term. After his resignation it contin-

ued, accelerating during the 1980s. In that decade the two major parties collaborated to deregulate industry and finance and to reduce taxes
on corporations and wealthy Americans. For a long season after 1974
American politics fostered a return to private affluence and public
squalor. By 1990 the years of retreat had left the nation much as Kennedy had found it, with "unconquered pockets of ignorance and prejudice, unanswered questions of poverty and surplus."

As they had before, those conditions would surely one day call for
correction. For that purpose the period 1961–1974, despite its failures,
provided an instructive legacy of achievement. The reforms of those
years had succeeded in reducing poverty and racial and sexual discrimination. They had demonstrated the effectiveness of constructive
federal social and economic policy.

And in foreign affairs Kennedy in his negotiations with Khrushchev
after 1962, Nixon in his negotiations with China and the Soviet Union
had opened the way to cooperative coexistence among the major powers. By the late 1980s even President Ronald Reagan, a notorious hawk,
had begun to understand the significance of that course. Cooperation,
not constant confrontation, fitted the needs of the United States in a
world where power had become diffused but nuclear rivalries still
threatened the survival of life on earth. The statesmen of the 1990s,
Soviet and American alike, began wisely to defuse those rivalries.

Survival was not enough. To create and sustain a just, distributive,
and free society, Americans had to start to build on the accomplishments of the years of discord. They had first to revive the liberal aspirations of that creative time. They had again to employ the state to make
those aspirations tangible.

Acknowledgments

This book, a work of synthesis and interpretation, rests continually on the basic narratives and analyses in the scholarship of others. As my notes indicate, I could not have proceeded without frequent and rewarding recourse to the studies of historians and political scientists, journalists, and memoirists, who have written on one aspect or another of the people and events I have discussed.

The Sterling Fund of Yale University defrayed most of my expenses for research. I am indebted, too, to the archivists who helped me find my way through the records of three presidents and their administrations. Among those archivists, three in particular provided indispensable guidance: Ronald E. Whealen at the John F. Kennedy Library in Boston, Massachusetts; Nancy Smith at the Lyndon B. Johnson Library in Austin, Texas; and Joan Howard at the Nixon Materials Project in Alexandria, Virginia.

Because of the hospitality of Ann Blum and Peter Taylor, of Michael Stoff, and of Janet Fesler, my sojourns in those cities were far more pleasant than they could otherwise have been. At one time or another three valiant women—Anne S. Bittker, Eliza Carlson, and Florence Thomas—translated my difficult handwriting into typescript. The resulting text profited from the criticisms of Edwin Barber, McGeorge Bundy (on Chapter 8), Alan Brinkley, Laura Kalman, Elting E. Morison, and James T. Patterson. All of them made useful and generous suggestions, which I incorporated in the book. But now and then, in spite of their comments, I persisted in what may have been my errors. Most important, during parts of recent years I was able to go ahead with my work only because of the solicitude of my selfless wife. More even than the rest of our family, I am the grateful beneficiary of her many acts of love.

Notes

Key: JFKL signifies the John F. Kennedy Library in Boston, Massachusetts.

LBJL signifies the Lyndon B. Johnson Library in Austin, Texas.

Within those archives, OH signifies Oral Histories:; POF signifies President's Office Files; NSF signifies National Security Files; WHCF signifies White House Central Files.

NPMS signifies Nixon Presidential Materials Staff, the designation preferred by the Nixon Materials Project in Alexandria, Virginia.

Unless I have otherwise indicated, my citations to NPMS are also to the White House Special Files, and within them also to the President's Office Files, and within them also to the President's Handwriting Files. Within that last category, I have used ANS to signify the Annotated News Summaries only where I have used that source.

PROLOGUE: 1960

On the idea of Franklin D. Roosevelt and Henry Luce, I drew upon my own *V Was for Victory* (New York, 1976). The relationship between those ideas and the mood of 1960 has received outstanding treatment in John W. Jeffries, "The Quest for National Purpose," *American Quarterly* XXX (Fall, 1978), pp. 451–70; and from a different perspective, in Godfrey Hodgson, *In Our Time* (London, 1977), Ch. 4. On the question of poverty, apart from the works cited in the text, there are two important studies, one historical—James T. Patterson, *America's Struggle against Poverty* (Cambridge: Mass., 1981)—the other contemporary—Gabriel Kolko, *Wealth and Power in America* (New York, 1962). The inquiries into national goals are cited and quoted in the text, but the statements of Kennan and Lippmann are from Jeffries, *op. cit.* On the relationship between Eisenhower and Nixon, I relied upon Stephen E. Ambrose, *Eisenhower: The President* (New York, 1984), and *Nixon: The Education of a Politician* (New York, 1987), cited hereafter as *Nixon I.* For Kennedy and his campaign, I found most useful two early biographies, both of which convey the flavor of the man better than do later, revisionistic accounts. Those early books are: Arthur Schlesinger, Jr., *A Thousand Days* (Boston, 1965), and Theodore C. Sorensen, *Kennedy* (New York, 1965), which contains most of the quotations I used. The others are "cool nonchalance" from Kenneth O'Connell and David Powers, *Johnny, We Hardly Knew Ye* (Boston, 1972), and the statement of Eleanor Roosevelt about Joseph P. Kennedy, at Hyde Park, to the late Herman Kahn, who repeated it to me. There is an elegant portrait of Kennedy "being himself" in John Kenneth Galbraith, *A Life in Our Times* (Boston, 1981); see, too, Herbert Parmet, *JFK: The Presidency* (New York, 1983). For an informed criticism of Kennedy and other "liberals," see Allen Matusow, *The Unraveling of America* (New York, 1984). For Harris Wofford on *The Strategy of Peace*, see Wofford's Oral History, JFKL, and his book *Of Kennedys and Kings* (New York, 1980).

1. LEGACIES

The prelude reflects my reading of Richard D. Mahoney, *JFK: Ordeal in Africa* (New York, 1983).

1. We Band of Brothers

On the transition, I drew largely from Ambrose, *Eisenhower: The President*; Schlesinger, *Thousand Days*; and Sorensen, *Kennedy*. The profile of Kennedy quotes Galbraith, *A Life*; Arthur M. Schlesinger, Jr., *Robert Kennedy and His Times* (Boston, 1978); and on Addison's disease, J. A. Nicholas et al., "Management of Adrenocortical Insufficiency During Surgery," *A.M.A. Archives of Surgery* v. 71 (1955), pp. 739–40. On activists, the quotation is from Roger Hilsman, OH, JFKL.

2. Impedance on the Hill

Kennedy on Panama is quoted in Galbraith, *A Life*. The balance of the section rests on Schlesinger, *Thousand Days*; Sorensen, *Kennedy*; and especially Tom Wicker, *JFK and LBJ* (New York, 1968).

3. False Starts

On counterinsurgency, I drew upon the folders on the "Special Group" in NSF, JFKL, especially the memo "Military Counterinsurgency" that General Lyman L. Lemnitzer received on July 4, 1962; see also the discussion in Parmet, *JFK: The Presidency*. On the disruptive nature of economic growth, I quoted Chester Bowles to J. K. Galbraith, September 15, 1961, Bowles Mss., Yale University Library. On the *Alianza* I relied upon Schlesinger, *Thousand Days*, and Richard N. Goodwin, *Remembering America* (Boston, 1988). The narrative about the Bay of Pigs derives largely from Sorensen, *Kennedy*, and Schlesinger, *Thousand Days*, as do the quotations, except as follows: a "beginner's credulity" from McGeorge Bundy, *New York Times*, June 10, 1985; "national interests" from Chester Bowles, *Promises to Keep* (New York, 1971). Examples of Bowles's views are from Bowles to W. W. Rostow, December 21, 1961 and to Dean Rusk, February 8, 1962, Bowles Mss., *loc. cit.* Also helpful were Parmet, *op. cit.*, and conversations with the late Tracy Barnes.

4. Vienna

Generally I drew upon Parmet, Schlesinger, and Sorensen, cited in the previous section. About Vienna, I quoted Charles Bohlen from his OH, JFKL. About Berlin, I quoted

Maxwell Taylor, memo to the president, September 4, 1961, POF, JFKL, and George Kennan to Chester Bowles, September 21, Bowles Mss. I also found useful Robert M. Susser, *The Berlin Crisis of 1961* (Baltimore, 1973).

5. A Can of Snakes

Later chapters cite the major sources I used on Vietnam. In this section I quoted from Schlesinger, *Thousand Days;* Roger Hilsman's OH, JFKL, including his quotation from Robert Kennedy; and Galbraith's letters to John F. Kennedy of May 10, October 9, and November 28, 1961, POF, JFKL.

2. PROBINGS

1. Introductory Economics

On the national and international economies, there is a wealth of material in folders 73 and 74 relating to the Council of Economic Advisers, POF, JFKL. I benefited even more from conversations with James Tobin and from his OH, JFKL. The quotations I used came from those sources, which also informed an incisive essay, "The Macroeconomic Education of John F. Kennedy," by Thomas R. Burke, 1985, Historical Manuscripts, Yale University Library.

2. Big Steel

My account, including most of the quotations I used, rests on an undated memo by Arthur Goldberg in Box 39 of the Theodore Sorensen Papers, JFKL. "Irresponsible defiance" is from Kennedy's press conference, April 11, 1962, in the White House Central Files, JFKL. "Dyspeptic" is from Walter Heller, memo for the president, November 2, 1962, POF, JFKL. The conversations with Mills are from Presidential Recordings, Transcript, Tax Cut Proposal, Audiotape 7, JFKL.

3. International Economics

On the Common Market, I relied upon the accounts in Schlesinger, *Thousand Days*, and Richard J. Barnet. *The Alliance* (New York, 1983), which contains the quotations from Charles de Gaulle.

4. Civil Rights

For this section and others relating to the same subject, I consulted the growing historical literature about civil rights. Two older books present the point of view of the Kennedy administration: Schlesinger, *Thousand Days*, and Carl M. Brauer, *John F. Kennedy and the Second Reconstruction* (New York, 1977). Two others, often critical of the Kennedys, provide useful accounts, episode by episode, of the civil rights movement: Harvard Sitkoff, *The Struggle for Black Equality* (New York, 1981), and Robert Weisbrot, *Freedom Bound* (New York, 1990). Another three focus on Martin Luther King, Jr., and the SCLC: Stephen B. Oates, *Let the Trumpet Sound* (New York, 1982); Taylor Branch, *Parting the Waters* (New York, 1988); and David C. Garrow, *Bearing the Cross*

(New York, 1986). Except as noted, quotations in this section are from the works just cited by Schlesinger, Brauer, Sitkoff, and Oates. "Clear moral expression" is in Harris Wofford, memo for the president, May 29, 1961, POF, JFKL; "had the good sense" is from a conversation with Kathleen Cleaver.

5. Ole Miss

For this section I found most useful the works cited above by Schlesinger, Brauer, Sitkoff, and Weisbrot. I also profited and regularly quoted from transcripts of Dictabelt 4A–4J in JFKL. Those transcripts recorded conversations between the Kennedys and Barnett and include Robert Kennedy's "shoot anybody . . ." from Transcript 26A, September 30, 1962.

3. APPEARANCE AND REALITY

1. Crisis

My narrative and interpretation of the missile crisis represent an effort to reconcile the points of view in several useful accounts. Those included the indispensable Robert F. Kennedy, *Thirteen Days* (New York, 1969), and two other early versions: Schlesinger, *Thousand Days*, and Sorensen, *Kennedy*. The quotations I used came from those three sources and from the transcript of the tape "Cuban Missile Crisis Meeting," October 17, 1962, JFKL, as well as "Messages Exchanged by President Kennedy and Chairman Kruschchev . . . October 1962," *Department of State Bulletin*, November 19, 1973, pp. 634–54. Also of the first importance for informing my account were Graham T. Allison, *Essence of Decision* (Boston, 1971); McGeorge Bundy, *Danger and Survival* (New York, 1988), ch. IX; J. Anthony Lukas, "Class Reunion," *New York Times Magazine*, August 30, 1987; and Albert and Roberta Wohlstetter, "Controlling the Risks in Cuba," *Adelphi Papers* no. 17 (April 1965), Institute for Strategic Studies, London.

2. Resolution

As above.

3. Skybolt

My account derives from Richard Neustadt, "Skybolt and Nassau," report for the president, November 15, 1963, NSF, JFKL. I also benefited from Alistair Horne, "The Macmillan Years and Afterwards," in W. R. Louis and H. Bull, eds. *The Special Relationship* (Oxford, 1986).

4. The SDS

Apart from observations of my own, this section is based upon Hal Draper, *Berkeley: The New Student Revolt* (New York, 1965), which includes an introduction by Mario Savio, from which I quoted; David Harris, *Dreams Die Hard* (New York, 1984); Allen J. Matusow, *The Unraveling of America* (New York, 1984); Jim Miller, *"Democracy Is in the Streets"* (New York, 1987), a history of a kind of the SDS; Theodore Roszak, *The*

Making of a Counter Culture (New York, 1968); and Malcolm Cowley, "Reconsideration: The '60s," *New Republic* (August 20 and 27, 1977), pp. 37–40.

4. NEITHER PEACE NOR TRANQUILLITY

The quotations in the prelude are from Martin Luther King, Jr., OH, JFKL, and from Brauer, *Kennedy and the Second Reconstruction.*

1. Birmingham

See the references about Chapter 2, part 4, above. The quotations I used relating to Birmingham are from Brauer, *op. cit.;* Sitkoff, *Struggle for Black Equality;* and newspaper clippings in "Civil Rights Alabama . . . ," Box 96, POF, JFKL. The quotations from the White House meetings are from my listening to the tapes "Civil Rights, 1963," *Presidential Recordings,* JFKL. For this section I used recordings 8612, 8814, and 8816. The account of Robert Kennedy's meeting with the black radicals is based upon Schlesinger, *Robert Kennedy,* and Clarence B. Jones to the editor, *New York Times,* June 7, 1963, in Burke Marshall Papers, JFKL. Kennedy's speech is from *Public Papers of the Presidents of the United States, John F. Kennedy, 1963* (Washington, D.C., 1964).

2. The Path to Peace

This section is based upon the accounts in Schlesinger, *Thousand Days;* Sorensen, *Kennedy;* and Glenn T. Seaborg, *Kennedy, Khrushchev, and the Test Ban* (Berkeley, 1981). The quotations are from those sources and from McGeorge Bundy to Averell Harriman, July 18 and July 22, 1963, NSF, JFKL.

3. Social Justice

The quotations relating to the March on Washington are from Sitkoff, *Struggle for Black Equality,* and Martin Luther King, Jr., "I Have a Dream," in A. Meier, E. Rudwick and F. L. Broderick, eds., *Black Protest Thought in the Twentieth Century* 2d ed. (Indianapolis, 1965). The legislative history of the civil rights bill is based on the detailed account in Charles and Barbara Whalen, *The Longest Debate* (Washington, D.C., 1985), which also provided the quotations I used. On blacks and poverty, I relied upon audiotape 108.2, "Civil Rights, 1963," *Presidential Recordings,* JFKL; Walter Heller, memo for the president, May 1, 1963, POF, JFKL; Schlesinger, *Thousand Days;* and an instructive essay, "The Evolution of Anti-Poverty Policy," Timothy P. Shriver, 1981, Historical Manuscripts, Yale University Library. On the poverty programs, I drew upon Patterson, *America's Struggle Against Poverty.*

4. Diem

The account in this section derives from William J. Rust et al., *Kennedy in Vietnam* (New York, 1985). The quotations are also from that source, as well as *The Pentagon Papers,* as published by the *New York Times* (New York, 1971), ch. 4. Exceptions are "replacing the French," in J. K. Galbraith to Kennedy, March 2, 1962, POF, JFKL; "to reduce involvement," in memorandum of a conversation of April 6, 1962, the president, Harriman, Forrestal, NSF, JFKL; "symbolized by Vietnam," in McGeorge Bundy, memo for the president, January 31, 1963, NSF, JFKL.

5. Dallas

The first paragraph is based on Sorensen, *Kennedy*. The ending quotation is from Charles Bohlen, OH, JFKL.

5. CONTINUATIONS

The prelude to the chapter, including the quotations, is from the *New York Times*, November 28, 1963.

1. LBJ

For Johnson's address, see Horace Busby, memo for the president and Mrs. Johnson, November 24, 1963, WHCF, LBJL. On Johnson's manner, I quoted from his memoir, Lyndon B. Johnson, *The Vantage Point* (New York, 1971); Doris Kearns, *Lyndon Johnson and the American Dream* (New York, 1976); and Rowland Evans and Robert Novak, *Lyndon B. Johnson and the Exercise of Power* (New York, 1966). On his life and career before 1963, I relied on those soruces and also Paul K. Conkin, *Big Daddy from the Pedernales* (Boston, 1986). Ronnie Dugger, *The Politician* (New York, 1982), is also informative.

2. Two Victories

O'Brien reported to the president in a memo of December 2, 1963, WHCF, LBJL. On the tax cut, I quoted from Walter Heller, memos for the president, November 23, 1963; December 3, 1963; January 9, 1964; and Heller, notes on meeting with the president, November 25, 1963, WHCF, LBJL. For the legislative history of the Civil Rights Act of 1964, I relied upon the accounts in Charles and Barbara Whalen, *The Longest Debate* (Washington, D.C., 1985) and James L. Sundquist, *Politics and Policy: The Eisenhower, Kennedy and Johnson Years* (Washington, 1968), as well as Lyndon Johnson, *Vantage Point*. Those were the sources for the quotations I used, as also was Foy Valentine to the president, March 30, 1964, WHCF, LBJL.

3. Attack on Poverty

The CEA report is from Walter Heller, memos to the president, November 23 and December 1, 1963, POF, JFKL and WHCF, LBJL. My account of the program is based upon Sundquist, *Politics and Policy*, and Patterson, *America's Struggle against Poverty*.

4. Bobby and Barry

The part of this section devoted to the Democrats is based largely on Johnson, *Vantage Point*, and Schlesinger, *Robert Kennedy*. "Relentless pursuit" is from Eric F. Goldman,

The Tragedy of Lyndon Johnson (New York, 1969), as is the quotation of Adlai Steven-son. On the Republicans, I relied in part on Theodore H. White, *The Making of the President, 1964* (New York, 1965), and, as the quotations in the text indicate, Barry Gold-water, *The Conscience of a Conservative* (New York, 1960). On Wallace and the election, I based my accounts on White, *op. cit.* and Johnson, *op. cit.*, and, for the Freedom Dem-ocrats, on Clayborne Carson, *In Struggle: SNCC and the Black Awakening of the 1960's* (Cambridge, Mass., 1981).

6. THE GREAT SOCIETY

The biography mentioned in the prelude is Doris Kearns, *Lyndon Johnson and the American Dream.*

1. The Right to Vote

In this section I have relied upon the books cited in connection with Chapter 2, section 4, and on Carson, *In Struggle: SNCC*—the sources also for the quotations I have used.

2. OEO

Much of this section derives from Patterson, *America's Struggle against Poverty*, which seems to me the outstanding work on the subjects it covers. Most of the quotations I used are from it. My assessment of the OEO reflects the ideas in his book and those, along with the data supporting them, in both Sar A. Levitan and Robert Taggart, *The Promise of Greatness* (Cambridge, Mass., 1976), and John E. Schwarz, *America's Hidden Success* (New York, 1983). I also used with profit the files on the OEO in WHCF, LBJL. From those files I quoted Harry McPherson, memo for the president, June 8, 1965, on the UMW; Joseph Califano, memo for the president, August 19, 1966, containing Shriver's comments on "the crisis of the city"; and Sargent Shriver, memo for the president, Jan-uary 8, 1968, on "a plan . . . to wipe out poverty."

3. An Extraordinary Record

On education, I used especially Douglass Cater, OH, LBJL, supplemented by John-son, *Vantage Point*, and Francis Keppel, as quoted in the *New York Times*, September 30, 1965. On the environment, I relied primarily on Sundquist, *Politics and Policy*, and Conkin, *Big Daddy*, supplemented by Lewis L. Gould, "First Lady as Catalyst: Lady Bird Johnson and Highway Beautification," *Environmental Review* X (Summer 1986), pp. 77–92.

4. Grandiosity

On Johnson's style, I drew upon Johnson, *Vantage Point*, which supplied most of my quotations, and Schlesinger, *Robert Kennedy.* "Elemental activist" was said by John Roche. "Nooks and crannies" is from Joseph Califano as quoted in the *New York Times*, April 17, 1985, which also quoted his "how many kids," which I used at the end of the chapter. That issue of the paper carried a retrospective on the Great Society.

7. THE POLITICS OF THE WARREN COURT

The biography quoted in the prelude is G. Edward White, *Earl Warren: A Public Life* (New York, 1982).

1. Preferred Freedoms

In this section and throughout the chapter, where I have cited in these notes the cases discussed in the text, I have quoted directly from the opinions, concurrences, and dissents of those cases, as published in *United States Reports*. Where these notes have not cited the cases, or where I have quoted views about the cases by contemporary or later commentators, I have used quotations in the works of history and analysis to which these notes refer. For this section, accordingly, I have quoted from *United States v. Carolene Products Co.*, 304 U.S. 144 (1938), and for the last paragraph from Alexander M. Bickel, *The Morality of Consent* (New Haven, 1975), and I profited from the analysis in Alpheus T. Mason, *Harlan Fiske Stone: Pillar of the Law* (New York, 1956).

2. From Brown to Green

Brown v. Board of Education, 347 U.S. 483 (1954), and discussions in Bickel, *Morality of Consent*; Richard Kluger, *Simple Justice* (New York, 1978); Paul L. Murphy, *The Constitution in Crisis Times* (New York, 1972); and J. Harvie Wilkinson III, *From Brown to Bakke* (New York, 1979). Also, *Green v. County School Board*, 391 U.S. 430 (1968), and the discussion in Jack Bass, *Unlikely Heroes* (New York, 1981).

3. Respecting an Establishment of Religion

Engel v. Vitale, 370 U.S. 421 (1961); *School District of Abington Township v. Schempp*, 374 U.S. 203 (1962); and the discussion in Murphy, *Constitution in Crisis Times*. Also *Griswold v. Connecticut*, 381 U.S. 479 (1964).

4. "One Person, One Vote"

Baker v. Carr, 369 U.S. 186 (1961); *Reynolds v. Sims*, 377 U.S. 533 (1963); and the discussions in Murphy, *Constitution in Crisis Times*, and John H. Ely, *Democracy and Distrust* (Cambridge, Mass., 1980).

5. From Mallory to Miranda

Mallory v. U.S., 354 U.S. 449 (1957); *Mapp v. Ohio*, 367 U.S. 643 (1961); *Gideon v. Wainwright*, 372 U.S. 335 (1963); *Escobedo v. Illinois*, 378 U.S. 478 (1964) and *Miranda v. Arizona*, 384 U.S. 486 (1966), as well as the excellent discussions in Liva Baker, *Miranda: Crime, Law and Politics* (New York, 1983); Anthony Lewis, *Gideon's Trumpet* (New York, 1964); and Murphy, *Constitution in Crisis Times*.

6. Law and Order

This section, including the quotations in it, is derived largely from the books by Baker and Murphy cited above.

7. Coda

The quotations are from Bickel, *Morality of Consent*, and Lawrence H. Tribe, *Abortion* (New York, 1990).

8. THE GREATEST POWER

1. Panama
2. The Dominican Republic

My chief reliance for these sections was on the eight reels of microfilm "Crises in Panama and the Dominican Republic, National Security Files and NSC Histories," University Publications of America, Frederick, Maryland, 1983. I also used and quoted from Johnson, *Vantage Point*, which provides the best case for the author's policy, and Schlesinger, *Robert Kennedy*, which ably presents the contrary view, as does George W. Ball, *The Past Has Another Pattern: Memoirs* (New York, 1982), from which I also quoted. On the Dominican episode, I found particularly helpful Laura Kalman, *Abe Fortas* (New Haven, 1990), and Tad Szulc, *Dominican Diary* (New York, 1965).

3. Tonkin Gulf

For this section, as for the rest of this chapter, I consulted some of the many books about the war in Vietnam. For my purposes, Johnson's *Vantage Point* and Schlesinger's *Robert Kennedy* served as they had in the previous sections. Frances FitzGerald, *Fire in the Lake* (New York, 1972), provided sensitive background for my account. That account drew most heavily on the *New York Times* paperback publication *The Pentagon Papers* (New York, 1971), which contains almost all the documents from which I quoted, as well as helpful analyses by the editors of the book. I found equally useful Stanley Karnow, *Vietnam: A History* (New York, 1983), which in my opinion presents the clearest narrative account of its subject, an account constantly and accurately informed by available public documents. I drew often on Karnow. Dean Rusk, *As I Saw It* (New York, 1990), seemed self-serving to me. For this section I benefited from Leslie H. Gelb and Richard F. Betts, *The Irony of Vietnam: The System Worked* (Washington, D.C., 1979). I also explored the Vietnam files in NSF, LBJL. For the period covered by this chapter, those files contain little of significance that was not published in the full edition of *The Pentagon Papers, loc. cit.* But I did profit from the meeting notes of John McCone and there found Johnson's "destroy their cities" from a meeting of August 4, 1964, NSF, LBJL.

4. Escalation

The section rests on the titles listed in connection with the previous section, supplemented by the valuable Larry Berman, *Planning a Tragedy: The Americanization of the War in Vietnam* (New York, 1982). For the later years of the Vietnam War, the same author's succeeding book is similarly important: Larry Berman, *Lyndon Johnson's War* (New York, 1989).

5. Brutalization

This section derives from the books listed in connection with section 3, above. The quotations from the soldiers are from Karnow, *Vietnam*, and from Kim Willenson, *The Bad War* (New York, 1987). The exchange between Hubert Humphrey and President Johnson is from McCone's meeting notes, February 24, 1966, NSF, LBJL.

6. Penumbras of War

This section rests in the books listed for section 3, and also Bundy, *Danger and Survival*.

9. POLARIZATION

The quotations in the prelude are from Oates, *Let the Trumpet Sound*, and Garrow, *Bearing the Cross*.

1. Watts

This section, including the quotations in it, rests on *The Report of the National Commission on Civil Disorders (New York Times* ed., New York, 1968), hereafter referred to as the Kerner Report. The exchange between King and the youths is quoted in Oates, cited above.

2. Black Power

Malcolm X is quoted from *The Autobiography of Malcolm X* (Grove Press ed., New York, 1966). On SNCC and CORE, I relied on Robert H. Brisbane, *Black Activism* (Valley Forge, Pa., 1974), and Weisbrot, *Freedom Bound*, as well as Frantz Fanon, *The Wretched of the Earth* (Grove Press ed., New York, 1965). On the march I also benefited from the account in Garrow, *Bearing the Cross*.

3. Chicago

This section is based upon Garrow, cited above; Sitkoff, *Struggle for Black Equality*; and the Kerner Report.

4. Cities on Fire

My account derives from the Kerner Report.

5. The Black Panthers

This section rests on Brisbane and Weisbrot, cited above, as well as Eldridge Cleaver, *Soul on Ice* (Dell ed., New York, 1968).

6. Backlash

This section is based on the Kerner Report. "Massive effect" is quoted in Schlesinger, *Robert Kennedy*. I also quoted TRB in the *New Republic* (October 22, 1966) and Bickel, *Morality of Consent*.

7. The New Left

"Unbearably moving," a statement of Staughton Lynd, is from Miller *"Democracy Is in the Streets."* That book, along with David Caute, *The Year of the Barricades* (New York, 1988), and Matusow, *Unraveling of America*, supplied the foundation for this section, as did William Chafe on feminism in *The Unfinished Journey* (New York, 1986). I have also quoted from Betty Friedan, *The Feminine Mystique* (Dell ed., New York, 1974), from Sara Evans, *Personal Politics* (Vintage ed., New York, 1979), and from the works of Robin Morgan and Herbert Marcuse cited in the text.

8. Confrontations

In this section I relied regularly on Miller, *"Democracy Is in the Streets,"* supplemented on McNamara and on the draft by the account and quotations in Steven Kelman, *Push Comes to Shove* (Boston, 1970), and, on the Pentagon episode, by Norman Mailer, *The Armies of the Night* (New York, 1968), and Matusow, *Unraveling of America*.

9. Fungus

This section, including the quotations, depends largely on *The Pentagon Papers*, as cited earlier, and Karnow, *Vietnam*, as supplemented by the indispensable "inside account" of Townsend Hoopes, *The Limits of Intervention* (New York, 1969). The quotations of Bill Moyers and of Robert Kennedy are from Schlesinger, *Robert Kennedy*.

10. The Politics of Discord

1. Enter Gene McCarthy

The first part of this section is based upon my own experience in the Connecticut McCarthy movement, as a contributor to the *New Republic*, and as a participant in the antiwar rally at Ascutney, Vermont, where J. K. Galbraith was the featured speaker. McCarthy's announcement is from Matusow, *Unraveling of America*. The rest of the section relies on Schlesinger, *Robert Kennedy*.

2. Tet

On Tet and its military sequel, I based my account largely on Karnow, *Vietnam*. On the American reaction, I relied primarily on Hoopes, *Limits of Intervention*, supplemented by the Vietnam files, Boxes 1–6, *Papers of Clark Clifford*, LBJL, which contain, inter alia, the important Hoopes, memo for the secretary of defense, March 14, 1968, and Maxwell Taylor, memo for the president, February 10, 1968. On Robert Kennedy's reaction to New Hampshire, I drew upon Schlesinger, *Robert Kennedy*. Matusow, *Unraveling of America*, provided useful background.

3. Exit Lyndon Johnson?

For this section I used the Hoopes book and Clifford Papers, cited above, supplemented by Schlesinger, *Robert Kennedy*, and the valuable memoir of Harry McPherson, *A Political Education* (Boston, 1972).

4. Memphis

This section is based upon Garrow, *Bearing the Cross* and Schlesinger, *Robert Kennedy*. The quotation at the end of the section is from Adam Walinsky, *New York Times*, June 5, 1988.

5. Los Angeles

This section rests on Schlesinger, *Robert Kennedy*, and Chafe, *Unfinished Journey*.

6. Chicago

My account, including the quotations, derives from Caute, *Year of the Barricades*; Miller, *"Democracy Is in the Streets"*; Matusow, *Unraveling of America*; and especially Theodore H. White, *The Making of the President, 1968* (New York, 1969).

7. Nixon Redux

This section rests upon White, cited above, supplemented by Stephen E. Ambrose, *Nixon: The Triumph of a Politician* (New York, 1989), hereafter cited as *Nixon II*, and Herbert S. Parmet, *Richard Nixon and His America* (Boston, 1990).

8. Verdict

This section rests primarily on White, cited above, and Johnson, *Vantage Point*, which contains the quotations "step by step" and "nervous and distrustful."

11. R N

The quotation in the prelude is from Barry M. Goldwater, *Goldwater* (New York, 1988).

1. Breakfast

In this section, as in the rest of this chapter and this book, I have relied again and again on the indispensable memoirs of Richard M. Nixon, *RN: The Memoirs of Richard Nixon* (New York, 1978), and of Henry Kissinger, *White House Years* (Boston, 1979), and the sequel to that volume, cited later. Those memoirs, as well as Nixon's *Six Crises* (Pyramid ed., New York, 1968, with a new preface), provide information nowhere else available and provide also, often inadvertently, important insights into the personalities of their authors. Both Nixon and Kissinger in their memoirs were constantly self-serving, as was Lyndon Johnson before them, and frequently inaccurate. Consequently, their memoirs have to be checked against other sources and corrected as necessary. For this section, I found the necessary correctives in the careful account of William Shawcross, *Sideshow* (New York, 1978). The quotations are from those sources except for the Rebozo-Getty episode, for which see H. R. Haldeman, memo for John Ehrlichman, February 17, 1969, Ehrlichman Files, Box 33, White House Special Files, NPMS.

2. Isolation

My account of Nixon's life before 1968 is based upon Nixon, *RN;* Ambrose, *Nixon I;* Roger Morris, *Richard Milhaus Nixon: The Rise of an American Politician* (New York, 1990); and Parmet, *Nixon.* The quotations about "unnecessary conversation" and Bebe Rebozo are from John Ehrlichman, *Witness to Power* (New York, 1981). On Nixon and trivia, see Bruce Oudes, ed., *From: The President: Richard Nixon's Secret Files* (New York, 1989). Ambrose, cited above, contains the quotation of Tom Wicker.

3. Southern Strategies

On the issue of crime, I drew upon A. James Reichley, *Conservatives in an Age of Change* (Washington, D.C., 1981), and Jonathan Schell, *The Time of Illusion* (New York, 1976). Nixon's instructions to Ehrlichman are on undated news analyses of early February and early March in Box 30 of NPMS-ANS (see legend preceding notes to this book). Reichley and Schell, just cited, were useful also on voting rights and on desegregation and contain the quotations I used. On the *Swann* case, I relied on Mason, *Supreme Court.* Nixon wrote about "low profile" on Leonard Garment, memo for the president, August 5, 1970, NPMS. Nixon's "personally to jump" is written on Edward L. Morgan, memo for the president, July 6, 1971, NPMS. "No never" is written on a news summary of January 9, 1970, NPMS-ANS. On Burger, Haynsworth, and Carswell, I relied heavily on Baker, *Miranda,* and the quotations therein, as well as on Nixon, *RN;* Chafe, *Unfinished Journey;* and Schell, *Time of Illusion.* Kalman, *Fortas,* provides the best account of Fortas's resignation. The quotations about Powell and Rehnquist I quoted from Baker, just cited.

4. FAP

On the issue of poverty before and during the Nixon years, and on the development of national policy to combat poverty, the outstanding study is Patterson, *America's Struggle against Poverty,* on which I have relied in this section. I found useful, too, Reichley, *Conservatism in an Age of Change,* and my quotations, unless otherwise indicated, are from those sources. Important for background and analysis were Nixon, *RN;* Daniel P. Moynihan, *The Politics of a Guaranteed Income* (New York, 1973); Ambrose, *Nixon II;* and Parmet, *Nixon and His America.* "Overstaffing, overlapping," and "the most fruitless" are respectively from draft memo to Secretary Shultz, undated, about February 1969, Box 1 NPMS, and TV news summary, May 19, 1969, NPMS-ANS. "I like the idea" is from Nixon's comment on Elliot Richardson, memo for the president on welfare, undated, Box 10, NPMS.

12. INCURSION

1. Vietnamization

My account in this section, including the quotations I have used, is based upon Nixon, *RN*, and Kissinger, *White House Years*, both tempered by Karnow, *Vietnam;* Reichley, *Conservatives in an Age of Change;* and Schell, *Time of Illusion.*

2. Diaspora on the Left

On conscription, see Ambrose, *Nixon II.* The findings about New Left leaders and Nixon's resulting instructions are in John Ehrlichman, memo for the president, June 5, 1969, NPMS, and T. C. Huston, memo for the president, June 18, 1969, NPMS. On the general disintegration of the left and the furor at the universities, I drew largely on Matusow, *Unraveling of America,* and Caute, *Year of the Barricades,* which was the source, too, of the quotations I used. The books of Roszak and Reich are cited in the text.

3. Pitiful Giant?

This section, including most of the quotations in it, rests largely on the Nixon and Kissinger memoirs, cited above, as modified by the accounts in Karnow, *Vietnam;* Schell, *Time of Illusion;* and Shawcross, *Sideshow.* Nixon wrote "anarchy in the air" on Patrick J. Buchanan, memo for the president, March 16, 1970, NPMS. "Feel so helpless" was said by Peggy Buttenheim, then a Yale junior, to the author on May 1, 1970.

4. Getting Tough

This section, including the quotations in it, derives from Nixon, *RN*, and Schell, *Time of Illusion,* except for "carried out by an elite group" which is from Daniel Patrick Moynihan, memo for the president, August 4, 1970, NPMS. On Nixon's desire to punish the universities, see also his comments on John Ehrlichman, memos for the president, undated and July 20, 1971, both in Box 12, POF, President's Handwriting Files, NPMS.

13. THE GLORIOUS BURDEN

1. A Structure of Peace

For background and quotations, this section derives from two unusually helpful sources: John L. Gaddis, *Strategies of Containment* (New York, 1982), an informed and thoughtful overview of the changing purposes of American foreign policy from Truman through Nixon, and Raymond L. Garthoff, *Detente and Confrontation* (Washington, D.C., 1985), a learned, detailed, persuasive account of American diplomacy and foreign policy, especially but not exclusively toward the Soviet Union, from Nixon through Carter.

2. The China Card
3. Accommodation or Confrontation?

Security restrictions still hamper research on the foreign policy of Nixon and Kissinger. Consequently, the memoirs of those two men, their biases notwithstanding, remain vital sources. But those biases need correction, and in these and ensuing sections on foreign policy, I have depended on Garthoff's reliable scholarship, cited above, to provide those corrections. The quotations in these sections are from the three works just mentioned.

4. Roller Coaster

On Laos, I relied on Kissinger, *White House Years*, modified by Karnow, *Vietnam*. On Calley, I leaned primarily on Schell, *Time of Illusion*, tempered by Nixon, *RN*. That last title speaks with unintentional eloquence to the question of the Plumbers. Indispensable on the Pentagon Papers is *New York Times v. United States*, 403 U.S. 713 (1971). On the Pentagon Papers the account in Ambrose, *Nixon II* is especially valuable, as is that book's discussion of Nixon and the Plumbers.

5. SALT

This section derives from Nixon, *RN*, and Kissinger, *White House Years*, as modified, corrected, and amplified by Garthoff, *Detente and Confrontation*.

6. Beijing

As in section 5, above, with Karnow, *Vietnam*, also helpful as a corrective to the memoirs cited.

7. Moscow

As in section 6, with an important additional discussion in Ambrose, *Nixon II*.

14. THE POLITICS OF CONNIVANCE

The quotation in the prelude is from Ehrlichman, *Witness to Power*.

1. Timely Conversions

This section, including the quotations in it, is based primarily on Nixon, *RN*, on Reichley, *Conservatives in an Age of Change*, up to the "spoof" by Herbert Stein, and then also on Edward R. Tufte, *Political Control of the Economy* (Princeton, 1978), with those works frequently supplemented by the material cited herewith: on ecology and related matters—"let's not go crazy"—Nixon's comment on Peter M. Flanagan, memo for the president, April 27, 1971; "boondoggle"—Nixon's comment on John C. Whitaker, memo for the president, May 25, 1971; "overboard"—Nixon's comment on John Ehrlichman, memo for the president, August 5, 1971; "very impractical"—John Ehrlichman, memo for the president, March 1, 1973, NPMS. On macroeconomic policy—"psychological recession"—Nixon comment on Paul W. McCracken, memo for the president, December 26, 1970; "disappointing"—Nixon comment on H. E. Houthakken, memo for the president, March 16, 1971; "intangible capital formation"—Nixon comment on Paul W. McCracken, memo for the president, April 14, 1971; "incline to move"—Nixon comment on Paul W. McCracken, memo for the president, June 1, 1971; "international bankers"—Nixon comment on Paul W. McCracken, memo for the president, September 13, 1971; Herbert Stein, memo for the president, November 10, 1971; George P. Schultz, memo for the president, December 18, 1971; "off their duffs"—Nixon comment on Herbert Stein, memo for the president, March 20, 1972, NPMS.

2. Social Issues

On busing, I drew from Schell, *Time of Illusion*. On the death penalty, I used Mason, *Supreme Court from Taft to Burger*, and Herman Schwartz, ed., *The Burger Years* (New York, 1987). On feminism, I quoted from Chafe, *Unfinished Journey*; on day care and otherwise, from Nixon comments on Robert H. Finch, memo for the president, April 15, 1971; and on Geoff Shepard, memo for the president, May 17, 1974, NPMS. On the Democratic party rules and their implications, I relied upon Byron E. Shafer, *Quiet Revolution* (New York, 1983). On Ulasewicz, Colson, and Wallace, I used Schell, *Time of Illusion*; on the White House, the social issues and Muskie, see Patrick Buchanan, memo for the president, April 19, 1971, NPMS.

3. Dirty Tricks

This section is based upon Nixon, *RN*, modified extensively by Schell, *Time of Illusion*; Sam J. Ervin, *The Whole Truth: The Watergate Conspiracy* (New York, 1980), especially on Stans; Elizabeth Drew, *Washington Journal* (New York, 1976), especially on ITT; and Carl Bernstein and Bob Woodward, *All the President's Men* (New York, 1974), especially on Segretti. On the ADA, I relied on Steven M. Gillon, *Politics and Vision* (New York, 1987). On Humphrey and Vietnam, and on Shultz and Daley, see respectively Daniel P. Moynihan, memo for the president, November 16, 1970, and George P. Shultz, memo to the president, May 1, 1972, NPMS.

4. McGovern

This section is based upon Nixon, *RN*; the excellent account in Chafe, *Unfinished Journey*; and my own recollection of McGovern in Connecticut.

5. Watergate

In this and later sections on Watergate, I have benefited constantly from J. Anthony Lukas, *Nightmare: The Underside of the Nixon Years* (Penguin ed., New York, 1988), and Theodore H. White, *Breach of Faith* (New York, 1975), which here and elsewhere provided many of the quotations I used. For this section, the works by Ervin, Bernstein and Woodward, and Schell, cited above, were also indispensable, respectively on the Patman committee, the *Washington Post*, and Henry Petersen. On the function of a trial, I quoted from that essential book on Watergate, John J. Sirica, *To Set the Record Straight* (New York, 1979).

6. "Peace Is at Hand"

As in sections 5 and 6 of Chapter 8.

15. DOUBLE TROUBLE

The quotations in the prelude are from Ehrlichman, *Witness to Power*, and Nixon, *RN*.

1. Rewards and Punishments

This section, along with the quotations in it, is based upon Nixon, *RN;* Kissinger, *White House Years;* and Reichley, *Conservatives in an Age of Change*.

2. Linebacker Two

This section, along with the quotations in it, is based upon Nixon, *RN*, and Henry Kissinger, *Years of Upheaval* (Boston, 1982), both as modified by Garthoff, *Detente and Confrontation.*

3. A Growing Cancer

This section, including the quotations in it, is based upon the books by White, Nixon, Sirica, Ervin, Drew, Bernstein and Woodward, and Schell, all cited in the note on section 4, Chapter 14.

4. Camouflage

As in section 2, above.

5. The Tapes

As in section 3, above.

6. Saturday Night Massacre

As in section 3, above, except Schell.

7. The Yom Kippur War

As in section 2, above; and on the economy, Lester C. Thurow, *The Zero-Sum Society* (New York, 1980); on abortion, *Roe v. Wade*, 410 U.S. 113 (1973).

16. THE RULE OF LAW

For this entire chapter, except for section 3, my account, including the quotations I have used, is based for foreign policy on the works cited for section 2, Chapter 15, and, for domestic issues, on the works cited for section 3, Chapter 15. Section 3 of this chapter, "To Say What the Law Is," is based upon the cases cited in it: *United States v. United States District Court*, 407 U.S. 297 (1972); and *United States v. Nixon*, 418 U.S. 683 (1974).

Illustration Credits

Index